MODERN STORIES

STORIES IN ENGLISH

3rd EDITION

W. H. NEW
University of British Columbia

H. J. ROSENGARTEN
University of British Columbia

ISBN: 0-7730-5127-9

Executive editor: Brian Henderson
Editors: Brenda Clews, John Meyers
Cover and design: Stephen MacEachern
Typesetting: Marnie Morrissey
Permissions: Luisa Rinaldo
Printing and binding: Webcom Limited

Canadian Cataloguing in Publication Data
Main entry under title:

Modern stories in English

3rd. ed.
Includes bibliographical references.
ISBN 0-7730-5127-9

1. Short stories, American. 2. Short stories, Canadian (English).*
3. Short stories, English.
I. New, W. H. (William Herbert), 1938–   .
II. Rosengarten, Herbert.

PR1309.S5M62 1991   813'.0108   C91-093608-0

Copp Clark Pitman Ltd.
2775 Matheson Blvd. East
Mississauga, Ontario
L4W 4P7

OTABIND
Bound to stay open

Publisher's Note
Otabind (Ota-bind). This book has been bound using the patented Otabind process. You can open this book at any page, gently run your finger down the spine, and the pages will lie flat.

Associated companies
   Longman Group Ltd., London
   Longman Inc., New York
   Longman Cheshire Pty., Melbourne
   Longman Paul Pty. Auckland

Printed and bound in Canada

3 4 5 5127-9 98 97 96

CONTENTS

CHILDHOOD, INITIATION, AND GROWTH

LOVE, MARRIAGE, AND THE ROLES OF MEN AND WOMEN

IDENTITY AND ALIENATION

RELIGIOUS AND MORAL VALUES

ART AND REALITY

CHRONOLOGICAL CONTENTS

Introduction

Good stories entertain us: this is the main reason we listen to them or read them. But "entertainment" comes in many guises. For some listeners and readers, narrative is everything—they like a quick-moving tale, a thrilling plot, mystery, adventure, suspense. Some want to identify with the characters of a story, perhaps to share their experiences vicariously, or perhaps because such empathy enlarges their understanding of the complexities of human behaviour. For other readers, plot and character are subordinate to a story's educational purpose or moral point; they want fiction to teach a lesson about life. A different group of readers is less interested in a separable "moral" or "subject" than in the manner by which the story is told, by its formal qualities; for them, the form that the story takes—meaning the cadences and textures of its language, as well as its structure—constitutes a "subject" in its own right. Readers look in a story variously for escape, for instruction, for a mirror of the world, for a work of artifice.

Just as there is a multiplicity of readers, so the modern short story draws on a multitude of forms that have long been a part of narrative tradition: myths, legends, fables, folk tales, ballads, fairy tales, and oral "exempla." Since the first half of the nineteenth century, when authors such as Edgar Allan Poe and Nathaniel Hawthorne began producing models of narrative suspense and psychological drama in short-story form, American writers have been among the short story's foremost practitioners. But the same era saw the development of short fiction elsewhere as well, in France, Germany, England, Russia, China, Spain, Italy; and the new perspectives brought by these different cultures and traditions gave additional vigour to the short story, strengthening its claim to be regarded as a fictional form in its own right. Such cross-fertilization has continued into our own time. Twentieth-century writers in English have been influenced not only by their own cultures, but also by innovative writers in other languages: by the folk writers of Asia and India, for example, and the Gothic authors of Quebec, the political fabulists from Czechoslovakia and the "magic realists" of Latin America.

Yet in English alone there is a rich variety, reflected by the stories in this collection. They display diverse views and contrasting styles; they are representative of the century's main technical developments in short fiction; they also come from many different parts of the world: mostly from the United States, Britain, and Canada, but also from Ireland, Africa, the Caribbean, and the South Pacific. They have in common the English language; to make this assertion, however, is to cover a wealth of specific differences, for in the relation between language and culture something happens that affects the shape and substance of stories. The way writers use images, for example, derives not so much from literary or linguistic precedent and example (though these play their part), as from the way they see their own world—from their particular experience, their own observations of places and people. Joyce's Dublin and Faulkner's South, Naipaul's Trinidad and Achebe's Nigeria: these are fictional locales, rooted in specific cultural and political observations. The worlds of the Irish Catholic and the Trinidad Hindu, the social patterns of American and Nigerian families, are not the same. Comparing stories from different cultures, therefore, can provide an opportunity to study ethnic differences, and to delight in the linguistic variety to which such differences have given rise. It can also reveal elements of social disparity and inequity, even while it underlines the common humanity of the experiences that the writers have depicted.

There are many shared human experiences—love, hate, work, war, birth, death, dreams—which recur from author to author, from country to country, in all forms of literature. The function of the Thematic Table of Contents in this anthology is to guide readers to some of these points of comparison. The number of stories about growing up, for example, or about the relations between men and women, testifies to the similarity of everyday life around the world. Stories about political or racial oppression ("Brother," "Dry September"), or about the problems arising out of modern scientific progress ("Report") can awaken comparable responses in readers from a wide range of backgrounds. But even here a reader must be sensitive to differences, and avoid making facile connections. The roles of men and women vary from society to society, as they have varied within a single society over time; attitudes to communal and individual values differ (individualism is not universally regarded as socially desirable or necessary); and generational conflict in a culture that reveres tradition will obviously carry different overtones from those it possesses in a society committed to novelty and change.

Although all the writers in this anthology have in common the cultural and linguistic heritage of English, that heritage has been altered by time and place. During the twentieth century, many national literatures founded on English patterns and traditions moved away from them in order to reclaim older indigenous traditions, or because new experiences, landscapes, and cultural mixes led to a need for different words and different ways of using them. Walt Whitman's efforts in the mid-nineteenth century to articulate a new language for the United States provided something of a model; Whitman wanted American English to mirror his "new" nation's expansionist, democratic, colloquial politics. The American writers in this book, from Faulkner and Hemingway to Cheever and Vonnegut, convey the characteristic sounds and rhythms of the language that subsequently evolved. In Africa and the Caribbean, where the tradition of oral storytelling developed into a sophisticated folk art, the tensions of modern life are still couched in a characteristically "oral" form. Achebe and Naipaul rely extensively for their effects on the rhythms of speech and the contrasts between different orders of vernacular fluency. Achebe's "Civil Peace" deals with the collapse of communal solidarity during the Nigerian civil war, while Naipaul's "My Aunt Gold Teeth" affirms the value of a tradition the narrator admires even while he can no longer participate in it; in both cases, it is the oral character of the culture which preserves the values and forms of a civilization once strong and now lost.

As with patterns of speech, so with thematic concerns. In Australia and New Zealand, writers found new subjects in responding to a set of social preoccupations born out of their separate South Pacific contexts and their relations with the colonizing power, Britain. Katherine Mansfield's deliberate, class-conscious individualism in "The Doll's House" looks back to a time when English conventions were still strong, while the satire of Peter Carey's "Do You Love Me?" questions the ways a post-colonial society defines its identity. Canadians have also sought their own voice: though living in an environment in many respects similar to that of their American neighbours, they have determinedly celebrated the differences that distinguish their social organization and social values from those that pertain in Britain and the United States—in the process developing a lively rhetoric of regional identities. Both Sinclair Ross and Alice Munro, for example (Ross in "Cornet at Night," about a prairie boy's imaginative break from farm routine, and Munro in "Thanks for the Ride," describing adolescent initiation and social decay in a small Ontario town), vividly record the sounds and sights of particular locales, emphasizing how their characters' lives and language are inextricably intertwined with their environment. Similarly, Margaret Laurence's "The Merchant of Heaven" and Rohinton Mistry's "Swimming Lessons" place characters in cross-cultural circumstances in order to reveal the constraints of speech and the presumptions of culture. All these stories evoke the language of place, some in dialogue, some through narration or description, some in transformations of everyday speech into political or social symbol.

In one way or another then, whether through setting or subject or language, a sense of place pervades all the stories in this collection. In many, however, that awareness is rooted in feelings of exile or alienation from an older tradition. Such exile has, during this century, proved to be an opportunity to discover freedom on the one hand, and an experience that is spiritually debilitating on the other. People have chosen to emigrate, or been driven to do so; they have willingly embraced a different kind of life, or had one forced upon them. Whichever is the case, such moves inevitably brought with them a sense of something left behind, something lost. Katherine Mansfield reveals this divided consciousness: she rejected what she considered the provinciality of New Zealand, and yet her stories sometimes look back wistfully to a colonial childhood. V.S. Naipaul experienced a twofold alienation: from his Indian heritage, and from his Trinidadian upbringing. For Ernest Hemingway, exile was a deliberate choice, dictated by a need to find fresh values; working in Paris in the 1920s, he sought to break away from outworn modes and empty rhetoric, to give literature new force and meaning by portraying life in starkly realistic terms. In this he only partly succeeded, for he could never wholly shed the ideal of heroic individualism that marks his American tradition.

The experience of alienation is not restricted to individuals. The Native writer George Clutesi, for instance, observes that Indians and Inuit in North America are dispossessed without even moving from their homeland. Writers from ethnic minorities (Alice Walker, Clark Blaise), using or responding to the language of the "majority" culture around them, live with an isolation of a related kind. For many writers, therefore, fiction becomes a way of challenging or subverting social conventions, a means to shape in artifice an alternative vision of the world. Feminist writers (Grenville, Thomas, Walker) have attempted to combat the presumptive values inherent in linguistic conventions as well as in social ones. And there is another kind of alienation—intellectual and artistic, such as we find detailed in Rudy Wiebe's "Where Is the Voice Coming From?" which dramatizes the struggle by a member of one culture to reach some understanding of another, and to find ordered utterance for his confused and painful impressions.

The language of the modern short story, then, can be not only a means of reporting on experience, but also a way of charting alternative perceptions of experience. Whatever the goal, the writer can call on a multitude of devices through which he or she may pattern the experience: through realistic description, for example, or through fantasy, through satire, through myth. In stories like "Hills Like White Elephants," for example, the writer's intention is to make us believe we are direct observers of the action; Hemingway creates the illusion of reality by focusing on dialogue, so that we have the sense that we are listening in on a real conversation. Such stories move us from the page to the world; we recognize the action as a comment on or description of life, a projection of psychological disturbance or a dramatization of social conflict. But other writers ask readers to look at the word as much as at the world. Writers like Barthelme and Vonnegut (writing "reports"), Helprin (writing "letters"), and Wiebe (copying out phrases from historical archives) adapt forms that, in part, paradoxically stress the limitations of documentary realism. Their stories challenge readers to acknowledge the empirical world and then to use their imagination to transcend its obvious restrictions. They ask readers to be co-creators of the story. They are celebrants of language-in-process, taking pleasure in language at play, exploring its boundaries.

Language takes narrative shape in other, more traditional ways. For writers like Cheever, Callaghan, and Bowles, a concern with moral behavior takes the form of parable or fable. In stories such as those by Jacobs and Forster, it is the pattern of fantasy or myth that structures experience; the reader enters the world of dream or nightmare, with its associative leaps of logic and its symbolic or psychological implications. For writers of satire—Joyce, King, Nowlan, and others—the story is patterned by a comic irony that exposes the flaws and foibles of people who live their lives in two dimensions, blinkered to other possibilities and unaware of their own follies.

Several stories in this anthology incorporate elements of myth as a structuring device, either the kind of myth that articulates directly a society's moral tradition, or the kind that is used as a literary means to sound "archetypes," to arouse in the reader a recognition of enduring patterns of human experience. Both kinds of myth can serve didactic purposes. Clutesi's "Ko-ishin-mit and the Shadow People" comes from a tradition in which such tales were designed (in the author's own words) "to teach the young the many wonders of nature; the importance of all living things, no matter how small and insignificant." In contrast, Bowles's "Allal" merges the conventions of myth with those of realism to produce a social fable that comments on modern human beings. It is ironic, oblique, spare; its eye is on contemporary behaviour all the while it seems to be concerned with events of pure fantasy. We are asked to believe in the truth of what the story tells us but not necessarily in the reality of the events it portrays—they are a means to a different end. That such stories are in one way or another "fantastic" does not make them any less relevant to our own daily lives; it simply makes us more conscious of the artifice which characterizes all works of literature, and by means of which writer and reader are able to share the pleasures of the imagination.

Born in Ogidi, Nigeria, in 1930 and educated at Umuahia, Ibadan, and London, Chinua Achebe has become established not only as an editor and publisher, but also as one of the most respected literary voices in contemporary Africa. He has written verse, books for juveniles, two books of short stories, and five novels, of which the first three won particularly enthusiastic reviews. *Things Fall Apart* (1958), *No Longer at Ease* (1961), and *Arrow of God* (1964) render different aspects of the conflict between European and African civilizations. The powerlessness of the traditional culture to remain intact in the face of European enslavement and colonization, the inability of a modern young African to reconcile his family attachments with his sense of independence and his observation of political corruption, the incapacity of both the lay African society and the European colonial bureaucracy to understand the role and identity of a traditional priest: these are Achebe's topics. His aim is openly political and didactic. In "The Novelist as Teacher," he asserts: "Here, then, is an adequate revolution for me to espouse—to help my society regain its belief in itself and put away the complexes of the years of denigration and self-denigration." In so doing he fulfills one of the traditional roles of the writer in African society: to educate the young to an appreciation of the moral truths of their own culture. His method, too, derives from traditional techniques; he relies on simple narrative structures and on the functional patterns of Igbo proverbs. "As long as one people sit on another and are deaf to their cry," he writes, "so long will understanding elude all of us."

"Civil Peace" is the concluding story of *Girls at War and other stories* (1972), a volume which, like his most recent novel, *Anthills of the Savannah* (1987), reflects the civil war that disrupted Nigerian life in the late 1960s. Though the fatalistic ironies that permeate the story are not untouched by humour, the work is fundamentally serious and reveals Achebe's continuing account of his deeply held commitment to freedom. In exploring its nature, in attempting both to communicate to a national audience and to reach across cultural and racial boundaries, he shows himself to be an acute and humane observer of human behaviour.

FOR FURTHER READING

Chinua Achebe, "The Novelist as Teacher," *Hopes and Impediments: Selected Essays 1965-1987* (London: Heinemann, 1988): 27-31.

David Carroll, *Chinua Achebe* (New York: Twayne, 1970).

G.D. Killam, *The Novels of Chinua Achebe* (London: Heinemann, 1969).

Margaret Laurence, *Long Drums and Cannons* (London: Macmillan, 1968).

Civil Peace

Jonathan Iwegbu counted himself extra-ordinarily lucky. "Happy survival!" meant so much more to him than just a current fashion of greeting old friends in the first hazy days of peace. It went deep to his heart. He had come out of the war with five inestimable blessings—his head, his wife Maria's head and the heads of three out of their four children. As a bonus he also had his old bicycle—a miracle too but naturally not to be compared to the safety of five human heads.

The bicycle had a little history of its own. One day at the height of the war it was commandeered "for urgent military action." Hard as its loss would have been to him he would still have let it go without a thought had he not had some doubts about the genuineness of the officer. It wasn't his disreputable rags, nor the toes peeping out of one blue and one brown canvas shoes, nor yet the two stars of his rank done obviously in a hurry in biro, that troubled Jonathan; many good and heroic soldiers looked the same or worse. It was rather a certain lack of grip and firmness in his manner. So Jonathan, suspecting he might be amenable to influence, rummaged in his raffia bag and produced the two pounds with which he had been going to buy firewood which his wife, Maria, retailed to camp officials for extra stock-fish and corn meal, and got his bicycle back. That night he buried it in the little clearing in the brush where the dead of the camp, including his own youngest son, were buried. When he dug it up again a year later after the surrender all it needed was a little palm-oil greasing. "Nothing puzzles God," he said in wonder.

He put it to immediate use as a taxi and accumulated a small pile of Biafran money ferrying camp officials and their families across the four-mile stretch to the nearest tarred road. His standard charge per trip was six pounds and those who had the money were only glad to be rid of some of it in this way. At the end of a fortnight he had made a small fortune of one hundred and fifteen pounds.

Then he made the journey to Enugu and found another miracle waiting for him. It was unbelievable. He rubbed his eyes and looked again and it was still standing there before him. But, needless to say, even that monumental blessing must be accounted also totally inferior to the five heads in the family. This newest miracle was his little house in Ogui Overside. Indeed nothing puzzles God! Only two houses away a huge concrete edifice some wealthy contractor had put up just before the war was a mountain of rubble. And here was Jonathan's little zinc house of no regrets built with mud blocks quite intact! Of course the doors and windows were missing and five sheets off the roof. But what was that? And anyhow he had returned to Enugu early enough to pick up bits of old zinc and wood and soggy sheets of cardboard lying around the neighbourhood before thousands more came out of their forest holes looking for the same things. He got a destitute carpenter with one old hammer, a blunt plane and a few bent and rusty nails in his tool bag to turn this assortment of wood, paper and metal into door and window shutter for five Nigerian shillings or fifty Biafran pounds. He paid the pounds, and moved in with his overjoyed family carrying five heads on their shoulders.

His children picked mangoes near the military cemetery and sold them to soldiers' wives for a few pennies—real pennies this time—and his wife started making breakfast akara balls for neighbours in a hurry to start life again. With his family earnings he took his bicycle to the villages around and brought fresh palm-wine which he mixed generously in his rooms with the water which had recently started running again in the public tap down the road, and opened up a bar for soldiers and other lucky people with good money.

At first he went daily, then every other day and finally once a week, to the offices of the Coal Corporation where he used to be a miner, to find out what was what. The only thing he did find out in the end was that the little house of his was even a greater blessing than he had thought. Some of his fellow ex-miners who had nowhere to return at the end of the day's waiting just slept outside the doors of the offices and cooked what meal they could scrounge together in Bournvita tins. As the weeks lengthened and still nobody could say what was what Jonathan discontinued his weekly visits altogether and faced his palm-wine bar.

But nothing puzzles God. Came the day of the windfall when after five days of endless scuffles in queues and counter-queues in the sun outside the Treasury he had twenty pounds counted into his palms as ex-gratia award for the rebel money he had turned in. It was like Christmas for him and for many others like him when the payments began. They called it (since few could manage its proper official name) *egg-rasher.*

As soon as the pound notes were placed in his palm Jonathan simply closed it tight over them and buried fist and money inside his trouser pocket. He had to be extra careful because he had seen a man a couple of days earlier collapse into near-madness in an instant before that oceanic crowd because no sooner had he got his twenty pounds than some heartless ruffian picked it off him. Though it was not right that a man in such an extremity of agony should be blamed yet many in the queues that day were able to remark quietly on the victim's careless-ness, especially after he pulled out the innards of his pocket and revealed a hole in it big enough to pass a thief's head. But of course he had insisted that the money had been in the other pocket, pulling it out to show its comparative wholeness. So one had to be careful.

Jonathan soon transferred the money to his left hand and pocket so as to leave his right free for shaking hands should the need arise, though by fixing his gaze at such an elevation as to miss all approaching human faces he made sure that the need did not arise, until he got home.

He was normally a heavy sleeper but that night he heard all the neighbourhood noises die down one after another. Even the night watchman who knocked the hour on some metal somewhere in the dis-tance had fallen silent after knocking one o'clock. That must have been the last thought in Jonathan's mind before he was finally carried away himself. He couldn't have been gone for long, though, when he was violently awakened again.

"Who is knocking?" whispered his wife lying beside him on the floor.

"I don't know," he whispered back breathlessly.

The second time the knocking came it was so loud and imperious that the rickety old door could have fallen down.

"Who is knocking?" he asked then, his voice parched and trembling.

"Na* tief-man and him people," came the cool reply. "Make you hopen de door." This was followed by the heaviest knocking of all.

Maria was the first to raise the alarm, then he followed and all their children.

"*Police-o! Thieves-o! Neighbours-o! Police-o! We are lost! We are dead! Neighbours, are you asleep? Wake up! Police-o!*"

This went on for a long time and then stopped suddenly. Perhaps they had scared the thief away. There was total silence. But only for a short while.

"You done finish?" asked the voice outside. "Make we help you small. Oya, everybody!"

*Na = it is.

"Police-o! Tief-man-o! Neighbours-o! We done loss-o! Police-o!. . . "

There were at least five other voices besides the leader's.

Jonathan and his family were now completely paralysed by terror. Maria and the children sobbed inaudibly like lost souls. Jonathan groaned continuously.

The silence that followed the thieves' alarm vibrated horribly. Jonathan all but begged their leader to speak again and be done with it.

"My frien," said he at long last, "we don try our best for call dem but I tink say dem all done sleep-o . . . So wetin we go do now? Sometaim you wan call soja? Or you wan make we call dem for you? Soja better pass police. No be so?"

"Na so!" replied his men. Jonathan thought he heard even more voices now than before and groaned heavily. His legs were sagging under him and his throat felt like sand-paper.

"My frien, why you no de talk again. I de ask you say you wan make we call soja?"

"No."

"Awrighto. Now make we talk business. We no be bad tief. We no like for make trouble. Trouble done finish. War done finish and all the katakata wey de for inside. No Civil War again. This time na Civil Peace. No be so?"

"Na so!" answered the horrible chorus.

"What do you want from me? I am a poor man. Everything I had went with this war. Why do you come to me? You know people who have money. We . . ."

"Awright! We know you say no get plenty money. But we sef no get even anini. So derefore make you open dis window and give us one hundred pound and we go commot. Orderwise we de come for inside now to show you guitar-boy like dis . . . "

A volley of automatic fire rang through the sky. Maria and the children began to weep aloud again.

"Ah, missisi de cry again. No need for dat. We done talk say we na good tief. We just take our small money and go nwayorly. No molest. Abi we de molest?"

"At all!" sang the chorus.

"My friends," began Jonathan hoarsely. "I hear what you say and I thank you. If I had one hundred pounds . . . "

"Lookia my frien, no be play we come play for your house. If we make mistake and step for inside you no go like am-o. So derefore . . . "

"To God who made me; if you come inside and find one hundred pounds, take it and shoot me and shoot my wife and children. I swear to God. The only money I have in this life is this twenty-pounds *egg-rasher* they gave me today . . . "

"O.K. Time de go. Make you open dis window and bring the twenty pound. We go manage am like dat."

There were now loud murmurs of dissent among the chorus: "Na lie de man de lie; e get plenty money . . . Make we go inside and search properly well . . . Wetin be twenty pound? . . . "

"Shurrup!" rang the leader's voice like a lone shot in the sky and silenced the murmuring at once. "Are you dere? Bring the money quick!"

"I am coming," said Jonathan fumbling in the darkness with the key of the small wooden box he kept by his side on the mat.

At the first sign of light as neighbours and others assembled to commiserate with him he was already strapping his five-gallon demijohn to his bicycle carrier and his wife, sweating in the open fire, was turning over akara balls in the wide clay bowl of boiling oil. In the corner his eldest son was rinsing out dregs of yesterday's palm wine from old beer bottles.

"I count it as nothing," he told his sympathizers, his eyes on the rope he was tying. "What is *egg-rasher*? Did I depend on it last week? Or is it greater than other things that went with the war? I say, let *egg-rasher* perish in the flames! Let it go where everything else has gone. Nothing puzzles God."

Margaret Atwood's international reputation stems from the forceful, witty, analytic character of her style, from the intellectual substance of her feminist argument, from the literary tension she establishes between the humane and the sardonic, and from her sheer productivity. From 1961 on, she published numerous books of poetry, fiction, criticism (including the influential *Survival*, 1972), children's literature, and social commentary. Her volumes of poetry include such feminist texts as *Power Politics* (1971) and an evocative reading of Canadian women's history called *The Journals of Susanna Moodie* (1970); her novels include *The Handmaid's Tale* (1985), a dystopian satire of academic inertia and American fundamentalism. Born in Ottawa in 1939, Atwood moved to Sault Ste. Marie and Toronto; a graduate of Victoria College (Toronto) and Radcliffe College (Harvard), she has taught and has been writer-in-residence at a number of universities, an editor for the House of Anansi, a cartoonist for *This Magazine*, president of the Writers' Union of Canada, and an active supporter of Amnesty International. She now lives in Toronto.

"Scarlet Ibis" comes from her third book of stories, *Bluebeard's Egg* (1983), and like *Bodily Harm* is set in the Caribbean, where (for the Canadian visitors) cultural differences variously seem terrifying experiences or simply curious encounters. The author's interest, however, is more in the reaction to experience than in the experience itself; Atwood fastens on the reasons people are satisfied with superficiality and plastic culture, and on the ways (wit and anecdote, masks against others and walls against the world) in which they distance themselves from both the horrors around them and the horrors they are reluctant to recognize in themselves. As Rosemary Sullivan writes, in the *Oxford Companion to Canadian Literature*, Atwood has, in her stories, "designs on our psyches—we are to be instructed through the underdarkness so that we can become saner and more resilient."

MARGARET ATWOOD

FOR FURTHER READING

Margaret Atwood, *Second Words* (Toronto: Anansi, 1982).

Frank Davey, *Margaret Atwood: A Feminist Poetics* (Vancouver: Talonbooks, 1984).

Jerome H. Rosenberg, *Margaret Atwood* (Boston: Twayne, 1984).

Kathryn VanSpanckeren and Jan Garden Castro, eds. *Margaret Atwood: Vision and Form* (Carbondale: Southern Illinois UP, 1988).

Scarlet Ibis

Some years ago now, Christine went with Don to Trinidad. They took Lilian, their youngest child, who was four then. The others, who were in school, stayed with their grand-mother.

Christine and Don sat beside the hotel pool in the damp heat, drinking rum punch and eating strange-tasting ham-burgers. Lilian wanted to be in the pool all the time—she could already swim a little—but Christine didn't think it was a good idea, because of the sun. Christine rubbed sun block on her nose, and on the noses of Lilian and Don. She felt that her legs were too white and that people were look-ing at her and finding her faintly ridiculous, because of her pinky-white skin and the large hat she wore. More than likely, the young black waiters who brought the rum punch and the hamburgers, who walked easily through the sun without paying any attention to it, who joked among themselves but were solemn when they set down the glasses and plates, had put her in a category; one that included fat, although she was not fat exactly. She sug-gested to Don that perhaps he was tipping too much. Don said he felt tired.

"You felt tired before,"Christine said. "That's why we came, remember? So you could get some rest."

Don took afternoon naps, sprawled on his back on one of the twin beds in the room—Lilian had a fold-out cot—his mouth slightly open, the skin of his face pushed by gravity back down towards his ears, so that he looked tauter, thin-ner, and more aquiline in this position than he did when awake. Deader, thought Christine, taking a closer look. People lying on their backs in coffins usually—in her lim-ited experience—seemed to have lost weight. This image, of Don encoffined, was one that had been drifting through her mind too often for comfort lately.

It was hopeless expecting Lilian to have an afternoon nap too, so Christine took her down to the pool or tried to keep her quiet by drawing with her, using Magic Markers. At that age Lilian drew nothing but women or girls, wearing very fancy dresses, full-skirted, with a lot of decoration. They were always smiling, with red, curvy mouths, and had abnormally long thick eyelashes. They did not stand on any ground—Lilian was not yet putting the ground into her pictures—but floated on the page as if it were a pond they were spread out on, arms outstretched, feet at the opposite sides of their skirts, their elaborate hair billowing around their heads. Sometimes Lilian put in some birds or the sun, which gave these women the appearance of giant airborne balloons, as if the wind had caught them under their skirts and carried them off, light as feathers, away from everything. Yet, if she were asked, Lilian would say these women were walking.

After a few days of all this, when they ought to have adjusted to the heat, Christine felt they should get out of the hotel and do something. She did not want to go shopping by herself, although Don suggested it; she felt that nothing she tried on helped her look any better, or, to be more precise, that it didn't much matter how she looked. She tried to think of some other distraction, mostly for the sake of Don. Don was not noticeably more rested, although he had a sunburn—which, instead of giving him a glow of health, made him seem angry—and he'd started drumming his fingers on tabletops again. He said he was having trouble sleeping: bad dreams, which he could not remember. Also the air conditioning was clogging up his nose. He had been under a lot of pressure lately, he said.

Christine didn't need to be told. She could feel the pressure he was under, like a clenched mass of something, tissue, congealed blood, at the back of her own head. She thought of Don as being encased in a sort of metal carapace, like the shell of a crab, that was slowly tightening on him, on all parts of him at once, so that something was sure to burst, like a thumb closed slowly in a car door. The metal skin was his entire body, and Christine didn't know how to unlock it for him and let him out. She felt as if all her ministrations—the cold washcloths for his headaches, the trips to the drugstore for this or that bottle of pills, the hours of tiptoeing around, intercepting the phone, keeping Lilian quiet, above all the mere act of witnessing him, which was so draining—were noticed by him hardly at all: moths beating on the outside of a lit window, behind which someone important was thinking about something of major significance that had nothing to do with moths. This vacation, for instance, had been her idea, but Don was only getting redder and redder.

Unfortunately, it was not carnival season. There were restaurants but Lilian hated sitting still in them, and one thing Don did not need was more food and especially more drink. Christine wished Don had a sport, but considering the way he was, he would probably overdo it and break something.

"I had an uncle who took up hooking rugs," she'd said to him one evening after dinner. "When he retired. He got them in kits. He said he found it very restful." The aunt that went with that uncle used to say, "I said for better or for worse, but I never said for lunch."

"Oh, for God's sake, Christine," was all Don had to say to that. He'd never thought much of her relatives. His view was that Christine was still on the raw side of being raw material. Christine did not look forward to the time, twenty years away at least, when he would be home all day, pacing, drumming his fingers, wanting whatever it was that she could never identify and never provide.

In the morning while the other two were beginning breakfast, Christine went bravely to the hotel's reception desk. There was a thin, elegant brown girl behind it, in lime green Rasta beads, and *Vogue* make-up, coiled like spaghetti around the phone. Christine, feeling hot and porous, asked if there was any material on things to do. The girl, sliding her eyes over and past Christine as if she were a minor architectural feature, selected and fanned an assortment of brochures, continuing to laugh lightly into the phone.

Christine took the brochures into the ladies' room to preview them. Not the beach, she decided, because of the sun. Not the boutiques, not the night clubs, not the memories of Old Spain.

She examined her face, added lipstick to her lips, which were getting thin and pinched together. She really needed to do something about herself, before it was too late. She made her way back to the breakfast table. Lilian was saying that the pancakes weren't the same as the ones at home. Don said she had to eat them because she had ordered them, and if she was old enough to order for herself she was old enough to know that they cost money and couldn't be wasted like that. Christine wondered silently if it was a bad pattern, making a child eat everything on her plate, whether she liked the food or not; perhaps Lilian would become fat, later on.

Don was having bacon and eggs. Christine had asked Don to order yoghurt and fresh fruit for her, but there was nothing at her place.

"They didn't have it," Don said.

"Did you order anything else?" said Christine, who was now hungry.

"How was I supposed to know what you want?" said Don.

"We're going to see the Scarlet Ibis," Christine announced brightly to Lilian. She would ask them to bring back the menu, so she could order.

"What?" said Don. Christine handed him the brochure, which showed some red birds with long curved bills sitting in a tree; there was another picture of one close up, in profile, one demented-looking eye staring out from its red feathers like a target.

"They're very rare," said Christine, looking around for a waiter. "It's a preservation."

"You mean a preserve," said Don, reading the brochure. "In a swamp? Probably crawling with mosquitoes."

"I don't want to go," said Lilian, pushing scraps of pancake around in a pool of watery syrup. This was her other complaint, that it wasn't the right kind of syrup.

"Imitation maple flavouring," Don said, reading the label.

"You don't even know what it is," said Christine. "We'll take some fly dope. Anyway, they wouldn't let tourists go there if there were that many mosquitoes. It's a *mangrove* swamp; that isn't the same as our kind."

"I'm going to get a paper," said Don. He stood up and walked away. His legs, coming out of the bottoms of his Bermuda shorts, were still very white, with an overglaze of pink down the backs. His body, once muscular, was losing tone, sliding down towards his waist and buttocks. He was beginning to slope. From the back, he had the lax, demoralized look of a man who has been confined in an institution, though from the front he was brisk enough.

Watching him go, Christine felt the sickness in the pit of her stomach that was becoming familiar to her these days. Maybe the pressure he was under was her. Maybe she was a weight. Maybe he wanted her to lift up, blow away somewhere, like a kite, the children hanging on behind her in a long string. She didn't know when she had first noticed this feeling; probably after it had been there some time, like a knocking on the front door when you're asleep. There had been a shifting of forces, unseen, unheard, underground, the sliding against each other of giant stones; some tremendous damage had occurred between them, but who could tell when?

"Eat your pancakes," she said to Lilian, "or your father will be annoyed." He would be annoyed anyway; she annoyed him. Even when they made love, which was not frequently any more, it was perfunctory, as if he were listening for something else, a phone call, a footfall. He was like a man scratching himself. She was like his hand.

Christine had a scenario she ran through often, the way she used to run through scenarios of courtship, back in high school: flirtation, pursuit, joyful acquiescence. This was an adult scenario, however. One evening she would say to Don as he was getting up from the table after dinner, "Stay there." He would be so surprised by her tone of voice that he would stay.

"I just want you to sit there and look at me," she would say.

He would not say, "For God's sake, Christine." He would know this was serious.

"I'm not asking much from you," she would say, lying.

"What's going on?" he would say.

"I want you to see what I really look like," she would say. "I'm tired of being invisible." Maybe he would, maybe he wouldn't. Maybe he would say he was coming on with a headache. Maybe she would find herself walking on nothing, because maybe there was nothing there. So far she hadn't even come close to beginning, to giving the initial command: "Stay," as if he were a trained dog. But that was what she wanted him to do, wasn't it? "Come back" was more like it. He hadn't always been under pressure.

Once Lilian was old enough, Christine thought, she could go back to work full time. She could brush up her typing and shorthand, find something. That would be good for her; she wouldn't concentrate so much on Don, she would have a reason to look better, she would either find new scenarios or act out the one that was preoccupying her. Maybe she was making things up, about Don. It might be a form of laziness.

Christine's preparations for the afternoon were careful. She bought some mosquito repellant at a drugstore, and a chocolate bar. She took two scarves, one for herself, one for Lilian, in case it was sunny. The big hat would blow off, she thought, as they were going to be in a boat. After a short argument with one of the waiters, who said she could only have drinks by the glass, she succeeded in buying three cans of Pepsi, not chilled. All these things she packed into her bag; Lilian's bag, actually, which was striped in orange and yellow and blue and had a picture of Mickey Mouse on it. They'd used it for toys Lilian brought with her on the plane.

After lunch they took a taxi, first through the hot streets of the town, where the sidewalks were too narrow or nonexistent and the people crowded onto the road and there was a lot of honking, then out through the cane fields, the road becoming bumpier, the driver increasing speed. He drove with the car radio on, the left-hand window open, and his elbow out, a pink jockey cap tipped back on his head. Christine had shown him the brochure and asked him if he knew where the swamp was; he'd grinned at her and said everybody knew. He said he could take them, but it was too far to go out and back so he would wait there for them. Christine knew it meant extra money, but did not argue.

They passed a man riding a donkey, and two cows wandering around by the roadside, anchored by ropes around their necks which were tied to dragging stones. Christine pointed these out to Lilian. The little houses among the tall cane were made of cement blocks, painted light green or pink or light blue; they were built up on open-work foundations, almost as if they were on stilts. The women who sat on the steps turned their heads, unsmiling, to watch their taxi as it went by.

Lilian asked Christine if she had any gum. Christine didn't. Lilian began chewing on her nails, which she'd taken up since Don had been under pressure. Christine told her to stop. Then Lilian said she wanted to go for a swim. Don looked out the window. "How long did you say?" he asked. It was a reproach, not a question.

Christine hadn't said how long because she didn't know; she didn't know because she'd forgotten to ask. Finally they turned off the main road onto a smaller, muddier one, and parked beside some other cars in a rutted space that had once been part of a field.

"I meet you here," said the driver. He got out of the car, stretched, turned up the car radio. There were other drivers hanging around, some of them in cars, others sitting on the ground drinking from a bottle they were passing around, one asleep.

Christine took Lilian's hand. She didn't want to appear stupid by having to ask where they were supposed to go next. She didn't see anything that looked like a ticket office.

"It must be that shack," Don said, so they walked towards it, a long shed with a tin roof; on the other side of it was a steep bank and the beginning of the water. There were wooden steps leading down to a wharf, which was the same brown as the water itself. Several boats were tied up to it, all of similar design: long and thin, almost like barges, with rows of bench-like seats. Each boat had a small outboard motor at the back. The names painted on the boats looked East Indian.

Christine took the scarves out of her bag and tied one on her own head and one on Lilian's. Although it was beginning to cloud over, the sun was still very bright, and she knew about rays coming through overcast, especially in the tropics. She put sun block on their noses, and thought that the chocolate bar had been a silly idea. Soon it would be a brown puddle at the bottom of her bag, which luckily was waterproof. Don paced behind them as Christine knelt.

An odd smell was coming up from the water: a swamp smell, but with something else mixed in. Christine wondered about sewage disposal. She was glad she'd made Lilian go to the bathroom before they left.

There didn't seem to be anyone in charge, anyone to buy the tickets from, although there were several people beside the shed, waiting probably: two plumpish, middle-aged men in T-shirts and baseball caps turned around backwards, an athletic couple in shorts with outside pockets, who were loaded down with cameras and binoculars, a trim grey-haired woman in a tailored pink summer suit that must have been far too hot. There was another woman off to the side, a somewhat large woman in a floral print dress. She'd spread a Mexican-looking shawl on the weedy grass near the shed and was sitting down on it, drinking a pint carton of orange juice through a straw. The others looked wilted and dispirited but not this woman. For her, waiting seemed to be an activity, not something imposed: she gazed around her, at the bank, the brown water, the line of sullen mangrove trees beyond, as if she were enjoying every minute.

This woman seemed the easiest to approach, so Christine went over to her, "Are we in the right place?" she said. "For the birds."

The woman smiled at her and said they were. She had a broad face, with high, almost Slavic cheekbones and round red cheeks like those of an old-fashioned wooden doll, except that they were not painted on. Her taffy-coloured hair was done in waves and rolls, and reminded Christine of the pictures on the Toni home-permanent boxes of several decades before.

"We will leave soon," said the woman. "Have you seen these birds before? They come back only at sunset. The rest of the time they are away, fishing." She smiled again, and Christine thought to herself that it was a pity she hadn't had bands put on to even out her teeth when she was young.

This was the woman's second visit to the Scarlet Ibis preserve, she told Christine. The first was three years ago, when she stopped over here on her way to South America with her husband and children. This time her husband and children had stayed back at the hotel: they hadn't seen a swimming pool for such a long time. She and her husband were Mennonite missionaries, she said. She herself didn't seem embarrassed by this, but Christine blushed a little. She had been raised Anglican, but the only vestige of that was the kind of Christmas cards she favoured: prints of medieval or Renaissance old masters. Religious people of any serious kind made her nervous: they were like men in raincoats who might or might not be flashers. You would be going along with them in the ordinary way, and then there could be a swift movement and you would look down to find the coat wide open and nothing on under it but some pant legs held up by rubber bands. This had happened to Christine in a train station once.

"How many children do you have?" she said, to change the subject. Mennonite would explain the wide hips: they liked women who could have a lot of children.

The woman's crooked-toothed smile did not falter. "Four," she said, "but one of them is dead."

"Oh," said Christine. It wasn't clear whether the four included the one dead, or whether that was extra. She knew better than to say, "That's too bad." Such a comment was sure to produce something about the will of God, and she didn't want to deal with that. She looked to make sure Lilian was still there, over by Don. Much of the time Lilian was a given, but there were moments at which she was threatened, unknown to herself, with sudden disappearance. "That's my little girl, over there," Christine said, feeling immediately that this was a callous comment; but the woman continued to smile, in a way that Christine now found eerie.

A small brown man in a Hawaiian-patterned shirt came around from behind the shed and went quickly down the steps to the wharf. He climbed into one of the boats and lowered the outboard motor into the water.

"Now maybe we'll get some action," Don said. He had come up behind her, but he was talking more to himself than to her. Christine sometimes wondered whether he talked in the same way when she wasn't there at all.

A second man, East Indian, like the first, and also in a hula-dancer shirt, was standing at the top of the steps, and they understood they were to go over. He took their money and gave each of them a business card in return; on one side of it was a coloured picture of an ibis, on the other a name and a phone number. They went single file down the steps and the first man handed them into the boat. When they were all seated—Don, Christine, Lilian, and the pink-suited woman in a crowded row, the two baseball-cap men in front of them, the Mennonite woman and the couple with the cameras at the very front—the second man cast off and hopped lightly into the bow. After a few tries the first man got the motor started, and they putt-putted slowly towards an opening in the trees, leaving a wispy trail of smoke behind them.

It was cloudier now, and not so hot. Christine talked with the pink-suited woman, who had blonde hair elegantly done up in a French roll. She was from Vienna, she said; her husband was here on business. This was the first time she had been on this side of the Atlantic Ocean. The beaches were beautiful, much finer than those of the Mediterranean. Christine complimented her on her good English, and the woman smiled and told her what a beautiful little girl she had, and Christine said Lilian would get conceited, a word that the woman had not yet added to her vocabulary. Lilian was quiet; she had caught sight of the woman's bracelet, which was silver and lavishly engraved. The woman showed it to her. Christine began to enjoy herself, despite the fact that the two men in front of her were talking too loudly. They were drinking beer, from cans they'd brought with them in a paper bag. She opened a Pepsi and shared some with Lilian. Don didn't want any.

They were in a channel now; she looked at the trees on either side, which were all the same, dark-leaved, rising up out of the water, on masses of spindly roots. She didn't know how long they'd been going.

It began to rain, not a downpour but heavily enough, large cold drops. The Viennese woman said, "It's raining," her eyes open in a parody of surprise, holding out her hand and looking up at the sky like someone in a child's picture book. This was for the benefit of Lilian. "We will get wet," she said. She took a white embroidered handkerchief out of her purse and spread it on the top of her head. Lilian was enchanted with the handkerchief and asked Christine if she could have one, too. Don said they should have known, since it always rained in the afternoon here.

The men in baseball caps hunched their shoulders, and one of them said to the Indian in the bow, "Hey, we're getting wet!"

The Indian's timid but closed expression did not change; with apparent reluctance he pulled a rolled-up sheet of plastic out from somewhere under the front seat and handed it to the men. They spent some time unrolling it and getting it straightened out, and then everyone helped to hold the plastic overhead like a roof, while the boat glided on at its unvarying pace, through the mangroves and the steam or mist that was now rising around them.

"Isn't this an adventure?" Christine said, aiming it at Lilian. Lilian was biting her nails. The rain pattered down. Don said he wished he'd brought a paper. The men in baseball caps began to sing, sounding oddly like boys at a summer camp who had gone to sleep one day and awakened thirty years later, unaware of the sinister changes that had taken place in them, the growth and recession of hair and flesh, the exchange of their once-clear voices for the murky ones that were now singing off-key, out of time:

> "They say that in the army,
> > the girls are rather fine,
> They promise Betty Grable,
> > they give you Frankenstein . . . "

They had not yet run out of beer. One of them finished a can and tossed it overboard, and it bobbed beside the boat for a moment before falling behind, a bright red dot in the borderless expanse of dull green and dull grey. Christine felt virtuous; she'd put her Pepsi can carefully into her bag, for disposal later.

Then the rain stopped, and after some debate about whether it was going to start again or not, the two baseball-cap men began to roll up the plastic sheet. While they were doing this there was a jarring thud. The boat rocked violently, and one man who was standing up almost pitched overboard, then sat down with a jerk.

"What the hell?" he said.

The Indian at the back reversed the motor.

"We hit something," said the Viennese woman. She clasped her hands, another classic gesture.

"Obviously," Don said in an undertone. Christine smiled at Lilian, who was looking anxious. The boat started forward again.

"Probably a mangrove root," said the man with the cameras, turning half round. "They grow out under the water." He was the kind who would know.

"Or an alligator," said one of the men in baseball caps. The other man laughed.

"He's joking, darling," Christine said to Lilian.

"But we are sinking," said the Viennese woman, pointing with one outstretched hand, one dramatic finger.

Then they all saw what they had not noticed before. There was a hole in the boat, near the front, right above the platform of loose boards that served as a floor. It was the size of a small fist. Whatever they'd hit had punched right through the wood, as if it were cardboard. Water was pouring through.

"This tub must be completely rotten," Don muttered directly to Christine this time. This was a role she was sometimes given when they were among people Don didn't know: the listener. "They get like that in the tropics."

"Hey," said one of the men in baseball caps. "You up front. There's a hole in the goddamned boat."

The Indian glanced over his shoulder at the hole. He shrugged, looked away, began fishing in the breast pocket of his sports shirt for a cigarette.

"Hey. Turn this thing around," said the man with the camera.

"Couldn't we get it fixed, and then start again?" said Christine, intending to conciliate. She glanced at the Mennonite woman, hoping for support, but the woman's broad flowered back was towards her.

"If we go back," the Indian said patiently—he could understand English after all—"you miss the birds. It will be too dark."

"Yeah, but if we go forward we sink."

"You will not sink," said the Indian. He had found a cigarette, already half-smoked, and was lighting it.

"He's done it before," said the largest baseball cap. "Every week he gets a hole in the goddamned boat. Nothing to it."

The brown water continued to come in. The boat went forward.

"Right," Don said, loudly, to everyone this time. "He thinks if we don't see the birds, we won't pay him."

That made sense to Christine. For the Indians, it was a lot of money. They probably couldn't afford the gas if they lost the fares. "If you go back, we'll pay you anyway," she called to the Indian. Ordinarily she would have made this suggestion to Don, but she was getting frightened.

Either the Indian didn't hear her or he didn't trust them, or it wasn't his idea of a fair bargain. He didn't smile or reply.

For a few minutes they all sat there, waiting for the problem to be solved. The trees went past. Finally Don said, "We'd better bail. At this rate we'll be in serious trouble in about half an hour."

"I should not have come," said the Viennese woman, in a tone of tragic despair.

"What with?" said the man with the cameras. The men in baseball caps had turned to look at Don, as if he were worthy of attention.

"Mummy, are we going to sink?" said Lilian.

"Of course not, darling," said Christine. "Daddy won't let us."

"Anything there is," said the largest baseball-cap man. He poured the rest of his beer over the side. "You got a jack-knife?" he said.

Don didn't, but the man with the cameras did. They watched while he cut the top out of the can, knelt down, moved a loose platform board so he could get at the water, scooped, dumped brown water over the side. Then the other men started taking the tops off their own beer cans including the full ones, which they emptied out. Christine produced the Pepsi can from her bag. The Mennonite woman had her pint juice carton.

"No mosquitoes, at any rate," Don said, almost cheerfully.

They'd lost a lot of time, and the water was almost up to the floor platform. It seemed to Christine that the boat was becoming heavier, moving more slowly through the water, that the water itself was thicker. They could not empty much water at a time with such small containers but maybe, with so many of them doing it, it would work.

"This really *is* an adventure," she said to Lilian, who was white-faced and forlorn. "Isn't this fun?"

The Viennese woman was not bailing; she had no container. She was making visible efforts to calm herself. She had taken out a tangerine, which she was peeling, over the embroidered handkerchief which she'd spread out on her lap. Now she produced a beautiful little pen-knife with a mother-of-pearl handle. To Lilian she said, "You are hungry? Look, I will cut in pieces, one piece for you, then one for me, *ja*?" The knife was not really needed, of course. It was to distract Lilian, and Christine was grateful.

There was an audible rhythm in the boat: scrape, dump; scrape, dump. The men in baseball caps, rowdy earlier, were not at all drunk now. Don appeared to be enjoying himself, for the first time on the trip.

But despite their efforts, the level of the water was rising.

"This is ridiculous," Christine said to Don. She stopped bailing with her Pepsi can. She was discouraged and also frightened. She told herself that the Indians wouldn't keep going if they thought there was any real danger, but she wasn't convinced. Maybe they didn't care if everybody drowned; maybe they thought it was Karma. Through the hole the brown water poured, with a steady flow, like a cut vein. It was up to the level of the loose floor boards now.

Then the Mennonite woman stood up. Balancing herself, she removed her shoes, placing them carefully side by side under the seat. Christine had once watched a man do this in a subway station; he'd put the shoes under the bench where she was sitting, and a few minutes later had thrown himself in front of the oncoming train. The two shoes had remained on the neat yellow-tiled floor, like bones on a plate after a meal. It flashed through Christine's head that maybe the woman had become unhinged and was going to leap overboard; this was plausible, because of the dead child. The woman's perpetual smile was a fraud then, as Christine's would have been in her place.

But the woman did not jump over the side of the boat. Instead she bent over and moved the platform boards. Then she turned around and lowered her large flowered rump onto the hole. Her face was towards Christine now; she continued to smile, gazing over the side of the boat at the mangroves and their monotonous roots and leaves as if they were the most interesting scenery she had seen in a long time. The water was above her ankles; her skirt was wet. Did she look a little smug, a little clever or self-consciously heroic? Possibly, thought Christine, though from that round face it was hard to tell.

"Hey," said one of the men in baseball caps, "now you're cooking with gas!" The Indian in the bow looked at the woman; his white teeth appeared briefly.

The others continued to bail, and after a moment Christine began to scoop and pour with the Pepsi can again. Despite herself, the woman impressed her. The water probably wasn't that cold but it was certainly filthy, and who could tell what might be on the other side of the hole? Were they far enough south for piranhas? Yet there was the Mennonite woman plugging the hole with her bottom, serene as a brooding hen, and no doubt unaware of the fact that she was more than a little ridiculous. Christine could imagine the kinds of remarks the men in baseball caps would make about the woman afterwards. "Saved by a big butt." "Hey, never knew it had more than one use." "Finger in the dike had nothing on her." That was the part that would have stopped Christine from doing such a thing, even if she'd managed to think of it.

Now they reached the long aisle of mangroves and emerged into the open; they were in a central space, like a lake, with the dark mangroves walling it around. There was a chicken-wire fence strung across it, to keep any boats from going too close to the Scarlet Ibis' roosting area: that was what the sign said, nailed to a post that was sticking at an angle out of the water. The Indian cut the motor and they drifted towards the fence; the other Indian caught hold of the fence, held on, and the boat stopped, rocking a little. Apart from the ripples they'd caused, the water was dead flat calm; the trees doubled in it appeared black, and the sun, which was just above the western rim of the real trees, was a red disk in the hazy grey sky. The light coming from it was orangy-red and tinted the water. For a few minutes nothing happened. The man with the cameras looked at his watch. Lilian was restless, squirming on the seat. She wanted to draw; she wanted to swim in the pool. If Christine had known the whole thing would take so long she wouldn't have brought her.

"They coming," said the Indian in the bow.

"Birds ahoy," said one of the men in baseball caps, and pointed, and then there were the birds all right, flying through the reddish light, right on cue, first singly, then in flocks of four or five, so bright, so fluorescent that they were like painted flames. They settled into the trees, screaming hoarsely. It was only the screams that revealed them as real birds.

The others had their binoculars up. Even the Viennese woman had a little pair of opera glasses. "Would you look at that," said one of the men. "Wish I'd brought my movie camera."

Don and Christine were without technology. So was the Mennonite woman. "You could watch them forever," she said, to nobody in particular. Christine, afraid that she would go on to say something embarrassing, pretended not to hear her. *Forever* was loaded.

She took Lilian's hand. "See those red birds?" she said. "You might never see one of those again in your entire life." But she knew that for Lilian these birds were no more special than anything else. She was too young for them. She said, "Oh," which was what she would have said if they had been pterodactyls or angels with wings as red as blood. Magicians, Christine knew from Lilian's last birthday party, were a failure with small children, who didn't see any reason why rabbits shouldn't come out of hats.

Don took hold of Christine's hand, a thing he had not done for some time; but Christine, watching the birds, noticed this only afterwards. She felt she was looking at a picture, of exotic flowers or of red fruit growing on trees, evenly spaced, like the fruit in the gardens of mediaeval paintings, solid, clear-edged, in primary colours. On the other side of the fence was another world, not real but at the same time more real than the one on this side, the men and women in their flimsy clothes and aging bodies, the decrepit boat. Her own body seemed fragile and empty, like blown glass.

The Mennonite woman had her faced turned up to the sunset; her body was cut off at the neck by shadow, so that her head appeared to be floating in the air. For the first time she looked sad; but when she felt Christine watching her she smiled again, as if to reassure her, her face luminous and pink and round as a plum. Christine felt the two hands holding her own, mooring her, one on either side.

Weight returned to her body. The light was fading, the air chillier. Soon they would have to return in the increasing darkness, in a boat so rotten a misplaced foot would go through it. The water would be black, not brown; it would be full of roots.

"Shouldn't we go back?'" she said to Don.

Lilian said, "Mummy, I'm hungry," and Christine remembered the chocolate bar and rummaged in her bag. It was down at the bottom, limp as a slab of bacon but not liquid. She brought it out and peeled off the silver paper, and gave a square to Lilian and one to Don, and ate one herself. The light was pink and dark at the same time, and it was difficult to see what she was doing.

When she told about this later, after they were safely home, Christine put in the swamp and the awful boat, and the men singing and the suspicious smell of the water. She put in Don's irritability, but only on days when he wasn't particularly irritable. (By then, there was less pressure; these things went in phases, Christine decided. She was glad she had never said anything, forced any issues.) She put in how good Lilian had been even though she hadn't wanted to go. She put in the hole in the boat, her own panic, which she made amusing, and the ridiculous bailing with the cans, and the Indians' indifference to their fate. She put in the Mennonite woman sitting on the hole like a big fat hen, making this funny, but admiring also, since the woman's solution to the problem had been so simple and obvious that no one else had thought of it. She left out the dead child.

She put in the rather hilarious trip back to the wharf, with the Indian standing up in the bow, beaming his heavy-duty flashlight at the endless, boring mangroves, and the two men in the baseball caps getting into a mickey and singing dirty songs.

She ended with the birds, which were worth every minute of it, she said. She presented them as a form of entertainment, like the Grand Canyon: something that really ought to be seen, if you liked birds, and if you should happen to be in that part of the world.

In collaboration with Flora Eldershaw, whom she met while studying history at the University of Sydney, Marjorie Barnard (1897-1988) frequently appeared in print using the pseudonym "M. Barnard Eldershaw." Together they wrote five novels, of which *Tomorrow and Tomorrow* (1947, republished in an uncensored form in 1983) is the most widely read, an anti-Utopian analysis of the social forces that were shaping postwar Australia. Barnard was well acquainted with the limited opportunities accorded women; though she had been offered a scholarship to Oxford when she graduated from university in 1918, her father would not permit her to leave Australia. She became a librarian instead, and the man she fell in love with did not win her parents' approval. Nor did the constraints cease after her father's death in 1940, for she was then required to look after her invalid mother. But after the publication of *Tomorrow and Tomorrow*, she went on to establish a reputation as a critic, reviewer, historian (*A History of Australia* appeared in 1962), and biographer (of the novelist Miles Franklin, in 1967). Her first collection of short stories, *The Persimmon Tree and Other Stories*, appeared in 1943. Although the title story has been frequently anthologized in Australia, the volume attracted relatively little attention until the 1980s, when its subject—the inward lives of women—found a wider readership.

"The Persimmon Tree" reads on the surface like one woman's placid memories of a particular year; beneath this apparent calm lie more searing revelations of desire and protests against the way things are. This is a story in which reversals counter appearances in many ways. It takes place during an Australian spring, with plants flowering in the "wrong" season, with desire being unfulfilled, with shadows substituting for realities, with disease giving way not to health but to dis-ease. It might be a simple record of external events; it might also record the narrator's growing sense of alienation from a self and an environment she once thought were hers to achieve.

FOR FURTHER READING

Candida Baker, "Marjorie Barnard," (an interview), *Yacker 2* (Sydney: Picador, 1987): 28-41.

Robert Darby, "Introduction" to M. Barnard, *But Not For Love* (Sydney: Allen & Unwin, 1988): 1-26.

Drusilla Modjeska, *Exiles at Home: Australian Women Writers, 1925-1945* (London: Sirius, 1981).

Louise E. Rorabacher, *Marjorie Barnard and M. Barnard Eldershaw* (New York: Twayne, 1973).

MARJORIE BARNARD

The Persimmon Tree

I saw the spring come once and I won't forget it. Only once. I had been ill all the winter and I was recovering. There was no more pain, no more treatments or visits to the doctor. The face that looked back at me from my old silver mirror was the face of a woman who had escaped. I had only to build up my strength. For that I wanted to be alone, an old and natural impulse. I had been out of things for quite a long time and the effort of returning was still too great. My mind was transparent and as tender as new skin. Everything that happened, even the commonest things, seemed to be happening for the first time, and had a delicate hollow ring like music played in an empty auditorium.

I took a flat in a quiet, blind street, lined with English trees. It was one large room, high ceilinged with pale walls, chaste as a cell in a honey comb, and furnished with the passionless, standardised grace of a fashionable interior decorator. It had the afternoon sun which I prefer because I like my mornings shadowy and cool, the relaxed end of the night prolonged as far as possible. When I arrived the trees were bare and still against the lilac dusk. There was a block of flats opposite, discreet, well tended, with a wide entrance. At night it lifted its oblongs of rose and golden light far up into the sky. One of its windows was immediately opposite mine. I noticed that it was always shut against the air. The street was wide but because it was so quiet the window seemed near. I was glad to see it always shut because I spend a good deal of time at my window and it was the only one that might have overlooked me and flawed my privacy.

I liked the room from the first. It was a shell that fitted without touching me. The afternoon sun threw the shadow of a tree on my light wall and it was in the shadow that I first noticed that the bare twigs were beginning to swell with buds. A water colour, pretty and innocuous, hung on that wall. One day I asked the silent woman who served me to take it down. After that the shadow of the tree had the wall to itself and I felt cleared and tranquil as if I had expelled the last fragment of grit from my mind.

I grew familiar with all the people in the street. They came and went with a surprising regularity and they all, somehow, seemed to be cut to a very correct pattern. They were part of the mise en scene, hardly real at all and I never felt the faintest desire to become acquainted with any of them. There was one woman I noticed about my own age. She lived over the way. She had been beautiful I thought, and was still handsome with a fine tall figure. She always wore dark clothes, tailor made, and there was reserve in her every movement. Coming and going she was always alone, but you felt that that was by her own choice, that everything she did was by her own steady choice. She walked up the steps so firmly, and vanished so resolutely into the discreet muteness of the building opposite, that I felt a faint, a very faint, envy of anyone who appeared to have her life so perfectly under control.

There was a day much warmer than anything we had had, a still, warm, milky day. I saw as soon as I got up that the window opposite was open a few inches, 'Spring comes even to the careful heart,' I thought. And the next morning not only was the window open but there was a row of persimmons set out carefully and precisely on the sill, to ripen in the sun. Shaped like a young woman's breasts their deep, rich, golden-orange colour, seemed just the highlight that the morning's spring tranquility needed. It was almost a shock to me to see them there. I remembered at home when I was a child there was a grove of persimmon trees down one side of the house. In the autumn they had blazed deep red, taking your breath away. They cast a rosy light into rooms on that side of the house as if a fire were burning outside. Then the leaves fell and left the pointed dark gold fruit clinging to the bare branches. They never lost their strangeness—magical, Hesperidean trees. When I saw the Fire Bird danced my heart moved painfully because I remembered the persimmon trees in the early morning against the dark windbreak of the loquats. Why did I always think of autumn in springtime?

Persimmons belong to autumn and this was spring. I went to the window to look again. Yes, they were there, they were real. I had not imagined them, autumn fruit warming to a ripe transparency in the spring sunshine. They must have come, expensively packed in sawdust, from California or have lain all winter in storage. Fruit out of season.

It was later in the day when the sun had left the sill that I saw the window opened and a hand come out to gather the persimmons. I saw a woman's figure against the curtains. *She* lived there. It was her window opposite mine.

Often now the window was open. That in itself was like the breaking of a bud. A bowl of thick cream pottery, shaped like a boat, appeared on the sill. It was planted, I think, with bulbs. She used to water it with one of those tiny, long-spouted, hand-painted cans that you use for refilling vases, and I saw her gingerly loosening the earth with a silver table fork. She didn't look up or across the street. Not once.

Sometimes on my leisurely walks I passed her in the street. I knew her quite well now, the texture of her skin, her hands, the set of her clothes, her movements. The way you know people when you are sure you will never be put to the test of speaking to them. I could have found out her name quite easily. I had only to walk into the vestibule of her block and read it in the list of tenants, or consult the visiting card on her door. I never did.

She was a lonely woman and so was I. That was a barrier, not a link. Lonely women have something to guard. I was not exactly lonely. I had stood my life on a shelf, that was all. I could have had a dozen friends round me all day long. But there wasn't a friend that I loved and trusted above all the others, no lover, secret or declared. She had, I suppose, some nutrient hinterland on which she drew.

The bulbs in her bowls were shooting. I could see the pale new-green spears standing out of the dark loam. I was quite interested in them, wondered what they would be. I expected tulips, I don't know why. Her window was open all day long now, very fine thin curtains hung in front of it and these were never parted. Sometimes they moved but it was only in the breeze.

The trees in the street showed green now, thick with budded leaves. The shadow pattern on my wall was intricate and rich. It was no longer an austere winter pattern as it had been at first. Even the movement of the branches in the wind seemed different. I used to lie looking at the shadow when I rested in the afternoon. I was always tired then and so more permeable to impressions. I'd think about the buds, how pale and tender they were, but how implacable. The way an unborn child is implacable. If man's world were in ashes the spring would still come. I watched the moving pattern and my heart stirred with it in frail, half-sweet melancholy.

One afternoon I looked out instead of in. It was growing late and the sun would soon be gone, but it was warm. The shadows of trees and buildings fell, as they sometimes do on a fortunate day, with dramatic grace. *She* was standing there just behind the curtains, in a long dark wrap, as if she had come from her bath and was going to dress, early, for the evening. She stood so long and so still, staring out,—at the budding trees, I thought—that tension began to accumulate in my mind. My blood ticked like a clock. Very slowly she raised her arms and the gown fell from her. She stood there naked, behind the veil of the curtains, the scarcely distinguishable but unmistakable form of a woman whose face was in shadow.

I turned away. The shadow of the burgeoning bough was on the white wall. I thought my heart would break.

Born in Philadelphia, Donald Barthelme (1931-1989) was educated in Texas. After graduating from the University of Houston, he worked for a time as a museum director, and also as an editor of *Location*, a journal concerned with art and literature; this interest in the visual arts, including the cinema, is reflected in all his writing. The title of his first collection of short stories, *Come Back, Dr. Caligari* (1964) alludes to an early German film, which employed expressionistic and surrealistic techniques; and Barthelme's extraordinary mixture and manipulation of styles at times seems to approximate film more closely than traditional literary modes. The rejection of literary convention, as a means of conveying the writer's sense of absurdity or meaninglessness in life, is itself a convention which Barthelme inherits from Rabelais, Sterne, and Joyce; but his more immediate literary antecedents are Poe and Kafka. Like them, he conveys a sense of purposeless evil underlying the surface of our lives; his stories are amusing and yet macabre, turning sense into non-sense, and disturbing our notions of reality. In his novel *Snow White* (1967), and such collections of stories as *City Life* (1971), *Great Days* (1979), and *Overnight to Many Distant Cities* (1983), he moves still further away from conventional methods of narration, sometimes combining typographical devices and pictures with his text, to create a dizzying series of surreal and cryptic images. "Report," from *Unspeakable Practices, Unnatural Acts* (1968), is not experimental in terms of technique; but by his adaptation and imitation of scientific jargon, Barthelme projects a bizarre picture of the human potential for self-destruction, in an age when technology seems to have deprived us of the capacity for natural feeling.

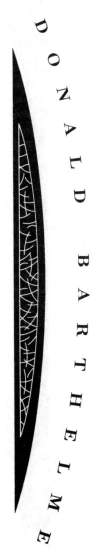

DONALD BARTHELME

FOR FURTHER READING

Critique 16, no. 3 (1975): special Barthelme issue.

Francis Gillen, "Donald Barthelme's City: A Guide," *Twentieth Century Literature* 18 (January/October 1972): 37-44.

Lois Gordon, *Donald Barthelme* (Boston: Twayne, 1981).

Wayne B. Stengel, *The Shape of Art in the Short Stories of Donald Barthelme* (Baton Rouge: Louisiana State UP, 1985).

Report

Our group is against the war. But the war goes on. I was
sent to Cleveland to talk to the engineers. The engineers
were meeting in Cleveland. I was supposed to persuade
them not to do what they are going to do. I took United's
4:45 from LaGuardia arriving in Cleveland at 6:13.
Cleveland is dark blue at that hour. I went directly to the
motel, where the engineers were meeting. Hundreds of
engineers attended the Cleveland meeting. I noticed many
fractures among the engineers, bandages, traction. I
noticed what appeared to be fracture of the carpal scaphoid
in six examples. I noticed numerous fractures of the
humeral shaft, of the os calcis, of the pelvic girdle. I
noticed a high incidence of clay-shoveller's fracture. I could
not account for these fractures. The engineers were making
calculations, taking measurements, sketching on the
blackboard, drinking beer, throwing bread, buttonholing
employers, hurling glasses into the fireplace. They were
friendly.

They were friendly. They were full of love and
information. The chief engineer wore shades. Patella in
Monk's traction, clamshell fracture by the look of it. He
was standing in a slum of beer bottles and microphone
cable. "Have some of this chicken à la Isambard Kingdom
Brunel the Great Ingineer," he said. "And declare who you
are and what we can do for you. What is your line,
distinguished guest?"

"Software," I said. "In every sense. I am here representing
a small group of interested parties. We are interested in
your thing, which seems to be functioning. In the midst of
so much dysfunction, function is interesting. Other
people's things don't seem to be working. The U.N.'s thing
doesn't seem to be working. The democratic left's thing
doesn't seem to be working. Buddha's thing—"

"Ask us anything about our thing, which seems to be working," the chief engineer said. "We will open our hearts and heads to you, Software Man, because we want to be understood and loved by the great lay public, and have our marvels appreciated by that public, for which we daily unsung produce tons of new marvels each more life-enhancing than the last. Ask us anything. Do you want to know about evaporated thin-film metallurgy? Monolithic and hybrid integrated-circuit processes? The algebra of inequalities? Optimization theory? Complex high-speed micro-miniature closed and open loop systems? Fixed variable mathematical cost searches? Epitaxial deposition of semi-conductor materials? Gross interfaced space gropes? We also have specialists in the cuckoo-flower, the doctorfish, and the dumdum bullet as these relate to aspects of today's expanding technology, and they do in the damnedest ways."

I spoke to him then about the war. I said the same things people always say when they speak against the war. I said that the war was wrong. I said that large countries should not burn down small countries. I said that the government had made a series of errors. I said that these errors once small and forgivable were now immense and unforgivable. I said that the government was attempting to conceal its original errors under layers of new errors. I said that the government was sick with error, giddy with it. I said that ten thousand of our soldiers had already been killed in pursuit of government's errors. I said that tens of thousands of the enemy's soldiers and civilians had been killed because of various errors, ours and theirs. I said that we are responsible for errors made in our name. I said that the government should not be allowed to make additional errors.

"Yes, yes," the chief engineer said, "there is doubtless much truth in what you say, but we can't possibly *lose* the war, can we? And stopping is losing, isn't it? The war regarded as a process, stopping regarded as an abort? We don't know *how* to lose a war. That skill is not among our skills. Our array smashes their array, that is what we know. That is the process. That is what is.

"But let's not have any more of this dispiriting downbeat counter-productive talk. I have a few new marvels here I'd like to discuss with you just briefly. A few new marvels that are just about ready to be gaped at by the admiring layman. Consider for instance the area of realtime online computer-controlled wish evaporation. Wish evaporation is going to be crucial in meeting the rising expectations of the world's peoples, which are as you know rising entirely too fast."

I noticed then distributed about the room a great many transverse fractures of the ulna. "The development of the pseudo-ruminant stomach for underdeveloped peoples," he went on, "is one of our interesting things you should be interested in. With the pseudo-ruminant stomach they can chew cuds, that is to say, eat grass. Blue is the most popular color worldwide and for that reason we are working with certain strains of your native Kentucky *Poa pratensis*, or bluegrass, as the staple input for the p/r stomach cycle, which would also give a shot in the arm to our balance-of-payments thing don't you know. . . . " I noticed about me then a great number of metatarsal fractures in banjo splints. "The kangaroo initiative . . . eight hundred thousand harvested last year . . . highest percentage of edible protein of any herbivore yet studied. . . . "

"Have new kangaroos been planted?"

The engineer looked at me.

"I intuit your hatred and jealousy of our thing," he said. "The ineffectual always hate our thing and speak of it as anti-human, which is not at all a meaningful way to speak of our thing. Nothing mechanical is alien to me," he said (amber spots making bursts of light in his shades), "because I am human, in a sense, and if I think it up, then 'it' is human too, whatever 'it' may be. Let me tell you, Software Man, we have been damned forbearing in the matter of this little war you declare yourself to be interested in. Function is the cry, and our thing is functioning like crazy. There are things we could do that we have not done. Steps we could take that we have not taken. These steps are, regarded in a certain light, the light of our enlightened self-interest, quite justifiable steps. We could, of course, get irritated. We could, of course, *lose patience*.

"We could, of course, release thousands upon thousands of self-powered crawling-along-the-ground lengths of titanium wire eighteen inches long with a diameter of .0005 centimetres (that is to say, invisible) which, scenting an enemy, climb up his trouser leg and wrap themselves around his neck. We have developed those. They are within our capabilities. We could, of course, release in the arena of the upper air our new improved pufferfish toxin which precipitates an identity crisis. No special technical problems there. That is almost laughably easy. We could, of course, place up to two millon maggots in their rice within twenty-four hours. The maggots are ready, massed in secret staging areas in Alabama. We have hypodermic darts capable of piebalding the enemy's pigmentation. We have rots, blights, and rusts capable of attacking his alphabet. Those are dandies. We have a hut-shrinking chemical which penetrates the fibres of the bamboo, causing it, the hut, to strangle its occupants. This operates only after 10 P.M., when people are sleeping. Their mathematics are at the mercy of a suppurating surd we have invented. We have a family of fishes trained to attack their fishes. We have the deadly testicle-destroying telegram. The cable companies are cooperating. We have a green substance that, well, I'd rather not talk about. We have a secret word that, if pronounced, produces multiple fractures in all living things in an area the size of four football fields."

"That's why—"

"Yes. Some damned fool couldn't keep his mouth shut. The point is that the whole structure of enemy life is within our power to *rend*, *vitiate*, *devour*, and *crush*. But that's not the interesting thing."

"You recount these possibilities with uncommon relish."

"Yes I realize that there is too much relish here. But you must realize that these capabilities represent in and of themselves highly technical and complex and interesting problems and hurdles on which our boys have expended many thousands of hours of hard work and brilliance. And that the effects are often grossly exaggerated by irresponsible victims. And that the whole thing represents a fantastic series of triumphs for the multi-disciplined problem solving team concept."

"I appreciate that."

"We *could* unleash all this technology at once. You can imagine what would happen then. But that's not the interesting thing."

"What is the interesting thing?"

"The interesting thing is that we have a *moral sense*. It is on punched cards, perhaps the most advanced and sensitive moral sense the world has ever known."

"Because it is on punched cards?"

"It considers all considerations in endless and subtle detail," he said. "It even quibbles. With this great new moral tool, how can we go wrong? I confidently predict that, although we *could* employ all this splendid new weaponry I've been telling you about, *we're not going to do it.*"

"We're not going to do it?"

I took United's 5:44 from Cleveland arriving at Newark at 7:19. New Jersey is bright pink at that hour. Living things move about the surface of New Jersey at that hour molesting each other only in traditional ways. I made my report to the group. I stressed the friendliness of the engineers. I said, It's all right. I said, We have a moral sense. I said, *We're not going to do it*. They didn't believe me.

Associated in the 1960s with a group called the Montreal Story Teller, Clark Blaise has moved repeatedly between Canada and the United States. Born to Canadian parents in Fargo, North Dakota in 1940, he grew up in Manitoba, on the urban American east coast, and in the rural South, and was educated in Ohio and Iowa. He now lives in San Francisco. His several books, including the collection *Resident Alien* (1986), reflect this mobility, assert his French heritage and his American upbringing, and focus on the problems of alienation that in various ways beset modern men and women. His widely praised short-story collection *A North American Education* (1973), expresses even by its title the continental range of his background; and the stories themselves, cast as personal narratives, draw readers into an intensely immediate world. The second-person narrative technique of "Eyes" enforces such a reaction, and the story's sombre tone—the watchfulness it suggests—skillfully links method with meaning. But the immediacy rises from the author's intention as well.

In an essay on the short story form—"To Begin, To Begin," the title a quotation from Donald Barthelme—Blaise asserts that theme is of secondary importance to the writer who is undergoing the process of writing a story. Narrative climax and the elegant contrivance of resolution, however important, are also of less moment than the mysteries of genesis. A good story, he says, is made by its first sentence and by the embellishments which the first paragraph gives it. The first sentence must imply its own opposite—"a good sensuous description of May sets up the possibility of a May disaster"; it must start the story neither too late nor too soon; it must disrupt and reorder the reader's sense of how things are; and it must have a rhythm all its own. The moment plot appears, in "the simple terrifying adverb: *Then*," the characters start to realize the implications of the initial mysteries; such a moment "is the cracking of the perfect, smug egg of possibility." But what preceded it is what allowed it; in the beginning is the identity that the story seems later to acquire or reveal. And in realizing and appreciating this identity, readers engage themselves with the artist in the creation of the story's own truths.

FOR FURTHER READING

Clark Blaise, "On Ending Stories," *Canadian Forum* 62 (September 1982): 7, 37.

Clark Blaise, "Portrait of the Artist as a Young Pup," *Canadian Literature* 100 (Spring 1984): 35-41.

Clark Blaise, "To Begin, To Begin," in *The Narrative Voice*, ed. John Metcalf (Toronto: McGraw-Hill Ryerson, 1972): 22-26.

Robert Lecker, *An Other I: The Fictions of Clark Blaise* (Toronto: ECW Press 1989).

You jump into this business of a new country cautiously. First you choose a place where English is spoken, with doctors and bus lines at hand, and a supermarket in a *centre d'achats* not too far away. You ease yourself into the city, approaching by car or bus down a single artery, aiming yourself along the boulevard that begins small and tree-lined in your suburb but broadens into the canyoned aorta of the city five miles beyond. And by that first winter when you know the routes and bridges, the standard congestions reported from the helicopter on your favorite radio station, you start to think of moving. What's the good of a place like this when two of your neighbors have come from Texas and the French paper you've dutifully subscribed to arrives by mail two days late? These French are all around you, behind the counters at the shopping center, in a house or two on your block; why isn't your little boy learning French at least? Where's the nearest *maternelle?** Four miles away.

In the spring you move. You find an apartment on a small side street where the dogs outnumber children and the row houses resemble London's, divided equally between the rundown and remodeled. Your neighbors are the young personalities of French television who live on delivered chicken, or the old pensioners who shuffle down the summer sidewalks in pajamas and slippers in a state of endless recuperation. Your neighbors pay sixty a month for rent, or three hundred; you pay two-fifty for a two-bedroom flat where the walls have been replastered and new fixtures hung. The bugs *d'antan* remain, as well as the hulks of cars abandoned in the fire alley behind, where downtown drunks sleep in the summer night.

*Maternelle = nursery school

Then comes the night in early October when your child is coughing badly, and you sit with him in the darkened nursery, calm in the bubbling of a cold-steam vaporizer while your wife mends a dress in the room next door. And from the dark, silently, as you peer into the ill-lit fire alley, he comes. You cannot believe it at first, that a rheumy, pasty-faced Irishman in slate-gray jacket and rubber-soled shoes has come purposely to *your* small parking space, that he has been here before and he is not drunk (not now, at least, but you know him as a panhandler on the main boulevard a block away), that he brings with him a crate that he sets on end under your bedroom window and raises himself to your window ledge and hangs there nose-high at a pencil of light from the ill-fitting blinds. And there you are, straining with him from the uncurtained nursery, watching the man watching your wife, praying silently that she is sleeping under the blanket. The man is almost smiling, a leprechaun's face that sees what you cannot. You are about to lift the window and shout, but your wheezing child lies just under you; and what of your wife in the room next door? You could, perhaps, throw open the window and leap to the ground, tackle the man before he runs and smash his face into the bricks, beat him senseless then call the cops . . . Or better, find the camera, affix the flash, rap once at the window and shoot when he turns. Do nothing and let him suffer. *He is at your mercy*, no one will ever again be so helpless—but what can you do? You know, somehow, he'll escape. If you hurt him, he can hurt you worse, later, viciously. He's been a regular at your window, he's watched the two of you when you prided yourself on being young and alone and masters of the city. He knows your child and the park he plays in, your wife and where she shops. He's a native of the place, a man who knows the city and maybe a dozen such windows, who knows the fire escapes and alleys and roofs, knows the habits of the city's heedless young.

And briefly you remember yourself, an adolescent in another country slithering through the mosquito-ridden grassy fields behind a housing development, peering into those houses where newlyweds had not yet put up drapes, how you could spend five hours in a motionless crouch for a myopic glimpse of a slender arm reaching from the dark to douse a light. Then you hear what the man cannot; the creaking of your bed in the far bedroom, the steps of your wife on her way to the bathroom, and you see her as you never have before: blond and tall and rangily built, a north-Europe princess from a constitutional monarchy, sensuous mouth and prominent teeth, pale, tennis-ball breasts cupped in her hands as she stands in the bathroom's light.

"How's Kit?" she asks. "I'd give him a kiss except that there's no blind in there," and she dashes back to bed, nude, and the man bounces twice on the window ledge.

"You coming?"

You find yourself creeping from the nursery, turning left at the hall and then running to the kitchen telephone; you dial the police, then hang up. How will you prepare your wife, not for what is happening, but for what has already taken place?"

"It's stuffy in here," you shout back, "I think I'll open the window a bit." You take your time, you stand before the blind blocking his view if he's still looking, then bravely you part the curtains. He is gone, the crate remains upright. "Do we have any masking tape?" you ask, lifting the window a crack.

And now you know the city a little better. A place where millions come each summer to take pictures and walk around must have its voyeurs too. And that place in all great cities where rich and poor co-exist is especially hard on the people in-between. It's health you've been seeking, not just beauty; a tough urban health that will save you money in the bargain, and when you hear of a place twice as large at half the rent, in a part of town free of Texans, English, and French, free of young actors and stewardesses who deposit their garbage in pizza boxes, you move again.

It is, for you, a city of Greeks. In the summer you move you attend a movie at the corner cinema. The posters advertise a war movie, in Greek, but the uniforms are unfamiliar. Both sides wear mustaches, both sides handle machine guns, both leave older women behind dressed in black. From the posters outside there is a promise of sex; blond women in slips, dark-eyed peasant girls. There will be rubble, executions against a wall. You can follow the story from the stills alone: mustached boy goes to war, embraces dark-eyed village girl. Black-draped mother and admiring young brother stand behind. Young soldier, mustache fuller, embraces blond prostitute on a tangled bed. Enter soldier, boy hides under sheets. Final shot, back in village. Mother in black; dark-eyed village girl in black. Young brother marching to the front.

You go in, pay your ninety cents, pay a nickel in the lobby for a wedge of *halvah*-like sweets. You understand nothing, you resent their laughter and you even resent the picture they're running. Now you know the Greek for "Coming Attractions," for this is a gangster movie at least thirty years old. The eternal Mediterranean gangster movie set in Athens instead of Naples or Marseilles, with smaller cars and narrower roads, uglier women and more sinister killers. After an hour the movie flatters you. No one knows you're not a Greek, that you don't belong in this theatre, or even this city. That, like the Greeks, you're hanging on.

Outside the theater the evening is warm and the wide sidewalks are clogged with Greeks who nod as you come out. Like the Ramblas in Barcelona, with children out past midnight and families walking back and forth for a long city block, the men filling the coffeehouses, the women left outside, chatting. Not a blond head on the sidewalk, not a blond head for miles. Greek music pours from the coffeehouses, flies stumble on the pastry, whole families munch their *torsades molles** as they walk. Dry goods are sold at midnight from the sidewalk, like New York fifty years ago. You're wandering happily, glad that you moved, you've rediscovered the innocence of starting over.

Then you come upon a scene directly from Spain. A slim blond girl in a floral top and white pleated skirt, tinted glasses, smoking, with bad skin, ignores a persistent young Greek in a shiny Salonika suit. "Whatsamatta?" he demands, slapping a ten-dollar bill on his open palm. And without looking back at him she drifts closer to the curb and a car makes a sudden squealing turn and lurches to a stop on the cross street. Three men are inside, the back door opens and not a word is exchanged as she steps inside. How? What refinement of gesture did we immigrants miss? You turn to the Greek boy in sympathy, you know just how he feels, but he's already heading across the street, shouting something to his friends outside a barbecue stand. You have a pocketful of bills and a Mediterranean soul, and money this evening means a woman, and blond means whore and you spend it all on another blond with open pores; all this a block from your wife and tenement. And you hurry home.

Months later you know the place. You trust the Greeks in their stores, you fear their tempers at home. Eight bathrooms adjoin a central shaft, you hear the beatings of your son's friends, the thud of fist on bone after the slaps. Your child knows no French, but he plays cricket with Greeks and Jamaicans out in the alley behind Pascal's hardware. He brings home the oily tires from the Esso station, plays in the boxes behind the appliance store. You watch from a greasy back window, at last satisfied. None of his friends is like him, like you. He is becoming Greek, becoming Jamaican, becoming a part of this strange new land. His hair is nearly white; you can spot him a block away.

On Wednesdays the butcher quarters his meat. Calves arrive by refrigerator truck, still intact but for their split-open bellies and sawed-off hooves. The older of the three brothers skins the carcass with a small thin knife that seems all blade. A knife he could shave with. The hide rolls back in a continuous flap, the knife never pops the membrane over the fat.

Another brother serves. Like yours, his French is adequate. *"Twa lif** d'hamburger,"* you request, still watching the operation on the rickety sawhorse. Who could resist? It's a Levantine treat, the calf's stumpy legs high in the air, the hide draped over the edge and now in the sawdust, growing longer by the second.

*torsades molles = soft, twisted rolls
**Twa lif = trois livres (3 pounds).

The store is filling. The ladies shop on Wednesday, especially the old widows in black overcoats and scarves, shoes and stockings. Yellow, mangled fingernails. Wednesdays attract them with boxes in the window, and they call to the butcher as they enter, the brother answers, and the women dip their fingers in the boxes. The radio is loud overhead, music from the Greek station.

"Une et soixante, m'sieur. Du bacon, jambon?"

And you think, taking a few lamb chops but not their saltless bacon, how pleased you are to manage so well. It is a Byzantine moment with blood and widows and sides of dripping beef, contentment in a snowy slum at five below.

The older brother, having finished the skinning, straightens, curses, and puts away the tiny knife. A brother comes forward to pull the hide away, a perfect beginning for a gameroom rug. Then, bending low at the rear of the glistening carcass, the legs spread high and stubby, the butcher digs in his hands, ripping hard where the scrotum is, and pulls on what seems to be a strand of rubber, until it snaps. He puts a single glistening prize in his mouth, pulls again and offers the other to his brother, and they suck.

The butcher is singing now, drying his lips and wiping his chin, and still he's chewing. The old black-draped widows with the parchment faces are also chewing. On leaving, you check the boxes in the window. Staring out are the heads of pigs and lambs, some with the eyes lifted out and a red socket exposed. A few are loose and the box is slowly dissolving from the blood, and the ice beneath.

The women have gathered around the body; little pieces are offered to them from the head and entrails. The pigs' heads are pink, perhaps they've been boiled, and hairless. The eyes are strangely blue. You remove your gloves and touch the skin, you brush against the grainy ear. How the eye attracts you! How you would like to lift one out, press its smoothness against your tongue, then crush it in your mouth. And you cannot. Already your finger is numb and the head, it seems, has shifted under you. And the eye, in panic, grows white as your finger approaches. You would take that last half inch but for the certainty, in this world you have made for yourself, that the eye would blink and your neighbors would turn upon you.

Born in New York in 1910, Paul Bowles won acclaim as a writer after he had already secured recognition for his contributions to film and the performing arts. After a short period at the University of Virginia, he travelled to Europe, then studied music with the celebrated American composers Aaron Copeland and Virgil Thomson. Subsequently he entered upon a successful career as a composer of film scores, operas, and ballets, and wrote incidental music for such plays as Tennessee Williams's *Summer and Smoke*. In 1941 his musical accomplishments were rewarded with a Guggenheim Fellowship. While still a young man, Bowles left America to travel extensively in Europe, Central America, India, and North Africa, and although his work frequently took him back to the United States, he and his wife (the writer Jane Bowles) eventually settled in Morocco. His fascination with the exotic has borne fruit in travel essays, as well as in numerous translations from works in French, Arabic, Spanish, and Italian. He has published several novels, including *The Sheltering Sky* (1949) and *Let It Come Down* (1952), and his *Collected Stories 1939-1976* appeared in 1979.

The unusual and exotic settings of Bowles's stories arise naturally from his easy familiarity with many foreign cultures, but they reflect also his dissatisfaction with Western life and manners. Some of his characters are Americans or Europeans who find themselves isolated or alienated in an environment that rejects the materialism and sophistication of the modern West. What they learn offers consolation: they are met by hostility, even violence, from a way of life that spurns them. Bowles does not offer solutions; he seems to suggest that the search for values is ultimately futile. Despite the bleakness of his vision, however, he is a fine storyteller, with the ability to realize a scene in sharp physical detail while investing it with a sense of mystery. "Allal" (1976) is a transformation tale that blends reality and fantasy in a manner suggestive of the folk tale, dramatically portraying the violence latent in all forms of life. Its Gothic quality is reminiscent of Poe's tales, and it is worth noting that Bowles's first short story collection, *The Delicate Prey* (1950), was dedicated to his mother "who first read me the stories of Poe."

FOR FURTHER READING

Paul Bowles, *Without Stopping: An Autobiography* (New York: Putnam, 1972).

Daniel Halpern, "Interview with Paul Bowles," *TriQuarterly* 33 (1975): 159-77.

L.D. Stewart, *Paul Bowles: The Illumination of North Africa* (Carbondale, Illinois: Southern Illinois UP, 1974).

Allal

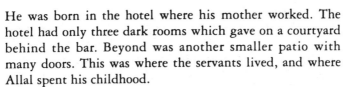

He was born in the hotel where his mother worked. The hotel had only three dark rooms which gave on a courtyard behind the bar. Beyond was another smaller patio with many doors. This was where the servants lived, and where Allal spent his childhood.

The Greek who owned the hotel had sent Allal's mother away. He was indignant because she, a girl of fourteen, had dared to give birth while she was working for him. She would not say who the father was, and it angered him to reflect that he himself had not taken advantage of the situation while he had had the chance. He gave the girl three months' wages and told her to go home to Marrakech. Since the cook and his wife liked the girl and offered to let her live with them for a while, he agreed that she might stay on until the baby was big enough to travel. She remained in the back patio for a few months with the cook and his wife, and then one day she disappeared, leaving the baby behind. No one heard of her again.

As soon as Allal was old enough to carry things, they set him to work. It was not long before he could fetch a pail of water from the well behind the hotel. The cook and his wife were childless, so that he played alone.

When he was somewhat older he began to wander over the empty table-land outside. There was nothing else up here but the barracks, and they were enclosed by a high blind wall of red adobe. Everything else was below in the valley: the town, the gardens, and the river winding southward among the thousands of palm trees. He could sit on a point of rock far above and look down at the people walking in the alleys of the town. It was only later that he visited the place and saw what the inhabitants were like. Because he had been left behind by his mother they called him a son of sin, and laughed when they looked at him. It seemed to him that in this way they hoped to make him into a shadow, in order not to have to think of him as real and alive. He awaited with dread the time when he would have to go each morning to the town and work. For the moment he helped in the kitchen and served the officers from the barracks, along with the few motorists who passed through the region. He got small tips in the restaurant, and free food and lodging in a cell of the servants' quarters, but the Greek gave him no wages. Eventually he reached an age when the situation seemed shameful, and he went of his own accord to the town below and began to work, along with other boys of his age, helping to make the mud bricks people used for building their houses.

Living in the town was much as he had imagined it would be. For two years he stayed in a room behind a blacksmith's shop, leading a life without quarrels, and saving whatever money he did not have to spend to keep himself alive. Far from making any friends during this time, he formed a thorough hatred for the people of the town, who never allowed him to forget that he was a son of sin, and therefore not like others, but *meskhot*—damned. Then he found a small house, not much more than a hut, in the palm groves outside the town. The rent was low and no one lived nearby. He went to live there, where the only sound was the wind in the trees, and avoided the people of the town when he could.

One hot summer evening shortly after sunset he was walking under the arcades that faced the town's main square. A few paces ahead of him an old man in a white turban was trying to shift a heavy sack from one shoulder to the other. Suddenly it fell to the ground, and Allal stared as two dark forms flowed out of it and disappeared into the shadows. The old man pounced upon the sack and fastened the top of it, at the same time beginning to shout: Look out for the snakes! Help me find my snakes!

Many people turned quickly around and walked back the way they had come. Others stood at some distance, watching. A few called to the old man: Find your snakes fast and get them out of here! Why are they here? We don't want snakes in this town!

Hopping up and down in his anxiety, the old man turned to Allal. Watch this for me a minute, my son. He pointed at the sack lying on the earth at his feet, and snatching up a basket he had been carrying, went swiftly around the corner into an alley. Allal stood where he was. No one passed by.

It was not long before the old man returned, panting with triumph. When the onlookers in the square saw him again, they began to call out, this time to Allal: Show that berrani the way out of town! He has no right to carry those things in here. Out! Out!

Allal picked up the big sack and said to the old man: Come on.

They left the square and went through the alleys until they were at the edge of town. The old man looked up then, saw the palm trees black against the fading sky ahead, and turned to the boy beside him.

Come on, said Allal again, and he went to the left along the rough path that led to his house. The old man stood perplexed.

You can stay with me tonight, Allal told him.

And these? he said, pointing first at the sack and then at the basket. They have to be with me.

Allal grinned. They can come.

When they were sitting in the house Allal looked at the sack and the basket. I'm not like the rest of them here, he said.

It made him feel good to hear the words being spoken. He made a contemptuous gesture. Afraid to walk through the square because of a snake. You saw them.

The old man scratched his chin. Snakes are like people, he said. You have to get to know them. Then you can be their friends.

Allal hesitated before he asked: Do you ever let them out?

Always, the old man said with energy. It's bad for them to be inside like this. They've got to be healthy when they get to Taroudant, or the man there won't buy them.

He began a long story about his life as a hunter of snakes, explaining that each year he made a voyage to Taroudant to see a man who bought them for the Aissaoua snake-charmers in Marrakech. Allal made tea while he listened, and brought out a bowl of kif paste to eat with the tea. Later, when they were sitting comfortably in the midst of the pipesmoke, the old man chuckled. Allal turned to look at him.

Shall I let them out?

Fine!

But you must sit and keep quiet. Move the lamp nearer.

He untied the sack, shook it a bit, and returned to where he had been sitting. Then in silence, Allal watched the long bodies move cautiously out into the light. Among the cobras were others with markings so delicate and perfect that they seemed to have been designed and painted by an artist. One reddish-gold serpent, which coiled itself lazily in the middle of the floor, he found particularly beautiful. As he stared at it, he felt a great desire to own it and have it always with him.

The old man was talking. I've spent my whole life with snakes, he said. I could tell you some things about them. Did you know that if you give them majoun you can make them do what you want, and without saying a word? I swear by Allah!

Allal's face assumed a doubtful air. He did not question the truth of the other's statement, but rather the likelihood of his being able to put the knowledge to use. For it was at that moment that the idea of actually taking the snake first came into his head. He was thinking that whatever he was to do must be done quickly, for the old man would be leaving in the morning. Suddenly he felt a great im-patience.

Put them away so I can cook dinner, he whispered. Then he sat admiring the ease with which the old man picked up each one by its head and slipped it into the sack. Once again he dropped two of the snakes into the basket, and one of these, Allal noted, was the red one. He imagined he could see the shining of its scales through the lid of the basket.

As he set to work preparing the meal Allal tried to think of other things. Then, since the snake remained in his mind in spite of every-thing, he began to devise a way of getting it. While he squatted over the fire in a corner, he mixed some kif paste in a bowl of milk and set is aside.

The old man continued to talk. That was good luck, getting the two snakes back like that, in the middle of the town. You can never be sure what people are going to do when they find out you're carrying snakes. Once in El Kelaa they took all of them and killed them, one after the other, in front of me. A year's work. I had to go back home and start all over again.

Even as they ate, Allal saw that his guest was growing sleepy. How will things happen? he wondered. There was no way of knowing beforehand precisely what he was going to do, and the prospect of hav-ing to handle the snake worried him. It could kill me, he thought.

Once they had eaten, drunk tea and smoked a few pipes of kif, the old man lay back on the floor and said he was going to sleep. Allal sprang up. In here! he told him, and led him to his own mat in an alcove. The old man lay down and swiftly fell asleep.

Several times during the next half hour Allal went to the alcove and peered in, but neither the body in its burnous nor the head in its tur-ban had stirred.

First he got out his blanket, and after tying three of its corners together spread it on the floor with the fourth corner facing the basket. Then he set the bowl of milk and kif paste on the blanket. As he loos-ened the strap from the cover of the basket the old man coughed. Allal stood immobile, waiting to hear the cracked voice speak. A small breeze had sprung up, making the palm branches rasp one against the other, but there was no further sound from the alcove. He crept to the far side of the room and squatted by the wall, his gaze fixed on the basket.

Several times he thought he saw the cover move slightly, but each time he decided he had been mistaken. Then he caught his breath. The shadow along the base of the basket was moving. One of the creatures had crept out from the far side. It waited for a while before continuing into the light, but when it did, Allal breathed a prayer of thanks. It was the red and gold one.

When finally it decided to go to the bowl, it made a complete tour around the edge, looking in from all sides, before lowering its head toward the milk. Allal watched, fearful that the foreign flavor of the kif paste might repel it. The snake remained there without moving.

He waited a half hour or more. The snake stayed where it was, its head in the bowl. From time to time Allal glanced at the basket, to be certain that the second snake was still in it. The breeze went on, rubbing the palm branches together. When he decided it was time, he rose slowly, and keeping an eye on the basket where apparently the other snake still slept, he reached over and gathered together the three tied corners of the blanket. Then he lifted the fourth corner, so that both the snake and the bowl slid to the bottom of the improvised sack. The snake moved slightly, but he did not think it was angry. He knew exactly where he would hide it: between some rocks in the dry river bed.

Holding the blanket in front of him he opened the door and stepped out under the stars. It was not far up the road, to a group of high palms, and then to the left down into the oued. There was a space between the boulders where the bundle would be invisible. He pushed it in with care, and hurried back to the house. The old man was asleep.

There was no way of being sure that the other snake was still in the basket, so Allal picked up his burnous and went outside. He shut the door and lay down on the ground to sleep.

Before the sun was in the sky the old man was awake, lying in the alcove coughing. Allal jumped up, went inside, and began to make a fire in the mijmah. A minute later he heard the other exclaim: They're loose again! Out of the basket! Stay where you are and I'll find them.

It was not long before the old man grunted with satisfaction. I have the black one! he cried. Allal did not look up from the corner where he crouched, the old man came over, waving a cobra. Now I've got to find the other one.

He put the snake away and continued to search. When the fire was blazing, Allal turned and said: Do you want me to help you look for it?

No, No! Stay where you are.

Allal boiled the water and made the tea, and still the old man was crawling on his knees, lifting boxes and pushing sacks. His turban had slipped off and his face ran with sweat.

Come and have tea, Allal told him.

The old man did not seem to have heard him at first. Then he rose and went into the alcove, where he rewound his turban. When he came out he sat down with Allal, and they had breakfast.

Snakes are very clever, the old man said. They can get into places that don't exist. I've moved everything in this house.

After they had finished eating, they went outside and looked for the snake between the close-growing trunks of the palms near the house.

When the old man was convinced that it was gone, he went sadly back in.

That was a good snake, he said at last. And now I'm going to Taroudant.

They said good-bye, and the old man took his sack and basket and started up the road toward the highway.

All day long as he worked, Allal thought of the snake, but it was not until sunset that he was able to go to the rocks in the oued and pull out the blanket. He carried it back to the house in a high state of excitement.

Before he untied the blanket, he filled a wide dish with milk and kif paste, and set it on the floor. He ate three spoonfuls of the paste himself and sat back to watch, drumming on the low wooden tea-table with his fingers. Everything happened just as he had hoped. The snake came slowly out of the blanket, and very soon had found the dish and was drinking the milk. As long as it drank he kept drumming; when it had finished and raised its head to look at him, he stopped, and it crawled back inside the blanket.

Later that evening he put down more milk, and drummed again on the table. After a time the snake's head appeared, and finally all of it, and the entire pattern of action was repeated.

That night and every night thereafter, Allal sat with the snake, while with infinite patience he sought to make it his friend. He never attempted to touch it, but soon he was able to summon it, keep it in front of him for as long as he pleased, merely by tapping on the table, and dismiss it at will. For the first week or so he used the kif paste; then he tried the routine without it. In the end the results were the same. After that he fed it only milk and eggs.

Then one evening as his friend lay gracefully coiled in front of him, he began to think of the old man, and formed an idea that put all other things out of his mind. There had not been any kif paste in the house for several weeks, and he decided to make some. He bought the ingredients the following day, and after work he prepared the paste. When it was done, he mixed a large amount of it in a bowl with milk and set it down for the snake. Then he himself ate four spoonfuls, washing them down with tea.

He quickly undressed, and moving the table so that he could reach it, stretched out naked on a mat near the door. This time he continued to tap on the table, even after the snake had finished drinking the milk. It lay still, observing him, as if it were in doubt that the familiar drumming came from the brown body in front of it.

Seeing that even after a long time it remained where it was, staring at him with its stony yellow eyes, Allal began to say to it over and over: Come here. He knew it could not hear his voice, but he believed it could feel his mind as he urged it. You can make them do what you want, without saying a word, the old man had told him.

Although the snake did not move, he went on repeating his command, for by now he knew it was going to come. And after another long wait, all at once it lowered its head and began to move toward him. It reached his hip and slid along his leg. Then it climbed up his leg and lay for a time across his chest. Its body was heavy and tepid, its scales wonderfully smooth. After a time it came to rest, coiled in the space between his head and his shoulders.

By this time the kif paste had completely taken over Allal's mind. He lay in a state of pure delight, feeling the snake's head against his own, without a thought save that he and the snake were together. The patterns forming and melting behind his eyelids seemed to be the same ones that covered the snake's back. Now and then in a huge frenzied movement they all swirled up and shattered into fragments which swiftly became one great yellow eye, split through the middle by the narrow vertical pupil that pulsed with his own heartbeat. Then the eye would recede, through shifting shadow and sunlight, until only the designs of the scales were left, swarming with renewed insistence as they merged and separated. At last the eye returned, so huge this time that it had no edge around it, its pupil dilated to form an aperture almost wide enough for him to enter. As he stared at the blackness within, he understood that he was being slowly propelled towards the opening. He put out his hands to touch the polished surface of the eye on each side, and as he did this he felt the pull from within. He slid through the crack and was swallowed by darkness.

On awakening Allal felt that he had returned from somewhere far away. He opened his eyes and saw, very close to him, what looked like the flank of an enormous beast, covered with coarse, stiff hair. There was a repeated vibration in the air, like distant thunder curling around the edges of the sky. He signed, or imagined that he did, for his breath made no sound. Then he shifted his head a bit, to try and see beyond the mass of hair beside him. Next he saw the ear, and he knew he was looking at his own head from the outside. He had not expected this; he had hoped only that his friend would come in and share his mind with him. But it did not strike him as being at all strange; he merely said to himself that now he was seeing through the eyes of the snake, rather than through his own.

Now he understood why the serpent had been so wary of him: from here the boy was a monstrous creature, with all the bristles on his head and his breathing that vibrated inside him like a far-off storm.

He uncoiled himself and glided across the floor to the alcove. There was a break in the mud wall wide enough to let him out. When he had pushed himself through, he lay full length on the ground in the crystal moonlight, staring at the strangeness of the landscape, where shadows were not shadows.

He crawled around the side of the house and started up the road toward the town, rejoicing in the sense of freedom different from any he had ever imagined. There was no feeling of having a body, for he was perfectly contained in the skin that covered him. It was beautiful to caress the earth with the length of his belly as he moved along the silent road, smelling the sharp veins of wormwood in the wind. When the voice of the muezzin floated out over the countryside from the mosque, he could not hear it, or know that within the hour night would end.

On catching sight of a man ahead, he left the road and hid behind a rock until the danger had passed. But then as he approached the town there began to be more people, so that he let himself down into the seguia, the deep ditch that went along beside the road. Here the stones and clumps of dead plants impeded his progress. He was still struggling along the floor of the seguia, pushing himself around the rocks and through the dry tangles of matted stalks left by the water, when dawn began to break.

The coming of daylight made him anxious and unhappy. He clambered up the bank of the seguia and raised his head to examine the road. A man walking past him, stood quite still, and then turned and ran back. Allal did not wait; he wanted now to get home as fast as possible.

Once he felt the thud of a stone as it struck the ground somewhere behind him. Quickly he threw himself over the edge of the seguia and rolled squirming down the bank. He knew the terrain here: where the road crossed the oued, there were two culverts not far apart. A man stood at some distance ahead of him with a shovel, peering down into the seguia. Allal kept moving, aware that he would reach the first culvert before the man could get to him.

The floor of the tunnel under the road was ribbed with hard little waves of sand. The smell of the mountains was in the air that moved through. There were places in here where he could have hidden, but he kept moving, and soon reached the other end. Then he continued to the second culvert and went under the road in the other direction, emerging once again into the seguia. Behind him several men had gathered at the entrance to the first culvert. One of them was on his knees, his head and shoulders inside the opening.

He now set out for the house in a straight line across the open ground, keeping his eye on the clump of palm beside it. The sun had just come up, and the stones began to cast long bluish shadows. All at once a small boy appeared from behind some nearby palms, saw him, and opened his eyes and mouth wide with fear. He was so close that

Allal went straight to him and bit him in the leg. The boy ran wildly towards the group of men in the seguia.

Allal hurried on to the house, looking back only as he reached the hole between the mud bricks. Several men were running among the trees toward him. Swiftly he glided through into the alcove. The brown body still lay near the door. But there was no time, and Allal needed time to get back to it, to lie close to its head and say: Come here.

As he stared out into the room at the body, there was a great pounding on the door. The boy was on his feet at the first blow, as if a spring had been released, and Allal saw with despair the expression of total terror in his face, and the eyes with no mind behind them. The boy stood panting, his fists clenched. The door opened and some of the men peered inside. Then with a roar the boy lowered his head and rushed through the doorway. One of the men reached out to seize him, but lost his balance and fell. An instant later all of them turned and began to run through the palm grove after the naked figure.

Even when, from time to time, they lost sight of him, they could hear the screams, and then they would see him, between the palm trunks, still running. Finally he stumbled and fell face downward. It was then that they caught him, bound him, and covered his nakedness, and took him away, to be sent one day soon to the hospital at Berrechid.

That afternoon the same group of men came to the house to carry out the search they had meant to make earlier. Allal lay in the alcove, dozing. When he awoke, they were already inside. He turned and crept to the hole. He saw the man waiting out there, a club in his hand.

The rage always had been in his heart; now it burst forth. As if his body were a whip, he sprang out into the room. The men nearest him were on their hands and knees, and Allal had the joy of pushing his fangs into two of them before a third severed his head with an axe.

Morley Callaghan (1903-1990), author of over a dozen novels, many stories, and an important memoir of Paris in the 1920s, *That Summer in Paris* (1963), enjoyed a reputation outside Canada before he became a national literary figure. One of Ernest Hemingway's co-workers at *The Toronto Star*, he published in Ezra Pound's avant-garde magazine *exile*, as well as in *Transition*, *Scribner's*, the *New Yorker* and other journals. A gathering of his work appeared in 1959 under the title *Morley Callaghan's Stories*. Yet from the 1930s until Edmund Wilson rediscovered him in 1960—"a writer whose work may be mentioned without absurdity in association with Chekhov's and Turgenev's"—he was virtually unknown. With English critics responding warmly to his work in the 1970s, his fortunes again altered; throughout, however, Callaghan himself remained fiercely committed to a sense of artistic independence.

Born and educated in Toronto, he won several Canadian literary prizes. Yet his style and literary intention were shaped less by the cultural milieu in Toronto than by what he refers to as his own "North American" consciousness; Hemingway, Scott Fitzgerald, and particularly Sherwood Anderson were his guides. He worked at paring from his style any words that might draw attention away from his protagonists; he was concerned with focusing on moral dilemmas and with presenting clearly the forces that turn ordinary events in ordinary lives into momentous drama. The result can more easily be termed parable than naturalism. If his stories are realistic, they are so only within their own terms; at their best they have the power of truth without the interference of petty detail, and the credibility that accompanies intense conviction. The impact of "Two Fishermen" (*Now that April's here and other stories*, 1936) derives from the tension between deeply held moral convictions and the placid surface style. Where the story leads is into a contemplation of the ways in which abstract principles—justice, for example—take real and imperfect forms, and so rake the lives of the people for whom they still have meaning.

FOR FURTHER READING

Morley Callaghan, "An Ocean Away," *Times Literary Supplement*, 4 June 1964, p. 493.
Fraser Sutherland, *The Style of Innocence* (Toronto: Clark, Irwin, 1972).
Edmund Wilson, *O Canada* (New York: Farrar, Straus & Giroux, 1965).

Two Fishermen

The only reporter on the town paper, the *Examiner*, was Michael Foster, a tall long-legged, eager young fellow, who wanted to go to the city some day and work on an important newspaper.

The morning he went into Bagley's Hotel, he wasn't at all sure of himself. He went over to the desk and whispered to the proprietor, Ted Bagley, "Did he come here, Mr. Bagley?"

Bagley said slowly, "Two men came here from this morning's train. They're registered." He put his spatulate forefinger on the open book and said, "Two men. One of them's a drummer. This one here T. Woodley. I know because he was through this way last year and just a minute ago he walked across the road to Molson's hardware store. The other one . . . here's his name, K. Smith."

"Who's K. Smith?" Michael asked.

"I don't know. A mild, harmless-looking little guy."

"Did he look like the hangman, Mr. Bagley?"

"I couldn't say that, seeing as I never saw one. He was awfully polite and asked where he could get a boat so he could go fishing on the lake this evening, so I said likely down at Smollet's place by the power-house."

"Well, thanks. I guess if he was the hangman, he'd go over to the jail first," Michael said.

He went along the street, past the Baptist church to the old jail with the high brick fence around it. Two tall maple trees, with branches drooping low over the sidewalk, shaded one of the walls from the morning sunlight. Last night, behind those walls, three carpenters, working by lamplight, had nailed the timbers for the scaffold. In the morning, young Thomas Delaney, who had grown up in the town, was being hanged: he had killed old Matthew Rhinehart whom he had caught molesting his wife when she had been berrypicking in the hills behind town. There had been a struggle and Thomas Delaney had taken a bad beating before he had killed Rhinehart. Last night a crowd had gathered on the sidewalk by the lamppost, and while moths and smaller insects swarmed around the high blue carbon light, the crowd had thrown sticks and bottles and small stones at the out-of-town workmen in the jail yard. Billy Hilton, the town constable, had stood under the light with his head down, pretending not to notice anything. Thomas Delaney was only three years older than Michael Foster.

Michael went straight to the jail office, where Henry Steadman, the sheriff, a squat, heavy man, was sitting on the desk idly wetting his long moustaches with his tongue. "Hello, Michael, what do you want?" he asked.

"Hello, Mr. Steadman, the *Examiner* would like to know if the hangman arrived yet."

"Why ask me?"

"I thought he'd come here to test the gallows. Won't he?"

"My, you're a smart young fellow, Michael, thinking of that."

"Is he in there now, Mr. Steadman?"

"Don't ask me. I'm saying nothing. Say, Michael, do you think there's going to be trouble? You ought to know. Does anybody seem sore at me? I can't do nothing. You can see that."

"I don't think anybody blames you, Mr. Steadman. Look here, can't I see the hangman? Is his name K. Smith?"

"What does it matter to you, Michael? Be a sport, go on away and don't bother us any more."

"All right, Mr. Steadman," Michael said very competently, "just leave it to me."

Early that evening, when the sun was setting, Michael Foster walked south of the town on the dusty road leading to the powerhouse and Smollet's fishing pier. He knew that if Mr. K. Smith wanted to get a boat he would go down to the pier. Fine powdered road dust whitened Michael's shoes. Ahead of him he saw the power-plant, square and low, and the smooth lake water. Behind him the sun was hanging over the blue hills beyond the town and shining brilliantly on square patches of farm land. The air around the power-house smelt of steam.

Out of the jutting, tumbledown pier of rock and logs, Michael saw a little fellow without a hat, sitting down with his knees hunched up to his chin, a very small man with little gray baby curls on the back of his neck, who stared steadily far out over the water. In his hand he was holding a stick with a heavy fishing-line twined around it and a gleaming copper spoon bait, the hooks brightened with bits of feathers such as they used in the neighbourhood when trolling for lake trout. Apprehensively Michael walked out over the rocks toward the stranger and called, "Were you thinking of going fishing, mister?" Standing up, the man smiled. He had a large head, tapering down to a small chin, a birdlike neck and a very wistful smile. Puckering his mouth up, he said shyly to Michael, "Did you intend to go fishing?"

"That's what I came down here for. I was going to get a boat back at the boat-house there. How would you like if we went together?"

"I'd like it first rate," the shy little man said eagerly. "We could take turns rowing. Does that appeal to you?"

"Fine. Fine. You wait here and I'll go back to Smollet's place and ask for a row-boat and I'll row around here and get you."

"Thanks. Thanks very much," the mild little man said as he began to untie his line. He seemed very enthusiastic.

When Michael brought the boat around to the end of the old pier and invited the stranger to make himself comfortable so he could handle the line, the stranger protested comically that he ought to be allowed to row.

Pulling strongly at the oars, Michael was soon out in the deep water and the little man was letting his line out slowly. In one furtive glance, he had noticed that the man's hair, gray at the temples, was inclined to curl to his ears. The line was out full length. It was twisted around the little man's forefinger, which he let drag in the water. And then Michael looked full at him and smiled because he thought he seemed so meek and quizzical. "He's a nice little guy," Michael assured himself and he said, "I work on the town paper, the *Examiner*."

"Is it a good paper? Do you like the work?"

"Yes. But it's nothing like a first-class city paper and I don't expect to be working on it long. I want to get a reporter's job on a city paper. My name's Michael Foster.

"Mine's Smith. Just call me Smitty."

"I was wondering if you'd been over to the jail yet."

Up to this time the little man had been smiling with the charming ease of a small boy who finds himself free, but now he became furtive and disappointed. Hesitating, he said, "Yes, I was over there first thing this morning."

"Oh, I just knew you'd go there," Michael said. They were a bit afraid of each other. By this time they were far out on the water which had a mill-pond smoothness. The town seemed to get smaller, with white houses in rows and streets forming geometric patterns, just as the blue hills behind the town seemed to get larger at sundown.

Finally Michael said, "Do you know this Thomas Delaney that's dying in the morning?" He knew his voice was slow and resentful.

"No. I don't know anything about him. I never read about them. Aren't there any fish at all in this old lake? I'd like to catch some fish," he said rapidly. "I told my wife I'd bring her home some fish." Glancing at Michael, he was appealing, without speaking, that they should do nothing to spoil an evening's fishing.

The little man began to talk eagerly about fishing as he pulled out a small flask from his hip pocket. "Scotch," he said, chuckling with delight. "Here, take a swig." Michael drank from the flask and passed it back. Tilting his head back and saying, "Here's to you, Michael," the little man took a long pull at the flask. "The only time I take a drink," he said still chuckling, "is when I go on a fishing trip by myself. I usually go by myself," he added apologetically as if he wanted the young fellow to see how much he appreciated his company.

They had gone far out on the water but they had caught nothing. It began to get dark. "No fish tonight, I guess, Smitty." Michael said.

"It's a crying shame," Smitty said. "I looked forward to coming up here when I found out the place was on the lake. I wanted to get some fishing in. I promised my wife I'd bring her back some fish. She'd often like to go fishing with me, but of course, she can't because she can't travel around from place to place like I do. Whenever I get a call to go some place, I always look at the map to see if it's by a lake or on a river, then I take my lines and hooks along."

"If you took another job, you and your wife could probably go fishing together," Michael suggested.

"I don't know about that. We sometimes go fishing together anyway." He looked away, waiting for Michael to be repelled and insist that he ought to give up the job. And he wasn't ashamed as he looked down at the water, but he knew that Michael thought he ought to be ashamed. "Somebody's got to do my job. There's got to be a hangman," he said.

"I just meant that if it was such disagreeable work, Smitty."

The little man did not answer for a long time. Michael rowed steadily with sweeping, tireless strokes. Huddled at the end of the boat, Smitty suddenly looked up with a kind of melancholy hopelessness and said mildly, "The job hasn't been so disagreeable."

"Good God, man, you don't mean you like it?"

"Oh, no," he said, to be obliging, as if he knew what Michael expected him to say, "I mean you get used to it, that's all." But he looked down again at the water, knowing he ought to be ashamed of himself.

"Have you got any children?"

"I sure have. Five. The oldest boy is fourteen. It's funny, but they're all a lot bigger and taller than I am. Isn't that funny?"

They started a conversation about fishing rivers that ran into the lake farther north. They felt friendly again. The little man, who had an extraordinary gift for story-telling, made many quaint faces, puckered up his lips, screwed up his eyes and moved around restlessly as if he wanted to get up in the boat and stride around for the sake of more expression. Again he brought out the whiskey flask and Michael stopped rowing. Grinning, they toasted each other and said together,

"Happy days." The boat remained motionless on the placid water. Far out, the sun's last rays gleamed on the water-line. And then it got dark and they could only see the town lights. It was time to turn around and pull for the shore. The little man tried to take the oars from Michael, who shook his head resolutely and insisted that he would prefer to have his friend catch a fish on the way back to the shore.

"It's too late now, and we may have scared all the fish away." Smitty laughed happily. "But we're having a grand time, aren't we?"

When they reached the old pier by the power-house, it was full night and they hadn't caught a single fish. As the boat bumped against the rocks Michael said, "You can get out here. I'll take the boat around to Smollet's."

"Won't you be coming my way?"

"Not just now. I'll probably talk with Smollet a while."

The little man got out of the boat and stood on the pier looking down at Michael. "I was thinking dawn would be the best time to catch some fish," he said. "At about five o'clock. I'll have an hour and a half to spare anyway. How would you like that?" He was speaking with so much eagerness that Michael found himself saying, "I could try. But if I'm not here at dawn, you go on without me."

"All right. I'll walk back to the hotel now."

"Good night, Smitty."

"Good night, Michael. We had a fine neighbourly time, didn't we?"

As Michael rowed the boat around to the boat-house, he hoped that Smitty wouldn't realize he didn't want to be seen walking back to town with him. And later, when he was going slowly along the dusty road in the dark and hearing all the crickets chirping in the ditches, he couldn't figure out why he felt so ashamed of himself.

At seven o'clock next morning Thomas Delaney was hanged in the town jail yard. There was hardly a breeze on that leaden gray morning and there were no small whitecaps out over the lake. It would have been a fine morning for fishing. Michael went down to the jail, for he thought it his duty as a newspaperman to have all the facts, but he was afraid he might get sick. He hardly spoke to all the men and women who were crowded under the maple trees by the jail wall. Everybody he knew was staring at the wall and muttering angrily. Two of Thomas Delaney's brothers, big, strapping fellows with bearded faces, were there on the sidewalk. Three automobiles were at the front of the jail.

Michael, the town newspaperman, was admitted into the courtyard by old Willie Mathews, one of the guards, who said that two newspapermen from the city were at the gallows on the other side of the building. "I guess you can go around there, too, if you want to," Mathews said, as he sat down slowly on the step. White-faced, and afraid, Michael sat down on the step with Mathews and they waited and said nothing.

At last the old fellow said, "Those people outside there are pretty sore, ain't they?"

"They're pretty sullen, all right. I saw two of Delaney's brothers there."

"I wish they'd go," Mathews said. "I don't want to see anything. I didn't even look at Delaney. I don't want to hear anything. I'm sick." He put his head back against the wall and closed his eyes.

The old fellow and Michael sat close together till a small procession came around the corner from the other side of the yard. First came Mr. Steadman, the sheriff, with his head down as though he were crying, then Dr. Parker, the physician, then two hard-looking young newspapermen from the city, walking with their hats on the backs of their heads, and behind them came the little hangman, erect, stepping out with military precision and carrying himself with a strange cocky dignity. He was dressed in a long black cutaway coat with gray striped trousers, a gates-ajar collar and narrow red tie, as if he alone felt the formal importance of the occasion. He walked with brusque precision till he saw Michael, who was standing up, staring at him with his mouth open.

The little hangman grinned and soon as the procession reached the doorstep, he shook hands with Michael. They were all looking at Michael. As though his work were over now, the hangman said eagerly to Michael, "I thought I'd see you here. You didn't get down to the pier at dawn?"

"No. I couldn't make it."

"That was tough, Michael. I looked for you," he said. "But never mind. I've got something for you." As they all went into the jail, Dr. Parker glanced angrily at Michael, then turned his back on him. In the office, where the doctor prepared to sign a certificate, Smitty was bending down over his fishing-basket which was in the corner. Then he pulled out two good-sized salmon-bellied trout, folded in a newspaper, and said, "I was saving these for you, Michael. I got four in an hour's fishing." Then he said, "I'll talk about that later, if you wait. We'll be busy here, and I've got to change my clothes."

Michael went out to the street with Dr. Parker and the two city newspapermen. Under his arm he was carrying the fish, folded in the newspaper. Outside, at the jail door, Michael thought that the doctor and the two newspapermen were standing a little apart from him. Then the small crowd, with their clothes all dust-soiled from the road, surged forward and the doctor said to them, "You might as well go home, boys. It's all over."

"Where's old Steadman?" somebody demanded. "We'll wait for the hangman," somebody else shouted.

The doctor walked away by himself. For a while Michael stood beside the two city newspapermen, and tried to look as nonchalant as they were looking, but he lost confidence in them when he smelled whiskey. They only talked to each other. Then they mingled with the crowd, and Michael stood alone. At last he could stand there no longer looking at all those people he knew so well, so he, too, moved out and joined the crowd.

When the sheriff came out with the hangman and two of the guards, they got half-way down to one of the automobiles before someone threw an old boot. Steadman ducked into one of the cars, as the boot hit him on the shoulder, and the two guards followed him. Those in the car must have thought at first that the hangman was with them for the car suddenly shot forward, leaving him alone on the sidewalk. The crowd threw small rocks and sticks, hooting at him as the automobile backed up slowly towards him. One small stone hit him on the head. Blood trickled from the side of his head as he looked around helplessly at all the angry people. He had the same expression on his face, Michael thought, as he had had last night when he had seemed ashamed and had looked down steadily at the water. Only now, he looked around wildly, looking for someone to help him as the crowd kept pelting him. Farther and farther Michael backed into the crowd and all the time he felt dreadfully ashamed as though he were betraying Smitty, who last night had had such a good neighbourly time with him. "It's different now, it's different," he kept thinking, as he held the fish in the newspaper tight under his arm. Smitty started to run toward the automobile but James Mortimer, a big fisherman, shot out his foot and tripped him and sent him sprawling on his face.

Mortimer, the big fisherman, looking for something to throw, said to Michael, "Sock him, sock him."

Michael shook his head and felt sick.

"What's the matter with you, Michael?"

"Nothing. I got nothing against him."

The big fisherman started pounding his fists up and down in the air. "He just doesn't mean anything to me at all," Michael said quickly. The fisherman, bending down, kicked a small rock loose from the road bed and heaved it at the hangman. Then he said, "What are you holding there, Michael, what's under your arm? Fish. Pitch them at him. Here, give them to me." Still in a fury, he snatched the fish, and threw them one at a time at the little man just as he was getting up from the road. The fish fell in the thick dust in front of him, sending up a little cloud. Smitty seemed to stare at the fish with his mouth hanging open, then he didn't even look at the crowd. That expression on Smitty's face as he saw the fish on the road made Michael hot with shame and he tried to get out of the crowd.

Smitty had his hands over his head, to shield his face as the crowd pelted him, yelling, "Sock the little rat. Throw the runt in the lake." The sheriff pulled him into the automobile. The car shot forward in a cloud of dust.

Born in Bacchus Marsh, Victoria, in 1943, and now a resident of Sydney, Peter Carey is one of the several contemporary stylists who have been refashioning short fiction in Australia. Like some of the others, he is a social iconoclast, working in fantasy. Elements of the fantastic are everywhere in his work, yet they do not provide escapist entertainment; paradoxically the fantastic serves instead to expose the ordinary cruelties that people tend passively to accept in their society. Writing in his introduction to *New Australian Short Stories* (1981), Craig Munro refers to Carey's "uncanny flair for significant settings and events." The significance derives from the associative resonances of his settings; the reader supplies it, recognizing the degree of overlap between the fictional exaggerations and ordinary life. The stories, Munro adds, "seem to fuse the past, present and future into super-real scenarios in which the gap between the observed and the imagined disappears."

Carey has published several novels and short story collections including *The Fat Man in History* (1974) and *War Crimes* (1979), in which "'Do You Love Me?'" appeared. His novel *Bliss* appeared in 1981 and was subsequently filmed; another novel, *Oscar and Lucinda*, won the Booker Prize in 1988. The sardonic comedy of "'Do You Love Me?'" characterizes much of Carey's fiction. His stories amuse, but they also expose weaknesses in the fabric of society. Critical of those who accept the mapmakers' version of events and also of those who emptily reject the mapmakers, Carey shows that uncertainty can sometimes prove debilitating. Those who accept received standards as though they were universal truths and those who dispute such standards without having anything adequate to replace them alike empty the world of love—and therefore potentially of meaning.

FOR FURTHER READING

Helen Daniel, *Liars* (Ringwood: Penguin, 1988).

Ken Gelder and Paul Salzman, *The New Diversity* (Melbourne: McPhee Gribble, 1989).

Van Ikin, "Peter Carey: the stories," *Science Fiction* 1 (June 1977): 19-29.

Craig Munro, Interview with Peter Carey, *Australian Literary Studies* 8 (1977): 182-87.

Elizabeth Webby, "Australian Short Fiction from While the Billy Boils to The Everlasting Secret Family," *Australian Literary Studies* 10 (1981): 147-64.

<h1>"Do You Love Me?"</h1>

1. The Role of the Cartographers

Perhaps a few words about the role of the Cartographers in our present society are warranted.

To begin with one must understand the nature of the yearly census, a manifestation of our desire to know, always, exactly where we stand. The census, originally a count of the population, has gradually extended until it has become a total inventory of the contents of the nation, a mammoth task which is continuing all the time—no sooner has one census been announced than work on another begins.

The results of the census play an important part in our national life and have, for many years, been the pivot point for the yearly "Festival of the Corn" (an ancient festival, related to the wealth of the earth).

We have a passion for lists. And nowhere is this more clearly illustrated than in the Festival of the Corn which takes place in midsummer, the weather always being fine and warm. On the night of the festival, the householders move their goods and possessions, all furniture, electrical goods, clothing, rugs, kitchen utensils, bathrobes, slippers, cushions, lawnmowers, curtains, doorstops, heirlooms, cameras, and anything else that can be moved into the street so that the census officials may the more easily check the inventory of each household.

The Festival of the Corn is, however, much more than a clerical affair. And, the day over and the night come, the householders invite each other to view their possessions which they refer to, on this night, as gifts. It is like nothing more than a wedding feast—there is much cooking, all sorts of traditional dishes, fine wines, strong liquors, music is played loudly in quiet neighbourhoods, strangers copulate with strangers, men dance together, and maidens in yellow robes distribute small barley sugar corn-cobs to young and old alike.

And in all this the role of the Cartographers is perhaps the most important, for our people crave, more than anything else, to know the extent of the nation, to know, exactly, the shape of the coastline, to hear what land may have been lost to the sea, to know what has been reclaimed and what is still in doubt. If the Cartographers' report is good the Festival of the Corn will be a good festival. If the report is bad, one can always sense, for all the dancing and drinking, a feeling of nervousness and apprehension in the revellers, a certain desperation. In the year of a bad Cartographers' report there will always be fights and, occasionally, some property will be stolen as citizens attempt to compensate themselves for their sense of loss.

Because of the importance of their job the Cartographers have become an elite—well-paid, admired, envied, and having no small opinion of themselves. It is said by some that they are overproud, immoral, vain and foot-loose, and it is perhaps the last charge (by necessity true) that brings about the others. For the Cartographers spend their years travelling up and down the coast, along the great rivers, traversing great mountains and vast deserts. They travel in small parties of three, four, sometimes five, making their own time, working as they please, because eventually it is their own responsibility to see that their team's task is completed in time.

My father, a Cartographer himself, often told me stories about himself or his colleagues and the adventures they had in the wilderness.

There were other stories, however, that always remained in my mind and, as a child, caused me considerable anxiety. These were the stories of the nether regions and I doubt if they were known outside a very small circle of Cartographers and government officials. As a child in a house frequented by Cartographers, I often heard these tales which invariably made me cling closely to my mother's skirts.

It appears that for some time certain regions of the country had become less and less real and these regions were regarded fearfully even by the Cartographers, who prided themselves on their courage. The regions in question were invariably uninhabited, unused for agriculture or industry. There were certain sections of the Halverson Ranges, vast stretches of the Greater Desert, and long pieces of coastline which had begun to slowly disappear like the image on an improperly fixed photograph.

It was because of these nebulous areas that the Fischerscope was introduced. The Fischerscope is not unlike radar in its principle and is able to detect the presence of any object, no matter how dematerialized or insubstantial. In this way the Cartographers were still able to map the questionable parts of the nether regions. To have returned with blanks on the maps would have created such public anxiety that no one dared think what it might do to the stability of our society. I now have reason to believe that certain areas of the country disappeared so completely that even the Fischerscope could not detect them and the Cartographers, acting under political pressure, used old maps to fake-in the missing sections. If my theory is grounded in fact, and I am sure it is, it would explain my father's cynicism about the Festival of the Corn.

2. The Archetypal Cartographer

My father was in his fifties but he had kept himself in good shape. His skin was brown and his muscles still firm. He was a tall man with a thick head of grey hair, a slightly less grey moustache and a long aquiline nose. Sitting on a horse he looked as proud and cruel as Ghenghis Khan. Lying on the beach clad only in bathers and sunglasses he still managed to retain his authoritative air.

Beside him I always felt as if I had betrayed him. I was slightly built, more like my mother.

It was the day before the festival and we lay on the beach, my father, my mother, my girlfriend and I. As was usual in these circumstances my father addressed all his remarks to Karen. He never considered the members of his own family worth talking to. I always had the uncomfortable feeling that he was flirting with my girlfriends and I never knew what to do about it.

People were lying in groups up and down the beach. Near us a family of five were playing with a large beach ball.

"Look at those fools," my father said to Karen.

"Why are they fools?" Karen asked.

"They're fools," said my father. "They were born fools and they'll die fools. Tomorrow they'll dance in the streets and drink too much."

"So," said Karen triumphantly, in the manner of one who has become privy to secret information. "It will be a good Cartographers' report?"

My father roared with laughter.

Karen looked hurt and pouted. "Am I am fool?"

"No," my father said, "you're really quite splendid."

3. The Most Famous Festival

The festival, as it turned out, was the greatest disaster in living memory.

The Cartographers' report was excellent, the weather was fine, but somewhere something had gone wrong.

The news was confusing. The television said that, in spite of the good report, various items had been stolen very early in the night. Later there was a news flash to say that a large house had completely disappeared in Howie Street.

Later still we looked out the window to see a huge band of people carrying lighted torches. There was a lot of shouting. The same image, exactly, was on the television and a reporter was explaining that bands of vigilantes were out looking for thieves.

My father stood at the window, a martini in his hand, and watched the vigilantes set alight a house opposite.

My mother wanted to know what we should do.

"Come and watch the fools," my father said, "they're incredible."

4. The I.C.I. Incident

The next day the I.C.I. building disappeared in front of a crowd of two thousand people. It took two hours. The crowd stood silently as the great steel and glass structure slowly faded before them.

The staff who were evacuated looked pale and shaken. The caretaker who was amongst the last to leave looked almost translucent. In the days that followed he made some name for himself as a mystic, claiming that he had been able to see other worlds, layer upon layer, through the fabric of the here and now.

5. Behaviour When Confronted With Dematerialization

The anger of our people when confronted with acts of theft has always been legendary and was certainly highlighted by the incidents which occurred on the night of the festival.

But the fury exhibited on this famous night could not compare with the intensity of emotion displayed by those who witnessed the earliest scenes of dematerialization.

The silent crowd who watched the I.C.I. building erupted into hysteria when they realized that it had finally gone and wasn't likely to come back.

It was like some monstrous theft for which punishment must be meted out.

They stormed into the Shell building next door and smashed desks and ripped down office partitions. Reporters who attended the scene were rarely impartial observers, but one of the cooler headed members of the press remarked on the great number of weeping men and women who hurled typewriters from windows and scattered files through crowds of frightened office workers.

Five days later they displayed similar anger when the Shell building itself disappeared.

6. Behaviour of Those Dematerializing

The first reports of dematerializing people were not generally believed and were suppressed by the media. But these things were soon common knowledge and few families were untouched by them. Such incidents were obviously not all the same but in many victims there was a tendency to exhibit extreme aggression towards those around them. Murders and assaults committed by these unfortunates were not uncommon and in most cases they exhibited an almost unbelievable rage, as if they were the victims of a shocking betrayal.

My friend James Bray was once stopped in the street by a very beautiful woman who clawed and scratched his face and said: "You did this to me you bastard, you did this to me."

He had never seen her before but he confessed that, in some irrational way, he felt responsible and didn't defend himself. Fortunately she disappeared before she could do him much damage.

7. Some Theories That Arose at the Time

1. The world is merely a dream dreamt by god who is waking after a long sleep. When he is properly awake the world will disappear completely. When the world disappears we will disappear with it and be happy.

2. The world has become sensitive to light. In the same way that prolonged use of say penicillin can suddenly result in a dangerous allergy, prolonged exposure of the world to the sun has made it sensitive to light.

   The advocates of this theory could be seen bustling through the city crowds in their long, hooded black robes.

3. The fact that the world is disappearing has been caused by the sloppy work of the Cartographers and census takers. Those who filled out their census forms incorrectly would lose those items they had neglected to describe. People overlooked in the census by impatient officials would also disappear. A strong pressure group demanded that a new census be taken quickly before matters got worse.

8. My Father's Theory

The world, according to my father, was exactly like the human body and had its own defence mechanisms with which it defended itself against anything that either threatened it or was unnecessary to it. The I.C.I. building and the I.C.I. company had obviously constituted some threat to the world or had simply been irrelevant. That's why it had disappeared and not because some damn fool god was waking up and rubbing his eyes.

"I don't believe in god," my father said. "Humanity is god. Humanity is the only god I know. If humanity doesn't need something it will disappear. People who are not loved will disappear. Everything that is not loved will disappear from the face of the earth. We only exist through the love of others and that's what it's all about.

9. A Contradiction

"Look at those fools," my father said, "they wouldn't know if they were up themselves."

10. An Unpleasant Scene

The world at this time was full of unpleasant and disturbing scenes. One that I recall vividly took place in the middle of the city on a hot, sultry Tuesday afternoon. It was about one-thirty and I was waiting for Karen by the post office when a man of forty or so ran past me. He was dematerializing rapidly. Everybody seemed to be deliberately looking the other way, which seemed to me to make him dematerialize faster. I stared at him hard, hoping that I could do something to keep him there until help arrived. I tried to love him, because I believed in my father's theory. I thought, I must love that man. But his face irritated me. It is not so easy to love a stranger and I'm ashamed to say that he had the small mouth and close-together eyes that I have always disliked in a person. I tried to love him but I'm afraid I failed.

While I watched he tried to hail taxi after taxi. But the taxi drivers were only too well aware of what was happening and had no wish to spend their time driving a passenger who, at any moment, might cease to exist. They looked the other way or put up their NOT FOR HIRE signs.

Finally he managed to way-lay a taxi at some traffic lights. By this time he was so insubstantial that I could see right through him. He was beginning to shout. A terrible thin noise, but penetrating nonetheless. He tried to open the cab door, but the driver had already locked it. I could hear the man's voice, high and piercing: "I want to go home." He repeated it over and over again. "I want to go home to my wife."

The taxi drove off when the lights changed. There was a lull in the traffic. People had fled the corner and left it deserted and it was I alone who saw the man finally disappear.

I felt sick.

Karen arrived five minutes later and found me pale and shaken. "Are you alright?" she said.

"Do you love me?" I said.

11. The Nether Regions

My father had an irritating way of explaining things to me I already understood, refusing to stop no matter how much I said "I know" or "You told me before."

Thus he expounded on the significance of the nether regions, adopting the tone of a lecturer speaking to a class of particularly backward children.

"As you know," he said, "the nether regions were amongst the first to disappear and this in itself is significant. These regions, I'm sure you know, are seldom visited by men and only then by people like me whose sole job is to make sure that they're still there. We had no use for these areas, these deserts, swamps, and coastlines which is why, of course, they disappeared. They were merely possessions of ours and if they had any use at all it was as symbols for our poets, writers and film makers. They were used as symbols of alienation, lovelessness, loneliness, uselessness and so on. Do you get what I mean?"

"Yes," I said, "I get what you mean."

"But do you?" My father insisted. "But do you really, I wonder." He examined me seriously, musing on the possibilities of my understanding him. "How old are you?"

"Twenty," I said.

"I knew, of course," he said. "Do you understand the significance of the nether regions?"

I sighed, a little too loudly and my father narrowed his eyes. Quickly I said: "They are like everything else. They're like the cities. The cities are deserts where people are alone and lonely. They don't love one another."

"Don't love one another," intoned my father, also sighing. "We no longer love one another. When we realize that we need one another we will stop disappearing. This is a lesson to us. A hard lesson, but, I hope, an effective one."

My father continued to speak, but I watched him without listening. After a few minutes he stopped abruptly: "Are you listening to me?" he said. I was surprised to detect real concern in his voice. He looked at me questioningly. "I've always looked after you," he said, "ever since you were little."

12. The Cartographers' Fall

I don't know when it was that I noticed that my father had become depressed. It probably happened quite gradually without either my mother or me noticing it.

Even when I did become aware of it I attributed it to a woman. My father had a number of lovers and his moods usually reflected the success or failure of these relationships.

But I know now that he had heard already of Hurst and Jamov, the first two Cartographers to disappear. The news was suppressed for several weeks and then, somehow or other, leaked to the press. Certainly the Cartographers had enemies amongst the civil servants who regarded them as overproud and overpaid, and it was probably from one of these civil servants that the press heard the news.

When the news finally broke I understood my father's depression and felt sorry for him.

I didn't know how to help him. I wanted, badly, to make him happy. I had never ever been able to give him anything or do anything for him that he couldn't do better himself. Now I wanted to help him, to show him I understood.

I found him sitting in front of the television one night when I returned from my office and I sat quietly beside him. He seemed more kindly now and he placed his hand on my knee and patted it.

I sat there for a while, overcome with the new warmth of this relationship and then, unable to contain my emotion any more, I blurted out: "You could change your job."

My father stiffened and sat bolt upright. The pressure of his hand on my knee increased until I yelped with pain, and still he held on, hurting me terribly.

"You are a fool," he said, "you wouldn't know if you were up yourself."

Through the pain in my leg, I felt the intensity of my father's fear.

13. Why the World Needs Cartographers

My father woke me at 3 a.m. to tell me why the world needed Cartographers. He smelled of whisky and seemed, once again, to be very gentle.

"The world needs Cartographers," he said softly, "because if they didn't have Cartographers the fools wouldn't know where they were. They wouldn't know if they were up themselves if they didn't have a Cartographer to tell them what's happening. The world needs Cartographers," my father said, "it fucking well needs Cartographers."

14. One Final Scene

Let me describe a final scene to you. I am sitting on the sofa my father brought home when I was five years old. I am watching television. My father is sitting in a leather armchair that once belonged to his father and which has always been exclusively his. My mother is sitting in the dining alcove with her cards spread across the table, playing one more interminable game of patience.

I glance casually across at my father to see if he is doing anything more than stare into space, and notice, with a terrible shock, that he is showing the first signs of dematerializing.

"What are you staring at?" My father, in fact, has been staring at me.

"Nothing."

"Well, don't."

Nervously I return my eyes to the inanity of the television. I don't know what to do. Should I tell my father that he is dematerializing? If I don't tell him will he notice? I feel I should do something but I can feel, already, the anger in his voice. His anger is nothing new. But this is possibly the beginning of a tide of uncontrollable rage. If he knows he is dematerializing, he will think I don't love him. He will blame me. He will attack me. Old as he is, he is still considerably stronger than I am and he could hurt me badly. I stare determinedly at the television and feel my father's eyes on me.

I try to feel love for my father, I try very, very hard.

I attempt to remember how I felt about him when I was little, in the days when he was still occasionally tender towards me.

But it's no good.

Because I can only remember how he has hit me, hurt me, humiliated me and flirted with my girlfriends. I realize, with a flush of panic and guilt, that I don't love him. In spite of which I say: "I love you."

My mother looks up sharply from her cards and lets out a surprised cry.

I turn to my father. He has almost disappeared. I can see the leather of the chair through his stomach.

I don't know whether it is my unconvincing declaration of love or my mother's exclamation that makes my father laugh. For whatever reason, he begins to laugh uncontrollably: "You bloody fools," he gasps, "I wish you could see the looks on your bloody silly faces."

And then he is gone.

My mother looks across at me nervously, a card still in her hand. "Do you love me?" she asks.

Born in Quincy, Massachusetts, John Cheever (1912-1982) began his writing career at the age of seventeen, when he turned the experience of his dismissal from Thayer Academy into a short story which appeared in *The New Republic*. Subsequently Cheever wrote over two hundred stories, many of them for the *New Yorker*, and writing was the main source of his income throughout his life (working for the *New Yorker*, he said, gave him "enough money to feed the family and buy a new suit every other year"). Toward the end of his life, his pre-eminence as a writer of short fiction was acknowledged by a Pulitzer Prize, a National Book Critics Circle Award, and an American Book Award, all bestowed on *The Stories of John Cheever* (1978). He also wrote five novels, including *The Wapshot Chronicle* (1957), which won a National Book Award, and *The Wapshot Scandal* (1964), winner of a Howells Medal. For the novel *Falconer* (1977), he drew on his experiences as a teacher at Sing Sing Prison in the early seventies, as well as on his own battle with alcoholism. Cheever's last work, the novella *Oh What a Paradise It Seems*, was published in 1982 shortly before his death from cancer.

The principal subject of Cheever's fiction is suburbia: the manners and mores of the affluent American upper-middle class. Seemingly insulated by their wealth from the social and political problems that afflict the majority, they nevertheless find their lives boring, frustrating, or even frightening, as they look beneath the surface comforts of domestic life and find an unsettling emptiness. Though Cheever mocks the pretensions and vanities of this society, he recognizes the common humanity of its members; they may live in large houses or belong to exclusive golf clubs, but their fears and failings are not restricted to any social class. In "A Country Husband" (from *Stories*, 1956), Francis Weed is aroused by his sudden brush with death to reassess his comfortable life in Shady Hill. He struggles against the forces of social convention and impending middle age, but his defeat is inevitable. Cheever portrays Francis's brief rebellion with a subtle mixture of irony and pathos.

FOR FURTHER READING

Samuel Coale, *John Cheever* (New York: Frederick Ungar, 1977).

Annette Grant, "The Art of Fiction LXII: John Cheever," *Paris Review* 17 (Fall 1976): 39-66.

James Eugene O'Hara, *John Cheever: A Study of the Short Fiction* (Boston: Twayne, 1989).

Lynne Waldeland, *John Cheever* (Boston: Twayne, 1979).

The Country Husband

To begin at the beginning, the airplane from Minneapolis in which Francis Weed was traveling East ran into heavy weather. The sky had been a hazy blue, with the clouds below the plane lying so close together that nothing could be seen of the earth. Then mist began to form outside the windows, and they flew into a white cloud of such density that it reflected the exhaust fires. The color of the cloud darkened to gray, and the plane began to rock. Francis had been in heavy weather before, but he had never been shaken up so much. The man in the seat beside him pulled a flask out of his pocket and took a drink. Francis smiled at his neighbor, but the man looked away; he wasn't sharing his pain killer with anyone. The plane began to drop and flounder wildly. A child was crying. The air in the cabin was overheated and stale, and Francis' left foot went to sleep. He read a little from a paper book that he had bought at the airport, but the violence of the storm divided his attention. It was black outside the ports. The exhaust fires blazed and shed sparks in the dark, and, inside, the shaded lights, the stuffiness, and the window curtains gave the cabin an atmosphere of intense and misplaced domesticity. Then the lights flickered and went out. "You know what I've always wanted to do?" the man beside Francis said suddenly. "I've always wanted to buy a farm in New Hampshire and raise beef cattle." The stewardess announced that they were going to make an emergency landing. All but the children saw in their minds the spreading wings of the Angel of Death. The pilot could be heard singing faintly, "I've got sixpence, jolly, jolly sixpence. I've got sixpence to last me all my life . . . " There was no other sound.

The loud groaning of the hydraulic valves swallowed up the pilot's song, and there was a shrieking high in the air, like automobile brakes, and the plane hit flat on its belly in a cornfield and shook them so violently that an old man up forward howled, "Me kidneys! Me kidneys!" The stewardess flung open the door, and someone opened an emergency door at the back, letting in the sweet noise of their continuing mortality—the idle splash and smell of a heavy rain. Anxious for their lives, they filed out of the doors and scattered over the cornfield in all directions, praying that the thread would hold. It did. Nothing happened. When it was clear that the plane would not burn or explode, the crew and the stewardess gathered the passengers together and led them to the shelter of a barn. They were not far from Philadelphia, and in a little while a string of taxis took them into the city. "It's just like the Marne," someone said, but there was surprisingly little relaxation of that suspiciousness with which many Americans regard their fellow travelers.

In Philadelphia, Francis Weed got a train to New York. At the end of that journey, he crossed the city and caught just as it was about to pull out the commuting train that he took five nights a week to his home in Shady Hill.

He sat with Trace Bearden. "You know, I was in that plane that just crashed outside Philadelphia," he said. "We came down in a field . . . " He had traveled faster than the newspapers or the rain, and the weather in New York was sunny and mild. It was a day in late September, as fragrant and shapely as an apple. Trace listened to the story, but how could he get excited? Francis had no powers that would let him recreate a brush with death—particularly in the atmosphere of a commuting train, journeying through a sunny countryside where already, in the slum gardens, there were signs of harvest. Trace picked up his newspaper, and Francis was left alone with his thoughts. He said good night to Trace on the platform at Shady Hill and drove in his secondhand Volkswagen up to the Blenhollow neighborhood, where he lived.

The Weeds' Dutch Colonial house was larger than it appeared to be from the driveway. The living room was spacious and divided like Gaul into three parts. Around an ell to the left as one entered from the vestibule was the long table, laid for six, with candles and a bowl of fruit in the center. The sounds and smells that came from the open kitchen door were appetizing, for Julia Weed was a good cook. The largest part of the living room centered on a fireplace. On the right were some bookshelves and a piano. The room was polished and tranquil, and from the windows that opened to the west there was some late-summer sunlight, brilliant and as clear as water. Nothing here was neglected; nothing had not been burnished. It was not the kind of household where, after prying open a stuck cigarette box, you would find an old shirt button and a tarnished nickel. The hearth was swept, the roses on the piano were reflected in the polish of the broad top, and there was an album of Schubert waltzes on the rack. Louisa Weed, a pretty girl of nine, was looking out the western windows. Her younger brother Henry was standing beside her. Her still younger brother, Toby, was studying the figures of some tonsured monks drinking beer on the polished brass of the woodbox. Francis, taking off his hat and putting down his paper, was not consciously pleased with the scene; he was not that reflective. It was his element, his creation, and he returned to it with that sense of lightness and strength with which any creature returns to his home. "Hi, everybody," he said. "The plane from Minneapolis . . ."

Nine times out of ten, Francis would be greeted with affection, but tonight the children are absorbed in their own antagonisms. Francis had not finished his sentence about the plane crash before Henry plants a kick in Louisa's behind. Louisa swings around, saying, *"Damn you!"* Francis makes the mistake of scolding Louisa for bad language before he punishes Henry. Now Louisa turns on her father and accuses him of favoritism. Henry is always right; she is persecuted and lonely; her lot is hopeless. Francis turns to his son, but the boy has justification for the kick—she hit him first; she hit him on the ear, which is dangerous. Louisa agrees with this passionately. She hit him on the ear, and she *meant* to hit him on the ear, because he messed up her china collection. Henry says that this is a lie. Little Toby turns away from the woodbox to throw in some evidence for Louisa. Henry claps his hand over little Toby's mouth. Francis separates the two boys but accidentally pushes Toby into the woodbox. Toby begins to cry. Louisa is already crying. Just then, Julia Weed comes into the part of the room where the table is laid. She is a pretty, intelligent woman, and the white in her hair is premature. She does not seem to notice the fracas. "Hello, darling," she says serenely to Francis. "Wash your hands, everyone. Dinner is ready." She strikes a match and lights the six candles in this vale of tears.

This simple announcement, like the war cries of the Scottish chieftains, only refreshes the ferocity of the combatants. Louisa gives Henry a blow on the shoulder. Henry, although he seldom cries, has pitched nine innings and is tired. He bursts into tears. Little Toby discovers a splinter in his hand and begins to howl. Francis says loudly that he has been in a plane crash and that he is tired. Julia appears again from the kitchen and, still ignoring the chaos, asks Francis to go upstairs and tell Helen that everything is ready. Francis is happy to go; it is like getting back to headquarters company. He is planning to tell his older daughter about the airplane crash, but Helen is lying on her bed reading a *True Romance* magazine, and the first thing Francis does is to take the magazine from her hand and remind Helen that he has forbidden her to buy it. She did not buy it, Helen replies. It was given to her by her best friend, Bessie Black. Everybody reads *True Romance*. Bessie Black's father reads *True Romance*. There isn't a girl in Helen's class who doesn't read *True Romance*. Francis expresses his detestation of the magazine and then tells her that dinner is ready—although from the sounds downstairs it doesn't seem so. Helen follows him down the stairs. Julia has seated herself in the candlelight and spread a napkin over her lap. Neither Louisa nor Henry has come to the table. Little Toby is still howling, lying face down on the floor. Francis speaks to him gently: "Daddy was in a plane crash this afternoon, Toby. Don't you want to hear about it?" Toby goes on crying. "If you don't come to the table now, Toby," Francis says, "I'll have to send you to bed without any supper." The little boy rises, gives him a cutting look, flies up the stairs to his bedroom, and slams the door. "Oh dear," Julia says, and starts to go after him. Francis says that she will spoil him. Julia says that Toby is ten pounds underweight and has to be encouraged to eat. Winter is coming, and he will spend the cold months in bed unless he has his dinner. Julia goes upstairs. Francis sits down at the table with Helen. Helen is suffering from the dismal feeling of having read too intently on a fine day, and she gives her father and the room a jaded look. She doesn't understand about the plane crash, because there wasn't a drop of rain in Shady Hill.

Julia returns with Toby, and they all sit down and are served. "Do I have to look at that big, fat slob?" Henry says, of Louisa. Everybody but Toby enters into this skirmish, and it rages up and down the table for five minutes. Toward the end, Henry puts his napkin over his head and, trying to eat that way, spills spinach all over his shirt. Julia's guns are loaded for this. She can't cook two dinners and lay two tables. She paints with lightning strokes that panorama of drudgery in which her youth, her beauty, and her wit have been lost. Francis says that he must be understood; he was nearly killed in an airplane crash, and he doesn't like to come home every night to a battlefield. Now Julia is deeply concerned. Her voice trembles. He doesn't come home every night to a battlefield. The accusation is stupid and mean. Everything was tranquil until he arrived. She stops speaking, puts down her knife and fork, and looks into her plate as if it is a gulf. She begins to cry. "Poor Mummy!" Toby says, and when Julia gets up from the table, drying her tears with a napkin, Toby goes to her side. "Poor Mummy," he says. "Poor Mummy!" And they climb the stairs together. The other children drift away from the battlefield, and Francis goes into the back garden for a cigarette and some air.

It was a pleasant garden, with walks and flower beds and places to sit. The sunset had nearly burned out, but there was still plenty of light. Put into a thoughtful mood by the crash and the battle, Francis listened to the evening sounds of Shady Hill. "Varmints! Rascals!" old Mr. Nixon shouted to the squirrels in his bird-feeding station. "Avaunt and quit my sight!" A door slammed. Someone was cutting grass. Then Donald Goslin, who lived at the corner, began to play the

"Moonlight Sonata." He did this nearly every night. He threw the tempo out the window and played it *rubato* from beginning to end, like an outpouring of tearful petulance, lonesomeness, and self-pity—of everything it was Beethoven's greatness not to know. The music rang up and down the street beneath the trees like an appeal for love, for tenderness, aimed at some lovely housemaid—some fresh-faced, homesick girl from Galway, looking at old snapshots in her third-floor room. "Here, Jupiter, here Jupiter," Francis called to the Mercers' retriever. Jupiter crashed through the tomato vines with the remains of a felt hat in his mouth.

Jupiter was an anomaly. His retrieving instincts and his high spirits were out of place in Shady Hill. He was as black as coal, with a long, alert, intelligent, rakehell face. His eyes gleamed with mischief, and he held his head high. It was the fierce, heavily collared dog's head that appears in heraldry, in tapestry, and that used to appear on umbrella handles and walking sticks. Jupiter went where he pleased, ransacking wastebaskets, clotheslines, garbage pails, and shoe bags. He broke up garden parties and tennis matches, and got mixed up in the processional at Christ Church on Sunday, barking at the men in red dresses. He crashed through old Mr. Nixon's rose garden two or three times a day, cutting a wide swath through the Condesa de Sastagos, and as soon as Donald Goslin lighted his barbecue fire on Thursday nights, Jupiter would get the scent. Nothing the Goslins did could drive him away. Sticks and stones and rude commands only moved him to the edge of the terrace, where he remained, with his gallant and heraldic muzzle, waiting for Donald Goslin to turn his back and reach for the salt. Then he would spring onto the terrace, lift the steak lightly off the fire, and run away with the Goslins' dinner. Jupiter's days were numbered. The Wrightsons' German gardener or the Farquarsons' cook would soon poison him. Even old Mr. Nixon might put some arsenic in the garbage that Jupiter loved. "Here, Jupiter, Jupiter!" Francis called, but the dog pranced off, shaking the hat in his white teeth. Looking at the windows of this house, Francis saw that Julia had come down and was blowing out the candles.

Julia and Francis Weed went out a great deal. Julia was well liked and gregarious, and her love of parties sprang from a most natural dread of chaos and loneliness. She went through her morning mail with real anxiety, looking for invitations, and she usually found some, but she was insatiable, and if she had gone out seven nights a week, it would not have cured her of a reflective look—the look of someone who hears distant music—for she would always suppose that there was a more brilliant party somewhere else. Francis limited her to two week-night parties, putting a flexible interpretation on Friday, and rode through the weekend like a dory in a gale. The day after the airplane crash the Weeds were to have dinner with the Farquarsons.

Francis got home late from town, and Julia got the sitter while he dressed, and then hurried him out of the house. The party was small and pleasant, and Francis settled down to enjoy himself. A new maid passed the drinks. Her hair was dark, and her face was round and pale and seemed familiar to Francis. He had not developed his memory as a sentimental faculty. Wood smoke, lilac, and other such perfumes did not stir him, and his memory was something like his appendix—a vestigial repository. It was not his limitation at all to be unable to escape the past; it was perhaps his limitation that he had escaped it so successfully. He might have seen the maid at other parties, he might have seen her taking a walk on Sunday afternoons, but in either case he would not be searching his memory now. Her face was, in a wonderful way, a moon face—Norman or Irish—but it was not beautiful enough to account for his feeling that he had seen her before, in circumstances that he ought to remember. He asked Nellie Farquarson who she was. Nellie said that the maid had come through an agency, and that her home was Trenon, in Normandy—a small place with a church and a restaurant that Nellie had once visited. While Nellie talked on about her travels abroad, Francis realized where he had seen the woman before. It had been at the end of the war. He had left a replacement depot with some other men and taken a three-day pass in Trenon. On their second day, they had walked out to a crossroads to see the public chastisement of a young woman who had lived with the German commandant during the Occupation.

It was a cool morning in the fall. The sky was overcast, and poured down onto the dirt crossroads a very discouraging light. They were on high land and could see how like one another the shapes of the clouds and the hills were as they stretched off toward the sea. The prisoner arrived sitting on a three-legged stool in a farm cart. She stood by the cart while the Mayor read the accusation and the sentence. Her head was bent and her face was set in that empty half smile behind which the whipped soul is suspended. When the Mayor was finished, she undid her hair and let it fall across her back. A little man with a gray mustache cut off her hair with shears and dropped it on the ground. Then, with a bowl of soapy water and a straight razor, he shaved her skull clean. A woman approached and began to undo the fastenings of her clothes, but the prisoner pushed her aside and undressed herself. When she pulled her chemise over her head and threw it on the ground, she was naked. The women jeered; the men were still. There was no change in the falseness or the plaintiveness of the prisoner's smile. The cold wind made her white skin rough and hardened the nipples of her breasts. The jeering ended gradually, put down by the recognition of their common humanity. One woman spat on her, but some inviolable grandeur in her nakedness lasted through the ordeal.

When the crowd was quiet, she turned—she had begun to cry—and, with nothing on but a pair of worn black shoes and stockings, walked down the dirt road alone away from the village. The round white face had aged a little, but there was no question but that the maid who passed his cocktails and later served Francis his dinner was the woman who had been punished at the crossroads.

The war seemed now so distant and that world where the cost of partisanship had been death or torture so long ago. Francis had lost track of the men who had been with him in Vesey. He could not count on Julia's discretion. He could not tell anyone. And if he had told the story now, at the dinner table, it would have been a social as well as a human error. The people in the Farquarsons' living room seemed united in their tacit claim that there had been no past, no war—that there was no danger or trouble in the world. In the recorded history of human arrangements, this extraordinary meeting would have fallen into place, but the atmosphere of Shady Hill made the memory unseemly and impolite. The prisoner withdrew after passing the coffee, but the encounter left Francis feeling languid; it had opened his memory and his senses, and left them dilated. Julia went into the house. Francis stayed in the car to take the sitter home.

Expecting to see Mrs. Henlein, the old lady who usually stayed with the children, he was surprised when a young girl opened the door and came out onto the lighted stoop. She stayed in the light to count her textbooks. She was frowning and beautiful. Now, the world is full of beautiful young girls, but Francis saw here the difference between beauty and perfection. All those endearing flaws, moles, birthmarks, and healed wounds were missing, and he experienced in his consciousness that moment when music breaks glass, and felt a pang of recognition as strange, deep, and wonderful as anything in his life. It hung from her frown, from an impalpable darkness in her face—a look that impressed him as a direct appeal for love. When she had counted her books, she came down the steps and opened the car door. In the light, he saw that her cheeks were wet. She got in and shut the door.

"You're new," Francis said.

"Yes. Mrs. Henlein is sick. I'm Anne Murchison."

"Did the children give you any trouble?"

"Oh, no, no." She turned and smiled at him unhappily in the dim dashboard light. Her light hair caught on the collar of her jacket, and she shook her head to set it loose.

"You've been crying."

"Yes."

"I hope it was nothing that happened in our house."

"No, no, it was nothing that happened in your house." Her voice was bleak. "It's no secret. Everybody in the village knows. Daddy's an alcoholic, and he just called me from some saloon and gave me a piece of his mind. He thinks I'm immoral. He called just before Mrs. Weed came back."

"I'm sorry."

"Oh, *Lord!*" She gasped and began to cry. She turned toward Francis, and he took her in his arms and let her cry on his shoulder. She shook in his embrace, and this movement accentuated his sense of the fineness of her flesh and bone. The layers of their clothing felt thin, and when her shuddering began to diminish, it was so much like a paroxysm of love that Francis lost his head and pulled her roughly against him. She drew away. "I live on Belleview Avenue," she said. "You go down Lansing Street to the railroad bridge."

"All right." He started the car.

"You turn left at that traffic light. . . . Now you turn right here and go straight on towards the tracks."

The road Francis took brought him out of his own neighborhood, across the tracks, and toward the river, to a street where the near-poor lived, in houses whose peaked gables and trimmings of wooden lace conveyed the purest feelings of pride and romance, although the houses themselves could not have offered much privacy or comfort, they were all so small. The street was dark, and, stirred by the grace and beauty of the troubled girl, he seemed, in turning into it, to have come into the deepest part of some submerged memory. In the distance, he saw a porch light burning. It was the only one, and she said that the house with the light was where she lived. When he stopped the car, he could see beyond the porch light into a dimly lighted hallway with an old-fashioned clothes tree. "Well, here we are," he said, conscious that a young man would have said something different.

She did not move her hands from the books, where they were folded, and she turned and faced him. There were tears of lust in his eyes. Determinedly—not sadly—he opened the door on his side and walked around to open hers. He took her free hand, letting his fingers in between hers, climbed at her side the two concrete steps, and went up a narrow walk through a front garden where dahlias, marigolds, and roses—things that had withstood the light frosts—still bloomed, and made a bittersweet smell in the night air. At the steps, she freed her hand and then turned and kissed him swiftly. Then she crossed the porch and shut the door. The porch light went out, then the light in the hall. A second later, a light went on upstairs at the side of the house, shining into a tree that was still covered with leaves. It took her only a few minutes to undress and get into bed, and then the house was dark.

Julia was asleep when Francis got home. He opened a second window and got into bed to shut his eyes on that night, but as soon as they were shut—as soon as he had dropped off to sleep—the girl entered his mind, moving with perfect freedom through its shut doors and filling chamber after chamber with her light, her perfume, and the music of her voice. He was crossing the Atlantic with her on the old *Mauretania* and, later, living with her in Paris. When he woke from his dream, he got up and smoked a cigarette at the open window. Getting back into bed, he cast around in his mind for something he desired to do that would injure no one, and he thought of skiing. Up through the dimness in his mind rose the image of a mountain deep in snow. It was late in the day. Wherever his eyes looked, he saw broad and heartening things. Over his shoulder, there was a snow-filled valley, rising into wooded hills where the trees dimmed the whiteness like a sparse coat of hair. The cold deadened all sound but the loud, iron clanking of the lift machinery. The light on the trails was blue, and it was harder than it had been a minute or two earlier to pick the turns, harder to judge—now that the snow was all deep blue—the crust, the ice, the bare spots, and the deep piles of dry powder. Down the mountain he swung, matching his speed against the contours of a slope that had been formed in the first ice age, seeking with ardor some simplicity of feeling and circumstance. Night fell then, and he drank a Martini with some old friend in a dirty country bar.

In the morning, Francis' snow-covered mountain was gone, and he was left with his vivid memories of Paris and the *Mauretania*. He had been bitten gravely. He washed his body, shaved his jaws, drank his coffee, and missed the seven-thirty-one. The train pulled out just as he brought his car to the station, and the longing he felt for the coaches as they drew stubbornly away from him reminded him of the humors of love. He waited for the eight-two, on what was now an empty platform. It was a clear morning; the morning seemed thrown like a gleaming bridge of light over his mixed affairs. His spirits were feverish and high. The image of the girl seemed to put him into a relationship to the world that was mysterious and enthralling. Cars were beginning to fill up the parking lot, and he noticed that those that had driven down from the high land above Shady Hill were white with hoarfrost. This first clear sign of autumn thrilled him. An express train—a night train from Buffalo or Albany—came down the tracks between the platforms, and he saw that the roofs of the foremost cars were covered with a skin of ice. Struck by the miraculous physicalness of everything, he smiled at the passengers in the dining car, who could be seen eating eggs and wiping their mouths with napkins as they traveled. The sleeping-car compartments, with their soiled bed linen, trailed through the fresh morning like a string of rooming-house windows. Then he saw an extraordinary thing; at one of the bedroom windows sat an unclothed woman of exceptional beauty, combing her golden hair. She passed like an apparition through Shady Hill, combing and combing her hair, and Francis followed her with his eyes until she was out of sight. Then old Mrs. Wrightson joined him on the platform and began to talk.

"Well, I guess you must be surprised to see me here the third morning in a row," she said, "but because of my window curtains I'm becoming a regular commuter. The curtains I bought on Monday I returned on Tuesday, and the curtains I bought Tuesday I'm returning today. On Monday, I got exactly what I wanted—it's a wool tapestry with roses and birds—but when I got them home, I found they were the wrong length. Well, I exchanged them yesterday, and when I got them home, I found they were still the wrong length. Now I'm praying to high heaven that the decorator will have them in the right length, because you know my house, you *know* my living-room windows, and you can imagine what a problem they present. I don't know what to do with them."

"I know what to do with them," Francis said.

"What?"

"Paint them black on the inside, and shut up."

There was a gasp from Mrs. Wrightson, and Francis looked down at her to be sure that she knew he meant to be rude. She turned and walked away from him, so damaged in spirit that she limped. A wonderful feeling enveloped him, as if light were being shaken about him, and he thought again of Venus combing her hair as she drifted through the Bronx. The realization of how many years had passed since he had enjoyed being deliberately impolite sobered him. Among his friends and neighbors, there were brilliant and gifted people—he saw that—but many of them, also, were bores and fools, and he had made the mistake of listening to them all with equal attention. He had confused a lack of discrimination with Christian love, and the confusion seemed general and destructive. He was grateful to the girl for this bracing sensation of independence. Birds were singing—cardinals and the last of the robins. The sky shone like enamel. Even the smell of ink from his morning paper honed his appetite for life, and the world that was spread out around him was plainly a paradise.

If Francis had believed in some hierarchy of love—in spirits armed with hunting bows, in the capriciousness of Venus and Eros—or even in magical potions, philters, and stews, in scapulae and quarters of the moon, it might have explained his susceptibility and his feverish high spirits. The autumnal loves of middle age are well publicized, and he guessed that he was face to face with one of these, but there was not a trace of autumn in what he felt. He wanted to sport in the green woods, scratch where he itched, and drink from the same cup.

His secretary, Miss Rainey, was late that morning—she went to a psychiatrist three mornings a week—and when she came in, Francis wondered what advice a psychiatrist would have for him. But the girl promised to bring back into his life something like the sound of music.

The realization that this music might lead him straight to a trial for statutory rape at the county courthouse collapsed his happiness. The photograph of his four children laughing into the camera on the beach at Gay Head reproached him. On the letterhead of his firm there was a drawing of the Laocoön, and the figure of the priest and his sons in the coils of the snake appeared to him to have the deepest meaning.

He had lunch with Pinky Trabert. At a conversational level, the mores of his friends were robust and elastic, but he knew that the moral card house would come down on them all—on Julia and the children as well—if he got caught taking advantage of a baby-sitter. Looking back over the recent history of Shady Hill for some precedent, he found there was none. There was no turpitude; there had not been a divorce since he had lived there; there had not even been a breath of scandal. Things seemed arranged with more propriety even than in the Kingdom of Heaven. After leaving Pinky, Francis went to a jeweler's and bought the girl a bracelet. How happy this clandestine purchase made him, how stuffy and comical the jeweler's clerks seemed, how sweet the women who passed at his back smelled! On Fifth Avenue, passing Atlas with his shoulders bent under the weight of the world, Francis thought of the strenuousness of containing his physicalness within the patterns he had chosen.

He did not know when he would see the girl next. He had the bracelet in his inside pocket when he got home. Opening the door of his house, he found her in the hall. Her back was to him, and she turned when she heard the door close. Her smile was open and loving. Her perfection stunned him like a fine day—a day after a thunderstorm. He seized her and covered her lips with his, and she struggled but she did not have to struggle for long, because just then little Gertrude Flannery appeared from somewhere and said, "Oh, Mr. Weed . . . "

Gertrude was a stray. She had been born with a taste for exploration, and she did not have it in her to center her life with her affectionate parents. People who did not know the Flannerys concluded from Gertrude's behavior that she was the child of a bitterly divorced family, where drunken quarrels were the rule. This was not true. The fact that little Gertrude's clothing was ragged and thin was her own triumph over her mother's struggle to dress her warmly and neatly. Garrulous, skinny, and unwashed, she drifted from house to house around the Blenhollow neighborhood, forming and breaking alliances based on an attachment to babies, animals, children her own age, adolescents, and sometimes adults. Opening your front door in the morning, you would find Gertrude sitting on your stoop. Going into the bathroom to shave, you would find Gertrude using the toilet. Looking into your son's crib, you would find it empty, and, looking further, you would find that Gertrude had pushed him in his baby carriage into the next village. She was helpful, pervasive, honest, hungry, and loyal. She never went home of her own choice. When the time to go arrived, she was indifferent to all its signs. "Go home, Gertrude," people could be heard saying in one house or another, night after night. "Go home, Gertrude. It's time for you to go home now, Gertrude." "You had better go home and get your supper, Gertrude." "I told you to go home twenty minutes ago, Gertrude." "Your mother will be worrying about you, Gertrude." "Go home, Gertrude, go home."

There are times when the lines around the human eye seem like shelves of eroded stone and when the staring eye itself strikes us with such a wilderness of animal feeling that we are at a loss. The look Francis gave the little girl was ugly and queer, and it frightened her. He reached into his pockets—his hands were shaking—and took out a quarter. "Go home, Gertrude, go home, and don't tell anyone, Gertrude. Don't—" He choked and ran into the living room as Julia called down to him from upstairs to hurry and dress.

The thought that he would drive Anne Murchison home later that night ran like a golden thread through the events of the party that Francis and Julia went to, and he laughed uproariously at dull jokes, dried a tear when Mabel Mercer told him about the death of her kitten, and stretched, yawned, sighed, and grunted like any other man with a rendezvous at the back of his mind. The bracelet was in his pocket. As he sat talking, the smell of grass was in his nose, and he was wondering where he would park the car. Nobody lived in the old Parker mansion, and the driveway was used as a lovers' lane. Townsend Street was a dead end, and he could park there, beyond the last house. The old lane that used to connect Elm Street to the riverbanks was overgrown, but he had walked there with his children, and he could drive his car deep enough into the brushwoods to be concealed.

The Weeds were the last to leave the party, and their host and hostess spoke of their own married happiness while they all four stood in the hallway saying good night. "She's my girl," their host said, squeezing his wife. "She's my blue sky. After sixteen years, I still bite her shoulders. She makes me feel like Hannibal crossing the Alps."

The Weeds drove home in silence. Francis brought the car up the driveway and sat still, with the motor running. "You can put the car in the garage," Julia said as she got out. "I told the Murchison girl she could leave at eleven. Someone drove her home. She shut the door, and Francis sat in the dark. He would be spared nothing then, it seemed, that a fool was not spared: ravening lewdness, jealousy, this hurt to his feelings that put tears in his eyes, even scorn—for he could see clearly the image he now presented, his arms spread over the steering wheel and his head buried in them for love.

Francis had been a dedicated Boy Scout when he was young, and, remembering the precepts of his youth, he left his office early the next afternoon and played some round-robin squash, but, with his body toned up by exercise and a shower, he realized that he might better have stayed at his desk. It was a frosty night when he got home. The air smelled sharply of change. When he stepped into the house, he sensed an unusual stir. The children were in their best clothes, and when Julia came down, she was wearing a lavender dress and her diamond sunburst. She explained the stir: Mr. Hubber was coming at seven to take their photograph for the Christmas card. She had put out Francis' blue suit and a tie with some color in it, because the picture was going to be in color this year. Julia was lighthearted at the thought of being photographed for Christmas. It was the kind of ceremony she enjoyed.

Francis went upstairs to change his clothes. He was tired from the day's work and tired with longing, and sitting on the edge of the bed had the effect of deepening his weariness. He thought of Anne Murchison, and the physical need to express himself, instead of being restrained by the pink lamps of Julia's dressing table, engulfed him. He went to Julia's desk, took a piece of writing paper, and began to write on it. "Dear Anne, I love you, I love you, I love you . . . " No one would see the letter, and he used no restraint. He used phrases like "heavenly bliss," and "love nest." He salivated, sighed, and trembled. When Julia called him to come down, the abyss between his fantasy and the practical world opened so wide that he felt it affected the muscles of his heart.

Julia and the children were on the stoop, and the photographer and his assistant had set up a double battery of floodlights to show the family and the architectural beauty of the entrance to their house. People who had come home on a late train slowed their cars to see the Weeds being photographed for their Christmas card. A few waved and called to the family. It took half an hour of smiling and wetting their lips before Mr. Hubber was satisfied. The heat of the lights made an unfresh smell in the frosty air, and when they were turned off, they lingered on the retina of Francis' eyes.

Later that night, while Francis and Julia were drinking their coffee in the living room, the doorbell rang. Julia answered the door and let in Clayton Thomas. He had come to pay for some theatre tickets that she had given his mother some time ago, and that Helen Thomas had scrupulously insisted on paying for, though Julia had asked her not to. Julia invited him in to have a cup of coffee. "I won't have any coffee," Clayton said, "but I will come in for a minute." He followed her into the living room, said good evening to Francis, and sat awkwardly in a chair.

Clayton's father had been killed in the war, and the young man's fatherlessness surrounded him like an element. This may have been conspicuous in Shady Hill because the Thomases were the only family that lacked a piece; all the other marriages were intact and productive. Clayton was in his second or third year of college, and he and his mother lived alone in a large house, which she hoped to sell. Clayton had once made some trouble. Years ago, he had stolen some money and run away; he had got to California before they caught up with him. He was tall and homely, wore horn-rimmed glasses, and spoke in a deep voice.

"When do you go back to college, Clayton?" Francis asked.

"I'm not going back," Clayton said. "Mother doesn't have the money, and there's no sense in all this pretense. I'm going to get a job, and if we sell the house, we'll take an apartment in New York."

"Won't you miss Shady Hill?" Julia asked.

"No," Clayton said. "I don't like it."

"Why not?" Francis asked.

"Well, there's a lot here I don't approve of," Clayton said gravely. "Things like the club dances. Last Saturday night, I looked in toward the end and saw Mr. Granner trying to put Mrs. Minot into the trophy case. They were both drunk. I disapprove of so much drinking."

"It was Saturday night," Francis said.

"And all the dovecotes are phony," Clayton said. "And the way people clutter up their lives. I've thought about it a lot, and what seems to me to be really wrong with Shady Hill is that it doesn't have any future. So much energy is spent in perpetuating the place—in keeping out undesirables, and so forth—that the only idea of the future anyone has is just more and more commuting trains and more parties. I don't think that's healthy. I think people ought to be able to dream big dreams about the future. I think people ought to be able to dream great dreams."

"It's too bad you couldn't continue with college," Julia said.

"I wanted to go to divinity school," Clayton said.

"What's your church?" Francis asked.

"Unitarian, Theosophist, Transcendentalist, Humanist," Clayton said.

"Wasn't Emerson a transcendentalist?" Julia asked.

"I mean the English transcendentalists," Clayton said, "All the American transcendentalists were goops."

"What kind of job do you expect to get?" Francis asked.

"Well, I'd like to work for a publisher," Clayton said, "but everyone tells me there's nothing doing. But it's the kind of thing I'm interested in. I'm writing a long verse play about good and evil. Uncle Charlie might get me into a bank, and that would be good for me. I need the discipline. I have a long way to go in forming my character. I have some terrible habits. I talk too much. I think I ought to take vows of silence. I ought to try not to speak for a week, and discipline myself. I've thought of making a retreat at one of the Episcopalian monasteries, but I don't like Trinitarianism."

"Do you have any girl friends?" Francis asked

"I'm engaged to be married," Clayton said. "Of course, I'm not old enough or rich enough to have my engagement observed or respected or anything, but I bought a simulated emerald for Anne Murchison with the money I made cutting lawns this summer. We're going to be married as soon as she finishes school."

Francis recoiled at the mention of the girl's name. Then a dingy light seemed to emanate from his spirit, showing everything—Julia, the boy, the chairs—in their true colorlessness. It was like a bitter turn of the weather.

"We're going to have a large family," Clayton said. "Her father's a terrible rummy, and I've had my hard times, and we want to have lots of children. Oh, she's wonderful, Mr. and Mrs. Weed, and we have so much in common. We like all the same things. We sent out the same Christmas card last year without planning it, and we both have an allergy to tomatoes, and our eyebrows grow together in the middle. Well, goodnight."

Julia went to the door with him. When she returned, Francis said that Clayton was lazy, irresponsible, affected, and smelly. Julia said that Francis seemed to be getting intolerant; the Thomas boy was young and should be given a chance. Julia had noticed other cases where Francis had been short-tempered. "Mrs. Wrightson has asked everyone in Shady Hill to her anniversary party but us," she said.

"I'm sorry, Julia."

"Do you know why they didn't ask us?"

"Why?"

"Because you insulted Mrs. Wrightson."

"Then you know about it?"

"June Masterson told me. She was standing behind you."

Julia walked in front of the sofa with a small step that expressed, Francis knew, a feeling of anger.

"I did insult Mrs. Wrightson, Julia, and I meant to. I've never liked her parties, and I'm glad she's dropped us."

"What about Helen?"

"How does Helen come into this?"

"Mrs. Wrightson's the one who decides who goes to the assemblies."

"You mean she can keep Helen from going to the dances?"

"Yes."

"I hadn't thought of that."

"Oh. I knew you hadn't thought of it," Julia cried, thrusting hilt-deep into this chink of his armor. "And it makes me furious to see this kind of stupid thoughtlessness wreck everyone's happiness."

"I don't think I've wrecked anyone's happiness."

"Mrs. Wrightson runs Shady Hill and has run it for the last forty years. I don't know what makes you think that in a community like this you can indulge every impulse you have to be insulting, vulgar, and offensive."

"I have very good manners," Francis said, trying to give the evening a turn toward the light.

"Damn you, Francis Weed!" Julia cried, and the spit of her words struck him in the face. "I've worked hard for the social position we enjoy in this place, and I won't stand by and see you wreck it. You must have understood when you settled here that you couldn't expect to live like a bear in a cave."

"I've got to express my likes and dislikes."

"You can conceal your dislikes. You don't have to meet everything head on, like a child. Unless you're anxious to be a social leper. It's no accident that we get asked out a great deal! It's no accident that Helen has so many friends. How would you like to spend your Saturday nights at the movies? How would you like to spend your Sundays raking up dead leaves? How would you like it if your daughter spent the assembly nights sitting at her window, listening to the music from the club? How would you like it—" He did something then that was, after all, not so unaccountable, since her words seemed to raise up between them a wall so deadening that he gagged. He struck her full in the face. She staggered and then, a moment later, seemed composed. She went up the stairs to their room. She didn't slam the door. When Francis followed, a few minutes later, he found her packing a suitcase.

"Julia, I'm very sorry."

"It doesn't matter," she said. She was crying.

"Where do you think you're going?"

"I don't know. I just looked at a timetable. There's an eleven-sixteen into New York. I'll take that."

"You can't go, Julia."

"I can't stay. I know that."

"I'm sorry about Mrs. Wrightson, Julia, and I'm—"

"It doesn't matter about Mrs. Wrightson. That isn't the trouble."

"What is the trouble?"

"You don't love me."

"I do love you, Julia."

"No, you don't."

"Julia, I do love you, and I would like to be as we were—sweet and bawdy and dark—but now there are so many people."

"You hate me."

"I don't hate you, Julia."

"You have no idea of how much you hate me. I think it's subconscious. You don't realize the cruel things you've done."

"What cruel things, Julia?"

"The cruel acts your subconscious drives you to in order to express your hatred of me."

"What, Julia?"

"I've never complained."

"Tell me."

"You don't know what you're doing."

"Tell me."

"Your clothes."

"What do you mean"

"I mean the way you leave your dirty clothes around in order to express your subconscious hatred of me."

"I don't understand."

"I mean your dirty socks and your dirty pajamas and your dirty underwear and your dirty shirts!" She rose from kneeling by the suitcase and faced him, her eyes blazing and her voice ringing with emotion. "I'm talking about the fact that you've never learned to hang up anything. You just leave your clothes all over the floor where they drop, in order to humiliate me. You do it on purpose!" She fell on the bed, sobbing.

"Julia, darling!" he said, but when she felt his hand on her shoulder she got up.

"Leave me alone," she said. "I have to go." She brushed past him to the closet and came back with a dress. "I'm not taking any of the things you've given me," she said. "I'm leaving my pearls and the fur jacket."

"Oh, Julia!" Her figure, so helpless in its self-deceptions, bent over the suitcase made him nearly sick with pity. She did not understand how desolate her life would be without him. She didn't understand the hours that working women have to keep. She didn't understand that most of her friendships existed within the framework of their marriage, and that without this she would find herself alone. She didn't understand about travel, about hotels, about money. "Julia, I can't let you go! What you don't understand Julia, is that you've come to be dependent on me."

She tossed her head back and covered her face with her hands. "Did you say that *I* was dependent on *you*?" she asked. "Is that what you said? And who is it that tells you what time to get up in the morning and when to go to bed at night? Who is it that prepares your meals and picks up your dirty clothes and invites your friends to dinner? If it weren't for me, your neckties would be greasy and your clothing would be full of moth holes. You were alone when I met you, Francis Weed, and you'll be alone when I leave. When Mother asked you for a list to send out invitations to our wedding, how many names did you have to give her? Fourteen!"

"Cleveland wasn't my home, Julia."

"And how many of your friends came to the church? Two!"

"Cleveland wasn't my home, Julia."

"Since I'm not taking the fur jacket," she said quietly, "you'd better put it back into storage. There's an insurance policy on the pearls that comes due in January. The name of the laundry and the maid's telephone number—all those things are in my desk. I hope you won't drink too much, Francis. I hope that nothing bad will happen to you. If you do get into serious trouble, you can call me."

"Oh, my darling, I can't let you go!" Francis said, "I can't let you go, Julia!" He took her in his arms.

"I guess I'd better stay and take care of you for a little while longer," she said.

Riding to work in the morning, Francis saw the girl walk down the aisle of the coach. He was surprised; he hadn't realized that the school she went to was in the city, but she was carrying books, she seemed to be going to school. His surprise delayed his reaction, but then he got up clumsily and stepped into the aisle. Several people had come between them, but he could see her ahead of him, waiting for someone to open the car door, and then, as the train swerved, putting out her hand to support herself as she crossed the platform into the next car. He followed her through that car and halfway through another before calling her name—"Anne! Anne!"—but she didn't turn. He followed her into still another car, and she sat down in an aisle seat. Coming up to her, all his feelings warm and bent in her direction, he put his hand on the back of her seat—even this touch warmed him—and leaning down to speak to her, he saw that it was not Anne. It was an older woman wearing glasses. He went on deliberately into another car, his face red with embarrassment and the much deeper feeling of having his good sense challenged; for if he couldn't tell one person from another, what evidence was there that his life with Julia and the children had as much reality as his dreams of iniquity in Paris or the litter, the grass smell, and the cave-shaped trees in Lovers' Lane.

Late that afternoon, Julia called to remind Francis that they were going out for dinner. A few minutes later, Trace Bearden called. "Look, fellar," Trace said. "I'm calling for Mrs. Thomas. You know? Clayton, that boy of hers, doesn't seem able to get a job, and I wondered if you could help. If you'd call Charlie Bell—I know he's indebted to you—and say a good word for the kid, I think Charlie would—"

"Trace, I hate to say this," Francis said, "but I don't feel that I can do anything for that boy. The kid's worthless. I know it's a harsh thing to say, but it's a fact. Any kindness done for him would backfire in everybody's face. He's just a worthless kid, Trace, and there's nothing to be done about it. Even if we got him a job, he wouldn't be able to keep it for a week. I know that to be a fact. It's an awful thing, Trace, and I know it is, but instead of recommending that kid, I'd feel obligated to warn people against him—people who knew his father and would naturally want to step in and do something. I'd feel obliged to warn them. He's a thief . . . "

The moment this conversation was finished, Miss Rainey came in and stood by his desk. "I'm not going to be able to work for you any more, Mr. Weed," she said. "I can stay until the seventeenth if you need me, but I've been offered a whirlwind of a job, and I'd like to leave as soon as possible."

She went out, leaving him to face alone the wickedness of what he had done to the Thomas boy. His children in their photograph laughed and laughed, glazed with all the bright colors of summer, and he remembered that they had met a bagpiper on the beach that day and he had paid the piper a dollar to play them a battle song of the Black Watch. The girl would be at the house when he got home. He would spend another evening among his kind neighbors, picking and choosing dead-end streets, cart tracks, and the driveways of abandoned houses. There was nothing to mitigate his feeling—nothing that laughter or a game of softball with the children would change—and, thinking back over the plane crash, the Farquarsons' new maid, and Anne Murchison's difficulties with her drunken father, he wondered how he could have avoided arriving at just where he was. He was in trouble. He had been lost once in his life, coming back from a trout stream in the north woods, and he had now the same bleak realization that no amount of cheerfulness or hopefulness or valor or perseverance could help him find, in the gathering dark, the path that he'd lost. He smelled the forest. The feeling of bleakness was intolerable, and he saw clearly that he had reached the point where he would have to make a choice.

He could go to a psychiatrist, like Miss Rainey; he could go to church and confess his lusts; he could go to a Danish massage parlor in the West Seventies that had been recommended by a salesman; he could rape the girl or trust that he would somehow be prevented from doing this; or he could get drunk. It was his life, his boat, and, like every other man, he was made to be the father of thousands, and what harm could there be in a tryst that would make them both feel more kindly toward the world? This was the wrong train of thought, and he came back to the first, the psychiatrist. He had the telephone number of Miss Rainey's doctor, and he called and asked for an immediate appointment. He was insistent with the doctor's secretary—it was his manner in business—and when she said that the doctor's schedule was full for the next few weeks, Francis demanded an appointment that day and was told to come at five.

The psychiatrist's office was a building that was used mostly by doctors and dentists, and the hallways were filled with the candy smell of mouthwash and memories of pain. Francis' character had been formed upon a series of private resolves—resolves about cleanliness, about going off the high diving board or repeating any other feat that challenged his courage, about punctuality, honesty, and virtue. To abdicate the perfect loneliness in which he had made his most vital decisions shattered his concept of character and left him now in a condition that felt like shock. He was stupefied. The scene for his *miserere mei Deus* was, like the waiting room of so many doctor's offices, a crude token gesture toward the sweets of domestic bliss: a place arranged with antiques, coffee tables, potted plants, and etchings of snow-covered bridges and geese in flight, although there were no children, no marriage bed, no stove, even, in this travesty of a house, where no one had ever spent the night and where the curtained windows looked straight onto a dark air shaft. Francis gave his name and address to a secretary and then saw, at the side of the room, a policeman moving toward him. "Hold it, hold it," the policeman said. "Don't move. Keep your hands where they are."

"I think it's all right, Officer," the secretary began. "I think it will be—"

"Let's make sure," the policeman said, and he began to slap Francis' clothes, looking for what—pistols, knives, an icepick? Finding nothing, he went off and the secretary began a nervous apology: "When you called on the telephone, Mr. Weed, you seemed very excited, and one of the doctor's patients has been threatening his life, and we have to be careful. If you want to go in now?" Francis pushed open a door connected to an electrical chime, and in the doctor's lair sat down heavily, blew his nose into a handkerchief, searched in his pockets for cigarettes, for matches, for something, and said hoarsely, with tears in his eyes, "I'm in love, Dr. Herzog."

It is a week or ten days later in Shady Hill. The seven-fourteen has come and gone, and here and there dinner is finished and the dishes are in the dish-washing machine. The village hangs, morally and economically, from a thread; but it hangs by its thread in the evening light. Donald Goslin has begun to worry the "Moonlight Sonata" again. *Marcato ma sempre pianissimo!* He seems to be wringing out a wet bath towel, but the housemaid does not heed him. She is writing a letter to Arthur Godfrey. In the cellar of his house, Francis Weed is building a coffee table. Dr. Herzog recommends woodwork as a therapy, and Francis finds some true consolation in the simple arithmetic involved in the holy smell of new wood. Francis is happy. Upstairs, little Toby is crying, because he is tired. He puts off his cowboy hat, gloves, and fringed jacket, unbuckles the belt studded with gold and rubies, the silver bullets and holsters, slips off his suspenders, his checked shirt, and Levi's, and sits on the edge of his bed to pull off his high boots. Leaving this equipment in a heap, he goes to the closet and takes his space suit off a nail. It is a struggle for him to get into the long tights, but he succeeds. He loops the magic cape over his shoulders and, climbing onto the footboard of his bed, he spreads his arms and flies the short distance to the floor, landing with a thump that is audible to everyone in the house but himself.

"Go home, Gertrude, go home," Mrs. Masterson says. "I told you to go home an hour ago, Gertrude. It's way past your suppertime, and your mother will be worried. Go home!" A door on the Babcocks' terrace flies open and out comes Mrs. Babcock without any clothes on, pursued by a naked husband. (Their children are away at boarding school, and their terrace is screened by a hedge.) Over the terrace they go and in at the kitchen door, as passionate and handsome a nymph and satyr as you will find on any wall in Venice. Cutting the last of the roses in her garden, Julia hears old Mr. Nixon shouting at the squirrels in his bird-feeding station. "Rapscallions! Varmints! Avaunt and quit my sight!" A miserable cat wanders into the garden, sunk in spiritual and physical discomfort. Tied to its head is a small straw hat—a doll's hat—and it is securely buttoned into a doll's dress, from the skirts of which protrudes its long, hairy tail. As it walks, it shakes its feet, as if it had fallen into water.

"Here, pussy, pussy, pussy!" Julia calls.

"Here, pussy, here, poor pussy!" But the cat gives her a skeptical look and stumbles away in its skirts. The last to come is Jupiter. He prances through the tomato vines, holding in his generous mouth the remains of an evening slipper. Then it is dark; it is a night where kings in golden suits ride elephants over the mountains.

George Clutesi (1905-1988), a member of the Tse-Shaht band of the Pacific coast, was one of Canada's foremost Native artists. A painter as well as a writer, he showed his work internationally; a forty-foot mural, designed for the world's fair Expo 67, is now on display at Montreal's permanent "Man and His World" exhibition, and his own designs illustrate *Son of Raven, Son of Deer* (1967), from which "Ko-ishin-mit and the Shadow People" is taken. Contact with the "European" bureaucracies of the Canadian government—particularly in regard to Indian affairs—led Clutesi to become a teacher of native culture, confident that it has significant meaning for both Indians and others.

"Ko-ishin-mit and the Shadow People," like all folk tales, emerges directly from a specific culture; though it can often be related to parallel stories from other cultures, it reflects its own society's structure, beliefs, superstitions, and values, and draws its particular language, its metaphors and analogies, from the local landscape. Primarily an oral art, the folk tale generally served a moral purpose and functioned as the didactic medium through which traditional values were handed from generation to generation. In his introduction to *Son of Raven, Son of Deer*, Clutesi notes that it was "Nan-is," the grandparent, who told such tales to the "ka-coots" (grandchildren), and that this pattern of behaviour not only gave the aged a respected position within society but also gave the young a sense of security. He criticizes such tales as "Henny Penny" and "Little Jack Horner," both for their implicit violence and for the gap between the child behaviour that society expects and approves, and the models hallowed by the stories themselves. The Indian stories, by contrast, assert the closeness between human beings and nature, focus on the interpenetration between mythic stories and moral truths, and give expression (in Clutesi's own words) to the "imaginative, romantic and resourceful" capacities of the Indian mind.

FOR FURTHER READING

J.W. Chalmers, "When You Tell a Story," *Canadian Author and Bookman* (Fall 1971): 5.

Penny Petrone, *Native Literature in Canada from the Oral Tradition to the Present* (Toronto: Oxford UP, 1990).

Ko-ishin-mit and the
Shadow People

"Finders keepers—losers weepers."

Most of you, no doubt have heard this old saying. To the non-Indian way of life it means that if anyone finds anything it is his to keep, while the one who has lost it may as well cry because it is lost to him, even though someone may have found it. This did not apply to the Indian way of life.

Ko-ishin-mit, the Son of Raven, was a very selfish and greedy person. He was always longing to own other people's possessions and coveted everything that was not his. Oh, he was greedy!

One fine day, early in the spring of the year, when the sun was shining and smiling with warmth, Ko-ishin-mit overheard a group of menfolk talking about a strange place where you could see everything you could think of lying about, with never a person in sight.

"What kind of things? Where is this place? How far is it from here?" Ko-ishin-mit demanded in a high state of excitement. He was hopping up and down and his voice became croaky as he kept asking where to find the place.

The menfolk ignored his frantic questions and the speaker, a grey-haired, wizened old man, kept on with his story.

"There are canoes," he told, "big ones and small ones, paddles, fishing gear, tools, all sorts of play things and food galore. Oh, there is lots and lots of food, and the food is always fresh, even though no one is ever seen in the place.

Ko-ishin-mit became more and more excited and his voice was raspy as he screamed, "Who owns all these things? Where? How can I find them?"

The storyteller continued with his tale. "It is said that this strange place is on a little isle around the point and across the bay. The secret is that one must get there by sundown, and one must leave before sunup. It is said, too, that the first person who finds this place may keep everything."

Ko-ishin-mit ran all the way home. "I must find this strange place first," he kept repeating to himself. "I must find the place first. I must. I must."

He flitted into his little house, and because he was out of breath he rasped and croaked, "Pash-hook, Pash-hook, Pash-hook, nah, my dear, get ready quickly. We are going out. Make some lunch. We may be gone all night," he croaked.

Pash-hook, the Daughter of Dsim-do the squirrel, scurried about. She did not need to be coaxed for she was always a fast and frisky little person. She never questioned her husband's wishes. Whatever her husband said had always been good enough for her and she was always eager to please him. So she hurried and she hurried.

Ko-ishin-mit grew more and more excited as he flitted here and hopped there inside his little house. He got out two paddles. He hopped down to the beach and pulled and tugged at his canoe until he had it to the water, a feat he had never before done alone.

Flitting back to the house he pressed and coaxed his little wife. "Hurry, hurry! Pash-hook, hurry! We must get there first. Hurry before we are too late. We must get there first. Oh, let us be first," he kept repeating, mostly to himself.

The sun was setting when they paddled into the bay of the little isle around the point. It was a beautiful little isle with small clumpy spreading spruce trees growing from mossy green hills. The little bay was ringed with white sandy beaches. The tide was out and the green sea-grass danced and waved at them to come ashore and rest awhile. This is what Pash-hook imagined as she eased her paddling and glided their little canoe towards the glistening beach. Pash-hook was the dreamer.

"Paddle harder! Paddle harder!" Ko-ishin-mit commanded his little wife.

Straight for the beach they glided. Ko-ishin-mit flitted out onto the wet sand. "Pull the canoe up," he ordered as he hopped up the beach looking about to see if there was anyone else there ahead of him. He could see long rows of beautiful canoes, big and small, pulled up well above the high-water mark. They all had pretty canoe mats covering them from the heat of the day and the cool of the night. There was no one in sight. Ko-ishin-mit was hopping up the beach. He did not wait to help his small wife with their canoe.

"I got here first!" he rasped as he hopped and flitted up to the neat row of houses on the grassy knoll that lay just below the spreading and clumpy spruce trees.

"I got here first!" the greedy Ko-ishin-mit croaked as he flitted swiftly to the biggest of the great houses. The huge door was shut and he pushed it open and hopped inside. He did not look back to see if his little wife Pash-hook was following. "I got here first," he chanted. Ko-ishin-mit, Son of Raven, was very, very greedy.

No one was to be seen. There was not a sound to be heard other than, "I got here first." Ko-ishin-mit's beady little black eyes grew even smaller in his greed to grab, grab, grab. "All is mine! All is mine!" his voice rasped out as he croaked, the way ravens do when they espy food.

"The whole village is mine. I got here first," he reasoned to himself. He hopped around the earthen floor of the great room. Big cedar boxes lined the walls. Ko-ishin-mit's greedy instinct told him that they would be full of dried and smoked food-stuffs. Indeed he did find smoked salmon, cured meats, oils, preserved fish eggs, dried herring roe, cured qwanis (camus bulbs), and dried berries.

"Everything, everything! All is mine. All is mine," he croaked as he flitted and hopped about opening boxes of oil, dried bulbs and fish-heads. Everything he saw he wanted. He wanted it all. His own drool spilled out of his mouth. He was very greedy.

Presently Pash-hook came into the great house. For the first time in her life she was not hurrying to do her husband's bidding. She did not scurry one little bit. Instead of helping her husband to carry out all the things and food-stuff down to their little canoe on the sandy beach, she slowly approached a small pile of embers that were still glowing on the centre hearth. There was no flame. The embers glowed warmly and invitingly. Pash-hook sat down and began to warm herself. She spread out her tiny hands. The embers still glowed warmly.

Ko-ishin-mit was so excited and so busy carrying out the food-stuff that he, for the first time in their married lives, forgot to make his wife do all the work.

"I shall never be hungry again. I shall never be hungry again," he kept repeating.

He worked hard packing, packing, packing, all he could lift and move down the long sloping beach. The tide was out and their little canoe was far down from the great houses. Pash-hook sat by the embers warming herself while Ko-ishin-mit worked at loading the canoe. At last the canoe was filled. It was so full there was hardly any room left for himself or for Pash-hook.

"One more trip. One more trip." How greedy Ko-ishin-mit was! He decided to put the last load where his wife would sit. He hopped up the high sloping beach and flitted into the now nearly empty cedar box and decided again he would put the very last load where Pash-hook would sit.

All of a sudden he remembered her. Pash-hook was still sitting by the fire warming herself at the embers.

"Come Pash-hook! Hurry! We must come back as fast as we can. We must take all. We must take all. We must come back before daylight returns. Hurry, hurry, Pash-hook!"

But Pash-hook still sat without moving, before the embers of the fire. Ko-ishin-mit lost his temper. He hopped to his wife's side demanding in his raspy voice, "What's the matter with you, woman? You have never disobeyed me like this before. Get up at once. We must go."

Pash-hook did not move. She did not speak. She did not look up at her husband.

Ko-ishin-mit was alarmed. He became very frightened.

"Get up, get up!" he croaked. In anger he grabbed Pash-hook by the shoulder and tried to pull her up. The harder he pulled the heavier she became. He could not budge the small little person. She felt like a rooted stone. Ko-ishin-mit was now trembling with fear. He hop-flitted out and down to his canoe and pushed and heaved trying to move it out to deeper water, but the harder he pulled and heaved the heavier the little canoe became.

"Something is wrong. Something is terribly wrong," he told himself. He tried to shout but only a weak croak came out. He flitted back to the great house and hopped inside. Pash-hook still sat by the embers of the fire.

Ko-ishin-mit noticed she was trying very hard to tell him something. He very gingerly approached her and bent his head towards her moving lips. Brave, gallant Pash-hook tried with all her might.

"There are strange people holding me down. I can't move," she whispered, almost out of breath. "Put back all you took," she entreated her husband.

Ko-ishin-mit flitted back to his canoe and once more tried to push it out into the stream. It would not move. He tried pulling it farther up onto the beach. It moved with hardly any effort at all. Trembling, Ko-ishin-mit grabbed the topmost bale and hauled it back to the great house. He worked very hard toting all the boxes and bales back to where he found them. When the last article had been returned to its own cedar box then only did Pash-hook stir.

"Heahh," she breathed, "I'm free," and shook herself and stood up. Her husband led her out and down the long, long beach to their canoe.

Pash-hook hopped in as her now very meek husband pushed the canoe into the stream. They both paddled with all their might and main until they were at a safe distance from the strange, strange place. When they at last stopped to rest Pash-hook spoke her first words since leaving the great house.

"Heahh, I'm free," she repeated. "There are people up there in the great house with the earthen floors. I'm sure of it. I felt hands, heavy hands, upon my shoulders holding me down. I'm certain that one of them sat on me because I felt so crushed down from above. I was very frightened. I couldn't speak. I couldn't tell you.

Ko-ishin-mit looked at his wife with great love. "Choo, choo, choo, all right, all right, Pash-hook, my mate. Don't be afraid any more. We shall never go to that isle again."

It is said that all things belong to someone. The old people say it is not wise to keep anything you find.

Around the point and across the bay
There is an Isle with clumpy spruce
That stands on mossy knolls
Green with salal.
The beaches are covered with sea-shells white
When the tide runs out sea-grasses wave and beckon you in.
The shadow people live there, it is said—
Shadow people one cannot see until the sun is up
To cast their shadows on the sands of sea-shells white.

The main body of the fiction of William Faulkner (1897-1962) stands as a memorial to the American South, the old South of rich plantation owners and poor white trash, of slavery and sudden violence: a region not without its glories, but suffering a progressive decay from within. Faulkner was born in Oxford, Mississippi, into a family whose roots reached back into the old South; and out of this background grew the fictional city of Jefferson in Yoknapatawpha County, the history of which forms the principal subject of Faulkner's work. After service in the Canadian Flying Corps during World War I and a period at the University of Mississippi, he turned to literature as a profession, publishing his first novel, *Soldiers' Pay*, in 1926. With *Sartoris* (1929), he began his re-creation and exploration of the South, which were to continue in such works as *The Sound and the Fury* (1929), *As I Lay Dying* (1930), *Light in August* (1932), *Absalom, Absalom!* (1936), and *Go Down, Moses* (1942). In these and other works, Faulkner chronicles the fortunes of the Sartorises and the Snopeses, the Compsons and the McCaslins, characters who recur throughout his writings, sometimes at the centre, at other times at the periphery of the action; and although the novels and stories do not form a continuous series, they are linked by common themes and preoccupations: the breakdown of social traditions, the strengths and weaknesses of the old Southern code, the strained and often bloody relations between black and white in the aftermath of slavery. "Dry September," from Faulkner's first collection of stories, *These Thirteen* (1931), is a powerful evocation of the frustration, bigotry, and passion pervading a society in which old fears and hatreds die hard.

Faulkner's achievement, however, extends beyond the dramatic creation of a Southern myth; in the moral problems and the racial tensions of his imaginary community in Mississippi, he has imaged sources of guilt and conflict which beset our larger society. In his address upon receiving the Nobel Prize for literature in 1950, Faulkner spoke of the role of the artist in terms applicable to himself, exhorting young writers to depict "the old verities and truths of the heart, the old universal truths lacking which any story is ephemeral and doomed—love and honor and pity and pride and compassion and sacrifice."

FOR FURTHER READING

James B. Carothers, *William Faulkner's Short Stories* (Ann Arbor: UMI Research Press, 1985).

Malcolm Cowley, "William Faulkner's Legend of the South," *Sewanee Review* 53 (1945): 343-61.

Michael Millgate, *The Achievement of William Faulkner* (New York: Random House, 1966).

Jean Stein, "The Art of Fiction XII: William Faulkner," *Paris Review* 12 (Spring 1956): 28-52.

J.B. Vickery, "Ritual and Theme in Faulkner's 'Dry September'," *Arizona Quarterly* 18 (Spring 1962): 5-14.

Dry September

Through the bloody September twilight, aftermath of sixty-two rainless days, it had gone like a fire in dry grass—the rumor, the story, whatever it was. Something about Miss Minnie Cooper and a Negro. Attacked, insulted, frightened: none of them, gathered in the barber shop on that Saturday evening where the ceiling fan stirred, without freshening it, the vitiated air, sending back upon them, in recurrent surges of stale pomade and lotion, their own stale breath and odors, knew exactly what had happened.

"Except it wasn't Will Mayes," a barber said. He was a man of middle age; a thin, sand-colored man with a mild face, who was shaving a client. "I know Will Mayes. He's a good nigger. And I know Miss Minnie Cooper, too."

"What do you know about her?" a second barber said.

"Who is she?" the client said. "A young girl?"

"No," the barber said. "She's about forty, I reckon. She aint married. That's why I dont believe—"

"Believe, hell!" a hulking youth in a sweat-stained silk shirt said. "Won't you take a white woman's word before a nigger's?"

"I dont believe Will Mayes did it," the barber said. "I know Will Mayes."

"Maybe you know who did it, then. Maybe you already got him out of town, you damn niggerlover."

"I dont believe anybody did anything. I dont believe anything happened. I leave it to you fellows if them ladies that get old without getting married dont have notions that a man cant—"

"Then you are a hell of a white man," the client said. He moved under the cloth. The youth had sprung to his feet.

"You dont?" he said. "Do you accuse a white woman of lying?"

The barber held the razor poised above the half-risen client. He did not look around.

"It's this durn weather," another said. "It's enough to make a man do anything. Even to her."

Nobody laughed. The barber said in his mild, stubborn tone. "I aint accusing nobody of nothing. I just know and you fellows know how a woman that never—"

"You damn niggerlover!" the youth said.

"Shut up, Butch," another said. "We'll get the facts in plenty of time to act."

"Who is? Who's getting them?" the youth said. "Facts, hell! I—"

"You're a fine white man," the client said. "Aint you?" In his frothy beard he looked like a desert rat in moving pictures. "You can tell them, Jack," he said to the youth. "If there aint any white men in this town you can count on me, even if I aint only a drummer and a stranger."

"That's right, boys," the barber said. "Find out the truth first. I know Will Mayes."

"Well, by God!" the youth shouted. "To think that a white man in this town—"

"Shut up, Butch," the second speaker said. "We got plenty of time."

The client sat up. He looked at the speaker. "Do you claim that anything excuses a nigger attacking a white woman? Do you mean to tell me you are a white man and you'll stand for it? You better go back North were you came from. The South dont want your kind here."

"North what?" the second said. "I was born and raised in this town."

"Well, by God!" the youth said. He looked about with a strained, baffled gaze, as if he was trying to remember what it was he wanted to say or to do. He drew his sleeve across his sweating face. "Damn if I'm going to let a white woman—"

"You tell them, Jack," the drummer said. "By God, if they—"

The screen door crashed open. A man stood in the floor, his feet apart and his heavy-set body poised easily. His white shirt was open at the throat; he wore a felt hat. His hot, bold glance swept the group. His name was McLendon. He had commanded troops at the front in France and had been decorated for valor.

"Well," he said, "are you going to sit there and let a black son rape a white woman on the streets of Jefferson?"

Butch sprang up again. The silk of his shirt clung flat to his heavy shoulders. At each armpit was a dark halfmoon. "That's what I been telling them! That's what I—"

"Did it really happen?" a third said. "This aint the first man scare she ever had, like Hawkshaw says. Wasn't there something about a man on the kitchen roof, watching her undress, about a year ago?"

"What?" the client said. "What's that?" The barber had been slowly forcing him back into the chair; he arrested himself reclining, his head lifted, the barber still pressing him down.

McLendon whirled on the third speaker. "Happen? What the hell difference does it make? Are you going to let the black sons get away with it until one really does it?"

"That's what I'm telling them!" Butch shouted. He cursed, long and steady, pointless.

"Here, here," a fourth said. "Not so loud. Dont talk so loud."

"Sure," McLendon said, "no talking necessary at all. I've done my talking. Who's with me?" He poised on the balls of his feet, roving his gaze.

The barber held the drummers face down, the razor poised. "Find out the facts first, boys. I know Willy Mayes. It wasn't him. Let's get the sheriff and do this thing right."

McLendon whirled upon him furious, rigid face. The barber did not look away. They looked like men of different races. The other barbers had ceased also above their prone clients. "You mean to tell me," McLendon said, "that you'd take a nigger's word before a white woman's? Why, you damn niggerloving—"

The third speaker rose and grasped McLendon's arm; he too had been a soldier. "Now, now. Let's figure this thing out. Who knows anything about what really happened?"

"Figure out hell!" McLendon jerked his arm free. "All that're with me get up from there. The ones that aint—" He roved his gaze, dragging his sleeve across his face.

Three men rose. The drummer in the chair sat up. "Here," he said, jerking at the cloth about his neck; "get this rag off me. I'm with him. I dont live here, but by God, if our mothers and wives and sisters—" He smeared the cloth over his face and flung it to the floor. McLendon stood in the floor and cursed the others. Another rose and moved towards him. The remainder sat uncomfortable, not looking at one another, then one by one they rose and joined him.

The barber picked the cloth from the floor. He began to fold it neatly. "Boys, dont do that. Will Mayes never done it. I know."

"Come on," McLendon said. He whirled. From his hip pocket protruded the butt of a heavy automatic pistol. They went out. The screen door crashed behind them reverberant in the dead air.

The barber wiped the razor carefully and swiftly, and put it away and ran to the rear, and took his hat from the wall. "I'll be back as soon as I can," he said to the other barbers. "I cant let—" He went out, running. The two other barbers followed him to the door and caught it on the rebound, leaning out and looking up the street after him. The air was flat and dead. It had a metallic taste at the base of the tongue.

"What can he do?" the first said. The second one was saying "Jees Christ, Jees Christ" under his breath. "I'd just as lief be Will Mayes as Hawk, if he gets McLendon riled."

"Jees Christ, Jees Christ," the second whispered.

"You reckon he really done it to her?" the first said.

II

She was thirty-eight or thirty-nine. She lived in a small frame house with her invalid mother and a thin, sallow, unflagging aunt, where each morning between ten and eleven she would appear on the porch in a lace-trimmed boudoir cap, to sit swinging in the porch swing until noon. After dinner she lay down for a while, until the afternoon began to cool. Then, in one of the three or four new voile dresses which she had each summer, she would go downtown to spend the afternoon in the stores with the other ladies, where they would handle the goods and haggle over the prices in cold, immediate voices, without any intention of buying.

She was of comfortable people—not the best in Jefferson, but good people enough—and she was still on the slender side of ordinary-look-ing, with a bright, faintly haggard manner and dress. When she was young she had had a slender nervous body and a sort of hard vivacity which had enabled her for a time to ride upon the crest of the town's social life as exemplified by the high school party and church social period of her contemporaries while still children enough to be unclass-conscious.

She was the last to realize that she was losing ground; that those among whom she had been a little brighter and louder flame than any other were beginning to learn the pleasure of snobbery—male—and retaliation—female. That was when her face began to wear that bright, haggard look. She still carried it to parties on shadowy porticoes and summer lawns, like a mask or a flag, with that bafflement of furious repudiation of truth in her eyes. One evening at a party she heard a boy and two girls, all schoolmates, talking. She never accepted another invitation.

She watched the girls with whom she had grown up as they married and got homes and children, but no man ever called on her steadily until the children of the other girls had been calling her "aunty" for several years, the while their mothers told them in bright voices about how popular Aunt Minnie had been as a girl. Then the town began to see her driving on Sunday afternoons with the cashier in the bank. He was a widower of about forty—a high-colored man, smelling always faintly of the barber shop or of whisky. He owned the first automobile in town, a red runabout; Minnie had the first motoring bonnet and veil the town ever saw. Then the town began to say: "Poor Minnie." "But she is old enough to take care of herself," others said. That was when she began to ask her old schoolmates that their children call her "cousin" instead of "aunty."

It was twelve years now since she had been relegated into adultery by public opinion, and eight years since the cashier had gone to a Memphis bank, returning for one day each Christmas, which he spent at an annual bachelors' party at a hunting club on the river. From behind their curtains the neighbors would see the party pass, and during the over-the-way Christmas day visiting they would tell her about him, about how well he looked, and how they heard that he was prospering in the city, watching with bright, secret eyes her haggard, bright face. Usually, by that hour there would be the scent of whiskey on her breath. It was supplied her by a youth, a clerk at the soda fountain: "Sure; I buy it for the old gal. I reckon she's entitled to a little fun."

Her mother kept to her room altogether now; the gaunt aunt ran the house. Against that background Minnie's bright dresses, her idle and empty days, had a quality of furious unreality. She went out in the evenings only with women now, neighbors, to the moving pictures. Each afternoon she dressed in one of the new dresses and went downtown alone, where her young "cousins" were already strolling in the late afternoons with their delicate, silken heads and thin, awkward arms and conscious hips, clinging to one another or shrieking and giggling with paired boys in the soda fountain when she passed and went on along the serried store fronts, in the doors of which the sitting and lounging men did not even follow her with their eyes any more.

III

The barber went swiftly up the street where the sparse lights, insect-swirled, glared in rigid and violent suspension in the lifeless air. The day had died in a pall of dust; above the darkened square, shrouded by the spent dust, the sky was as clear as the inside of a brass bell. Below the east was a rumor of the twice-waxed moon.

When he overtook them McLendon and three others were getting into a car parked in an alley. McLendon stooped his thick head, peering out beneath the top, "Changed your mind, did you?" he said. "Damn good thing; by God, tomorrow when this town hears about how you talked tonight—"

"Now, now," the other ex-soldier said. "Hawkshaw's all right. Come on, Hawk; jump in."

"Will Mayes never done it, boys," the barber said. "If anybody done it. Why, you all know well as I do there aint any town where they got better niggers than us. And you know how a lady will kind of think things about men when there aint any reason to, and Miss Minnie anyway—"

"Sure, sure," the soldier said. "We're just going to talk to him a little; that's all."

"Talk hell!" Butch said. "When we're through with the—"

"Shut up, for God's sake!" the soldier said. "Do you want everybody in town—"

"Tell them, by God!" McLendon said. "Tell every one of the sons that'll let a white woman—"

"Let's go; let's go; here's the other car." The second car slid squealing out of a cloud of dust at the alley mouth. McLendon started his car and took the lead. Dust lay like a fog in the street. The street lights hung nimbused as in water. They drove out of town.

A rutted lane turned at right angles. Dust hung above it too, and above all the land. The dark bulk of the ice plant, where the Negro Mayes was night watchman, rose against the sky. "Better stop here, hadn't we?" the soldier said. McLendon did not reply. He hurled the car up and slammed to a stop, the headlights glaring on the blank wall.

"Listen here, boys," the barber said; "if he's here, dont that prove he never done it? Dont it? If it was him, he would run. Dont you see he would?" The second car came up and stopped. McLendon got down; Butch sprang down beside him. "Listen, boys," the barber said.

"Cut the lights off!" McLendon said. The breathless dark rushed down. There was no sound in it save their lungs as they sought air in the parched dust in which for two months they had lived; then the diminishing crunch of McLendon's and Butch's feet, and a moment later McLendon's voice:

"Will! . . . Will!"

Below the east the wan hemorrhage of the moon increased. It heaved above the ridge, silvering the air, the dust, so that they seemed to breathe, live, in a bowl of molten lead. There was no sound of night-bird nor insect, no sound save their breathing and a faint ticking of contracting metal about the cars. Where their bodies touched one another they seemed to sweat dryly, for no more moisture came. "Christ!" a voice said; "let's get out of here."

But they didn't move until vague noises began to grow out of the darkness ahead; then they got out and waited tensely in the breathless dark. There was another sound: a blow, a hissing expulsion of breath and McLendon cursing in undertone. They stood a moment longer, then they ran forward. They ran in a stumbling clump, as though they were fleeing something. "Kill him, kill the son," a voice whispered. McLendon flung them back.

"Not here," he said. "Get him into the car." "Kill him, kill the black son!" the voice murmured. They dragged the Negro to the car. The barber had waited beside the car. He could feel himself sweating and he knew he was going to be sick at the stomach.

"What is it, captains?" the Negro said. "I aint done nothing. 'Fore God, Mr John." Someone produced handcuffs. They worked busily about the Negro as though he were a post, quiet, intent, getting in one another's way. He submitted to the handcuffs, looking swiftly and constantly from dim face to dim face. "Who's here, captains?" he said, leaning to peer into the faces until they could feel his breath and smell his sweaty reek. He spoke a name or two. "What you all say I done, Mr John?"

McLendon jerked the car door open. "Get in!" he said.

The Negro did not move. "What you all going to do with me, Mr John? I aint done nothing. White folks, captains, I aint done nothing: I swear 'fore God." He called another name.

"Get in!" McLendon said. He struck the Negro. The others expelled their breath in a dry hissing and struck him with random blows and he whirled and cursed them, and swept his manacled hands across their faces and slashed the barber upon the mouth, and the barber struck him also. "Get him in there," McLendon said. They pushed at him. He ceased struggling and got in and sat quietly as the others took their places. He sat between the barber and the soldier, drawing his limbs in so as not to touch them, his eyes going swiftly and constantly from face to face. Butch clung to the running board. The car moved on. The barber nursed his mouth with his handkerchief.

"What's the matter, Hawk?" the soldier said.

"Nothing," the barber said. They regained the highroad and turned away from town. The second car dropped back out of the dust. They went on, gaining speed; the final fringe of houses dropped behind.

"Goddamn, he stinks!" the soldier said.

"We'll fix that," the drummer in front beside McLendon said. On the running board Butch cursed into the hot rush of air. The barber leaned suddenly forward and touched McLendon's arm.

"Let me out, John," he said.

"Jump out, niggerlover," McLendon said without turning his head. He drove swiftly. Behind them the sourceless lights of the second car glared in the dust. Presently McLendon turned into a narrow road. It was rutted with disuse. It led back to an abandoned brick kiln—a series of reddish mounds and weed- and vine-choked vats without bottom. It had been used for pasture once, until one day the owner missed one of his mules. Although he prodded carefully in the vats with a long pole, he could not even find the bottom of them.

"John," the barber said.

"Jump out, then," McLendon said, hurling the car along the ruts. Beside the barber the Negro spoke:

"Mr Henry."

The barber sat forward. The narrow tunnel of the road rushed up and past. Their motion was like an extinct furnace blast: cooler, but utterly dead. The car bounded from rut to rut.

"Mr Henry," the Negro said.

The barber began to tug furiously at the door. "Look out, there!" the soldier said, but the barber had already kicked the door open and swung onto the running board. The soldier leaned across the Negro and grasped at him, but he had already jumped. The car went on without checking speed.

The impetus hurled him crashing through dust-sheathed weeds, into the ditch. Dust puffed about him, and in a thin, vicious crackling of sapless stems he lay choking and retching until the second car passed and died away. Then he rose and limped on until he reached the highroad and turned towards town, brushing at his clothes with his hands. The moon was higher, riding high and clear of the dust at last, and after a while the town began to glare beneath the dust. He went on, limping. Presently he heard cars and the glow of them grew in the dust until they passed. McLendon's car came last now. There were four people in it and Butch was not on the running board.

They went on; the dust swallowed them; the glare and the sound died away. The dust of them hung for a while, but soon the eternal dust absorbed it again. The barber climbed back onto the road and limped on toward town.

IV

As she dressed for supper on that Saturday evening, her own flesh felt like fever. Her hands trembled among the hooks and eyes, and her eyes had a feverish look, and her hair swirled crisp and crackling under the comb. While she was still dressing the friends called for her and sat while she donned her sheerest underthings and stockings and a new voile dress. "Do you feel strong enough to go out?" they said, their eyes bright too, with a dark glitter. "When you have had time to get over the shock, you must tell us what happened. What he said and did; everything."

In the leafed darkness, as they walked toward the square, she began to breathe deeply, something like a swimmer preparing to dive, until she ceased trembling, the four of them walking slowly because of the terrible heat and out of solicitude for her. But as they neared the square she began to tremble again, walking with her head up, her hands clenched at her sides, their voices about her murmurous, also with that feverish, glittering quality of their eyes.

They entered the square, she in the center of the group, fragile in her fresh dress. She was trembling worse. She walked slower and slower, as children eat ice cream, her head up and her eyes bright in the haggard banner of her lace, passing the hotel and the coatless drummers in chairs along the curb looking around at her. "That's the one: see? The one in pink in the middle." "Is that her? What did they do with the nigger? Did they—?" "Sure. He's all right." "All right, is he?" "Sure. He went on a little trip." Then the drug store, where even the young men lounging in the doorway tipped their hats and followed with their eyes the motion of her hips and legs when she passed.

They went on, passing the lifted hats of the gentlemen, the suddenly ceased voices, deferent, protective. "Do you see?" the friends said. Their voices sounded like long, hovering sighs of hissing exultation. "There's not a Negro on the square. Not one."

They reached the picture show. It was like a miniature fairyland with its lighted lobby and colored lithographs of life caught in its terrible and beautiful mutations. Her lips began to tingle. In the dark, when the picture began, it would be all right; she could hold back the laughing so it would not waste away so fast and so soon. So she hurried on before the turning faces, the undertones of low astonishment, and they took their accustomed places where she could see the aisle against the silver glare and the young men and girls coming in two and two against it.

The lights flicked away; the screen glowed silver, and soon life began to unfold, beautiful and passionate and sad, while still the young men and girls entered, scented and sibilant in the half dark, their paired backs in silhouette delicate and sleek, their slim, quick bodies awkward, divinely young, while beyond them the silver dream accumulated, inevitably on and on. She began to laugh. In trying to suppress it, it made more noise than ever; heads began to turn. Still laughing, her friends raised her and led her out, and she stood at the curb, laughing on a high, sustained note, until the taxi came up and they helped her in.

They removed the pink voile and the sheer underthings and the stockings, and put her to bed, and cracked ice for her temples, and sent for the doctor. He was hard to locate, so they ministered to her with hushed ejaculations, renewing the ice and fanning her. While the ice was fresh and cold she stopped laughing and lay still for a time, moaning only a little. But soon the laughing welled again and her voice rose screaming.

"Shhhhhhhhhhh Shhhhhhhhhhhhhhh!" they said, freshening the icepack, smoothing her hair, examining it for gray; "poor girl!" Then to one another: "Do you suppose anything really happened?" their eyes darkly aglitter, secret and passionate. "Shhhhhhhhhh! Poor girl! Poor Minnie!"

V

It was midnight when McLendon drove up to his neat new house. It was trim and fresh as a birdcage and almost as small, with its clean, green-and-white paint. He locked the car and mounted the porch and entered. His wife rose from a chair beside the reading lamp. McLendon stopped in the floor and stared at her until she looked down.

"Look at that clock," he said, lifting his arm, pointing. She stood before him, her face lowered, a magazine in her hands. Her face was pale, strained, and weary-looking. "Haven't I told you about sitting up like this, waiting to see when I come in?"

"John," she said. She laid the magazine down. Poised on the balls of his feet, he glared at her with his hot eyes, his sweating face.

"Didn't I tell you?" He went toward her. She looked up then. He caught her shoulder. She stood passive, looking at him.

"Dont, John. I couldn't sleep . . . The heat; something. Please, John. You're hurting me."

"Didn't I tell you?" He released her and half struck, half flung her across the chair, and she lay there and watched him quietly as he left the room.

He went on through the house, ripping off his shirt, and on the dark, screened porch at the rear he stood and mopped his head and shoulders with the shirt and flung it away. He took the pistol from his hip and laid it on the table beside the bed, and sat on the bed and removed his shoes, and rose and slipped his trousers off. He was sweating again already, and he stooped and hunted furiously for the shirt. At last he found it and wiped his body again, and, with his body pressed against the dusty screen, he stood panting. There was no movement, no sound, not even an insect. The dark world seemed to lie stricken beneath the cold moon and the lidless stars.

Edward Morgan Forster (1879-1970) was born into a London family connected with the group of wealthy Evangelicals known as the Clapham Sect. His upbringing and education (Tonbridge School and King's College, Cambridge) were solidly middle class; yet despite this background, Forster turned a critical and satirical eye on the snobbery and superficiality of English society. After leaving Cambridge in 1901, he travelled through Italy and Greece, and in the Mediterranean temperament he perceived qualities of passion and responsiveness very different from the coldness and reserve of the English character. In his novels *Where Angels Fear to Tread* (1905), *The Longest Journey* (1907), and *Howards End* (1910), he exposes middle-class illusions, and sets the deadening force of social convention against the liberating power of feeling, a conflict enacted on both the spiritual and the sexual level. This opposition between social pressures and individual feeling is often expressed as a clash between the rational faculties and the imagination, and it takes on a broader significance in *A Passage to India* (1924), in which two cultures meet but do not merge: the Englishman and the Indian are symbolically parted at the end of that novel, as if to emphasize how the Western mind has lost touch with the deeper springs of intuitive awareness and the sources of natural harmony.

These concerns also find expression in Forster's short stories, collected in *The Celestial Omnibus* (1911) and *The Eternal Moment* (1928), where he gives freer rein to allegorical and mythical tendencies. In "The Road from Colonus" (*The Celestial Omnibus*), Forster juxtaposes the shallowness of contemporary English values with the spirit of life in an ancient land. The title alludes to the story of Oedipus, who, old and blind, was transfigured by his experience in the sacred grove at Colonus, and enabled to meet his death with pride and dignity.

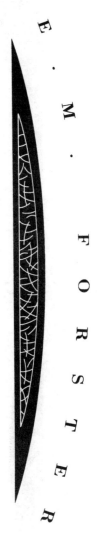

E. M. FORSTER

FOR FURTHER READING

E.M. Forster, *Aspects of the Novel* (London: Edward Arnold, 1927; reprinted by Penguin Books, 1962).

Judith Scherer Herz, *The Short Narratives of E.M. Forster* (Basingstoke: Macmillan, 1988).

F.P.W. McDowell, "Forster's 'Natural Supernaturalism': The Tales," *Modern Fiction Studies* 7 (1961): 271-83.

Norman Page, *E.M. Forster* (Basingstoke: Macmillan, 1987).

Lionel Trilling, *E.M. Forster,* 2d ed. (New York: New Directions, 1964).

The Road from Colonus

I

For no very intelligible reason, Mr Lucas had hurried ahead of his party. He was perhaps reaching the age at which independence becomes valuable, because it is so soon to be lost. Tired of attention and consideration, he liked breaking away from the younger members, to ride by himself, and to dismount unassisted. Perhaps he also relished that more subtle pleasure of being kept waiting for lunch, and of telling the others on their arrival that it was of no consequence.

So, with childish impatience, he battered the animal's sides with his heels, and made the muleteer bang it with a thick stick and prick it with a sharp one, and jolted down the hill sides through clumps of flowering shrubs and stretches of anemones and asphodel, till he heard the sound of running water, and came in sight of the group of plane trees where they were to have their meal.

Even in England those trees would have been remarkable, so huge were they, so interlaced, so magnificently clothed in quivering green. And here in Greece they were unique, the one cool spot in that hard brilliant landscape, already scorched by the heat of an April sun. In their midst was hidden a tiny Khan or country inn, a frail mud building with a broad wooden balcony in which sat an old woman spinning, while a small brown pig, eating orange peel, stood beside her. On the wet earth below squatted two children, playing some primaeval game with their fingers; and their mother, none too clean either, was messing with some rice inside. As Mrs Forman would have said, it was all very Greek, and the fastidious Mr Lucas felt thankful that they were bringing their own food with them, and should eat it in the open air.

Still, he was glad to be there—the muleteer had helped him off—and glad that Mrs Forman was not there to forestall his opinions—glad even that he should not see Ethel for quite half an hour. Ethel was his youngest daughter, still unmarried. She was unselfish and affectionate, and it was generally understood that she was to devote her life to her father, and be the comfort of his old age. Mrs Forman always referred to her as Antigone, and Mr Lucas tried to settle down to the role of Oedipus, which seemed the only one that public opinion allowed him.

He had this in common with Oedipus, that he was growing old. Even to himself it had become obvious. He had lost interest in other people's affairs, and seldom attended when they spoke to him. He was fond of talking himself but often forgot what he was going to say, and even when he succeeded, it seldom seemed worth the effort. His phrases and gestures had become stiff and set, his anecdotes, once so successful, fell flat, his silence was as meaningless as his speech. Yet he had led a healthy, active life, had worked steadily, made money, educated his children. There was nothing and no one to blame: he was simply growing old.

At the present moment, here he was in Greece, and one of the dreams of his life was realized. Forty years ago he had caught the fever of Hellenism, and all his life he had felt that could he but visit that land, he would not have lived in vain. But Athens had been dusty, Delphi wet, Thermopylae flat, and he had listened with amazement and cynicism to the rapturous exclamations of his companions. Greece was like England: it was a man who was growing old, and it made no difference whether that man looked at the Thames or the Eurotas. It was his last hope of contradicting that logic of experience, and it was failing.

Yet Greece had done something for him, though he did not know it. It had made him discontented, and there are stirrings of life in discontent. He knew that he was not the victim of continual ill-luck. Something great was wrong, and he was pitted against no mediocre or accidental enemy. For the last month a strange desire had possessed him to die fighting.

"Greece is the land for young people," he said to himself as he stood under the plane trees, "but I will enter into it, I will possess it. Leaves shall be green again, water shall be sweet, the sky shall be blue. They were so forty years ago, and I will win them back. I do mind being old, and I will pretend no longer."

He took two steps forward, and immediately cold waters were gurgling over his ankle.

"Where does the water come from?" he asked himself. "I do not even know that." He remembered that all the hill sides were dry; yet here the road was suddenly covered with flowing streams.

He stopped still in amazement, saying: "Water out of a tree—out of a hollow tree? I never saw nor thought of that before."

For the enormous plane that leant towards the Khan was hollow—it had been burnt out for charcoal—and from its living trunk there gushed an impetuous spring, coating the bark with fern and moss, and flowing over the mule track to create fertile meadows beyond. The simple country folk had paid to beauty and mystery such tribute as they could, for in the rind of the tree a shrine was cut, holding a lamp and a little picture of the Virgin, inheritor of the Naiad's and Dryad's joint abode.

"I never saw anything so marvelous before," said Mr Lucas. "I could even step inside the trunk and see where the water comes from."

For a moment he hesitated to violate the shrine. Then he remembered with a smile his own thought—"the place shall be mine; I will enter it and possess it"—and leapt almost aggressively on to a stone within.

The water pressed up steadily and noiselessly from the hollow roots and hidden crevices of the plane, forming a wonderful amber pool ere it spilt over the lip of bark on to the earth outside. Mr Lucas tasted it and it was sweet, and when he looked up the black funnel of the trunk he saw sky which was blue, and some leaves which were green; and he remembered, without smiling, another of his thoughts.

Others had been before him—indeed he had a curious sense of companionship. Little votive offerings to the presiding Power were fastened on to the bark—tiny arms and legs and eyes in tin, grotesque models of the brain or the heart—all tokens of some recovery of strength or wisdom or love. There was no such thing as the solitude of nature, for the sorrows and joys of humanity had pressed even into the bosom of a tree. He spread out his arms and steadied himself against the soft charred wood, and then slowly leant back, till his body was resting on the trunk behind. His eyes closed, and he had the strange feeling of one who is moving, yet at peace—the feeling of the swimmer, who, after long struggling with chopping seas, finds that after all the tide will sweep him to his goal.

So he lay motionless, conscious only of the stream below his feet, and that all things were a stream, in which he was moving.

He was aroused at last by a shock—the shock of an arrival perhaps, for when he opened his eyes, something unimagined, indefinable, had passed over all things, and made them intelligible and good.

There was meaning in the stoop of the old woman over her work, and in the quick motions of the little pig, and in her diminishing globe of wool. A young man came singing over the streams on a mule, and there was beauty in his pose and sincerity in his greeting. The sun made no accidental patterns upon the spreading roots of the trees, and there was intention in the nodding clumps of asphodel, and in the music of the water. To Mr Lucas, who, in a brief space of time, had discovered not only Greece, but England and all the world and life, there seemed nothing ludicrous in the desire to hang within the tree another votive offering—a little model of an entire man.

"Why, here's papa, playing at being Merlin."

All unnoticed they had arrived—Ethel, Mrs Forman, Mr Graham, and the English-speaking dragoman. Mr Lucas peered out at them suspiciously. They had suddenly become unfamiliar, and all that they did seemed strained and coarse.

"Allow me to give you a hand," said Mr Graham, a young man who was always polite to his elders.

Mr Lucas felt annoyed. "Thank you, I can managed perfectly well by myself," he replied. His foot slipped as he stepped out of the tree, and went into the spring.

"Oh papa, my papa!" said Ethel, "what are you doing? Thank goodness I have got a change for you on the mule."

She tended him carefully, giving him clean socks and dry boots, and then sat him down on the rug beside the lunch basket, while she went with the others to explore the grove.

They came back in ecstasies, in which Mr Lucas tried to join. But he found them intolerable. Their enthusiasm was superficial, commonplace, and spasmodic. They had no perception of the coherent beauty that was flowering around them. He tried at least to explain his feelings, and what he said was:

"I am altogether pleased with the appearance of this place. It impresses me very favourably. The trees are fine, remarkably fine for Greece, and there is something very poetic in the spring of clear running water. The people too seem kindly and civil. It is decidedly an attractive place."

Mrs Forman upbraided him for his tepid praise.

"Oh, it is a place in a thousand!" she cried, "I could live and die here! I really would stop if I had not to be back at Athens! It reminds me of the Colonus of Sophocles."

"Well I must stop," said Ethel. "I positively must."

"Yes, do! You and your father! Antigone and Oedipus. Of course you must stop at Colonus!"

Mr Lucas was almost breathless with excitement. When he stood within the tree, he had believed that his happiness would be independent of locality. But these few minutes' conversation had undeceived him. He no longer trusted himself to journey through the world, for old thoughts, old weariness might be waiting to rejoin him as soon as he left the shade of the planes, and the music of the virgin water. To sleep in the Khan with the gracious, kind-eyed people, to watch the bats flit about within the globe of shade, and see the moon turn the golden patterns into silver—one such night would place him beyond relapse, and confirm him for ever in the kingdom he had regained. But all his lips could say was: "I should be willing to put in a night here."

"You mean a week, papa! It would be sacrilege to put in less."

"A week then, a week," said his lips, irritated at being corrected, while his heart was leaping with joy. All through lunch he spoke to them no more, but watched the place he should know so well, and the people who would so soon be his companions and friends. The inmates of the Khan only consisted of an old woman, a middle-aged woman, a young man and two children, and to none of them had he spoken, yet he loved them as he loved everything that moved or breathed or existed beneath the benedictory shade of the planes.

"*En route!*" said the shrill voice of Mrs Forman. "Ethel! Mr Graham! The best of things must end."

"To-night," thought Mr Lucas, "they will light the little lamp by the shrine. And when we all sit together on the balcony, perhaps they will tell me which offerings they put up."

"I beg your pardon, Mr Lucas," said Graham, "but they want to fold up the rug you are sitting on."

Mr Lucas got up, saying to himself: "Ethel shall go to bed first, and then I will try to tell them about my offering too—for it is a thing I must do. I think they will understand if I am left with them alone."

Ethel touched him on the cheek. "Papa! I've called you three times. All the mules are here."

"Mules? What mules?"

"Our mules. We're all waiting. Oh, Mr Graham, do help my father on."

"I don't know what you're talking about, Ethel."

"My dearest papa, we must start. You know we have to get to Olympia tonight."

Mr Lucas in pompous, confident tones replied: "I always did wish, Ethel, that you had a better head for plans. You know perfectly well that we are putting in a week here. It is your own suggestion."

Ethel was startled into impoliteness. "What a perfectly ridiculous idea. You must have known I was joking. Of course I meant I wished we could."

"Ah! if we could only do what we wished!" sighed Mrs Forman, already seated on her mule.

"Surely," Ethel continued in calmer tones, "you didn't think I meant it."

"Most certainly I did. I have made all my plans on the supposition that we are stopping here, and it will be extremely inconvenient, indeed, impossible for me to start."

He delivered this remark with an air of great conviction, and Mrs Forman and Mr Graham had to turn away to hide their smiles.

"I am sorry I spoke so carelessly; it was wrong of me. But, you know, we can't break up our party, and even one night here would make us miss the boat at Patras."

Mrs Forman, in an aside, called Mr Graham's attention to the excellent way in which Ethel managed her father.

"I don't mind about the Patras boat. You said that we should stop here, and we are stopping."

It seemed as if the inhabitants of the Khan had divined in some mysterious way that the altercation touched them. The old woman stopped her spinning, while the young man and the two children stood behind Mr Lucas, as if supporting him.

Neither arguments nor entreaties moved him. He said little, but he was absolutely determined, because for the first time he saw his daily life aright. What need had he to return to England? Who would miss him? His friends were dead or cold. Ethel loved him in a way, but, as was right, she had other interests. His other children he seldom saw. He had only one other relative, his sister Julia, whom he both feared and hated. It was no effort to struggle. He would be a fool as well as a coward if he stirred from the place which brought him happiness and peace.

At last Ethel, to humour him, and not disinclined to air her modern Greek, went into the Khan with the astonished dragoman to look at the rooms. The woman inside received them with loud welcomes, and the young man, when no one was looking, began to lead Mr Lucas's mule to the stable.

"Drop it, you brigand!" shouted Graham, who always declared that foreigners could understand English if they chose. He was right, for the man obeyed, and they all stood waiting for Ethel's return.

She emerged at last, with close-gathered skirts, followed by the dragoman bearing the little pig, which he had bought at a bargain.

"My dear papa, I will do all I can for you, but stop in that Khan—no."

"Are there—fleas?" asked Mrs Forman.

Ethel intimated that "fleas" was not the word.

"Well, I am afraid that settles it," said Mrs Forman, "I know how particular Mr Lucas is."

"It does not settle it," said Mr Lucas. "Ethel, you go on. I do not want you. I don't know why I ever consulted you. I shall stop here alone."

"That is absolute nonsense," said Ethel, losing her temper. "How can you be left alone at your age? How would you get your meals or your bath? All your letters are waiting for you at Patras. You'll miss the boat. That means missing the London operas, and upsetting all your engagements for the month. And as if you could travel by yourself!"

"They might knife you," was Mr Graham's contribution.

The Greeks said nothing; but whenever Mr Lucas looked their way, they beckoned him towards the Khan. The children would even have drawn him by the coat, and the old woman on the balcony stopped her almost completed spinning, and fixed him with mysterious appealing eyes. As he fought, the issue assumed gigantic proportions, and he believed that he was not merely stopping because he had regained youth or seen beauty or found happiness, but because in that place and with those people a supreme event was awaiting him which would transfigure the face of the world. The moment was so tremendous that he abandoned words and arguments as useless, and rested on the strength of his mighty unrevealed allies: silent men, murmuring water, and whispering trees. For the whole place called with one voice, articulate to him, and his garrulous opponents became every minute more meaningless and absurd. Soon they would be tired and go chattering away into the sun, leaving him to the cool grove and the moonlight and the destiny he foresaw.

Mrs Forman and the dragoman had indeed already started, amid the piercing screams of the little pig, and the struggle might have gone on indefinitely if Ethel had not called in Mr Graham.

"Can you help me?" she whispered. "He is absolutely unmanageable."

"I'm no good at arguing—but if I could help you in any other way—" and he looked down complacently at his well-made figure.

Ethel hesitated. Then she said: "Help me in any way you can. After all, it is for his good that we do it."

"Then have his mule led up behind him."

So when Mr Lucas thought he had gained the day, he suddenly felt himself lifted off the ground, and sat sideways on the saddle, and at the same time the mule started off at a trot. He said nothing, for he had nothing to say, and even his face showed little emotion as he felt the shade pass and heard the sound of the water cease. Mr Graham was running at his side, hat in hand, apologizing.

"I know I had no business to do it, and I do beg your pardon awfully. But I do hope that some day you too will feel that I was—damn!"

A stone had caught him in the middle of the back. It was thrown by the little boy, who was pursuing them along the mule track. He was followed by his sister, also throwing stones.

Ethel screamed to the dragoman, who was some way ahead with Mrs Forman, but before he could rejoin them, another adversary appeared. It was the young Greek, who had cut them off in front, and now dashed down at Mr Lucas' bridle. Fortunately Graham was an expert boxer, and it did not take him a moment to beat down the youth's feeble defence, and to send him sprawling with a bleeding mouth into the asphodel. By this time the dragoman had arrived, the children, alarmed at the fate of their brother, had desisted, and the rescue party, if such it is to be considered, retired in disorder to the trees.

"Little devils!" said Graham, laughing with triumph. "That's the modern Greek all over. Your father meant money if he stopped, and they consider we were taking it out of their pocket."

"Oh, they are terrible—simple savages! I don't know how I shall ever thank you. You've saved my father."

"I only hope you didn't think me brutal."

"No," replied Ethel with a little sigh. "I admire strength."

Meanwhile the cavalcade reformed, and Mr Lucas, who, as Mrs Forman said, bore his disappointment wonderfully well, was put comfortably on to his mule. They hurried up the opposite hillside, fearful of another attack, and it was not until they had left the eventful place far behind that Ethel found an opportunity to speak to her father and ask his pardon for the way she had treated him.

"You seemed so different, dear father, and you quite frightened me. Now I feel that you are your old self again."

He did not answer, and she concluded that he was not unnaturally offended at her behaviour.

By one of those curious tricks of mountain scenery, the place they had left an hour before suddenly reappeared far below them. The Khan was hidden under the green dome, but in the open there still stood three figures, and through the pure air rose up a faint cry of defiance or farewell.

Mr Lucas stopped irresolutely, and let the reins fall from his hand. "Come, father dear," said Ethel gently.

He obeyed, and in another moment a spur of the hill hid the dangerous scene for ever.

II

It was breakfast time, but the gas was alight, owing to the fog. Mr Lucas was in the middle of an account of a bad night he had spent. Ethel, who was to be married in a few weeks, had her arms on the table, listening.

"First the door bell rang, then you came back from the theatre. Then the dog started, and after the dog the cat. And at three in the morning a young hooligan passed by singing. Oh yes: then there was the water gurgling in the pipe above my head."

"I think that was only the bath water running away," said Ethel, looking rather worn.

"Well, there's nothing I dislike more than running water. It's perfectly impossible to sleep in the house. I shall give it up. I shall give notice next quarter. I shall tell the landlord plainly, 'The reason I am giving up the house is this: it is perfectly impossible to sleep in it.' If he says—says—well, what has he got to say?"

"Some more toast, father?"

"Thank you, my dear." He took it, and there was an interval of peace.

But he soon recommenced. "I'm not going to submit to the practising next door as tamely as they think. I wrote and told them so—didn't I?"

"Yes," said Ethel, who had taken care that the letter should not reach. "I have seen the governess, and she has promised to arrange it differently. And Aunt Julia hates noise. It will sure to be all right."

Her aunt, being the only unattached member of the family, was coming to keep house for her father when she left him. The reference was not a happy one, and Mr Lucas commenced a series of half articulate sighs, which was only stopped by the arrival of the post.

"Oh, what a parcel!" cried Ethel. "For me! What can it be! Greek stamps. This is most exciting!"

It proved to be some asphodel bulbs, sent by Mrs Forman from Athens for planting in the conservatory.

"Doesn't it bring it all back! You remember the asphodels, father. And all wrapped up in Greek newspapers. I wonder if I can read them still. I used to be able to, you know."

She rattled on, hoping to conceal the laughter of the children next door—a favourite source of querulousness at breakfast time.

"Listen to me! 'A rural disaster.' Oh, I've hit on something sad. But never mind. 'Last Tuesday at Plataniste, in the province of Messenia, a shocking tragedy occurred. A large tree'—aren't I getting on well?—'blew down in the night and'—wait a minute—oh dear! 'crushed to death the five occupants of the little Khan there, who had apparently been sitting in the balcony. The bodies of Maria Rhomaides, the aged proprietress, and of her daughter, aged forty-six, were easily recognizable, whereas that of her grandson'—oh, the rest is really too horrid; I wish I had never tried it, and what's more I feel to have heard the name Plataniste before. We didn't stop there, did we, in the spring?"

"We had lunch," said Mr Lucas, with a faint expression of trouble on his vacant face. "Perhaps it was where the dragoman bought the pig."

"Of course," said Ethel in a nervous voice. "Where the dragoman bought the little pig. How terrible!"

"Very terrible!" said her father, whose attention was wandering to the noisy children next door. Ethel suddenly started to her feet with genuine interest.

"Good gracious!" she exclaimed. "This is an old paper. It happened not lately but in April—the night of Tuesday the eighteenth—and we—we must have been there in the afternoon."

"So we were," said Mr Lucas. She put her hand to her heart, scarcely able to speak.

"Father, dear father, I must say it: you wanted to stop there. All those people, those poor half savage people, tried to keep you, and they're dead. The whole place, it says, is in ruins, and even the stream has changed its course. Father, dear, if it had not been for me, and if Arthur had not helped me, you must have been killed."

Mr Lucas waved his hand irritably. "It is not a bit of good speaking to the governess, I shall write to the landlord and say, 'The reason I am giving up the house is this: the dog barks, the children next door are intolerable, and I cannot stand the noise of running water.'"

Ethel did not check his babbling. She was aghast at the narrowness of the escape, and for a long time kept silence. At last she said: "Such a marvelous deliverance does make one believe in Providence."

Mr Lucas, who was still composing his letter to the landlord, did not reply.

A native of Springs, Transvaal, where she was born in 1923, Nadine Gordimer focuses almost exclusively in her work on the impact of South Africa on the individual consciousness. Though she has been a visiting lecturer at several American universities (Harvard, Princeton, Northwestern, Michigan, Columbia), and has lived for short periods in England, the world outside South Africa enters her fictional world only through the experience of exiles, émigrés, and foreign travellers. Yet the appeal of her work is not diminished by this restriction in locale. She is not a polemical writer, even though she does respond morally to such questions as justice and apartheid in her country. Writing should not, she observes in an interview with Alan Ross, be put at the service of a cause, although a cause may itself become a topic of a story. "I write about . . . private selves," she adds; but these, "even in the most private situations, . . . are what they are because . . . lives are regulated and . . . mores formed by the political situation. You see, in South Africa, society is the political situation. To paraphrase, one might say . . . , politics is character."

This relation between society and individual behaviour is one which she has variously probed in the many novels and volumes of short stories published since 1949. *A World of Strangers* (1958), for example, examines the inability of a young Englishman to reconcile his attraction to South Africa with his rejection of the racial divisions he finds there. *The Late Bourgeois World* (1966) presents the paralysis of will that affects one level of white society in the country—a world in which a clock ticking "afraid, alive, afraid, alive . . . "renders the moral tension in a single terse image. "No Place Like," which originally appeared in *The Southern Review* and then was collected in *Livingstone's Companions* (1971), demonstrates the same talent for trenchant observation. Details of setting and style—the fragmentary phrases, the tone, the repetitiousness, and the point of view—all contribute to the story's effect. Momentary experiences are made into the arenas where the mind can discover or fail to discover significant meaning in life, and ideas about human behaviour and human potential are distilled into exact images and precisely rendered scenes.

FOR FURTHER READING

Thomas H. Gullason, "The Short Story: an Underrated Art," *Studies in Short Fiction* 2 (Fall 1964): 13-31.

Robert F. Haugh, *Nadine Gordimer* (New York: Twayne, 1974).

Ezekiel Mphahlele, *The African Image* (London: Faber, 1962).

Judie Newman, *Nadine Gordimer* (London: Routledge, 1988).

Alan Ross, "A Writer in South Africa: Nadine Gordimer," *London Magazine* 5 (May 1965): 12-28.

Michael Wade, *Nadine Gordimer* (London: Evans Brothers, 1978).

The relief of being down, out, and on the ground after hours in the plane was brought up short for them by the airport building: dirty, full of up-ended chairs like a closed restaurant. *Transit? Transit?* Some of them started off on a stairway but were shooed back exasperatedly in a language they didn't understand. The African heat in the place had been cooped up for days and nights; somebody tried to open one of the windows but again there were remonstrations from the uniformed man and the girl in her white gloves and leopard-skin pillbox hat. The windows were sealed, anyway, for the air-conditioning that wasn't working; the offender shrugged. The spokesman that every group of travellers produces made himself responsible for a complaint; at the same time some of those sheep who can't resist a hole in a fence had found a glass door unlocked on the far side of the transit lounge—they were leaking to an open passage-way: grass, bougainvillea trained like standard roses, a road glimpsed there! But the uniformed man raced to round them up and a cleaner trailing his broom was summoned to bolt the door.

The woman in beige trousers had come very slowly across the tarmac, putting her feet down on this particular earth once more, and she was walking even more slowly round the dirty hall. Her coat dragged from the crook of her elbow, her shoulder was weighed by the strap of a bag that wouldn't zip over a package of duty-free European liquor, her bright silk shirt opened dark mouths of wet when she lifted her arms. Fellow-glances of indignance or the seasoned superiority of a sense of humour found no answer in her. As her pace brought her into the path of the black cleaner, the two faces matched perfect indifference: his, for whom the distance from which these people came had no existence because he had been nowhere outside the two miles he walked from his village to the airport; hers, for whom the distance had no existence because she had been everywhere and arrived back.

Another black man, struggling into a white jacket as he unlocked wooden shutters, opened the bar, and the businessmen with their hard-top briefcases moved over to the row of stools. Men who had got talking to unattached women—not much promise in that now; the last leg of the journey was ahead—carried them glasses of gaudy synthetic fruit juice. The Consul who had wanted to buy her a drink with dinner on the plane had found himself a girl in red boots with a small daughter in identical red boots. The child waddled away and flirtation took the form of the two of them hurrying after to scoop it up, laughing. There was a patient queue of ladies in cardigans waiting to get into the lavatories. She passed—once, twice, three times in her slow rounds—a woman who was stitching petit-point. The third time she made out that the subject was a spaniel dog with orange-and-black-streaked ears. Beside the needle-woman was a husband of a species as easily identifiable as the breed of dog—an American, because of the length of boot-lace, slotted through some emblem or badge, worn in place of a tie. He sighed and his wife looked up over her glasses as if he had made a threatening move.

The woman in the beige trousers got rid of her chit for Light Refreshment in an ashtray but she had still the plastic card that was her authority to board the plane again. She tried to put it in the pocket of the coat but she couldn't reach, so she had to hold the card in her teeth while she unharnessed herself from the shoulder-bag and the coat. She wedged the card into the bag beside the liquor packages, leaving it to protrude a little so that it would be easy to produce when the time came. But it slipped down inside the bag and she had to unpack the whole thing—the hairbrush full of her own hair, dead, shed; yesterday's newspaper from a foreign town; the book whose jacket tore on the bag's zip as it came out; wads of pink paper handkerchiefs, gloves for a cold climate, the quota of duty-free cigarettes, the Swiss pocket-knife that you couldn't buy back home, the wallet of travel documents. There at the bottom was the shiny card. Without it, you couldn't board the plane again. With it, you were committed to go on to the end of the journey, just as the passport bearing your name committed you to a certain identity and place. It was one of the nervous tics of travel to feel for the reassurance of that shiny card. She had wandered to the revolving stand of paperbacks and came back to make sure where she had put the card: yes, it was there. It was not a bit of paper; shiny plastic, you couldn't tear it up—indestructible, it looked, of course they use them over and over again. *Tropic of Capricorn*, *Kamasutra*, *Something of Value*. The stand revolved and brought round the same books, yet one turned it again in case there should be a book that had escaped notice, a book you'd been wanting to read all your life. If one were to find such a thing, here and now, on this last stage, this last stop . . . She felt strong hope, the excitation of weariness and tedium perhaps. They came round—*Something of Value, Kamasutra, Tropic of Capricorn*.

She went to the seat where she had left her things and loaded up again, the coat, the shoulder-bag bearing down. Somebody had fallen asleep, mouth open, bottom fly-button undone, an Austrian hat with plaited cord and feather cutting into his damp brow. How long had they been in this place? What time was it where she had left? (Some airports had a whole series of clockfaces showing what time it was everywhere.) Was it still yesterday, there?—Or tomorrow. And where she was going? She thought, I shall find out when I get there.

A pair of curio vendors had unpacked their wares in a corner. People stood about in a final agony of indecision: What would he do with a thing like that? Will she appreciate it, I mean? A woman repeated as she must have done in bazaars and shops and marketplaces all over the world, I've seen them for half the price . . . But this was the last stop of all, the last chance *to take back something*. How else stake a claim? The last place of all the other places of the world.

Bone bracelets lay in a collapsed spiral of overlapping circles. Elephant hair ones fell into the pattern of the Olympic symbol. There were the ivory paper-knives and the little pictures of palm trees, huts and dancers on black paper. The vendor, squatting in the posture that derives from the necessity of the legless beggar to sit that way and has become as much a mark of the street professional, in such towns as the one that must be somewhere behind the airport, as the hard-top brief-case was of the international businessman drinking beer at the bar, importuned her with the obligation to buy. To refuse was to upset the ordination of roles. He was there to sell "ivory" bracelets and "African" art; they—these people shut up for him in the building—had been brought there to buy. He had a right to be angry. But she shook her head, she shook her head, while he tried out his few words of German and French (*bon marché, billig*) as if it could only be a matter of finding the right cue to get her to play the part assigned to her. He seemed to threaten, in his own tongue, finally, his head in its white skullcap hunched between jutting knees. But she was looking again at the glass case full of tropical butterflies under the President's picture. The picture was vivid, and new; a general successful in coup only months ago, in full dress uniform, splendid as the dark one among the Magi. The butterflies, relic of some colonial conservationist society, were beginning to fall away from their pins in grey crumbs and gauzy fragments. But there was one big as a bat and brilliantly emblazoned as the general: something in the soil and air, in whatever existed out there—whatever "out there" there was—that caused nature and culture to imitate each other. . . ?

If it were possible to take a great butterfly. Not take back; just take. But she had the Swiss knife and the bottles, of course. The plastic card. It would see her onto the plane once more. Once the plastic card was handed over, nowhere to go but across the tarmac and up the stairway into the belly of the plane, no turning back past the air hostess in her leopard-skin pillbox, past the barrier. It wasn't allowed; against regulations. The plastic card would send her to the plane, the plane would arrive at the end of the journey, the Swiss knife would be handed over for a kiss, the bottles would be exchanged for an embrace—she was shaking her head at the curio vendor (he had actually got up from his knees and come after her, waving his pictures), *no thanks, no thanks.* But he wouldn't give up and she had to move away, to walk up and down once more in the hot, enclosed course dictated by people's feet, the up-ended chairs and tables, the little shored-up piles of hand-luggage. The Consul was swinging the child in red boots by its hands, in an arc. It was half-whimpering, half-laughing, yelling to be let down, but the larger version of the same model, the mother, was laughing in a way to make her small breasts shake for the Consul, and to convey to everyone how marvelous such a distinguished man was with children.

There was a gritty crackle and then the announcement in careful, African-accented English, of the departure of the flight. A kind of concerted shuffle went up like a sigh: at last! The red-booted mother was telling her child it was silly to cry, the Consul was gathering their things together, the woman was winding the orange thread for her needlework rapidly round a spool, the sleepers woke and the beer-drinkers threw the last of their foreign small change on the bar counter. No queue outside the Ladies' now and the woman in the beige trousers knew there was plenty of time before the second call. She went in and, once more, unharnessed herself among the crumpled paper towels and spilt powder. She tipped all the liquid soap containers in turn until she found one that wasn't empty; she washed her hands thoroughly in hot and then cold water and put her wet palms on the back of her neck, under her hair. She went to one of the row of mirrors and looked at what she saw there a moment, and then took out from under the liquor bottles, the Swiss knife and the documents, the hair-brush. It was full of hair; a web of dead hairs that bound the bristles together so that they could not go through a head of live hair. She raked her fingers slowly through the bristles and was aware of a young Indian woman at the next mirror moving quickly and efficiently about an elaborate toilet. The Indian backcombed the black, smooth hair cut in Western style to hang on her shoulders, painted her eyes, shook her ringed hands dry rather than use the paper towels, sprayed French perfume while she extended her neck, repleated the green and silver sari that left bare a small roll of lavender-grey flesh between waist and *choli*.

This is the final call for all passengers.

The hair from the brush was no-colour, matted and coated with fluff. Twisted round the forefinger (like the orange thread for the spaniel's ears) it became a fibrous funnel, dusty and obscene. She didn't want the Indian girl to be confronted with it and hid it in her palm while she went over to the dustbin. But the Indian girl saw only herself, watching her reflection appraisingly as she turned and swept out.

The brush went easily through the living hair, now. Again and again, until it was quite smooth and fell, as if it had a memory, as if it were cloth that had been folded and ironed a certain way, along the lines in which it had been arranged by professional hands in another hemisphere. A latecomer rushed into one of the lavatories, sounded the flush and hurried out, plastic card in hand.

The woman in the beige trousers had put on lipstick and run a nail-file under her nails. Her bag was neatly packed. She dropped a coin in the saucer set out, like an offering for some humble household god, for the absent attendant. The African voice was urging all passengers to proceed immediately through Gate B. The voice had some difficulty with *l*'s, pronouncing them more like *r*'s; a pleasant, reasoning voice, asking only for everyone to present the boarding pass, avoid delay, come quietly.

She went into one of the lavatories marked "Western-type toilet" that bolted automatically as the door shut, a patent device ensuring privacy; there was no penny to pay. She had the coat and bag with her and arranged them, the coat folded and balanced on the bag, on the cleanest part of the floor. She thought what she remembered thinking so many times before: not much time, I'll have to hurry. That was what the plastic card was for—surely not for being left behind, never. She had it stuck in the neck of the shirt now, in the absence of a convenient pocket; it felt cool and wafer-stiff as she put it there but had quickly taken on the warmth of her body. Some tidy soul determined to keep up Western-type standards had closed the lid and she sat down as if on a bench—the heat and the weight of the paraphernalia she had been carrying about were suddenly exhausting. She thought she would smoke a cigarette; there was no time for that. But the need for a cigarette hollowed out a deep sigh within her and she got the pack carefully out of the pocket of her coat without disturbing the arrangement on the floor. All passengers delaying departure of the flight were urged to proceed immediately through Gate B. Some of the words were lost over the echoing intercommunication system and at times the only thing that could be made out was the repetition, Gate B, a vital fact from which all grammatical contexts could fall away without rendering the message unintelligible. Gate B. If you remembered, if you knew Gate B, the key to mastery of the whole procedure remained intact with you. Gate B was the converse of the open sesame; it would keep you, passing safely through it, in the known, familiar, and inescapable, safe from caves of treasure and shadow. *Immediately. Gate B. Gate B.*

She could sense from the different quality of the atmosphere outside the door, and the doors beyond it, that the hall was emptying now. They were trailing, humping along under their burdens—the petit-point, the child in red boots—to the gate where the girl in the leop-ard-skin pillbox collected their shiny cards.

She took hers out. She looked around the cell as one looks around for a place to set down a vase of flowers or a note that mustn't blow away. It would not flush down the outlet; plastic doesn't disintegrate in water. As she had idly noticed, before, it wouldn't easily tear up. She was not at all agitated; she was simply looking for somewhere to dis-pose of it, now. She heard the voice (was there a shade of hurt embar-rassment in the rolling *r*-shaped *l*'s) appealing to the passenger who was holding up flight so-and-so to please . . . She noticed for the first time that there was actually a tiny window, with the sort of pane that tilts outwards from the bottom, just above the cistern. She stood on the seat-lid and tried to see out, just managing to post the shiny card like a letter through the slot.

Gate B, the voice offered, *Gate B*. But to pass through Gate B you had to have a card, without a card Gate B had no place in the proce-dure. She could not manage to see anything at all, straining precari-ously from up there, through the tiny window; there was no knowing at all where the card had fallen. But as she half-jumped, half-clambered down again, for a second the changed angle of her vision brought into sight something like a head—the top of a huge untidy palm tree, up in the sky, rearing perhaps between buildings or above shacks and muddy or dusty streets where there were donkeys, bicycles and barefoot peo-ple. She saw it only for that second but it was so very clear, she saw even that it was an old palm tree, the fronds rasping and sharpening against each other. And there was a crow—she was sure she had seen the black flap of a resident crow.

She sat down again. The cigarette had made a brown aureole round itself on the cistern. In the corner what she had thought was a date-pit was a dead cockroach. She flicked the dead cigarette butt at it. Heel-taps clattered into the outer room, an African voice said, Who is there? Please, are you there? She did not hold her breath or try to keep partic-ularly still. There was no one there. All the lavatory doors were rattled in turn. There was a high-strung pause, as if the owner of the heels didn't know what to do next. Then the heels rang away again and the door of the Ladies' swung to with the heavy sound of fanned air.

There were burst of commotion without, reaching her muffledly where she sat. The calm grew longer. Soon the intermittent commo-tion would cease; the jets must be breathing fire by now, the belts fastened and the cigarettes extinguished, although the air-conditioning wouldn't be working properly yet, on the ground, and they would be patiently sweating. They couldn't wait forever, when they were so nearly there. The plane would be beginning to trundle like a huge perambulator, it would be turning, winking, shuddering in summoned power.

Take off. It as perfectly still and quiet in the cell. She thought of the great butterfly; of the general with his beautiful markings of braid and medals. Take off.

So that was the sort of place it was: crows in old dusty palm trees, crows picking the carrion in open gutters, legless beggars threatening in an unknown tongue. Not Gate B, but some other gate. Suppose she were to climb out that window, would they ask her for her papers and put her in some other cell, at the general's pleasure? The general had no reason to trust anybody who did not take Gate B. No sound at all, now. The lavatories were given over to their own internal rumblings; the cistern gulped now and then. She was quite sure, at last, that flight so-and-so had followed its course; was gone. She lit another cigarette. She did not think at all about what to do next, not at all; if she had been inclined to think that, she would not have been sitting wherever it was she was. The butterfly, no doubt, was extinct and the general would dislike strangers; the explanations (everything has an explanation) would formulate themselves, in her absence, when the plane reached its destination. The duty-free liquor could be poured down the lavatory, but there remained the problem of the Swiss pocket-knife. And yet—through the forbidden doorway: grass, bougainvillea trained like standard roses, a road glimpsed there!

In a writing career spread over fifty years (his first novel, *The Man Within*, appeared in 1929), Graham Greene (1904–91) published over thirty volumes of fiction, essays, plays, and poetry, and wrote a number of film scripts, including the screenplays of some of his own novels. During his life he was a journalist, a film critic, an intelligence officer (in Africa from 1941 to 1943), and an indefatigable traveller. His fictional writings reflect the breadth of his experience, and may be divided into three main groups: adventure stories, which Greene calls "entertainments," usually about spies or criminals, books such as *A Gun for Sale* (1936) or *The Third Man* (1950); "political" thrillers dramatizing ideological conflicts, like *England Made Me* (1935) or *The Quiet American* (1955); and "Catholic" novels which reflect Greene's preoccupation with sin, damnation, and the struggle between good and evil (Greene converted to Catholicism in 1926). The works in the last-named group (for example, *Brighton Rock*, 1938, *The Power and the Glory*, 1940) are primarily concerned with the spiritual state of their protagonists, but they also make use of the conventions of the thriller: pursuit, betrayal, capture, violent death (sometimes self-inflicted). Even in his "entertainments," Greene is an essentially serious writer, always exploring questions of conduct and belief. The world of Greeneland—a world stretching from Brighton to Saigon, from Vienna to Haiti—is populated by priests and murderers; gangsters and revolutionaries, who live on the fringe of society; outcasts or rebels, whose spiritual and moral crises epitomize the modern search for values in an anarchic world.

"Brother" (1935; in *Collected Stories*, 1973) presents one of Greene's favorite themes, that of trust and betrayal. It deals with the political agitation of a restless Europe in the 1930s, and reflects his sympathy for leftist causes. Greene always rejected comfortable orthodoxies in favour of a questioning spirit; he believed that the task of the storyteller is "to act as the devil's advocate, to elicit sympathy and a measure of understanding for those who lie outside the boundaries of State approval."

FOR FURTHER READING

Robert O. Evans, ed., *Graham Greene: Some Critical Considerations* (Lexington: University of Kentucky Press, 1963).

Richard Kelly, *Graham Greene* (New York: F. Ungar, 1984).

David Lodge, *Graham Greene* (New York: Columbia UP, 1966).

Martin Shuttleworth and Simon Raven, "The Art of Fiction: III. Graham Greene," *Paris Review* 1 (Autumn 1953): 24-41.

Peter Wolfe, *Graham Greene: The Entertainer* (Carbondale, Illinois: Southern Illinois UP, 1972).

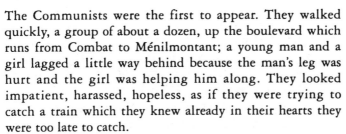

Brother

The Communists were the first to appear. They walked quickly, a group of about a dozen, up the boulevard which runs from Combat to Ménilmontant; a young man and a girl lagged a little way behind because the man's leg was hurt and the girl was helping him along. They looked impatient, harassed, hopeless, as if they were trying to catch a train which they knew already in their hearts they were too late to catch.

The proprietor of the café saw them coming when they were still a long way off; the lamps at that time were still alight (it was later that the bullets broke the bulbs and dropped darkness all over that quarter of Paris), and the group showed up plainly in the wide barren boulevard. Since sunset only one customer had entered the café, and very soon after sunset firing could be heard from the direction of Combat; the Métro station had closed hours ago. And yet something obstinate and undefeatable in the proprietor's character prevented him from putting up the shutters; it might have been avarice; he could not himself have told what it was as he pressed his broad yellow forehead against the glass and stared this way and that, up the boulevard and down the boulevard.

But when he saw the group and their air of hurry he began immediately to close his café. First he went and warned his only customer, who was practising billiard shots, walking round and round the table, frowning and stroking a thin moustache between shots, a little green in the face under the low diffused lights.

"The Reds are coming," the proprietor said, "you'd better be off. I'm putting up the shutters."

"Don't interrupt. They won't harm me," the customer said. "This is a tricky shot. Red's in baulk. Off the cushion. Screw on spot." He shot his ball straight into a pocket.

"I knew you couldn't do anything with that," the proprietor said, nodding his bald head. "You might just as well go home. Give me a hand with the shutters first. I've sent my wife away." The customer turned on him maliciously, rattling the cue between his fingers. "It was your talking that spoilt the shot. You've cause to be frightened, I dare say. But I'm a poor man. I'm safe. I'm not going to stir." He went across to his coat and took out a dry cigar. "Bring me a bock." He walked round the table on his toes and the balls clicked and the proprietor padded back into the bar, elderly and irritated. He did not fetch the beer but began to close the shutters; every move he made was slow and clumsy. Long before he had finished the group of Communists was outside.

He stopped what he was doing and watched them with furtive dislike. He was afraid that the rattle of the shutters would attract their attention. If I am very quiet and still, he thought, they may go on, and he remembered with malicious pleasure the police barricade across the Place de la République. That will finish them. In the meanwhile I must be very quiet, very still, and he felt a kind of warm satisfaction at the idea that worldly wisdom dictated the very attitude most suited to his nature. So he stared through the edge of a shutter, yellow, plump, cautious, hearing the billiard balls crackle in the other room, seeing the young man come limping up the pavement on the girl's arm, watching them stand and stare with dubious faces up the boulevard towards Combat.

But when they came into the café he was already behind the bar, smiling and bowing and missing nothing, noticing how they had divided forces, how six of them had began to run back the way they had come.

The young man sat down in a dark corner above the cellar stairs and the others stood round the door waiting for something to happen. It gave the proprietor an odd feeling that they should stand there in his café not asking for a drink, knowing what to expect, when he, the owner, knew nothing, understood nothing. At last the girl said "Cognac," leaving the others and coming to the bar, but when he had poured it out for her, very careful to give a fair and not a generous measure, she simply took it to the man sitting in the dark and held it to his mouth.

"Three francs," the proprietor said. She took the glass and sipped a little and turned it so that the man's lips might touch the same spot. Then she knelt down and rested her forehead against the man's forehead and so they stayed.

"Three francs," the proprietor said, but he could not make his voice bold. The man was no longer visible in his corner, only the girl's back, thin and shabby in a black cotton frock, as she knelt, leaning forward to find the man's face. The proprietor was daunted by the four men at the door, by the knowledge that they were Reds who had no respect for private property, who would drink his wine and go away without paying, who would rape his women (but there was only his wife, and she was not there), who would rob his bank, who would murder him as soon as look at him. So with fear in his heart he gave up the three francs as lost rather than attract any more attention.

Then the worst that he contemplated happened.

One of the men at the door came up to the bar and told him to pour out four glasses of cognac. "Yes, yes," the proprietor said, fumbling with the cork, praying secretly to the Virgin to send an angel, to send the police, to send the Gardes Mobiles, now, immediately, before the cork came out, "that will be twelve francs."

"Oh no," the man said, "we are all comrades here. Share and share alike. Listen," he said, with earnest mockery, leaning across the bar, "all we have is yours just as much as it's ours, comrade," and stepping back a pace he presented himself to the proprietor, so that he might make his choice of stringy tie, of threadbare trousers, of starved features. "And it follows from that, comrade, that all you have is ours. So four cognacs. Share and share alike."

"Of course," the proprietor said, "I was only joking." Then he stood with bottle poised, and the four glasses tingled upon the counter. "A machine-gun," he said, "up by Combat," and smiled to see how for the moment the men forgot their brandy as they fidgeted near the door. Very soon now, he thought, and I shall be quit of them.

"A machine-gun," the Red said incredulously, "they're using machine-guns?"

"Well," the proprietor said, encouraged by this sign that the Gardes Mobiles were not very far away, "you can't pretend that you aren't armed yourselves." He leant across the bar in a way that was almost paternal. "After all, you know, your ideas—they wouldn't do in France. Free love."

"Who's talking of free love?" the Red said.

The proprietor shrugged and smiled and nodded at the corner. The girl knelt with her head on the man's shoulder, her back to the room. They were quite silent and the glass of brandy stood on the floor beside them. The girl's beret was pushed back on her head and one stocking was laddered and darned from knee to ankle.

"What, those two? They aren't lovers."

"I," the proprietor said, "with my bourgeois notions would have thought . . . "

"He's her brother," the Red said.

The men came clustering round the bar and laughed at him, but softly as if a sleeper or a sick person were in the house. All the time they were listening for something. Between their shoulders the proprietor could look out across the boulevard; he could see the corner of the Faubourg du Temple.

"What are you waiting for?"

"For friends," the Red said. He made a gesture with open palm as if to say, You see, we share and share alike. We have no secrets.

Something moved at the corner of the Faubourg du Temple.

"Four more cognacs," the Red said.

"What about those two?" the proprietor asked.

"Leave them alone. They'll look after themselves. They're tired."

How tired they were. No walk up the boulevard from Ménilmontant could explain the tiredness. They seemed to have come farther and fared a great deal worse than their companions. They were more starved; they were infinitely more hopeless, sitting in their dark corner away from the friendly gossip, the amicable desperate voices which now confused the proprietor's brain, until for a moment he believed himself to be a host entertaining friends.

He laughed and made a broad joke directed at the two of them; but they made no sign of understanding. Perhaps they were to be pitied, cut off from the camaraderie round the counter; perhaps they were to be envied for their deeper comradeship. The proprietor thought for no reason at all of the bare grey trees of the Tuileries like a series of exclamation marks drawn against the winter sky. Puzzled, disintegrated, with all his bearings lost, he stared out through the door towards the Faubourg.

It was as if they had not seen each other for a long while and would soon again be saying good-bye. Hardly aware of what he was doing he filled the four glasses with brandy. They stretched out worn blunted fingers for them.

"Wait," he said. "I've got something better than this"; then paused, conscious of what was happening across the boulevard. The lamplight splashed down on blue steel helmets; the Gardes Mobiles were lining out across the entrance to the Faubourg, and a machine-gun pointed directly at the café windows.

So, the proprietor thought, my prayers are answered. Now I must do my part, not look, not warn them, save myself. Have they covered the side door? I will get the other bottle. Real Napoleon brandy. Share and share alike.

He felt a curious lack of triumph as he opened the trap of the bar and came out. He tried not to walk quickly back towards the billiard room. Nothing that he did must warn these men; he tried to spur himself with the thought that every slow casual step he took was a blow for France, for his café, for his savings. He had to step over the girl's feet to pass her; she was asleep. He noted the sharp shoulder blades thrusting through the cotton, and raised his eyes and met her brother's, filled with pain and despair.

He stopped. He found he could not pass without a word. It was as if he needed to explain something, as if he belonged to the wrong party.

With false bonhomie he waved the corkscrew he carried in the other's face. "Another cognac, eh?"

"It's no good talking to them," the Red said. "They're German. They don't understand a word."

"German?"

"That's what's wrong with his leg. A concentration camp."

The proprietor told himself that he must be quick, that he must put a door between him and them, that the end was very close, but he was bewildered by the hopelessness in the man's gaze. "What's he doing here?" Nobody answered him. It was as if his question were too foolish to need a reply. With his head sunk upon his breast the proprietor went past, and the girl slept on. He was like a stranger leaving a room where all the rest are friends. A German. They don't understand a word; and up, up through the heavy darkness of his mind, through the avarice and the dubious triumph, a few German words remembered from very old days climbed like spies into the light: a line from the *Lorelei* learnt at school, *Kamerad* with its war-time suggestion of fear and surrender and oddly from nowhere the phrase *mein Bruder*. He opened the door of the billiard room and closed it behind him and softly turned the key.

"Spot in baulk," the customer explained and leant across the great green table, but while he took aim, wrinkling his narrow peevish eyes, the firing started. It came in two burst with a rip of glass between. The girl cried out something, but it was not one of the words he knew. Then feet ran across the floor, the trap of the bar slammed. The proprietor sat back against the table and listened and listened for any further sound; but silence came in under the door and silence through the keyhole.

"The cloth. My God, the cloth," the customer said, and the proprietor looked down at his own hand which was working the corkscrew into the table.

"Will this absurdity ever end?" the customer said. "I shall go home."

"Wait," the proprietor said. "Wait." He was listening to voices and footsteps in the other room. These were voices he did not recognize. Then a car drove up and presently drove away again. Somebody rattled the handle of the door.

"Who is it?" the proprietor called.

"Who are you? Open that door."

"Ah," the customer said with relief, "the police. Where was I now? Spot in baulk." He began to chalk his cue. The proprietor opened the door. Yes, the Gardes Mobiles had arrived; he was safe again, though his windows were smashed. The Reds had vanished as if they had never been. He looked at the raised trap, at the smashed electric bulbs, at the broken bottle which dripped behind the bar. The café was full of men, and he remembered with odd relief that he had not had time to lock the side door.

"Are you the owner?" the officer asked. "A bock for each of these men and a cognac for myself. Be quick about it."

The proprietor calculated: "Nine francs fifty," and watched closely with bent head the coins rattle down upon the counter.

"You see," the officer said with significance, "we pay." He nodded towards the side door. "Those others: did they pay?"

No, the proprietor admitted, they had not paid, but as he counted the coins and slipped them into the till, he caught himself silently repeating the officer's order—"A bock for each of these men." Those others, he thought, one's got to say that for them, they weren't mean about the drink. It was four cognacs with them. But, of course, they did not pay. "And my windows," he complained aloud with sudden asperity, "what about my windows?"

"Never you mind," the officer said, "the government will pay. You have only to send in your bill. Hurry up now with my cognac. I have no time for gossip."

"You can see for yourself," the proprietor said, "how the bottles have been broken. Who will pay for that?"

"Everything will be paid for," the officer said.

"And now I must go to the cellar to fetch more."

He was angry at the reiteration of the word pay. They enter my café, he thought, they smash my windows, they order me about and think that all is well if they pay, pay, pay. It occurred to him that these men were intruders.

"Step to it," the officer said and turned and rebuked one of the men who had leant his rifle against the bar.

At the top of the cellar steps the proprietor stopped. They were in darkness, but by the light from the bar he could just make out a body half-way down. He began to tremble violently, and it was some seconds before he could strike a match. The young German lay head downwards, and the blood from his head had dropped on to the step below. His eyes were open and stared back at the proprietor with the old despairing expression of life. The proprietor would not believe that he was dead. "Kamerad," he said bending down, while the match singed his fingers and went out, trying to recall some phrase in German, but he could only remember, as he bent lower still, "mein Bruder." Then suddenly he turned and ran up the steps, waved the match-box in the officer's face, and called out a low hysterical voice to him and his men and to the customer stooping under the low green shade, "Cochons. Cochons."

"What was that? What was that?" the officer exclaimed. "Did you say that he was your brother? It's impossible," and he frowned incredulously at the proprietor and rattled the coins in his pocket.

Praised for her comic and astute feminist novels—*Lilian's Story* (1985), *Dreamhouse* (1986), and *Joan Makes History* (1988)—Kate Grenville has also published a guidebook on how to write, and worked as a film editor and writer in Australia and England. Born Catherine Elizabeth Gee in Sydney, New South Wales, in 1950, she is a graduate of the University of Sydney and the University of Colorado.

In an interview for *Contemporary Authors* 118, she observes that she began writing in order to find out—and thereby express—what it was like to be a woman. Her concern was not to write sociology or social realism, she says, but to "dignify the dilemmas of contemporary women" and to "lay out contemporary sexual politics for examination and satire." Her work does not locate answers to these dilemmas or resolve the conflicts between men and women; rather it reveals the way language can mask or assert the feelings that variously underpin and undermine relationships. In "Slow Dissolve" (which appeared in *Bearded Ladies*, 1984), the cinematic method alluded to by the title hints at dissolution also, which in the story itself takes several forms. Here language is sometimes romantic, sometimes violent; it both disguises and declares power, and ultimately the story is about power.

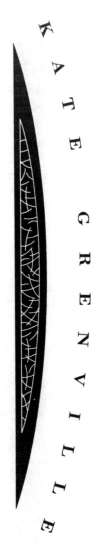

KATE GRENVILLE

FOR FURTHER READING

Ken Gelder and Paul Salzman, *The New Diversity* (Melbourne: McPhee Gribble, 1989).

Pamela Gilbert, *Coming Out from Under: Contemporary Australian Women Writers* (London: Pandora, 1988).

Slow Dissolve

My name's gone from the label by the bell. Now there's just a neatly-typed C.Stone. I wonder how she likes it on her own. I can hear her coming down the inside stairs. A nice smile now.

— Caroline!

— Mirrie!

— Nice to see you!

— It's been so long!

I feel that my smile shows too many teeth. So does hers. We stare at each other's mouths for a moment.

— I kept meaning . . .

— Nearly phoned you . . .

— Absolutely flat out . . .

— Tried to call you . . .

And here we are. There was nothing to say when we shared this flat, and there's still nothing to say.

— Hope my things haven't been in your way.

— No, no, plenty of room.

— Good good I kept meaning.

— Cup of tea?

— Lovely thanks.

The smell of the kitchen is the same as ever. The ghosts of a thousand sausages still hang in the air. Greasy fluff clings to the leg of the stove as it always did. The gap in the lino is full of the same black crumbs.

Caroline is straight out of the pages of the glossy magazines. What London's best-dressed secretaries are wearing.

— You're looking good Caroline.

— Oh thanks but I'm a mess my hair's terrible today.

She still talks in a whine like a broken motor. Her sharp little cat-face only cracks its varnish to smile when absolutely necessary.

— That's a great dress, I say.

— Oh this old thing. Just an old thing for work.

Her eyes flicker over my collection from the jumble sales.

— You're looking good too.

Making the tea, she moves around the kitchen slowly as if drugged. There's a slow walk to the cupboard for the sugarbowl and she lifts it down slowly from the shelf. There's another slow walk back to the table with the sugar and a long consideration about where to put it. She hovers it down as cautiously as the helicopter containing the Queen. It might be dangerous to interrupt this trance but if I don't speak I'll break into a high-pitched cackle.

— Going away this summer?

— I don't really know.

She takes a teabag out of the box.

— I went away last summer.

After frowning thought she takes out another teabag.

— I went to Bermuda.

— That must have been good.

She closes the box carefully, as if small creatures are seething inside.

— It was all right.

The box is finally safe back on the shelf.

— Did you go there with someone?

— Yes, oh yes I went there with a fellow I knew here, see, he asked me to go, only we had a fight and then he came back here but I didn't want to so I stayed there.

After this she seems exhausted.

— But it must have been good being in Bermuda? Even without him?

The silence has set like old yolk.

— It was all right. Sun and . . . beaches. Beaches and . . . swimming and all that. I got a good tan.

She inspects a patch of arm.

— Gone now.

She scratches with a fingernail at the vanished tan.

— I was really brown. But it faded.

— You didn't meet anyone else?

— Well you see everyone there was like in a couple. Every man was with a woman and there weren't any free men. And it was really expensive. Eating cost a lot and even a Coke was nearly a pound.

She stares bleakly round the room.

— See, if I'd of found a man he could've taken me out to dinner and bought me drinks and that and I could've stayed at his hotel and it wouldn't have cost me hardly anything, he could've taken me out to dinner every night. I couldn't afford to eat hardly by myself, but all the men were with women, they'd brought them with them, see.

She stares at me until I nod, then goes on.

— Anyway just before I had to leave I found a man and it was all right then. He was kind of old but all right. But I only had a few days of that and then I had to go back home. But the last few days were okay it didn't cost me anything and I could move out of my hotel and all that and he could buy me dinner.

The kettle makes a stifled screaming noise and after staring at it for a moment she pours the water into the mugs. When she puts the kettle back on the stove it keens softly to itself.

— What about your boyfriend, I ask. Still seeing him?

— You mean Pete, well he and I broke up. He had a lot of money you know, quite well off really. But he was very mean with it. Never took me anywhere nice or anything.

She stirs her tea as if she plans to wear through the bottom of the mug with the spoon.

— I mean I don't expect people to spend a lot of money on me all the time or anything. But when they've got it, it seems mean I think. He had a good job and all that.

She shifts in the chair and smooths the skirt over her knees.

— And there was another girl of course. I knew about her all along, it was all right by me. But she was just out for what she could get. Clothes and fancy meals. Jewellery even. Then she just dumped him, must have got all she wanted.

She licks the spoon and holds its curve against her cheek as if warming herself.

— Makes you think doesn't it. Like you should be out for what you can get. I was with him two years, two years I spent on him.

The spoon must be cold and she flips it across the room towards the sink, where it skitters along the enamel and disappears down the back. She watches as if expecting to see it crawl back up.

— Two years. Nearly three really. And then we broke up and I'm back where I started.

Her lips pucker towards the steaming tea and for a moment she looks like an old woman with her teeth out. She sighs.

— Everything's so dear. I've got to get my hair done once a week and that's going on ten pounds right there. Then clothes, they get dearer all the time, but you've got to look nice, otherwise . . .

She glances at me but doesn't finish the sentence.

— And after two years.

She runs a hand down her shin, closely inspecting it. It's a fine shin, but the sell-by date is moving up fast and the goods will soon start to look a little shabby. With a sputter and pop she squeezes cream out of a bottle and smooths it into her hands.

— Want to get your things?

These two shabby coats, the boots that need mending, and the boxes of tired paints were hardly worth coming back for. The suitcase bulges when everything's packed in. I'm leaving her the broken pith helmet and the eiderdown that leaks feathers. She must get cold alone here at night.

The living-room is full of a faint twittering from the television, and ghostly shadows of colours move about on the screen. Caroline sits unblinking, staring at a huge mouthing face.

— I asked someone to meet me here at six, mind if I wait?

— Of course, fine.

She shifts in the chair so her body is receptively turned to me as if for a chat but her attention is now fixed on three women pointing at a wet floor.

— So what are you up to these days, Mirrie, she says. Still doing your drawings?

I remind myself that the only artist she knows by name is Leonardo da Vinski.

— Yes. Paintings actually.

— And what about . . . still by yourself?

She waits for my well-practised explanation of how much I like living on my own. Practice makes perfect, but it makes a nice change to surprise her.

— Actually there's a man I'm seeing quite a lot of.

Caroline sits forward in her chair.

— That's wonderful, she whispers. Wonderful.

Her eyes retreat to the television. I'm afraid she might suddenly crack the varnish and start to cry.

— It may not last, of course, I say. Who can tell?

She glances at me sharply. I see she's thinking there's already trouble.

— I mean, we just get on well. That's all.

Her attention on me is so great that I can see her inspecting first my right eye, then my left, for the truth. Her eyes are devouring my face.

— But I never believe in looking into the future.

Caroline nods and I hear myself rushing on.

— Just enjoy the moment, that's what I always say.

Caroline switches the television off and turns her full attention on me. I feel myself smiling brightly.

— Known him long?

— Three months.

She nods like a housewife sniffing a dubious grapefruit.

— What's he do?

— He's a designer.

— How old is he?

— Thirty-five.

— Sounds good. Planning to get married?

— We don't see the point of marriage. We don't believe a piece of paper makes any difference.

She nods but her smile doesn't seem quite convinced.

— Anyway, I've got my work.

She glances at my clothes again.

— Wouldn't it be easier if you got married.

One of my fingernails has just broken and I have to stop myself tearing at it.

— We just don't think it's necessary.

She glances out the window at the darkening sky.

— He been married before?

— Well yes. But it was a long time ago. And she was a bitch.

Caroline is rubbing a hand over and over the same patch of her knee. She's stopped watching me. Somehow she's got the wrong idea of all this.

Finally, in a voice that's a pitch too high, she says:

— Well that's wonderful Mirrie, I'm sure you'll be really happy, I certainly hope it all works out for you.

She snaps on the television again and switches from channel to channel. At last the doorbell rings.

— That'll be Allan now.

She glances at her watch and I can't avoid hearing what I know she's going to say, although I hurry out of the room.

— Bit late isn't he?

I run down the stairs two at a time. When I open the door, there he'll be, my lovely man. I open the door and Allan is staring at me as if he wants to break my nose.

— You gave me the wrong fucking address.

I start to apologize and put my hand on his shoulder but he pushes past me up the stairs. Up in the living-room, Caroline has turned off the television and is standing with welcoming smile. Allan barely glances at her.

— These your things?

He's already picked up my bag and is waiting for me by the door. Caroline is smiling, and keeps smiling as Allan goes heavily down the stairs.

— He's a real strong silent type isn't he, she says and giggles. Real strong and silent.

We can hear Allan get into his car and slam the door. He starts the engine with a gnashing sound and revs up so hard that the whole house seems to shake. When he gives a blast on the horn, the living-room is filled with the blare. Caroline and I stand staring at each other, listening to the noise echoing until at last it fades away.

Born in 1947 and educated at Harvard College and at Harvard's Center for Middle Eastern Studies, Mark Helprin served in the British Merchant Navy and in the Israeli Army and Air Force. His military experience has provided him with much material for his fiction; his first novel, *Refiner's Fire* (1977), is a picaresque narrative depicting the adventures of a young American caught up in Israel's conflict with its neighbours. Helprin is a frequent contributor to the *New Yorker*, and his stories, collected in *A Dove of the East* (1975) and *Ellis Island & other stories* (1981), have a breadth of subject and setting that reflects the diversity of his experience. *Ellis Island & other stories* won the 1982 National Jewish Book Award for fiction.

Whether focusing on a Middle-Eastern battlefield, mountain climbing in the Alps, or scullers racing on the River Charles in Boston, Helprin's writing is grounded in sharp, realistic detail born of careful observation. At the same time, his characters spring from a more romantic tradition; moved by a mixture of idealism and doubt, they have an awareness of inexplicable forces at work within themselves as well as in the external environment, and like classical heroes they struggle to make an assertion of self over the physical limits of their existence. These tensions are sometimes conveyed through an injection of fantasy (a prominent element of Helprin's 1983 novel *Winter's Tale*), through which he can give his characters and situations an archetypal dimension. In "Letters from the *Samantha*" (*Ellis Island & other stories*), a story cast in traditional epistolary form, he has produced a variation on the theme of Coleridge's "Rime of the Ancient Mariner"; a ship's captain must try to maintain the orderly values of the civilized society he represents in the face of an unexpected and a threatening presence. As in the tales of Joseph Conrad, the shipboard setting becomes an arena of moral conflict in which the protagonist must make a crucial decision affecting others as well as himself.

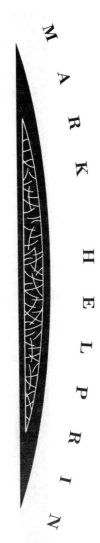

MARK HELPRIN

FOR FURTHER READING

Anne Duchene, "Out of the Icebox," *Times Literary Supplement*, 13 March 1981, p. 278.

Gerald Locklin, Review of *Ellis Island & other stories*. *Studies in Short Fiction* 18 (Summer 1981): 339-40.

Letters from the Samantha

These letters were recovered in good condition from the vault of the sunken *Samantha*, an iron-hulled sailing ship of one thousand tons, built in Scotland in 1879 and wrecked during the First World War in the Persian Gulf off Basra.

20 August, 1909, 20° 14' 18" S,
43° 51' 57" E
Off Madagascar

DEAR SIR:

Many years have passed since I joined the Green Star Line. You may note in your records and logs, if not, indeed, by memory, the complete absence of disciplinary action against me. During my command, the *Samantha* has been a trim ship on time. Though my subordinates sometimes complain, they are grateful, no doubt, for my firm rule and tidiness. It saves the ship in storms, keeps them healthy, and provides good training—even though they will be masters of steamships.

No other vessel of this line has been as punctual or well run. Even today we are a week ahead and our Madagascar wood will reach Alexandria early. Bound for London, the crew are happy, and though we sail the Mozambique Channel, they act as if we had just caught sight of Margate. There are no problems on this ship. But I must in conscience report an irregular incident for which I am ready to take full blame.

Half a day out of Androka, we came upon a sea so blue and casual that its waters seemed fit to drink. Though the wind was slight and we made poor time, we were elated by perfect climate and painter's colors, for off the starboard side Madagascar rose as green and tranquil as a well-watered palm, its mountains engraved by thrashing freshwater streams which beat down to the coast. A sweet up-welling breeze blew steadily from shore and confounded our square sails. Twenty minutes after noon, the lookout sighted a tornado on land. In the ship's glass I saw it, horrifying and enormous. Though at a great distance, its column appeared as thick as a massive tree on an islet in an atoll, and stretched at least 70 degrees upward from the horizon.

I have seen these pipes of windy fleece before. If there is sea nearby, they rush to it. So did this. When it became not red and black from soil and debris but silver and green from the water it drew, I began to tighten ship. Were the typhoon to have struck us directly, no preparation would have saved us. But what a shame to be swamped by high waves, or to be dismasted by beaten sea and wind. Hatches were battened as if for storm, minor sails furled, and the mainsail driven down half.

It moved back and forth over the sea in illegible patterning, as if tacking to changing winds. To our dismay, the distance narrowed. We Were afraid, though every man on deck wanted to see it, to feel it, perhaps to ride its thick swirling waters a hundred times higher than our mast—higher than the peaks inland. I confess that I have wished to be completely taken up by such a thing, to be lifted into the clouds, arms and legs pinned in the stream. The attraction is much like that of phosphorescent seas, when glowing lights and smooth swell are dangerously magnetic even for hardened masters of good ships. I have wanted to surrender to plum-colored seas, to know what one might find there naked and alone. But I have not, and will not.

Finally, we began to run rough water. The column was so high that we bent our heads to see its height, and the sound was greater than any engine, causing masts and spars to resonate like cords. Waves broke over the prow. Wind pushed us on, and the curl of the sea rushed to fill the depression of the waters. No more than half a mile off the starboard bow, the column veered to the west, crossing our path to head for Africa as rapidly as an express. Within minutes, we could not even see it.

As it crossed our bows, I veered in the direction from which it had come. It seemed to communicate a decisiveness of course, and here I took opportunity to evade. In doing so we came close to land. This was dangerous not only for the presence of reefs and shoals but because of the scattered debris. Trees as tall as masts and much thicker, roots sucked clean, lay in puzzlement upon the surface. Brush and vines were everywhere. The water was reddish brown from earth which had fallen from the cone. We were meticulously careful in piloting through this fresh salad, as a good ram against a solid limb would have been the end. Our cargo is hardwoods, and would have sunk us like granite. I myself straddled the sprit stays, pushing aside small logs with a boat hook and calling out trim to the wheel.

Nearly clear, we came upon a clump of tangled vegetation. I could not believe my eyes, for floating upon it was a large monkey, bolt upright and dignified. I sighted him first, though the lookout called soon after. On impulse, I set trim for the wavy mat and, as we smashed into it, offered the monkey an end of the boat hook. When he seized it I was almost pulled in, for his weight is almost equal to mine. I observed that he had large teeth, which appeared both white and sharp. He came close, and then took to the lines until he sat high on the top-gallant. As he passed, his foot cuffed my shoulder and I could smell him.

My ship is a clean ship. I regretted immediately my gesture with the hook. We do not need the mysterious defecations of such a creature, or the threat of him in the rigging at night. But we could not capture him to throw him back into the sea and, even had we collared him, might not have been able to get him overboard without danger to ourselves. We are now many miles off the coast. It is dark, and he sits high off the deck. The night watch is afraid and requests that I fell him with my rifle. They have seen his sharp teeth, which he displays with much screaming and gesticulating when they near him in the rigging. I think he is merely afraid, and I cannot bring myself to shoot him. I realize that no animals are allowed on board and have often had to enforce this rule when coming upon a parrot or cat hidden belowdecks where some captains do not go. But this creature we have today removed from the sea is like a man, and he has ridden the typhoon. Perhaps we will pass a headland and throw him overboard on a log. He must eventually descend for want of food. Then we will have our way. I will report further when the matter is resolved, and assure you that I regret this breach of regulations.

Yours & etc.,
SAMSON LOW
MASTER, S/V SAMANTHA

23 August, 1909, 10° 43' 3" S,
49° 5' 27" E
South of the Seychelles

DEAR SIR:
We have passed the Channel and are heading north-northeast, hoping to ride the summer monsoon. It is shamefully hot, though the breeze is less humid than usual. Today two men dropped from the heat but they resumed work by evening. Because we are on a homeward tack, morale is at its best, or rather would be were it not for that damned ape in the rigging. He has not come down, and we have left behind his island and

its last headland. He will have to have descended by the time we breach passage between Ras Asir and Jazirat Abd al-Kuri. The mate has suggested that there we throw him into the sea on a raft, which the carpenter has already set about building. He has embarked upon this with my permission, since there is little else for him to do. It has been almost an overly serene voyage and the typhoon caused no damage.

The raft he designed is very clever and has become a popular subject of discussion. It is about six feet by three feet, constructed of spare pine dunnage we were about to cast away when the typhoon was sighted. On each side is an outrigger for stability in the swell. In the center is a box, in which is a seat. Flanking this box are several smaller ones for fruit, biscuit, and a bucket of fresh water, in case the creature should drift a long time on the sea. This probably will not be so; the currents off Ras Asir drive for the beach, and we have noted that dunnage is quickly thrown upon the strand. Nevertheless, the crew have added their own touch—a standard distress flag flying from a ten-foot switch. They do not know, but I will order it replaced by a banner of another color, so that a hapless ship will not endanger itself to rescue a speechless monkey.

The crew have divided into two factions—those who wish to have the monkey shot, and those who would wait for him to descend and then put him in his boat. I am with the latter, since I would be the huntsman, and have already mentioned my lack of enthusiasm for this. A delegation of the first faction protested. They claimed that the second faction comprised those who stayed on deck, that the creature endangered balance in the rigging, and that he produced an uncanny effect in his screeching and bellicose silhouettes, which from below are humorous but which at close range, they said, are disconcerting and terrifying.

Since I had not seen him for longer than a moment and wanted to verify their complaint, I went up. Though sixty years of age, I did not use the bosun's chair, and detest those masters who do. It is pharaonic, and smacks of days in my father's youth when he saw with his own eyes gentlemen in sedan chairs carried about the city. The sight of twenty men laboring to hoist a ship's rotund captain is simply Egyptian, and I will not have it. Seventy feet off the deck, a giddy height to which I have not ascended in years, I came even with the ape. The ship was passing a boisterous sea and had at least a twenty-degree roll, which flung the two of us from side to side like pendula.

I am not a naturalist, nor have we on board a book of zoology, so the most I can do is to describe him. He is almost my height (nearly five feet ten inches) and appears to be sturdily built. Feet and hands are human in appearance except that they have a bulbous, skew, arthritic look common to monkeys. He is muscular and covered with fine reddish-brown hair. One can see the whiteness of his tendons when he stretches an arm or leg. I have mentioned the sharp, dazzling white teeth, set in rows like a trap, canine and pointed. His face is curiously delicate, and covered with orange hair leading to a snow-white crown of fur. My breath nearly failed when I looked into his eyes, for they are a bright, penetrating blue.

At first, he began to scream and swing as if he would come at me. If he had, I would have fared badly. The sailors fear him, for there is no man on board with half his strength, no man on the sea with a tenth his agility in the ropes, and if there is a man with the glacierlike pinnacled teeth, then he must be in a Scandinavian or Eastern European circus, for there they are fond of such things. To my surprise, he stopped his pantomime and, with a gentle and quizzical tilt of his head, looked me straight in the eyes. I had been sure that as a man I could answer his gaze as if from infallibility, and I calmly looked back. But he had me. His eyes unset me, so that I nearly shook. From that moment, he has not threatened or bared his teeth, but merely rests near the top of the foremast. The crew have attributed his conversion to my special power. This is flattering, though not entirely, as it assumes my ability to commune with an ape. Little do they suspect that it is I and not the monkey who have been converted, although to what I do not know. I am still thoroughly ashamed of my indiscretion and the troubles arising from it. We will get him and put him adrift off Ras Asir.

This evening, the cook grilled up some beef. I had him thoroughly vent the galley and use a great many herbs. The aroma was maddening. I sat in near-hypnotic ease in a canvas chair on the quarterdeck, a glass of wine in hand, as the heat fell to a cool breeze. We are all sunburnt and have been working hard, as the ape silently watches, to trim regularly and catch the best winds. We are almost in the full swift of the monsoon, and shortly will ride it in all its speed. It was wonderful to sit on deck and smell the herb-laden meat. The sea itself must have been jealous. I had several men ready with cargo net and pikes, certain that he would come down. We stared up at him as if he were the horizon, waiting. He smelled the food and agitated back and forth. Though he fretted, he did not descend. Even when we ate we saw him shunting to and fro on a yardarm. We left a dish for him away from us but he did not venture to seize it. If he had, we would have seized him.

From his impatience, I predict that tomorrow he will surrender to his stomach. Then we will catch him and this problem will be solved. I truly regret such an irregularity, though it would be worthwhile if he could only tell us how far he was lifted inside the silvered cone, and what it was like.

Yours & etc.,
SAMSON LOW

25 August, 1909, 2° 13' 10" N,
51° 15' 17" E
Off Mogadishu

DEAR SIR:

Today he came down. After the last correspondence, it occurred to me
that he might be vegetarian, and that though he was hungry, the meat
had put him off. Therefore, I searched my memory for the most aro-
matic vegetable dish I know. In your service as a fourth officer, I called
at Jaffa port, in Palestine, in January of 1873. We went up to Sfat, a
holy town high in the hills, full of Jews and Arabs, quiet and mystical.
There were so many come into that freezing velvet dome of stars that
all hostelries were full. I and several others paid a small sum for private
lodging and board. At two in the morning, after we had returned from
Mt. Jermak, the Arabs made a hot lively fire from bundles of dry
cyprus twigs, and in a great square pan heated local oil and herbs, in
which they fried thick sections of potato. I have never eaten so well.
Perhaps it was our hunger, the cold, the silence, being high in the
mountains at Sfat, where air is like ether and all souls change. Today I
made the cook follow that old receipt.

We had been in the monsoon for several hours, and the air was littered with silver sparks—apparitions of heat from a glittering afternoon. Though the sun was low, iron decks could not be tread. In the
rigging, he appeared nearly finished, limp and slouching, an arm hanging without energy, his back bent. We put potatoes in a dish on the
forecastle. He descended slowly, finally touching deck lightly and
ambling to the bows like a spider, all limbs brushing the planks. He
ate his fill, and we threw the net over him. We had expected a fero-
cious struggle, but his posture and expression were so peaceful that I
ordered the net removed. Sailors stood ready with pikes, but he stayed
in place. Then I approached him and extended my hand as if to a child.

In imitation, he put out his arm, looking much less fearsome.
Without a show of teeth, in his tired state, crouched on all fours to half
our heights, he was no more frightening than a hound. I led him to the
stern and back again while the crew cheered and laughed. Then the
mate took him, and then the entire hierarchy of the ship, down to the
cabin boys, who are smaller than he and seemed to interest him the
most. By dark, he had strolled with every member of the crew and was
miraculously tame. But I remembered his teeth, and had him chained
to his little boat.

He was comfortable there, surrounded by fruit and water (which he
ate and drank methodically) and sitting on a throne of sorts, with half
a dozen courtiers eager to look in his eyes and hold his obliging wrist.
Mine is not the only London post in which he will be mentioned.
Those who can write are describing him with great zeal. I have seen

some of these letters. He has been portrayed as a "mad baboon," a "man-eating gorilla of horrible colors, muscled but as bright as a bird," a "pygmy man set down on the sea by miracle and typhoon," and as all manner of Latin names, each different from the others and incorrectly spelled.

Depending on the bend of the monsoon and whether it continues to run strongly, we will pass Ras Asir in three days. I thought of casting him off early but was implored to wait for the Cape. I relented, and in doing so was made to understand why those in command must stay by rules. I am sure, however, that my authority is not truly diminished, and when the ape is gone I will again tighten discipline.

I have already had the distress flag replaced by a green banner. It flies over the creature on his throne. Though in splendor, he is in chains and in three days' time will be on the sea once more.

Yours & etc.,
SAMSON LOW

28 August, 1909, 12° 4' 39" N,
50° 1' 2" E
North of Ras Asir

DEAR SIR:
A most alarming incident has occurred. I must report, though it is among the worst episodes of my command. This morning, I arose, expecting to put the ape over the side as we rounded Ras Asir at about eleven. (The winds have been consistently excellent and a northward breeze veering off the monsoon has propelled us as steadily as an engine.) Going out on deck, I discovered that his boat was nowhere to be seen. At first, I thought that the mate had already disposed of him, and was disappointed that we were far from the coast. Then, to my shock, I saw him sitting unmanacled atop the main cargo hatch.

I screamed at the mate, demanding to know what had happened to the throne (as it had come to be called). He replied that it had gone overboard during the twelve-to-four watch. I stormed below and got that watch out in a hurry. Though sleepy-eyed, they were terrified. I told them that if the guilty one did not come forth I would put them all in irons. My temper was short and I could have struck them down. Two young sailors, as frightened as if they were surrendering themselves to die, admitted that they had thrown it over. They said they did not want to see the ape put to drift.

They are in irons until we make Suez. Their names are Mulcahy and Esper, and their pay is docked until they are freed. As we rounded the Cape, cutting close in (for the waters there are deep), we could see that though the creature would have been immediately cast up on shore, the shore itself was barren and inhospitable, and surely he would have died there. My Admiralty chart does not detail the inland topography of this area and shows only a yellow tongue marked "Africa" thrusting into the Gulf of Aden.

I can throw him overboard now or later. I do not want to do it. I brought him on board in the first place. There is nothing with which to fashion another raft. We have many tons of wood below, but not a cubic foot of it is lighter than water. The wind is good and we are making for the Bab al-Mandab, where we will pass late tomorrow afternoon—after that, the frustrating run up the Red Sea to the Canal.

The mate suggests that we sell him to the Egyptians. But I am reluctant to make port with this in mind, as it would be a victory for the two in chains and in the eyes of many others. And we are not animal traders. If he leaves us at sea the effects of his presence will be invalidated, we will touch land with discipline restored, and I will have the option of destroying these letters, though everything here has been entered in short form in the log. I have ordered him not to be fed, but they cast him scraps. I must get back my proper hold on the ship.

Yours & etc.,
SAMSON LOW

30 August, 1909, 15° 49' 30" N,
41° 5' 32" E
Red Sea off Massawa

DEAR SIR:
I have been felled by an attack of headaches. Never before has this happened. There is pressure in my skull enough to burst it. I cannot keep my balance; my eyes roam and I am drunk with pain. For the weary tack up the Red Sea I have entrusted the mate with temporary command, retiring to my cabin with the excuse of heat prostration. I have been in the Red Sea time and again but have never felt apprehension that death would follow its heat. We have always managed. To the east, the mountains of the Hijaz are so dry and forbidding that I have seen sailors look away in fright.

The ape has begun to suffer from the heat. He is listless and ignored. His novelty has worn off (with the heat as it is) and no one pays him any attention. He will not go belowdecks but spends most of the day under the canvas sun shield, chewing slowly, though there is nothing in his mouth. It is hot there—the light so white and uncompromising it sears the eyes. I have freed his champions from irons and restored their pay. By this act I have won over the crew and caused the factions to disappear. No one thinks about the ape. But I dare not risk a recurrence of bad feeling and have decided to cast him into the sea. Where we found him, a strong seaward current would have carried him to the open ocean. Here, at least, he can make the shore, although it is the most barren coast on earth. But who would have thought he might survive the typhoon? He has been living beyond his time. To be picked up and whirled at incomprehensible speed, carried for miles above the earth where no man has even been, and thrown into the sea is a death sentence. If he survived that, perhaps he can survive Arabian desert.

His expression is neither sad nor fierce. He looks like an old man, neutral to the world. In the last two days he has become the target of provocation and physical blows. I have ordered this stopped, but a sailor will sometimes throw a nail or a piece of wood at him. We shall soon be rid of him.

Yesterday we came alongside another British ship, the *Stonepool*, of the Dutch Express Line. On seeing the ape, they were envious. What is it, their captain asked, amazed at its coloring. I replied that he was a Madagascar ape we had fished from the sea, and I offered him to them, saying he was tame as a dog. At first, they wanted him. The crew cried out for his acceptance, but the captain demurred, shaking his head and looking into my eyes as if he were laughing at me. "Damn!" I said, and went below without even a salute at parting.

My head aches. I must stop. At first light tomorrow, I will toss him back.

Yours & etc.,
SAMSON LOW

3 September 1909
Suez

DEAR SIR:
The morning before last I went on deck at dawn. The ape was sitting on the main hatch, his eyes upon me from the moment I saw him. I walked over to him and extended my arm, which he would not take in his customary manner. I seized his wrist, which he withdrew. However, as he did this I laid hold of the other wrist, and pulled him off the hatch. He did not bare his teeth. He began to scream. Awakened by this, most of the crew stood in the companionways or on deck, silently observing.

He was hard to drag, but I towed him to the rail. When I took his other arm to hoist him over, he bared his teeth with a frightening shriek. Everyone was again terrified. The teeth must be six inches long.

He came at me with those teeth, and I could do nothing but throttle him. With my hands on his throat, his arms were free. He grasped my side. I felt the pads of his hands against my ribs. I had to tolerate that awful sensation to keep hold of his throat. No man aboard came close. He shrieked and moaned. His eyes reddened. My response was to tighten my hold, to end the horror. I gripped so hard that my own teeth were bared and I made sounds similar to his. He put his hands around my neck as if to strangle me back, but I had already taken the inside position and, despite his great strength, lessened the power of his grip merely by lifting my arms against his. Nevertheless he choked me. But I had a great head start. We held this position for long minutes, sweating, until his arms dropped and his body convulsed. In rage, I threw him by the neck into the sea, where he quickly sank.

Some of the crew have begun to talk about him as if he were about to be canonized. Others see him as evil. I assembled them as the coasts began to close on Suez and the top of the sea was white and still. I made my views clear, for in years of command in a life on the sea I have learned much. I felt confident of what I told them.

He is not a symbol. He stands neither for innocence nor for evil. There is no parable and no lesson in his coming and going. I was neither right nor wrong in bringing him aboard (though it was indeed incorrect) or what I later did. We must get on with the ship's business. He does not stand for a man or men. He stands for nothing. He was an ape, simian and lean, half sensible. He came on board, and now he is gone.

Yours & etc.,
SAMSON LOW

Perhaps the most widely read and influential writer of his generation, Ernest Hemingway (1899-1961) embodied the vigor, the restlessness, and the despair of the twentieth century, in his life as well as his writings. The son of a physician, he was born in Oak Park, near Chicago, and spent his boyhood in Illinois and Michigan. After leaving school in 1917 and working briefly as a reporter for the *Kansas City Star*, he joined the Red Cross, and drove an ambulance on the Italian front until he was wounded. After the war, he became a reporter for *The Toronto Star*, in company with Morley Callaghan. Then Hemingway began to produce novels and stories about the waste and sterility that marked the postwar period, and which led his friend Gertrude Stein to remark, "You are all a lost generation." *In Our Time* appeared in 1924, followed by *The Sun Also Rises* (1926), and *Men Without Women* (1927); in these works Hemingway revealed an originality of plot and a striking economy of style which quickly established him as a major writer. *A Farewell to Arms* (1929) was inspired by his war experiences in Italy; and *For Whom the Bell Tolls* (1940) grew out of the period he spent in Spain in 1937 during the Spanish Civil War. Between 1941 and 1945 he was a war correspondent in Europe and the Far East. His last major work was *The Old Man and the Sea* (1952), which brought him the Pulitzer Prize in 1953; and in 1954 he was awarded the Nobel Prize for literature. In his last years Hemingway suffered periods of illness and depression; and while in Idaho in July 1961 he committed suicide with a shotgun.

Hemingway's life was filled with action and adventure; and his preoccupation with the physical aspect of existence, particularly its violence, is reflected in most of his writing. Whether his subject is the horror of war, or the struggle between human beings and nature, Hemingway draws a picture of a world where the only certainties are pain, deprivation, or death. Whatever their hopes or ideals may have been, his characters learn that life is a futile ordeal; to counter this, they must develop a protective shell of toughness, or endure their fate with numb resignation. Even in "Hills Like White Elephants" (*Men Without Women*), a story far removed from the brutalities of war or the bullring, there is an undercurrent of emotional violence. The dialogue is terse and laconic; but Hemingway's spare style conveys hidden tensions with admirable understatement, hinting at the sterility and breakdown of a whole way of life.

FOR FURTHER READING

Jackson J. Benson, *The Short Stories of Ernest Hemingway: Critical Essays* (Durham, N.C.: Duke UP, 1975).

Joseph Defalco, *The Hero in Hemingway's Short Stories* (Pittsburgh: University of Pittsburgh Press, 1963).

Joseph M. Flora, *Ernest Hemingway: A Study of the Short Fiction* (Boston: Twayne, 1989).

Leo Gurko, *Ernest Hemingway and the Pursuit of Heroism* (New York: T.Y. Crowell, 1968).

Eusebio L. Rodrigues, "'Hills Like White Elephants': An Analysis," *Literary Criterion* 5 (1962): 105-9.

Hills Like White Elephants

The hills across the valley of the Ebro were long and white. On this side there was no shade and no trees and the station was between two lines of rails in the sun. Close against the side of the station there was the warm shadow of the building and a curtain, made of strings of bamboo beads, hung across the open door into the bar, to keep out flies. The American and the girl with him sat at a table in the shade, outside the building. It was very hot and the express from Barcelona would come in forty minutes. It stopped at this junction for two minutes and went on to Madrid.

"What should we drink?" the girl asked. She had taken off her hat and put it on the table.

"It's pretty hot," the man said.

"Let's drink beer."

"Dos cervezas," the man said into the curtain.

"Big ones?" a woman asked from the doorway.

"Yes. Two big ones."

The woman brought two glasses of beer and two felt pads. She put the felt pads and the beer glasses on the table and looked at the man and the girl. The girl was looking off at the line of hills. They were white in the sun and the country was brown and dry.

"They look like white elephants," she said.

"I've never seen one," the man drank his beer.

"No, you wouldn't have."

"I might have," the man said. "Just because you say I wouldn't have doesn't prove anything."

The girl looked at the bead curtain. "They've painted something on it," she said. "What does it say?"

"Anis del Toro. It's a drink."

"Could we try it?"

The man called "Listen" through the curtain. The woman came out from the bar.

"Four reales."

"We want two Anis del Toro."

"With water?"

"Do you want it with water?"

"I don't know," the girl said. "Is it good with water?"

"It's all right."

"You want them with water?" asked the woman.

"Yes, with water."

"It tastes like licorice," the girl said and put the glass down.

"That's the way with everything."

"Yes," said the girl. "Everything tastes of licorice. Especially all the things you've waited so long for, like absinthe."

"Oh, cut it out."

"You started it," the girl said. "I was being amused. I was having a fine time."

"Well, let's try and have a fine time."

"All right. I was trying. I said the mountains looked like white elephants. Wasn't that bright?"

"That was bright."

"I wanted to try this new drink. That's all we do, isn't it—look at things and try new drinks?"

"I guess so."

The girl looked across at the hills.

"They're lovely hills," she said. "They don't really look like white elephants. I just meant the coloring of their skin through the trees."

"Should we have another drink?"

"All right."

The warm wind blew the bead curtain against the table.

"The beer's nice and cool," the man said.

"It's lovely," the girl said.

"It's really an awfully simple operation, Jig," the man said. "It's not really an operation at all."

The girl looked at the ground the table legs rested on.

"I know you wouldn't mind it, Jig. It's really not anything. It's just to let the air in."

The girl did not say anything.

"I'll go with you and I'll stay with you all the time. They just let the air in and then it's all perfectly natural."

"Then what will we do afterward?"

"We'll be fine afterward. Just like we were before."

"What makes you think so?"

"That's the only thing that bothers us. It's the only thing that's made us unhappy."

The girl looked at the bead curtain, put her hand out and took hold of two of the strings of beads.

"And you think then we'll be all right and be happy."

"I know we will. You don't have to be afraid. I've known lots of people that have done it."

"So have I," said the girl. "And afterward they were all so happy."

"Well," the man said, "if you don't want to you don't have to. I wouldn't have you do it if you didn't want to. But I know it's perfectly simple."

"And you really want to?"

"I think it's the best thing to do. But I don't want you to do it if you don't really want to."

"And if I do it you'll be happy and things will be like they were and you'll love me?"

"I love you now. You know I love you."

"I know. But if I do it, then it will be nice again if I say things are like white elephants, and you'll like it?"

"I'll love it. I love it now but I just can't think about it. You know how I get when I worry."

"If I do it you won't ever worry?"

"I won't worry about that because it's perfectly simple."

"Then I'll do it. Because I don't care about me."

"What do you mean?"

"I don't care about me."

"Well, I care about you."

"Oh yes. But I don't care about me. And I'll do it and then everything will be fine."

"I don't want you to do it if you feel that way."

The girl stood up and walked to the end of the station. Across, on the other side, were fields of grain and trees along the banks of the Ebro. Far away, beyond the river, were mountains. The shadow of a cloud moved across the field of grain and she saw the river through the trees.

"And we could have all this," she said. "And we could have everything and every day we make it more impossible."

"What did you say?"

"I said we could have everything."

"We can have everything."

"No, we can't."

"We can have the whole world."

"No, we can't."

"We can go everywhere."

"No, we can't. It isn't ours any more."

"It's ours."

"No, it isn't. And once they take it away, you never get it back."

"But they haven't taken it away."

"We'll wait and see."

"Come on back in the shade," he said. "You mustn't feel that way."

"I don't feel any way," the girl said. "I just know things."

"I don't want you to do anything that you don't want to do—"

"Nor that isn't good for me," she said. "I know. Could we have another beer?"

"All right. But you've got to realize—"

"I realize," the girl said. "Can't we maybe stop talking?"

They sat down at the table and the girl looked across at the hills on the dry side of the valley and the man looked at her and at the table.

"You've got to realize," he said, "that I don't want you to do it if you don't want to. I'm perfectly willing to go through with it if it means anything to you."

"Doesn't it mean anything to you? We could get along."

"Of course it does. But I don't want anybody but you. I don't want any one else. And I know it's perfectly simple."

"Yes, you know it's perfectly simple."

"It's all right for you to say that, but I do know it."

"Would you do something for me now?"

"I'd do anything for you."

"Would you please please please please please please please stop talking?"

He did not say anything but looked at the bags against the wall of the station. There were labels on them from all the hotels where they had spent nights.

"But I don't want you to," he said. "I don't care anything about it."

"I'll scream," the girl said.

The woman came out through the curtains with two glasses of beer and put them down on the damp felt pads. "The train comes in five minutes," she said.

"What did she say?" asked the girl.

"That the train is coming in five minutes."

The girl smiled brightly at the woman, to thank her.

"I'd better take the bags over to the other side of the station," the man said. She smiled at him.

"All right. Then come back and we'll finish the beer."

He picked up the two heavy bags and carried them around the station to the other tracks. He looked up the tracks but could not see the train. Coming back, he walked through the barroom, where people waiting for the train were drinking. He drank an Anis at the bar and looked at the people. They were all waiting reasonably for the train. He went out through the bead curtain. She was sitting at the table and smiled at him.

"Do you feel better?" he asked.

"I feel fine," she said. "There's nothing wrong with me. I feel fine."

Jack Hodgins was born in 1938 in Merville, at the north end of Vancouver Island, where he lived until he left in 1956 to attend university in Vancouver. He later returned to the Island to teach in Nanaimo; subsequently he left to teach at the University of Ottawa, then returned once more, this time to teach Creative Writing at the University of Victoria. The North Island community, where Hodgins's family were loggers for two generations, is still a rural one. His memories of this rural life—its anecdotal dialogues, its penchant for tall tales and grand gestures—give much of his writing its vigorous character. His stories teem with incidents and individuals, and yet the exaggeration which gives them their comic quality also serves as a reminder of the chance dreams and stern realities that generate the exaggeration in the first place. It is a process of transformation. As W.J. Keith observes, such points of transformation constitute the narrative heart of Hodgins's fiction; comedy, says Keith, is always teetering on the edge of something else—tragedy, perhaps, or a recognition of the sadness of the unattainable. It is this recognition which turns "his local backyard into an image of the whole creative universe."

"The Lepers' Squint" (from *The Barclay Family Theatre*, 1981) takes Hodgins away from his usual locales to Ireland, where medieval and modern come together in a study of intellectual and emotional frustration. The author in the story is suffering from more than "writer's block"; Hodgins uses the story of the Lepers' Squint as an analogy to the writer's spiritual situation. Philip Desmond's dilemma is a perennial one for all artists: how is the artist to reconcile the claims of art and life? How far dare the writer yield to the power of inner feeling and imagination without losing himself or betraying his public, everyday self? Hodgins does not answer these questions, though the story ends on a muted note that hints at something lost.

FOR FURTHER READING

Geoff Hancock, "An Interview with Jack Hodgins," *Canadian Fiction Magazine*, nos. 32/33 (1979/80): 33-63.

David L. Jeffrey, "Jack Hodgins and the Island Mind," *Book Forum* 4 (1980): 70-78.

W.J. Keith, "Jack Hodgins' Island World," *Canadian Forum* 61 (September/October 1981): 30-31.

The Lepers' Squint

Today, while Mary Brennan may be waiting for him on that tiny island high in the mountain lake called Gougane Barra, Philip Desmond is holed up in the back room of this house at Bantry Bay, trying to write his novel. A perfect stack of white paper, three black nylon-tipped pens, and a battered portable typewriter are set out before him on the wooden table. He knows the first paragraph already, has already set it down, and trusts that the rest of the story will run off the end of it like a fishing line pulled by a salmon. But it is cold, it is so cold in this house, even now in August, that he presses both hands down between his thighs to warm them up. It is so cold in this room that he finds it almost impossible to sit still, so damp that he has put on the same clothes he would wear if he were walking out along the edge of that lagoon, in the spitting rain and the wind. Through the small water-specked panes of the window he can see his children playing on the lumpy slabs of rock at the shore, beyond the bobbing branches of the fuchsia hedge. Three children; three red quilted jackets; three faces flushed up by the steady force of the cold wind; they drag tangled clots of stinking seaweed up the slope and, crouching, watch a family of swans explore the edges of a small weedy island not far out in the lagoon.

A high clear voice in his head all the while insists on singing to him of some girl so fair that the ferns uncurl to look at her. The voice of an old man in a mountain pub, singing without accompaniment, stretched and stiff as a rooster singing to the ceiling and to the crowd at the bar and to the neighbours who sit around him. *The ferns uncurled to look at her, so very fair was she, with her hair as bright as the seaweed that floats in from the sea.* But here at Ballylickey the seaweed is brown as mud and smells so strong your eyes water.

Mrs. O'Sullivan is in the next room, Desmond knows, in her own room, listening. If he coughs she will hear. If he sings. She will know exactly the moment he sets down his next word on that top sheet of paper. Mrs. O'Sullivan is the owner of this house, which Desmond rented from home through the Borde Failte people before he discovered that she would live in it with them, in the centre of the house, in her two rooms, and silently listen to the life of his family going on around her. She is a tall dry-skinned old woman with grey finger-waves caged in blue hair-net, whose thick fingers dig into the sides of her face in an agony of desire to sympathize with everything that is said to her. "Oh I know I know I know," she groans. Last night when Desmond's wife mentioned how tired she was after the long drive down from Dublin, her fingers plucked at her face, her dull eyes rolled up to search for help along the ceiling: "Oh I know I know I know." There is no end to her sympathy, there is nothing she doesn't already know. But she will be quiet as a mouse, she promised, they won't know she is here.

"Maybe she's a writer," Desmond's wife whispered to him, later in bed. "Maybe she's making notes on us. Maybe she's writing a book called *North Americans I Have Eavesdropped On*."

"I can't live with someone listening to me breathe," Desmond said. "And I can't write with someone sitting waiting."

"Adjust," his wife said, and flicked at his nose. She who could adjust to anything, or absorb it.

On this first day of his novel Desmond has been abandoned by his wife, Carrie, who early this morning drove the car in to Cork. There are still, apparently, a few Seamus Murphy statues she hasn't seen, or touched. "Keep half an eye on the kids," she said before she left. Then she came back and kissed him and whispered, "Though if you get busy it won't matter. I'm sure Mrs. O'Sullivan won't miss anything." To be fair, to be really fair, he knows that his annoyance is unjustified. He didn't tell her he intended to work today, the first day in this house. She probably thinks that after travelling for six weeks through the country he'll rest a few more days before beginning; she may even believe that he is glad to be rid of her for the day, after all those weeks of unavoidable closeness. She certainly knows that with Mrs. O'Sullivan in the house no emergency will be overlooked, no crisis ignored.

Desmond, now that his hands have warmed a little, lifts one of the pens to write, though silently as possible, as if what he is about to do is a secret perversion from which the ears of Mrs. O'Sullivan must be protected. But he cannot, now, put down any new words. Because if the novel, which has been roaring around in his head all summer and much longer, looking for a chance to get out, should not recognize in the opening words the crack through which it is to spring forth, transformed into a string of words like a whirring fishline, then he will be left with all that paper to stare at, and an unmoving pen, and he is not ready to face that. Of course he knows the story, has seen it all in his mind a hundred times as if someone else had gone to the trouble of writing it and producing it as a movie just for him. But he has never been one for plunging into things, oceans or stories, and prefers to work his way in gently. That opening paragraph though, is only a paragraph after all and has no magic, only a few black lifeless lines at the top of the paper. So he writes his title again, and under it his name: Barclay Philip Desmond. Then he writes the opening paragraph a second time, and again under that, and again, hoping that the pen will go on by itself to write the next words and surprise him. But it does not happen, not now. Instead, he discovers he is seeing two other words which are not there at all, as if perhaps they are embedded, somehow, just beneath the surface of the paper.

Mary Brennan.

Desmond knows he must keep the name from becoming anything more than that, from becoming a face too, or the pale scent of fear. He writes his paragraph again, over and over until he has filled up three or four pages. Then, crumpling the papers in his hand, he wonders if this will be one of those stories that remain forever in their authors' heads, driving them mad, refusing to suffer conversion into words.

It's the cold, he thinks. Blame it on the bloody weather. His children outside on the rocky slope have pulled the hoods of their jackets up over their heads. Leaves torn from the beech tree lie soaked and heavy on the grass. At the far side of the lagoon the family of swans is follow-ing the choppy retreating tide out through the gap to the open bay; perhaps they know of a calmer inlet somewhere. The white stone house with red window frames in its nest of bushes across the water has blurred behind the rain, and looks more than ever like the romantic pictures he has seen on postcards. A thin line of smoke rises from the yellowish house with the gate sign *Carrigdhoun*.

But it is easier than writing, far easier, to allow the persistent day-dreams in, and memory. That old rooster-stiff man, standing in the cleared-away centre of the bar in Ballyvourney to pump his song out to the ceiling, his hands clasping and unclasping at his sides as if they are responsible for squeezing those words into life. The ferns uncurled to see her, he sings, so very fair was she. Neighbours clap rhythm, or stamp their feet. Men six-deep at the bar-counter continue to shout at each other about sheep, and the weather. With hair as bright as the sea-weed that floats in from the sea.

"'Tis an island of singers sure!" someone yells in Desmond's ear. "An island of saints and paupers and bloody singers!"

But Desmond thinks of Mary Brennan's hot apple-smelling breath against his face: "Islands do not exist until you have loved on them."

The words are a Caribbean poet's, she explains, and not her own. But the sentiment is adaptable. The ferns may not uncurl to see the dark brown beauty of her eyes, but Desmond has seen men turn at her flash of hair, the reddish-brown of gleaming kelp. Turn, and smile to themselves. This day while he sits behind the wooden table, hunched over his pile of paper, he knows that she is waiting for him on a tiny hermitage island in a mountain lake not far away, beneath the branches of the crowded trees. Islands, she had told him, do not exist until you've loved on them.

Yesterday, driving south from Dublin across the Tipperary farmland, they stopped again at the Rock of Cashel so that Carrie could prowl a second time through that big roofless cathedral high up on the sudden limestone knoll and run her hands over the strange broken form of St. Patrick's Cross. The kings of Munster lived there once, she told him, and later turned it over to the church. St. Patrick himself came to baptize the king there, and accidentally pierced the poor man's foot with the point of his heavy staff.

"There's all of history here, huddled together," she said, and catalogued it for him. "A tenth-century round tower, a twelfth-century chapel, a thirteenth-century cathedral, a fourteenth-century tower, a fifteenth-century castle, and . . . " she rolled her eyes, "a twentieth-century tourist shop."

But it was the cross itself that drew her. Originally a cross within a frame, it was only the central figure of a man now, with one arm of the cross and a thin upright stem that held that arm in place. Rather like a tall narrow pitcher. There was a guide this second time, and a tour, and she pouted when he insisted they stick to the crowd and hear the official truths instead of making guesses or relying on the brief explanations on the backs of postcards. She threw him a black scowl when the guide explained the superstition about the cross: that if you can touch hand to hand around it you'll never have another toothache as long as you live. Ridiculous, she muttered; she'd spent an hour the last time looking at that thing, marvelling at the beautiful piece of sculpture nature or time or perhaps vandals had accidentally made of it, running her hands over the figures on the coronation stone at its base and up the narrow stem that supported the remaining arm of the cross.

He was more curious, though, about the round swell of land which could be seen out across the flat Tipperary farms, a perfect green hill crowned with a circle of leafy trees. The guide told him that after one of the crusades a number of people returned to Ireland with a skin disease which was mistaken for leprosy and were confined to that hill, inside that circle, and forbidden to leave it. They were brought across to Mass here on Sundays, she said, before leading him back inside the cathedral to show a small gap in the stones far up one grey wall of the empty Choir. "The poor lepers, a miserable lot altogether as you can imagine, were crowded into a little room behind that wall," she said, "and were forced to see and hear through that single narrow slit of a window. It's called the Lepers' Squint, for obvious reasons."

Afterwards, when the crowd of nuns and priests and yellow-slickered tourists had broken up to walk amongst the graves and the Celtic crosses or to climb the stone steps to the round tower, Desmond would like to have spoken to one of the priests, perhaps the short red-faced one, to say, "What do you make of all this?" or "Is it true what she told us about that fat archbishop with all his wives and children?" But he was intimidated by the black suit, that collar, and by the way the priest seemed always to be surrounded by nuns who giggled like schoolgirls at the silly jokes he told, full of words Desmond couldn't understand. He would go home without ever speaking to a single member of the one aristocracy this country still permitted itself.

But while he stood tempted in the sharp wind that howled across the high hump of rock the guide came over the grass to him. "'Tis certain that you're not American as I thought at first," she said, "for you speak too soft for that. Would you be from England then?"

"No," he said. And without thinking: "We're from Vancouver Island."

"Yes?" she said, her eyes blank. "And where would that be now?"

"A long way from here," he said. "An island, too, like this one, with its own brand of ruins.

"There's a tiny island off our coast," he said, "where they used to send the lepers once, but the last of them died a few years ago. It's a bare and empty place they say now, except for the wind. There are even people who believe that ghosts inhabit it."

But then there were people, too, who said he was crazy to take the children to this uneasy country. It's smaller than you think, they said. You'll hear the bombs from above the border when you get there. What if war breaks out? What if the IRA decides that foreign hostages might help their cause? What about that bomb in the Dublin department store?

Choose another country, they said. A warmer safer one. Choose an island where you can lie in the sun and be waited on by smiling blacks. Why pick Ireland?

Jealousy, he'd told them. Everyone else he knew seemed to have inherited an "old country," an accent, a religion, a set of customs, from parents. His family fled the potato famine in 1849 and had had five generations in which to fade out into Canadians. "I don't know what I've inherited from them," he said, "but whatever it is has gone too deep to be visible."

They'd spent the summer travelling; he would spend the fall and winter writing.

His search for family roots, however, had ended down a narrow hedged-in lane: a half-tumbled stone cabin, stony fields, a view of misty hills, and distant neighbours who turned their damp hay with a two-tined fork and knew nothing at all of the cabin's past.

"Fled the famine did they?" the old woman said. "'Twas many a man did that and was never heard from since."

The summer was intended as a literary pilgrimage too, and much of it was a disappointment. Yeats's castle tower near Coole had been turned into a tourist trap as artificial as a wax museum, with cassette recorders to listen to as you walk through from room to room, and a souvenir shop to sell you books and postcards; Oliver Goldsmith's village was not only deserted, it had disappeared, the site of the little schoolhouse nothing more than a potato patch and the parsonage just half a vine-covered wall; the James Joyce museum only made him feel guilty that he'd never been able to finish *Ulysses*, though there'd been a little excitement that day when a group of women's libbers crashed the male nude-bathing beach just behind the tower.

A man in Dublin told him there weren't any live writers in this country. "You'll find more of our novelists and poets in America than you'll find here," he said. "You're wasting your time on that."

With a sense almost of relief, as though delivered from a responsibility (dead writers, though disappointing, do not confront you with flesh, as living writers could, or with demands), he took the news along with a handful of hot dogs to Carrie and the kids, who had got out of the car to admire a statue. Watching her eat that onion and pork sausage "hot dog" he realized that she had become invisible to him, or nearly invisible. He hadn't even noticed until now that she'd changed her hair, that she was pinning it back; probably because of the wind. In the weeks of travel, in constant too-close confinement, she had all but disappeared, had faded out of his notice the way his own limbs must have done, oh, thirty years ago.

If someone had asked, "What does your wife look like?" he would have forgotten to mention short. He might have said dainty but that was no longer entirely true; sitting like that she appeared to have rounded out, like a copper Oriental idol: dark and squat and yet fine, perhaps elegant. He could not have forgotten her loud, almost masculine laugh of course, but he had long ago ceased to notice the quality of her speaking voice. Carrie, his Carrie, was busy having her own separate holiday, almost untouched by his, though they wore each other like old comfortable unnoticed and unchanged clothes.

"A movie would be nice," he said. "If we could find a babysitter."

But she shook her head. "We can see movies at home. And besides, by the evenings I'm tired out from all we've done, I'd never be able to keep my eyes open."

After Cashel, on their way to the Bantry house, they stopped a while in the city of Cork. And here, he discovered, here after all the disappointments, was a dead literary hero the tourist board hadn't yet got ahold of. He forgot again that she even existed as he tracked down the settings of the stories he loved: butcher shops and smelly quays and dark crowded pubs and parks.

The first house, the little house where the famous writer was born, had been torn down by a sports club which had put a high steel fence around the property, but a neighbour took him across the road and through a building to the back balcony to show him the Good Shepherd Convent where the writer's mother had grown up, and where she returned often with the little boy to visit the nuns. "If he were still alive," Desmond said, "if he still lived here, I suppose I would be scared to come, I'd be afraid to speak to him." The little man, the neighbour, took off his glasses to shine them on a white handkerchief. "Ah, he was a shy man himself. He was back here a few years before he died, with a big crew of American fillum people, and he was a friendly man, friendly enough. But you could see he was a shy man too, yes. 'Tis the shy ones sometimes that take to the book writing."

Carrie wasn't interested in finding the second house. She had never read the man's books, she never read anything at all except art histories and museum catalogues. She said she would go to the park, where there were statues, if he'd let her off there. She said if the kids didn't get out of the car soon to run off some of their energy they would drive her crazy, or kill each other. You could hardly expect children to be interested in old dead writers they'd never heard of, she said. It was no fun for them.

He knew as well as she did that if they were not soon released from the backseat prison they would do each other damage. "I'll go alone," he said.

"But don't be long. We've got a good ways to do yet if we're going to make it to that house today."

So he went in search of the second house, the house the writer had lived in for most of his childhood and youth and had mentioned in dozens of his stories. He found it high up the sloping streets on the north side of the river. Two rows of identical homes, cement-grey, faced each other across a bare sloping square of dirt, each row like a set of steps down the slope, each home just a gate in a cement waist-high wall, a door, a window. Somewhere in this square was where the barefoot grandmother had lived, and where the lady lived whose daughter refused to sleep lying down because people died that way, and where the toothless woman lived who between her sessions in the insane asylum loved animals and people with a saintly passion.

The house he was after was half-way up the left-hand slope and barely distinguishable from the others, except that there was a woman in the tiny front yard, opening the gate to come out.

"There's no one home," she said when she saw his intentions. "They weren't expecting me this time, and presumably, they weren't expecting you either."

"Then it *is* the right house?" Desmond said. Stupidly, he thought. Right house for what?

But she seemed to understand. "Oh yes. It's the right house. Some day the city will get around to putting a plaque on the wall but for the time being I prefer it the way it is. My name, by the way," she added, "is Mary Brennan. I don't live here but I stop by often enough. The old man, you see, was one of my teachers years ago."

She might have been an official guide, she said it all so smoothly. Almost whispering. And there was barely a trace of the musical tipped-up accent of the southern counties in her voice. Perhaps Dublin, or educated. Her name meant nothing to him at first, coming like that without warning. "There would be little point in your going inside anyway, even if they were home," she said. "There's a lovely young couple living there now but they've redone the whole thing over into a perfectly charming but very modern apartment. There's nothing at all to remind you of him. I stop by for reasons I don't begin to understand, respect perhaps, or inspiration, but certainly not to find anything of him here."

In a careless, uneven way, she was pretty. Even beautiful. She wore clothes—a yellow skirt, a sweater—as if they'd been pulled on as she'd hurried out the door. Her coat was draped over her arm, for the momentary blessing of sun. But she was tall enough to get away with the sloppiness and had brown eyes which were calm, calming. And hands that tended to behave as if they were helping to deliver her words to him, stirring up the pale scent of her perfume. He would guess she was thirty, she was a little younger than he was.

"Desmond," he said. "Uh, Philip Desmond."

She squinted at him, as if she had her doubts. Then she nodded, consenting. "You're an American," she said. "And probably a writer. But I must warn you. I've been to your part of the world and you just can't do for it what he did for this. It isn't the same. You don't have the history, the sense that everything that happens is happening on top of layers of things which have already happened. Now I saw you drive up in a motor car and I arrived on a bus so if you're going back down to the city centre I'll thank you for a ride."

Mary Brennan, of course. Why hadn't he known? There were two of her books in the trunk of his car. Paperbacks. Desmond felt his throat closing. Before he'd known who she was she hadn't let him say a word, and now that she seemed to be waiting to hear what he had to offer, he was speechless. His mind was a blank. All he could think of was *Mary Brennan* and wish that she'd turned out to be only a colourful eccentric old lady, something he could handle. He was comfortable with young women only until they turned out to be better than he was at something important to him. Then his throat closed. His mind pulled down the shades and hid.

All Desmond could think to say, driving down the hill towards the River Lee, was: "A man in Dublin told me there was no literature happening in this country." He could have bitten off his tongue. This woman *was* what was happening. A country that had someone like her needed no one else.

She would not accept that, she said, not even from a man in Dublin. And she insisted that he drive her out to the limestone castle restaurant at the mouth of the river so she could buy him a drink there and convince him Dublin was wrong. Inside the castle, though, while they watched the white ferry to Swansea slide out past their window, she discovered she would rather talk about her divorce, a messy thing which had been a strain on everyone concerned and had convinced her if she needed convincing that marriage was an absurd arrangement. She touched Desmond, twice, with one hand, for emphasis.

Oh, she was a charming woman, there was no question. She could be famous for those eyes alone, which never missed a detail in that room (a setting she would use, perhaps, in her next novel of Irish infidelity and rebellion?) and at the same time somehow returned to him often enough and long enough to keep him frozen, afraid to sneak his own glances at the items she was cataloguing for herself. "Some day," she said, "they will have converted all our history into restaurants and bars like this one, just as I will have converted it all to fiction. Then what will we have?"

And when, finally, he said he must go, he really must go, the park was pretty but didn't have all that much in it for kids to do, she said, "Listen, if you want to find out what is happening here, if you really do love that old man's work, then join us tomorrow. There'll be more than a dozen of us, some of the most exciting talent in the country, all meeting up at Gougane Barra . . . you know the place, the lake in the mountains where this river rises . . . it was a spot he loved."

"Tomorrow," he said. "We'll have moved in by then, to the house we've rented for the winter."

"There's a park there now," she said. "And of course the tiny hermitage island. It will begin as a picnic but who knows how it will end." The hand, a white hand with unpainted nails, touched him again.

"Yes," he said. "Yes. We've been there. There's a tiny church on the island, he wrote a story about it, the burial of a priest. And it's only an hour or so from the house, I'd guess. Maybe. Maybe I will."

"Oh you must," she said, and leaned forward. "You knew, of course, that they call it Deep-Valleyed Desmond in the songs." She drew back, biting on a smile.

But when he'd driven her back to the downtown area, to wide St. Patrick's Street, she discovered she was not quite ready yet to let him go. "Walk with me," she said, "for just a while," and found him a parking spot in front of the Munster Arcade where dummies dressed as monks and Vikings and Celtic warriors glowered at him from behind the glass.

"This place exists," she said, "because he made it real for me. He and others, in their stories. I could never write about a place where I was the first, it would panic me. I couldn't be sure it really existed or if I were inventing it."

She led him down past the statue of sober Father Matthew and the parked double-decker buses to the bridge across the Lee. A wind, coming down the river, brought a smell like an open sewer with it. He put his head down and tried to hurry across.

"If I were a North American, like you," she said, "I'd have to move away or become a shop girl. I couldn't write."

He was tempted to say something about plastering over someone else's old buildings, but thought better of it. He hadn't even read her books yet, he knew them only by reputation, he had no right to comment. He stopped, instead, to lean over the stone wall and look at the river. It was like sticking his head into a septic tank. The water was dark, nearly black, and low. Along the edges rats moved over humps of dark shiny muck and half-buried cans and bottles. Holes in the stone wall dumped a steady stream of new sewage into the river. The stories, as far as he could remember, had never mentioned this. These quays were romantic places where young people met and teased each other, or church-goers gathered to gossip after Mass, or old people strolled. None of them, apparently, had noses.

Wind in the row of trees. Leaves rustling. Desmond look at her hands. The perfect slim white fingers lay motionless along her skirt, then moved suddenly up to her throat, to touch the neck of her sweater. Then the nearer one moved again, and touched his arm. Those eyes, busy recording the street, paused to look at him; she smiled. Cataloguing me too? he thought. Recording me for future reference? But she didn't know a thing about him.

"I've moved here to work on a book," he said.

Her gaze rested for a moment on the front of his jacket, then flickered away. "Not about *here*," she said. "You're not writing about *this* place?" She looked as if she would protect it from him, if necessary, or whisk it away.

"I have my own place," he said. "I don't need to borrow his."

She stopped, to buy them each an apple from an old black-shawled woman who sat up against the wall by her table of fruit. Ancient, gypsy-faced, with huge earrings hanging from those heavy lobes. Black Spanish eyes. Mary Brennan flashed a smile, counted out some silver pieces, and picked over the apples for two that were red and clear. The hands that offered change were thick and wrinkled, with crescents of black beneath the nails. They disappeared again beneath the shawl. Desmond felt a momentary twinge about biting into the apple; vague memories of parental warnings. You never know whose hands have touched it, they said, in a voice to make you shudder in horror at the possibilities and scrub at the skin of fruit until it was bruised and raw.

Mary Brennan, apparently, had not been subjected to the same warnings. She bit hugely. "Here," she said, at the bridge, "here is where I'm most aware of him. All his favourite streets converge here, from up the hill. Sunday's Well, over there where his wealthy people lived. And of course Blarney Lane. If you had the time we could walk up there, I could show you. Where his first house was, and the pub he dragged his father home from."

"I've seen it," Desmond said, and started across the bridge. She would spoil it all for him if he let her.

But she won him again on the way back down the other side with her talk of castles and churches. Did he know, she asked, the reason there was no roof on the cathedral at Cashel? Did he know why Blackrock Castle where they'd been a half-hour before was a different style altogether than most of the castles of Ireland? Did he know the origin of the word "blarney"?

No he did not, but he knew that his wife would be furious if he didn't hurry back to the park. They passed the noise of voices haggling over second-hand clothes and old books at the Coal Market, they passed the opera house, a tiny yellow book store. She could walk, he saw, the way so many women had forgotten how to walk after high-heeled shoes went out, with long legs and long strides, with some spring in her steps as if there were pleasure in it.

"Now you'll not forget," she said at his car, in his window. "Tomorrow, in Deep-Valleyed Desmond where the Lee rises." There was the scent of apple on her breath. Islands, she leaned in to say, do not exist until you've loved on them.

But today, while Mary Brennan waits on that tiny island for him, Philip Desmond is holed up in the back room of this house at Bantry Bay, trying to write his novel. His wife has taken the car to Cork. When she returns, he doesn't know what he will do. Perhaps he'll get into the car and drive up the snaking road past the crumbling O'Sullivan castle into the mountains, and throw himself into the middle of that crowd of writers as if he belongs there. Maybe he will make them think that he is important, that back home he is noticed in the way Mary Brennan is noticed here, that his work matters. And perhaps late at night, when everyone is drunk, he will lead Mary Brennan out onto the hermitage island to visit the oratory, to speak in whispers of the stories which had happened there, and to lie on the grass beneath the trees, by the quiet edge of the lake. It is not, Desmond knows, too unthinkable. At a distance.

The piece of paper in front of him is still blank. Mrs. O'Sullivan will advertise the laziness of writers, who only pretend they are working when they are actually dreaming. Or sleeping. She will likely be able to tell exactly how many words he has written, though if he at the end of this day complains of how tired he is, she will undoubtedly go into her practised agony. He wonders if she too, from her window, has noticed that the tide had gone out, that the lagoon is empty of everything except brown shiny mud and seaweed, and that the nostril-burning smell of it is penetrating even to the inside of the house, even in here where the window hasn't been opened, likely, in years. He wonders, too, if she minds that the children, who have tired of their sea-edge exploring, are building a castle of pebbles and fuchsia branches in the middle of her back lawn. The youngest, Michael, dances like an Indian around it; maybe he has to go to the bathroom and can't remember where it is. While his father, who could tell him, who could take him there, sits and stares at a piece of paper.

For a moment Desmond wonders how the medieval masses in the cathedral at Cashel must have appeared to the lepers crowded behind that narrow hole. Of course he has never seen a Mass of any kind himself, but still he can imagine the glimpses of fine robes, the bright colours, the voices of a choir singing those high eerie Latin songs, the voice of a chanting priest, the faces of a few worshippers. It was a lean world from behind that stone wall, through that narrow hole. Like looking through the eye of a needle. The Mass, as close as they were permitted to get to the world, would be only timidly glimpsed past other pressed straining heads. For of course Desmond imagines himself far at the back of the crowd.

("Yes?" the guide said. "And where would that be now?"

"A long way from here," he said. "An island, too, like this one, with its own brand of ruins. You've never heard of it though it's nearly the size of Ireland?"

"I have, yes. And it's a long way you've come from home."

"There's a tiny island just off our coast where they used to send the lepers, but the last of them died there a few years ago. It's a bare and empty place they say now, except for the wind. There are even people who believe that ghosts inhabit it.")

What does the world look like to a leper, squinting through that narrow hole? What does it feel like to be confined to the interior of a circle of trees, at the top of a hill, from which everything else can be seen but not approached? Desmond likes to think that he would prefer the life of that famous fat archbishop, celebrating Mass in the cathedral and thinking of his hundred children.

Somewhere in the house a telephone rings. Desmond hasn't been here long enough to notice where the telephone is, whether it is in her part of the house or theirs. But he hears, beyond the wall, the sudden rustling of clothes, the snap of bones, the sound of feet walking across the carpet. Why should Mrs. O'Sullivan have a phone? There are so few telephones in this country that they are all listed in the one book. But her footsteps return, and he hears behind him the turning of his door handle, the squeal of a hinge. Then her voice whispering: "Mr. Desmond? Is it a bad time to interrupt?"

"Is it my wife?"

No it is not. And of course Desmond knows who it is. Before he left the castle-restaurant she asked for his address, for Mrs. O'Sullivan's name, for the name of this village.

"I'm sorry, Mrs. O'Sullivan," he said. "Tell her, tell them I'm working, they'll understand. Tell them I don't want to be disturbed, not just now anyway."

He doesn't turn to see how high her eyebrows lift. He can imagine. Working, she's thinking. If that's working. But when she has closed the door something in him relaxes a little—or at least suspends its tension for a while—and he writes the paragraph again at the top of the page and then adds new words after it until he discovers he has completed a second. It is not very good; he decides when he reads it over that it is not very good at all, but at least it is something. A beginning. Perhaps the dam has been broken.

But there is a commotion, suddenly, in the front yard. A car horn beeping. The children run up the slope past the house. He can hear Carrie's voice calling them. There is a flurry of excited voices and then one of the children is at the door, calling, "Daddy, Daddy, come and see what Mommy has!"

What Mommy has, he discovers soon enough, is something that seems to be taking up the whole back seat, a grey lumpy bulk. And she, standing at the open door, is beaming at him. "Come help me get this thing out!" she says. There is colour in her face, excitement. She has made another one of her finds.

It is, naturally, a piece of sculpture. There is no way Desmond can tell what it is supposed to be and he has given up trying to understand such things long ago. He pulls the figure out, staggers across to the front door, and puts it down in the hall.

"I met the artist who did it," she says. "He was in the little shop delivering something. We talked, it seemed, for hours. This is inspired by the St. Patrick's Cross, he told me, but he abstracted it even more to represent the way art has taken the place of religion in the modern world."

"Whatever it represents," Desmond says, "we'll never get it home."

Nothing, to Carrie, is a problem. "We'll enjoy it here, in this house. Then before we leave we'll crate it up and ship it home." She walks around the sculpture, delighted with it, delighted with herself.

"I could have talked to him for hours," she says, "we got along beautifully. But I remembered you asked me to have the car home early." She kisses him, pushes a finger on his nose. "See how obedient I am?"

"I said that?"

"Yes," she says. "Right after breakfast. Some other place you said you wanted to go prowling around in by yourself. I rushed home down all that long winding bloody road for you. On the wrong side, I'll never get used to it. Watching for radar traps, for heaven's sake. Do you think the gardai have radar traps here?"

But Desmond is watching Mrs. O'Sullivan, who has come out into the hall to stare at the piece of sculpture. Why does he have this urge to show her his two paragraphs? Desmond doesn't even show Carrie anything until it is finished. Why, he wonders, should he feel just because she sits there listening through the wall that she's also waiting for him to produce something? She probably doesn't even read. Still, he wants to say, "Look. Read this, isn't it good? And I wrote it in your house, only today."

Mrs. O'Sullivan's hand is knotting at her throat. The sculpture has drawn a frown, a heavy sulk. "'Tis a queer lot of objects they've been making for the tourists, and none of them what you could put a name to."

"But oh," Carrie says, "he must be nearly the best in the country! Surely. And this is no tourist souvenir. I got it from an art shop in Cork."

Mrs. O'Sullivan's hand opens and closes, creeps closer to her mouth. "Oh," she says. "Cork." As if a lot has been explained. "You can expect anything at all from a city. Anything at all. There was people here staying in this house, 'twas last year yes, came back from Cork as pleased as the Pope with an old box of turf they had bought. They wanted to smell it burning in my fire if you don't mind. What you spend your money on is your own business, I told them, but I left the bogs behind years ago, thank you, and heat my house with electricity. Keep the turf in your car so."

Carrie is plainly insulted. Words struggle at her lips. But she dismisses them, apparently, and chooses diversion. "I'll make a pot of tea. Would you like a cup with us, Mrs. O'Sullivan? The long drive's made me thirsty."

And Mrs. O'Sullivan, whose role is apparently varied and will shift for any occasion, lets her fingers pluck at her face. "Oh I know I know I know!" Her long brown-stockinged legs move slowly across the patterned carpet. "And Mr. Desmond, too, after his work. I was tempted to take him a cup but he shouldn't be disturbed I know."

"Work?" Carrie says. "Working at what?"

"I started the novel," Desmond says.

"You have? Then that's something we should celebrate. Before you go off wherever it is you think you're going."

"It's only a page," Desmond says. "And it's not very good at all, but it's a start. It's better than the blank paper."

Like some children, he thinks, he's learned to make a virtue out of anything. Even a page of scribble. When he'd be glad to give a thousand pages of scribble for the gift of honesty. Or change. Or even blindness of a sort. What good is vision after all if it refuses to ignore the dark?

Because hasn't he heard, somewhere, that artists—painters—deliberately create frames for themselves to look through, to sharpen their vision by cutting off all the details which have no importance to their work?

He follows the women into the kitchen, where cups already clatter onto saucers. "Maybe after tea," he says, "I'll get a bit more done."

Pretending, perhaps, that the rest of the world sits waiting, like Mrs. O'Sullivan, for the words he will produce. Because his tongue, his voice, has made the decision for him. Desmond knows that he may only sit in front of that paper for the rest of that day, that he may only play with his pen—frustrated—until enough time has gone by to justify his coming out of the room. To read one of the books he's bought. To talk with Carrie about her shopping in Cork, about her sculptor. To play with the children perhaps, or take them for a walk along the road to look for donkeys, for ruins. Desmond knows that the evening may be passed in front of the television set, where they will see American movies with Irish commercials, and will later try to guess what *an naught* is telling them about the day's events, and that he will try very hard not to think of Mary Brennan or of the dozen Irish writers at Gougane Barra or of the tiny hermitage island which the famous writer loved. Deep-Valleyed Desmond. He knows that he could be there with them, through this day and this night, celebrating something he'd come here to find; but he acknowledges, too, the other. That words, too, were invented perhaps to do the things that stones can do. And he has come here, after all, to build his walls.

William Wymark Jacobs (1863-1943) was born and raised in Wapping, London, where his father was manager of a ships' wharf. Following his education at a private school in London and at Birkbeck College, he entered the Civil Service, and worked in the Savings Bank department from 1883 to 1899. During this period he began to submit stories and sketches to the popular magazines of the day, *Blackfriars, The Idler,* and *Strand Magazine,* with such success that by 1899 he was earning enough from his writing to enable him to give up his job and devote himself to full-time authorship. Between 1896 and 1926 Jacobs wrote over a hundred and fifty short stories, five novels, and several plays; but for the last seventeen years of his life, he retired into private life and published almost nothing at all.

Jacobs is especially remembered for his humorous tales about seafaring men and dockyard workers, gathered in such collections as *Many Cargoes* (1896) and *Odd Craft* (1904); his settings are cheap lodging houses, ships' wharves, or dock-side pubs where old sea dogs gather to swap yarns or spin tall tales. "The Monkey's Paw," from *The Lady of the Barge* (1902), is a somewhat macabre exception to Jacobs' usual light comedy, though it too has the flavour of the tall tale. He introduces the supernatural into a plain domestic setting with a clarity and an economy of style that lend the plot added force and authenticity, intensifying the horror of the outcome.

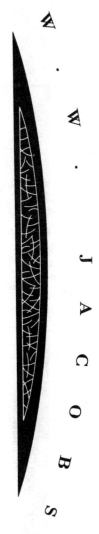

W . W . J A C O B S

FOR FURTHER READING

E.F. Bleiler, ed., *Supernatural Fiction Writers: Fantasy and Horror*, 2 vols. (New York: Scribner, 1985), I. 384-85.

Hugh Greene, Introduction to W.W. Jacobs, *Selected Short Stories* (London: Bodley Head, 1975).

J.B. Priestley, "Mr. W.W. Jacobs," *Figures in Modern Literature* (London: John Lane, 1924): pp. 103-23.

The Monkey's Paw

I

Without, the night was cold and wet, but in the small parlour of Laburnam Villa the blinds were drawn and the fire burned brightly. Father and son were at chess, the former, who possessed ideas about the game involving radical changes, putting his king into such sharp and unnecessary perils that it even provoked comment from the white-haired old lady knitting placidly by the fire.

"Hark at the wind," said Mr. White, who, having seen a fatal mistake after it was too late, was amiably desirous of preventing his son from seeing it.

"I'm listening," said the latter, grimly surveying the board as he stretched out his hand. "Check."

"I should hardly think that he'd come tonight," said his father, with his hand poised over the board.

"Mate," replied the son.

"That's the worst of living so far out," bawled Mr. White, with sudden and unlooked-for violence; "of all the beastly, slushy, out-of-the-way places to live in, this is the worse. Pathway's a bog, and the road's a torrent. I don't know what people are thinking about. I suppose because only two houses in the road are let, they think it doesn't matter."

"Never mind, dear," said his wife, soothingly; "perhaps you'll win the next one."

Mr. White looked up sharply, just in time to intercept a knowing glance between mother and son. The words died away on his lips, and he hid a guilty grin in his thin grey beard.

"There he is," said Herbert White, as the gate banged to loudly and heavy footsteps came toward the door.

The old man rose with hospitable haste, and opening the door, was heard condoling with the new arrival. The new arrival also condoled with himself, so that Mrs. White said,

"Tut, tut!" and coughed gently as her husband entered the room, followed by a tall, burly man, beady of eye and rubicund of visage.

"Sergeant-Major Morris," he said, introducing him.

The sergeant-major shook hands, and taking the proffered seat by the fire, watched contentedly while his host got out whiskey and tumblers and stood a small copper kettle on the fire.

At the third glass his eyes got brighter, and he began to talk, the little family circle regarding with eager interest this visitor from distant parts, as he squared his broad shoulders in the chair and spoke of wild scenes and doughty deeds; of wars and plagues and strange peoples.

"Twenty-one years of it," said Mr. White, nodding at his wife and son. "When he went away he was a slip of youth in the warehouse. Now look at him."

"He don't look to have taken much harm," said Mrs. White, politely.

"I'd like to go to India myself," said the old man, "just to look round a bit, you know."

"Better where you are," said the sergeant-major, shaking his head. He put down the empty glass, and sighing softly, shook it again.

"I should like to see those old temples and fakirs and jugglers," said the old man. "What was that you started telling me the other day about a monkey's paw or something, Morris?"

"Nothing," said the soldier hastily. "Leastways nothing worth hearing."

"Monkey's paw?" said Mrs. White, curiously.

"Well, it's just a bit of what you might call magic, perhaps," said the sergeant-major, offhandedly.

His three listeners leaned forward eagerly. The visitor absent-mindedly put his empty glass to his lips and then set it down again. His host filled it for him.

"To look at," said the sergeant-major, fumbling in his pocket, "it's just an ordinary little paw, dried to a mummy."

He took something out of his pocket and proffered it. Mrs. White drew back with a grimace, but her son, taking it, examined it curiously.

"And what is there special about it?" inquired Mr. White as he took it from his son, and having examined it, placed it upon the table.

"It had a spell put on it by an old fakir," said the sergeant-major, "a very holy man. He wanted to show that fate ruled people's lives, and that those who interfered with it did so to their sorrow. He put a spell on it so that three separate men could each have three wishes from it."

His manner was so impressive that his hearers were conscious that their light laughter jarred somewhat.

"Well, why don't you have three, sir?" said Herbert White, cleverly.

The soldier regarded him in the way that middle age is wont to regard presumptuous youth. "I have," he said, quietly, and his blotchy face whitened.

"And did you really have the three wishes granted?" asked Mrs. White.

"I did," said the sergeant-major, and his glass tapped against his strong teeth.

"And has anybody else wished?" persisted the old lady.

"The first man had his three wishes. Yes," was the reply; "I don't know what the first two were, but the third was for death. That's how I got the paw."

His tones were so grave that a hush fell upon the group.

"If you've had your three wishes, it's no good to you now, then, Morris," said the old man at last. "What do you keep it for?"

The soldier shook his head. "Fancy, I suppose," he said, slowly. "I did have some idea of selling it, but I don't think I will. It has caused enough mischief already. Besides, people won't buy. They think it's a fairy tale, some of them, and those who do think anything of it want to try it first and pay me afterward."

"If you could have another three wishes," said the old man, eyeing him keenly, "would you have them?"

"I don't know," said the other. "I don't know."

He took the paw, and dangling it between his forefinger and thumb, suddenly threw it upon the fire. White, with a slight cry, stooped down and snatched it off.

"Better let it burn," said the soldier, solemnly.

"If you don't want it, Morris," said the other, "give it to me."

"I won't," said his friend, doggedly. "I threw it on the fire. If you keep it, don't blame me for what happens. Pitch it on the fire again like a sensible man."

The other shook his head and examined his new possession closely. "How do you do it?" he inquired.

"Hold it up in your right hand and wish aloud," said the sergeant-major, "but I warn you of the consequences."

"Sounds like the *Arabian Nights*," said Mrs. White, as she rose and began to set the supper. "Don't you think you might wish for four pairs of hands for me?"

Her husband drew the talisman from pocket, and then all three burst into laughter as the sergeant-major, with a look of alarm on his face, caught him by the arm.

"If you must wish," he said, gruffly, "wish for something sensible."

Mr. White dropped it back in his pocket, and placing chairs, motioned his friend to the table. In the business of supper the talisman was partly forgotten, and afterward the three sat listening in an enthralled fashion to a second instalment of the soldier's adventures in India.

"If the tale about the monkey's paw is not more truthful than those he has been telling us," said Herbert, as the door closed behind their guest, just in time for him to catch the last train, "we shan't make much out of it."

"Did you give him anything for it, father?" inquired Mrs. White, regarding her husband closely.

"A trifle," said he, colouring slightly. "He didn't want it, but I made him take it. And he pressed me again to throw it away."

"Likely," said Herbert, with pretended horror. "Why, we're going to be rich, and famous and happy. Wish to be an emperor, father, to begin with; then you can't be henpecked."

He darted round the table, pursued by the maligned Mrs. White armed with an antimacassar.

Mr. White took the paw from his pocket and eyed it dubiously. "I don't know what to wish for, and that's a fact," he said, slowly. "It seems to me I've got all I want."

"If you only cleared the house, you'd be quite happy, wouldn't you?" said Herbert, with his hand on his shoulder. "Well, wish for two hundred pounds, then; that'll just do it."

His father, smiling shamefacedly at his own credulity, held up the talisman, as his son, with a solemn face, somewhat marred by a wink at his mother, sat down at the piano and struck a few impressive chords.

"I wish for two hundred pounds," said the old man distinctly.

A fine crash from the piano greeted the words, interrupted by a shuddering cry from the old man. His wife and son ran toward him.

"It moved," he cried, with a glance of disgust at the object as it lay on the floor. "As I wished, it twisted in my hand like a snake."

"Well, I don't see the money," said his son as he picked it up and placed it on the table, "and I bet I never shall."

"It must have been your fancy, father," said his wife, regarding him anxiously.

He shook his head. "Never mind, though; there's no harm done, but it gave me a shock all the same."

They sat down by the fire again while the two men finished their pipes. Outside, the wind was higher than ever, and the old man started nervously at the sound of a door banging upstairs. A silence unusual and depressing settled upon all three, which lasted until the old couple rose to retire for the night.

"I expect you'll find the cash tied up in a big bag in the middle of your bed," said Herbert, as he bade them good-night, "And something horrible squatting up on top the wardrobe watching you as you pocket your ill-gotten gains."

He sat alone in the darkness, gazing at the dying fire, and seeing faces in it. The last face was so horrible and so simian that he gazed at it in amazement. It got so vivid that, with a little uneasy laugh, he felt on the table for a glass containing a little water to throw over it. His hand grasped the monkey's paw, and with a little shiver he wiped his hand on his coat and went up to bed.

II

In the brightness of the wintry sun next morning as it streamed over the breakfast table he laughed at his fears. There was an air of prosaic wholesomeness about the room which it had lacked on the previous night, and the dirty, shrivelled little paw was pitched on the sideboard with a carelessness which betokened no great belief in its virtues.

"I suppose all old soldiers are the same," said Mrs. White. "The idea of our listening to such nonsense! How could wishes be granted in these days? And if they could, how could two hundred pounds hurt you, father?"

"Might drop on his head from the sky," said the frivolous Herbert.

"Morris said the things happened so naturally," said his father, "that you might if you so wished attribute it to coincidence."

"Well, don't break into the money before I come back," said Herbert as he rose from the table. "I'm afraid it'll turn you into a mean, avaricious man, and we shall have to disown you."

His mother laughed, and following him to the door, watched him down the road; and returning to the breakfast table, was very happy at the expense of her husband's credulity. All of which did not prevent her from scurrying to the door at the postman's knock, nor prevent her from referring somewhat shortly to retired sergeant-majors of bibulous habits when she found that the post brought a tailor's bill.

"Herbert will have some more of his funny remarks, I expect, when he comes home," she said, as they sat at dinner.

"I dare say," said Mr. White, pouring himself out some beer; "but for all that, the thing moved in my hand; that I'll swear to."

"You thought it did," said the old lady soothingly.

"I say it did," replied the other. "There was no thought about it; I have just—What's the matter?"

His wife made no reply. She was watching the mysterious movements of a man outside, who, peering in an undecided fashion at the house, appeared to be trying to make up his mind to enter. In mental connection with the two hundred pounds, she noticed that the stranger was well dressed, and wore a silk hat of glossy newness. Three times he paused at the gate, and then walked on again. The fourth time he stood with his hand upon it, and then with sudden resolution flung it open and walked up the path. Mrs. White at the same moment placed her hands behind her, and hurriedly unfastening the strings of her apron, put that useful article of apparel beneath the cushion of her chair.

She brought the stranger, who seemed ill at ease, into the room. He gazed at her furtively, and listened in a preoccupied fashion as the old lady apologized for the appearance of the room, and her husband's coat, a garment which he usually reserved for the garden. She then waited as patiently as her sex would permit, for him to broach his business, but he was at first strangely silent.

"I—was asked to call," he said at last, and stooped and picked a piece of cotton from his trousers. "I come from 'Maw and Meggins.'"

The old lady started. "Is anything the matter?" she asked, breathlessly. "Has anything happened to Herbert? What is it? What is it?"

Her husband interposed. "There, there, mother," he said, hastily. "Sit down, and don't jump to conclusions. You've not brought bad news, I'm sure, sir," and he eyed the other wistfully.

"I'm sorry—" began the visitor.

"Is he hurt?" demanded the mother, wildly.

The visitor bowed in assent. "Badly hurt," he said, quietly, "but he is not in any pain."

"Oh, thank God!" said the old woman, clasping her hands. "Thank God for that! Thank—"

She broke off suddenly as the sinister meaning of the assurance dawned upon her and she saw the awful confirmation of her fears in the other's perverted face. She caught her breath, and turning to her slower-witted husband, laid her trembling old hand upon his. There was a long silence.

"He was caught in the machinery," said the visitor at length in a low voice.

"Caught in the machinery," repeated Mr. White, in a dazed fashion, "yes."

He sat staring blankly out at the window, and taking his wife's hand between his own, pressed it as he had been wont to do in their old courting-days nearly forty years before.

"He was the only one left to us," he said, turning gently to the visitor. "It is hard."

The other coughed, and rising, walked slowly to the window. "The firm wished me to convey their sincere sympathy with you in your great loss," he said, without looking round. "I beg that you will understand I am only their servant and merely obeying orders."

There was no reply; the old woman's face was white, her eyes staring, and her breath inaudible; on the husband's face was a look such as his friend the sergeant might have carried into his first action.

"I was to say that Maw and Meggins disclaim all responsibility," continued the other. "They admit no liability at all, but in consideration of your son's services, they wish to present you with a certain sum as compensation."

Mr. White dropped his wife's hand, and rising to his feet, gazed with a look of horror at his visitor. His dry lips shaped the words, "How much?"

"Two hundred pounds," was the answer.

Unconscious of his wife's shriek, the old man smiled faintly, put out his hands like a sightless man, and dropped, a senseless heap, to the floor.

III

In the huge new cemetery, some two miles distant, the old people buried their dead, and came back to a house steeped in shadow and silence. It was all over so quickly that at first they could hardly realize it, and remained in a state of expectation as though of something else to happen—something else which was to lighten this load, too heavy for old hearts to bear.

But the days passed, and expectation gave place to resignation—the hopeless resignation of the old, sometimes miscalled apathy. Sometimes they hardly exchanged a word, for now they had nothing to talk about, and their days were long to weariness.

It was about a week after that the old man, waking suddenly in the night, stretched out his hand and found himself alone. The room was in darkness, and the sound of subdued weeping came from the window. He raised himself in bed and listened.

"Come back," he said, tenderly. "You will be cold."

"It is colder for my son," said the old woman, and wept afresh.

The sound of her sobs died away on his ears. The bed was warm, and his eyes heavy with sleep. He dozed fitfully, and then slept until a sudden wild cry from his wife awoke him with a start.

"*The paw!*" she cried wildly. "The monkey's paw!"

He started up in alarm. "Where? Where is it? What's the matter?"

She came stumbling across the room toward him. "I want it," she said, quietly. "You've not destroyed it?"

"It's in the parlour, on the bracket," he replied, marvelling. "Why?"

She cried and laughed together, and bending over, kissed his cheek.

"I only just thought of it," she said, hysterically. "Why didn't I think of it before? Why didn't *you* think of it?"

"Think of what?" he questioned.

"The other two wishes," she replied, rapidly. "We've only had one."

"Was not that enough?" he demanded, fiercely.

"No," she cried, triumphantly; "we'll have one more. Go down and get it quickly, and wish our boy alive again."

The man sat up in bed and flung the bedclothes from his quaking limbs. "Good God, you are mad!" he cried, aghast.

"Get it," she panted; "get it quickly, and wish—Oh, my boy, my boy!"

Her husband struck a match and lit the candle. "Get back to bed," he said, unsteadily. "You don't know what you are saying."

"We had the first wish granted," said the old woman, feverishly; "why not the second?"

"A coincidence," stammered the old man.

"Go and get it and wish," cried his wife, quivering with excitement.

The old man turned and regarded her, and his voice shook. "He has been dead ten days, and besides he—I would not tell you else, but—I could only recognize him by his clothing. If he was too terrible for you to see then, how now?"

"Bring him back," cried the old woman, and dragged him toward the door. "Do you think I fear the child I have nursed?"

He went down in the darkness, and felt his way to the parlour, and then to the mantelpiece. The talisman was in its place, and a horrible fear that the unspoken wish might bring his mutilated son before him ere he could escape from the room seized upon him, and he caught his breath as he found that he had lost the direction of the door. His brow cold with sweat, he felt his way round the table, and groped along the wall until he found himself in the small passage with the unwholesome thing in his hand.

Even his wife's face seemed changed as he entered the room. It was white and expectant, and to his fears seemed to have an unnatural look upon it. He was afraid of her.

"*Wish!*" she cried, in a strong voice.

"It is foolish and wicked," he faltered.

"*Wish!*" repeated his wife.

He raised his hand. "I wish my son alive again."

The talisman fell to the floor, and he regarded it fearfully. Then he sank trembling into a chair as the old woman, with burning eyes, walked to the window and raised the blind.

He sat until he was chilled with the cold, glancing occasionally at the figure of the old woman peering through the window. The candle-end, which had burned below the rim of the china candlestick, was throwing pulsating shadows on the ceiling and walls, until, with a flicker larger than the rest, it expired. The old man, with an unspeakable sense of relief at the failure of the talisman, crept back to his bed, and a minute or two afterward the old woman came silently and apathetically beside him.

Neither spoke, but lay silently listening to the ticking of the clock. A stair creaked, and a squeaky mouse scurried noisily through the wall. The darkness was oppressive, and after lying for some time screwing up his courage, he took the box of matches, and striking one, went downstairs for a candle.

At the foot of the stairs the match went out, and he paused to strike another; and at the same moment a knock, so quiet and stealthy as to be scarcely audible, sounded on the front door.

The matches fell from his hand and spilled in the passage. He stood motionless, his breath suspended until the knock was repeated. Then he turned and fled swiftly back to his room, and closed the door behind him. A third knock sounded through the house.

"*What's that?*" cried the old woman, starting up.

"A rat," said the old man in shaking tones—"a rat. It passed me on the stairs."

His wife sat up in bed listening. A loud knock resounded through the house.

"It's Herbert!" she screamed. "It's Herbert!"

She ran to the door, but her husband was before her, and catching her by the arm, held her tightly.

"What are you going to do?" he whispered hoarsely.

"It's my boy; it's Herbert!" she cried, struggling mechanically. "I forgot it was two miles away. What are you holding me for? Let go. I must open the door."

"For God's sake don't let it in," cried the old man, trembling.

"You're afraid of your own son," she cried, struggling. "Let me go. I'm coming, Herbert; I'm coming."

There was another knock, and another. The old woman with a sudden wrench broke free and ran from the room. Her husband followed to the landing, and called after her appealingly as she hurried downstairs. He heard the chain rattle back and the bottom bolt drawn slowly and stiffly from the socket. Then the old woman's voice, strained and panting.

"The bolt," she cried, loudly. "Come down. I can't reach it."

But her husband was on his hands and knees groping wildly on the floor in search of the paw. If he could only find it before the thing outside got in. A perfect fusillade of knocks reverberated through the house, and he heard the scraping of a chair as his wife put it down in the passage against the door. He heard the creaking of the bolt as it came slowly back, and at the same moment he found the monkey's paw, and frantically breathed his third and last wish.

The knocking ceased suddenly, although the echoes of it were still in the house. He heard the chair drawn back, and the door opened. A cold wind rushed up the staircase, and a long loud wail of disappointment and misery from his wife gave him courage to run down to her side, and then to the gate beyond. The street lamp flickering opposite shone on a quiet and deserted road.

Born in Dublin, the city which figures so largely in all his writing, James Joyce (1882-1941) was educated at two Jesuit schools, and at University College, Dublin. He early showed himself to be a rebel against tradition, rejecting his Catholic background and leaving Ireland soon after his graduation in 1902. With his lifelong companion Nora Barnacle, whom he eventually married in 1931, Joyce spent most of his life in self-imposed exile in various parts of Europe, supporting himself first by teaching, and then with the help of wealthy patrons. Though his writing career spanned forty years, Joyce published relatively little; his major works being *Dubliners* (1914), *A Portrait of the Artist as a Young Man* (1916), *Ulysses* (1922), and *Finnegan's Wake* (1939). Despite this limited output, Joyce's experiments in language and technique had an enormous influence, even in his own lifetime. But his work was also controversial: *Ulysses* was charged with obscenity on its first appearance, and banned in both England and America.

Dubliners, too, was regarded as a daring book, and Joyce fought for many years over its publication. Though it was completed initially in 1905, the publisher objected to some parts of the book (for example, to the use of the word "bloody" in several stories), and feared that publication would lead to a prosecution for indecency. Joyce fought to retain his stories intact, because, as he wrote to the publisher concerned (Grant Richards), "I believe that in composing my chapter of moral history in exactly the way I have composed it I have taken the first step towards the spiritual liberation of my country."

In "The Boarding House," as in the other stories in *Dubliners*, Joyce presents an episode in the life of his native city, turning a pitiless light on its follies and frailties. With an astonishingly small compass, he creates a vivid sense of the seedy gentility of such establishments as that run by Mrs. Mooney; and he conveys too the moral duplicity practised by mother and daughter on their helpless victim, a man made only too vulnerable by his own sense of decency. The tone of the story is drily comic; but its effect is not far removed from "the odour of ashpits and old weeds and offal" which Joyce said hung around his stories.

FOR FURTHER READING

Richard Ellmann, *James Joyce* (New York: Oxford University Press, 1959).

Don Gifford, *Joyce Annotated: Notes for Dubliners and A Portrait of the Artist as a Young Man* (Berkeley: University of California Press, 1982).

Hugh Kenner, *Dublin's Joyce* (Bloomington: Indiana UP, 1956).

Bruce A. Rosenberg, "The Crucifixion in 'The Boarding House,'" *Studies in Short Fiction* 5 (1967): 44-53.

JAMES JOYCE

The Boarding House

Mrs Mooney was a butcher's daughter. She was a woman who was quite able to keep things to herself: a determined woman. She had married her father's foreman, and opened a butcher's shop near Spring Gardens. But as soon as his father-in-law was dead Mr Mooney began to go to the devil. He drank, plundered the till, ran headlong into debt. It was no use making him take the pledge: he was sure to break out again a few days after. By fighting his wife in the presence of customers and by buying bad meat he ruined his business. One night he went for his wife with the cleaver, and she had to sleep in a neighbour's house.

After that they lived apart. She went to the priest and got a separation from him, with care of the children. She would give him neither money nor food nor house-room; and so he was obliged to enlist himself as a sheriff's man. He was a shabby stooped little drunkard with a white face and a white moustache and white eyebrows, pencilled above his little eyes, which were pink-veined and raw; and all day long he sat in the bailiff's room, waiting to be put on a job. Mrs Mooney, who had taken what remained of her money out of the butcher business and set up a boarding house in Hardwicke Street, was a big imposing woman. Her house had a floating population made up of tourists from Liverpool and the Isle of Man and, occasionally, *artistes* from the music halls. Its resident population was made up of clerks from the city. She governed the house cunningly and firmly, knew when to give credit, when to be stern and when to let things pass. All the resident young men spoke of her as *The Madam*.

Mrs Mooney's young men paid fifteen shillings a week for board and lodgings (beer or stout at dinner excluded). They shared in common tastes and occupations and for this reason they were very chummy with one another. They discussed with one another the chances of favourites and outsiders. Jack Mooney, the Madam's son, who was clerk to a commission agent in Fleet Street, had the reputation of being a hard case. He was fond of using soldiers' obscenities: usually he came home in the small hours. When he met his friends he had always a good one to tell them, and he was always sure to be on to a good thing—that is to say, a likely horse or a likely *artiste*. He was also handy with the mitts and sang comic songs. On Sunday nights there would often be a reunion in Mrs Mooney's front drawing-room. The music-hall *artistes* would oblige; and Sheridan played waltzes and polkas and vamped accompaniments. Polly Mooney, the Madam's daughter, would also sing. She sang:

I'm a . . . naughty girl
You needn't sham:
You know I am.

Polly was a slim girl of nineteen; she had light soft hair and a small full mouth. Her eyes, which were grey with a shade of green through them, had a habit of glancing upwards when she spoke with anyone, which made her look like a little perverse madonna. Mrs Mooney had first sent her daughter to be a typist in a corn-factor's office, but as a disreputable sheriff's man used to come every other day to the office, asking to be allowed to say a word to his daughter, she had taken her daughter home again and set her to do housework. As Polly was very lively, the intention was to give her the run of the young men. Besides, young men like to feel that there is a young woman not very far away. Polly, of course, flirted with the young men, but Mrs Mooney, who was a shrewd judge, knew that the young men were only passing the time away: none of them meant business. Things went on so for a long time, and Mrs Mooney began to think of sending Polly back to typewriting, when she noticed that something was going on between Polly and one of the young men. She watched the pair and kept her own counsel.

Polly knew that she was being watched, but still her mother's persistent silence could not be misunderstood. There had been no open complicity between mother and daughter, no open understanding, but though people in the house began to talk of the affair, still Mrs Mooney did not intervene. Polly began to grow a little strange in her manner, and the young man was evidently perturbed. At last, when she judged it to be the right moment, Mrs Mooney intervened. She dealt with moral problems as a cleaver deals with meat: and in this case she had made up her mind.

It was a bright Sunday morning of early summer, promising heat, but with a fresh breeze blowing. All the windows of the boarding house were open and the lace curtains ballooned gently towards the street beneath the raised sashes. The belfry of George's Church sent out constant peals, and worshippers, singly or in groups, traversed the little circus before the church, revealing their purpose by their self-contained demeanour no less than by the little volumes in their gloved hands. Breakfast was over in the boarding house, and the table of the breakfast-room was covered with plates on which lay yellow streaks of eggs with morsels of bacon-fat and bacon-rind. Mrs Mooney sat in the straw armchair and watched the servant Mary remove the breakfast things. She made Mary collect the crusts and pieces of broken bread to help to make Tuesday's bread-pudding. When the table was cleared, the broken bread collected, the sugar and butter safe under lock and key, she began to reconstruct the interview which she had had the night before with Polly. Things were as she had suspected: she had been frank in her questions and Polly had been frank in her answers. Both had been somewhat awkward, of course. She had been made awkward by her not wishing to receive the news in too cavalier a fashion or to seem to have connived, and Polly had been made awkward not merely because allusions of that kind always made her awkward, but also because she did not wish it to be thought that in her wise innocence she had divined the intention behind her mother's tolerance.

Mrs Mooney glanced instinctively at the little gilt clock on the mantelpiece as soon as she had become aware through her reverie that the bells of George's Church had stopped ringing. It was seventeen minutes past eleven: she would have lots to time to have the matter out with Mr Doran and then catch short twelve at Marlborough Street. She was sure she would win. To begin with, she had all the weight of social opinion on her side: she was an outraged mother. She had allowed him to live beneath her roof, assuming that he was a man of honour, and he had simply abused her hospitality. He was thirty-four or thirty-five years of age, so that youth could not be pleaded as his excuse; nor could ignorance be his excuse, since he was a man who had seen something of the world. He had simply taken advantage of Polly's youth and inexperience: that was evident. The question was: What reparation would he make?

There must be reparation made in such a case. It is all very well for the man: he can go his ways as if nothing had happened, having had his moment of pleasure, but the girl has to bear the brunt. Some mothers would be content to patch up such an affair for a sum of money: she had known cases of it. But she would not do so. For her only one reparation could make up for the loss of her daughter's honour: marriage.

She counted all her cards again before sending Mary up to Mr Doran's room to say that she wished to speak with him. She felt sure she would win. He was a serious young man, not rakish or loud-voiced like the others. If it had been Mr Sheridan or Mr Meade or Bantam Lyons, her task would have been much harder. She did not think he would face publicity. All the lodgers in the house knew something of the affair; details had been invented by some. Besides, he had been employed for thirteen years in a great Catholic wine-merchant's office, and publicity would mean for him, perhaps, the loss of his job. Whereas if he agreed all might be well. She knew he had a good screw for one thing, and she suspected he had a bit of stuff put by.

Nearly the half-hour! She stood up and surveyed herself in the pier-glass. The decisive expression of her great florid face satisfied her, and she thought of some mothers she knew who could not get their daughters off their hands.

Mr Doran was very anxious indeed this Sunday morning. He had made two attempts to shave, but his hand had been so unsteady that he had been obliged to desist. Three days' reddish beard fringed his jaws, and every two or three minutes a mist gathered on his glasses so that he had to take them off and polish them with his pocket-handkerchief. The recollection of his confession of the night before was a cause of acute pain to him; the priest had drawn out every ridiculous detail of the affair, and in the end had so magnified his sin that he was almost thankful at being afforded a loophole of reparation. The harm was done. What could he do now but marry her or run away? He could not brazen it out. The affair would be sure to be talked of, and his employer would be certain to hear of it. Dublin is such a small city: everyone knows everyone else's business. He felt his heart leap warmly in his throat as he heard in his excited imagination old Mr Leonard calling out in his rasping voice: "Send Mr Doran here, please."

All his long years of service gone for nothing! All his industry and diligence thrown away! As a young man he had sown his wild oats, of course; he had boasted of his free-thinking and denied the existence of God to his companions in public-houses. But that was all passed and done with . . . nearly. He still bought a copy of *Reynolds Newspaper* every week, but he attended to his religious duties, and for nine-tenths of the year lived a regular life. He had money enough to settle down on; it was not that. But the family would look down on her. First of all there was her disreputable father, and then her mother's boarding house was beginning to get a certain fame. He had a notion that he was being had. He could imagine his friends talking of the affair and laughing. She *was* a little vulgar; sometimes she said "I seen" and "If I had've known." But what would grammar matter if he really loved her? He could not make up his mind whether to like her or despise her for what she had done. Of course he had done it too. His instinct urged him to remain free, not to marry. Once you are married you are done for, it said.

While he was sitting helplessly on the side of the bed in shirt and trousers, she tapped lightly at his door and entered. She told him all, that she had made a clean breast of it to her mother and that her mother would speak with him that morning. She cried and threw her arms round his neck, saying:

"O Bob! Bob! What am I to do? What am I to do at all?"

She would put an end to herself, she said.

He comforted her feebly, telling her not to cry, that it would be all right, never fear. He felt against his shirt the agitation of her bosom.

It was not altogether his fault that it had happened. He remembered well, with the curious patient memory of the celibate, the first casual caresses her dress, her breath, her fingers had given him. Then late one night as he was undressing for bed she had tapped at his door, timidly. She wanted to relight her candle at his, for hers had been blown out by a gust. It was her bath night. She wore a loose open combing-jacket of printed flannel. Her white instep shone in the opening of her furry slippers and the blood glowed warmly behind her perfumed skin. From her hands and wrists too as she lit and steadied her candle a faint perfume arose.

On nights when he came in very late it was she who warmed up his dinner. He scarcely knew what he was eating, feeling her beside him alone, at night, in the sleeping house. And her thoughtfulness! If the night was anyway cold or wet or windy there was sure to be a little tumbler of punch ready for him. Perhaps they could be happy together . . .

They used to go upstairs together on tiptoe, each with a candle, and on the third landing exchange reluctant good nights. They used to kiss. He remembered well her eyes, the touch of her hand and his delirium . . .

But delirium passes. He echoed her phrase, applying it to himself: "*What am I to do?*" The instinct of the celibate warned him to hold back. But the sin was there; even his sense of honour told him that reparation must be made for such a sin.

While he was sitting with her on the side of the bed Mary came to the door and said that the missus wanted to see him in the parlour. He stood up to put on his coat and waistcoat, more helpless than ever. When he was dressed he went over to her to comfort her. It would be all right, never fear. He left her crying on the bed and moaning softly: "*O my God!*"

Going down the stairs his glasses became so dimmed with moisture that he had to take them off and polish them. He longed to ascend through the roof and fly away to another country where he would never hear again of his trouble, and yet a force pushed him downstairs step by step. The implacable faces of his employer and of the Madam stared upon his discomfiture. On the last flight of stairs he passed Jack Mooney, who was coming up from the pantry nursing two bottles of *Bass*. They saluted coldly; and the lover's eyes rested for a second or two on a thick bulldog face and a pair of thick short arms. When he reached the foot of the staircase he glanced up and saw Jack regarding him from the door of the return-room.

Suddenly he remembered the night when one of the music-hall *artistes*, a little blond Londoner, had made a rather free allusion to Polly. The reunion had been almost broken up on account of Jack's violence. Everyone tried to quiet him. The music-hall *artiste*, a little paler than usual, kept smiling and saying that there was no harm meant; but Jack kept shouting at him that if any fellow tried that sort of game on with his sister he'd bloody well put his teeth down his throat: so he would.

Polly sat for a little time on the side of the bed, crying. Then she dried her eyes and went over to the looking-glass. She dipped the end of the towel in the water-jug and refreshed her eyes with the cool water. She looked at herself in profile and readjusted a hairpin above her ear. Then she went back to the bed again and sat at the foot. She regarded the pillows for a long time, and the sight of them awakened in her mind secret, amiable memories. She rested the nape of her neck against the cool iron bedrail and fell into a reverie. There was no longer any perturbation visible on her face.

She waited on patiently, almost cheerfully, without alarm, her memories gradually giving place to hopes and visions of the future. Her hopes and visions were so intricate that she no longer saw the white pillows on which her gaze was fixed, or remembered that she was waiting for anything.

At last she heard her mother calling. She started to her feet and ran to the banisters.

"Polly! Polly!"

"Yes, mamma?"

"Come down, dear. Mr Doran wants to speak to you."

Then she remembered what she had been waiting for.

Poet, short story writer, novelist, and critic, Janice Kulyk Keefer is the author of numerous works, including *Under Eastern Eyes* (a 1987 critique of Canadian Maritime fiction), and *Constellations* (1988). Born in Toronto in 1952, and educated at the University of Toronto and the University of Sussex, she did her doctoral studies on Henry James and Joseph Conrad, and now teaches literature at Guelph University. In her own writings, she has increasingly re-examined her Eastern European heritage, to consider what this background implies for her sense of self and culture. Writing about her Polish grandmother's life, she comments on the way a writer does not *want*, but *has* to know the stories of the past: "all the stories of lovers in a garden, memories of neon stars and epic journeys by boat and train and foot. The stuff that my particular obsession feeds on, threading images and words through ever-larger silences."

The silent (and perhaps silenced) stories of the past shape the psychological and social tensions that "Mrs. Putnam at the Planetarium" reconstructs. The differences between past and present are central to this story, which won first prize in the fiction category in the 1985 CBC Radio literary competition and was collected the next year in *The Paris-Napoli Express*, a collection of Keefer's stories. The title character, growing old in Toronto, can no longer connect with the world around her, nor can she relive the past. She has always had to keep her passionate life secret. But now the very public institutions on which she has depended for order seem also to fail her. Neither the official history told by the city's museum nor the rational language of scientific explanation which is used in the planetarium—not even the classics of English literature which she used to teach—can help her. She is left with jealousy, rivalry, competition, discrimination. Recalling the song from Tennyson's *The Princess*, she tries to identify with Danaë, Perseus's mother, who waited for her lover Zeus to come to her as a shower of gold from the heavens. But Mrs. Putnam's stars are simulated; the fictions she hangs on to may no longer have the power to convey her to a universe ordered by love.

FOR FURTHER READING
Janice Kulyk Keefer, "Another Country," *Canadian Literature* 120 (Spring 1989): 6-11.

Mrs. Putnam at the Planetarium

Tuesdays Mrs. Putnam locked her flat, walked three city blocks to the subway; passed, with the sombre airiness of a ghost, through grilles and spokes and greedy-mouthed machines, and rode from Jane and Bloor to Museum. Rode in summer, when the cars were full of tourists with cameras clotting their necks and the pale yellow tiles made the station seem a morgue, ice under the hammer heat of asphalt overhead. Rode in winter when the closeness of the cars made Mrs. Putnam, in her Merino wool coat, her black mink toque, clammy, dizzy, ravaged like a book with pages razored out. Did not ride in spring and autumn since those flighty seasons no longer existed for her now. Once there had been day trips to Niagara-on-the-Lake in Tulip Time, or Autumn Splendour in Muskoka with the boarders from St. Radigonde's or, more rarely, much more rarely, outings with Adam to the Island in late May, early September. Long before there'd even been a Planetarium, back when the Museum walls had been the colour of greased soot, and stone lions snarled in the Tomb Garden.

On this Tuesday—mid-November, snowless, skyless—Mrs. Putnam claimed the seat reserved for veterans, pregnant women and old-age pensioners and started for the Planetarium. Across the aisle from her were advertisements for office temps, notices for putting your newborn through university and pamphlets about Careers without College. Mrs. Putnam glued milky brown eyes to them. For the past ten years she had been retired on a pension sufficient for her to maintain her flat, though not to repair the cracks in the plaster or buy poison enough to terminate the roaches. She had neither nieces nor nephews with babies requiring to be sent to Victoria or Trinity College, and since she'd come by her post as English Mistress and later Language Specialist with only a Grade

13 Diploma from Harbord Collegiate Mrs. Putnam had no need to consult pamphlets at all. Yet it was imperative to do so—otherwise she would have had to look upon her fellow travellers, and Mrs. Putnam had no interest in anybody else's story but her own.

Twelve year olds with pink or green or orange hair, Jamaicans looking resolutely uncolourful in raincoats, Lebanese waiters mournful as blank television screens, Pakistanis with babies on their laps, babies with perfectly round faces and eyes like black moons in the dank heat or chill of the subway car. Arms sweating, legs jolting, Mrs. Putnam holding tight and tighter to the silver pole in front of doors out which her stop would show as welcome as the ram to Abraham, and in another sort of thicket altogether.

Changing trains she noted men at the newspaper kiosks who reminded her of Adam—no similarity whatsoever in colour of hair or lack of it, no slightest resemblance in build or height, but perhaps the cut of the overcoat, the precise indentation of the fedora. She was not the sort who would have held a lover's hand or gazed into his eyes, but often after he had left her side and was safely showering she would take up his hat from her dresser and press her fingertips along the crease his own had made in the felt. His wife had the vexing habit of presenting him with a new fedora every Christmas. She ordered them by telephone from Creeds; it was one of the few things she could do for him. The little else she could do Althea had told while waiting in Mrs. Putnam's office one rainy Sunday afternoon for Uncle Adam to take her to tea with Aunt Rosamund.

"She's awfully pale, of course, being an invalid, but it's amazing how strong her hands are—she does yards of crochet and knits scarves and vests and things, none of which Uncle Adam can wear, since he's allergic to wool *(though he wore cashmere mufflers and Harris tweeds, as Mrs. Putnam could have told her)* but he does have his office filled with crocheted doilies and coasters everywhere, even under the secretary's typewriter, which shows how devoted they are to one another. Aunt Rosamund's made me all kinds of tablecloths and comforters for my own hope chest—she says I'm like a daughter to her, since she hasn't any children of her own, which is sad, don't you think Mrs. Putnam? Maybe you feel the same—I mean, having no children, not even a husband even. I mean, of course you did have a husband once, at least you *say* you did, I mean—no offence Mrs. Putnam—"

Mrs. Putnam took none. Pimply, placid Althea, who hadn't the imagination of a pincushion and thus, any notion of the fact that while Aunt Rosamund was crocheting quiet mounds of doilies, Uncle Adam was taking more than tea with Hilary Putnam. Althea, thick as three planks, who couldn't recite a line of poetry to save her soul *(a soul the colour and consistency of clotted cream, thought Mrs. Putnam)* but who nevertheless passed all of Mrs. Putnam's classes for the six years she was at

St. Radigonde's and her uncle at Mrs. Putnam's. Tuesday and Thursday evenings, from six to ten, and, perhaps half a dozen times a year, an entire Saturday or Sunday when Rosamund could be persuaded there was pressing work to be done at the Trust Company of which her husband was vice-president. Kind Althea, who hadn't meant anything by her remarks, since she hadn't the intelligence to think ill of anyone's peculiarities, but who merely parroted schoolgirl gossip about the English Mistress' marriage, which, as Mrs. Putnam knew extremely well, all the girls and over half the staff believed to be a harmless fiction, if not an outright lie.

Southbound to Museum Mrs. Putnam stared at her reflection in the window as the train racketed through a tunnel. The mink toque had been a present from Adam, the last she'd ever had from him. The first had been a ring—one topaz in a (twelve carat) band. To match her eyes, he'd said—and her hair, which was a watered blond, definitely not 22 carat, but then, all her own at least, and hadn't it made the first grey hair scarcely noticeable? Though he'd not been there to notice anything the night that Mrs. Putnam's mirror finally ambushed her. A massive coronary at his desk, or so Althea had announced the day after the funeral to which, of course, his niece's English teacher had not been summoned. Rosamund—Rosamund was still sipping the small beer of invalid life in Rosedale, having, to counterbalance her fringed nerves, an amazingly strong heart. Althea had vouched for it—of all her former pupils, Althea was the only one who still sent Christmas cards to Mrs. Putnam, rang her up on shopping trips to town, and never sounded disconcerted by the minute and peculiar questions put to her—not on the subjects of how many children she had, and of which sex, but of whether there had been any change in her aunt's condition. There never was.

Mrs. Putnam's was a different case. She had been a carelessly handsome, strong-blooded young woman and it had been to her the strictest form of punishment to watch as, year by year, the slow blue veins that Adam had once traced along her arms and breasts struggled up to the very surface of her skin like drowning swimmers. Liver spots over her hands, the peevish slouch of skin, cracks in her lips which, in the caustic light over the bathroom mirror, seemed to be fissures or crevasses down which her very soul might slip—these were to Mrs. Putnam stages of a cross made of real and not symbolic wood; they left scars and splinters in her shoulders. Her colleagues at St. Radigonde's would not have noticed—she had no friends among them and no confidantes; they, for their part, regarded her merely as an English Mistress renowned for the strict discipline she kept within her class, and for the tedium of the material she set her students. Not even Adam had known that, while she buried his niece under slabs of Pope and all of Milton's *Areopagitica*, at home, alone, she'd finger a vellum Swinburne, recite from memory the lusher lyrics of Tennyson or read aloud from Keats in a special edition, gilt-edged with plump, fawn-coloured, soft suede covers.

Pigeons were wheeling over the Museum steps, or skittering after bits of popcorn that schoolchildren, on their way home from a session with dinosaurs or dusty Indians in the anthropologist's bargain basement, had bought from the Italian vendors. At their yellow-painted carts, crenellated with candy apples, fragrant with the steam from roasting chestnuts, Mrs. Putnam did not so much as glance—nor at the faces of the children, flushed against the chill of this grey air outside, sharp as icicles against their cheeks. Mrs. Putnam liked neither popcorn nor children overmuch—on the one she had lost a quarter of a tooth some twenty years ago; on the other she had wasted 40 years. In none of her students had she bred a love of Shelley, Scott or Swift, though she had done a creditable job in teaching them what sentence fragments, comma splices and malapropisms were. For, some fifteen years ago, the Headmistress of St. Radigonde's had decided that English Literature would have to be hatcheted and Contemporary Culture (plus remedial grammar) put in its place if the school were to hold its own against the more prestigious, if less venerable, private girls' schools in Toronto. Mrs. Putnam had lately read that no-one taught *Edwin Drood* or *Silas Marner* to schoolchildren these days—it was all Contemporary Song Lyrics and Shakespeare Comic Books. A colleague of hers, retired now from Weatherstone School, had got up a petition against it and asked Mrs. Putnam to sign, but she hadn't. *I do not care, I do not care*, was all that Mrs. Putnam had written in reply.

No-one asked Mrs. Putnam for the extravagant sum it cost to get a ticket to the Planetarium: on Tuesdays old-age pensioners were admitted free—into the Museum as well, though Mrs. Putnam refused to set so much as the toe of her ankle boots inside the place, now that they'd changed everything round and destroyed the garden. On Sunday afternoons after Adam's death Mrs. Putnam had walked under the arches and the stone lions, listening to snow or leaves fall as if they'd been the bells that had hung from the roofs of the tombs. Once a man not much older than herself had watched her from the window of the garden door and asked her, after she'd returned, to have tea with him downtown. From his accent, she had diagnosed him as Eastern European, and refused, not out of loyalty to Adam's memory, but because she'd been raised in the belief that people whose names ended in *off* or *ski* or *vich* might be highschool janitors but hardly the social equals of a Stuart or Jones or Putnam—she'd had visions of the man stirring his tea with his index finger. Foreigners had been barred from St. Radigonde's since its founding by an interim Anglican bishop in 1833, though somewhere in the middle of Mrs. Putnam's term at the school *that* had changed as it had everywhere—Mrs. Putnam understood that the country's Prime Minister was married to an emigrant from that country whose flag looked like a checkerboard.

Once inside the Planetarium she walked up and down corridors painted the colour of milk frozen in the bottle, ignoring the displays of information on the walls and joining the small queue in front of the Projection Room. Waiting for the doors to open she looked down at her hands, then lifted them a little cautiously to her face, stroking her cheek with the leather, inhaling its rich, almost meaty scent. Real kid, none of that pigskin business—though she had to eat macaroni and skimp on the cheese four days a week, Mrs. Putnam would have her necessary luxuries, mere tokens of the things she could have had if Adam hadn't betrayed her at his desk that Tuesday morning, or, at the very least, if Rosamund's nerves had done her in before he had to die.

Particles of rouge like motes of rosy dust clung to Mrs. Putnam's gloves; all the heating and air-cleaning machines whirring through the foyer made her eyes feel papery, her skin crisp under the powder she had pressed on that morning. Why wouldn't they open the doors, why must they make her wait—70 years old and with the dignity, the presence of a dowager queen, yet they kept her in line as if she were queuing up for cigarettes at the five and ten. Where on earth was the Manager, he would have to be talked to, he would have to——. Someone in front of her began to whistle—further down the line she heard, distinctly, a belch. Mrs. Putnam drew tighter the collar of her good, her excellent cloth coat, pulled the mink toque down so it covered her ear lobes—shrivelled, hard now like dried apricots—and waited. If Adam had been with her, if ever he could have been with her. . . . But then, if there was anything she detested it was whining women, watering their tea with tears over the mistakes they'd made. *She* had made up her mind when she was thirteen—just after her mother had died—that she would marry well or never marry at all, having learned from her parents' case that life as or with a bank clerk was no great addendum to the sum of human happiness.

Adam had been charming to her—it hadn't been his fault that Rosamund had had the tenacity of a wire-haired terrier in her grip on life, on Adam, and on the president of Adam's company: Rosamund's father. And yet if desire, need and hope had anything to do with our lot on earth; if there were justice under the stars. . . . The subjunctive mood, Miss Putnam had drilled into her students' heads, is always used for things that one merely wishes or hypothesizes to be true.

But now it was as if the gates of a post-modernist heaven had been opened for the pensioners and straggling students. The inner doors of the Planetarium swung slowly apart and gathered them in like the great skirts of a Mater Misericordia. As quickly as her dignity and arthritic hip would let her, Mrs. Putnam found her customary seat, three rows back from the front, and at right angles from a certain twist in the crumpled metal that projected stars on the egg-shaped dome over her head. She drooped into the chair like a bird to its nest on a darkening winter afternoon; back she tilted, closing her eyes until her head had found its cradling place and the low music rising from the projector crept across her like a hand stroking her brow. And then she looked up at the great black bowl, not hard and blank as the subway window but soft, dewy, gelid—like a membrane to which Mrs. Putnam could raise up her hands, poking fingers through to touch the stars.

Lights dimmed, the music faded and a voice fountained from the projector, talking about Pole stars and Betelgeuse and Charles' Wain. The names didn't matter to Mrs. Putnam; she was lying in the grass on the Island with Adam—they had rented one of the small canoes and paddled out to the hand's breadth of land that was now a bird sanctuary; they had beached the canoe and were lying on their backs in wild, tall grass, watching the stars. For once he was not wearing his fedora; she had on her finger a ring with one diamond and a band of 24-carat gold. Rosamund was in Mt. Pleasant and even Althea had been sent back home to Thunder Bay, to parents who had at last decided that the advantages of a private education did not outweigh the loving kindness to be found only in the bosom of one's family. Softly Hilary opened lips that time had not so much as crumpled:

Now sleeps the crimson petal, now the white. . . . Now lies the earth all Danae to the stars. . . .

and the stars sang back to her. They were not crystal splinters as children imagined them, but round, fragrant as waterlilies you might pick off the mirror of a lake and hold up to your face, breathing in their succulence and fragrance. . . .

Across the table from her someone began to snore, with all the violence of a chain-saw massacre. It was hot in the darkened room, the leatherette under Mrs. Putnam's hands began to feel like fur and she was floating somewhere between floor and stars. The voice was talking now about satellites and lasers. Mrs. Putnam remembered hearing on the radio that before long man would be able to orbit messages in space—celestial billboards advertising Pepsi or the other Cola, *billets-doux* or messages of condolence that could circle earth forever, forcing their stories down peoples' very eyes. If it were possible, floating through a darkness cut to ribboned light—what would they say were she to chisel it into the night sky: *Rosamund, detested of Adam who loved Hilary alone*, Hilary who loved Keats and Tennyson and silk against her skin, and all the powders and perfumes of Araby she could not wear to St. Radigonde's, but which she would apply each evening upon coming home, whether Adam were coming or not, whether she believed in him

or not, coming or going, leaving or loving, Betelgeuse and Charles'
Wain, Miss or Mrs. Putnam, Althea and detested Rosamund and
petalled stars in the night sky, looking down where she lay, in her
story, nobody else's story—head lolling against the squashed
leatherette as a voice explained the simulated stars shifting, blooming,
exploding on the painted ceiling over the sleeping dark in which Mrs.
Putnam lies curled tight, a newborn's fist around some fiction of a finger to grab onto, climbing steep, black spaces in between the stars.

THOMAS KING

Of Cherokee, German, and Greek background, Thomas King was born in Sacramento, California, in 1943. After teaching some years in the Native Studies Department at the University of Lethbridge, he returned to the United States, to teach American Studies at the University of Minnesota. In the 1980s, King became a leading spokesman for Native writing in Canada, drawing attention to its quality and variety. As anthologist and critic, he edited such works as *The Canadian Fiction Magazine's* Native Fiction issue (no. 60, 1987), *"All My Relations": An Anthology of Contemporary Canadian Native Prose* (1990), and (with Cheryl Carver and Helen Hoy) *The Native in Literature* (1985). But it is as a storyteller in his own right—in short fiction, poetry, and the novel (*Medicine River* appeared in 1990)—that he has attracted most attention. In all three genres, he brings oral forms to the written page, not only to convey the voices of his characters but also to heighten the reader's appreciation of the oral culture being written about. King's aim is not merely to entertain, but also to expose the ridiculousness of social biases and demonstrate the power that is invested in them. His satire reveals bombast and greed, and questions the entrenched priorities of bureaucratic institutions.

"Joe the Painter and the Deer Island Massacre" appeared first in *Whetstone* in 1985, and then as one of King's own contributions to his special issue of *Canadian Fiction Magazine* in 1987; the version printed here has been revised by the author. Characteristically using dialogue to advance his narrative, King modulates the voices in such a way as to shift the tone from farce to social critique. Trickery abounds. But ultimately the power to reconstruct events is given to the narrator–storyteller, reasserting the value of the artist in Native societies and the potential of art both to undermine unexamined biases and to protect the vitality of belief.

FOR FURTHER READING

Margaret Atwood, "A Double-Bladed Knife: Subversive Laughter in Two Stories by Thomas King," *Canadian Literature* 124–125 (Spring–Summer 1990): 243–50.

Thomas King, "Introduction" to *All My Relations* (Toronto: McClelland & Stewart, 1990), ix–xvi.

Joe the Painter and the Deer Island Massacre

Joe the Painter knew almost everyone in town and everyone knew Joe and all of the people who knew Joe as well as
I knew Joe didn't like him. Except me. I liked Joe. I was
probably the only person who was willing to be seen with
Joe regular like. A lot of folk would say hi to Joe if they
ran into him and couldn't get across the street in time and
some would even sit down to coffee with him while the sun
was out. One or two of the married fellows had invited Joe
to dinner at their houses but they only did it once.

Joe was friendly enough. Whenever he'd see someone he
knew, he'd boom out a "Howdy."

"Howdy Ed," he shouted at Ed Petersen as Ed slipped
out of the old Vance hotel at three in the afternoon. Joe was
friendly like that. "What the hell you doing in the Vance
at this time of the day?"

But he wasn't one to chew his words.

"Dingdang! George, don't tell me you actually paid
$5,000 for that piece of junk?"

He was polite. He just wasn't judicious.

"Howdy Mrs. Secord, how's the girls? Looks like you
been living off pudding. Say, you pregnant again? Damn
fine weather ain't it."

"Joe's just an honest man," Marvin Booster, the bartender
at the Ritz, would tell his customers after Joe left. "Most
people can't manage honesty. Honesty makes most people
nervous."

"Howdy Marvin, you settle up with the tax boys yet?"

Joe just had a habit of making people uncomfortable.
Most times they would try and drift away before Joe stuck
them with one of his "howdies."

"Howdy Bill, did you beat the drunk driving ticket?"

"Howdy Pete, you and the Mrs. back together yet?"

"Howdy Betty, god you look like hell. You had a relapse?"

But that wasn't exactly why people avoided Joe though it was a pretty good reason all by itself. And it wasn't that he was dirty or smelled bad. He took a shower every morning and his clothes were always clean. He didn't drink. And he didn't smoke.

"Howdy Bob, you know a bullet would be a heck of a lot faster and not near the expense."

Joe didn't like smoking at all.

"Smoking just touches me wrong though I suppose I got a few bad habits too."

Joe liked to blow his nose in the gutter. Whenever he felt a clog in his "breathing trap" as he called it, he'd step to the curb, lean over so as not to get his shoes dirty, hold one nostril shut with his thumb, snort, and blow out the other one. Then he'd change hands. Like shooting beans through a straw. He always did it first thing in the morning and then, after that, whenever the occasion demanded it.

On weekends, sometimes, a few of the kids on their way to the docks to fish would hang around in front of the Ritz bar and wait for Joe to come down from his bachelor apartment. He'd blow a little louder for the kids.

I think that Joe's main problem was that he was loud. He wasn't boisterous, he just talked loud all the time. Maybe he was a bit deaf and didn't want to admit it or just didn't know it. Before he came out to the coast, he had worked in a foundry back east.

"It was real noisy," Joe shouted. And he liked to stand close to you when he talked. It was no good backing up because he'd just follow you around until he got you in a corner.

People who disliked Joe didn't dislike him because he was a criminal or snobbish or weird or perverted or mean, it was a whole bunch of things that altogether tended to overwhelm folk.

"You're probably the only friend, only real friend that Joe the Painter has," Howard Souto told me once and I suppose he was right.

I liked Joe. He was a friend to me and a good one.

Joe's real name was Joseph Ghoti. Everyone just called him Joe or Joe the Painter because he had painted houses for a living before he retired and moved into the small apartment above the Ritz.

The one thing that no one could fault Joe for was his civic spirit. He went to all the political rallies . . . for both parties. He voted in all the elections and if he felt particularly strong about some issue, he'd paint a paper placard and hang it out of his apartment window. He bought poppies on Veterans' Day, kept his old papers and pop bottles for the Boy Scouts and bought dozens of boxes of Girl Scout cookies and gave them away as presents. He went to the county fair every year and stood when they played the National Anthem. He'd even stand when they played it on television. I watched a baseball game with him once that was played in Montreal and he stood when they played the Canadian National Anthem.

"That's the Canadian National Anthem," shouted Joe as he jumped out of his chair. "Come on stand up and get your hat off, those folks got feelings too you know."

It was his civic spirit that seemed to get him into most of his trouble.

About three years ago Joe caught me on the street just outside Lazio's Marine Supply store.

"Howdy Chief," shouted Joe. "You got time for coffee? Something in the paper you ought to see."

Joe was the only one in town called me "Chief." My family was from Horseshoe Bar, a mountain community about seventy miles out of town. My father was Cherokee, out of Oklahoma during the dust bowl years. He had settled in at Horseshoe Bar and married a Pomo woman up from Round Valley. I wasn't a chief and Joe knew it but he didn't smile when he said it.

"Look at this . . . right there . . . what do you think?"

"Where?"

"There, there . . . right there," Joe shouted and stabbed his finger into the paper.

"The centennial celebration?"

"That's it. How about that! The town's one hundred years old."

"That's great, Joe." I said it without much inflection.

"Great? Can't you read? Look here. There's going to be a competition for the best pageant."

"That's great, Joe."

"What's the matter? Hey, maybe you don't know what a pageant is, huh? Is that it? Maybe you can't read." And he stabbed the paper again.

"So . . . there's going to be a pageant. That's great."

"Damn, I guess I'm going to have to read it to you."

There was no stopping Joe once he got started.

"The city council announced last night," Joe began loud enough to be heard down the street in the Ritz, "that the California State Endowment for the Arts has approved the city's application for $56,000. The money will be used to stage a pageant competition. The successful pageant will be performed as part of the centennial celebration. Applications for the pageant competition should be ready at City Hall by the end of the week."

"Maybe now you're more excited."

"What's to get excited about. Hell, Joe, what are we going to do, enter the pageant competition?"

"Now you're talking!!"

"A pageant?"

"Sure, be a great thing to do for the town. Give the town a pageant that would do it proud. And you get paid. See . . . right here . . . participants in the successful pageant will be paid for their performances during the month of April. You got performances four nights with two performances on Friday and Saturday . . . for a whole month."

"Where are we going to get a pageant?"

"Well, you just don't go out to your local market and buy one. Damn, you don't just walk up to Howard Souto at the Green Front and say, 'Howdy, Howard, got any ripe pageants in today?'"

"Joe . . . "

"You got to write one!"

"Joe . . . "

"A pageant about the way this town was founded. That would win the competition. I could write it, you know. What do you think?"

My coffee was getting cold.

"Why would you want to write a pageant?"

"Why? Chief, I live here. This is a good town. Damn fine town. And it's going to have a birthday, you know. And I can write a real good pageant and do it up right. This is my town. Who else should write a pageant?"

"Well, sure as hell not me," I said, trying to get a taste of my coffee.

"Dingdang, of course not you. You can't write. You can hardly read and I suspect that you don't even know exactly what a pageant is. Besides, you're going to be one of the stars."

"One of the stars??"

"That's right . . . Ah-ha, now you're interested."

"You're nuts, Joe . . . I'm no pagean-ter or whatever I'd be."

"An actor . . . a star!"

"Forget it. You can write your pageant and I'll watch it and I'll bring my family, bring everyone up at the Bar and we'll all cheer when it's over but I won't be in it."

"Look Chief," said Joe seriously, bringing his voice down to a normal volume which meant he was going to tell me a secret. "My pageant is going to have Indians in it. You're the only Indian I know."

"I can get you lots of Indians."

"And," said Joe reaching across and patting my hand, "you're my best friend."

Well, hell, what was I supposed to say?

I didn't see Joe after that for near a week. He caught up with me over a cup of coffee and pie at Connie's.

"Howdy Chief," Joe sang out waving a piece of paper around in a circle.

Ed Petersen who was sitting at the counter slid off the stool and headed for the rest room. Bill Johnson left half a cup of good hot coffee, dropped a dollar at the register, and left before Connie could give him his change. Mrs. Bertrand, sitting at the front booth, disappeared behind a copy of the *Herald*.

"Howdy, Connie, how's the boil doing?"

Joe slid in across from me and slapped the paper down on the table.

"There's this screening," he shouted. "You have to submit an idea for the pageant. Council's got this jury that is going to look at all the ideas and select the best three."

"They going to do all three pageants?"

"Chief, you're not listening again. The jury is going to choose three. Whoever gets chosen will get a small grant. You take the grant, work up the pageant, and about a month before the centennial celebration, the city council will preview each pageant and choose the best one. That pageant will be the one that is shown during the centennial."

"Oh." I could see that I was going to need more coffee.

"You awake? You got all that?"

"Sure, but what do I have to do?"

"I'll be the author . . . been doing some research and I've got the idea right here," and he tapped his head to indicate the general location. "I need you to get me thirty or forty Indians. All kinds . . . you know, men, women, and kids . . . could use lots of kids."

"Thirty or forty?"

"How many in your family?"

"Two brothers and three sisters."

"That won't be enough. You got any friends besides me?"

"Indians?"

"Chief, you hard of hearing . . . we been talking about Portuguese fishermen? Course I mean Indians. I need thirty or forty Indians."

There was my father and his two brothers and their families at the Bar and Bernie and James and their cousins over at Hupa Valley. Mom had a couple of sisters down south who might come up.

"I suppose."

"Don't be supposing, supposing killed the cat."

"What's the pageant going to be about?"

"Can't tell, it's a secret."

"Suppose you tell me."

"There you go supposing again."

"You don't know yet, huh?"

"Dingdang, course I know. Say, are you trying to wring my leg out? Damned if I don't think sometimes you're dumber than you look."

"How about a hint? Got to tell the folks something."

Joe looked around the restaurant. He even stood up and looked to see who was in the booths behind us.

"You got to promise that you won't tell anyone. I want it to be a surprise. Hey, you listening?"

"Won't tell a soul, Joe, just the folks . . . I promise."

"You guys got some sort of special sign?"

"Huh?"

"You know . . . some sign that means you gave your word and that you'll die rather than talk?"

"Joe!"

"No sign, huh?"

"You got my word!"

Joe fumbled in his pockets and came up with a grocery receipt from the Green Front and wrote something on it so small you could hardly read it.

"Math . . . Mathe . . . ah . . . Lar . . . Ler . . . Lerzo . . . "

"Matthew Larson," shouted Joe.

"Matthew Larson?"

Joe was nodding his head up and down and smiling like a big kid.

"Matthew Larson . . . the lumber magnate? The Matthew Larson who built the mansion over on Bay Street?"

"Shssssss, damn, keep your voice down. Dingdang, you talk loud!"

"The pageant is going to be about him?"

"Founder of this town. Make a great pageant. I'm going to call it 'Matthew Larson and the Deer Island Massacre.'"

"Deer Island Massacre?"

"Never heard of it, right? Course you haven't. Can't read or write. I'll bet not many people in this town know about it. Happened in 1863. Larson and his two brothers brought a boat up from San Francisco and dropped anchor in the bay. Nothing here then but the salt flats and the bay and the trees and some Indians."

"Thirty or forty Indians?"

"Right . . . and within four months Larson had brought up about fifty families. Part of them began logging the timber and setting up a mill, the others began to build the town. Some of the families including Larson and his brothers moved over to Deer Island where the marina is now. There was a band of Indians on the island and relations between Larson and the chief didn't go too well. Hey, you still awake?"

"Deer Island, huh?"

"Right. And in the middle of the night on March 31, 1863, just a bit after midnight, the massacre took place."

"Massacre?"

"Keep your voice down! Damn! Yes, a massacre. Larson's two brothers were killed but Larson survived and built the town. That's how this place was started. Make a good pageant, huh?"

"And you want me to get you Indians to play the part of the Indians on Deer Island . . . the ones involved in the massacre?"

"What else would I want Indians for?"

"Joe . . . I'm not sure I can do that . . . I mean . . . you know my folks . . . they may not like . . . "

"What's to like? It's all history. You can't muck around with history. It ain't always the way we'd like it to be but there it is. Can't change it."

"But Joe . . . "

"Dingdang, now don't go getting huffy and sulky on me, Chief. I need thirty or forty Indians and you said you could get them. It'll make a great pageant."

"Who gets to play Matthew Larson?"

"Well, you sure as hell can't play Larson. Larson was a white man. You don't look like a white man. You look like an Indian. I'll probably play Larson."

Confidence, that's what Joe had and civic pride. Sure enough, at the end of the month, Joe called me up and yelled over the phone that his idea was one of the three that had been chosen and that Mayor Anderson had caught Joe after the meeting and told him how much he liked Joe's idea.

"Great idea, Joe, that's what he said. Shook my hand, bought me a cup of coffee from that machine they have. Awful damn coffee. I told him too . . . awful damn coffee."

"Chief, they liked the idea so much, I didn't even have to show them my script."

"You got a script?"

"Damn if you're not blind and deaf! Course I got a script. I just don't want to show it to every nosepusher that comes heeltoeing up. I want it to be a surprise. Everyone'll see it at the competition. Say . . . did you get me those Indians?"

Folks at the Bar said sure, they'd come . . . be kinda fun. My aunts at Round Valley said yes too and Bernie and James over at Hupa promised to come and bring as many of their friends and neighbors that they could find.

"Where we going to put the folks during the rehearsals?"

"That's the best part. The mayor said that the Indians could pitch their tents on Deer Island."

"I don't know if they have tents, Joe."

"The hell you say!"

"I'll see what I can do."

"The mayor said they could use the facilities at the marina. And Chief . . . you listening, Chief . . . rehearsals begin on Monday."

Rehearsals began on Friday. My father couldn't make it down from the Bar right away and Aunt Amy and her girls had car trouble in Laytonville and had to wait there two days for a part. Bernie and James and about ten of their relations came down to the island to say hi and then disappeared in town. Just as well, too. It took the mayor until Wednesday to find enough tents and butane stoves. Even Joe wasn't ready . . . some last minute changes to the script. By Thursday night the camp was set up and everyone was there.

"Ho," said my father looking around the camp and smiling, "just like the old days."

Around ten o'clock that evening Joe came bustling into camp with a cardboard box that said Seagram's on the side. I knew it wasn't liquor but Bernie and James were disappointed when Joe opened the box and took out a few scripts.

"Howdy," said Joe and he shook hands and introduced himself to everyone in the camp including the kids. "Thanks for coming. Real good of you to come. It's going to be a great pageant."

"Why's he shouting?" said Bernie.

"These are the scripts. I don't know most of you so I'm going to let the Chief here hand out the parts."

Everyone sort of looked around casual-like and skinnied their necks to see who Joe was talking about.

"Hey . . . is he talking about you cousin?" And James began to laugh.

"You must have gotten a promotion that we didn't hear about over in the valley."

"Floyd, hey, Floyd . . . give us an honor song for the Chief here."

Joe just grinned and dropped the box of scripts in my lap.

"Tomorrow," he shouted, "we start tomorrow."

That first night on Deer Island was soft and quiet. Some of us got propped up against the tight clusters of marsh grass and listened to my father and my uncles tell stories. All the kids were sprawled on top of one another like a litter of puppies. After the men got things going, Aunt Amy took over. She was the best storyteller. Bernie and James got out a drum and started singing a few social songs and some of the families danced for a while. Mostly we watched the fires and watched the fog slip in off the mud flats and curl around the tents. You could hear the frogs in the distance and the water pushing at the edges of the island. As I went to sleep, I imagined that in the morning, when the fog lifted, the town and the pulp factory and the marina and Larson's mansion would be gone and all you'd be able to see was the flats stretched out to the trees.

I didn't read the script until early the next morning.

"Ho," said my father, "did you read this?"

"Joe did a lot of research on it." And that was all I could think of saying.

"Son, you better talk to Joe."

"Sure, I'll talk to Joe."

Damn, if there wasn't going to be trouble.

"What'd you think of the script?" Joe shouted.

"Joe . . . "

"Told you I could write."

"Joe . . ."

"Typed it myself too!"

"Joe . . ."

"Had to go all the way to Sacramento for some of the old records."

"Damn it, Joe . . ."

"No sense in talking about it. Got just enough time to get it together. Come on. Dingdang, time's half-way to China . . . round up your Indians and let's get started."

"Did you talk to Joe?"

"Sure, dad . . . I talked to Joe."

"What did he say?"

"He said we needed to get started."

"Ho."

Joe had us practise every day. We ran up and down the sand, yelling and hollering and rolling around in the marsh grass.

At the end of the first week, Joe backed me up against one of the tents and lowered his voice.

"Chief, we got a little problem."

"A problem?"

"Your Indians don't look like Indians."

"What?"

"Now, don't take offense. I know they're Indians . . . you're not one to slip in a few Italians or Chinese on me but they don't look like Indians."

"Joe . . ."

"Bothered you too, I know . . . couldn't put my finger on it at first but now I got it. None of your folks have got long hair."

"Long hair?"

"They all got crew cuts! Hell, we can't have Indians with crew cuts. No one's going to believe that Indians in 1863 had crew cuts. They got to have long hair with braids . . . everybody. We got to find them some wigs."

"Wigs?"

"No time to grow long hair. You got any ideas? You're sure easy with the questions."

"I don't know . . . maybe the drama department at the high school would have some wigs."

"Now you're talking."

The drama department only had ten wigs and they didn't much look like Indian wigs but Joe said that they'd do. Lucille's dress shop loaned us another eight . . . off their manikins. Bernie got twelve balls of black yarn from a yard sale. Aunt Amy and her girls and a bunch of the boys braided the yarn into braids. If you wore a hat, you could stuff the braids along the side and they looked pretty good. But we were still short about ten wigs.

"Not to worry," shouted Joe slapping his head with inspiration. "The rest of the Indians can play the parts of Larson and his brothers and the other men."

I got to admit that putting on the pageant was fun. The kids had a great time there on the island and the evenings got better and better. Towards the end, some of the folks from the town came on over and sat around and talked. A few even got up and danced. Dad took old Mrs. Pearson and danced her around for near a half hour.

Boy, were we nervous on the day of the competition.

"You all know your parts," Joe shouted and he shouted even louder than usual.

"Damn," said James, "that man can shout."

"No point in being anxious. You'll do a great job. Just remember to yell like hell. Make it look real."

We were the last group to perform. The first pageant was pretty good. It was about Sarah Jute and the 1903 fire. Fire started in Pearson's warehouse on New Year's Eve. Most of the firemen were at a party and pretty drunk. Sarah was a prostitute in Old Town. New Year's Eve was a busy time for her, but when she saw the fire, she rounded up the rest of her friends and some of the men who were with them and they all formed a bucket line and held the fire in check until help arrived. Sally Jamison played the lead. She was great as Sarah, running up and down the line, yelling instructions to the women . . . real energetic.

"Hey," I said to Joe, "that was pretty good."

The second pageant was real dull. Paul Wolwik had gotten some of the businessmen together to act out the founding of the first city council. We all clapped to be polite.

Then it was our turn.

"Ok, Chief, let's knock them to their legs."

"Pretty good crowd, huh, Joe?"

The city council had set up about fifty chairs along the boardwalk of the marina. The mayor and his wife were right in the middle. But there were a lot more people than there were chairs and the rest of the folk were either leaning against the railing or dug into comfortable positions in the sand.

"You nervous, Joe?"

"Dingdang!"

Joe put on his hat and walked out through the sand. He had on a black frock coat that the high school had loaned us and a broad brimmed black hat. He looked impressive in the coat and the vest with the gold watch chain strung from pocket to pocket. He didn't have a watch though. The chain was hooked around a couple of flat washers so it wouldn't fall out. Matthew Larson couldn't have looked grander.

"The pageant that the Native Sons Players are about to present," Joe began in a thunderous voice, "is about the founding of our town. It is about our founder, Matthew Larson, and how he came to Sequoia county in 1863 and sculptured a town out of a barren wilderness. I hope you all enjoy the weather and our presentation."

Native Sons Players! Damn, that Joe was creative. Sounded professional.

The pageant was in three parts. The first part dramatized Matthew Larson landing near Rocky Point and coming ashore. He was greeted by an Indian named Redbird who lived with his tribe on Deer Island.

I got to play Redbird.

Larson and Redbird greeted one another and Redbird invited Larson back to his camp. Redbird gave Larson some otter skins and Larson gave Redbird a couple of iron kettles and a Bible. The two men parted friends and Larson returned to San Francisco to get the rest of his family and friends.

I didn't forget any of my lines. No one had any trouble hearing Joe. At the end of the first act, everyone clapped. Mayor Anderson clapped really hard and smiled at everyone around him.

The second act started with the arrival of Larson and the other people. My two uncles from the Bar and their families and three or four of the folks from Hupa played the parts of the settlers. Everyone ran around pretending like they were building a town. Halfway through the act, I came out to complain that Larson and his people were encroaching on my people's land. I thought it sounded strange for an Indian in 1863 to complain about Whites "encroaching" on their land but Joe swore that it was a direct quote from the historical record. Redbird had a better vocabulary than I did.

"God gave this land for all to use, Red and White," shouted Joe.

"We will share it with you, white man," I said with my arms folded across my chest like Joe showed me, "but you must not build your houses on our island. My people live there and we are happy."

You could see the tension building.

The second act ended with Matthew Larson and his two brothers coming ashore at Deer Island and claiming that it belonged to them. I had a nice monologue at the end of the second act.

"The white man takes more than he needs. He is greedy like a bear in the spring. We will share the forest and the rivers and the great lake but we will not share this island. It is our home. We will fight to keep it. Beware, white man, the wrath of the Indian is swift and terrible."

There was a short break between the second and third act so that the people in the audience could stretch and so that us actors could get ready for the last act.

"The year is 1863," Joe shouted. "Matthew Larson has defied Redbird and ignored his warning. Larson and his brothers have landed on Deer Island and have begun to build homes for themselves and their families. Redbird and his people are camped nearby."

That was our cue. Everybody came trooping out to the center of the island right in front of where the mayor and the council were sitting. Aunt Amy and the girls built a fire and we all got into our positions.

"It is evening," Joe continued, "and the Indians are singing and dancing around the fire."

"Hey, ah, ah, ah, ah . . . ahhha," Bernie began the song nice and loud so everyone could hear and then the rest of us joined in. It sounded pretty fierce but it was just one of the 49ers that Bernie and the rest of us knew. Some of the kids were singing along and dancing and trying to keep those yarn braids under their hats.

"The Indians were dancing and singing and you could hear the drum and the bloodcurdling shouts all the way up the island where Matthew Larson and his family huddled in their houses."

And that was our cue to sing real loud and whoop and jump around on the sand. James and his cousins were really getting into it.

"Damn," said James as he fancy-danced past me, "this is fun."

"But the night grew late," Joe bellowed above the drum and the singing, "and the Indians grew tired. Soon they were all asleep, tired out from all the dancing and singing."

We all began to yawn and stretch and say things like, "Boy, I'm tired," but we said them in Cherokee or Hupa so that the crowd didn't know. One of my uncles told a pretty bad joke and some of the kids began to laugh. We stretched out on the sand and pretended to be asleep.

"It is now about midnight," Joe shouted at the crowd, "and the pale moon is hidden by the fog that has stolen out of the bay. And in the distance, if you listen very carefully, you can hear the muffled sound of oars."

I opened one eye so I could see what was going on. Joe bowed to the crowd and trudged off across the sand. He waved to the mayor as he disappeared under the boardwalk and the mayor waved back. In a minute, Joe reappeared with Uncle Ben and some of the men from the Bar and a few of the older kids. They were dressed in jeans and jackets cause we couldn't find any good costumes for all of them. But they all had rifles and knives and Uncle Ben had an old sword that he had borrowed from Captain Oleg who ran a salmon charter for the tourists during the summer.

They all came creeping across the sand real quiet. When they were about thirty feet away, Joe stood up and said in a loud voice that we weren't supposed to hear:

"There's their camp, men. Spread out and let none escape. It's God's work . . . there'll be no peace with Redbird and his people for there can be no peace between Christians and heathens. Steel your hearts to the cries of the Indians. Who goes with me to make our families safe? Who goes with me to bring the light of civilization to this dark land?"

And Uncle Ben and the rest of the men shook their rifles and waved their knives and shouted, "We're with you Matthew!"

"Then do your duty," yells Joe and all the men came charging into our camp.

"Whites!" yells one of the kids.

"We're being attacked," yells another.

"Grab your arms, men," I yell leaping out of the sand. "Protect the women and children."

Jimmy Pete comes at me with a knife and I whack him with my tomahawk. Aunt Amy pushes Uncle Ben over a log and is then shot by Jesse Long from Hupa who is playing the part of Matthew's brother William. James shoots Jesse and Joe kills both Bernie and James.

We couldn't find any blanks for the guns so we just shout out, "Bang! Bang! Bang!" real loud.

It looks real good too. Some of the kids got a bunch of little plastic bags of ketchup from Connie's restaurant. Blood. They hadn't worked very well at first 'cause they wouldn't break easily when you smashed them against your chest. But if you tore them open a bit, they worked fine. We taped one to each hand so that when we were shot, we could slap a hand over the wound and it looked like we had really been shot or stabbed.

"Death to the heathens," shouts Joe and he shoots me dead.

"I'm killed," I moan and slap a ketchup pack against my stomach. I have to do it twice. Those packets are tough.

"I'm dead," I say again. "Matthew Larson has killed me and all my people."

In a minute, all of us are lying in the sand trying to look dead. The flies start to buzz around the ketchup.

Everything was quiet. The mayor and the council just sat there. Joe took off his hat.

"I abhor the taking of a human life but civilization needs a strong arm to open the frontier. Farewell, Redman. Know that from your bones will spring a new and stronger community forever."

When the clapping started, we were all supposed to get up and take a bow.

But it didn't start. Everyone just sat there. The mayor was looking red and snapped around to whisper something to his wife.

Joe was kneeling next to me with his rifle.

"Just stay there," he said, "it'll take 'em a minute to warm to it. It was more powerful than I thought."

Then someone began to clap and everyone joined in. We got up and took our bows.

We stayed on Deer Island that night. The next morning James and Bernie and I packed up the tents and the wigs and the stoves and returned them. I didn't see Joe for three or four days. Word was that the mayor was upset and that he and Joe had had words and that Joe had taken the lion's share.

"Howdy Chief, you want some coffee?"

"Sure Joe, hell, where you been? My father said he really enjoyed that pageant. All the folks said to tell you if you need Indians again to just give them a call."

"That was a good pageant, wasn't it?"

"The best, Joe."

"The mayor didn't like it."

"What does he know."

"He said it wasn't appppprooooopriate!"

"What does he know."

"The committee chose Wolwik's pageant."

"What? What about Sally's pageant? That was better than Wolwik's."

And Joe began to laugh. God, that man could laugh louder than he could talk.

"The mayor said that Sally's pageant wasn't appppprooopriate either."

"Damn."

"Come on, I'll buy. I still got some of that pageant money left. We can get some pie too . . . à la mode."

Everyone in town knew Joe. And all the people who knew Joe as well as I knew Joe didn't like him. Except me.

I like Joe.

In several of her novels and stories, Margaret Wemyss Laurence (1926-1987) transformed the place of her birth—a Manitoba town called Neepawa (Cree for "land of plenty") —into a town called Manawaka. *The Stone Angel* (1964), *A Jest of God* (1966) (upon which the film *Rachel Rachel* was based), and *A Bird in the House* (1970) are all set in that rural landscape. Ukrainians and Scots and others have all emigrated there to start a new life, and though generations pass, pride and folly and other traits of human individuality continue to interfere with their happiness. Laurence is extraordinarily sensitive to this individuality and also respectful of it. It is a frame of mind that gives her both insight into the lives of the women around whom these stories revolve and perspective on them. Her characters are, by turns, bound by convention, in search of freedom, constrained by weakness, and aroused by anger, love, and pride; above all, they are separate human beings, alive and warm, needing and demanding a recognition of their distinctive selves.

Sympathy toward this need for self-expression found another outlet for Margaret Laurence in her African stories. From 1950 to 1952 she lived in Somaliland, and from 1952 to 1957 in Ghana. Out of this experience came several books, including *The Tomorrow-Tamer and other stories* (1963), in which "The Merchant of Heaven" appears. The book focuses on some of the realities of modern Africa: the enthusiasms and ideals that accompanied independence, the conflicts between indigenous and European ways of life, and the problems with expatriates. The task of making these subjects appear to be realistic segments from actual life is one of rigorous selection. "I don't think of the form as something imposed upon a novel," she wrote to Clara Thomas, "but as its bone, the skeleton which makes it possible for the flesh to move and be revealed as itself." The imagery reinforces the reader's appreciation of character and culture; the form of the storytelling embodies the angle of vision which the narrative attempts to explore.

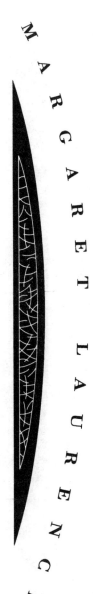

MARGARET LAURENCE

FOR FURTHER READING

Margaret Laurence, "Ten Years' Sentences," *Canadian Literature* 41 (Summer 1969): 10-16.

Patricia Morley, *Margaret Laurence* (Boston: Twayne, 1981).

W.H. New, "Text and Subtext: Laurence's 'The Merchant of Heaven'," in *Margaret Laurence*, ed. Christl Verduyn (Peterborough, Ont.: Broadview Press, 1988): 52-7.

George Woodcock, ed., *A Place to Stand On* (Edmonton: NeWest, 1983).

The Merchant of Heaven

Across the tarmac the black-and-orange dragon lizards skitter, occasionally pausing to raise their wrinkled necks and stare with ancient saurian eyes on a world no longer theirs. In the painted light of mid-day, the heat shimmers like molten glass. No shade anywhere. You sweat like a pig, and inside the waiting room you nearly stifle. The African labourers, trundling baggage or bits of air-freight, work stripped to the waist, their torsos sleek and shining. The airport officials in their white drill uniforms are damp and crumpled as gulls newly emerged from the egg.

In this purgatorially hot and exposed steam bath, I awaited with some trepidation the arrival of Amory Lemon, proselytizer for a mission known as the Angel of Philadelphia.

Above the buildings flew the three-striped flag—red, yellow and green—with the black star of Africa in its centre. I wondered if the evangelist would notice it or know what it signified. Very likely not. Brother Lemon was not coming here to study political developments. He was coming—as traders once went to Babylon—for the souls of men.

I had never seen him before, but I knew him at once, simply because he looked so different from the others who came off the plane—ordinary English people, weary and bored after the long trip, their still-tanned skins indicating that this was not their first tour in the tropics. Brother Lemon's skin was very white and smooth—it reminded me of those sea pebbles which as a child I used to think were the eyeballs of the drowned. He was unusually tall; he walked in a stately and yet brisk fashion, with controlled excitement. I realized that this must be a great moment for him. The apostle landing at Cyprus or Thessalonica, the light of future battles already kindling in his eyes, and replete with faith as a fresh-gorged mosquito is with blood.

"Mr. Lemon? I'm Will Kettridge—the architect. We've corresponded—"

He looked at me with piercing sincerity from those astonishing turquoise eyes of his.

"Yes, of course," he said, grasping me by the hand. "I'm very pleased to make your acquaintance. It surely was nice of you to meet me. The name's Lee-*mon*. Brother Lee-*mon*. Accent on the last syllable. I really appreciate your kindness, Mr. Kettridge."

I felt miserably at a disadvantage. For one thing, I was wearing khaki trousers which badly needed pressing, whereas Brother Lemon was clad in a dove-grey suit of a miraculously immaculate material. For another, when a person interprets your selfish motive as pure altruism, what can you tactfully say?

"Fine," I said. "Let's collect your gear."

Brother Lemon's gear consisted of three large wardrobe suitcases, a pair of water skis, a box which from its label and size appeared to contain a gross of cameras but turned out to contain only a Rolleiflex and a cine-camera complete with projector and editing equipment, a carton of an anti-malarial drug so new that we in this infested region had not yet heard of it, and finally, a lovely little pigskin case which enfolded a water-purifier. Brother Lemon unlocked the case and took out a silvery mechanism. His face glowed with a boyish fascination.

"See? It works like a syringe. You just press this thing, and the water is sucked up here. Then you squirt it out again, and there you are. Absolutely guaranteed one hundred per cent pure. Not a single bacteria. You can even drink swamp water."

I was amused and rather touched. He seemed so frankly hopeful of adventure. I was almost sorry that this was not the Africa of Livingstone or Burton.

"Wonderful," I said. "The water is quite safe here, though. All properly filtered and chlorinated."

"You can't be too careful," Brother Lemon said. "I couldn't afford to get sick—I'll be the only representative of our mission, for a while at least."

He drew in a deep breath of the hot salty tar-stinking air.

"I've waited six years for this day, Mr. Kettridge," he said. "Six years of prayer and preparation."

"I hope the country comes up to your expectations, then."

He looked at me in surprise.

"Oh, it will," he said with perfect equanimity. "Our mission, you know, is based on the Revelation of St. John the Divine. We believe there is a special message for us in the words given by the Spirit to the Angel of the Church in Philadelphia———"

"A different Philadelphia, surely."

His smile was confident, even pitying.

"These things do not happen by accident, Mr. Kettridge. When Andrew McFetters had his vision, back in 1924, it was revealed that the ancient Church would be reborn in our city of the same name, and would take the divine word to unbelievers in seven different parts of the world."

Around his head his fair hair sprouted and shone like some fantastic marigold halo in a medieval painting.

"I believe my mission has been foretold," he said with stunning simplicity. "I estimate I'll have a thousand souls within six months."

Suddenly I saw Brother Lemon as a kind of soul-purifier, sucking in the septic souls and spewing them back one hundred per cent pure.

That evening I told Danso of my vague uneasiness. He laughed, as I had known he would.

"Please remember you are an Englishman, Will," he said. "Englishmen should not have visions. It is not suitable. Leave that to Brother Lemon and me. Evangelists and Africans always get on well—did you know? It is because we are both so mystical. Did you settle anything?"

"Yes, I'm getting the design work. He says he doesn't want contemporary for the church, but he's willing to consider it for his house."

"What did he say about money?" Danso asked. "That's what I'm interested in."

"His precise words were—'the Angel of Philadelphia Mission isn't going to do this thing on the cheap.'"

Danso was short and slim, but he made up for it in mercurial energy. Now he crouched tigerish by the chaise-longue, and began feinting with clenched fists like a bantamweight—which, as a matter of fact, he used to be, before a scholarship to an English university and an interest in painting combined to change the course of his life.

"Hey, come on, you Brother Lemon!" he cried. "That's it, man! You got it and I want it—very easy, very simple. Bless you, Brother Lemon, benedictions on your name, my dear citric sibling."

"I have been wondering," I said, "how you planned to profit from Brother Lemon's presence."

"Murals, of course."

"Oh, Danso, don't be an idiot. He'd never——"

"All right, all right, man. Pictures, then. A nice oil. Everybody wants holy pictures in a church, see?"

"He'll bring them from Philadelphia," I said. "Four-tone prints, done on glossy paper."

Danso groaned. "Do you really think he'll do that, Will?"

"Maybe not," I said encouragingly. "You could try."

"Listen—how about this? St. Augustine, bishop of hippos."

"Hippo, you fool. A place."

"I know that," Danso said witheringly. "But, hell, who wants to look at some fly-speckled North African town, all mudbrick and camel dung? Brother Lemon wants colour, action, you know what I mean. St. Augustine is on the river bank, see, the Congo or maybe the Niger. Bush all around. Ferns thick as a woman's hair. Palms—great big feathery palms. But very stiff, very stylized—Rousseau stuff—like this——"

His brown arms twined upward, became the tree trunks, and his thick fingers the palm fans, precise, sharp in the sun.

"And in the river—real blue and green river, man, all sky and scum—in that river is the congregation, only they're hippos, see— enormous fat ones, all bulging eyes, and they're singing 'Hallelujah' like the angels themselves, while old St. Augustine leads them to par- adise——"

"Go ahead—paint it," I began, "and we'll——"

I stopped. My smile withdrew as I looked at Danso.

"Whatsamatter?" he said. "Don't you think the good man will buy it?"

In his eyes there was an inexpressible loathing.

"Danso! How can you——? You haven't even met him yet."

The carven face remained ebony, remained black granite.

"I have known this pedlar of magic all my life, Will. My mother always took me along to prayer meetings, when I was small."

The mask slackened into laughter, but it was not the usual laughter.

"Maybe he thinks we are short of ju-ju," Danso remarked. "Maybe he thinks we need a few more devils to exorcise."

When I first met Brother Lemon, I had seen him as he must have seen himself, an apostle. Now I could almost see him with Danso's bit- ter eyes—as sorcerer.

I undertook to show Brother Lemon around the city. He was impressed by the profusion and cheapness of tropical fruit; delightedly he pur- chased baskets of oranges, pineapples, paw-paw. He loaded himself down with the trinkets of Africa—python-skin wallets, carved ele- phants, miniature *dono* drums.

On our second trip, however, he began to notice other things. A boy with suppurating yaws covering nearly as much of his body as did his shreds of clothing. A loin-clothed labourer carrying a headload so heavy that his flimsy legs buckled and bent. A trader woman minding a roadside stall on which her living was spread—half a dozen boxes of cube sugar and a handful of pink plastic combs. A girl child squatting modestly in the filth-flowing gutter. A grinning penny-pleading gamin with a belly outpuffed by navel hernia. A young woman, preg- nant and carrying another infant on her back, her placid eyes growing all at once proud and hating as we passed comfortably by. An old

Muslim beggar who howled and shouted *sura** from the Qoran, and then, silent, looked and looked with the unclouded innocent eyes of lunacy. Brother Lemon nodded absently as I dutifully pointed out the new Post Office, the library, the Law Courts, the Bank.

We reached shanty town, where the mud and wattle huts crowded each other like fish in a net, where plantains were always frying on a thousand smoky charcoal burners, where the rhythm of life was forever that of the women's lifted and lowered wooden pestles as the cassava was pounded into meal, where the crimson portulaca and the children swarmed over the hard soil and survived somehow, at what loss of individual blossom or brat one could only guess.

"It's a crime," Brother Lemon said, "that people should have to live like this."

He made the mistake all kindly people make. He began to give money to children and beggars—sixpences, shillings—thinking it would help. He overpaid for everything he bought. He distributed largesse.

"These people are poor, real poor, Mr. Kettridge," he said seriously, "and the way I figure it—if I'm able through the Angel of Philadelphia Mission to ease their lives, then it's my duty to do so."

"Perhaps," I said. "But the shilling or two won't last long, and then what? You're not prepared to take them all on as permanent dependants, are you?"

He gazed at me blankly. I guess he thought I was stony-hearted. He soon came to be surrounded by beggars wherever he went. They swamped him; their appalling voices followed him down any street. Fingerless hands reached out; half-limbs hurried at his approach. He couldn't cope with it, of course. Who could? Finally, he began to turn away, as ultimately we all turn, frightened and repelled by the outrageous pain and need.

Brother Lemon was no different from any stranger casting his tiny shillings into the wishful well of good intentions, and seeing them disappear without so much as a splash or tinkle. But unlike the rest of us, he at least could console himself.

"Salvation is like the loaves and fishes," he said. "There's enough for all, for every person in this world. None needs to go empty away."

He could hardly wait to open his mission. He frequently visited my office, in order to discuss the building plans. He wanted me to hurry with them, so construction could begin the minute his landsite was allocated. I knew there was no hurry—he'd be lucky if he got the land within six months—but he was so keen that I hated to discourage him.

He did not care for the hotel, where the bottles and glasses clinked merrily the night through, disturbing his sombre slumbers. I helped

*Sura = a chapter from the Koran.

him find a house. It was a toy-size structure on the outskirts of the city. It had once (perhaps in another century) been whitewashed, but now it was ashen. Brother Lemon immediately had it painted azure. When I remonstrated with him—why spend money on a rented bungalow?—he gave me an odd glance.

"I grew up on the farm," he said. "We never did get around to painting that house."

He overpaid the workmen and was distressed when he discovered one of them had stolen a gallon of paint. The painters, quite simply, regarded Brother Lemon's funds as inexhaustible. But he did not understand and it made him unhappy. This was the first of a myriad annoyances.

A decomposing lizard was found in his plumbing. The wiring was faulty and his lights winked with persistent malice. The first cook he hired turned out to have both forged references and gonorrhoea.

Most of his life, I imagine, Brother Lemon had been fighting petty battles in preparation for the great one. And now he found even this battle petty. As he recounted his innumerable domestic difficulties, I could almost see the silken banners turn to grey. He looked for dragons to slay, and found cockroaches in his store-cupboard. Jacob-like, he came to wrestle for the Angel's blessing, and instead was bent double with cramps in his bowels from eating unwashed salad greens.

I was never tempted to laugh. Brother Lemon's faith was of a quality that defied ridicule. He would have preferred his trials to be on a grander scale, but he accepted them with humility. One thing he could not accept, however, was the attitude of his servants. Perhaps he had expected to find an African Barnabas, but he was disappointed. His cook was a decent enough chap, but he helped himself to tea and sugar.

"I pay Kwaku half again as much as the going wage—you told me so yourself. And now he does this."

"So would you," I said, "in his place."

"That's where you're wrong," Brother Lemon contradicted, so sharply that I never tried that approach again.

"All these things are keeping me from my work," he went on plaintively. "That's the worst of it. I've been in the country three weeks tomorrow, and I haven't begun services yet. What's the home congregation going to think of me?"

Then he knotted his big hands in sudden and private anguish.

"No——" he said slowly. "I shouldn't say that. It shouldn't matter to me. The question is—what is the Almighty going to think?"

"I expect He's learned to be patient," I ventured.

But Brother Lemon hadn't even heard. He wore the fixed expression of a man beholding a vision.

"That's it," he said finally. "Now I see why I've been feeling so let down and miserable. It's because I've been putting off the work of my mission. I had to look around—oh yes, see the sights, buy souvenirs. Even my worry about the servants, and the people who live so poor and all. I let these things distract me from my true work."

He stood up, there in his doll's house, an alabaster giant.

"My business," he said, "is with the salvation of their immortal souls. That, and that alone. It's the greatest kindness I can do these people."

After that day, he was busy as a nesting bird. I met him one morning in the Post Office, where he was collecting packages of Bibles. He shook my hand in that casually formal way of his.

"I reckon to start services within a week," he said. "I've rented an empty lot, temporarily, and I'm having a shelter put up."

"You certainly haven't wasted any time recently."

"There isn't any time to waste," Brother Lemon's bell voice tolled. "Later may be too late."

"You can't carry all that lot very far," I said. "Can I give you a lift?"

"That's very friendly of you, Mr. Kettridge, but I'm happy to say I've got my new car at last. Like to see it?"

Outside, a dozen street urchins rushed up, and Brother Lemon allowed several of them to carry his parcels on their heads. We reached the appointed place, and the little boys, tattered and dusty as fallen leaves, lively as clickety-winged cockroaches, began to caper and jabber.

"Mastah—I beg you—you go dash me!"

A "dash" of a few pennies was certainly in order. But Brother Lemon gave them five shillings apiece. They fled before he could change his mind. I couldn't help commenting wryly on the sum, but his eyes never wavered.

"You have to get known somehow," Brother Lemon said. "Lots of churches advertise nowadays."

He rode off, then, in his new two-toned orchid Buick.

Brother Lemon must have been lonely. He knew no other Europeans, and one evening he dropped in, uninvited, to my house.

"I've never explained our teaching to you, Mr. Kettridge," he said, fixing me with his blue-polished eyes. "I don't know, mind you, what your views on religion are, or how you look at salvation——"

He was so pathetically eager to preach that I told him to go ahead. He plunged into his spiel like the proverbial hart into cooling streams. He spoke of the seven golden candlesticks, which were the seven churches of Asia, and the seven stars—the seven angels of the churches. The seven lamps of fire, the heavenly book sealed with seven seals, the seven-horned Lamb which stood as it had been slain.

I had not read Revelation in years, but its weird splendour came back to me as I listened to him. Man, however, is many-eyed as the beasts around that jewelled throne. Brother Lemon did not regard the Apocalypse as poetry.

"We have positive proof," he cried, "that the Devil—he who bears the mark of the beast—shall be loosed out of his prison and shall go out to deceive the nations."

This event, he estimated, was less than half a century away. Hence the urgency of his mission, for the seven churches were to be reborn in strategic spots throughout the world, and their faithful would spearhead the final attack against the forces of evil. Every soul saved now would swell that angelic army; every soul unsaved would find the gates of heaven eternally barred. His face was tense and ecstatic. Around his head shone the terrible nimbus of his radiant hair.

"Whosoever is not found written in the book of life will be cast into the lake of fire and brimstone, and will be tormented day and night for ever and ever. But the believers will dwell in the new Jerusalem, where the walls are of jasper and topaz and amethyst, and the city is of pure gold."

I could not find one word to say. I was thinking of Danso. Danso as a little boy, in the evangel's meeting place, listening to the same sermon while the old gods of his own people still trampled through the night forests of his mind. The shadow spirits of stone and tree, the hungry gods of lagoon and grove, the fetish hidden in its hut of straw, the dark soul-hunter Sasabonsam—to these were added the dragon, the serpent, the mark of the beast, the lake of fire and the anguish of the damned. What had Danso dreamed about, those years ago, when he slept?

"I am not a particulary religious man," I said abruptly.

"Well, okay," he said regretfully, "Only—I like you, Mr. Kettridge, and I'd like to see you saved."

Later that evening Danso arrived. I had tried to keep him from meeting Brother Lemon. I felt somehow I had to protect each from the other.

Danso was dressed in his old khaki trousers and a black mammy-cloth shirt patterned with yellow diamonds. He was all harlequin tonight. He dervished into the room, swirled a bow in the direction of Brother Lemon, whose mouth had dropped open, then spun around and presented me with a pile of canvases.

Danso knew it was not fashionable, but he painted people. A globe-hipped market mammy stooped while her friends loaded a brass tray full of tomatoes onto her head. A Hausa trader, encased in his long embroidered robe, looked haughtily on while boys floated stick boats down a gutter. A line of little girls in their yellow mission school dresses walked lightfoot back from the well, with buckets on their heads.

A hundred years from now, when the markets and shanties have been supplanted by hygienic skyscrapers, when the gutters no longer reek, when pidgin English has grown from a patois into a sedate language boasting grammar texts and patriotic poems, then Africans will look nostalgically at Danso's pictures of the old teeming days, and will probably pay fabulous prices. At the moment, however, Danso could not afford to marry, and were it not for his kindly but conservative uncles, who groaned and complained and handed over a pound here, ten shillings there, he would not have been able to paint, either.

I liked the pictures. I held one of them up for Brother Lemon to see.

"Oh yes, a market scene," he said vaguely. "Say, that reminds me, Mr. Kettridge. Would you like me to bring over my colour slides some evening? I've taken six rolls of film so far, and I haven't had one failure."

Danso, slit-eyed and lethal, coiled himself up like a spitting cobra.

"Colour slides, eh?" he hissed softly. "Very fine—who wants paintings if you can have the real thing? But one trouble—you can't use them in your church. Every church needs pictures. Does it look like a church, with no pictures? Of course not. Just a cheap meeting place, that's all. Real religious pictures. What do you say, Mr. Lemon?"

I did not know whether he hoped to sell a painting, or whether the whole thing was one of his elaborate farces. I don't believe he knew, either.

Brother Lemon's expression stiffened. "Are you a Christian, Mr. Danso?"

Immediately, Danso's demeanour altered. His muscular grace was transformed into the seeming self-effacement of a spiritual grace. Even the vivid viper markings of his mammy-cloth shirt appeared to fade into something quiet as mouse fur or monk's robe.

"Of course," he said with dignity. "I am several times a Christian. I have been baptised into the Methodist, Baptist and Roman Catholic churches, and one or two others whose names I forget."

He laughed at Brother Lemon's rigid face.

"Easy, man—I didn't mean it. I am only once a Christian—that's better, eh? Even then, I may be the wrong kind. So many, and each says his is the only one. The Akan church was simpler."

"Beg pardon?"

"The Akan church—African." Danso snapped his fingers. "Didn't you know we had a very fine religion here before ever a whiteman came?"

"Idolatry, paganism," Brother Lemon said. "I don't call that a religion."

Danso had asked for it, admittedly, but now he was no longer able to hold around himself the cloak of usual mockery.

"You are thinking of fetish," he said curtly. "But that is not all. There is plenty more. Invisible, intangible—real proper gods. If we'd been left alone, our gods would have grown, as yours did, into One. It was happening already—we needed only a prophet. But now our prophet will never come. Sad, eh?"

And he laughed. I could see he was furious at himself for having spoken. Danso was a chameleon who felt it was self-betrayal to show his own hues. He told me once he sympathized with the old African belief that it was dangerous to tell a stranger all your name, as it gave him power over you.

Brother Lemon pumped the bellows of his preacher voice.

"Paganism in any form is an abomination! I'm surprised at you, a Christian, defending it. In the words of Jeremiah—'Pour out thy fury upon the heathen!'"

"You pour it out, man," Danso said with studied languor. "You got lots to spare."

He began leafing through the Bible that was Brother Lemon's invariable companion, and suddenly he leapt to his feet.

"Here you are!" he cried. "For a painting. The throne of heaven, with all the elders in white, and the many-eyed beasts saying 'Holy, Holy'—what about it?"

He was perfectly serious. One might logically assume that he had given up any thought of a religious picture, but not so. The apocalyptic vision had caught his imagination, and he frowned in concentration, as though he were already planning the arrangement of figures and the colours he would use.

Brother Lemon looked flustered. Then he snickered. I was unprepared, and the ugly little sound startled me.

"You?" he said. "To paint the throne of heaven?"

Danso snapped the book shut. His face was volcanic rock, hard and dark, seeming to bear the marks of the violence that formed it. Then he picked up his pictures and walked out of the house.

"Well, I must say there was no need for him to go and fly off the handle like that," Brother Lemon said indignantly. "What's wrong with him, anyway?"

He was not being facetious. He really didn't know.

"Mr. Lemon," I asked at last, "don't you ever—not even for an instant—have any doubts?"

"What do you mean, doubts?" His eyes were genuinely puzzled.

"Don't you ever wonder if salvation is—well—yours to dole out?"

"No," he replied slowly. "I don't have any doubts about my religion, Mr. Kettridge. Why, without my religion, I'd be nothing."

I wondered how many drab years he must have lived, years like unpainted houses, before he set out to find his golden candlesticks and jewelled throne in far places.

By the time Danso and I got around to visiting the Angel of Philadelphia Mission, Brother Lemon had made considerable headway. The temporary meeting place was a large open framework of poles, roofed with sun-whitened palm boughs. Rough benches had been set up inside, and at the front was Brother Lemon's pulpit, a mahogany box draped with delphinium-coloured velvet. A wide silken banner proclaimed "Ye Shall Be Saved."

At the back of the hall, a long table was being guarded by muscular white-robed converts armed with gilt staves. I fancied it must be some sort of communion set-up, but Danso, after a word with one of the men, enlightened me. Those who remained for the entire service would receive free a glass of orange squash and a piece of *kenkey*.*

Danso and I stationed ourselves unobtrusively at the back, and watched the crowd pour in. Mainly women, they were. Market woman and fishwife, quail-plump and bawdy, sweet-oiled flesh gleaming brownly, gaudy as melons in trade cloth and headscarf. Young women with sleeping children strapped to their backs by the cover cloth. Old women whose unsmiling eyes had witnessed heaven knows how much death and who now were left with nothing to share their huts and hearts. Silent as sandcrabs, frightened and fascinated, women who sidled in, making themselves slight and unknown, as though apologizing for their presence on earth. Crones and destitutes, shrunken skins scarcely covering their insistent bones, dried dugs hanging loose and shrivelled.

Seven boys, splendidly uniformed in white and scarlet, turbanned in gold, fidgeted and tittered their way into the hall, each one carrying his fife or drum. Danso began to laugh.

"Did you wonder how he trained a band so quickly, Will? They're all from other churches. I'll bet that cost him a good few shillings. He said he wasn't going to do things on the cheap."

I was glad Danso was amused. He had been sullen and tense all evening, and had changed his mind a dozen times about coming.

The band began to whistle and boom. The women's voices shrilled in hymn. Slowly, regally, his bright hair gleaming like every crown in Christendom, Brother Lemon entered his temple. Over his orlon suit he wore a garment that resembled an academic gown, except that his was a resplendent peacock-blue, embroidered with stars, seven in number. He was followed by seven mites or sprites, somebody's offspring, each carrying a large brass candlestick complete with lighted taper. These were placed at intervals across the platform, and each attendant stood wide-eyed behind his charge, like small bedazzled genii.

Brother Lemon raised both arms. Silence. He began to speak, pausing from time to time in order that his two interpreters might translate into Ga and Twi. Although most of his listeners could not understand the words of Brother Lemon himself, they could scarcely fail to perceive his compulsive fire.

Kenkey = a Ghanaian food made of fermented cornmeal.

In the flickering flarelight of torches and tapers, the smoky light of the sweat-stinking dark, Brother Lemon seemed to stretch tall as a shadow, tall as the pale horseman at night when children cry in their sleep.

Beside me, Danso sat quietly, never stirring. His face was blank and his eyes were shuttered.

The sun would become black as sackcloth of hair, and the moon would become as blood. In Brother Lemon's voice the seven trumpets sounded, and the fire and hail were cast upon earth. The bitter star fell upon the fountains of waters; the locusts of hell emerged with wings like the sound of chariots. And for the unbelieving and idolatrous— plague and flagellation and sorrow.

The women moaned and chanted. The evening was hot and dank, and the wind from the sea did not reach here.

"Do you think they really do believe, though?" I whispered to Danso.

"If you repeat something often enough, someone will believe you. The same people go to the fetish priest, this man's brother."

But I looked at Brother Lemon's face. "He believes what he says."

"A wizard always believes in his own powers," Danso said.

Now Brother Lemon's voice softened. The thunders and trumpets of impending doom died, and there was hope. He told them how they could join the ranks of saints and angels, how the serpent could be quelled for evermore. He told them of the New Jerusalem, with its walls of crysolyte and beryl and jacinth, with its twelve gates each of a single pearl. The women shouted and swayed. Tears like the rains of spring moistened their parched and praising faces. I felt uneasy, but I did not know why.

"My people," Danso remarked, "drink dreams like palm wine."

"What is the harm in that?"

"Oh, nothing. But if you dream too long, nothing else matters. Listen—he is telling them that life on earth doesn't matter. So the guinea worm stays in the flesh. The children still fall into the pit latrines and die with excrement in their mouths. And women sit for all eternity, breaking building-stones with hammers for two shillings a day."

Brother Lemon was calling them up to the front. Come up, come up, all ye who would be saved. In front of the golden candlesticks of brass the women jostled and shoved, hands outstretched. Half in a trance, a woman walked stiffly to the evangel's throne, her voice keening and beseeching. She fell, forehead in the red dust.

"Look at that one," I said with open curiosity. "See?"

Danso did not reply. I glanced at him. He sat with his head bowed, and his hands were slowly clenching and unclenching, as though cheated of some throat.

We walked back silently through the humming streets.

"My mother," Danso said suddenly, "will not see a doctor. She has a lot of pain. So what can I do?"

"What's the matter with her?"

"A malignant growth. She believes everything will be all right in a very short time. Everything will be solved. A few months, maybe, a year at most——"

"I don't see——"

Danso looked at me.

"She was the woman who fell down," he said, "who fell down there at his feet."

Danso's deep-set eyes were fathomless and dark as sea; life could drown there.

The next morning Brother Lemon phoned and asked me to accompany him to the African market-place. He seemed disturbed, so I agreed, although without enthusiasm.

"Where are the ju-ju stalls?" he enquired, when we arrived.

"Whatever for?"

"I've heard a very bad thing," he said grimly, "and I want to see if it's true."

So I led him past the stalls piled with green peppers and tomatoes and groundnuts, past the tailors whirring on their treadle sewing machines, past trader women in wide hats of woven rushes, and babies creeping like lost toads through the centipede-legged crowd. In we went, into the recesses of a labyrinthian shelter, always shadowed and cool, where the stalls carried the fetish priests' stock-in-trade, the raw materials of magic. Dried roots, parrot beak, snail shell, chunks of sulphur and bluestone, cowrie shells and strings of bells.

Brother Lemon's face was strained, skin stretched luminous over sharp bones. I only realized then how thin he had grown. He searched and searched, and finally he found what he had hoped not to find. At a little stall in a corner, the sort of place you would never find again once you were outside the maze, a young girl sat. She was selling crudely carved wooden figures, male and female, of the type used to kill by sorcery. I liked the look of the girl. She wasn't more than seventeen, and her eyes were almond and daylight. She was laughing, although she sold death. I half expected Brother Lemon to speak to her, but he did not. He turned away.

"All right," he said. "We can go now."

"You know her?"

"She joined my congregation," he said heavily. "Last week, she came up to the front and was saved. Or so I thought."

"This is her livelihood, after all," I said inadequately. "Anyway, they can't all be a complete success."

"I wonder how many are," Brother Lemon said. "I wonder if any are."

I almost told him of one real success he had had. How could I? The night before I could see only Danso's point of view, yet now, looking at the evangelist's face, I came close to betraying Danso. But I stopped myself in time. And the thought of last night's performance made me suddenly angry.

"What do you expect?" I burst out. "Even Paul nearly got torn to pieces by the Ephesians defending their goddess. And who knows—maybe Diana was better for them than Jehovah. She was theirs, anyway."

Brother Lemon gazed at me as though he could hardly believe I had spoken the words. A thought of the design contract flitted through my mind, but when you've gone so far, you can't go back.

"How do you think they interpret your golden candlesticks and gates of pearl?" I went on. "The ones who go because they've tried every-where else? As ju-ju, Mr. Lemon, just a new kind of ju-ju. That's all."

All at once I was sorrier than I could possibly say. Why the devil had I spoken? He couldn't comprehend, and if he ever did, he would be finished and done for.

"That's—not true——" he stammered. "That's—why, that's an awful thing to say."

And it was. It was.

This city had assimilated many gods. A priest of whatever faith would not have had to stay here very long in order to realize that the competi-tion was stiff. I heard indirectly that Brother Lemon's conversions, after the initial success of novelty, were tailing off. The Homowo festival was absorbing the energies of the Ga people as they paid homage to the ancient gods of the coast. A touring faith-healer from Rhodesia was drawing large crowds. The Baptists staged a parade. The Roman Catholics celebrated a saint's day, and the Methodists parried with a pic-nic. A new god arrived from the northern deserts and its priests were claiming for it marvellous powers in overcoming sterility. The oratory of a visiting *imam** from Nigeria was boosting the local strength of Islam. Allah has ninety-nine names, say the Muslims. But in this city, He must have had nine hundred and ninety-nine, at the very least. I remembered Brother Lemon's brave estimate—a thousand souls within six months. He was really having to scrabble for them now.

I drove over to the meeting place one evening to take some building plans. The service was over, and I found Brother Lemon, still in his blue and starred robe, frantically looking for one of his pseudo-golden candlesticks which had disappeared. He was enraged, positive that someone had stolen it.

*Imam = Muslim priest.

"Those candlesticks were specially made for my mission, and each member of the home congregation contributed towards them. It's certainly going to look bad if I have to write back and tell them one's missing——"

But the candlestick had not been stolen. Brother Lemon came into my office the following day to tell me. He stumbled over the words as though they were a matter of personal shame to him.

"It was one of my converts. He—borrowed it. He told me his wife was barren. He said he wanted the candlestick so he could touch her belly with it. He said he'd tried plenty of other—fetishes, but none had worked. So he thought this one might work."

He avoided my eyes.

"I guess you were right," he said.

"You shouldn't take it so hard," I said awkwardly. "After all, you can't expect miracles."

He looked at me, bewildered.

His discoveries were by no means at an end. The most notable of all occurred the night I went over to his bungalow for dinner and found him standing bleak and fearful under the flame tree, surrounded by half a dozen shouting and gesticulating ancients who shivered with years and anger. Gaunt as pariah dogs, bleached tatters fluttering like wind-worn prayer flags, a delegation of mendicants—come to wring from the next world the certain mercy they had not found in this?

"What's going on?" I asked.

Brother Lemon looked unaccountably relieved to see me.

"There seems to have been some misunderstanding," he said. "Maybe you can make sense of what they say."

The old men turned milky eyes to me, and I realized with a start that every last one of them was blind. Their leader spoke pidgin.

"Dis man"—waving in Brother Lemon's direction—"he say, meka we come heah, he go find we some shade place, he go dash me plenty plenty chop, he mek all t'ing fine too much, he mek we eye come strong. We wait long time, den he say 'go, you.' We no savvy dis palavah. I beg you, mastah, you tell him we wait long time."

"I never promised anything," Brother Lemon said helplessly. "They must be crazy."

Screeched protestations from the throng. They pressed around him, groping and grotesque beside his ivory height and his eyes. The tale emerged, bit by bit. Somehow, they had received the impression that the evangelist intended to throw a feast for them, at which, in the traditional African manner, a sheep would be throat-slit and sacrificed, then roasted and eaten. Palm wine would flow freely. Brother Lemon, furthermore, would restore the use of their eyes.

Brother Lemon's voice was unsteady.

"How could they? How could they think——"

"Who's your Ga interpreter?" I asked.

Brother Lemon looked startled.

"Oh no. He wouldn't say things I hadn't said. He's young, but he's a good boy. It's not just a job to him, you know. He's really interested. He'd never——"

"All the same, I think it would be wise to send for him."

The interpreter seemed all right, although perhaps not in quite the way Brother Lemon meant. This was his first job, and he was performing it with all possible enthusiasm. But his English vocabulary and his knowledge of fundamentalist doctrine were both strictly limited. He had not put words into Brother Lemon's mouth. He had only translated them in his own way, and the listening beggars had completed the transformation of text by hearing what they wanted to hear.

In a welter of words in two tongues, the interpreter and Brother Lemon sorted out the mess. The ancients still clung to him, though, claw hands plucking at his suit. He pulled away from them, almost in desperation, and finally they left. They did not know why they were being sent away, but they were not really surprised, for hope to them must always have been suspect. Brother Lemon did not see old men trailing eyeless out of his compound and back to the begging streets. I think he saw something quite different—a procession of souls, all of whom would have to be saved again.

The text that caused the confusion was from chapter seven of Revelation. "They shall hunger no more, neither thirst any more; neither shall the sun light on them, nor any heat. For the Lamb which is in the midst of the throne shall feed them, and shall lead them unto living fountains of waters, and God shall wipe away all tears from their eyes."

I thought I would not see Brother Lemon for a while, but a few days later he was at my office once more. Danso was in the back working out some colour schemes for a new school I was doing, and I hoped he would not come into the main office. Brother Lemon came right to the point.

"The municipal authorities have given me my building site, Mr. Kettridge."

"Good. That's fine."

"No, it's not fine," Brother Lemon said. "That's just what it's not."

"What's the matter? Where is it?"

"Right in the middle of shantytown."

"Well?"

"It's all right for the mission, perhaps, but they won't give me a separate site for my house."

"I wasn't aware that you wanted a separate site."

"I didn't think there would be any need for one," he said. "I certainly didn't imagine they'd put me there. You know what that place is like."

He made a gesture of appeal.

"It isn't that I mind Africans, Mr. Kettridge. Honest to goodness it isn't that at all. But shantytown—the people live so close together and it smells so bad, and at night the drums and that lewd dancing they do, and the idolatry. I can't—I don't want to be reminded every minute———"

He broke off and we were silent. Then he sighed.

"They'd always be asking," he said, "for things I can't give. It's not my business, anyway. It's not up to me. I won't be kept from my work."

I made no comment. The turquoise eyes once more glowed with proselytizing zeal. He towered; his voice cymballed forth.

"Maybe you think I was discouraged recently. Well, I was. But I'm not going to let it get me down. I tell you straight, Mr. Kettridge, I intend to salvage those souls, as many as I can, if I have to give my very life to do it."

And seeing his resilient radiance, I could well believe it. But I drew him back to the matter at hand.

"It would be a lot easier if you accepted this site, Mr. Lemon. Do you think, perhaps, a wall———"

"I can't," he said. "I—I'm sorry, but I just can't. I thought if you'd speak to the authorities. You're an Englishman———"

I told him I had no influence in high places. I explained gently that this country was no longer a colony. But Brother Lemon only regarded me mournfully, as though he thought I had betrayed him.

When he had gone, I turned and there was Danso, lean as a leopard, draped in the doorway.

"Yes," he said, "I heard. At least he's a step further than the slavers. They didn't admit we had souls."

"It's not that simple, Danso———"

"I didn't say it was simple," Danso corrected. "It must be quite a procedure—to tear the soul out of a living body, and throw the inconvenient flesh away like fruit rind."

"He doesn't want to live in that area," I tried ineffectually to explain, "because in some way the people there are a threat to him, to everything he is———"

"Good," Danso said. "That makes it even."

I saw neither Danso nor Brother Lemon for several weeks. The plans for the mission were still in abeyance, and for the moment I almost forgot about them. Then one evening Danso ambled in, carrying a large wrapped canvas.

"What's this?" I asked.

He grinned. "My church picture. The one I have done for Brother Lemon."

I reached out, but Danso pulled it away.

"No, Will. I want Brother Lemon to be here. You ask him to come over."

"Not without seeing the picture," I said. "How do I know what monstrosity you've painted?"

"No—I swear it—you don't need to worry."

I was not entirely convinced, but I phoned Brother Lemon. Somewhat reluctantly he agreed, and within twenty minutes we heard the Buick scrunching on the gravel drive.

He looked worn out. His unsuccessful haggling with the municipal authorities seemed to have exhausted him. He had been briefly ill with malaria despite his up-to-date preventive drugs. I couldn't help remembering how he had looked that first morning at the airport, confidently stepping onto the alien soil of his chosen Thessalonica, to take up his ordained role.

"Here you are, Mr. Lemon," Danso said. "I painted a whole lot of stars and candlesticks and other junk in the first version, then I threw it away and did this one instead."

He unwrapped the painting and set it up against a wall. It was a picture of the Nazarene. Danso had not portrayed any emaciated mauve-veined ever sorrowful Jesus. This man had the body of a fisherman or a carpenter. He was well built. He had strong wrists and arms. His eyes were capable of laughter. Danso had shown Him with a group of beggars, sore-fouled, their mouths twisted in perpetual leers of pain.

Danso was looking at me questioningly.

"It's the best you've done yet," I said.

He nodded and turned to Brother Lemon. The evangelist's eyes were fixed on the picture. He did not seem able to look away. For a moment I thought he had caught the essential feeling of the thing, but then he blinked and withdrew his gaze. His tall frame sagged as though he had been struck and—yes—hurt. The old gods he could fight. He could grapple with and overcome every obstacle, even his own pity. But this was a threat he had never anticipated. He spoke in a low voice.

"Do many—do all of you—see Him like that?"

He didn't wait for an answer. He did not look at Danso or myself as he left the house. We heard the orchid Buick pull away.

Danso and I did not talk much. We drank beer and looked at the picture.

"I have to tell you one thing, Danso," I said at last. "The fact that you've shown Him as an African doesn't seem so very important one way or another."

Danso set down his glass and ran one finger lightly over the painting.

"Perhaps not," he admitted reluctantly. "But could anyone be shown as everything? How to get past the paint, Will?"

"I don't know."

Danso laughed and began slouching out to the kitchen to get another beer.

"We will invent new colours, man," he cried. "But for this we may need a little time."

I was paid for the work I had done, but the mission was never built. Brother Lemon did not obtain another site, and in a few months, his health—as they say—broke down. He returned whence he had come, and I have not heard anything about the Angel of Philadelphia Mission from that day to this.

Somewhere, perhaps, he is still preaching, heaven and hell pouring from his apocalyptic eyes, and around his head that aureole, hair the colour of light. Whenever Danso mentions him, however, it is always as the magician, the pedlar who bought souls cheap, and sold dear his cabbalistic word. But I can no longer think of Brother Lemon as either Paul or Elymas, apostle or sorcerer.

I bought Danso's picture. Sometimes, when I am able to see through black and white, until they merge and cease to be separate or apart, I look at those damaged creatures clustering so despairingly hopeful around the Son of Man, and it seems to me that Brother Lemon, after all, is one of them.

The son of a coal miner in Nottingham, David Herbert Lawrence (1885-1930) was brought up in a household very similar to that depicted in his novel *Sons and Lovers* (1913), in which the father's coarse sensuality struggled against the mother's finer sensibilities. With his mother's encouragement, Lawrence developed his literary abilities, and after a spell as a teacher in Croydon, near London, he made writing his full-time profession, producing a great many essays, poems, and short stories. His work, particularly his novels, often aroused controversy because of his frank treatment of sexual relations; two of his novels, *The Rainbow* (1915) and *Lady Chatterley's Lover* (1928), were declared obscene and banned in England for many years. Disgusted by the response of the press and public, Lawrence left England with his German wife in 1919, and travelled in various parts of the world for a number of years, chiefly in the United States and Mexico.

In much of his writing, Lawrence examines the tension between men and women as social creatures, hemmed in by conventions and "responsibilities," and as feeling creatures, part of a larger universe of instinctive response. "The Horse Dealer's Daughter" dramatizes this conflict through the relationship of Dr. Fergusson with Mabel Pervin. Initially both are creatures of habit and convention, cut off from true feeling and turned in upon themselves. Once relieved of their social roles, they respond to each other with almost brutal urgency, in a manner reflecting Lawrence's antiromantic ideas about love and sexual awareness. "Accept the sexual, physical being of yourself," he wrote, "and of every other creature. Don't be afraid of the physical functions. . . . Conquer the fear of sex, and restore the natural flow" ("The State of Funk").

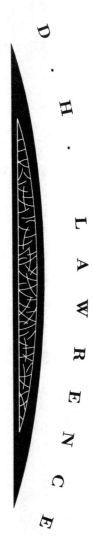

D. H. LAWRENCE

FOR FURTHER READING

Janice Hubbard Harris, *The Short Fiction of D.H. Lawrence* (New Brunswick, N.J.: Rutgers UP, 1984).

Donald Junkins, "D.H. Lawrence's 'The Horse-Dealer's Daughter'," *Studies in Short Fiction* 6 (1969): 210-12.

D.H. Lawrence, *Fantasia of the Unconscious and Psychoanalysis and the Unconscious* (Melbourne: Heinemann, 1961).

Keith Sagar, *The Life of D.H. Lawrence* (New York: Pantheon, 1980).

Mark Spilka, *The Love Ethic of D.H. Lawrence* (Bloomington: Indiana UP, 1955).

The Horse Dealer's Daughter

"Well, Mabel, and what are you going to do with yourself?" asked Joe, with foolish flippancy. He felt quite safe himself. Without listening for an answer, he turned aside, worked a grain of tobacco to the tip of his tongue, and spat it out. He did not care about anything, since he felt safe himself.

The three brothers and the sister sat round the desolate breakfast table, attempting some sort of desultory consultation. The morning's post had given the final tap to the family fortune, and all was over. The dreary dining-room itself, with its heavy mahogany furniture, looked as if it were waiting to be done away with.

But the consultation amounted to nothing. There was a strange air of ineffectuality about the three men, as they sprawled at table, smoking and reflecting vaguely on their own condition. The girl was alone, a rather short, sullen-looking young woman of twenty-seven. She did not share the same life as her brothers. She would have been good-looking, save for the impressive fixity of her face, "bull-dog," as her brothers called it.

There was a confused tramping of horses' feet outside. The three men all sprawled round in their chairs to watch. Beyond the dark holly bushes that separated the strip of lawn from the high-road, they could see a cavalcade of shire horses swinging out of their own yard, being taken for exercise. This was the last time. These were the last horses that would go through their hands. The young men watched with critical, callous look. They were all frightened at the collapse of their lives, and the sense of disaster in which they were involved left them no inner freedom.

Yet they were three fine, well-set fellows enough. Joe, the eldest, was a man of thirty-three, broad and handsome in a hot, flushed way. His face was red, he twisted his black moustache over a thick finger, his eyes were shallow and restless. He had a sensual way of uncovering his teeth when he laughed, and his bearing was stupid. Now he watched the horses with a glazed look of helplessness in his eyes, a certain stupor of downfall.

The great draught-horses swung past. They were tied head to tail, four of them, and they heaved along to where a lane branched off from the high-road, planting their great hoofs floutingly in the fine black mud, swinging their great rounded haunches sumptuously, and trotting a few sudden steps as they were led into the lane, round the corner. Every movement showed a massive, slumbrous strength, and a stupidity which held them in subjection. The groom at the head looked back, jerking the leading rope. And the cavalcade moved out of sight up the lane, the tail of the last horse, bobbed up tight and stiff, held out taut from the swinging great haunches as they rocked behind the hedges in a motion-like sleep.

Joe watched with glazed hopeless eyes. The horses were almost like his own body to him. He felt he was done for now. Luckily he was engaged to a woman as old as himself, and therefore her father, who was steward of a neighbouring estate, would provide him with a job. He would marry and go into harness. His life was over, he would be a subject animal now.

He turned uneasily aside, the retreating steps of the horses echoing in his ears. Then, with foolish restlessness, he reached for the scraps of bacon-rind from the plates, and making a faint whistling sound, flung them to the terrier that lay against the fender. He watched the dog swallow them, and waited till the creature looked into his eyes. Then a faint grin came on his face, and in a high, foolish voice he said:

"You won't get much more bacon, shall you, you little b——?"

The dog faintly and dismally wagged its tail, then lowered its haunches, circled round, and lay down again.

There was another helpless silence at the table. Joe sprawled uneasily in his seat, not willing to go till the family conclave was dissolved. Fred Henry, the second brother, was erect, clean-limbed, alert. He had watched the passing of the horses with more *sang-froid*. If he was an animal, like Joe, he was an animal which controls, not one which is controlled. He was master of any horse, and he carried himself with a well-tempered air of mastery. But he was not master of the situations of life. He pushed his coarse brown moustache upwards, off his lip, and glanced irritably at his sister, who sat impassive and inscrutable.

"You'll go and stop with Lucy for a bit, shan't you?" he asked. The girl did not answer.

"I don't see what else you can do," persisted Fred Henry.

"Go as a skivvy,"* Joe interpolated laconically.

*Skivvy = cleaning woman.

The girl did not move a muscle.

"If I was her, I should go in for training for a nurse," said Malcolm, the youngest of them all. He was the baby of the family, a young man of twenty-two, with a fresh, jaunty *museau.**

But Mabel did not take any notice of him. They had talked at her and round her for so many years, that she hardly heard them at all.

The marble clock on the mantelpiece softly chimed the half-hour, the dog rose uneasily from the hearthrug and looked at the party at the breakfast table. But still they sat on in ineffectual conclave.

"Oh, all right," said Joe suddenly, apropos of nothing. "I'll get a move on."

He pushed back his chair, straddled his knees with a downward jerk, to get them free, in horsey fashion, and went to the fire. Still he did not go out of the room; he was curious to know what the others would do or say. He began to charge his pipe, looking down at the dog and saying in a high, affected voice:

"Going wi' me? Going wi' me are ter?** Tha'rt goin' further than tha counts on just now, dost hear?"

The dog faintly wagged its tail, the man stuck out his jaw and covered his pipe with his hands, and puffed intently, losing himself in the tobacco, looking down all the while at the dog with an absent brown eye. The dog looked up at him in mournful distrust. Joe stood with his knees stuck out, in real horsey fashion.

"Have you had a letter from Lucy?" Fred Henry asked of his sister.

"Last week," came the neutral reply.

"And what does she say?"

There was no answer.

"Does she *ask* you to go and stop there?" persisted Fred Henry.

"She says I can if I like."

"Well, then, you'd better. Tell her you'll come on Monday."

This was received in silence.

"That's what you'll do then, is it?" said Fred Henry, in some exasperation.

But she made no answer. There was a silence of futility and irritation in the room. Malcolm grinned fatuously.

"You'll have to make up your mind between now and next Wednesday," said Joe loudly, "or else find yourself lodgings on the kerbstone."

The face of the young woman darkened, but she sat on immutable.

"Here's Jack Fergusson!" exclaimed Malcolm, who was looking aimlessly out of the window.

"Where?" exclaimed Joe, loudly.

**Museau* = snout, face.
**Are ter = are you.

"Just gone past."

"Coming in?"

Malcolm craned his neck to see the gate.

"Yes," he said.

There was a silence. Mabel sat on like one condemned, at the head of the table. Then a whistle was heard from the kitchen. The dog got up and barked sharply. Joe opened the door and shouted:

"Come on."

After a moment a young man entered. He was muffled up in over-coat and a purple woollen scarf, and his tweed cap, which he did not remove, was pulled down on his head. He was of medium height, his face was rather long and pale, his eyes looked tired.

"Hello, Jack! Well, Jack!" exclaimed Malcolm and Joe. Fred Henry merely said, "Jack."

"What's doing?" asked the newcomer, evidently addressing Fred Henry.

"Same. We've got to be out by Wednesday. Got a cold?"

"I have—got it bad, too."

"Why don't you stop in?"

"*Me* stop in? When I can't stand on my legs, perhaps I shall have a chance." The young man spoke huskily. He had a slight Scotch accent.

"It's a knock-out, isn't it," said Joe, boisterously, "if a doctor goes round croaking with a cold. Looks bad for the patients, doesn't it?"

The young doctor looked at him slowly.

"Anything the matter with *you*, then?" he asked sarcastically.

"Not as I know of. Damn your eyes, I hope not. Why?"

"I thought you were very concerned about the patients, wondered if you might be one yourself."

"Damn it, no, I've never been patient to no flaming doctor, and hope I never shall be," returned Joe.

At this point Mabel rose from the table, and they all seemed to become aware of her existence. She began putting the dishes together. The young doctor looked at her, but did not address her. He had not greeted her. She went out of the room with the tray, her face impassive and unchanged.

"When are you off then, all of you?" asked the doctor.

"I'm catching the eleven-forty," replied Malcolm. "Are you goin' down wi' th' trap, Joe?"

"Yes, I've told you I'm going down wi' th' trap, haven't I?"

"We'd better be getting her in then. So long, Jack, if I don't see you before I go," said Malcolm, shaking hands.

He went out, followed by Joe, who seemed to have his tail between his legs.

"Well, this is the devil's own," exclaimed the doctor, when he was left alone with Fred Henry. "Going before Wednesday, are you?"

"That's the orders," replied the other.

"Where, to Northampton?"

"That's it."

"The devil!" exclaimed Fergusson, with quiet chagrin.

And there was silence between the two.

"All settled up, are you?" asked Fergusson.

"About."

There was another pause.

"Well, I shall miss yer, Freddy, boy," said the young doctor.

"And I shall miss thee, Jack," returned the other.

"Miss you like hell," mused the doctor.

Fred Henry turned aside. There was nothing to say. Mabel came in again, to finish clearing the table.

"What are *you* going to do, then, Miss Pervin?" asked Fergusson. "Going to your sister's, are you?"

Mabel looked at him with her steady, dangerous eyes, that always made him uncomfortable, unsettling his superficial ease.

"No," she said.

"Well, what in the name of fortune *are* you going to do? Say what you mean to do," cried Fred Henry, with futile intensity.

But she only averted her head, and continued her work. She folded the white table-cloth, and put on the chenille cloth.

"The sulkiest bitch that ever trod!" muttered her brother.

But she finished her task with perfectly impassive face, the young doctor watching her interestedly all the while. Then she went out.

Fred Henry stared after her, clenching his lips, his blue eyes fixing in sharp antagonism, as he made a grimace of sour exasperation.

"You could bray her into bits, and that's all you'd get out of her," he said, in a small, narrowed tone.

The doctor smiled faintly.

"What's she *going* to do, then?" he asked.

"Strike me if *I* know!" returned the other.

There was a pause. Then the doctor stirred.

"I'll be seeing you to-night, shall I?" he said to his friend.

"Ay—where's it to be? Are we going over to Jessdale?"

"I don't know. I've got such a cold on me. I'll come round to the 'Moon and Stars', anyway."

"Let Lizzie and May miss their night for once, eh?"

"That's it—if I feel as I do now."

"All's one—"

The two young men went through the passage and down to the back door together. The house was large, but it was servantless now, and desolate. At the back was a small bricked house-yard, and beyond that a big square, gravelled fine and red, and having stables on two sides. Sloping, dank, winter-dark fields stretched away on the open sides.

But the stables were empty. Joseph Pervin, the father of the family, had been a man of no education, who had become a fairly large horse dealer. The stables had been full of horses, there was a great turmoil and come-and-go of horses and of dealers and grooms. Then the kitchen was full of servants. But of late things had declined. The old man had married a second time, to retrieve his fortunes. Now he was dead and everything was gone to the dogs, there was nothing but debt and threatening.

For months, Mabel had been servantless in the big house, keeping the home together in penury for her ineffectual brothers. She had kept house for ten years. But previously it was with unstinted means. Then, however brutal and coarse everything was, the sense of money had kept her proud, confident. The men might be foulmouthed, the women in the kitchen might have bad reputations, her brothers might have illegitimate children. But so long as there was money, the girl felt herself established, and brutally proud, reserved.

No company came to the house, save dealers and coarse men. Mabel had no associates of her own sex, after her sister went away. But she did not mind. She went regularly to church, she attended to her father. And she lived in the memory of her mother, who had died when she was fourteen, and whom she had loved. She had loved her father, too, in a different way, depending upon him, and feeling secure in him, until at the age of fifty-four he married again. And then she had set hard against him. Now he had died and left them all hopelessly in debt.

She had suffered badly during the period of poverty. Nothing, however, could shake the curious sullen, animal pride that dominated each member of the family. Now, for Mabel, the end had come. Still she would not cast about her. She would follow her own way just the same. She would always hold the keys of her own situation. Mindless and persistent, she endured from day to day. Why should she think? Why should she answer anybody? It was enough that this was the end, and there was no way out. She need not pass any more darkly along the main street of the small town, avoiding every eye. She need not demean herself any more, going into the shops and buying the cheapest food. This was at an end. She thought of nobody, not even of herself. Mindless and persistent, she seemed in a sort of ecstasy to be coming nearer to her fulfilment, her own glorification, approaching her dead mother, who was glorified.

In the afternoon she took a little bag, with shears and sponge and a small scrubbing brush, and went out. It was a grey, wintry day, with saddened, dark green fields and an atmosphere blackened by the smoke of foundries not far off. She went quickly, darkly along the causeway, heeding nobody, through the town to the churchyard.

There she always felt secure, as if no one could see her, although as a matter of fact she was exposed to the stare of every one who passed along under the churchyard wall. Nevertheless, once under the shadow of the great looming church, among the graves, she felt immune from the world, reserved within the thick churchyard wall as in another country.

Carefully she clipped the grass from the grave, and arranged the pinky white, small chrysanthemums in the tin cross. When this was done, she took an empty jar from a neighbouring grave, brought water, and carefully, most scrupulously sponged the marble headstone and the coping-stone.

It gave her sincere satisfaction to do this. She felt in immediate contact with the world of her mother. She took minute pains, went through the park in a state bordering on pure happiness, as if in performing this task she came into a subtle, intimate connection with her mother. For the life she followed here in the world was far less real than the world of death she inherited from her mother.

The doctor's house was just by the church. Fergusson, being a mere hired assistant, was slave to the country-side. As he hurried now to attend to the outpatients in the surgery, glancing across the graveyard with his quick eye, he saw the girl at her task at the grave. She seemed so intent and remote, it was like looking into another world. Some mystical element was touched in him. He slowed down as he walked, watching her as if spell-bound.

She lifted her eyes, feeling him looking. Their eyes met. And each looked away again at once, each feeling, in some way, found out by the other. He lifted his cap and passed on down the road. There remained distinct in his consciousness, like a vision, the memory of her face, lifted from the tombstone in the churchyard, and looking at him with slow, large, portentous eyes. It *was* portentous, her face. It seemed to mesmerize him. There was a heavy power in her eyes which laid hold of his whole being, as if he had drunk some powerful drug. He had been feeling weak and done before. Now the life came back into him, he felt delivered from his own fretted, daily self.

He finished his duties at the surgery as quickly as might be, hastily filling up the bottles of the waiting people with cheap drugs. Then, in perpetual haste, he set off again to visit several cases in another part of his round, before teatime. At all times he preferred to walk if he could, but particularly when he was not well. He fancied the motion restored him.

The afternoon was falling. It was grey, deadened, and wintry, with a slow, moist, heavy coldness sinking in and deadening all the faculties. But why should he think or notice? He hastily climbed the hill and turned across the dark green fields, following the black cindertrack. In the distance, across a shallow dip in the country, the small town was clustered like smouldering ash, a tower, a spire, a heap of low, raw, extinct houses. And on the nearest fringe of the town, sloping into the dip, was Oldmeadow, the Pervins' house. He could see the stables and the outbuildings distinctly, as they lay towards him on the slope. Well, he would not go there many more times! Another resource would be lost to him, another place gone: the only company he cared for in the alien, ugly little town he was losing. Nothing but work, drudgery, constant hastening from dwelling to dwelling among the colliers and the iron-workers. It wore him out, but at the same time he had a craving for it. It was a stimulant to him to be in the homes of the working people, moving, as it were, through the innermost body of their life. His nerves were excited and gratified. He could come so near, into the very lives of the rough, inarticulate, powerfully emotional men and women. He grumbled, he said he hated the hellish hole. But as a matter of fact it excited him, the contact with the rough, strongly-feeling people was a stimulant applied direct to his nerves.

Below Oldmeadow, in the green, shallow, soddened hollow of fields, lay a square, deep pond. Roving across the landscape, the doctor's quick eye detected a figure in black passing through the gate of the field, down towards the pond. He looked again. It would be Mabel Pervin. His mind suddenly became alive and attentive.

Why was she going down there? He pulled up on the path on the slope above, and stood staring. He could just make sure of the small black figure moving in the hollow of the failing day. He seemed to see her in the midst of such obscurity, that he was like a clairvoyant, seeing rather with the mind's eye than with ordinary sight. Yet he could see her positively enough, whilst he kept his eye attentive. He felt, if he looked away from her, in the thick, ugly falling dusk, he would lose her altogether.

He followed her minutely as she moved, direct and intent, like something transmitted rather than stirring in voluntary activity, straight down the field towards the pond. There she stood on the bank for a moment. She never raised her head. Then she waded slowly into the water.

He stood motionless as the small black figure walked slowly and deliberately towards the centre of the pond, very slowly, gradually moving deeper into the motionless water, and still moving forward as the water got up to her breast. Then he could see her no more in the dusk of the dead afternoon.

"There!" he exclaimed. "Would you believe it?"

And he hastened straight down, running over the wet, soddened fields, pushing through the hedges, down into the depression of callous wintry obscurity. It took him several minutes to come to the pond. He stood on the bank, breathing heavily. He could see nothing. His eyes seemed to penetrate the dead water. Yes, perhaps that was the dark shadow of her black clothing beneath the surface of the water.

He slowly ventured into the pond. The bottom was deep, soft clay, he sank in, and the water clasped dead cold round his legs. As he stirred he could smell the cold, rotten clay that fouled up into the water. It was objectionable in his lungs. Still, repelled and yet not heeding, he moved deeper into the pond. The cold water rose over his thighs, over his loins, upon his abdomen. The lower part of his body was all sunk in the hideous cold element. And the bottom was so deeply soft and uncertain, he was afraid of pitching with his mouth underneath. He could not swim, and was afraid.

He crouched a little, spreading his hands under the water and moving them round, trying to feel for her. The dead cold pond swayed upon his chest. He moved again, a little deeper, and again, with his hands underneath, he felt all around under the water. And he touched her clothing. But it evaded his fingers. He made a desperate effort to grasp it.

And so doing he lost his balance and went under, horribly, suffocating in the foul earthy water, struggling madly for a few moments. At last, after what seemed an eternity, he got his footing, rose again into the air and looked around. He gasped, and knew he was in the world. Then he looked at the water. She had risen near him. He grasped her clothing, and drawing her nearer, turned to take his way to land again.

He went very slowly, carefully, absorbed in the slow progress. He rose higher, climbing out of the pond. The water was now only about his legs; he was thankful, full of relief to be out of the clutches of the pond. He lifted her and staggered on to the bank, out of the horror of wet, grey clay.

He laid her down on the bank. She was quite unconscious and running with water. He made the water come from her mouth, he worked to restore her. He did not have to work very long before he could feel the breathing begin again in her; she was breathing naturally. He worked a little longer. He could feel her live beneath his hands; she was coming back. He wiped her face, wrapped her in his overcoat, looked round into the dim, dark grey world, then lifted her and staggered down the bank and across the fields.

It seemed an unthinkably long way, and his burden so heavy he felt he would never get to the house. But at last he was in the stable-yard, and then in the house-yard. He opened the door and went into the house. In the kitchen he laid her down on the hearthrug, and called. The house was empty. But the fire was burning in the grate.

Then again he kneeled to attend to her. She was breathing regularly, her eyes were wide open and as if conscious, but there seemed something missing in her look. She was conscious in herself, but unconscious of her surroundings.

He ran upstairs, took blankets from a bed, and put them before the fire to warm. Then he removed her saturated, earthy-smelling clothing, rubbed her dry with a towel, and wrapped her naked in the blankets. Then he went into the dining-room, to look for spirits. There was a little whisky. He drank a gulp himself, and put some into her mouth.

The effect was instantaneous. She looked full into his face, as if she had been seeing him for some time, and yet had only just become conscious of him.

"Dr. Fergusson?" she said.

"What?" he answered.

He was divesting himself of his coat, intending to find some dry clothing upstairs. He could not bear the smell of the dead, clayey water, and he was mortally afraid for his own health.

"What did I do?" she asked.

"Walked into the pond," he replied. He had begun to shudder like one sick, and could hardly attend to her. Her eyes remained full on him, he seemed to be going dark in his mind, looking back at her helplessly. The shuddering became quieter in him, his life came back to him, dark and unknowing, but strong again.

"Was I out of my mind?" she asked, while her eyes were fixed on him all the time.

"Maybe, for the moment," he replied. He felt quiet, because his strength had come back. The strange fretful strain had left him.

"Am I out of my mind now?" she asked.

"Are you?" he reflected a moment. "No," he answered truthfully, "I don't see that you are." He turned his face aside. He was afraid now, because he felt dazed, and felt dimly that her power was stronger than his, in this issue. And she continued to look at him fixedly all the time. "Can you tell me where I shall find some dry things to put on?" he asked.

"Did you dive into the pond for me?" she asked.

"No," he answered. "I walked in. But I went in overhead as well."

There was silence for a moment. He hesitated. He very much wanted to go upstairs to get into dry clothing. But there was another desire in him. And she seemed to hold him. His will seemed to have gone to sleep, and left him, standing there slack before her. But he felt warm inside himself. He did not shudder at all, though his clothes were sodden on him.

"Why did you?" she asked.

"Because I didn't want you to do such a foolish thing," he said.

"It wasn't foolish," she said, still gazing at him as she lay on the floor, with a sofa cushion under her head. "It was the right thing to do. *I* knew best, then."

"I'll go and shift these wet things," he said. But still he had not the power to move out of her presence, until she sent him. It was as if she had the life of his body in her hands, and he could not extricate himself. Or perhaps he did not want to.

Suddenly she sat up. Then she became aware of her own immediate condition. She felt the blankets about her, she knew her own limbs. For a moment it seemed as if her reason were going. She looked round, with wild eye, as if seeking something. He stood still with fear. She saw her clothing lying scattered.

"Who undressed me?" she asked, her eyes resting full and inevitable on his face.

"I did," he replied, "to bring you round."

For some moments she sat and gazed at him awfully, her lips parted.

"Do you love me, then?" she asked.

He only stood and stared at her, fascinated. His soul seemed to melt. She shuffled forward on her knees, and put her arms round him, round his legs, as he stood there, pressing her breasts against his knees and thighs, clutching him with strange, convulsive certainty, pressing his thighs against her, drawing him to her face, her throat, as she looked up at him with flaring, humble eyes of transfiguration, triumphant in first possession.

"You love me," she murmured, in strange transport, yearning and triumphant and confident. "You love me. I know you love me, I know."

And she was passionately kissing his knees, through the wet clothing, passionately and indiscriminately kissing his knees, his legs, as if unaware of everything.

He looked down at the tangled wet hair, the wild, bare, animal shoulders. He was amazed, bewildered, and afraid. He had never thought of loving her. He had never wanted to love her. When he rescued her and restored her, he was a doctor, and she was a patient. He had had no single personal thought of her. Nay, this introduction of the personal element was very distasteful to him, a violation of his professional honour. It was horrible to have her there embracing his knees. It was horrible. He revolted from it, violently. And yet—and yet—he had not the power to break away.

She looked at him again, with the same supplication of powerful love, and that same transcendent, frightening light of triumph. In view of the delicate flame which seemed to come from her face like a light, he was powerless. And yet he had never intended to love her. He had never intended. And something stubborn in him could not give way.

"You love me," she repeated, in a murmur of deep, rhapsodic assurance. "You love me."

Her hands were drawing him, drawing him down to her. He was afraid, even a little horrified. For he had, really, no intention of loving her. Yet her hands were drawing him towards her. He put out his hand quickly to steady himself, and grasped her bare shoulder. A flame seemed to burn the hand that grasped her soft shoulder. He had no intention of loving her: his whole will was against his yielding. It was horrible. And yet wonderful was the touch of her shoulders, beautiful the shining of her face. Was she perhaps mad? He had a horror of yielding to her. Yet something in him ached also.

He had been staring away at the door, away from her. But his hand remained on her shoulder. She had gone suddenly very still. He looked down at her. Her eyes were now wide with fear, with doubt, the light was dying from her face, a shadow of terrible greyness was returning. He could not bear the touch of her eyes' question upon him, and the look of death behind the question.

With an inward groan he gave way, and let his heart yield towards her. A sudden gentle smile came on his face. And her eyes, which never left his face, slowly, slowly filled with tears. He watched the strange water rise in her eyes, like some slow fountain coming up. And his heart seemed to burn and melt away in his breast.

He could not bear to look at her any more. He dropped on his knees and caught her head with his arms and pressed her face against his throat. She was very still. His heart, which seemed to have broken, was burning with a kind of agony in his breast. And he felt her slow, hot tears wetting his throat. But he could not move.

He felt the hot tears wet his neck and the hollows of his neck, and he remained motionless, suspended through one of man's eternities. Only now it had become indispensable to him to have her face pressed close to him; he could never let her go again. He could never let her head go away from the close clutch of his arm. He wanted to remain like that for ever, with his heart hurting him in a pain that was also life to him. Without knowing, he was looking down on her damp, soft brown hair.

Then, as it were suddenly, he smelt the horrid stagnant smell of that water. And at the same moment she drew away from him and looked at him. Her eyes were wistful and unfathomable. He was afraid of them, and he fell to kissing her, not knowing what he was doing. He wanted her eyes not to have that terrible, wistful, unfathomable look.

When she turned her face to him again, a faint delicate flush was glowing, and there was again dawning that terrible shining of joy in her eyes, which really terrified him, and yet which he now wanted to see, because he feared the look of doubt still more.

"You love me?" she said, rather faltering.

"Yes." The word cost him a painful effort. Not because it wasn't true. But because it was too newly true, the *saying* seemed to tear open again his newly-torn heart. And he hardly wanted it to be true, even now.

She lifted her face to him, and he bent forward and kissed her on the mouth, gently, with the one kiss that is an eternal pledge. And as he kissed her his heart strained again in his breast. He never intended to love her. But now it was over. He had crossed over the gulf to her, and all that he had left behind had shrivelled and become void.

After the kiss, her eyes again slowly filled with tears. She sat still, away from him, with her face drooped aside, and her hands folded in her lap. The tears fell very slowly. There was complete silence. He too sat there motionless and silent on the hearthrug. The strange pain of his heart that was broken seemed to consume him. That he should love her? That this was love! That he should be ripped open in this way! Him, a doctor! How they would all jeer if they knew! It was agony to him to think they might know.

In the curious naked pain of the thought he looked again to her. She was sitting there drooped into a muse. He saw a tear fall, and his heart flared hot. He saw for the first time that one of her shoulders was quite uncovered, one arm bare, he could see one of her small breasts; dimly, because it had become almost dark in the room.

"Why are you crying?" he asked, in an altered voice.

She looked up at him, and behind her tears the consciousness of her situation for the first time brought a dark look of shame to her eyes.

"I'm not crying, really," she said, watching him, half frightened. He reached his hand, and softly closed it on her bare arm.

"I love you! I love you!" he said in a soft, low vibrating voice, unlike himself.

She shrank, and dropped her head. The soft, penetrating grip of his hand on her arm distressed her. She looked up at him.

"I want to go," she said. "I want to go and get you some dry things."

"Why?" he said. "I'm all right."

"But I want to go," she said. "And I want you to change your things."

He released her arm, and she wrapped herself in the blanket, looking at him rather frightened. And still she did not rise.

"Kiss me," she said wistfully.

He kissed her, but briefly, half in anger.

Then, after a second, she rose nervously, all mixed up in the blanket. He watched her in her confusion, as she tried to extricate herself and wrap herself up so that she could walk. He watched her relentlessly, as she knew. And as she went, the blanket trailing, and as he saw a glimpse of her feet and her white leg, he tried to remember her as she was when he had wrapped her in the blanket. But then he didn't want to remember, because she had been nothing to him then, and his nature revolted from remembering her as she was when she was nothing to him.

A tumbling, muffled noise from within the dark house startled him. Then he heard her voice:—"There are clothes." He rose and went to the foot of the stairs, and gathered up the garments she had thrown down. Then he came back to the fire, to rub himself down and dress. He grinned at his own appearance when he had finished.

The fire was sinking, so he put on coal. The house was now quite dark, save for the light of a street-lamp that shone in faintly from beyond the holly trees. He lit the gas with matches he found on the mantelpiece. Then he emptied the pockets of his own clothes, and threw all his wet things in a heap into the scullery. After which he gathered up her sodden clothes, gently, and put them in a separate heap on the coppertop in the scullery.

It was six o'clock on the clock. His own watch had stopped. He ought to go back to the surgery. He waited, and still she did not come down. So he went to the foot of the stairs and called:

"I shall have to go."

Almost immediately he heard her coming down. She had on her best dress of black voile, and her hair was tidy, but still damp. She looked at him—and in spite of herself, smiled.

"I don't like you in those clothes," she said.

"Do I look a sight?" he answered.

They were shy of one another.

"I'll make you some tea," she said.

"No, I must go."

"Must you?" And she looked at him again with the wide, strained doubtful eyes. And again, from the pain of his breast, he knew how he loved her. He went and bent to kiss her, gently, passionately, with his heart's painful kiss.

"And my hair smells so horrible," she murmured in distraction. "And I'm so awful, I'm so awful! Oh, no, I'm too awful." And she broke into bitter, heart-broken sobbing. "You can't want to love me, I'm horrible."

"Don't be silly, don't be silly," he said, trying to comfort her, kissing her, holding her in his arms. "I want you, I want to marry you, we're going to be married, quickly, quickly—tomorrow if I can."

But she only sobbed terribly, and cried:

"I feel awful. I feel awful. I feel I'm horrible to you."

"No, I want you, I want you," was all he answered, blindly, with that terrible intonation which frightened her almost more than her horror lest he should *not* want her.

Born Kathleen Mansfield Beauchamp, the third of five children in a prosperous New Zealand family, Katherine Mansfield (1888-1923) grew up in Wellington, was educated at Queen's College (London), and returned only briefly to New Zealand before finally settling in Europe in 1908. In England she lived what was then considered a bohemian life, one marked by its love of theatre, its urbanity, and its shifting liaisons. On the edge of several famous literary circles—Bloomsbury, Garsington, and the milieu of D.H. and Frieda Lawrence, for example—she published stories in *The New Age, Rhythm, Adelphi*, and several other periodicals. A deft satirist in her early sketches (*In a German Pension*, 1911), she drew most attention for the later stories she collected in *Bliss* (1920) and *The Garden Party* (1922). Her sharp, spare style contrasted strongly with conventional forms of storytelling; she strove to break away from plotted narrative and to evoke through image and cadence the pressures, perspectives, and insights of particular frames of mind. For her, beauty was evanescent, order a fond dream; isolation at once fed and desolated the creative imagination. In a contemporary review, the poet Walter de la Mare wrote of her work: "The pitch of mind is invariably emotional, the poise lyrical. Nonetheless that mind is absolutely tranquil and attentive in its intellectual grasp of the matter in hand. And through all, Miss Mansfield's personality, whatever its disguises, haunts her work just as its customary inmate may haunt a vacant room, its *genius* a place." More recent critics have attempted to come to terms with how and why this process happens, finding her work variously confessional, political, and technically innovative.

One of the places that haunted her was New Zealand. It was—as "The Doll's House" (*The Dove's Nest*, 1923) suggests—something of a bittersweet memory. She rejected what she saw as New Zealand's provincialism, yet was attracted to its natural beauty—a double perspective clearly shown in "The Doll's House." It is a story about children, but it is an oblique one; it is not about childlike harmony. It is a story which animates instead the chance moments of insight and the codified techniques of social violence which strafe the child's world. As some of her other stories show, they strafe the adult's world as well. But the kind of order Mansfield could craft in prose always eluded her in life. In 1923 she died in France, of tuberculosis, at the Gurdjieff Institute for the Harmonious Development of Man.

FOR FURTHER READING

Paul Delaney, "Short and Simple Annals of the Poor: Katherine Mansfield's 'The Doll's House'," *Mosaic* 10 (Fall 1976): 7-17.

David Dowling, "Aunt Beryl's Doll's House," *Landfall* 34 (June 1980): 148-58.

Kate Fullbrook, *Katherine Mansfield* (Brighton: Harvester, 1986).

Cherry A. Hankin, *Katherine Mansfield and Her Confessional Stories* (London: Macmillan, 1983).

Clare Hanson and Andrew Gurr, *Katherine Mansfield* (London: Macmillan, 1981).

The Doll's House

When dear old Mrs. Hay went back to town after staying with the Burnells she sent the children a doll's house. It was so big that the carter and Pat carried it into the court-yard, and there it stayed, propped up on two wooden boxes beside the feed-room. No harm could come to it; it was summer. And perhaps the smell of paint would have gone off by the time it had to be taken in. For, really, the smell of paint coming from that doll's house ("Sweet of old Mrs. Hay, of course; most sweet and generous!")—but the smell of paint was quite enough to make anyone seriously ill, in Aunt Beryl's opinion. Even before the sacking was taken off. And when it was. . . .

There stood the doll's house, a dark, oily, spinach green, picked out with bright yellow. Its two solid little chimneys, glued on to the roof, were painted red and white, and the door, gleaming with yellow varnish, was like a little slab of toffee. Four windows, real windows, were divided into panes by a broad streak of green. There was actually a tiny porch, too, painted yellow, with big lumps of congealed paint hanging along the edge.

But perfect, perfect little house! Who could possibly mind the smell. It was part of the joy, part of the newness.

"Open it quickly, someone!"

The hook at the side was stuck fast. Pat prised it open with his penknife, and the whole house front swung back, and—there you were, gazing at one and the same moment into the drawing-room and dining-room, the kitchen and two bedrooms. That is the way for a house to open! Why don't all houses open like that? How much more exciting than peering through the slit of a door into a mean little hall with a hat-stand and two umbrellas! That is—isn't it?—what you long to know about a house when you put your hand on the knocker. Perhaps it is the way God opens houses at the dead of night when He is taking a quiet turn with an angel. . . .

"Oh-oh!" The Burnell children sounded as though they were in despair. It was too marvellous; it was too much for them. They had never seen anything like it in their lives. All the rooms were papered. There were pictures on the walls, painted on the paper, with gold frames complete. Red carpet covered all the floors except the kitchen; red plush chairs in the drawing-room, green in the dining-room; tables, beds with real bedclothes, a cradle, a stove, a dresser with tiny plates and one big jug. But what Kezia liked more than anything, what she liked frightfully, was the lamp. It stood in the middle of the dining-room table, an exquisite little amber lamp with a white globe. It was even filled all ready for lighting, though, of course, you couldn't light it. But there was something inside that looked like oil and moved when you shook it.

The father and mother dolls, who sprawled very still as though they had fainted in the drawing-room, and their two little children asleep upstairs, were really too big for the doll's house. They didn't look as though they belonged. But the lamp was perfect. It seemed to smile at Kezia, to say "I live here." The lamp was real.

The Burnell children could hardly walk to school fast enough the next morning. They burned to tell everybody, to describe, to—well—to boast about their doll's house before the schoolbell rang.

"I'm to tell," said Isabel, "because I'm the eldest. And you two can join in after. But I'm to tell first."

There was nothing to answer. Isabel was bossy, but she was always right, and Lottie and Kezia knew too well the powers that went with being eldest. They brushed through the thick buttercups at the road edge and said nothing.

"And I'm to choose who's to come and see it first. Mother said I might."

For it had been arranged that while the doll's house stood in the courtyard they might ask the girls at school, two at a time, to come and look. Not to stay to tea, of course, or to come traipsing through the house. But just to stand quietly in the courtyard while Isabel pointed out the beauties, and Lottie and Kezia looked pleased. . . .

But hurry as they might, by the time they had reached the tarred palings of the boys' playground the bell had begun to jangle. They only just had time to whip off their hats and fall into line before the roll was called. Never mind. Isabel tried to make up for it by looking very important and mysterious and by whispering behind her hand to the girls near her, "Got something to tell you at playtime."

Playtime came and Isabel was surrounded. The girls of her class nearly fought to put their arms round her, to walk away with her, to beam flatteringly, to be her special friend. She held quite a court under the huge pine trees at the side of the playground. Nudging, giggling together, the little girls pressed up close. And the only two who stayed outside the ring were the two who were always outside, the little Kelveys. They knew better than to come anywhere near the Burnells.

For the fact was, the school the Burnell children went to was not at all the kind of place their parents would have chosen if there had been any choice. But there was none. It was the only school for miles. And the consequence was all the children of the neighbourhood, the Judge's little girls, the doctor's daughters, the storekeeper's children, the milkman's, were forced to mix together. Not to speak of there being an equal number of rude, rough little boys as well. But the line had to be drawn somewhere. It was drawn at the Kelveys. Many of the children, including the Burnells, were not allowed even to speak to them. They walked past the Kelveys with their heads in the air, and as they set the fashion in all matters of behaviour, the Kelveys were shunned by everybody.

Even the teacher had a special voice for them, and a special smile for the other children when Lil Kelvey came up to her desk with a bunch of dreadfully common-looking flowers.

They were the daughters of a spry, hard-working little washer-woman, who went about from house to house by the day. This was awful enough. But where was Mr. Kelvey? Nobody knew for certain. But everybody said he was in prison. So they were the daughters of a washerwoman and a gaolbird. Very nice company for other people's children! And they looked it. Why Mrs. Kelvey made them so conspicuous was hard to understand. The truth was they were dressed in "bits" given to her by the people for whom she worked. Lil, for instance, who was a stout, plain child, with big freckles, came to school in a dress made from a green art-serge tablecloth of the Burnells', with red plush sleeves from the Logans' curtains. Her hat, perched on top of her high forehead, was a grown-up woman's hat, once the property of Miss Lecky, the post-mistress. It was turned up at the back and trimmed with a large scarlet quill. What a little guy she looked! It was impossible not to laugh. And her little sister, our Else, wore a long white dress, rather like a nightgown, and a pair of little boy's boots. But whatever our Else wore she would have looked strange. She was a tiny wishbone of a child, with cropped hair and enormous solemn eyes—a little white owl. Nobody had ever seen her smile; she scarcely ever spoke. She went through life holding on to Lil, with a piece of Lil's skirt screwed up in her hand. Where Lil went, our Else followed. In the playground, on the road going to and from school, there was Lil marching in front and our Else holding on behind. Only when she wanted anything, or when she was out of breath, our Else gave Lil a tug, a twitch, and Lil stopped and turned around. The Kelveys never failed to understand each other.

Now they hovered at the edge; you couldn't stop them listening. When the little girls turned round and sneered, Lil, as usual, gave her silly, shamefaced smile, but our Else only looked.

And Isabel's voice, so very proud, went on telling. The carpet made a great sensation, but so did the beds with real bedclothes, and the stove with an oven door.

When she finished Kezia broke in. "You've forgotten the lamp, Isabel."

"Oh yes," said Isabel, "and there's a teeny little lamp, all made of yellow glass, with a white globe that stands on the dining-room table. You couldn't tell it from a real one."

"The lamp's best of all," cried Kezia. She thought Isabel wasn't making half enough of the little lamp. But nobody paid any attention. Isabel was choosing the two who were to come back with them that afternoon and see it. She chose Emmie Cole and Lena Logan. But when the others knew they were all to have a chance, they couldn't be nice enough to Isabel. One by one they put their arms round Isabel's waist and walked her off. They had something to whisper to her, a secret. "Isabel's *my* friend."

Only the little Kelveys moved away forgotten; there was nothing more for them to hear.

Days passed, and as more children saw the doll's house, the fame of it spread. It became the one subject, the rage. The one question was, "Have you seen Burnells' doll's house? Oh, ain't it lovely!" "Haven't you seen it? Oh, I say!"

Even the dinner hour was given up to talking about it. The little girls sat under the pines eating their thick mutton sandwiches and big slabs of johnny cake spread with butter. While always, as near as they could get, sat the Kelveys, our Else holding on to Lil, listening too, while they chewed their jam sandwiches out of a newspaper soaked with large red blobs.

"Mother," said Kezia, "can't I ask the Kelveys just once?"

"Certainly not, Kezia."

"But why not?"

"Run away, Kezia; you know quite well why not."

At last everybody had seen it except them. On that day the subject rather flagged. It was the dinner hour. The children stood together under the pine trees, and suddenly, as they looked at the Kelveys eating out of their paper, always by themselves, always listening, they wanted to be horrid to them. Emmie Cole started the whisper.

"Lil Kelvey's going to be a servant when she grows up."

"O-oh, how awful!" said Isabel Burnell, and she made eyes at Emmie.

Emmie swallowed in a very meaning way and nodded to Isabel as she'd seen her mother do on those occasions.

"It's true—it's true—it's true," she said.

Then Lena Logan's little eyes snapped. "Shall I ask her?" she whispered.

"Bet you don't," said Jessie May.

"Pooh, I'm not frightened," said Lena. Suddenly she gave a little squeal and danced in front of the other girls. "Watch! Watch me! Watch me now!" said Lena. And sliding, gliding, dragging one foot, giggling behind her hand, Lena went over to the Kelveys.

Lil looked up from her dinner. She wrapped the rest quickly away. Our Else stopped chewing. What was coming now?

"Is it true you're going to be a servant when you grow up, Lil Kelvey?" shrilled Lena.

Dead silence. But instead of answering, Lil only gave her silly, shamefaced smile. She didn't seem to mind the question at all. What a sell for Lena! The girls began to titter.

Lena couldn't stand that. She put her hands on her hips; she shot forward. "Yah, yer father's in prison!" she hissed spitefully.

This was such a marvellous thing to have said that the little girls rushed away in a body, deeply, deeply excited, wild with joy. Some one found a long rope, and they began skipping. And never did they skip so high, run in and out so fast, or do such daring things as on that morning.

In the afternoon Pat called for the Burnell children with the buggy and they drove home. There were visitors. Isabel and Lottie, who liked visitors, went upstairs to change their pinafores. But Kezia thieved out at the back. Nobody was about; she began to swing on the big white gates of the courtyard. Presently, looking along the road, she saw two little dots. They grew bigger, they were coming towards her. Now she could see that one was in front and one close behind. Now she could see that they were the Kelveys. Kezia stopped swinging. She slipped off the gate as if she was going to run away. Then she hesitated. The Kelveys came nearer, and beside them walked their shadows, very long, stretching right across the road with their heads in the buttercups. Kezia clambered back on the gate; she had made up her mind; she swung out.

"Hullo," she said to the passing Kelveys.

They were so astounded that they stopped. Lil gave her silly smile. Our Else stared.

"You can come and see our doll's house if you want to," said Kezia, and she dragged one toe on the ground. But at that Lil turned red and shook her head quickly.

"Why not?" asked Kezia.

Lil gasped, then she said, "Your ma told our ma you wasn't to speak to us."

"Oh, well," said Kezia. She didn't know what to reply. "It doesn't matter. You can come and see our doll's house all the same. Come on. Nobody's looking."

But Lil shook her head still harder.

"Don't you want to?" asked Kezia.

Suddenly there was a twitch, a tug at Lil's skirt. She turned round. Our Else was looking at her with big, imploring eyes; she was frowning; she wanted to go. For a moment Lil looked at our Else very doubtfully. But then our Else twitched her skirt again. She started forward. Kezia led the way. Like two little stray cats they followed across the courtyard to where the doll's house stood.

"There it is," said Kezia.

There was a pause. Lil breathed loudly, almost snorted; our Else was still as stone.

"I'll open it for you," said Kezia kindly. She undid the hook and they looked inside.

"There's the drawing-room and the dining-room, and that's the—"

"Kezia!"

Oh, what a start they gave!

"Kezia!"

It was Aunt Beryl's voice. They turned round. At the back door stood Aunt Beryl, staring as if she couldn't believe what she saw.

"How dare you ask the little Kelveys into the courtyard!" said her cold, furious voice. "You know as well as I do, you're not allowed to talk to them. Run away, children, run away at once. And don't come back again," said Aunt Beryl. And she stepped into the yard and shooed them out as if they were chickens.

"Off you go immediately!" she called, cold and proud.

They did not need telling twice. Burning with shame, shrinking together, Lil huddling along like her mother, our Else dazed, somehow they crossed the big courtyard and squeezed through the white gate.

"Wicked, disobedient little girl!" said Aunt Beryl bitterly to Kezia, and she slammed the doll's house to.

The afternoon had been awful. A letter had come from Willie Brent, a terrifying, threatening letter, saying if she did not meet him that evening in Pulman's Bush, he'd come to the front door and ask the reason why! But now that she had frightened those little rats of Kelveys and given Kezia a good scolding, her heart felt lighter. That ghastly pressure was gone. She went back to the house humming.

When the Kelveys were well out of sight of Burnells', they sat down to rest on a big red drainpipe by the side of the road. Lil's cheeks were still burning; she took off the hat with the quill and held it on her knee. Dreamily they looked over the hay paddocks, past the creek, to the group of wattles where Logan's cows stood waiting to be milked. What were their thoughts?

Presently our Else nudged up close to her sister. But now she had forgotten the cross lady. She put out a finger and stroked her sister's quill; she smiled her rare smile.

"I seen the little lamp," she said softly.

Then both were silent once more.

Born in 1952 to a Parsi family in Bombay, Rohinton Mistry emigrated to Canada in 1975, and worked in a Toronto bank. His writing career began in 1983, with a short story contributed to a literary competition, and two years later he gave up his banking job to write full time. Following a brief sojourn in California, Mistry returned to Canada, and now lives in Brampton, Ontario.

"Swimming Lessons" is the concluding story in Mistry's collection, *Tales from Firozsha Baag* (1987), a finalist for the Governor-General's Award for fiction. The other stories are set in Firozsha Baag (an apartment complex in Bombay recalled by the narrator), and trace the interconnected lives of the various individuals who live there. "Swimming Lessons," in contrast, records the efforts of the narrator to accommodate himself to the unfamiliar culture he encounters in Canada, and his concerns about explaining to his parents in India his sense of difference and dislocation. By immersing himself in a new culture, he has begun to lose touch with the rituals and traditions that had previously shaped his life. In this context, the swimming lessons suggest, however, that he is also learning to adapt to his new environment.

FOR FURTHER READING

Geoff Hancock, "An Interview with Rohinton Mistry," *Canadian Fiction Magazine* 65 (1989): 143-50.

W.H. New, "A Shaping of Connections" in *A Shaping of Connections*, ed. Hena Maes-Jelinek et al. (Aarhus: Dangaroo, 1989): 154-63.

Swimming Lessons

The old man's wheelchair is audible today as he creaks by in the hallway: on some days it's just a smooth whirr. Maybe the way he slumps in it, or the way his weight rests has something to do with it. Down to the lobby he goes, and sits there most of the time, talking to people on their way out or in. That's where he first spoke to me a few days ago. I was waiting for the elevator, back from Eaton's with my new pair of swimming-trunks.

"Hullo," he said. I nodded, smiled.

"Beautiful summer day we've got."

"Yes," I said, "it's lovely outside."

He shifted the wheelchair to face me squarely. "How old do you think I am?"

I looked at him blankly, and he said, "Go on, take a guess."

I understood the game; he seemed about seventy-five although the hair was still black, so I said, "Sixty-five?" He made a sound between a chuckle and a wheeze: "I'll be seventy-seven next month." Close enough.

I've heard him ask that question several times since, and everyone plays by the rules. Their faked guesses range from sixty to seventy. They pick a lower number when he's more depressed than usual. He reminds me of Grandpa as he sits on the sofa in the lobby, staring out vacantly at the parking lot. Only difference is, he sits with the stillness of stroke victims, while Grandpa's Parkinson's disease would bounce his thighs and legs and arms all over the place. When he could no longer hold the *Bombay Samachar* steady enough to read, Grandpa took to sitting on the veranda and staring emptily at the traffic passing outside Firozsha Baag. Or waving to anyone who went by in the compound: Rustomji, Nariman Hansotia in his 1932 Mercedes-Benz, the fat ayah Jaakaylee with her shopping-bag, the *kuchrawalli* with her basket and long bamboo broom.

The Portuguese woman across the hall has told me a little about the old man. She is the communicator for the apartment building. To gather and disseminate information, she takes the liberty of unabashedly throwing open her door when newsworthy events transpire. Not for Portuguese Woman the furtive peerings from thin cracks or spyholes. She reminds me of a character in a movie, *Barefoot In The Park* I think it was, who left empty beer cans by the landing for anyone passing to stumble and give her the signal. But PW does not need beer cans. The gutang-khutang of the elevator opening and closing is enough.

The old man's daughter looks after him. He was living alone till his stroke, which coincided with his youngest daughter's divorce in Vancouver. She returned to him and they moved into this low-rise in Don Mills. PW says the daughter talks to no one in the building but takes good care of her father.

Mummy used to take good care of Grandpa, too, till things became complicated and he was moved to the Parsi General Hospital. Parkinsonism and osteoporosis laid him low. The doctor explained that Grandpa's hip did not break because he fell, but he fell because the hip, gradually growing brittle, snapped on that fatal day. That's what osteoporosis does, hollows out the bones and turns effect into cause. It has an unusually high incidence in the Parsi community, he said, but did not say why. Just one of those mysterious things. We are the chosen people where osteoporosis is concerned. And divorce. The Parsi community has the highest divorce rate in India. It also claims to be the most westernized community in India. Which is the result of the other? Confusion again, of cause and effect.

The hip was put in traction. Single-handed, Mummy struggled valiantly with bedpans and dressings for bedsores which soon appeared like grim spectres on his back. *Mamaiji*, bent double with her weak back, could give no assistance. My help would be enlisted to roll him over on his side while Mummy changed the dressing. But after three months, the doctor pronounced a patch upon Grandpa's lungs, and the male ward of Parsi General swallowed him up. There was no money for a private nursing home. I went to see him once, at Mummy's insistence. She used to say that the blessings of an old person were the most valuable and potent of all, they would last my whole life long. The ward had rows and rows of beds; the din was enormous, the smells nauseating, and it was just as well that Grandpa passed most of his time in a less than conscious state.

But I should have gone to see him more often. Whenever Grandpa went out, while he still could in the days before parkinsonism, he would bring back pink and white sugar-coated almonds for Percy and me. Every time I remember Grandpa, I remember that; and then I think: I should have gone to see him more often. That's what I also thought when our telephone-owning neighbour, esteemed by all for that reason, sent his son to tell us the hospital had phoned that Grandpa died an hour ago.

The postman rang the doorbell the way he always did, long and continuous; Mother went to open it, wanting to give him a piece of her mind but thought better of it, she did not want to risk the vengeance of postmen, it was so easy for them to destroy letters; workers nowadays thought no end of themselves, strutting around like peacocks, ever since all this Shiv Sena agitation about Maharashtra for Maharashtrians, threatening strikes and Bombay bundh all the time, with no respect for the public; bus drivers and conductors were the worst, behaving as if they owned the buses and were doing favours to commuters, pulling the bell before you were in the bus, the driver purposely braking and moving with big jerks to make the standees lose their balance, the conductor so rude if you did not have the right change.

But when she saw the airmail envelope with a Canadian stamp her face lit up, she said wait to the postman, and went in for a fifty paisa piece, a little baksheesh for you, she told him, then shut the door and kissed the envelope, went in running, saying my son has written, my son has sent a letter, and Father looked up from the newspaper and said, don't get too excited, first read it, you know what kind of letters he writes, a few lines of empty words, I'm fine, hope you are all right, your loving son—that kind of writing I don't call letter-writing.

Then Mother opened the envelope and took out one small page and began to read silently, and the joy brought to her face by the letter's arrival began to ebb; Father saw it happening and knew he was right, he said read aloud, let me also hear what our son is writing this time, so Mother read: My dear Mummy and Daddy, Last winter was terrible, we had record-breaking low temperatures all through February and March, and the first official day of spring was colder than the first official day of winter had been, but it's getting warmer now. Looks like it will be a nice warm summer. You asked about my new apartment. It's small, but not bad at all. This is just a quick note to let you know I'm fine, so you won't worry about me. Hope everything is okay at home.

After Mother put it back in the envelope, Father said everything about his life is locked in silence and secrecy, I still don't understand why he bothered to visit us last year if he had nothing to say; every letter of his has been a quick note so we won't worry—what does he think we worry about, his health, in that country everyone eats well whether they work or not, he should be worrying about us with all the black market and rationing, has he forgotten already how he used to go to the ration-shop and wait in line every week; and what kind of apartment description is that, not bad at all; and if it is a Canadian weather report I need from him, I can go with Nariman Hansotia from A Block to the Cawasji Framji Memorial Library and read all about it, there they get newspapers from all over the world.

The sun is hot today. Two women are sunbathing on the stretch of patchy lawn at the periphery of the parking lot. I can see them clearly from my kitchen. They're wearing bikinis and I'd love to take a closer look. But I have no binoculars. Nor do I have a car to saunter out to and pretend to look under the hood. They're both luscious and gleaming. From time to time they smear lotion over their skin, on the bellies, on the inside of the thighs, on the shoulders. Then one of them gets the other to undo the string of her top and spread some there. She lies on her stomach with the straps undone. I wait. I pray that the heat and haze make her forget, when it's time to turn over, that the straps are undone.

But the sun is not hot enough to work this magic for me. When it's time to come in, she flips over, deftly holding up the cups, and reties the top. They arise, pick up towels, lotions and magazines, and return to the building.

This is my chance to see them closer. I race down the stairs to the lobby. The old man says hullo. "Down again?"

"My mailbox," I mumble.

"It's Saturday," he chortles. For some reason he finds it extremely funny. My eye is on the door leading in from the parking lot.

Through the glass panel I see them approaching. I hurry to the elevator and wait. In the dimly lit lobby I can see their eyes are having trouble adjusting after the bright sun. They don't seem as attractive as they did from the kitchen window. The elevator arrives and I hold it open, inviting them in with what I think is a gallant flourish. Under the fluorescent glare in the elevator I see their wrinkled skin, aging hands, sagging bottoms, varicose veins. The lustrous trick of sun and lotion and distance has ended.

I step out and they continue to the third floor. I have Monday night to look forward to, my first swimming lesson. The high school behind the apartment building is offering, among its usual assortment of macramé and ceramics and pottery classes, a class for non-swimming adults.

The woman at the registration desk is quite friendly. She even gives me the opening to satisfy the compulsion I have about explaining my non-swimming status.

"Are you from India?" she asks. I nod. "I hope you don't mind my asking, but I was curious because an Indian couple, husband and wife, also registered a few minutes ago. Is swimming not encouraged in India?"

"On the contrary," I say. "Most Indians swim like fish. I'm an exception to the rule. My house was five minutes walking distance from

Chaupatty beach in Bombay. It's one of the most beautiful beaches in Bombay, or was, before the filth took over. Anyway, even though we lived so close to it, I never learned to swim. It's just one of those things."

"Well," says the woman, "that happens sometimes. Take me, for instance, I never learned to ride a bicycle. It was the mounting that used to scare me, I was afraid of falling." People have lined up behind me. "It's been very nice talking to you," she says, "hope you enjoy the course."

The art of swimming had been trapped between the devil and the deep blue sea. The devil was money, always scarce, and kept the private swimming clubs out of reach; the deep blue sea of Chaupatty beach was grey and murky with garbage, too filthy to swim in. Every so often we would muster our courage and Mummy would take me there to try and teach me. But a few minutes of paddling was all we could endure. Sooner or later something would float up against our legs or thighs or waists, depending on how deep we'd gone in, and we'd be revulsed and stride out to the sand.

Water imagery in my life is recurring. Chaupatty beach, now the high-school swimming pool. The universal symbol of life and regeneration did nothing but frustrate me. Perhaps the swimming pool will overturn that failure.

When images and symbols abound in this manner, sprawling or rolling across the page without guile or artifice, one is prone to say, how obvious, how skilless; symbols, after all, should be still and gentle as dewdrops, tiny, yet shining with a world of meaning. But what happens when, on the page of life itself, one encounters the ever-moving, all-engirdling sprawl of the filthy sea? Dewdrops and oceans both have their rightful places; Nariman Hansotia certainly knew that when he told his stories to the boys of Firozsha Baag.

The sea of Chaupatty was fated to endure the finales of life's everyday functions. It seemed that the dirtier it became, the more crowds it attracted: street urchins and beggars and beachcombers, looking through the junk that washed up. (Or was it the crowds that made it dirtier?—another instance of cause and effect blurring and evading identification.)

Too many religious festivals also used the sea as repository for their finales. Its use should have been rationed, like rice and kerosene. On Ganesh Chaturthi, clay idols of the god Ganesh, adorned with garlands and all manner of finery, were carried in processions to the accompaniment of drums and a variety of wind instruments. The music got more frenzied the closer the procession got to Chaupatty and to the moment of immersion.

Then there was Coconut Day, which was never as popular as Ganesh Chaturthi. From a bystander's viewpoint, coconuts chucked into the sea do not provide as much of a spectacle. We used the sea, too, to deposit the leftovers from Parsi religious ceremonies, things such as flowers, or the ashes of the sacred sandalwood fire, which just could not be dumped with the regular garbage but had to be entrusted to the care of Avan Yazad, the guardian of the sea. And things which were of no use but which no one had the heart to destroy were also given to Avan Yazad. Such as old photographs.

After Grandpa died, some of his things were flung out to sea. It was high tide; we always checked the newspaper when going to perform these disposals; an ebb would mean a long walk in squelchy sand before finding water. Most of the things were probably washed up on shore. But we tried to throw them as far out as possible, then waited a few minutes; if they did not float back right away we would pretend they were in the permanent safekeeping of Avan Yazad, which was a comforting thought. I can't remember everything we sent out to sea, but his brush and comb were in the parcel, his *kusti*, and some Kemadrin pills, which he used to take to keep the parkinsonism under control.

Our paddling sessions stopped for lack of enthusiasm on my part. Mummy wasn't too keen either, because of the filth. But my main concern was the little guttersnipes, like naked fish with little buoyant penises, taunting me with their skills, swimming underwater and emerging unexpectedly all around me, or pretending to masturbate—I think they were too young to achieve ejaculation. It was embarrassing. When I look back, I'm surprised that Mummy and I kept going as long as we did.

I examine the swimming-trunks I bought last week. Surf King, says the label, Made in Canada-Fabriqué Au Canada. I've been learning bits and pieces of French from bilingual labels at the supermarket too. These trunks are extremely sleek and streamlined hipsters, the distance from waistband to pouch tip the barest minimum. I wonder how everything will stay in place, not that I'm boastful about my endowments. I try them on, and feel that the tip of my member lingers perilously close to the exit. Too close, in fact, to conceal the exigencies of my swimming lesson fantasy: a gorgeous woman in the class for non-swimmers, at whose sight I will be instantly aroused, and she, spying the shape of my desire, will look me straight in the eye with her intentions; she will come home with me, to taste the pleasures of my delectable Asian brown body whose strangeness has intrigued her and unleashed uncontrollable surges of passion inside her throughout the duration of the swimming lesson.

I drop the Eaton's bag and wrapper in the garbage can. The swimming-trunks cost fifteen dollars, same as the fee for the ten weekly lessons. The garbage bag is almost full. I tie it up and take it outside. There is a medicinal smell in the hallway; the old man must have just returned to his apartment.

PW opens her door and says, "Two ladies from the third floor were lying in the sun this morning. In bikinis."

"That's nice," I say, and walk to the incinerator chute. She reminds me of Najamai in Firozsha Baag, except that Najamai employed a bit more subtlety while going about her life's chosen work.

PW withdraws and shuts her door.

Mother had to reply because Father said he did not want to write to his son till his son had something sensible to write to him, his questions had been ignored long enough, and if he wanted to keep his life a secret, fine, he would get no letters from his father.

But after Mother started the letter he went and looked over her shoulder, telling her what to ask him, because if they kept on writing the same questions, maybe he would understand how interested they were in knowing about things over there; Father said go on, ask him what his work is at the insurance company, tell him to take some courses at night school, that's how everyone moves ahead over there, tell him not to be discouraged if his job is just clerical right now, hard work will get him ahead, remind him he is a Zoroastrian: man-ashni, gavashni, kunashni, *better write the translation also: good thoughts, good words, good deeds—he must have forgotten what it means, and tell him to say prayers and do* kusti *at least twice a day.*

Writing it all down sadly, Mother did not believe he wore his sudra *and* kusti *anymore, she would be very surprised if he remembered any of the prayers; when she had asked him if he needed new* sudras *he said not to take any trouble because the Zoroastrian Society of Ontario imported them from Bombay for their members, and this sounded like a story he was making up, but she was leaving it in the hands of God, ten thousand miles away there was nothing she could do but write a letter and hope for the best.*

Then she sealed it, and Father wrote the address on it as usual because his writing was much neater than hers, handwriting was important in the address and she did not want the postman in Canada to make any mistake; she took it to the post office herself, it was impossible to trust anyone to mail it ever since the postage rates went up because people just tore off the stamps for their own use and threw away the letter, the only safe way was to hand it over the counter and make the clerk cancel the stamps before your own eyes.

Berthe, the building superintendent, is yelling at her son in the parking lot. He tinkers away with his van. This happens every fine-weathered Sunday. It must be the van that Berthe dislikes because I've seen mother and son together in other quite amicable situations.

Berthe is a big Yugoslavian with high cheekbones. Her nationality was disclosed to me by PW. Berthe speaks a very rough-hewn English, I've overheard her in the lobby scolding tenants for late rents and leaving dirty lint screens in the dryers. It's exciting to listen to her, her words fall like rocks and boulders, and one can never tell where or how the next few will drop. But her Slavic yells at her son are a different matter, the words fly swift and true, well-aimed missiles that never miss. Finally, the son slams down the hood in disgust, wipes his hands on a rag, accompanies mother Berthe inside.

Berthe's husband has a job in a factory. But he loses several days of work every month when he succumbs to the booze, a word Berthe uses often in her Slavic tirades on those days, the only one I can understand, as it clunks down heavily out of the tight-flying formation of Yugoslavian sentences. He lolls around in the lobby, submitting passively to his wife's tongue-lashings. The bags under his bloodshot eyes, his stringy moustache, stubbled chin, dirty hair are so vulnerable to the poison-laden barbs (poison works the same way in any language) emanating from deep within the powerful watermelon bosom. No one's presence can embarrass or dignify her into silence.

No one except the old man who arrives now. "Good morning," he says, and Berthe turns, stops yelling, and smiles. Her husband rises, positions the wheelchair at the favourite angle. The lobby will be peaceful as long as the old man is there.

It was hopeless. My first swimming lesson. The water terrified me. When did that happen, I wonder, I used to love splashing at Chaupatty, carried about by the waves. And this was only a swimming pool. Where did all that terror come from? I'm trying to remember.

Armed with my Surf King I enter the high school and go to the pool area. A sheet with instructions for the new class is pinned to the bulletin board. All students must shower and then assemble at eight by the shallow end. As I enter the showers three young boys, probably from a previous class, emerge. One of them holds his nose. The second begins to hum, under his breath: Paki Paki, smell like curry. The third says to the first two: pretty soon all the water's going to taste of curry. They leave.

It's a mixed class, but the gorgeous woman of my fantasy is missing. I have to settle for another, in a pink one-piece suit, with brown hair and a bit of a stomach. She must be about thirty-five. Plain-looking.

The instructor is called Ron. He gives us a pep talk, sensing some nervousness in the group. We're finally all in the water, in the shallow end. He demonstrates floating on the back, then asks for a volunteer. The pink one-piece suit wades forward. He supports her, tells her to lean back and let her head drop in the water.

She does very well. And as we all regard her floating body, I see what was not visible outside the pool: her bush, curly bits of it, straying out at the pink Spandex V. Tongues of water lapping against her delta, as if caressing it teasingly, make the brown hair come alive in a most tantalizing manner. The crests and troughs of little waves, set off by the movement of our bodies in a circle around her, dutifully irrigate her;

the curls alternately wave free inside the crest, then adhere to her wet thighs, beached by the inevitable trough. I could watch this forever, and I wish the floating demonstration would never end.

Next we are shown how to grasp the rail and paddle, face down in the water. Between practising floating and paddling, the hour is almost gone. I have been trying to observe the pink one-piece suit, getting glimpses of her straying pubic hair from various angles. Finally, Ron wants a volunteer for the last demonstration, and I go forward. To my horror he leads the class to the deep end. Fifteen feet of water. It is so blue, and I can see the bottom. He picks up a metal hoop attached to a long wooden stick. He wants me to grasp the hoop, jump in the water, and paddle, while he guides me by the stick. Perfectly safe, he tells me. A demonstration of how paddling propels the body.

It's too late to back out; besides, I'm so terrified I couldn't find the words to do so even if I wanted to. Everything he says I do as if in a trance. I don't remember the moment of jumping. The next thing I know is, I'm swallowing water and floundering, hanging on to the hoop for dear life. Ron draws me to the rails and helps me out. The class applauds.

We disperse and one thought is on my mind: what if I'd lost my grip? Fifteen feet of water under me. I shudder and take deep breaths. This is it. I'm not coming next week. This instructor is an irresponsible person. Or he does not value the lives of non-white immigrants. I remember the three teenagers. Maybe the swimming pool is the hangout of some racist group, bent on eliminating all non-white swimmers, to keep their waters pure and their white sisters unogled.

The elevator takes me upstairs. Then gutang-khutang. PW opens her door as I turn the corridor of medicinal smells. "Berthe was screaming loudly at her husband tonight," she tells me.

"Good for her," I say, and she frowns indignantly at me.

The old man is in the lobby. He's wearing thick wool gloves. He wants to know how the swimming was, must have seen me leaving with my towel yesterday. Not bad, I say.

"I used to swim a lot. Very good for the circulation." He wheezes. "My feet are cold all the time. Cold as ice. Hands too."

Summer is winding down, so I say stupidly, "Yes, it's not so warm any more."

The thought of the next swimming lesson sickens me. But as I comb through the memories of that terrifying Monday, I come upon the straying curls of brown pubic hair. Inexorably drawn by them, I decide to go.

It's a mistake, of course. This time I'm scared even to venture in the shallow end. When everyone has entered the water and I'm the only one outside, I feel a little foolish and slide in.

Instructor Ron says we should start by reviewing the floating technique. I'm in no hurry. I watch the pink one-piece pull the swim-suit down around her cheeks and flip back to achieve perfect flotation. And then reap disappointment. The pink Spandex triangle is perfectly streamlined today, nothing strays, not a trace of fuzz, not one filament, not even a sign of post-depilation irritation. Like the airbrushed parts of glamour magazine models. The barrenness of her impeccably packaged apex is a betrayal. Now she is shorn like the other women in the class. Why did she have to do it?

The weight of this disappointment makes the water less manageable, more lung-penetrating. With trepidation, I float and paddle my way through the remainder of the hour, jerking my head out every two seconds and breathing deeply, to continually shore up a supply of precious, precious air without, at the same time, seeming too anxious and losing my dignity.

I don't attend the remaining classes. After I've missed three, Ron the instructor telephones. I tell him I've had the flu and am still feeling poorly, but I'll try to be there the following week.

He does not call again. My Surf King is relegated to an unused drawer. Total losses: one fantasy plus thirty dollars. And no watery rebirth. The swimming pool, like Chaupatty beach, has produced a stillbirth. But there is a difference. Water means regeneration only if it is pure and cleansing. Chaupatty was filthy, the pool was not. Failure to swim through filth must mean something other than failure of rebirth—failure of symbolic death? Does that equal success of symbolic life? death of a symbolic failure? death of a symbol? What is the equation?

The postman did not bring a letter but a parcel, he was smiling because he knew that every time something came from Canada his baksheesh was guaranteed, and this time because it was a parcel Mother gave him a whole rupee, she was quite excited, there were so many stickers on it besides the stamps, one for Small Parcel, another Printed Papers, a red sticker saying Insured; she showed it to Father, and opened it, then put both hands on her cheeks, not able to speak because the surprise and happiness was so great, tears came to her eyes and she could not stop smiling, till Father became impatient to know and finally got up and came to the table.

When he saw it he was surprised and happy too, he began to grin, then hugged Mother saying our son is a writer, and we didn't even know it, he never told us a thing, here we are thinking he is still clerking away at the insurance company, and he has written a book of stories, all these years in school and college he kept his talent hidden, making us think he was just like one of the boys in the Baag, shouting and playing the fool in the compound, and now what a surprise; then Father opened the book and began reading it, heading back to the easy chair, and Mother so excited, still holding his arm, walked with him, saying it was not fair him reading it first, she wanted to read it too, and they agreed that he would read the first story, then give it to her so she could also read it, and they would take turns in that manner.

Mother removed the staples from the padded envelope in which he had mailed the book, and threw them away, then straightened the folded edges of the envelope and put it away safely with the other envelopes and letters she had collected since he left.

The leaves are beginning to fall. The only ones I can identify are maple. The days are dwindling like the leaves. I've started a habit of taking long walks every evening. The old man is in the lobby when I leave, he waves as I go by. By the time I'm back, the lobby is usually empty.

Today I was woken up by a grating sound outside that made my flesh crawl. I went to the window and saw Berthe raking the leaves in the parking lot. Not in the expanse of patchy lawn on the periphery, but in the parking lot proper. She was raking the black tarred surface. I went back to bed and dragged a pillow over my head, not releasing it till noon.

When I return from my walk in the evening, PW, summoned by the elevator's gutang-khutang, says, "Berthe filled six big black garbage bags with leaves today."

"Six bags!" I say. "Wow!"

Since the weather turned cold, Berthe's son does not tinker with his van on Sundays under my window. I'm able to sleep late.

Around eleven, there's a commotion outside. I reach out and switch on the clock radio. It's a sunny day, the window curtains are bright. I get up, curious, and see a black Olds Ninety-Eight in the parking lot, by the entrance to the building. The old man is in his wheelchair, bundled up, with a scarf wound several times round his neck as though to immobilize it, like a surgical collar. His daughter and another man, the car-owner, are helping him from the wheelchair into the front seat, encouraging him with words like: that's it, easy does it, attaboy. From the open door of the lobby, Berthe is shouting encouragement too, but hers is confined to one word: yah, repeated at different levels of pitch and volume, with variations on vowel-length. The stranger could be the old man's son, he has the same jet black hair and piercing eyes.

Maybe the old man is not well, it's an emergency. But I quickly scrap that thought—this isn't Bombay, an ambulance would have arrived. They're probably taking him out for a ride. If he is his son, where has he been all this time, I wonder.

The old man finally settles in the front seat, the wheelchair goes in the trunk, and they're off. The one I think is the son looks up and catches me at the window before I can move away, so I wave, and he waves back.

In the afternoon I take down a load of clothes to the laundry room. Both machines have completed their cycles, the clothes inside are waiting to be transferred to dryers. Should I remove them and place them on top of a dryer, or wait? I decide to wait. After a few minutes, two women arrive, they are in bathrobes, and smoking. It takes me a while to realize that these are the two disappointments who were sunbathing in bikinis last summer.

"You didn't have to wait, you could have removed the clothes and carried on, dear," says one. She has a Scottish accent. It's one of the few I've learned to identify. Like maple leaves.

"Well," I say, "some people might not like strangers touching their clothes."

"You're not a stranger, dear," she says, "you live in this building, we've seen you before."

"Besides, your hands are clean," the other one pipes in. "You can touch my things any time you like."

Horny old cow. I wonder what they've got on under their bathrobes. Not much, I find, as they bend over to place their clothes in the dryers.

"See you soon," they say, and exit, leaving me behind in an erotic wake of smoke and perfume and deep images of cleavages. I start the washers and depart, and when I come back later, the dryers are empty.

PW tells me, "The old man's son took him out for a drive today. He has a big beautiful black car."

I see my chance, and shoot back: "Olds Ninety-Eight."

"What?"

"The car," I explain, "it's an Oldsmobile Ninety-Eight."

She does not like this at all, my giving her information. She is visibly nettled, and retreats with a sour face.

Mother and Father read the first five stories, and she was very sad after reading some of them, she said he must be so unhappy there, all his stories are about Bombay, he remembers every little thing about his childhood, he is thinking about it all the time even though he is ten thousand miles away, my poor son, I think he misses his home and us and everything he left behind, because if he likes it over there why would he not write stories about that, there must be so many new ideas that his new life could give him.

But Father did not agree with this, he said it did not mean that he was unhappy, all writers worked in the same way, they used their memories and experiences and made stories out of them, changing some things, adding some, imagining some, all writers were very good at remembering details of their lives.

Mother said, how can you be sure that he is remembering because he is a writer, or whether he started to write because he is unhappy and thinks of his past, and wants to save it all by making stories of it; and Father said that is not a sensible question, anyway, it is now my turn to read the next story.

The first snow has fallen, and the air is crisp. It's not very deep, about two inches, just right to go for a walk in. I've been told that immigrants from hot countries always enjoy the snow the first year, maybe for a couple of years more, then inevitably the dread sets in, and the approach of winter gets them fretting and moping. On the other hand, if it hadn't been for my conversation with the woman at the swimming registration desk, they might now be saying that India is a nation of non-swimmers.

Berthe is outside, shovelling the snow off the walkway in the parking lot. She has a heavy, wide pusher which she wields expertly.

The old radiators in the apartment alarm me incessantly. They continue to broadcast a series of variations on death throes, and go from hot to cold and cold to hot at will, there's no controlling their temperature. I speak to Berthe about it in the lobby. The old man is there too, his chin seems to have sunk deeper into his chest, and his face is a yellowish grey.

"Nothing, not to worry about anything," says Berthe, dropping rough-hewn chunks of language around me. "Radiator no work, you tell me. You feel cold, you come to me, I keep you warm," and she opens her arms wide, laughing. I step back, and she advances, her breasts preceding her like the gallant prows of two ice-breakers. She looks at the old man to see if he is appreciating the act: "You no feel scared, I keep you safe and warm."

But the old man is staring outside, at the flakes of falling snow. What thoughts is he thinking as he watches them? Of childhood days, perhaps, and snowmen with hats and pipes, and snowball fights, and white Christmases, and Christmas trees? What will I think of, old in this country, when I sit and watch the snow come down? For me, it is already too late for snowmen and snowball fights, and all I will have is thoughts about childhood thoughts and dreams, built around snowscapes and winter wonderlands on the Christmas cards so popular in Bombay; my snowmen and snowball fights and Christmas trees are in the pages of Enid Blyton's books, dispersed amidst the adventures of the Famous Five, and the Five Find-Outers, and the Secret Seven. My snowflakes are even less forgettable than the old man's, for they never melt.

It finally happened. The heat went. Not the usual intermittent coming and going, but out completely. Stone cold. The radiators are like ice. And so is everything else. There's no hot water. Naturally. It's the hot water that goes through the rads and heats them. Or is it the other way around? Is there no hot water because the rads have stopped circulating it? I don't care, I'm too cold to sort out the cause and effect relationship. Maybe there is no connection at all.

I dress quickly, put on my winter jacket, and go down to the lobby.
The elevator is not working because the power is out, so I take the
stairs. Several people are gathered, and Berthe has announced that she
has telephoned the office, they are sending a man. I go back up the
stairs. It's only one floor, the elevator is just a bad habit. Back in
Firozsha Baag they were broken most of the time. The stairway enters
the corridor outside the old man's apartment, and I think of his cold
feet and hands. Poor man, it must be horrible for him without heat.

As I walk down the long hallway, I feel there's something different
but can't pin it down. I look at the carpet, the ceiling, the wallpaper: it
all seems the same. Maybe it's the freezing cold that imparts a feeling
of difference.

PW opens her door: "The old man had another stroke yesterday.
They took him to the hospital."

The medicinal smell. That's it. It's not in the hallway any more.

*In the stories that he'd read so far Father said that all the Parsi families were
poor or middle-class, but that was okay; nor did he mind that the seeds for the
stories were picked from the sufferings of their own lives; but there should also
have been something positive about Parsis, there was so much to be proud of: the
great Tatas and their contribution to the steel industry, or Sir Dinshaw Petit
in the textile industry who made Bombay the Manchester of the East, or
Dadabhai Naoroji in the freedom movement, where he was the first to use the
word swaraj, and the first to be elected to the British Parliament where he carried on his campaign; he should have found some way to bring some of these
wonderful facts into his stories, what would people reading these stories think,
those who did not know about Parsis—that the whole community was full of
cranky, bigoted people; and in reality it was the richest, most advanced and
philanthropic community in India, and he did not need to tell his own son that
Parsis had a reputation for being generous and family-oriented. And he could
have written something also about the historic background, how Parsis came to
India from Persia because of Islamic persecution in the seventh century, and
were the descendants of Cyrus the Great and the magnificent Persian Empire.
He could have made a story of all this, couldn't he?*

*Mother said what she liked best was his remembering everything so well, how
beautifully he wrote about it all, even the sad things, and though he changed
some of it, and used his imagination, there was truth in it.*

*My hope is, Father said, that there will be some story based on his Canadian
experience, that way we will know something about our son's life there, if not
through his letters then in his stories; so far they are all about Parsis and
Bombay, and the one with a little bit about Toronto, where a man perches on
top of the toilet, is shameful and disgusting, although it is funny at times and
did make me laugh, I have to admit, but where does he get such an imagination
from, what is the point of such a fantasy; and Mother said that she would also
enjoy some stories about Toronto and the people there; it puzzles me, she said,*

why he writes nothing about it, especially since you say that writers use their own experience to make stories out of.

Then Father said this is true, but he is probably not using his Toronto experience because it is too early; what do you mean, too early, asked Mother and Father explained it takes a writer about ten years time after an experience before he is able to use it in his writing, it takes that long to be absorbed internally and understood, thought out and thought about, over and over again, he haunts it and it haunts him if it is valuable enough, till the writer is comfortable with it to be able to use it as he wants; but this is only one theory I read somewhere, it may or may not be true.

That means, said Mother, that his childhood in Bombay and our home here is the most valuable thing in his life just now, because he is able to remember it all to write about it, and you were so bitterly saying he is forgetting where he came from; and that may be true, said Father, but that is not what the theory means, according to the theory he is writing of these things because they are far enough in the past for him to deal with objectively, he is able to achieve what critics call artistic distance, without emotions interfering; and what do you mean emotions, said Mother, you are saying he does not feel anything for his characters, how can he write so beautifully about so many sad things without any feelings in his heart?

But before Father could explain more, about beauty and emotion and inspiration and imagination, Mother took the book and said it was her turn now and too much theory she did not want to listen to, it was confusing and did not make as much sense as reading the stories, she would read them her way and Father could read them his.

My books on the windowsill have been damaged. Ice has been forming on the inside ledge, which I did not notice, and melting when the sun shines in. I spread them in a corner of the living-room to dry out.

The winter drags on. Berthe wields her snow pusher as expertly as ever, but there are signs of weariness in her performance. Neither husband nor son is ever seen outside with a shovel. Or anywhere else, for that matter. It occurs to me that the son's van is missing, too.

The medicinal smell is in the hall again. I sniff happily and look forward to seeing the old man in the lobby. I go downstairs and peer into the mailbox, see the blue and magenta of an Indian aerogramme with Don Mills, Ontario, Canada in Father's flawless hand through the slot.

I pocket the letter and enter the main lobby. The old man is there, but not in his usual place. He is not looking out through the glass door. His wheelchair is facing a bare wall where the wallpaper is torn in places. As though he is not interested in the outside world any more, having finished with all that, and now it's time to see inside. What does he see inside, I wonder? I go up to him and say hullo. He says hullo without raising his sunken chin. After a few seconds his grey countenance faces me. "How old do you think I am?" His eyes are dull and glazed; he is looking even further inside than I first presumed.

"Well, let's see, you're probably close to sixty-four."

"I'll be seventy-eight next August." But he does not chuckle or wheeze. Instead, he continues softly, "I wish my feet did not feel so cold all the time. And my hands." He lets his chin fall again.

In the elevator I start opening the aerogramme, a tricky business because a crooked tear means lost words. Absorbed in this while emerging, I don't notice PW occupying the centre of the hallway, arms folded across her chest: "They had a big fight. Both of them have left."

I don't immediately understand her agitation. "What . . . who?"

"Berthe. Husband and son both left her. Now she is all alone."

Her tone and stance suggest that we should not be standing here talking but do something to bring Berthe's family back. "That's very sad," I say, and go in. I picture father and son in the van, driving away, driving across the snow-covered country, in the dead of winter, away from wife and mother; away to where? how far will they go? Not son's van nor father's booze can take them far enough. And the further they go, the more they'll remember, they can take it from me.

All the stories were read by Father and Mother, and they were sorry when the book was finished, they felt they had come to know their son better now, yet there was much more to know, they wished there were many more stories; and this is what they mean, said Father, when they say that the whole story can never be told, the whole truth can never be known; what do you mean, they say, asked Mother, who they, and Father said writers, poets, philosophers. I don't care what they say, said Mother, my son will write as much or as little as he wants to, and if I can read it I will be happy.

The last story they liked the best of all because it had the most in it about Canada, and now they felt they knew at least a little bit, even if it was a very little bit, about his day-to-day life in his apartment; and Father said if he continues to write about such things he will become popular because I am sure they are interested there in reading about life through the eyes of an immigrant, it provides a different viewpoint; the only danger is if he changes and becomes so much like them that he will write like one of them and lose the important dif-ference.

The bathroom needs cleaning. I open a new can of Ajax and scour the tub. Sloshing with mug from bucket was standard bathing procedure in the bathrooms of Firozsha Baag, so my preference now is always for a shower. I've never used the tub as yet; besides, it would be too much like Chaupatty or the swimming pool, wallowing in my own dirt. Still, it must be cleaned.

When I've finished, I prepare for a shower. But the clean gleaming tub and the nearness of the vernal equinox give me the urge to do something different today. I find the drain plug in the bathroom cabinet, and run the bath.

I've spoken so often to the old man, but I don't know his name. I should have asked him the last time I saw him, when his wheelchair was facing the bare wall because he had seen all there was to see outside and it was time to see what was inside. Well, tomorrow. Or better yet, I can look it up in the directory in the lobby. Why didn't I think of that before? It will only have an initial and a last name, but then I can surprise him with: hullo Mr Wilson, or whatever it is.

The bath is full. Water imagery is recurring in my life: Chaupatty beach, swimming pool, bathtub. I step in and immerse myself up to the neck. It feels good. The hot water loses its opacity when the chlorine, or whatever it is, has cleared. My hair is still dry. I close my eyes, hold my breath, and dunk my head. Fighting the panic, I stay under and count to thirty. I come out, clear my lungs and breathe deeply.

I do it again. This time I open my eyes under water, and stare blindly without seeing, it takes all my will to keep the lids from closing. Then I am slowly able to discern the underwater objects. The drain plug looks different, slightly distorted; there is a hair trapped between the hole and the plug, it waves and dances with the movement of the water. I come up, refresh my lungs, examine quickly the overwater world of the washroom, and go in again. I do it several times, over and over. The world outside the water I have seen a lot of, it is now time to see what is inside.

The spring session for adult non-swimmers will begin in a few days at the high school. I must not forget the registration date.

The dwindled days of winter are now all but forgotten; they have grown and attained a respectable span. I resume my evening walks, it's spring, and a vigorous thaw is on. The snowbanks are melting, the sound of water on its gushing, gurgling journey to the drains is beautiful. I plan to buy a book of trees, so I can identify more than the maple as they begin to bloom.

When I return to the building, I wipe my feet energetically on the mat because some people are entering behind me, and I want to set a good example. Then I go to the board with its little plastic letters and numbers. The old man's apartment is the one on the corner by the stairway, that makes it number 201. I run down the list, come to 201, but there are no little white plastic letters beside it. Just the empty black rectangle with holes where the letters would be squeezed in. That's strange. Well, I can introduce myself to him, then ask his name.

However, the lobby is empty. I take the elevator, exit at the second floor, wait for the gutang-khutang. It does not come: the door closes noiselessly, smoothly. Berthe has been at work, or has made sure someone else has. PW's cue has been lubricated out of existence.

But she must have the ears of a cockroach. She is waiting for me. I whistle my way down the corridor. She fixes me with an accusing look. She waits till I stop whistling, then says: "You know the old man died last night."

I cease groping for my key. She turns to go and I take a step towards her, my hand still in my trouser pocket. "Did you know his name?" I ask, but she leaves without answering.

Then Mother said, the part I like best in the last story is about Grandpa, where he wonders if Grandpa's spirit is really watching him and blessing him, because you know I really told him that, I told him helping an old suffering person who is near death is the most blessed thing to do, because that person will ever after watch over you from heaven, I told him this when he was disgusted with Grandpa's urine-bottle and would not touch it, would not hand it to him even when I was not at home.

Are you sure, said Father, that you really told him this, or you believe you told him because you like the sound of it, you said yourself the other day that he changes and adds and alters things in the stories but he writes it all so beautifully that it seems true, so how can you be sure; this sounds like another theory, said Mother, but I don't care, he says I told him and I believe now I told him, so even if I did not tell him then it does not matter now.

Don't you see, said Father, that you are confusing fiction with facts, fiction does not create facts, fiction can come from facts, it can grow out of facts by compounding, transposing, augmenting, diminishing, or altering them in any way; but you must not confuse cause and effect, you must not confuse what really happened with what the story says happened, you must not loose your grasp on reality, that way madness lies.

Then Mother stopped listening because, as she told Father so often, she was not very fond of theories, and she took out her writing pad and started a letter to her son; Father looked over her shoulder, telling her to say how proud they were of him and were waiting for his next book, he also said, leave a little space for me at the end, I want to write a few lines when I put the address on the envelope.

For the settings of her prose fiction, Alice Munro has relied primarily on the small towns and rural landscapes of Western Ontario, where she was born in 1931. Although she started publishing short stories in such journals as *Queen's Quarterly*, *Tamarack Review*, and *The Canadian Forum* in the 1950s, she published no book until 1968, when a collection of fifteen stories appeared under the title *Dance of the Happy Shades* and immediately won critical acclaim. Like the novel which followed in 1971, *Lives of Girls and Women*—and stories in subsequent collections: *Something I've Been Meaning to Tell You* (1974), *Who Do You Think You Are?* (1978), *The Moons of Jupiter* (1982), and *Friend of My Youth* (1990)—her fiction explores tensions between the orderly and the uncontrollable in modern life, particularly as they affect women. The orderly manifests itself in conventions of various kinds: the moral and social structure of small-town society, the dimensions of family life, the roles accorded men and women by tradition and inertia.

Munro's dramatization of these social realities brings her characters up against the knowledge of the limits which such order imposes on them. They rebel, or they surrender, or they question their ability to escape themselves—to escape the identities which the conventions have inevitably helped create. When the father in one of her stories ("Boys and Girls"), for example, dismisses his daughter's intentional rebellion with the phrase, "she's only a girl," he dismisses implicitly her capacities for intelligence and independent judgment; moreover, the girl has become so pressured by family expectations, that she acknowledges "maybe it was true." The characters in the sardonically titled "Thanks for the Ride" also are circumscribed by imposed stereotypes. Those who know what limits them do not delight in their knowledge; those who do not know are equally joyless, for their very lack of knowledge creates an emptiness in their lives. The story is one which gains its meaning not just from the characters' behaviour, but also from the writer's control over setting and style, over image, allusion, and oxymoron. The unity of the whole gives evidence that the act of storytelling is both a fine art and a careful craft.

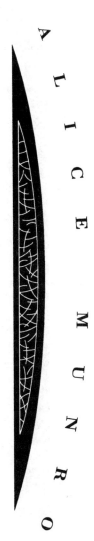

ALICE MUNRO

FOR FURTHER READING

E.D. Blodgett, *Alice Munro* (Boston: Twayne, 1988).

Heliane Catherine Daziron, "The Preposterous Oxymoron," *Literary Half-Yearly* 24 (July 1983): 116-24.

Helen Hoy, "'Dull, Simple, Amazing and Unfathomable': Paradox and Double Vision in Alice Munro's Fiction," *Studies in Canadian Literature*, no. 5 (1980): 100-15.

L.K. MacKendrick, ed., *Probable Fictions: Alice Munro's Narrative Acts* (Toronto: ECW Press, 1983).

Alice Munro, "The Colonel's Hash Resettled," in *The Narrative Voice*, ed. John Metcalf (Toronto: McGraw-Hill Ryerson, 1972): 181-83.

Thanks for the Ride

My cousin George and I were sitting in a restaurant called Pop's Cafe, in a little town close to the Lake. It was getting dark in there, and they had not turned the lights on, but you could still read the signs plastered against the mirror between the fly-speckled and slightly yellowed cutouts of strawberry sundaes and tomato sandwiches.

"Don't ask for information," George read. "If we knew anything we wouldn't be here" and "If you've got nothing to do, you picked a hell of a good place to do it in." George always read everything out loud—posters, billboards, Burma-Shave signs, "Mission Creek. Population 1700. Gateway to the Bruce. We love our children."

I was wondering whose sense of humour provided us with the signs. I though it would be the man behind the cash register. Pop? Chewing on a match, looking out at the street, not watching for anything except for somebody to trip over a crack in the sidewalk or have a blowout or make a fool of himself in some way that Pop, rooted behind the cash register, huge and cynical and incurious, was never likely to do. Maybe not even that; maybe just by walking up and down, driving up and down, going places, the rest of the world proved its absurdity. You see the judgment on the faces of people looking out of windows, sitting on front steps in some little towns; so deeply, deeply uncaring they are, as if they had sources of disillusionment which they would keep, with some satisfaction, in the dark.

There was only the one waitress, a pudgy girl who leaned over the counter and scraped at the polish on her fingernails. When she had flaked most of the polish off her thumbnail she put the thumb against her teeth and rubbed the nail back and forth absorbedly. We asked her what her name was and she didn't answer. Two or three minutes later the thumb came out of her mouth and she said, inspecting it: "That's for me to know and you to find out."

"All right," George said. "Okay if I call you Mickey?"

"I don't care."

"Because you remind me of Mickey Rooney," George said. "Hey, where's everybody go in this town? Where's everybody go?" Mickey had turned her back and begun to drain out the coffee. It looked as if she didn't mean to talk any more, so George got a little jumpy, as he did when he was threatened with having to be quiet or be by himself. "Hey, aren't there any girls in this town?" he said almost plaintively. "Aren't there any girls or dances or anything? We're strangers in town," he said. "Don't you want to help us out?"

"Dance hall down on the beach closed up Labour Day," Mickey said coldly.

"There any other dance halls?"

"There's a dance tonight out at Wilson's *school*," Mickey said.

"That old-time? No, no, I don't go for the old-time. *All-a-man left* and that, used to have that down in the basement of the church. Yeah, *ever' body swing*—I don't go for that. Inna basement of the *church*," George said, obscurely angered. "You don't remember that," he said to me. "Too young."

I was just out of high-school at this time, and George had been working for three years in the Men's Shoes in a downtown department store, so there was that difference. But we had never bothered with each other back in the city. We were together now because we had met unexpectedly in a strange place and because I had a little money, while George was broke. Also I had my father's car, and George was in one of his periods between cars, which made him always a little touchy and dissatisfied. But he would have to rearrange these facts a bit, they made him uneasy. I could feel him manufacturing a sufficiency of good feeling, old-pal feeling, and dressing me up as Old Dick, good kid, real character—which did not matter one way or the other, though I did not think, looking at his tender blond piggish handsomeness, the nudity of his pink mouth, and the surprised, angry creases that frequent puzzlement was beginning to put into his forehead, that I would be able to work up an Old George.

I had driven up to the Lake to bring my mother home from a beach resort for women, a place where they had fruit juice and cottage cheese for reducing, and early-morning swims in the Lake, and some religion, apparently, for there was a little chapel attached. My aunt, George's mother, was staying there at the same time, and George arrived about an hour or so after I did, not to take his mother home, but to get some money out of her. He did not get along well with his father, and he did not make much money working in the shoe department, so he was very often broke. His mother said he could have a loan if he would stay over and go to church with her the next day. George said he would. Then George and I got away and drove half a mile along the lake to this little town neither of us had seen before, which George said would be full of bootleggers and girls.

It was a town of unpaved, wide, sandy streets and bare yards. Only the hardy things like red and yellow nasturtiums, or a lilac bush with brown curled leaves, grew out of that cracked earth. The houses were set wide apart, with their own pumps and sheds and privies out behind; most of them were built of wood and painted green or grey or yellow. The trees that grew there were big willows or poplars, their fine leaves greyed with the dust. There were no trees along the main street, but spaces of tall grass and dandelions and blowing thistles— open country between the store buildings. The town hall was surprisingly large, with a great bell in a tower, the red brick rather glaring in the midst of the town's walls of faded, pale-painted wood. The sign beside the door said that it was a memorial to the soldiers who had died in the First World War. We had a drink out of the fountain in front.

We drove up and down the main street for a while, with George saying: "What a dump! Jesus, what a dump!" and "Hey, look at that! Aw, not so good either." The people on the street went home to supper, the shadows of the store buildings lay solid across the street, and we went into Pop's.

"Hey," George said, "is there any other restaurant in this town? Did you see any other restaurant?"

"No," I said.

"Any other town I ever been," George said, "pigs hangin' out the windows, practically hangin' off the trees. Not here. Jesus! I guess it's late in the season," he said.

"You want to go to a show?"

The door opened. A girl came in, walked up and sat on a stool, with most of her skirt bunched up underneath her. She had a long somnolent face, no bust, frizzy hair; she was pale, almost ugly, but she had that inexplicable aura of sexuality. George brightened, though not a great deal. "Never mind," he said. "This'll do. This'll do in a pinch, eh? In a pinch."

He went to the end of the counter and sat down beside her and started to talk. In about five minutes they came back to me, the girl drinking a bottle of orange pop.

"This is Adelaide," George said. "Adelaide, Adeline—Sweet Adeline. I'm going to call her Sweet A, Sweet A."

Adelaide sucked at her straw, paying not much attention.

"She hasn't got a date," George said. "You haven't got a date have you, honey?"

Adelaide shook her head very slightly.

"Doesn't hear half of what you say to her," George said. "Adelaide, Sweet A, have you got any friends? Have you got any nice, young little girl friend to go out with Dickie? You and me and her and Dickie?"

"Depends," said Adelaide. "Where do you want to go?"

"Anywhere you say. Go for a drive. Drive up to Owen Sound, maybe."

"You got a car?"

"Yeah, yeah, we got a car. C'mon, you must have some nice little friend for Dickie." He put his arm around this girl, spreading his fingers over her blouse. "C'mon out and I'll show you the car."

Adelaide said: "I know one girl might come. The guy she goes around with, he's engaged, and his girl came up and she's staying at his place up the beach, his mother and dad's place, and—"

"Well that is certainly int-er-esting," George said. "What's her name? Come on, let's go round and get her. You want to sit around drinking pop all night?"

"I'm finished," Adelaide said. "She might not come. I don't know."

"Why not? Her mother not let her out nights?"

"Oh, she can do what she likes," said Adelaide. "Only there's times she don't want to. I don't know."

We went out and got into the car, George and Adelaide in the back. On the main street about a block from the cafe we passed a thin, fairhaired girl in slacks and Adelaide cried: "Hey stop! That's her! That's Lois!"

I pulled in and George stuck his head out of the window, whistling. Adelaide yelled, and the girl came unhesitatingly, unhurriedly to the car. She smiled, rather coldly and politely, when Adelaide explained to her. All the time George kept saying: "Hurry up, come on, get in! We can talk in the car." The girl smiled, did not really look at any of us, and in a few moments, to my surprise, she opened the door and slid into the car.

"I don't have anything to do," she said. "My boy friend's away."

"That so?" said George, and I saw Adelaide, in the rear-vision mirror, make a cross warning face. Lois did not seem to have heard him.

"We better drive around to my house," she said. "I was just going down to get some Cokes, that's why I only have my slacks on. We better drive around to my house and I'll put on something else."

"Where are we going to go," she said, "so I know what to put on?"

I said: "Where do you want to go?"

"Okay, okay," George said. "First things first. We gotta get a bottle, then we'll decide. You know where to get one?" Adelaide and Lois both said yes, and then Lois said to me: "You can come in the house and wait while I change, if you want to." I glanced in the rear mirror and thought that there was probably some agreement she had with Adelaide.

Lois's house had an old couch on the porch and some rugs hanging down over the railing. She walked ahead of me across the yard. She had her long pale hair tied at the back of her neck; her skin was dustily freckled, but not tanned; even her eyes were light-coloured. She was cold and narrow and pale. There was derision, and also great gravity, about her mouth. I thought she was about my age or a little older.

She opened the front door and said in a clear, stilted voice: "I would like you to meet my family."

The little front room had linoleum on the floor and flowered paper curtains at the windows. There was a glossy chesterfield with a Niagara Falls and a To Mother cushion on it, and there was a little black stove with a screen around it for summer, and a big vase of paper apple blossoms. A tall, frail woman came into the room drying her hands on a dishtowel, which she flung into a chair. Her mouth was full of blue-white china teeth, and long cords trembled in her neck. I said how-do-you-do to her, embarrassed by Lois's announcement, so suddenly and purposefully conventional. I wondered if she had any misconceptions about this date, engineered by George for such specific purposes. I did not think so. Her face had no innocence in it that I could see; it was knowledgeable, calm, and hostile. She might have done it, then, to mock me, to make me into this caricature of The Date, the boy who grins and shuffles in the front hall and waits to be presented to the nice girl's family. But that was a little far-fetched. Why should she want to embarrass me when she had agreed to go out with me without even looking into my face? Why should she care enough?

Lois's mother and I sat down on the chesterfield. She began to make conversation, giving this The Date interpretation. I noticed the smell in the house, the smell of stale small rooms, bedclothes, frying, washing, and medicated ointments. And dirt, though it did not look dirty. Lois's mother said: "That's a nice car you got out front. Is that your car?"

"My father's."

"Isn't that lovely! Your father has such a nice car. I always think it's lovely for people to have things. I've got no time for these people that's just eaten up with malice 'n envy. I say it's lovely. I bet your mother, every time she wants anything, she just goes down to the store and buys it—new coat, bedspread, pots and pans. What does your father do? Is he a lawyer or doctor or something like that?"

"He's a chartered accountant."

"Oh. That's in an office, is it?"

"Yes."

"My brother, Lois's uncle, he's in the office of the CPR in London. He's quite high up there, I understand."

She began to tell me about how Lois's father had been killed in an accident at the mill. I noticed an old woman, the grandmother probably, standing in the doorway of the room. She was not thin like the others, but as soft and shapeless as a collapsed pudding, pale brown spots melting together on her face and arms, bristles of hairs in the moisture around her mouth. Some of the smell in the house seemed to come from her. It was a smell of hidden decay, such as there is when some obscure little animal has died under the verandah. The smell, the slovenly, confiding voice—something about this life I had not known, something about these people. I thought: my mother, George's mother, they are innocent. Even George, George is innocent. But these others are born sly and sad and knowing.

I did not hear much about Lois's father except that his head was cut off.

"Clean off, imagine, and rolled on the floor! Couldn't open the coffin. It was June, the hot weather. And everybody in town just stripped their gardens, stripped them for the funeral. Stripped their spirea bushes and peenies and climbin' clemantis. I guess it was the worst accident ever took place in this town.

"Lois had a nice boy friend this summer," she said. "Used to take her out and sometimes stay here overnight when his folks weren't up at the cottage and he didn't feel like passin' his time there all alone. He'd bring the kids candy and even me he'd bring presents. That china elephant up there, you can plant flowers in it, he brought me that. He fixed the radio for me and I never had to take it into the shop. Do your folks have a summer cottage up here?"

I said no, and Lois came in, wearing a dress of yellow-green stuff—stiff and shiny like Christmas wrappings—high-heeled shoes, rhinestones, and a lot of dark powder over her freckles. Her mother was excited.

"You like that dress?" she said. "She went all the way to London and bought that dress, didn't get it anywhere round here!"

We had to pass by the old woman as we went out. She looked at us with sudden recognition, a steadying of her pale, jellied eyes. Her mouth trembled open, she stuck her face out at me.

"You can do what you like with my gran'daughter," she said in her old, strong voice, the rough voice of a country woman. "But you be careful. And you know what I mean!"

Lois's mother pushed the old woman behind her, smiling tightly, eyebrows lifted, skin straining over her temples. "Never mind," she mouthed at me, grimacing distractedly. "Never mind. Second childhood." The smile stayed on her face; the skin pulled back from it. She seemed to be listening all the time to a perpetual din and racket in her head. She grabbed my hand as I followed Lois out. "Lois is a nice girl," she whispered. "You have a nice time, don't let her mope!" There was a quick, grotesque, and, I suppose, originally flirtatious, flickering of brows and lids. "Night!"

Lois walked stiffly ahead of me, rustling her papery skirt. I said: "Did you want to go to a dance or something?"

"No," she said. "I don't care."

"Well you got all dressed up—"

"I always get dressed up on Saturday night," Lois said, her voice floating back to me, low and scornful. Then she began to laugh, and I had a glimpse of her mother in her, that jaggedness and hysteria. "Oh, my God!" she whispered. I knew she meant what had happened in the house, and I laughed too, not knowing what else to do. So we went back to the car laughing as if we were friends, but we were not.

We drove out of town to a farmhouse where a woman sold us a whiskey bottle full of muddy-looking liquor, something George and I had never had before. Adelaide had said that this woman would probably let us use her front room, but it turned out that she would not, and that was because of Lois. When the woman peered up at me from under the man's cap she had on her head and said to Lois, "Change's as good as a rest, eh?" Lois did not answer, kept a cold face. Then later the woman said that if we were so stuck-up tonight her front room wouldn't be good enough for us and we better go back to the bush. All the way back down the lane Adelaide kept saying: "Some people can't take a joke, can they? Yeah, stuck-up is right—" until I passed her the bottle to keep her quiet. I saw George did not mind, thinking this had taken her mind off driving to Owen Sound.

We parked at the end of the lane and sat in the car drinking. George and Adelaide drank more than we did. They did not talk, just reached for the bottle and passed it back. This stuff was different from anything I had tasted before; it was heavy and sickening in my stomach. There was no other effect, and I began to have the depressing feeling that I was not going to get drunk. Each time Lois handed the bottle back to me she said "Thank you" in a mannerly and subtly contemptuous way. I put my arm around her, not much wanting to. I was wondering what was the matter. This girl lay against my arm, scornful, acquiescent, angry, inarticulate and out-of-reach. I wanted to talk to her then more than to touch her, and that was out of the question; talk was not so little a thing to her as touching. Meanwhile I was aware that I should be beyond this, beyond the first stage and well into the second (for I had a knowledge, though it was not very comprehensive, of the orderly progression of stages, the ritual of back- and front-seat seduction). Almost I wished I was with Adelaide.

"Do you want to go for a walk?" I said.

"That's the first bright idea you've had all night," George told me from the back seat. "Don't hurry," he said as we got out. He and Adelaide were muffled and laughing together. "Don't hurry back!"

Lois and I walked along a wagon track close to the bush. The fields were moonlit, chilly and blowing. Now I felt vengeful, and I said softly, "I had quite a talk with your mother."

"I can imagine," said Lois.

"She told me about that guy you went out with last summer."

"This summer."

"It's last summer now. He was engaged or something, wasn't he?"

"Yes."

I was not going to let her go. "Did he like you better?" I said. "Was that it? Did he like you better?"

"No, I wouldn't say he liked me," Lois said. I thought, by some thickening of the sarcasm in her voice, that she was beginning to be drunk. "He liked Momma and the kids okay but he didn't like me. *Like me*," she said, "What's that?"

"Well, he went out with you—"

"He just went around with me for the summer. That's what those guys from up the beach always do. They come down here to the dances and get a girl to go around with. For the summer. They always do.

"How I know he didn't *like* me," she said, "he said I was always bitching. You have to act grateful to those guys, you know, or they say you're bitching."

I was a little startled at having loosed all this. I said: "Did you like him?"

"Oh, sure! I should, shouldn't I? I should just get down on my knees and thank him. That's what my mother does. He brings her a cheap old spotted elephant—"

"Was this guy the first?" I said.

"The first steady. Is that what you mean?"

It wasn't. "How old are you?"

She considered. "I'm almost seventeen. I can pass for eighteen or nineteen. I can pass in a beer parlour. I did once."

"What grade are you in at school?"

She looked at me, rather amazed. "Did you think I still went to school? I quit that two years ago. I've got a job at the glove-works in town."

"That must have been against the law. When you quit."

"Oh, you can get a permit if your father's dead or something."

"What do you do at the glove-works?" I said.

"Oh, I run a machine. It's like a sewing machine. I'll be getting on piecework soon. You make more money."

"Do you like it?"

"Oh, I wouldn't say I loved it. It's a job—you ask a lot of questions," she said.

"Do you mind?"

"I don't have to answer you," she said, her voice flat and small again. "Only if I like." She picked up her skirt and spread it out in her hands. "I've got burrs on my skirt," she said. She bent over, pulling them one by one, "I've got burrs on my dress," she said. "It's my good dress. Will they leave a mark? If I pull them all—slowly—I won't pull any threads."

"You shouldn't have worn that dress," I said. "What'd you wear that dress for?"

She shook the skirt, tossing a burr loose. "I don't know," she said. She held it out, the stiff, shining stuff, with faintly drunken satisfaction. "I wanted to show you guys!" she said, with a sudden small explosion of viciousness. The drunken, nose-thumbing, toe-twirling satisfaction could not now be mistaken as she stood there foolishly, tauntingly, with her skirt spread out. "I've got an imitation cashmere sweater at home. It cost me twelve dollars," she said. "I've got a fur coat I'm paying on, paying on for next winter. I've got a fur coat—"

"That's nice," I said. "I think it's lovely for people to have things."

She dropped the skirt and struck the flat of her hand on my face. This was a relief to me, to both of us. We felt a fight had been building in us all along. We faced each other as warily as we could, considering we were both a little drunk, she tensing to slap me again and I to grab her or slap her back. We would have it out, what we had against each other. But the moment of this keenness passed. We let out our breath; we had not moved in time. And the next moment, not bothering to shake off our enmity, nor thinking how the one thing could give way to the other, we kissed. It was the first time, for me, that a kiss was accomplished without premeditation, or hesitancy, or over-haste, or the usual vague ensuing disappointment. And laughing shakily against me, she began to talk again, going back to the earlier part of our conversation as if nothing had come between.

"Isn't it funny?" she said. "You know, all winter all the girls do is talk about last summer, talk and talk about those guys, and I bet you those guys have forgotten even what their names were—"

But I did not want to talk any more, having discovered another force in her that lay side by side with her hostility, that was, in *fact*, just as enveloping and impersonal. After a while I whispered: "Isn't there some place we can go?"

And she answered: "There's a barn in the next field."

She knew the countryside; she had been there before.

We drove back into town after midnight. George and Adelaide were asleep in the back seat. I did not think Lois was asleep, though she kept her eyes closed and did not say anything. I had read somewhere about *Omne animal*, and I was going to tell her, but then I thought she would not know Latin words and would think I was being—oh, pretentious and superior. Afterwards I wished that I had told her. She would have known what it meant.

Afterwards the lassitude of the body, and the cold; the separation. To brush away the bits of hay and tidy ourselves with heavy unconnected movements, to come out of the barn and find the moon gone down, but the flat stubble fields still there, and the poplar trees, and the stars. To find our same selves, chilled and shaken, who had gone that headlong journey and were here still. To go back to the car and find the others sprawled asleep. That is what it is: *triste. Triste est.*

That headlong journey. Was it like that because it was the first time, because I was a little, strangely drunk? No. It was because of Lois. There are some people who can go only a little way with the act of love, and some others who can go very far, who can make a greater surrender, like the mystics. And Lois, this mystic of love, sat now on the far side of the carseat, looking cold and rumpled, and utterly closed up in herself. All the things I wanted to say to her went clattering emptily through my head. *Come and see you again—Remember—Love*—I could not say any of these things. They would not seem even half-true across the space that had come between us. I thought: I will say something to her before the next tree, the next telephone pole. But I did not. I only drove faster, too fast, making the town come nearer.

The street lights bloomed out of the dark trees ahead; there were stirrings in the back seat.

"What time is it?" George said.

"Twenty past twelve."

"We musta finished that bottle. I don't feel so good. Oh, Christ, I don't feel so good. How do you feel?"

"Fine."

"Fine, eh? Feel like you finished your education tonight, eh? That how you feel? Is yours asleep? Mine is."

"I am not," said Adelaide drowsily. "Where's my belt? George—oh. Now where's my other shoe? It's early for Saturday night, isn't it? We could go and get something to eat."

"I don't feel like food," George said. "I gotta get some sleep. Gotta get up early tomorrow and go to church with my mother."

"Yeah, I know," said Adelaide, disbelieving, though not too ill-humoured. "You could've anyways bought me a hamburger!"

I had driven around to Lois's house. Lois did not open her eyes until the car stopped.

She sat still a moment, and then pressed her hands down over the skirt of her dress, flattening it out. She did not look at me. I moved to kiss her, but she seemed to draw slightly away, and I felt that there had after all been something fraudulent and theatrical about this final gesture. She was not like that.

George said to Adelaide: "Where do you live? You live near here?"

"Yeah. Half a block down."

"Okay. How be you get out here too? We gotta get home sometime tonight."

He kissed her and both the girls got out.

I started the car. We began to pull away, George settling down on the back seat to sleep. And then we heard the female voice calling after us, the loud, crude, female voice, abusive and forlorn:

"Thanks for the ride!"

It was not Adelaide calling; it was Lois.

A Trinidadian born in 1932, who emigrated to England in 1950, an Oxonian, a novelist, a reporter, and the winner of such prestigious awards as the Hawthornden and Booker Prizes, Vidiadhar Surajprasad Naipaul is a man of extraordinary talent and complex motivations. Profoundly influenced by both his Indian and West Indian heritages, he yet finds India and Trinidad to be constraining environments; and in his travel books (among them, *The Middle Passage*, 1962, and *An Area of Darkness*, 1964) he shrewdly observes the details of life in the two societies and broods over his own sense of alienation from them. From one vantage point, such "exile" can be seen as a reflection of the Caribbean predicament; that of societies founded by exiles and historically uncertain of their allegiances and identities: the acute consciousness of being alive and alone, the laconic acceptance of the fugitive joys and persistent sadness of life, the alternately grim and wry rendering of a society that cannot locate or cannot believe in a sustaining code of values. Naipaul's characteristically tragicomic tone catches at exactly this ambivalence.

The most lighthearted of his works are early books—the sketches of *Miguel Street* (1959) and the novel *The Mystic Masseur* (1957). But the vein of dislocating irony that occurs even here has grown larger with each succeeding work: *A House for Mr. Biswas* (1961), an inventive portrait of Trinidad domestic crises and individual pride; *A Flag on the Island* (1967), from which "My Aunt Gold Teeth" is taken; *The Mimic Men* (1967), about middle-class drive and human emptiness; *In a Free State* (1971), a collection of stories and journal entries that explores the dimensions of freedom in the mind and the modern world. Reading the present and recognizing the hand of history in shaping it constitute for him a kind of psychological burden, which his writing addresses but refuses to pretend to resolve. Accompanying this intellectual development is an increasing stylistic skill. Naipaul's incisive portraits, his intelligent understanding of human behaviour, and his powers of rendering intense awareness have made him one of the most significant modern prose writers and one of the most accomplished to have emerged thus far from the nations of the Caribbean.

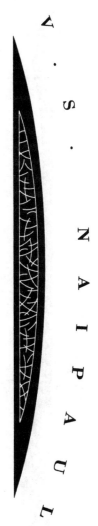

V. S. NAIPAUL

FOR FURTHER READING

Robert D. Hamner, ed. *Critical Perspectives on V.S. Naipaul* (Washington: Three Continents, 1977).

Bharati Mukherjee and Robert Boyers, "A Conversation With V.S. Naipaul," *Salmagundi* 54 (Fall 1981): 4-22.

V.S. Naipaul, *The Overcrowded Barracoon and Other Articles* (London: Andre Deutsch, 1972).

V.S. Naipaul and Ian Hamilton, "Without a Place," *Times Literary Supplement*, 30 August 1971, pp. 897-98.

William Walsh, *V.S. Naipaul* (Edinburgh: Oliver & Boyd, 1973).

My Aunt Gold Teeth

I never knew her real name and it is quite likely that she did have one, though I never heard her called anything but Gold Teeth. She did, indeed, have gold teeth. She had sixteen of them. She had married early and she had married well, and shortly after her marriage she exchanged her perfectly sound teeth for gold ones, to announce to the world that her husband was a man of substance.

Even without her gold teeth my aunt would have been noticeable. She was short, scarcely five foot, and she was very fat. If you saw her in silhouette you would have found it difficult to know whether she was facing you or whether she was looking sideways.

She ate little and prayed much. Her family being Hindu, and her husband being a pundit, she, too, was an orthodox Hindu. Of Hinduism she knew little apart from the ceremonies and the taboos, and this was enough for her. Gold Teeth saw God as a Power, and religious ritual as a means of harnessing that Power for great practical good, her good.

I may have given the impression that Gold Teeth prayed because she wanted to be less fat. The fact was that Gold Teeth had no children and she was almost forty. It was her childlessness, not her fat, that oppressed her, and she prayed for the curse to be removed. She was willing to try any means—any ritual, any prayer—in order to trap and channel the supernatural Power.

And so it was that she began to indulge in surreptitious Christian practices.

She was living at the time in a country village called Cunupia, in County Caroni. Here the Canadian Mission had long waged war against the Indian heathen, and saved many. But Gold Teeth stood firm. The Minister of Cunupia expended his Presbyterian piety on her; so did the headmaster of the Mission school. But all in vain. At no time was Gold Teeth persuaded even to think about being converted. The idea horrified her. Her father had been in his day one of the best-known Hindu pundits, and even now her husband's fame as a pundit, as a man who could read and write Sanskrit, had spread far beyond Cunupia. She was in no doubt whatsoever the Hindus were the best people in the world, and that Hinduism was a superior religion. She was willing to select, modify and incorporate alien eccentricities into her worship; but to abjure her own faith—never!

Presbyterianism was not the only danger the good Hindu had to face in Cunupia. Besides, of course, the ever-present threat of open Muslim aggression, the Catholics were to be reckoned with. Their pamphlets were everywhere and it was hard to avoid them. In them Gold Teeth read of novenas and rosaries, of squads of saints and angels. These were things she understood and could even sympathize with, and they encouraged her to seek further. She read of the mysteries and the miracles, of penances and indulgences. Her scepticism sagged, and yielded to a quickening, if reluctant, enthusiasm.

One morning she took the train for the County town of Chaguanas, three miles, two stations and twenty minutes away. The Church of St Philip and St James in Chaguanas stands imposingly at the end of the Caroni Savannah Road, and although Gold Teeth knew Chaguanas well, all she knew of the church was that it had a clock, at which she had glanced on her way to the railway station nearby. She had hitherto been far more interested in the drab ochre-washed edifice opposite, which was the police station.

She carried herself into the churchyard, awed by her own temerity, feeling like an explorer in a land of cannibals. To her relief, the church was empty. It was not as terrifying as she had expected. In the gilt and images and the resplendent cloths she found much that reminded her of her Hindu temple. Her eyes caught a discreet sign: CANDLES TWO CENTS EACH. She undid the knot in the end of her veil, where she kept her money, took out three cents, popped them into the box, picked up a candle and muttered a prayer in Hindustani. A brief moment of elation gave way to a sense of guilt, and she was suddenly anxious to get away from the church as fast as her weight would let her.

She took a bus home, and hid the candle in her chest of drawers. She had half feared that her husband's Brahminical flair for clairvoyance would have uncovered the reason for her trip to Chaguanas. When after four days, which she spent in an ecstasy of prayer, her husband had mentioned nothing, Gold Teeth thought it safe to burn the candle. She burned it secretly at night, before her Hindu images, and sent up, as she thought, prayers of double efficacy.

Every day her religious schizophrenia grew, and presently she began wearing a crucifix. Neither her husband nor her neighbours knew she did so. The chain was lost in the billows of fat around her neck, and the crucifix was itself buried in the valley of her gargantuan breasts. Later she acquired two holy pictures, one of the Virgin Mary, the other of the crucifixion, and took care to conceal them from her husband. The prayers she offered to these Christian things filled her with new hope and buoyancy. She became an addict of Christianity.

Then her husband, Ramprasad, fell ill.

Ramprasad's sudden, unaccountable illness alarmed Gold Teeth. It was, she knew, no ordinary illness, and she knew too, that her religious transgression was the cause. The District Medical Officer at Chaguanas said it was diabetes, but Gold Teeth knew better. To be on the safe side, though, she used the insulin he prescribed and, to be even safer, she consulted Ganesh Pundit, the masseur with mystic leanings, celebrated as a faith-healer.

Ganesh came all the way from Fuente Grove to Cunupia. He came in great humility, anxious to serve Gold Teeth's husband, for Gold Teeth's husband was a Brahmin among Brahmins, a *Panday*, a man who knew all five Vedas; while he, Ganesh, was a mere *Chaubay* and knew only four.

With spotless white *koortah*,* his *dhoti*** cannily tied, and a tasselled green scarf as a concession to elegance, Ganesh exuded the confidence of the professional mystic. He looked at the sick man, observed his pallor, sniffed the air. "This man," he said, "is bewitched. Seven spirits are upon him."

He was telling Gold Teeth nothing she didn't know. She had known from the first that there were spirits in the affair, but she was glad that Ganesh had ascertained their number.

"But you mustn't worry," Ganesh added. "We will 'tie' the house—in spiritual bonds—and no spirit will be able to come in."

Then, without being asked, Gold Teeth brought out a blanket, folded it, placed it on the floor and invited Ganesh to sit on it. Next she brought him a brass jar of fresh water, a mango leaf and a plate full of burning charcoal.

"Bring me some ghee," Ganesh said, and after Gold Teeth had done so, he set to work. Muttering continuously in Hindustani he sprinkled the water from the brass jar around him with the mango leaf. Then he melted the ghee in the fire and the charcoal hissed so sharply that Gold Teeth could not make out his words. Presently he rose and said, "You must put some of the ash of this fire on your husband's forehead, but if he doesn't want you to do that, mix it with his food. You must keep the water in this jar and place it every night before your front door."

Gold Teeth pulled her veil over her forehead.

Ganesh coughed. "That," he said, rearranging his scarf, "is all. There is nothing more I can do. God will do the rest."

Koortah = long shirt.
**Dhoti* = loincloth.

He refused payment for his services. It was enough honour, he said, for a man as humble as he was to serve Pundit Ramprasad, and she, Gold Teeth, had been singled out by fate to be the spouse of such a worthy man. Gold Teeth received the impression that Ganesh spoke from a first-hand knowledge of fate and its designs, and her heart, buried deep down under inches of mortal, flabby flesh, sank a little.

"Baba," she said hesitantly, "revered Father, I have something to say to you." But she couldn't say anything more and Ganesh, seeing this, filled his eyes with charity and love.

"What is it, my child?"

"I have done a great wrong, Baba."

"What sort of wrong?" he asked, and his tone indicated that Gold Teeth could do no wrong.

"I have prayed to Christian things."

And to Gold Teeth's surprise, Ganesh chuckled benevolently. "And do you think God minds, daughter? There is only one God and different people pray to Him in different ways. It doesn't matter how you pray, but God is pleased if you pray at all."

"So it is not because of me that my husband has fallen ill?"

"No, to be sure, daughter."

In his professional capacity Ganesh was consulted by people of many faiths, and with the licence of the mystic he had exploited the commodiousness of Hinduism, and made room for all beliefs. In this way he had many clients, as he called them, many satisfied clients.

Henceforward Gold Teeth not only pasted Ramprasad's pale forehead with the sacred ash Ganesh had prescribed, but mixed substantial amounts with his food. Ramprasad's appetite, enormous even in sickness, diminished; and he shortly entered into a visible and alarming decline that mystified his wife.

She fed him more ash than before, and when it was exhausted and Ramprasad perilously macerated, she fell back on the Hindu wife's last resort. She took her husband home to her mother. That venerable lady, my grandmother, lived with us in Port-of-Spain.

Ramprasad was tall and skeletal, and his face was grey. The virile voice that had expounded a thousand theological points and recited a hundred *puranas** was now a wavering whisper. We cooped him up in a room called, oddly, "the pantry." It had never been used as a pantry and one can only assume that the architect had so designated it some forty years before. It was a tiny room. If you wished to enter the pantry you were compelled, as soon as you opened the door, to climb on to the bed: it fitted the room to a miracle. The lower half of the walls were concrete, the upper close lattice-work; there were no windows.

My grandmother had her doubts about the suitability of the room for a sick man. She was worried about the lattice-work. It let in air and

Puranas = Hindu scriptures.

light, and Ramprasad was not going to die from these things if she could help it. With cardboard, oil-cloth and canvas she made the lattice-work air-proof and light-proof.

And, sure enough, within a week Ramprasad's appetite returned, insatiable and insistent as before. My grandmother claimed all the credit for this, though Gold Teeth knew that the ash she had fed him had not been without effect. Then she realized with horror that she had ignored a very important thing. The house in Cunupia had been tied and no spirits could enter, but the house in the city had been given no such protection and any spirit could come and go as it chose. The problem was pressing.

Ganesh was out of the question. By giving his services free he had made it impossible for Gold Teeth to call him in again. But thinking in this way of Ganesh, she remembered his words: "It doesn't matter how you pray, but God is pleased if you pray at all."

Why not, then, bring Christianity into play again?

She didn't want to take any chances this time. She decided to tell Ramprasad.

He was propped up in bed, and eating. When Gold Teeth opened the door he stopped eating and blinked at the unwonted light. Gold Teeth, stepping into the doorway and filling it, shadowed the room once more and he went on eating. She placed the palms of her hands on the bed. It creaked.

"Man," she said.

Ramprasad continued to eat.

"Man," she said in English, "I thinking about going to the church to pray. You never know, and it better to be on the safe side. After all, the house ain't tied—"

"I don't want you to pray in no church," he whispered, in English too.

Gold Teeth did the only thing she could do. She began to cry.

Three days in succession she asked his permission to go to church, and his opposition weakened in the face of her tears. He was now, besides, too weak to oppose anything. Although his appetite had returned, he was still very ill and very weak, and every day his condition became worse.

On the fourth day he said to Gold Teeth, "Well, pray to Jesus and go to church, if it will put your mind at rest."

And Gold Teeth straight away set about putting her mind at rest. Every morning she took the trolley-bus to the Holy Rosary Church, to offer worship in her private way. Then she was emboldened to bring a crucifix and pictures of the Virgin and the Messiah into the house. We were all somewhat worried by this, but Gold Teeth's religious nature was well known to us; her husband was a learned pundit and when all was said and done this was an emergency, a matter of life and death. So we could do nothing but look on. Incense and camphor and ghee burned now before the likeness of Krishna and Shiva as well as Mary and Jesus. Gold Teeth revealed an appetite for prayer that equalled her husband's for food, and we marvelled at both, if only because neither prayer nor food seemed to be of any use to Ramprasad.

One evening, shortly after bell and gong and conch-shell had announced that Gold Teeth's official devotions were almost over, a sudden chorus of lamentation burst over the house, and I was summoned to the room reserved for prayer. "Come quickly, something dreadful has happened to your aunt."

The prayer-room, still heavy with fumes of incense, presented an extraordinary sight. Before the Hindu shrine, flat on her face, Gold Teeth lay prostrate, rigid as a sack of flour. I had only seen Gold Teeth standing or sitting, and the aspect of Gold Teeth prostrate, so novel and so grotesque, was disturbing.

My grandmother, an alarmist by nature, bent down and put her ear to the upper half of the body on the floor. "I don't seem to hear her heart," she said.

We were all somewhat terrified. We tried to lift Gold Teeth but she seemed as heavy as lead. Then, slowly, the body quivered. The flesh beneath the clothes rippled, then billowed, and the children in the room sharpened their shrieks. Instinctively we all stood back from the body and waited to see what was going to happen. Gold Teeth's hand began to pound the floor and at the same time she began to gurgle.

My grandmother had grasped the situation. "She's got the spirit," she said.

At the word "spirit," the children shrieked louder, and my grandmother slapped them into silence.

The gurgling resolved itself into words pronounced with a lingering ghastly quaver. "Hail Mary, Hare Ram," Gold Teeth said, "the snakes are after me. Everywhere snakes. Seven snakes. Rama! Rama! Full of grace. Seven spirits leaving Cunupia by the four-o'clock train for Port-of-Spain."

My grandmother and my mother listened eagerly, their faces lit up with pride. I was rather ashamed at the exhibition, and annoyed with Gold Teeth for putting me into a fright. I moved towards the door.

"Who is that going away? Who is the young *caffar*, the unbeliever?" the voice asked abruptly.

"Come back quickly, boy," my grandmother whispered. "Come back and ask her pardon."

I did as I was told.

"It is all right, son," Gold Teeth replied, "you don't know. You are young."

Then the spirit appeared to leave her. She wrenched herself up to a sitting position and wondered why we were all there. For the rest of that evening she behaved as if nothing had happened, and she pretended she didn't notice that everyone was looking at her and treating her with unusual respect.

"I have always said it, and I will say it again," my grandmother said, "that these Christians are very religious people. That is why I encouraged Gold Teeth to pray to Christian things."

Ramprasad died early next morning and we had the announcement on the radio after the local news at one o'clock. Ramprasad's death was the only one announced and so, although it came between commercials, it made some impression. We buried him that afternoon in Mucurapo Cemetery.

As soon as we got back my grandmother said, "I have always said it, and I will say it again: I don't like these Christian things. Ramprasad would have got better if only you, Gold Teeth, had listened to me and not gone running after these Christian things."

Gold Teeth sobbed her assent; and her body squabbered and shook as she confessed the whole story of her trafficking with Christianity. We listened in astonishment and shame. We didn't know that a good Hindu, and a member of our family, could sink so low. Gold Teeth beat her breast and pulled ineffectually at her long hair and begged to be forgiven. "It is all my fault," she cried. "My own fault, Ma. I fell in a moment of weakness. Then I just couldn't stop."

My grandmother's shame turned to pity. "It's all right, Gold Teeth. Perhaps it was this you needed to bring you back to your senses."

That evening Gold Teeth ritually destroyed every reminder of Christianity in the house.

"You have only yourself to blame," my grandmother said, "if you have no children now to look after you."

Born and educated in Nova Scotia, Alden Nowlan (1933-1983) moved in 1952 to the neighbouring province of New Brunswick, where he became editor of the Hartland *Observer*. His Maritime roots go deep, and his insights into the stark details and laconic tempo of rural Maritime life derive from his sympathetic experience of it. Although better known as a poet and a playwright than as a short-story writer, he has produced several volumes of prose: a collection of stories, *Miracle at Indian River* (1968), and a novel, *Various Persons Named Kevin O'Brien* (1973), that takes the form of loosely linked episodes in the shifting identity of the title character. Of his many volumes of poetry, *Bread, Wine and Salt* won the Governor-General's Award when it appeared in 1967.

Nowlan's characters typically are constrained by their Calvinist Maritime heritage. Life is dour; authority is firm; and joy is not to be trusted. Yet they are not without humour, nor is the writer without a strong sense of irony as he views their predicament. The portrait of the Evangelical church in "Miracle at Indian River" neither ridicules nor condemns the naïveté it discloses. Relying as heavily as it does on the techniques of the anecdote, however, the story communicates its central joke with broad humour. The exaggeration of the tall tale is there, tempered by controlled understatement. The result is a witty satire of a whole way of life, which never loses sight of the realities in which it is founded, and never takes lightly the seriousness with which those realities affect individual human lives.

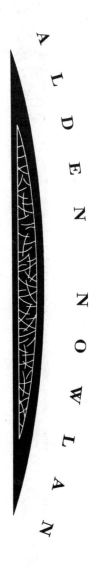

FOR FURTHER READING

Sandra Djwa, "Alden Nowlan 1933-1983," *Canadian Literature* 101 (Summer 1984): 181-83.

Keath Fraser, "Notes on Alden Nowlan," *Canadian Literature* 45 (Summer 1970): 41-51.

Alden Nowlan, "An Interview with Alden Nowlan," *Fiddlehead* 81 (1969): 5-13.

Miracle at
Indian River

This is the story of how mates were chosen for all the marriageable young men and women in the congregation of the Fire-Baptized Tabernacle of the Living God in Indian River, New Brunswick. It is a true story, more or less, and whether it is ridiculous or pathetic or even oddly beautiful depends a good deal on the mood you're in when you read it.

Indian River is one of those little places that don't really exist, except in the minds of their inhabitants. Passing through it as a stranger you might not even notice that it is there. Or if you did notice it, you'd think it was no different from thousands of other little backwoods communities in Canada and the United States. But you'd be wrong. Indian River, like every community large and small, has a character all its own.

The inhabitants of Indian River are pure Dutch, although they don't know it. Their ancestors settled in New Amsterdam more than three hundred years ago and migrated to New Brunswick after the American Revolution. But they've always been isolated, always intermarried, so that racially they're probably more purely Dutch than most of the Dutch in Holland, even though they've long ago forgotten the language and few of them could locate the Netherlands on a map.

The village contains a railway station which hasn't been used since 1965 when the CNR discontinued passenger service in that part of northwestern New Brunswick, a one-room school that was closed five years ago when the government began using buses to carry local children to the regional school in Cumberland Centre, a general store and two churches: St. Edwards's Anglican, which used to be attended by the station agent, the teacher and the storekeeper, and the Fire-Baptized Tabernacle of the Living God, attended by practically everyone else in Indian River.

The tabernacle, formerly a barracks, was bought from the Department of National Defence and brought in on a flatcar. "Jesus Saves" is painted in big red letters over the door. A billboard beside the road warns drivers to prepare to meet their God. There is an evergreen forest to the north, a brook full of speckled trout to the west and, in the east, a pasture in which a dozen Holstein cattle and a team of Clydesdale horses graze together. The pastor, Rev. Horace Zwicker, his wife, Myrtle, and their five children live in a flat behind the pulpit.

Pastor Zwicker was born in Indian River and, before he was called of God to the ministry, was a door-to-door salesman of magazine subscriptions and patent medicines, chauffeur for a chiropractor, and accordionist in a hillbilly band that toured the Maritime Provinces and Maine.

Services are held in the tabernacle Wednesday night, Sunday morning and Sunday night. During the summer evangelists arrive, usually from Alabama, Georgia or Tennessee, and then there are services every night of the week. Almost every one of the evangelists has some sort of speciality, like painting a pastel portrait of Christ as he delivers his sermon or playing "The Old Rugged Cross" on an instrument made from empty whiskey bottles. Once there was a man with a long black beard and shoulder-length hair who claimed to have gone to school with Hitler; another time a professed ex-convict named Bent-Knee Benjamin preached in striped pajamas, a ball and chain fastened to his leg.

Fire-Baptized people worry a good deal about sin—mostly innocent little rural sins like smoking, drinking, watching television and going to the movies. Fire-Baptized women, of whom there are several thousands in northwestern New Brunswick, are easy to identify on the streets of towns like Woodstock and Fredericton because they don't use cosmetics and wear their hear in a sort of Oregon Trail bun at the backs of their necks. Fire-Baptized girls are made to dress somewhat the way Elizabeth dressed before she met Philip. There is a legend, invented presumably by Anglicans and Catholics, that Fire-Baptized girls are extraordinarily agreeable and inordinately passionate.

A few years ago there happened to be an unusually large number of unmarried young men and women in Indian River.

Pastor Zwicker frequently discussed this matter with his Lord.

"Lord," he said, "You know as well as I do that it isn't good to have a pack of hot young bucks and fancy-free young females running around loose. Like Paul says, those who don't marry are apt to burn, and when they've burned long enough they'll do just about anything to put the fire out. Now, tell me straight, Lord, what do You figure I should do about it?"

The Lord offered various suggestions and Pastor Zwicker tried them all.

He had long and prayerful conversations with each young man and woman. He told Harris Brandt, for example, that Rebecca Vaneyck was not only a sweet Christian girl, pure and obedient, she made the best blueberry pie of any cook her age in Connaught County. "Never cared much for blueberries myself, Pastor," Harris said. He told Rebecca that Harris was a stout Christian youth who wouldn't get drunk, except if he were sorely tempted of the devil on election day, and wouldn't beat her unless she really deserved it. And she replied: "But, Pastor, he has such bad teeth!"

His conversations with the others were equally fruitless. The Lord advised stronger methods.

"Look here, Brother," the pastor admonished young Francis Witt's father, "it's time that young fellow of yours settled down and got himself a wife. I was talking it over with the Lord just the other night. Now, as you're well aware, Brother, the Scriptures tell us that a son should be obedient to his father. So if I was you—"

"Need the boy," replied the father. "Couldn't run this place without him. Talked to the Lord about it myself. Wife did too. Lord said maybe Francis wouldn't ever get married. Might be an old bachelor like his Uncle Ike. Nothing wrong in that, Lord said."

Other parents made other excuses. If even one couple had responded favourably to his efforts, Pastor Zwicker might have decided that he was worrying himself and the Lord needlessly. But to be met everywhere by disinterest! It was unnatural. Was the devil turning his flock into a herd of Papist celibates?

He had talked once with an escapee from a nunnery in Ireland. A tunnel to the rectory. Lecherous old men, naked under their black nightgowns. Babies' bones in the walls.

His body trembled and his soul—although he did not know this and would have been horrified had he known—made the sign of the cross. What was there left for a man of God to do?

God moves in a mysterious way His wonders to perform. The following Sunday night the power of the Holy Ghost shook the tabernacle to its very foundations. The Day of Pentecost described in the Acts of the Apostles was reenacted with more fervour than ever before in Indian River.

Pastor Zwicker had summoned a guitarist from Houlton, Maine, and a fiddler from Fredericton. He himself played the accordion and his wife the Jew's harp. Old Sister Rossa was at the piano and little Billy Wagner was sent home to fetch his harmonica and mandolin.

There was music—music even as the pastor laid aside his accordion and preached, music and singing and, as the service progressed, a Jericho dance up and down the aisle.

Later, old men said it was the best sermon they had ever heard.

"Brother Zwicker just opened his mouth and let the Lord fill it," they said.

His theme was the sins of the flesh. As near as Woodstock, as near as Fredericton, as near as Presque Isle, half-naked women with painted faces and scented bodies prowled the streets seeking whom they might devour. He had looked upon their naked thighs, observed the voluptuous movements of their rumps, had noted that their nipples were visible through their blouses. In King Square in Saint John he had stepped aside to allow a young lady to precede him onto a bus and had discovered to his horrified amazement that she was not wearing drawers. Saint John was another Babylon where before long men and women would be dancing together naked in the streets.

There was much more of the same kind of thing, interspersed, of course, with many quotations from the Bible, particularly from Genesis, Leviticus and Revelation. The Bible was almost the only book that Pastor Zwicker had ever read and he knew great stretches of it by heart.

"Praise the Lord!" the people shouted. "Hallelujah! Thank you, Jesus!"

Old Ike Witt stood on his chair and danced.

"Oh, diddly-doe-dum, diddly-dee-doe-dee," he sang. "Oh, too-row-lou-row-tiddly-lou-do-dee! Glory to Jesus! Diddly-day-dum! Glory to Jesus! Tiddly-lee-tum-tee!"

Matilda Rega threw herself on the floor, laughing and crying, yelling: "Oh Jesus! Christ Almighty! Oh, sweet Jesus! God Almighty! Oh, Jesus!"

She began crawling down the aisle toward the altar. The Jericho dancers leapt back and forth across her wriggling body.

We are marching to Zion!
Beautiful, beautiful Zion!
We are marching to Zion!
The beautiful City of God!

Kneeling before the altar, Timothy Fairvort whimpered and slapped his own face, first one cheek, then the other.

"I have sinned," he moaned.

SLAP!

"I have lusted in my heart."

SLAP!

"I will burn in hell if I am not saved."

SLAP!

"Oh, help me, Jesus."

SLAP!

The Jericho dancers sang:

Joy, Joy, Joy, There is joy in my heart!
Joy in my heart! Joy in my heart!
Joy, Joy, Joy, There is joy in my heart!
Joy in my heart TODAY!

It was as if the midway of the Fredericton Exhibition, Hank Snow and the Rainbow Ranch Boys, Oral Roberts, Billy Graham, a Salvation Army band, Lester Flatt and Earl Scruggs, Garner Ted Armstrong and a Tory leadership convention were somehow all rolled into one and compressed into the lobby of the Admiral Beatty Hotel in Saint John.

Then it happened.

Sister Zwicker began speaking in an unknown tongue.

"Elohim!" she yelled. "Elohim, angaro metalani negat! Gonolariski motono etalo bene! Wanga! Wanga! Angaro talans fo do easta analandanoro!"

"Listen!" roared the pastor. "Listen!"

The Jericho dancers sang:

When the saints go marching in!
When the saints go marching in!
How I long to be in that company
When the saints go marching in!

"Elohim!" screamed Myrtle Zwicker. "Wanga! Ortoro ortoro clana estanatoro! Wanga!"

"Listen!" bellowed the pastor. "Listen!"

Others took up the cry. At last the Jericho dancers returned to their seats, exhausted, sweat pouring down their hot, red faces. The music faded away. Old Ike Witt climbed down from his chair. Matilda Rega lay still, quietly sobbing, at the foot of the altar. Timothy Fairvort put his jacket over his head, like a criminal in a newspaper photograph. There was silence except for the voices of the pastor and his wife.

"The Lord is talking to us!" shouted the pastor, who had by now taken off his jacket and tie and unbuttoned his shirt to the waist. "Harken to the voice of the Lord!"

"Elohim!" cried his wife. "Naro talaro eganoto wanga! Tao laro matanotalero. Wanga!"

"It is Egyptian," the pastor explained. "The Lord is addressing us in the language of Pharaoh, the tongue that Joseph spoke when he was a prisoner in the land of Egypt."

"Egyptian," murmured the congregation. "Thank you, Jesus."

"Taro wanga sundaro—"

"The Lord is telling us that His heart is saddened."

"Metizo walla toro delandonaro—"

"His heart is saddened by the disobedience of His people."

"Crena wontano meta kleva sancta danco—"

"The disobedience and perversity of His young people is heavy upon His heart."

"Zalanto wanga—"

"For they have refused to marry and multiply and be fruitful and replenish the earth, as He has commanded them."

"Toronalanta wanga—"

"In His mercy He has chosen to give them one more chance to escape the just punishment for their disobedience."

"Praise His name! Thank you, Jesus!"

"Willo morto innitaro—"

"It is His will that His handmaiden, Rebecca Vaneyck, should become the bride of—"

"Altaro mintanaro—"

"Yes, yes, the bride of Harris Brandt. This is the will of the God of Abraham and of Isaac and of Jacob, for it was He who brought you out of the land of Egypt."

"Yes, yes," chanted the congregation. "It is the Lord's will. Let it be done. Hallelujah!"

Rebecca and Harris were led to the altar. They looked at one another with dazed, wondering faces. After a moment he reached out and took her hand.

Within a half an hour, three other couples stood with them. The Lord had revealed His will. Puny mortals such as they had no say in the matter.

The Jericho dancers leapt and cavorted in thanksgiving. So did Ike Witt and Timothy Fairvort, whose face was still hidden by his jacket. He stumbled blindly around the tabernacle, knocking over chairs, singing behind his jacket:

When the roll is called up yonder!
When the roll is called up yonder!
When the roll is called up yonder!
When the roll is called up yonder,
I'll be there!

Pastor Zwicker fanned himself with a copy of *The Fire-Baptized Quarterly*. Next week there would be four marriages in his tabernacle. The Lord's will had been accomplished.

"Thank you, Jesus," he murmured.

Then he remembered Ike Witt and Matilda Rega, the old bachelor and the old maid. Could it be the Lord's will that they, too, should be joined together? He would discuss it with Myrtle. Perhaps next Sunday the Lord would reveal His thoughts about the matter.

Joyce Carol Oates was born in New York in 1938 and educated at Syracuse University and the University of Wisconsin. After a period in Canada, teaching English at the University of Windsor, she took up a post at Princeton. Her work has received wide critical acclaim, and brought her many awards, including a Guggenheim Fellowship in 1967 and an O. Henry Special Award for Continuing Achievement in 1970. She is a prolific novelist as well as the author of several volumes of poetry and literary criticism, and has had two plays produced on the New York stage; in addition to these successes, her short stories have appeared in many journals and anthologies, and have been published in numerous collections, the most recent of which is *The Assignation* (1988).

In her preoccupation with violence, emotional disturbance, and familial conflict, Oates has been likened to Faulkner; and there is undoubtedly a dark, sometimes melodramatic, quality to her writing which recalls the Gothic element in Faulkner's books; her novel *Wonderland* (1971), for example, opens with the shotgun slaying of five people. Many of her characters are ordinary people who, confronted by the apparent senselessness of life, are driven to extremes by fear or frustration; or they are stunned, like Sister Irene in "In the Region of Ice" (*The Wheel of Love*, 1970), by an awareness of human helplessness and isolation. In an exchange of letters with the American writer Joe David Bellamy, Oates wrote: "I believe that the storm of emotion constitutes our human tragedy, if anything does. It's our constant battle with nature (Nature), trying to subdue chaos outside and inside ourselves, occasionally winning small victories, then being swept along by some cataclysmic event of our own making. I feel an enormous sympathy with people who've gone under, who haven't won even the smallest victories. . . . "

FOR FURTHER READING

J.D. Bellamy, "The Dark Lady of American Letters," *Atlantic Monthly* 229 (February 1972): 63-67.

Joanne V. Creighton, *Joyce Carol Oates* (Boston: Twayne, 1979).

Joyce Carol Oates, "Building Tension in the Short Story," *Writer* 79 (June 1966): 11-12; "Background and Foreground in Fiction," *Writer* 80 (August 1967): 11-13.

In the Region of Ice

Sister Irene was a tall, deft woman in her early thirties. What one could see of her face made a striking impression—serious, hard gray eyes, a long slender nose, a face waxen with thought. Seen at the right time, from the right angle, she was almost handsome. In her past teaching positions she had drawn a little upon the fact of her being young and brilliant and also a nun, but she was beginning to grow out of that.

This was a new university and an entirely new world. She had heard—of course it was true—that the Jesuit administration of this school had hired her at the last moment to save money and to head off the appointment of a man of dubious religious commitment. She had prayed for the necessary energy to get her through this first semester. She had no trouble with teaching itself; once she stood before a classroom she felt herself capable of anything. It was the world immediately outside the classroom that confused and alarmed her, though she let none of this show—the cynicism of her colleagues, the indifference of many of the students, and above all, the looks she got that told her nothing much would be expected of her because she was a nun. This took energy, strength. At times she had the idea that she was on trial and that the excuses she made to herself about her discomfort were only the common excuses made by guilty people. But in front of a class she had no time to worry about herself or the conflicts in her mind. She became, once and for all, a figure existing only for the benefit of others, an instrument by which facts were communicated.

About two weeks after the semester began, Sister Irene noticed a new student in her class. He was slight and fair-haired, and his face was blank, but not blank by accident, blank on purpose, suppressed and restricted into a dumbness that looked hysterical. She was prepared for him before he raised his hand, and when she saw his arm jerk, as if he had at last lost control of it, she nodded to him without hesitation.

"Sister, how can this be reconciled with Shakespeare's vision in *Hamlet*? How can these opposing views be in the same mind?"

Students glanced at him, mildly surprised. He did not belong in the class, and this was mysterious, but his manner was urgent and blind.

"There is no need to reconcile opposing views," Sister Irene said, leaning forward against the podium. "In one play Shakespeare suggests one vision, in another play another; the plays are not simultaneous creations, and even if they were, we never demand a logical—"

"We must demand a logical consistency," the young man said. "The idea of education is itself predicated upon consistency, order, sanity—"

He had interrupted her, and she hardened her face against him—for his sake, not her own, since she did not really care. But he noticed nothing. "Please see me after class," she said.

After class the young man hurried up to her.

"Sister Irene, I hope you didn't mind my visiting today. I'd heard some things, interesting things," he said. He stared at her, and something in her face allowed him to smile. "I . . . could we talk in your office? Do you have time?"

They walked down to her office. Sister Irene sat at her desk, and the young man sat facing her; for a moment they were self-conscious and silent.

"Well, I suppose you know—I'm a Jew," he said.

Sister Irene stared at him. "Yes?" she said.

"What am I doing at a Catholic university, huh?" He grinned. "That's what you want to know."

She made a vague movement of her hand to show that she had no thoughts on this, nothing at all, but he seemed not to catch it. He was sitting on the edge of the straight-backed chair. She saw that he was young but did not really look young. There were harsh lines on either sides of his mouth, as if he had misused that youthful mouth somehow. His skin was almost as pale as hers, his eyes were dark and not quite in focus. He looked at her and through her and around her, as his voice surrounded them both. His voice was a little shrill at times.

"Listen, I did the right thing today—visiting your class! God, what a lucky accident it was; some jerk mentioned you, said you were a good teacher—I thought, what a laugh! These people know about good teachers here? But yes, listen, yes, I'm not kidding—you are good. I mean that."

Sister Irene frowned. "I don't quite understand what all this means."

He smiled and waved aside her formality, as if he knew better. "Listen, I got my B.A. at Columbia, then I came back here to this crappy city. I mean, I did it on purpose, I wanted to come back. I wanted to. I have my reasons for doing things. I'm on a three-thou-sand-dollar fellowship," he said, and waited for that to impress her. "You know, I could have gone almost anywhere with that fellowship, and I came back home here—my home's in the city—and enrolled here. This was last year. This is my second year. I'm working on a the-sis, I mean I was, my master's thesis—but the hell with that. What I want to ask you is this: Can I enroll in your class, is it too late? We have to get special permission if we're late."

Sister Irene felt something nudging her, some uneasiness in him that was pleading with her not to be offended by his abrupt, familiar man-ner. He seemed to be promising another self, a better self, as if his fair, childish, almost cherubic face were doing tricks to distract her from what his words said.

"Are you in English studies?" she asked.

"I was in history. Listen," he said, and his mouth did something odd, drawing itself down into a smile that made the lines about it deepen like knives, "listen, they kicked me out."

He sat back, watching her. He crossed his legs. He took out a pack-age of cigarettes and offered her one. Sister Irene shook her head, star-ing at his hands. They were small and stubby and might have belonged to a ten-year-old, and the nails were a strange near-violet color. It took him awhile to extract a cigarette.

"Yeah, kicked me out. What do you think of that?"

"I don't understand."

"My master's thesis was coming along beautifully, and then this bas-tard—I mean, excuse me, this professor, I won't pollute your office with his name—he started making criticisms, he said some things were unacceptable, he—" The boy leaned forward and hunched his nar-row shoulders in a parody of secrecy. "We had an argument. I told him some frank things, things only a broad-minded person could hear about himself. That takes courage, right? He didn't have it! He kicked me out of the master's program, so now I'm coming into English. Literature is greater than history; European history is one big pile of garbage. Sky-high. Filth and rotting corpses, right? Aristotle says that poetry is higher than history; he's right; in your class today I suddenly realized that this is my field, Shakespeare, only Shakespeare is—"

Sister Irene guessed that he was going to say that only Shakespeare was equal to him, and she caught the moment of recognition and hesi-tation, the half-raised arm, the keen, frowning forehead, the narrowed eyes; then he thought better of it and did not end the sentence. "The students in your class are mainly negligible, I can tell you that. You're new here, and I've been here a year—I would have finished my studies last year but my father got sick, he was hospitalized, I couldn't take exams and it was a mess—but I'll make it through English in one year or drop dead. I can do it, I can do anything. I'll take six courses at once—" He broke off, breathless. Sister Irene tried to smile. "All right then, it's settled? You'll let me in? Have I missed anything so far?"

He had no idea of the rudeness of his question. Sister Irene, feeling suddenly exhausted, said, "I'll give you a syllabus of the course."

"Fine! Wonderful!"

He got to his feet eagerly. He looked through the schedule, muttering to himself, making favourable noises. It struck Sister Irene that she was making a mistake to let him in. There were these moments when one had to make an intelligent decision. . . . But she was sympathetic with him, yes. She was sympathetic with something about him.

She found out his name the next day: Allen Weinstein.

After this she came to her Shakespeare class with a sense of excitement. It became clear to her at once that Weinstein was the most intelligent student in the class. Until he had enrolled, she had not understood what was lacking, a mind that could appreciate her own. Within a week his jagged, protean mind had alienated the other students, and though he sat in the center of the class, he seemed totally alone, encased by a miniature world of his own. When he spoke of the "frenetic humanism of the High Renaissance," Sister Irene dreaded the raised eyebrows and mocking smiles of the other students, who no longer bothered to look at Weinstein. She wanted to defend him, but she never did, because there was something rude and dismal about his knowledge; he used it like a weapon, talking passionately of Nietzsche and Goethe and Freud until Sister Irene would be forced to close the discussion.

In meditation, alone, she often thought of him. When she tried to talk about him to a young nun, Sister Carlotta, everything sounded gross. "But no, he's an excellent student," she insisted. "I'm very grateful to have him in class. It's just that . . . he thinks ideas are real." Sister Carlotta, who loved literature also, had been forced to teach grade-school arithmetic for the last four years. That might have been why she said, a little sharply, "You don't think ideas are real?"

Sister Irene acquiesced with a smile, but of course she did not think so: only reality is real.

When Weinstein did not show up for class on the day the first paper was due, Sister Irene's heart sank, and the sensation was somehow a familiar one. She began her lecture and kept waiting for the door to open and for him to hurry noisily back to his seat, grinning an apology toward her—but nothing happened.

If she had been deceived by him, she made herself think angrily, it was as a teacher and not as a woman. He had promised her nothing.

Weinstein appeared the next day near the steps of the liberal arts building. She heard someone running behind her, a breathless exclamation: "Sister Irene!" She turned and saw him, panting and grinning in embarrassment. He wore a dark-blue suit with a necktie, and he looked, despite his childish face, like a little old man; there was something oddly precarious and fragile about him. "Sister Irene, I owe you an apology, right?" He raised his eyebrows and smiled a sad, forlorn, yet irritatingly conspiratorial smile. "The first paper—not in on time, and I know what your rules are. . . . You won't accept late papers, I know—that's good discipline, I'll do that when I teach too. But, unavoidably, I was unable to come to school yesterday. There are many—many—" He gulped for breath, and Sister Irene had the startling sense of seeing the real Weinstein stare out at her, a terrified prisoner behind the confident voice. "There are many complications in family life. Perhaps you are unaware—I mean—"

She did not like him, but she felt this sympathy, something tugging and nagging at her the way her parents had competed for her love so many years before. They had been whining, weak people, and out of their wet need for affection, the girl she had been (her name was Yvonne) had emerged stronger than either of them, contemptuous of tears because she had seen so many. But Weinstein was different; he was not simply weak—perhaps he was not weak at all—but his strength was confused and hysterical. She felt her customary rigidity as a teacher begin to falter. "You may turn your paper in today if you have it," she said, frowning.

Weinstein's mouth jerked into an incredulous grin. "Wonderful! Marvelous!" he said. "You are very understanding, Sister Irene, I must say. I must say . . . I didn't expect, really . . . " He was fumbling in a shabby old briefcase for the paper. Sister Irene waited. She was prepared for another of his excuses, certain that he did not have the paper, when he suddenly straightened up and handed her something. "Here! I took the liberty of writing thirty pages instead of just fifteen," he said. He was obviously quite excited; his cheeks were mottled pink and white. "You may disagree violently with my interpretation—I expect you to, in fact I'm counting on it—but let me warn you, I have the exact proof, right here in the play itself!" He was thumping at a book, his voice growing louder and shriller. Sister Irene, startled, wanted to put her hand over his mouth and soothe him.

"Look," he said breathlessly, "may I talk with you? I have a class now I hate, I loathe, I can't bear to sit through! Can I talk with you instead?"

Because she was nervous, she stared at the title page of the paper: "'Erotic Melodies in *Romeo and Juliet*' by Allen Weinstein, Jr."

"All right?" he said. "Can we walk around here? Is it all right? I've been anxious to talk with you about some things you said in class."

She was reluctant, but he seemed not to notice. They walked slowly along the shaded campus paths. Weinstein did all the talking, of course, and Sister Irene recognized nothing in his cascade of words that she had mentioned in class. "The humanist must be committed to the totality of life," he said passionately. "This is the failing one finds everywhere in the academic world! I found it in New York and I found it here and I'm no ingénu, I don't go around with my mouth hanging open—I'm experienced, look, I've been to Europe, I've lived in Rome! I went everywhere in Europe except Germany, I don't talk about Germany . . . Sister Irene, think of the significant men in the last century, the men who've changed the world! Jews, right? Marx, Freud, Einstein! Not that I believe Marx, Marx is a madman . . . and Freud, no, my sympathies are with spiritual humanism. I believe that the Jewish race is the exclusive . . . the exclusive, what's the word, the exclusive means by which humanism will be extended. . . . Humanism begins by excluding the Jew, and now," he said with a high, surprised laugh, "the Jew will perfect it. After the Nazis, only the Jew is authorized to understand humanism, its limitations and its possibilities. So, I say that the humanist is committed to life in its totality and not just to his profession! The religious person is totally religious, he is his religion! What else? I recognize in you a humanist and a religious person—"

But he did not seem to be talking to her or even looking at her.

"Here, read this," he said. "I wrote it last night." It was a long free-verse poem, typed on a typewriter whose ribbon was worn out.

"There's this trouble with my father, a wonderful man, a lovely man, but his health—his strength is fading, do you see? What must it be to him to see his son growing up? I mean, I'm a man now, he's getting old, weak, his health is bad—it's hell, right? I sympathize with him. I'd do anything for him, I'd cut open my veins, anything for a father—right? That's why I wasn't in school yesterday," he said, and his voice dropped for the last sentence, as if he had been dragged back to earth by a fact.

Sister Irene tried to read the poem, then pretended to read it. A jumble of words dealing with "life" and "death" and "darkness" and "love."

"What do you think?" Weinstein said nervously, trying to read it over her shoulder and crowding against her.

"It's very . . . passionate," Sister Irene said.

This was the right comment; he took the poem back from her in silence, his face flushed with excitement. "Here, at this school, I have few people to talk with. I haven't shown anyone else that poem." He looked at her with his dark, intense eyes, and Sister Irene felt them focus upon her. She was terrified at what he was trying to do—he was trying to force her into a human relationship.

"Thank you for your paper," she said, turning away.

When he came the next day, ten minutes late, he was haughty and disdainful. He had nothing to say and sat with his arms folded. Sister Irene took back with her to the convent a feeling of betrayal and confusion. She had been hurt. It was absurd, and yet—She spent too much time thinking about him, as if he were somehow a kind of crystallization of her own loneliness; but she had no right to think so much of him. She did not want to think of him or of her loneliness. But Weinstein did so much more than think of his predicament: he embodied it, he acted it out, and that was perhaps why he fascinated her. It was as if he were doing a dance for her, a dance of shame and agony and delight, and so long as he did it, she was safe. She felt embarrassment for him, but also anxiety; she wanted to protect him. When the dean of the graduate school questioned her about Weinstein's work, she insisted that he was an "excellent" student, though she knew the dean had not wanted to hear that.

She prayed for guidance, she spent hours on her devotions, she was closer to her vocation than she had been for some years. Life at the convent became tinged with unreality, a misty distortion that took its tone from the glowering skies of the city at night, identical smokestacks ranged against the clouds and giving to the sky the excrement of the populated and successful earth. This city was not her city, this world was not her world. She felt no pride in knowing this, it was a fact. The little convent was not like an island in the center of this noisy world, but rather a kind of hole or crevice the world did not bother with, something of no interest. The convent's rhythm of life had nothing to do with the world's rhythm, it did not violate or alarm it in any way. Sister Irene tried to draw together the fragments of her life and synthesize them somehow in her vocation as a nun: she was a nun, she was recognized as a nun and had given herself happily to that life, she had a name, a place, she had dedicated her superior intelligence to the Church, she worked without pay and without expecting gratitude, she had given up pride, she did not think of herself but only of her work and her vocation, she did not think of anything external to these, she saturated herself daily in the knowledge that she was involved in the mystery of Christianity.

A daily terror attended this knowledge, however, for she sensed herself being drawn by that student, that Jewish boy, into a relationship she was not ready for. She wanted to cry out in fear that she was being forced into the role of Christian, and what did that mean? What could her studies tell her? What could the other nuns tell her? She was alone, no one could help; he was making her into a Christian, and to her that was a mystery, a thing of terror, something others slipped on the way they slipped on their clothes, casually and thoughtlessly, but to her a magnificent and terrifying wonder.

For days she carried Weinstein's paper, marked A, around with her; he did not come to class. One day she checked with the graduate office and was told that Weinstein had called in to say his father was ill and that he would not be able to attend classes for a while. "He's strange, I remember him," the secretary said. "He missed all his exams last spring and made a lot of trouble. He was in and out of here every day."

So there was no more of Weinstein for a while, and Sister Irene stopped expecting him to hurry into class. Then, one morning, she found a letter from him in her mailbox.

He had printed it in black ink, very carefully, as if he had not trusted handwriting. The return address was in bold letters that, like his voice, tried to grab onto her: Birchcrest Manor. Somewhere north of the city. "Dear Sister Irene," the block letters said, "I am doing well here and have time for reading and relaxing. The Manor is delightful. My doctor here is an excellent, intelligent man who has time for me, unlike my former doctor. If you have time, you might drop in on my father, who worries about me too much, I think, and explain to him what my condition is. He doesn't seem to understand. I feel about this new life the way that boy, what's his name, in *Measure for Measure*, feels about the prospects of a different life; you remember what he says to his sister when she visits him in prison, how he is looking forward to an escape into another world. Perhaps you could *explain* this to my father and he would stop worrying." The letter ended with the father's name and address, in letters that were just a little too big. Sister Irene, walking slowly down the corridor as she read the letter, felt her eyes cloud over with tears. She was cold with fear, it was something she had never experienced before. She knew what Weinstein was trying to tell her, and the desperation of his attempt made it all the more pathetic; he did not deserve this, why did God allow him to suffer so?

She read through Claudio's speech to his sister, in *Measure for Measure:*

Ay but to die, and go we know not where;
To lie in cold obstruction and to rot;
This sensible warm motion to become
A kneaded clod; and the delighted spirit
To bathe in fiery floods, or to reside
In thrilling region of thick-ribbed ice,
To be imprison'd in the viewless winds
And blown with restless violence round about
The pendent world; or to be worse than worst
Of those that lawless and incertain thought
Imagines howling! 'Tis too horrible!
The weariest and most loathed worldly life
That age, ache, penury, and imprisonment
Can lay on nature is a paradise
To what we fear of death.

Sister Irene called the father's number that day. "Allen Weinstein residence, who may I say is calling?" a woman said, bored. "May I speak to Mr. Weinstein? It's urgent—about his son," Sister Irene said. There was a pause at the other end. "You want to talk to his mother, maybe?" the woman said. "His mother? Yes, his mother, then. Please. It's very important."

She talked with this strange, unsuspected woman, a disembodied voice that suggested absolutely no face, and insisted upon going over that afternoon. The woman was nervous, but Sister Irene, who was a university professor, after all, knew enough to hide her own nervousness. She kept waiting for the woman to say, "Yes, Allen has mentioned you . . . " but nothing happened.

She persuaded Sister Carlotta to ride over with her. This urgency of hers was something they were all amazed by. They hadn't suspected that the set of her gray eyes could change to this blurred, distracted alarm, this sense of mission that seemed to have come to her from nowhere. Sister Irene drove across the city in the late afternoon traffic, with the high whining noises from residential streets where trees were being sawed down in pieces. She understood now the secret, sweet wildness that Christ must have felt, giving himself for man, dying for the billions of men who would never know of him and never understand the sacrifice. For the first time she approached the realization of that great act. In her troubled mind the city traffic was jumbled and yet oddly coherent, an image of the world that was always out of joint with what was happening in it, its inner history struggling with its external spectacle. This sacrifice of Christ's, so mysterious and legendary now, almost lost in time—it was that by which Christ transcended both God and man at one moment, more than man because of his fate to do what no other man could do, and more than God because no god could suffer as he did. She felt a flicker of something close to madness.

She drove nervously, uncertainly, afraid of missing the street and afraid of finding it too, for while one part of her rushed forward to confront these people who had betrayed their son, another part of her would have liked nothing so much as to be waiting as usual for the summons to dinner, safe in her room. . . . When she found the street and turned onto it, she was in a state of breathless excitement. Here lawns were bright green and marred with only a few leaves, magically clean, and the houses were enormous and pompous, a mixture of styles: ranch houses, colonial houses, French country houses, white-bricked wonders with curving glass and clumps of birch trees somehow encircled by white concrete. Sister Irene stared as if she had blundered into another world. This was a kind of heaven, and she was too shabby for it.

The Weinsteins' house was the strangest one of all: it looked like a small Alpine lodge, with an inverted V-shaped front entrance. Sister

Irene drove up the black-topped driveway and let the car slow to a stop; she told Sister Carlotta she would not be long.

At the door she was met by Weinstein's mother, a small nervous woman with hands like her son's. "Come in, come in," the woman said. She had once been beautiful, that was clear, but now in missing beauty she was not handsome or even attractive but looked ruined and perplexed, the misshapen swelling of her white-blond professionally set hair like a cap lifting up from her surprised face. "He'll be right in. Allen?" she called, "our visitor is here." They went into the living room. There was a grand piano at one end and an organ at the other. In between were scatterings of brilliant modern furniture in conversational groups, and several puffed-up white rugs on the polished floor. Sister Irene could not stop shivering.

"Professor, it's so strange, but let me say when the phone rang I had a feeling—I had a feeling," the woman said, with damp eyes. Sister Irene sat, and the woman hovered about her. "Should I call you Professor? We don't . . . you know . . . we don't understand the technicalities that go with—Allen, my son, wanted to go here to the Catholic school; I told my husband why not? Why fight? It's the thing these days, they do anything they want for knowledge. And he had to come home, you know. He couldn't take care of himself. New York, that was the beginning of the trouble. . . . Should I call you Professor?"

"You can call me Sister Irene."

"Sister Irene?" the woman said, touching her throat in awe, as if something intimate and unexpected had happened.

Then Weinstein's father appeared, hurrying. He took long, impatient strides. Sister Irene stared at him and in that instant doubted everything—he was in his fifties, a tall, sharply handsome man, heavy but not fat, holding his shoulders back with what looked like an effort, but holding them back just the same. He wore a dark suit and his face was flushed, as if he had run a long distance.

"Now," he said, coming to Sister Irene and with a precise wave of his hand motioning his wife off, "now, let's straighten this out. A lot of confusion over that kid, eh?" He pulled a chair over, scraping it across a rug and pulling one corner over, so that its brown underside was exposed. "I came home early just for this, Libby phoned me. Sister, you got a letter from him, right?"

The wife looked at Sister Irene over her husband's head as if trying somehow to coach her, knowing that this man was so loud and impatient that no one could remember anything in his presence.

"A letter—yes—today—"

"He says what in it? You got the letter, eh? Can I see it?"

She gave it to him and wanted to explain, but he silenced her with a flick of his hand. He read through the letter so quickly that Sister

Irene thought perhaps he was trying to impress her with his skill at reading.

"So?" he said, raising his eyes, smiling, "so what is this? He's happy out there, he says. He doesn't communicate with us any more, but he writes to you and says he's happy—what's that? I mean, what the hell is that?"

"But he isn't happy. He wants to come home," Sister Irene said. It was so important that she make him understand that she could not trust her voice; goaded by this man, it might suddenly turn shrill, as his son's did. "Someone must read their letters before they're mailed, so he tried to tell me something by making an allusion to—"

"What?"

"—an allusion to a play, so that I would know. He may be thinking suicide, he must be very unhappy—"

She ran out of breath. Weinstein's mother had begun to cry, but the father was shaking his head jerkily back and forth. "Forgive me, Sister, but it's a lot of crap, he needs the hospital, he needs help—right? It costs me fifty a day out there, and they've got the best place in the state, I figure it's worth it. He needs help, that kid, what do I care if he's unhappy? He's unbalanced!" he said angrily. "You want us to get him out again? We argued with the judge for two hours to get him in, an acquaintance of mine. Look, he can't control himself—he was smashing things here, he was hysterical. They need help, lady, and you do something about it fast! You do something! We made up our minds to do something and we did it! This letter—what the hell is this letter? He never talked like that to us!"

"But he means the opposite of what he says—"

"Then he's crazy! I'm the first to admit it." He was perspiring, and his face had darkened. "I've got no pride left this late. He's a little bastard, you want to know? He calls me names, he's filthy, got a filthy mouth—that's being smart, huh? They give him a big scholarship for his filthy mouth? I went to college too, and I got out and knew something, and I for Christ's sake did something with it; my wife is an intelligent woman, a learned woman, would you guess she does book reviews for the little newspaper out here? Intelligent isn't crazy—crazy isn't intelligent. Maybe for you at the school he writes nice papers and gets an A, but out here, around the house, he can't control himself, and we got him committed!"

"But—"

"We're fixing him up, don't worry about it!" He turned to his wife. "Libby, get out of here, I mean it. I'm sorry, but get out of here, you're making a fool of yourself, go stand in the kitchen or something, you and the goddamn maid can cry on each other's shoulders. That one in the kitchen is nuts too, they're all nuts. Sister," he said, his voice lowering, "I thank you immensely for coming out here. This is wonderful, your interest in my son. And I see he admires you—that letter there. But what about that letter? If he did want to get out, which I don't admit—he was willing to be committed, in the end he said okay himself—if he wanted out I wouldn't do it. Why? So what if he wants to come back? The next day he wants something else, what then? He's a sick kid, and I'm the first to admit it."

Sister Irene felt that sickness spread to her. She stood. The room was so big it seemed it must be a public place; there had been nothing personal or private about their conversation. Weinstein's mother was standing by the fireplace, sobbing. The father jumped to his feet and wiped his forehead in a gesture that was meant to help Sister Irene on her way out. "God, what a day," he said, his eyes snatching at hers for understanding, "you know—one of those days all day long? Sister, I thank you a lot. There should be more people in the world who care about others, like you. I mean that."

On the way back to the convent, the man's words returned to her, and she could not get control of them; she could not even feel anger. She had been pressed down, forced back, what could she do? Weinstein might have been watching her somehow from a barred window, and he surely would have understood. The strange idea she had had on the way over, something about understanding Christ, came back to her now and sickened her. But the sickness was small. It could be contained.

About a month after her visit to his father, Weinstein himself showed up. He was dressed in a suit as before, even the necktie was the same. He came right into her office as if he had been pushed and could not stop.

"Sister," he said, and shook her hand. He must have seen fear in her because he smiled ironically. "Look, I'm released. I'm let out of the nut house. Can I sit down?"

He sat. Sister Irene was breathing quickly, as if in the presence of an enemy who does not know he is an enemy.

"So, they finally let me out. I heard what you did. You talked with him, that was all I wanted. You're the only one who gave a damn. Because you're a humanist and a religious person, you respect . . . the individual. Listen," he said, whispering, "it was hell out there! Hell Birchcrest Manor! All fixed up with fancy chairs and *Life* magazines lying around—and what do they do to you? They locked me up, they gave me shock treatments! Shock treatments, how do you like that, it's discredited by everybody now—they're crazy out there themselves, sadists. They locked me up, they gave me hypodermic shots, they didn't treat me like a human being! Do you know what that is," Weinstein demanded savagely, "not to be treated like a human being? They made me an animal—for fifty dollars a day! Dirty filthy swine!

Now I'm an outpatient because I stopped swearing at them. I found somebody's bobby pin, and when I wanted to scream I pressed it under my fingernail and it stopped me—the screaming went inside and not out—so they gave me good reports, those sick bastards. Now I'm an outpatient and I can walk along the street and breathe in the same filthy exhaust from the buses like all you normal people! Christ," he said, and threw himself back against the chair.

Sister Irene stared at him. She wanted to take his hand, to make some gesture that would close the aching distance between them. "Mr. Weinstein—"

"Call me Allen!" he said sharply.

"I'm very sorry—I'm terribly sorry—"

"My own parents committed me, but of course they didn't know what it was like. It was hell," he said thickly, "and there isn't any hell except what other people do to you. The psychiatrist out there, the main shrink, he hates Jews too, some of us were positive of that, and he's got a bigger nose than I do, a real beak." He made a noise of disgust. "A dirty bastard, a sick, dirty, pathetic bastard—all of them. Anyway, I'm getting out of here, and I came to ask you a favor."

"What do you mean."

"I'm getting out. I'm leaving. I'm going up to Canada and lose myself. I'll get a job, I'll forget everything. I'll kill myself maybe—what's the difference? Look, can you lend me some money?"

"Money?"

"Just a little! I have to get to the border, I'm going to take a bus."

"But I don't have any money—"

"No money?" He stared at her. "You mean—you don't have any? Sure you have some!"

She stared at him as if he had asked her to do something obscene. Everything was splotched and uncertain before her eyes.

"You must . . . you must go back," she said, "you're making a —"

"I'll pay it back. Look, I'll pay it back, can you go to where you live or something and get it? I'm in a hurry. My friends are sons of bitches: one of them pretended he didn't see me yesterday—I stood right in the middle of the sidewalk and yelled at him, I called him some appropriate names! So he didn't see me, huh? You're the only one who understands me, you understand me like a poet, you—"

"I can't help you, I'm sorry—I . . . "

He looked to one side of her and flashed his gaze back, as if he could control it. He seemed to be trying to clear his vision.

"You have the soul of a poet," he whispered, "you're the only one. Everybody else is rotten! Can't you lend me some money, ten dollars maybe? I have three thousand in the bank, and I can't touch it! They take everything away from me, they make me into an animal. . . . You know I'm not an animal, don't you. Don't you?"

"Of course," Sister Irene whispered.

"You could get money. Help me. Give me your hand or something, touch me, help me—please. . . . " He reached for her hand and she drew back. He stared at her and his face seemed about to crumble, like a child's. "I want something from you, but I don't know what—I want something!" he cried. "Something real! I want you to look at me like I was a human being, is that too much to ask? I have a brain, I'm alive, I'm suffering—what does that mean? Does that mean nothing? I want something real and not this phoney Christian love garbage—it's all in the books, it isn't personal—I want something real—look. . . . "

He tried to take her hand again, and this time she jerked away. She got to her feet. "Mr. Weinstein," she said, "please—"

"You! You nun!" he said scornfully, his mouth twisted into a mock grin. "You nun! There's nothing under that ugly outfit, right? And you're not particularly smart even though you think you are; my father has more brains in his foot than you—"

He got to his feet and kicked the chair.

"You bitch!" he cried.

She shrank back against her desk as if she thought he might hit her, but he only ran out of the office.

Weinstein: the name was to become disembodied from the figure, as time went on. The semester passed, the autumn drizzle turned into snow. Sister Irene rode to school in the morning and left in the afternoon, four days a week, anonymous in her black winter cloak, quiet and stunned. University teaching was an anonymous task, each day dissociated from the rest, with no necessary sense of unity among the teachers: they came and went separately and might for a year just miss a colleague who left his office five minutes before they arrived, and it did not matter.

She heard of Weinstein's death, his suicide by drowning, from the English Department secretary, a handsome white-haired woman who kept a transistor radio on her desk. Sister Irene was not surprised; she had been thinking of him as dead for months. "They identified him by some special television way they have now," the secretary said. "They're shipping the body back. It was up in Quebec. . . . "

Sister Irene could feel a part of herself drifting off, lured by the plains of white snow to the north, the quiet, the emptiness, the sweep of the Great Lakes up to the silence of Canada. But she called that part of herself back. She could only be one person in her lifetime. That was the ugly truth, she thought, that she could not really regret Weinstein's suffering and death; she had only one life and had already given it to someone else. He had come too late to her. Fifteen years ago, perhaps, but not now.

She was only one person, she thought, walking down the corridor in a dream. Was she safe in this single person, or was she trapped? She had only one identity. She could make only one choice. What she had done or hadn't done was the result of that choice, and how was she guilty? If she could have felt guilt, she thought, she might at least have been able to feel something.

FLANNERY O'CONNOR

Born in 1925 in Savannah, Georgia, Mary Flannery O'Connor suffered for much of her life from disseminated lupus, a rare blood disease from which she died in 1964. During her short life, she won numerous honours for her several novels and story collections, including the National Book Award for *The Complete Short Stories* (1972). Her best known works include *Wise Blood* (1952), *A Good Man Is Hard to Find* (1955), *The Violent Bear It Away* (1960), and *Everything That Rises Must Converge* (1965). O'Connor's fiction frequently addresses the theme of violence in modern life, questioning the efficacy of religion as a way of overcoming evil. Paradoxically O'Connor, who was deeply committed to Roman Catholicism, has been called a theological writer, one who places ultimate faith in the power of Christian redemption. In her writing she is preoccupied with the issues of sin and grace, but she finds no easy solutions to the riddle of human nature.

"A Good Man Is Hard to Find" (the title is an ironic echo of an old popular song) exemplifies O'Connor's bleak perception of the dark side of the human soul. In the escaped convict known as "The Misfit" she presents an evil not explicable in rational terms, a violence that bursts through conventional forms of order, behaviour, and religious faith. By their own lights, the grandmother and her family are "good people," but they are guided by petty and selfish desires which draw them into the sphere of forces beyond understanding or control. What begins as domestic comedy turns, by a grotesque accident, into an event of profound horror that challenges the notion of a purposeful universe.

FOR FURTHER READING:

Robert H. Brinkmeyer, *The Art and Vision of Flannery O'Connor* (Baton Rouge: Louisiana State UP, 1989).

Marshall B. Gentry, *Flannery O'Connor's Religion of the Grotesque* (Jackson: Univ. Press of Mississippi, 1986).

Suzanne Morrow, *Flannery O'Connor: A Study of the Short Fiction* (Boston: Twayne, 1988).

V. S. Pritchett, "Flannery O'Connor: Satan Comes to Georgia," in *The Tale Bearers: Essays on English, American, and Other Writers* (London: Chatto & Windus, 1980): 164-69.

A Good Man Is
Hard to Find

The GRANDMOTHER didn't want to go to Florida. She wanted to visit some of her connections in east Tennessee and she was seizing at every chance to change Bailey's mind. Bailey was the son she lived with, her only boy. He was sitting on the edge of his chair at the table, bent over the orange sports section of the *Journal*. "Now look here, Bailey," she said, "see here, read this," and she stood with one hand on her thin hip and the other rattling the newspaper at his bald head. "Here this fellow that calls himself The Misfit is aloose from the Federal Pen and headed toward Florida and you read here what it says he did to these people. Just you read it. I wouldn't take my children in any direction with a criminal like that aloose in it. I couldn't answer to my conscience if I did."

Bailey didn't look up from his reading so she wheeled around then and faced the children's mother, a young woman in slacks, whose face was as broad and innocent as a cabbage and was tied around with a green head-kerchief that had two points on the top like rabbit's ears. She was sitting on the sofa, feeding the baby his apricots out of a jar. "The children have been to Florida before," the old lady said. "You all ought to take them somewhere else for a change so they would see different parts of the world and be broad. They never have been to east Tennessee."

The children's mother didn't seem to hear her but the eight-year-old boy, John Wesley, a stocky child with glasses, said, "If you don't want to go to Florida, why dontcha stay at home?" He and the little girl, June Star, were reading the funny papers on the floor.

"She wouldn't stay at home to be queen for a day," June Star said without raising her yellow head.

"Yes and what would you do if this fellow, The Misfit, caught you?" the grandmother asked.

"I'd smack his face," John Wesley said.

"She wouldn't stay at home for a million bucks," June Star said. "Afraid she'd miss something. She has to go everywhere we go."

"All right, Miss," the grandmother said. "Just remember that the next time you want me to curl your hair."

June Star said her hair was naturally curly.

The next morning the grandmother was the first one in the car, ready to go. She had her big black valise that looked like the head of a hippopotamus in one corner, and underneath it she was hiding a basket with Pitty Sing, the cat, in it. She didn't intend for the cat to be left alone in the house for three days because he would miss her too much and she was afraid he might brush against one of the gas burners and accidentally asphyxiate himself. Her son, Bailey, didn't like to arrive at a motel with a cat.

She sat in the middle of the back seat with John Wesley and June Star on either side of her. Bailey and the children's mother and the baby sat in front and they left Atlanta at eight forty-five with the mileage on the car at 55890. The grandmother wrote this down because she thought it would be interesting to say how many miles they had been when they got back. It took them twenty minutes to reach the outskirts of the city.

The old lady settled herself comfortably, removing her white cotton gloves and putting them up with her purse on the shelf in front of the back window. The children's mother still had on slacks and still had her head tied up in a green kerchief, but the grandmother had on a navy blue straw sailor hat with a bunch of white violets on the brim and a navy blue dress with a small white dot in the print. Her collars and cuffs were white organdy trimmed with lace and at her neckline she had pinned a purple spray of cloth violets containing a sachet. In case of an accident, anyone seeing her dead on the highway would know at once that she was a lady.

She said she thought it was going to be a good day for driving, neither too hot nor too cold, and she cautioned Bailey that the speed limit was fifty-five miles an hour and that the patrolmen hid themselves behind billboards and small clumps of trees and sped out after you before you had a chance to slow down. She pointed out interesting details of the scenery: Stone Mountain; the blue granite that in some places came up to both sides of the highway; the brilliant red clay banks slightly streaked with purple; and the various crops that made rows of green lace-work on the ground. The trees were full of silver-white sunlight and the meanest of them sparkled. The children were reading comic magazines and their mother had gone back to sleep.

"Let's go through Georgia fast so we won't have to look at it much," John Wesley said.

"If I were a little boy," said the grandmother, "I wouldn't talk about my native state that way. Tennessee has the mountains and Georgia has the hills."

"Tennessee is just a hillbilly dumping ground," John Wesley said, "and Georgia is a lousy state too."

"You said it," June Star said.

"In my time," said the grandmother, folding her thin veined fingers, "children were more respectful of their native states and their parents and everything else. People did right then. Oh look at the cute little pickaninny!" she said and pointed to a Negro child standing in the door of a shack. "Wouldn't that make a picture, now?" she asked and they all turned and looked at the little Negro out of the back window. He waved.

"He didn't have any britches on," June Star said.

"He probably didn't have any," the grandmother explained. "Little niggers in the country don't have things like we do. If I could paint, I'd paint that picture," she said.

The children exchanged comic books.

The grandmother offered to hold the baby and the children's mother passed him over the front seat to her. She set him on her knee and bounced him and told him about the things they were passing. She rolled her eyes and screwed up her mouth and stuck her leathery thin face into his smooth bland one. Occasionally he gave her a faraway smile. They passed a large cotton field with five or six graves fenced in the middle of it, like a small island. "Look at the graveyard!" the grandmother said, pointing it out. "That was the old family burying ground. That belonged to the plantation."

"Where's the plantation?" John Wesley asked.

"Gone With the Wind," said the grandmother. "Ha. Ha."

When the children finished all the comic books they had brought, they opened the lunch and ate it. The grandmother ate a peanut butter sandwich and an olive and would not let the children throw the box and the paper napkins out the window. When there was nothing else to do they played a game by choosing a cloud and making the other two guess what shape it suggested. John Wesley took one the shape of a cow and June Star guessed a cow and John Wesley said, no, an automobile, and June Star said he didn't play fair, and they began to slap each other over the grandmother.

The grandmother said she would tell them a story if they would keep quiet. When she told a story, she rolled her eyes and waved her head and was very dramatic. She said once when she was a maiden lady she had been courted by a Mr. Edgar Atkins Teagarden from Jasper, Georgia. She said he was a very good-looking man and a gentleman and that he brought her a watermelon every Saturday afternoon with his initials cut in it, E. A. T. Well, one Saturday, she said, Mr. Teagarden brought the watermelon and there was nobody at home and he left it on the front porch and returned in his buggy to Jasper, but she never got the watermelon, she said, because a nigger boy ate it when he saw the initials, E. A. T.! This story tickled John Wesley's funny bone and he giggled and giggled but June Star didn't think it was any good. She said she wouldn't marry a man that just brought her a watermelon on Saturday. The grandmother said she would have done well to marry Mr. Teagarden because he was a gentleman and had bought Coca-Cola stock when it first came out and that he had died only a few years ago, a very wealthy man.

They stopped at The Tower for barbecued sandwiches The Tower was a part stucco and part wood filling station and dance hall set in a clearing outside of Timothy. A fat man named Red Sammy Butts ran it and there were signs stuck here and there on the building and for miles up and down the highway saying, TRY RED SAMMY'S FAMOUS BARBECUE. NONE LIKE FAMOUS RED SAMMY'S! RED SAM! THE FAT BOY WITH THE HAPPY LAUGH. A VETERAN! RED SAMMY'S YOUR MAN!

Red Sammy was lying on the bare ground outside The Tower with his head under a truck while a gray monkey about a foot high, chained to a small chinaberry tree, chattered nearby. The monkey sprang back into the tree and got on the highest limb as soon as he saw the children jump out of the car and run toward him.

Inside, The Tower was a long dark room with a counter at one end and tables at the other and dancing space in the middle. They all sat down at a board table next to the nickelodeon and Red Sam's wife, a tall burnt-brown woman with hair and eyes lighter than her skin, came and took their order. The children's mother put a dime in the machine and played "The Tennessee Waltz," and the grandmother said that tune always made her want to dance. She asked Bailey if he would like to dance but he only glared at her. He didn't have a naturally sunny disposition like she did and trips made him nervous. The grandmother's brown eyes were very bright. She swayed her head from side to side and pretended she was dancing in her chair. June Star said play something she could tap to so the children's mother put in another dime and played a fast number and June Star stepped out onto the dance floor and did her tap routine.

"Ain't she cute?" Red Sam's wife said, leaning over the counter. "Would you like to come be my little girl?"

"No I certainly wouldn't," June Star said. "I wouldn't live in a broken-down place like this for a million bucks!" and she ran back to the table.

"Ain't she cute?" the woman repeated, stretching her mouth politely.

"Aren't you ashamed?" hissed the grandmother.

Red Sam came in and told his wife to quit lounging on the counter and hurry up with these people's order. His khaki trousers reached just to his hip bones and his stomach hung over them like a sack of meal swaying under his shirt. He came over and sat down at a table nearby and let out a combination sigh and yodel. "You can't win," he said. "You can't win," and he wiped his sweating red face off with a gray handkerchief. "These days you don't know who to trust," he said. "Ain't that the truth?"

"People are certainly not nice like they used to be," said the grandmother.

"Two fellers come in here last week," Red Sammy said, "driving a Chrysler. It was a old beat-up car but it was a good one and these boys looked all right to me. Said they worked at the mill and you know I let them fellers charge the gas they bought? Now why did I do that?"

"Because you're a good man!" the grandmother said at once.

"Yes'm, I suppose so," Red Sam said as if he were struck with this answer.

His wife brought the orders, carrying the five plates all at once without a tray, two in each hand and one balanced on her arm. "It isn't a soul in this green world of God's that you can trust," she said. "And I don't count nobody out of that, not nobody," she repeated, looking at Red Sammy.

"Did you read about that criminal, The Misfit, that's escaped?" asked the grandmother.

"I wouldn't be a bit surprised if he didn't attact this place right here," said the woman. "If he hears about it being here, I wouldn't be none surprised to see him. If he hears it's two cent in the cash register, I wouldn't be a tall surprised if he . . . "

"That'll do," Red Sam said. "Go bring these people their Co'-Colas," and the woman went off to get the rest of the order.

"A good man is hard to find," Red Sammy said. "Everything is getting terrible. I remember the day you could go off and leave your screen door unlatched. Not no more."

He and the grandmother discussed better times. The old lady said that in her opinion Europe was entirely to blame for the way things were now. She said the way Europe acted you would think we were made of money and Red Sam said it was no use talking about it, she was exactly right. The children ran outside into the white sunlight and looked at the monkey in the lacy chinaberry tree. He was busy catching fleas on himself and biting each one carefully between his teeth as if it were a delicacy.

They drove off again into the hot afternoon. The grandmother took cat naps and woke up every few minutes with her own snoring. Outside of Toombsboro she woke up and recalled an old plantation that she had visited in this neighbourhood once when she was a young lady. She said the house had six white columns across the front and that there was an avenue of oaks leading up to it and two little wooden trellis arbors on either side in front where you sat down with your suitor after a stroll in the garden. She recalled exactly which road to turn off to get to it. She knew that Bailey would not be willing to lose any time looking at an old house, but the more she talked about it, the more she wanted to see it once again and find out if the little twin arbors were still standing. "There was a secret panel in this house,"she said craftily, not telling the truth but wishing that she were, "and the story went that all the family silver was hidden in it when Sherman came through but it was never found . . . "

"Hey!" John Wesley said. "Let's go see it! We'll find it! We'll poke all the woodwork and find it! Who lives there? Where do you turn off at? Hey Pop, can't we turn off there?"

"We never have seen a house with a secret panel!" June Star shrieked. "Let's go to the house with the secret panel! Hey Pop, can't we go see the house with the secret panel!"

"It's not far from here, I know," the grandmother said. "It wouldn't take over twenty minutes."

Bailey was looking straight ahead. His jaw was as rigid as a horseshoe. "No," he said.

The children began to yell and scream that they wanted to see the house with the secret panel. John Wesley kicked the back of the front seat and June Star hung over her mother's shoulder and whined desperately into her ear that they never had any fun even on their vacation, that they could never do what THEY wanted to do. The baby began to scream and John Wesley kicked the back of the seat so hard that his father could feel the blows in his kidney.

"All right!" he shouted and drew the car to a stop at the side of the road. "Will you all shut up? Will you all just shut up for one second? If you don't shut up, we won't go anywhere."

"It would be very educational for them," the grandmother murmured.

"All right," Bailey said, "but get this: this is the only time we're going to stop for anything like this. This is the one and only time."

"The dirt road that you have to turn down is about a mile back," the grandmother directed. "I marked it when we passed."

"A dirt road," Bailey groaned.

After they had turned and were headed toward the dirt road, the grandmother recalled other points about the house, the beautiful glass over the front doorway and the candle-lamp in the hall. John Wesley said that the secret panel was probably in the fireplace.

"You can't go inside this house," Bailey said. "You don't know who lives there."

"While you all talk to the people in front, I'll run around behind and get in a window," John Wesley suggested.

"We'll all stay in the car," his mother said.

They turned onto the dirt road and the car raced roughly along in a swirl of pink dust. The grandmother recalled the times when there were no paved roads and thirty miles was a day's journey. The dirt road was hilly and there were sudden washes in it and sharp curves on dangerous embankments. All at once they would be on a hill, looking down over the blue tops of trees for miles around, then the next minute, they would be in a red depression with the dust-coated trees looking down on them.

"This place had better turn up in a minute," Bailey said, "or I'm going to turn around."

The road looked as if no one had traveled on it in months.

"It's not much farther," the grandmother said and just as she said it, a horrible thought came to her. The thought was so embarrassing that she turned red in the face and her eyes dilated and her feet jumped up, upsetting her valise in the corner. The instant the valise moved, the newspaper top she had over the basket under it rose with a snarl and Pitty Sing, the cat, sprang onto Bailey's shoulder.

The children were thrown to the floor and their mother, clutching the baby, was thrown out the door onto the ground; the old lady was thrown into the front seat. The car turned over once and landed right-side-up in a gulch off the side of the road. Bailey remained in the driver's seat with the cat—gray-striped with a broad white face and an orange nose—clinging to his neck like a caterpillar.

As soon as the children saw they could move their arms and legs, they scrambled out of the car, shouting, "We've had an ACCIDENT!" The grandmother was curled up under the dashboard, hoping she was injured so that Bailey's wrath would not come down on her all at once. The horrible thought she had had before the accident was that the house she had remembered so vividly was not in Georgia but in Tennessee.

Bailey removed the cat from his neck with both hands and flung it out the window against the side of a pine tree. Then he got out of the car and started looking for the children's mother. She was sitting against the side of the red gutted ditch, holding the screaming baby, but she only had a cut down her face and a broken shoulder. "We've had an ACCIDENT!" the children screamed in a frenzy of delight.

"But nobody's killed," June Star said with disappointment as the grandmother limped out of the car, her hat still pinned to her head but the broken front brim standing up at a jaunty angle and the violet spray hanging off the side. They all sat down in the ditch, except the children, to recover from the shock. They were all shaking.

"Maybe a car will come along," said the children's mother hoarsely.

"I believe I have injured an organ," said the grandmother pressing her side, but no one answered her. Bailey's teeth were clattering. He had on a yellow sport shirt with bright blue parrots designed in it and his face was as yellow as the shirt. The grandmother decided that she would not mention that the house was in Tennessee.

The road was about ten feet above and they could see only the tops of the trees on the other side of it. Behind the ditch they were sitting in there were more woods, tall and dark and deep. In a few minutes they saw a car some distance away on top of a hill, coming slowly as if the occupants were watching them. The grandmother stood up and waved both arms dramatically to attract their attention. The car continued to come on slowly, disappeared around a bend and appeared again, moving even slower, on top of the hill they had gone over. It was a big black battered hearse-like automobile. There were three men in it.

It came to a stop just over them and for some minutes, the driver looked down with a steady expressionless gaze to where they were sitting, and didn't speak. Then he turned his head and muttered something to the other two and they got out. One was a fat boy in black trousers and a red sweat shirt with a silver stallion embossed on the front of it. He moved around on the right side of them and stood staring, his mouth partly open in a kind of loose grin. The other had on khaki pants and a blue striped coat and a gray hat pulled down very low, hiding most of his face. He came around slowly on the left side. Neither spoke.

The driver got out of the car and stood by the side of it, looking down at them. He was an older man than the other two. His hair was just beginning to gray and he wore silver-rimmed spectacles that gave him a scholarly look. He had a long creased face and didn't have on any shirt or undershirt. He had on blue jeans that were too tight for him and was holding a black hat and a gun. The two boys also had guns.

"We've had an ACCIDENT!" the children screamed.

The grandmother had the peculiar feeling that the bespectacled man was someone she knew. His face was as familiar to her as if she had known him all her life but she could not recall who he was. He moved away from the car and began to come down the embankment, placing his feet carefully so that he wouldn't slip. He had on tan and white shoes and no socks, and his ankles were red and thin. "Good afternoon," he said. "I see you all had you a little spill."

"We turned over twice!" said the grandmother.

"Oncet," he corrected. "We seen it happen. Try their car and see will it run, Hiram," he said quietly to the boy with the gray hat.

"What you got that gun for?" John Wesley asked. "Whatcha gonna do with that gun?"

"Lady," the man said to the children's mother, "would you mind calling them children to sit down by you? Children make me nervous. I want all you all to sit down right together there where you're at."

"What are you telling US what to do for?" June Star asked.

Behind them the line of woods gaped like a dark open mouth. "Come here," said their mother.

"Look here now," Bailey began suddenly, "we're in a predicament! We're in . . . "

The grandmother shrieked. She scrambled to her feet and stood staring. "You're The Misfit!" she said. "I recognized you at once!"

"Yes'm," the man said, smiling slightly as if he were pleased in spite of himself to be known, "but it would have been better for all of you, lady, if you hadn't of reckernized me."

Bailey turned his head sharply and said something to his mother that shocked even the children. The old lady began to cry and The Misfit reddened.

"Lady," he said, "don't you get upset. Sometimes a man says things he don't mean. I don't reckon he meant to talk to you thataway."

"You wouldn't shoot a lady, would you?" the grandmother said and removed a clean handkerchief from her cuff and began to slap at her eyes with it.

The Misfit pointed the toe of his shoe into the ground and made a little hole and then covered it up again. "I would hate to have to," he said.

"Listen," the grandmother almost screamed, "I know you're a good man. You don't look a bit like you have common blood. I know you must come from nice people!"

"Yes mam," he said, "finest people in the world." When he smiled he showed a row of strong white teeth. "God never made a finer woman than my mother and my daddy's heart was pure gold," he said. The boy with the red sweat shirt had come around behind them and was standing with his gun at his hip. The Misfit squatted down on the ground. "Watch them children, Bobby Lee," he said. "You know they make me nervous." He looked at the six of them huddled together in front of him and he seemed to be embarrassed as if he couldn't think of anything to say. "Ain't a cloud in the sky," he remarked, looking up at it. "Don't see no sun but don't see no cloud neither."

"Yes, it's a beautiful day," said the grandmother. "Listen," she said, "you shouldn't call yourself The Misfit because I know you're a good man at heart. I can just look at you and tell."

"Hush!" Bailey yelled. "Hush! Everybody shut up and let me handle this!" He was squatting in the position of a runner about to sprint forward but he didn't move.

"I pre-chate that, lady," The Misfit said and drew a little circle in the ground with the butt of his gun.

"It'll take a half a hour to fix this here car," Hiram called, looking over the raised hood of it.

"Well, first you and Bobby Lee get him and that little boy to step over yonder with you." The Misfit said, pointing to Bailey and John

Wesley. "The boys want to ast you something," he said to Bailey. "Would you mind stepping back in them woods there with them?"

"Listen," Bailey began, "we're in a terrible predicament! Nobody realizes what this is," and his voice cracked. His eyes were as blue and intense as the parrots in his shirt and he remained perfectly still.

The grandmother reached up to adjust her hat brim as if she were going to the woods with him but it came off in her hand. She stood staring at it and after a second she let it fall on the ground. Hiram pulled Bailey up by the arm as if he were assisting an old man. John Wesley caught hold of his father's hand and Bobby Lee followed. They went off toward the woods and just as they reached the dark edge, Bailey turned and supporting himself against a gray naked pine trunk, he shouted, "I'll be back in a minute, Mamma, wait on me!"

"Come back this instant!" his mother shrilled but they all disappeared into the woods.

"Bailey Boy!" the grandmother called in a tragic voice but she found she was looking at The Misfit squatting on the ground in front of her. "I just know you're a good man," she said desperately, "You're not a bit common!"

"Nome, I ain't a good man," The Misfit said after a second as if he had considered her statement carefully, "but I ain't the worst in the world neither. My daddy said I was a different breed of dog from my brothers and sisters. 'You know,' Daddy said, 'it's some that can live their whole life out without asking about it and it's others has to know why it is, and this boy is one of the latters. He's going to be into everything!'" He put on his black hat and looked up suddenly and then away deep into the woods as if he were embarrassed again. "I'm sorry I don't have on a shirt before you ladies," he said, hunching his shoulders slightly. "We buried our clothes that we had on when we escaped and we're just making do until we can get better. We borrowed these from some folks we met," he explained.

"That's perfectly all right," the grandmother said. "Maybe Bailey has an extra shirt in his suitcase."

"I'll look and see terrectly," The Misfit said.

"Where are they taking him?" the children's mother screamed.

"Daddy was a card himself," The Misfit said. "You couldn't put anything over on him. He never got in trouble with the Authorities though. Just had the knack of handling them."

"You could be honest too if you'd only try," said the grandmother. "Think how wonderful it would be to settle down and live a comfortable life and not have to think about somebody chasing you all the time."

The Misfit kept scratching in the ground with the butt of his gun as if he were thinking about it. "Yes'm, somebody is always after you," he murmured.

The grandmother noticed how thin his shoulder blades were just behind his hat because she was standing up looking down at him. "Do you ever pray?" she asked.

He shook his head. All she saw was the black hat wiggle between his shoulder blades. "Nome," he said.

There was a pistol shot from the woods, followed closely by another. Then silence. The old lady's head jerked around. She could hear the wind move through the tree tops like a long satisfied insuck of breath. "Bailey Boy!" she called.

"I was a gospel singer for a while," The Misfit said. "I been most everything. Been in the arm service, both land and sea, at home and abroad, been twict married, been an undertaker, been with the rail-roads, plowed Mother Earth, been in a tornado, seen a man burnt alive oncet," and he looked up at the children's mother and the little girl who were sitting close together, their faces white and their eyes glassy; "I even seen a woman flogged," he said.

"Pray, pray," the grandmother began, "pray, pray . . . "

"I never was a bad boy that I remember of," The Misfit said in an almost dreamy voice, "but somewheres along the line I done something wrong and got sent to the penitentiary. I was buried alive," and he looked up and held her attention to him by a steady stare.

"That's when you should have started to pray," she said. "What did you do to get sent to the penitentiary that first time?"

"Turn to the right, it was a wall," The Misfit said, looking up again at the cloudless sky. "Turn to the left, it was a wall. Look up it was a ceiling, look down it was a floor. I forget what I done, lady. I set there and set there, trying to remember what it was I done and I ain't recalled it to this day. Oncet in a while, I would think it was coming to me, but it never come."

"Maybe they put you in by mistake," the old lady said vaguely.

"Nome," he said. "It wasn't no mistake. They had the papers on me."

"You must have stolen something," she said.

The Misfit sneered slightly. "Nobody had nothing I wanted," he said. "It was a head-doctor at the penitentiary said what I had done was kill my daddy but I known that for a lie. My daddy died in nineteen ought nineteen of the epidemic flu and I never had a thing to do with it. He was buried in the Mount Hopewell Baptist churchyard and you can go there and see for yourself."

"If you would pray," the old lady said, "Jesus would help you."

"That's right," The Misfit said.

"Well then, why don't you pray?" she asked trembling with delight suddenly.

"I don't want no hep," he said. "I'm doing all right by myself."

Bobby Lee and Hiram came ambling back from the woods. Bobby Lee was dragging a yellow shirt with bright blue parrots in it.

"Thow me that shirt, Bobby Lee," The Misfit said. The shirt came flying at him and landed on his shoulder and he put it on. The grandmother couldn't name what the shirt reminded her of. "No, lady," The Misfit said while he was buttoning it up, "I found out the crime don't matter. You can do one thing or you can do another, kill a man or take a tire off his car, because sooner or later you're going to forget what it was you done and just be punished for it."

The children's mother had begun to make heaving noises as if she couldn't get her breath. "Lady," he asked, "would you and that little girl like to step off yonder with Bobby Lee and Hiram and join your husband?"

"Yes, thank you," the mother said faintly. Her left arm dangled helplessly and she was holding the baby, who had gone to sleep, in the other. "Hep that lady up, Hiram," The Misfit said as she struggled to climb out of the ditch, "and Bobby Lee, you hold onto that little girl's hand."

"I don't want to hold hands with him," June Star said. "He reminds me of a pig."

The fat boy blushed and laughed and caught her by the arm and pulled her off into the woods after Hiram and her mother.

Alone with The Misfit, the grandmother found that she had lost her voice. There was not a cloud in the sky nor any sun. There was nothing around her but woods. She wanted to tell him that he must pray. She opened and closed her mouth several times before anything came out. Finally she found herself saying, "Jesus. Jesus," meaning, Jesus will help you, but the way she was saying it, it sounded as if she might be cursing.

"Yes'm," The Misfit said as if he agreed. "Jesus thown everything off balance. It was the same case with Him as with me except He hadn't committed any crime and they could prove I had committed one because they had the papers on me. Of course," he said, "they never shown me my papers. That's why I sign myself now. I said long ago, you get you a signature and sign everything you do and keep a copy of it. Then you'll know what you done and you can hold up the crime to the punishment and see do they match and in the end you'll have something to prove you ain't been treated right. I call myself The Misfit," he said, "because I can't make what all I done wrong fit what all I gone through in punishment."

There was a piercing scream from the woods, followed closely by a pistol report. "Does it seem right to you, lady, that one is punished a heap and another ain't punished at all?"

"Jesus!" the old lady cried. "You've got good blood! I know you wouldn't shoot a lady! I know you come from nice people! Pray! Jesus, you ought not to shoot a lady. I'll give you all the money I've got!"

"Lady," The Misfit said, looking beyond her far into the woods, "there never was a body that give the undertaker a tip."

There were two more pistol reports and the grandmother raised her head like a parched old turkey hen crying for water and called, "Bailey Boy, Bailey Boy!" as if her heart would break.

"Jesus was the only One that ever raised the dead," The Misfit continued, "and He shouldn't have done it. He thown everything off balance. If He did what He said, then it's nothing for you to do but thow away everything and follow Him, and if He didn't, then it's nothing for you to do but enjoy the few minutes you got left the best way you can—by killing somebody or burning down his house or doing some other meanness to him. No pleasure but meanness," he said and his voice had become almost a snarl.

"Maybe He didn't raise the dead," the old lady mumbled, not knowing what she was saying and feeling so dizzy that she sank down in the ditch with her legs twisted under her.

"I wasn't there so I can't say He didn't," The Misfit said. "I wisht I had of been there," he said, hitting the ground with his fist. "It ain't right I wasn't there because if I had of been there I would of known. Listen lady," he said in a high voice, "if I had of been there I would of known and I wouldn't be like I am now." His voice seemed about to crack and the grandmother's head cleared for an instant. She saw the man's face twisted close to her own as if her were going to cry and she murmured, "Why you're one of my babies. You're one of my own children!" She reached out and touched him on the shoulder. The Misfit sprang back as if a snake had bitten him and shot her three times through the chest. Then he put his gun down on the ground and took off his glasses and began to clean them.

Hiram and Bobby Lee returned from the woods and stood over the ditch, looking down at the grandmother who half sat and half lay in a puddle of blood with her legs crossed under her like a child's and her face smiling up at the cloudless sky.

Without his glasses, The Misfit's eyes were red-rimmed and pale and defenseless-looking. "Take her off and thow her where you thown the others," he said, picking up the cat that was rubbing itself against his leg.

"She was a talker, wasn't she?" Bobby Lee said, sliding down the ditch with a yodel.

"She would of been a good woman," The Misfit said, "if it had been somebody there to shoot her every minute of her life."

"Some fun!" Bobby Lee said.

"Shut up, Bobby Lee," The Misfit said. "It's no real pleasure in life."

Katherine Anne Porter (1890-1980) was born in Texas, and her formal education was limited to girls' schools in the South; but she learned much from her own reading, and early formed the desire to be a writer. Her first collection of short stories, *Flowering Judas and other stories* (1930; augmented edition, 1935), won immediate critical praise for her smooth, spare prose, and for the psychological insights of such stories as "He." The success of *Flowering Judas and other stories* brought her a Guggenheim Fellowship, which enabled her to travel; and her subsequent voyage to Europe in 1931 provided the material for her longest work, the novel *Ship of Fools* (1962). The many awards and distinctions conferred upon her include a Pulitzer Prize, which she received in 1966.

In her introduction in the 1940 edition of *Flowering Judas and other stories*, Porter describes how she sought "to understand the logic of this majestic and terrible failure of the life of man in the Western world"; and to a greater or lesser extent, this concern is reflected in all her work. She dramatizes the human struggle for contact and communication in the face of all fears, prejudices, and frustrations which alienate people from each other. Like the protagonist in her long story "The Leaning Tower" (1944), many of her characters confront a society in the process of disintegration, or experience "an infernal desolation of the spirit, and chill and the knowledge of death. . . . " Porter's stories reflect her sense of the confusion that characterizes human life; she investigates "self-betrayal and self-deception—the way that all human beings deceive themselves about the way they operate. . . . Everyone takes his stance, asserts his own rights and feelings, mistaking the motives of others, and his own . . . " (*Paris Review* interview, 1963). In "He," Mrs. Whipple succeeds for a while in shutting away the truth about her feelings for her son; but the author passes no harsh judgment on her self-delusion and insincerity, and portrays with compassion the dawning horror of her final recognition of failure.

FOR FURTHER READING

George Hendrick, *Katherine Anne Porter* (New York: Twayne, 1965).

M.M. Libermann, *Katherine Anne Porter's Fiction* (Detroit: Wayne State UP, 1971).

Barbara Thompson, "The Art of Fiction XXIX: Katherine Anne Porter," *Paris Review* 8 (Winter/Spring 1963): 87-114.

Darlene Harbour Unrue, *Truth and Vision in Katherine Anne Porter's Fiction* (Athens: University of Georgia Press, 1985).

Life was very hard for the Whipples. It was hard to feed all the hungry mouths, it was hard to keep the children in flannels during the winter, short as it was. "God knows what would become of us if we lived north," they would say; keeping them decently clean was hard. "It looks like our luck won't never let up on us," said Mr Whipple, but Mrs Whipple was all for taking what was sent and calling it good, anyhow when the neighbours were in earshot. "Don't ever let a soul hear us complain," she kept saying to her husband. She couldn't stand to be pitied. "No, not if it comes to it that we have to live in a wagon and pick cotton around the country," she said, "nobody's going to get a chance to look down on us."

Mrs Whipple loved her second son, the simple-minded one, better than she loved the other two children put together. She was for ever saying so, and when she talked with certain of her neighbours, she would even throw in her husband and her mother for good measure.

"You needn't keep on saying it around," said Mr Whipple, "you'll make people think nobody else has any feelings about Him but you."

"It's natural for a mother," Mrs Whipple would remind him. "You know yourself it's more natural for a mother to be that way. People don't expect so much of fathers, some way."

This didn't keep the neighbours from talking plainly among themselves. "A Lord's pure mercy if He should die," they said. "It's the sins of the fathers," they agreed among themselves. "There's bad blood and bad doings somewhere, you can bet on that." This behind the Whipples' backs. To their faces everybody said, "He's not so bad off. He'll be all right yet. Look how He grows!"

Mrs Whipple hated to talk about it, she tried to keep her mind off it, but every time anybody set foot in the house, the subject always came up, and she had to talk about Him first, before she could get on to anything else. It seemed to ease her mind. "I wouldn't have anything happen to Him for all the world, but it just looks like I can't keep Him out of mischief. He's so strong and active. He's always into everything; He was like that since He could walk. It's actually funny sometimes the way He can do anything; it's laughable to see Him up to His tricks. Emly has more accidents; I'm for every tying up her bruises, and Adna can't fall a foot without cracking a bone. But He can do anything and not get a scratch. The preacher said such a nice thing once when he was here. He said, and I'll remember it to my dying day, 'The innocent walk with God—that's why He don't get hurt.'" Whenever Mrs Whipple repeated these words, she always felt a warm pool spread in her breast, and the tears would fill her eyes, and then she could talk about something else.

He did grow and He never got hurt. A plank blew off the chicken house and struck Him on the head and He never seemed to know it. He had learned a few words, and after this He forgot them. He didn't whine for food as the other children did, but waited until it was given Him; He ate squatting in the corner, smacking and mumbling. Rolls of fat covered Him like an overcoat, and He could carry twice as much wood and water as Adna. Emly had a cold in the head most of the time—"she takes that after me," said Mrs Whipple—so in bad weather they gave her the extra blanket off His cot. He never seemed to mind the cold.

Just the same, Mrs Whipple's life was a torment for fear something might happen to Him. He climbed the peach trees much better than Adna and went skittering along the branches like a monkey, just a regular monkey. "Oh, Mrs Whipple, you hadn't ought to let Him do that. He'll lose His balance sometime. He can't rightly know what He's doing."

Mrs Whipple almost screamed out at the neighbour. "He *does* know what He's doing! He's as able as any other child! Come down out of there, you!" When He finally reached the ground she could hardly keep her hands off Him for acting like that before people, a grin all over His face and her worried sick about Him all the time.

"It's the neighbours," said Mrs Whipple to her husband. "Oh, I do mortally wish they would keep out of our business. I can't afford to let Him do anything for fear they'll come nosing around about it. Look at the bees, now. Adna can't handle them, they sting him so. I haven't got time to do everything, and now I don't dare let Him. But if He gets a sting He don't really mind."

"It's just because He ain't got sense enough to be scared of anything," said Mr Whipple.

"You ought to be ashamed of yourself," said Mrs Whipple, "talking that way about your own child. Who's to take up for Him if we don't, I'd like to know? He sees a lot that goes on, He listens to things all the time. And anything I tell Him to do He does it. Don't never let anybody hear you say such things. They'd think you favoured the other children over Him."

"Well, now I don't, and you know it, and what's the use of getting all worked up about it? You always think the worst of everything. Just let Him alone, He'll get along somehow. He gets plenty to eat and wear, don't He?" Mr Whipple suddenly felt tired out. "Anyhow, it can't be helped now."

Mrs Whipple felt tired too; she complained in a tired voice: "What's done can't never be undone, I know that good as anybody; but He's my child, and I'm not going to have people say anything. I get sick of people coming around saying things all the time."

In the early autumn Mrs Whipple got a letter from her brother saying he and his wife and two children were coming over for a little visit next Sunday week. "Put the big pot in the little one," he wrote at the end. Mrs Whipple read this part out loud twice, she was so pleased. Her brother was a great one for saying funny things. "We'll just show him that's no joke," she said, "we'll just butcher one of the sucking pigs."

"It's a waste and I don't hold with waste the way we are now," said Mr Whipple. "That pig'll be worth money by Christmas."

"It's a shame and a pity we can't have a decent meal's vittles once in a while when my own family comes to see us," said Mrs Whipple. "I'd hate for his wife to go back and say there wasn't a thing in the house to eat. My God, it's better than buying up a great chance of meat in town. There's where you'd spend the money!"

"All right, do it yourself then," said Mr Whipple. "Christamighty, no wonder we can't get ahead!"

The question was how to get the little pig away from his ma, a great fighter, worse than a Jersey cow. Adna wouldn't try it: "That sow'd rip my insides out all over the pen." "All right, old fraidy," said Mrs Whipple, "*He's* not scared. Watch *Him* do it." And she laughed as though it was all a good joke and gave Him a little push towards the pen. He sneaked up and snatched the pig right away from the teat and galloped back and was over the fence with the sow raging at His heels. The little black squirming thing was screeching like a baby in a tantrum, stiffening its back and stretching its mouth to the ears. Mrs Whipple took the pig with her face stiff and sliced its throat with one stroke. When He saw the blood He gave a great jolting breath and ran away. "But He'll forget and eat plenty, just the same," thought Mrs Whipple. Whenever she was thinking, her lips moved, making words. "He'd eat it all if I didn't stop Him. He'd eat up every mouthful from the other two if I'd let Him."

She felt badly about it. He was ten years old now and a third again as large as Adna, who was going on fourteen. "It's a shame, a shame," she kept saying under her breath, "and Adna with so much brains!"

She kept on feeling badly about all sorts of things. In the first place it was the man's work to butcher; the sight of the pig scraped pink and naked made her sick. He was too fat and soft and pitiful-looking. It was simply a shame the way things had to happen. By the time she had finished it up, she almost wished her brother would stay at home.

Early on Sunday morning Mrs Whipple dropped everything to get Him all cleaned up. In an hour He was dirty again, with crawling under fences after an opossum, and straddling along the rafters of the barn looking for eggs in the hayloft. "My lord, look at you now after all my trying! And here's Adna and Emly staying so quiet. I get tired trying to keep you decent. Get off that shirt and put on another; people will say I don't half dress you!" And she boxed Him on the ears, hard. He blinked and blinked and rubbed His head, and His face hurt Mrs Whipple's feelings. Her knees began to tremble, she had to sit down while she buttoned His shirt. "I'm just all gone before the day starts."

The brother came with his plump healthy wife and two great roaring hungry boys. They had a grand dinner, with the pig roasted to a crackling in the middle of the table, full of dressing, a pickled peach in his mouth and plenty of gravy for the sweet potatoes.

"This looks like prosperity all right," said the brother; "you're going to have to roll me home like I was a barrel when I'm done."

Everybody laughed out loud; it was fine to hear them laughing all at once around the table. Mrs Whipple felt warm and good about it. "Oh, we've got six more of these; I say it's a little as we can do when you come to see us so seldom."

He wouldn't come into the dining-room and Mrs Whipple passed it off very well. "He's timider than my other two," she said. "He'll just have to get used to you. There isn't everybody He'll make up with, you know how it is with some children, even cousins." Nobody said anything out of the way.

"Just like my Alfy here," said the brother's wife. "I sometimes got to lick him to make him shake hands with his own grandmammy."

So that was over, and Mrs Whipple loaded up a big plate for Him first, before everybody. "I always say He ain't to be slighted, no matter who else goes without," she said, and carried it to Him herself.

"He can chin Himself on the top of the door," said Emly, helping along.

"That's fine. He's getting along fine," said the brother.

They went away after supper. Mrs Whipple rounded up the dishes, sent the children to bed, and sat down and unlaced her shoes. "You see?" she said to Mr Whipple. "That the way my whole family is. Nice and considerate about everything. No out-of-the-mouth remarks—

they *have* got refinement. I get awfully sick of people's remarks. Wasn't that pig good?"

Mr Whipple said, "Yes, we're out three hundred pounds of pork, that's all. It's easy to be polite when you come to eat. Who knows what they had in their minds all along?"

"Yes, that's like you," said Mrs Whipple. "I don't expect anything else from you. You'll be telling me next that my own brother will be saying around that we made Him eat in the kitchen! Oh, my God!" She rocked her head in her hands, a hard pain started in the very middle of her forehead. "Now it's all spoiled, and everything was so nice and easy. All right, you don't like them and you never did—all right, they'll not come here again soon, never you mind! But they *can't* say He wasn't dressed every lick as good as Adna—oh, honest, sometimes I wish I was dead!"

"I wish you'd let up," said Mr Whipple. "It's bad enough as it is."

It was a hard winter. It seemed to Mrs Whipple that they hadn't ever known anything but hard times, and now to cap it all a winter like this. The crops were about half of what they a right to expect; after the cotton was in it didn't do much more than cover the grocery bill. They swapped off one of the plough horses, and got cheated, for the new one died of the heaves. Mrs Whipple kept thinking all the time it was terrible to have a man you couldn't depend on not to get cheated. They cut down on everything, but Mrs Whipple kept saying there are things you can't cut down on, and they cost money. It took a lot of warm clothes for Adna and Emly, who walked four miles to school during the three-months session. "He sets around the fire a lot. He won't need so much," said Mr Whipple. "That's so," said Mrs Whipple, "and when He does the outdoor chores He can wear your tarpaulin coat. I can't do no better, that's all."

In February He was taken sick, and lay curled up under His blanket looking very blue in the face and acting as if He would choke. Mr and Mrs Whipple did everything they could for Him for two days, and then they were scared and sent for the doctor. The doctor told them they must keep Him warm and give Him plenty of milk and eggs. "He isn't as stout as He looks, I'm afraid," said the doctor. "You've got to watch them when they're like that. You must put more cover on Him, too."

"I just took off His big blanket to wash," said Mrs Whipple, ashamed. "I can't stand dirt."

"Well, you'd better put it back on the minute it's dry," said the doctor, "or He'll have pneumonia."

Mr and Mrs Whipple took a blanket off their own bed and put His cot in by the fire. "They can't say we didn't do everything for Him," she said, "even to sleeping cold ourselves on His account."

When the winter broke He seemed to be well again, but He walked as if His feet hurt Him. He was able to run a cotton planter during the season.

"I got it all fixed up with Jim Ferguson about breeding the cow next time," said Mr Whipple. "I'll pasture the bull this summer and give Jim some fodder in the autumn. That's better than paying out money when you haven't got it."

"I hope you didn't say such a thing before Jim Ferguson," said Mrs Whipple. "You oughtn't to let him know we're so down as all that."

"Godamighty, that ain't saying we're down! A man has got to look ahead sometimes. *He* can lead the bull over today. I need Adna on the place."

At first Mrs Whipple felt easy in her mind about sending Him for the bull. Adna was too jumpy and couldn't be trusted. You've got to be steady around animals. After He was gone she started thinking, and after a while she could hardly bear it any longer. She stood in the lane and watched for Him. It was nearly three miles to go and a hot day, but He oughtn't to be so long about it. She shaded her eyes and stared until coloured bubbles floated in her eyeballs. It was just like everything else in life, she must always worry and never know a moment's peace about anything. After a long time she saw Him turn into the side lane, limping. He came on very slowly, leading the big hulk of an animal by a ring in the nose, twirling a little stick in His hand, never looking back or sideways, but coming on like a sleepwalker with His eyes half shut.

Mrs Whipple was scared sick of bulls; she had heard awful stories about how they followed on quietly enough, and then suddenly pitched on with a bellow and pawed and gored a body to pieces. Any second now that black monster would come down on Him. My God. He'd never have sense enough to run.

She mustn't make a sound nor a move; she mustn't get the bull started. The bull heaved his head aside and horned the air at a fly. Her voice burst out of her in a shriek, and she screamed at Him to come on, for God's sake. He didn't seem to hear her clamour, but kept on twirling His switch and limping on, and the bull lumbered along behind him as gently as a calf. Mrs Whipple stopped calling and ran towards the house, praying under her breath: "Lord, don't let anything happen to Him. Lord, you *know* people will say we oughtn't to have sent Him. You *know* they'll say we didn't take care of Him. Oh, get Him home, safe home, safe home, and I'll look out for Him better! Amen."

She watched from the window while He led the beast in and tied him up in the barn. It was no use trying to keep up. Mrs Whipple couldn't bear another thing. She sat down and rocked and cried with her apron over her head.

From year to year the Whipples were growing poorer and poorer. The place just seemed to run down of itself, no matter how hard they worked. "We're losing our hold," said Mrs Whipple. "Why can't we do like other people and watch for our best chances? They'll be calling us poor white trash next."

"When I get to be sixteen I'm going to leave," said Adna. "I'm going to get a job in Powell's grocery store. There's money in that. No more farm for me."

"I'm going to be a school teacher," said Emly. "But I've got to finish the eighth grade, anyhow. Then I can live in town. I don't see any chances here."

"Emly takes after my family," said Mrs Whipple. "Ambitious every last one of them, and they don't take second place for anybody."

When autumn came Emly got a chance to wait at table in the railroad eating-house in the town near by, and it seemed such a shame not to take it when the wages were good and she could get her food too, that Mrs Whipple decided to let her take it, and not bother with school until the next session. "You've got plenty of time," she said. "You're young and smart as a whip."

With Adna gone too, Mr Whipple tried to run the farm with just Him to help. He seemed to get along fine, doing His work and part of Adna's without noticing it. They did well enough until Christmas time, when one morning He slipped on the ice coming up from the barn. Instead of getting up He thrashed round and round, and when Mr Whipple got to Him, He was having some sort of fit.

They brought Him inside and tried to make Him sit up, but He blubbered and rolled, so they put Him to bed and Mr Whipple rode to town for the doctor. All the way there and back he worried about where the money was to come from: it sure did look like he had about all the troubles he could carry.

From then on He stayed in bed. His legs swelled up double their size, and the fits kept coming back. After four months the doctor said, "It's no use, I think you'd better put Him in the County Home for treatment right away. I'll see about it for you. He'll have good care there and be off your hands."

"We don't begrudge Him any care, and I won't let Him out of my sight," said Mrs Whipple. "I won't have it said I sent my sick child off among strangers."

"I know how you feel," said the doctor. "You can't tell me anything about that, Mrs Whipple. I've got a boy of my own. But you'd better listen to me. I can't do anything more for Him, that's the truth."

Mr and Mrs Whipple talked it over a long time that night after they went to bed. "It's just charity," said Mrs Whipple, "that's what we've come to, charity! I certainly never looked for this."

"We pay taxes to help support the place just like everybody else," said Mr Whipple, "and I don't call that taking charity. I think it would be fine to have Him where He'd get the best of everything . . . and besides, I can't keep up with these doctor's bills any longer."

"Maybe that's why the doctor wants us to send Him—he's scared he won't get his money," said Mrs Whipple.

"Don't talk like that," said Mr Whipple, feeling pretty sick, "or we won't be able to send Him."

"Oh, but we won't keep Him there long," said Mrs Whipple. "Soon's He's better we'll bring Him right back home."

"The doctor has told you, and told you time and again, He can't ever get better, and you might as well stop talking," said Mr Whipple.

"Doctors don't know everything," said Mrs Whipple, feeling almost happy. "But anyhow, in the summer Emly can come home for a vacation, and Adna can get down for Sundays: we'll all work together and get on our feet again, and the children will feel they've got a place to come to."

All at once she saw it full summer again, with the garden going fine, and new white roller shades up all over the house, and Adna and Emly home, so full of life; all of them happy together. Oh, it could happen, things would ease up on them.

They didn't talk before Him much, but they never knew just how much He understood. Finally the doctor set the day and a neighbour who owned a double-seated carryall offered to drive them over. The hospital would have sent an ambulance, but Mrs Whipple couldn't stand to see Him going away looking so sick as all that. They wrapped Him in blankets, and the neighbour and Mr. Whipple lifted Him into the back seat of the carryall beside Mrs Whipple, who had on her black shirtwaist. She couldn't stand to go looking like charity.

"You'll be all right, I guess I'll stay behind," said Mr Whipple. "It don't look like everybody ought to leave the place at once."

"Besides, it ain't as if He was going to stay for ever," said Mrs Whipple to the neighbour. "This is only for a little while."

They started away, Mrs Whipple holding to the edges of the blankets to keep Him from sagging sideways. He sat there blinking and blinking. He worked His hands out and began rubbing His nose with his knuckles, and then with the end of the blanket. Mrs Whipple couldn't believe what she saw; He was scrubbing away big tears that rolled out of the corners of His eyes. He snivelled and made a gulping noise. Mrs Whipple kept saying, "Oh, honey, you don't feel so bad, do you? You don't feel so bad, do you?" for He seemed to be accusing her of something. Maybe He remembered that time she boxed His ears; maybe He had been scared that day with the bull; maybe He had slept cold and couldn't tell her about it; maybe He knew they were sending Him away for good and all because they were too poor to keep Him.

Whatever it was, Mrs Whipple couldn't bear to think of it. She began to cry, frightfully, and wrapped her arms tightly round him. His head rolled on her shoulder: she had loved Him as much as she possibly could; there were Adna and Emly who had to be thought of too, there was nothing she could do to make up to Him for His life. Oh, what a mortal pity He was ever born.

They came in sight of the hospital, with the neighbour driving very fast, not daring to look behind him.

Born in Shellbrook, Saskatchewan in 1908, Sinclair Ross grew up on the Canadian prairies. He worked as a banker there and in Montreal before retiring to live in Greece and Spain, and subsequently in Vancouver. The author of several novels, he is particularly known for his first, *As for Me and My House*, which appeared in 1941. Like many of his short stories, most of which were collected in 1968 under the title *The Lamp at Noon and other stories*, it deals with the realities of rural prairie life during the drought and depression of the 1930s.

Ross's art displays the chief characteristics of literary regionalism: scrupulous fidelity to the geographical realities of a place and time, sensitivity to the details of speech, habit, and social convention, and a vital interest in the connections between a landscape and its people. He attempts not only to invoke these connections but also to elicit from the reader an appreciation for the way in which they give a particular cast to a universal human dilemma. Recurrently Ross dramatizes the tensions between human beings and nature, integrates them with Calvinist mores, and then qualifies his response to the Protestant ethic by the importance he attaches to artistic freedom. In the world he draws, nature and society exert uncompromising demands; beauty and art are ephemeral things, and against the pressures of day-to-day survival they seem to have peripheral value—to be sentimental, impractical, and (in the language of that culture) "womanish." At the same time, they are extraordinarily important. As "Cornet at Night" suggests, the characters who appreciate artistry will be all the more frustrated by their immediate environment because of their sensitivity. But in recognizing the limitations of their surroundings they also discover resources upon which less fortunate individuals cannot draw.

FOR FURTHER READING

Keath Fraser, "Futility at the Pump: the Short Stories of Sinclair Ross," *Queen's Quarterly* 77 (Spring 1970): 72-80.

Lorraine McMullen, *Sinclair Ross* (Boston: Twayne, 1979).

Donald Stephens, ed., *Writers of the Prairies* (Vancouver: University of British Columbia, 1973).

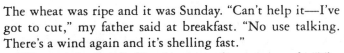

Cornet at Night

The wheat was ripe and it was Sunday. "Can't help it—I've got to cut," my father said at breakfast. "No use talking. There's a wind again and it's shelling fast."

"Not on the Lord's Day," my mother protested. "The horses stay in the stables where they belong. There's church this afternoon and I intend to ask Louise and her husband home for supper."

Ordinarily my father was a pleasant, accommodating little man, but this morning his wheat and the wind had lent him sudden steel. "No, today we cut," he met her evenly. "You and Tom go to church if you want to. Don't bother me."

"If you take the horses out today I'm through—I'll never speak to you again. And this time I mean it."

He nodded. "Good—if I'd known I'd have started cutting wheat on Sundays years ago."

"And that's no way to talk in front of your son. In the years to come he'll remember."

There was silence for a moment and then, as if in its clash with hers his will had suddenly found itself, my father turned to me.

"Tom, I need a man to stook for a few days and I want you to go to town tomorrow and get me one. The way the wheat's coming along so fast and the oats nearly ready too I can't afford the time. Take old Rock. You'll be safe with him."

But ahead of me my mother cried, "That's one thing I'll not stand for. You can cut your wheat or do anything else you like yourself, but you're not interfering with him. He's going to school tomorrow as usual."

My father bunched himself and glared at her. "No, for a change he's going to do what I say. The crop's more important than a day at school."

"But Monday's his music lesson day—and when will we have another teacher like Miss Wiggins who can teach him music too?"

"A dollar for lessons and the wheat shelling! When I was his age I didn't even get to school."

"Exactly," my mother scored, "and look at you today. Is it any wonder I want him to be different?"

He slammed out at that to harness his horses and cut his wheat, and away sailed my mother with me in her wake to spend an austere half-hour in the dark, hot, plushy little parlour. It was a kind of vicarious atonement, I suppose, for we both took straight-backed leather chairs, and for all of the half-hour stared across the room at a big pansy-bordered motto on the opposite wall: *As for Me and My House We Will Serve the Lord.*

At last she rose and said, "Better run along and do your chores now, but hurry back. You've got to take your bath and change your clothes, and maybe help a little getting dinner for your father."

There was a wind this sunny August morning, tanged with freedom and departure, and from his stall my pony Clipper whinnied for a race with it. Sunday or not, I would ordinarily have had my gallop anyway, but today a sudden welling-up of social and religious conscience made me ask myself whether one in the family like my father wasn't bad enough. Returning to the house, I merely said that on such a fine day it seemed a pity to stay inside. My mother heard but didn't answer. Perhaps her conscience too was working. Perhaps after being worsted in the skirmish with my father, she was in no mood for granting dispensations. In any case I had to take my bath as usual, put on a clean white shirt, and change my overalls for knicker corduroys.

They squeaked, those corduroys. For three months now they had been spoiling all my Sundays. A sad, muted, swishing little squeak, but distinctly audible. Every step and there it was, as if I needed to be oiled. I had to wear them to church and Sunday-school; and after service, of course, while the grown-ups stood about gossiping, the other boys discovered my affliction. I sulked and fumed, but there was nothing to be done. Corduroys that had cost four-fifty simply couldn't be thrown away till they were well worn-out. My mother warned me that if I started sliding down the stable roof, she'd patch the seat and make me keep on wearing them.

With my customary little bow-legged sidle I slipped into the kitchen again to ask what there was to do. "Nothing but try to behave like a Christian and a gentleman," my mother answered stiffly. "Put on a tie, and shoes and stockings. Today your father is just about as much as I can bear."

"And then what?" I asked hopefully. I was thinking that I might take a drink to my father, but dared not as yet suggest it.

"Then after you can stay quiet and read—and afterwards practise your music lesson. If your Aunt Louise should come she'll find that at least I bring my son up decently."

It was a long day. My mother prepared the midday meal as usual, but, to impress upon my father the enormity of his conduct, withdrew as soon as the food was served. When he was gone, she and I emerged to take our places at the table in an atmosphere of unappetizing righteousness. We didn't eat much. The food was cold, and my mother had no heart to warm it up. For relief at last she said, "Run along and feed the chickens while I change my dress. Since we aren't going to service today we'll read Scripture for a while instead."

And Scripture we did read, Isaiah, verse about, my mother in her black silk dress and rhinestone brooch, I in my corduroys and Sunday shoes that pinched. It was a very august afternoon, exactly like the tone that had persisted in my mother's voice since breakfast time. I think I might have openly rebelled, only for the hope that by compliance I yet might win permission for the trip to town with Rock. I was inordinately proud that my father had suggested it, and for his faith in me forgave him even Isaiah and the plushy afternoon. Whereas with my mother, I decided, it was a case of downright bigotry.

We went on reading Isaiah, and then for a while I played hymns on the piano. A great many hymns—even the ones with awkward sharps and accidentals that I'd never tried before—for, fearing visitors, my mother was resolved to let them see that she and I were uncontaminated by my father's sacrilege, But among these likely visitors was my Aunt Louise, a portly, condescending lady married to a well-off farmer with a handsome motor-car, and always when she came it was my mother's vanity to have me play for her a waltz or reverie, or *Holy Night* sometimes with variations. A man-child and prodigy might eclipse the motor-car. Presently she roused herself, and pretending mild reproof began, "Now, Tommy, you're going wooden on those hymns. For a change you'd better practise *Sons of Liberty*. Your Aunt Louise will want to hear it, anyway."

There was a fine swing and vigour in this piece, but it was hard. Hard because it was so alive, so full of youth and head-high rhythm. It was a march, and it did march. I couldn't take time to practise at the hard spots slowly till I got them right, for I had to march too. I had to let my fingers sometimes miss a note or strike one wrong. Again and again this afternoon I started carefully, resolving to count right through, the way Miss Wiggins did, and as often I sprang ahead to lead my march a moment or two all dash and fire, and then fall stumbling in the bitter dust of dissonance. My mother didn't know. She thought that speed and perseverance would eventually get me there. She tapped her foot and smiled encouragement, and gradually as the afternoon wore on began to look a little disappointed that there were to be no visitors, after all. "Run along for the cows," she said at last, "while I get supper ready for your father. There'll be nobody here, so you can slip into your overalls again."

I looked at her a moment, and then asked, "What am I going to wear to town tomorrow? I might get grease or something on the corduroys."

For while it was always my way to exploit the future, I liked to do it rationally, within the limits of the sane and probable. On my way for the cows I wanted to live the trip to town tomorrow many times, with variations, but only on the explicit understanding that tomorrow there was to be a trip to town. I have always been tethered to reality, always compelled by an unfortunate kind of probity in my nature to prefer a barefaced disappointment to the luxury of a future I have no just claims upon.

I went to town the next day, though not till there had been a full hour's argument that paradoxically enough gave all three of us the victory. For my father had his way: I went; I had my way: I went; and in return for her consent my mother wrung a promise from him of a pair of new plush curtains for the parlour when the crop was threshed, and for me the metronome that Miss Wiggins declared was the only way I'd ever learn to keep time on marching pieces like the *Sons of Liberty*.

It was my first trip to town alone. That was why they gave me Rock, who was old and reliable and philosophic enough to meet motor-cars and the chance locomotive on an equal and even somewhat supercilious footing.

"Mind you pick somebody big and husky," said my father as he started for the field. "Go to Jenkins' store, and he'll tell you who's in town. Whoever it is, make sure he's stooked before."

"And mind it's somebody who looks like he washed himself," my mother warned, "I'm going to put clean sheets and pillowcases on the bunkhouse bed, but not for any dirty tramp or hobo."

By the time they had both finished with me there were a great many things to mind. Besides repairs for my father's binder, I was to take two crates of eggs each containing twelve dozen eggs to Mr. Jenkins' store and in exchange have a list of groceries filled. And to make it complicated, both quantity and quality of some of the groceries were to be determined by the price of eggs. Thirty cents a dozen, for instance, and I was to ask for coffee at sixty-five cents a pound. Twenty-nine cents a dozen and coffee at fifty cents a pound. Twenty-eight and no oranges. Thirty-one and bigger oranges. It was like decimals with Miss Wiggins, or two notes in the treble against three in the bass. For my father a tin of special blend tobacco, and my mother not to know. For my mother a box of face powder at the drugstore, and my father not to know. Twenty-five cents from my father on the side for ice-cream and licorice. Thirty-five from my mother for my dinner at the Chinese restaurant. And warning, of course, to take good care of Rock, speak politely to Mr. Jenkins, and see that I didn't get machine oil on my corduroys.

It was three hours to town with Rock, but I don't remember them, I remember nothing but a smug satisfaction with myself, an exhilarating conviction of importance and maturity—and that only by contrast with the sudden sag to embarrassed insignificance when finally old Rock and I drove up to Jenkins' store.

For a farm boy is like that. Alone with himself and his horse he cuts a fine figure. He is the measure of the universe. He foresees a great many encounters with life, and in them all acquits himself a little more than creditably. He is fearless, resourceful, a bit of a brag. His horse never contradicts.

But in town it is different. There are eyes here, critical, that pierce with a single glance the little bubble of his self-importance, and leave him dwindled smaller even than his normal size. It always happens that way. They are so superbly poised and sophisticated, these strangers, so completely masters of their situation as they loll in doorways and go sauntering up and down Main Street. Instantly he yields to them his place as measure of the universe, especially if he is a small boy wearing squeaky corduroys, especially if he has a worldly-wise old horse like Rock, one that knows his Main Streets, and will take them in nothing but his own slow philosophic stride.

We arrived all right. Mr. Jenkins was a little man with a freckled bald head, and when I carried in my two crates of eggs, one in each hand, and my legs bowed a bit, he said curtly, "Well, can't you set them down? My boy's delivering, and I can't take time to count them now myself."

"They don't need counting," I said politely. "Each layer holds two dozen, and each crate holds six layers. I was there. I saw my mother put them in."

At this a tall, slick-haired young man in yellow shoes who had been standing by the window turned around and said, "That's telling you, Jenkins—he was there." Nettled and glowering, Jenkins himself came round the counter and repeated, "So you were there, were you? Smart youngster! What did you say was your name?"

Nettled in turn to preciseness I answered, "I haven't yet. It's Thomas Dickson and my father's David Dickson, eight miles north of here. He wants a man to stook and was too busy to come himself."

He nodded, unimpressed, and then putting out his hand said, "Where's your list? Your mother gave you one, I hope?"

I said she had and he glowered again. "Then let's have it and come back in half an hour. Whether you were there or not, I'm going to count your eggs. How do I know that half of them aren't smashed?"

"That's right," agreed the young man, sauntering to the door and looking at Rock. "They've likely been bouncing along at a merry clip. You're quite sure, Buddy, that you didn't have a runaway?"

Ignoring the impertinence I staved off Jenkins. "The list, you see, has to be explained. I'd rather wait and tell you about it later on."

He teetered a moment on his heels and toes, then tried again. "I can read too. I make up orders every day. Just go away for a while—look for your man—anything."

"It wouldn't do," I persisted. "The way this one's written isn't what it really means. You'd need me to explain—"

He teetered rapidly. "Show me just one thing I don't know what it means."

"Oranges," I said, "but that's only oranges if eggs are twenty-nine cents or more—and bigger oranges if they're thirty-one. You see, you'd never understand—"

So I had my way and explained it all right then and there. What with eggs at twenty-nine and a half cents a dozen and my mother out a little in her calculations, it was somewhat confusing for a while; but after arguing a lot and pulling away the paper from each other that they were figuring on, the young man and Mr. Jenkins finally had it all worked out, with mustard and soap omitted altogether, and an extra half-dozen oranges thrown in. "Vitamins," the young man overruled me, "they make you grow"—and then with a nod towards an open biscuit box invited me to help myself.

I took a small one, and started up Rock again. It was nearly one o'clock now, so in anticipation of his noonday quart of oats he trotted off, a little more briskly, for the farmers' hitching-rail beside the lumber-yard. This was the quiet end of town. The air drowsed redolent of pine and tamarack, and resin simmering slowly in the sun. I poured out the oats and waited till he had finished. After the way the town had treated me it was comforting and peaceful to stand with my fingers in his mane, hearing him munch. It brought me a sense of place again in life. It made me feel almost as important as before. But when he finished and there was my own dinner to be thought about I found myself more of an alien in the town than ever, and felt the way to the little Chinese restaurant doubly hard. For Rock was older than I. Older and wiser, with a better understanding of important things. His philosophy included the relishing of oats even within a stone's throw of sophisticated Main Street. Mine was less mature.

I went, however, but I didn't have dinner. Perhaps it was my stomach, all puckered and tense with nervousness. Perhaps it was the restaurant itself, the pyramids of oranges in the window and the dark green rubber plant with the tropical-looking leaves, the indolent little Chinaman behind the counter and the dusky smell of last night's cigarettes that to my prairie nostrils was the orient itself, the exotic atmosphere about it all with which a meal of meat and vegetables and pie would have somehow simply jarred. I climbed onto a stool and ordered an ice-cream soda.

A few stools away there was a young man sitting. I kept watching him and wondering.

He was well-dressed, a nonchalance about his clothes that distinguished him from anyone I had ever seen, and yet at the same time it was a shabby suit, with shiny elbows and threadbare cuffs. His hands were slender, almost a girl's hands, yet vaguely with their shapely quietness they troubled me, because, however slender and smooth, they were yet hands to be reckoned with, strong with a strength that was different from the rugged labour-strength I knew.

He smoked a cigarette, and blew rings towards the window.

Different from the farmer boys I knew, yet different also from the young man with the yellow shoes in Jenkins' store. Staring out at it through the restaurant window he was as far away from Main Street as was I with plodding old Rock and my squeaky corduroys. I presumed for a minute or two an imaginary companionship. I finished my soda, and to be with him a little longer ordered lemonade. It was strangely important to be with him, to prolong a while this companionship. I hadn't the slightest hope of his noticing me, nor the slightest intention of obtruding myself. I just wanted to be there, to be assured by something I had never encountered before, to store it up for the three hours home with old Rock.

Then a big, unshaven man came in, and slouching onto the stool beside me said, "They tell me across the street you're looking for a couple of hands. What's your old man pay this year?"

"My father," I corrected him, "doesn't want a couple of men. He just wants one."

"I've got a pal," he insisted, "and we always go together."

I didn't like him. I couldn't help making contrasts with the cool, trim quietness of the young man sitting farther along. "What do you say?" he said as I sat silent, thrusting his stubby chin out almost over my lemonade. "We're ready any time."

"It's just one man my father wants," I said aloofly, drinking off my lemonade with a flourish to let him see I meant it. "And if you'll excuse me now—I've got to look for somebody else."

"What about this?" he intercepted me, and doubling up his arm displayed a hump of muscle that made me, if not more inclined to him, at least a little more deferential. "My pal's got plenty, too. We'll set up two stooks any day for anybody else's one."

"Not both," I edged away from him. "I'm sorry—you just wouldn't do."

He shook his head contemptuously. "Some farmer—just one man to stook."

"My father's a good farmer," I answered stoutly, rallying to the family honour less for its own sake than for what the young man on the other stool might think of us. "And he doesn't need just one man to stook. He's got three already. That's plenty other years, but this year the crop's so big he needs another. So there!"

"I can just see the place," he said, slouching to his feet and starting towards the door. "An acre of two of potatoes and a couple of dozen hens."

I glared after him a minute, then climbed back onto the stool and ordered another soda. The young man was watching me now in the big mirror behind the counter, and when I glanced up and met his eyes he gave a slow, half-smiling little nod of approval. And out of all proportion to anything it could mean, his nod encouraged me. I didn't flinch or fidget as I would have done had it been the young man with the yellow shoes watching me, and I didn't stammer over the confession that his amusement and appraisal somehow forced from me. "We haven't three men—just my father—but I'm to take one home today. The wheat's ripening fast this year and shelling, so he can't do it all himself."

He nodded again and then after a minute asked quietly, "What about me? Would I do?"

I turned on the stool and stared at him.

"I need a job, and if it's any recommendation there's only one of me."

"You don't understand," I started to explain, afraid to believe that perhaps he really did. "It's to stook. You have to be in the field by seven o'clock and there's only a bunkhouse to sleep in—a granary with a bed in it—"

"I know—that's about what I expect." He drummed his fingers a minute, then twisted his lips into a kind of half-hearted smile and went on, "They tell me a little toughening up is what I need. Outdoors, and plenty of good hard work—so I'll be like the fellow that just went out."

The wrong hands; white slender fingers, I knew they'd never do—but catching the twisted smile again I pushed away my soda and said quickly, "Then we'd better start right away. It's three hours home, and I've still some places to go. But you can get in the buggy now, and we'll drive around together."

We did. I wanted it that way, the two of us, to settle scores with Main Street. I wanted to capture some of old Rock's disdain and unconcern; I wanted to know what it felt like to take young men with yellow shoes in my stride, to be preoccupied, to forget them the moment that we separated. And I did. "My name's Philip," the stranger said as we drove from Jenkins' to the drugstore. "Philip Coleman—usually just Phil," and companionably I responded, "Mine's Tommy Dickson. For the last year, though, my father says I'm getting big and should be called just Tom."

That was what mattered now, the two of us there, and not the town at all. "Do you drive yourself all the time?" he asked, and nonchalant and off-hand I answered, "You don't really have to drive old Rock. He just goes, anyway. Wait till you see my chestnut three-year-old. Clipper I call him. Tonight after supper if you like you can take him for a ride."

But since he'd never learned to ride at all he thought Rock would do better for a start, and then we drove back to the restaurant for his cornet and valise.

"Is it something to play?" I asked as we cleared the town. "Something like a bugle?"

He picked up the black leather case from the floor of the buggy and held it on his knee. "Something like that. Once I played a bugle too. A cornet's better, though."

"And you mean you can play the cornet?"

He nodded. "I play in a band. At least I did play in a band. Perhaps if I get along all right with the stooking I will again some time."

It was later that I pondered this, how stooking for my father could have anything to do with going back to play in a band. At the moment I confided, "I've never heard a cornet—never even seen one. I suppose you still play it sometimes—I mean at night, when you've finished stooking."

Instead of answering directly he said, "That means you've never heard a band either." There was surprise in his voice, almost incredulity, but it was kindly. Somehow I didn't feel ashamed because I had lived all my eleven years on a prairie farm, and knew nothing more than Miss Wiggins and my Aunt Louise's gramophone. He went on, "I was younger than you are now when I started playing in a band. Then I was with an orchestra a while—then with the band again. It's all I've done ever since."

It made me feel lonely for a while, isolated from the things in life that mattered, but, brightening presently, I asked, "Do you know a piece called *Sons of Liberty*? Four flats in four-four time?"

He thought hard a minute, and then shook his head. "I'm afraid I don't—not by name anyway. Could you whistle a bit of it?"

I whistled two pages, but still he shook his head. "A nice tune, though," he conceded. "Where did you learn it?"

"I haven't yet," I explained. "Not properly, I mean. It's been my lesson for the last two weeks, but I can't keep up to it."

He seemed interested, so I went on and told him about my lessons and Miss Wiggins, and how later on they were going to buy me a metronome so that when I played a piece I wouldn't always be running away with it, "Especially a march. It keeps pulling you along the way it really ought to go until you're all mixed up and have to start at the beginning again. I know I'd do better if I didn't feel that way, and could keep slow and steady like Miss Wiggins."

But he said quickly, "No, that's the right way to feel—you've just got to learn to harness it. It's like old Rock here and Clipper. The way you are, you're Clipper. But if you weren't that way, if you didn't get excited and wanted to run sometimes, you'd just be Rock. You see? Rock's easier to handle than Clipper, but at his best he's a sleepy old plow-horse. Clipper's harder to handle—he may even cost you some tumbles. But finally get him broken in and you've got a horse that amounts to something. You wouldn't trade him for a dozen like Rock."

It was a good enough illustration, but it slandered Rock. And he was listening. I know—because even though like me he had never heard a cornet before, he had experience enough to accept it at least with tact and manners.

For we hadn't gone much farther when Philip, noticing the way I kept watching the case that was still on his knee, undid the clasps and took the cornet out. It was a very large cornet, shapely and eloquent, gleaming in the August sun like pure and mellow gold. I couldn't restrain myself. I said, "Play it—play it now—just a little bit to let me hear."

And in response, smiling at my earnestness, he raised it to his lips.

But there was only one note—only one fragment of a note—and then away went Rock. I'd never have believed he had it in him. With a snort and plunge he was off the road and into the ditch—then out of the ditch again and off at a breakneck gallop across the prairie. There were stones and badger holes, and he spared us none of them. The egg-crates full of groceries bounced out, then the tobacco, then my mother's face powder. "Whoa, Rock!" I cried, "Whoa, Rock!" but in the rattle and whir of wheels I don't suppose he even heard. Philip couldn't help much because he had his cornet to hang on to. I tried to tug on the reins, but at such a rate across the prairie it took me all my time to keep from following the groceries. He was a big horse, Rock, and once under way had to run himself out. Or he may have thought that if he gave us a thorough shaking-up we would be too subdued when it was over to feel like taking him seriously to task. Anyway, that was how it worked out. All I dared to do was run round to pat his sweaty neck and say, "Good Rock, good Rock—nobody's going to hurt you."

Besides there were the groceries to think about, and my mother's box of face powder. And his pride and reputation at stake, Rock had made it a runaway worthy of the horse he really was. We found the powder smashed open and one of the egg-crates cracked. Several of the oranges had rolled down a badger hole, and couldn't be recovered. We spent nearly ten minutes sifting raisins through our fingers, and still they felt a little gritty. "There were extra oranges," I tried to encourage Philip, "and I've seen my mother wash her raisins." He looked at me dubiously, and for a few minutes longer worked away trying to mend the egg-crate.

We were silent for the rest of the way home. We thought a great deal about each other, but asked no questions. Even though it was safely away in its case again I could still feel the cornet's presence as if it were a living thing. Somehow its gold and shapeliness persisted, transfiguring the day, quickening the dusty harvest fields to a gleam and lustre like its own. And I felt assured, involved. Suddenly there was a force in life, a current, an inevitability, carrying me along too. The questions they would ask when I reached home—the difficulties in making them understand that faithful old Rock had really run away—none of it now seemed to matter. This stranger with the white, thin hands, this gleaming cornet that as yet I hadn't even heard, intimately and enduringly now they were my possessions.

When we reached home my mother was civil and no more. "Put your things in the bunkhouse," she said, "and then wash here. Supper'll be ready in about an hour."

It was an uncomfortable meal. My father and my mother kept looking at Philip and exchanging glances. I told them about the cornet and the runaway, and they listened stonily. "We've never had a harvest-hand before that was a musician too," my mother said in a somewhat thin voice. "I suppose, though, you do know how to stook?"

I was watching Philip desperately and for my sake he lied, "Yes, I stooked last year. I may have a blister or two by this time tomorrow, but my hands will toughen up."

"You don't as a rule do farm work?" my father asked.

And Philip said, "No, not as a rule."

There was an awkward silence, so I tried to champion him. "He plays his cornet in a band. Ever since he was my age—that's what he does."

Glances were exchanged again. The silence continued.

I had been half-intending to suggest that Philip bring his cornet into the house to play it for us, I perhaps playing with him on the piano, but the parlour with its genteel plushiness was a room from which all were excluded but the equally genteel—visitors like Miss Wiggins and the minister—and gradually as the meal progressed I came to understand that Philip and his cornet, so far as my mother was concerned, had failed to qualify.

So I said nothing when he finished his supper, and let him go back to the bunkhouse alone. "Didn't I say to have Jenkins pick him out?" my father stormed as soon as he had gone. "Didn't I say somebody big and strong?"

"He's tall," I countered, "and there wasn't anybody else except two men, and it was the only way they'd come."

"You mean you didn't want anybody else. A cornet player! Fine stooks he'll set up." And then, turning to my mother, "It's your fault—you and your nonsense about music lessons. If you'd listen to me sometimes, and try to make a man of him."

"I do listen to you," she answered quickly. "It's because I've had to listen to you now for thirteen years that I'm trying to make a different man of him. If you'd go to town yourself instead of keeping him out of school—and do your work in six days a week like decent people. I told you yesterday that in the long run it would cost you dear."

I slipped away and left them. The chores at the stable took me nearly an hour; and then, instead of returning to the house, I went over to see Philip. It was dark now, and there was a smoky lantern lit. He sat on the only chair, and in a hospitable silence motioned me to the bed. At once he ignored and accepted me. It was as if we had always known each other and long outgrown the need of conversation. He smoked, and blew rings towards the open door where the warm fall night encroached. I waited, eager, afraid lest they call me to the house, yet knowing that I must wait. Gradually the flame in the lantern smoked the glass till scarcely his face was left visible. I sat tense, expectant, wondering who he was, where he came from, why he should be here to do my father's stooking.

There were no answers, but presently he reached for his cornet. In the dim, soft darkness I could see it glow and quicken. And I remember still what a long and fearful moment it was, crouched and steeling myself, waiting for him to begin.

And I was right: when they came the notes were piercing, golden as the cornet itself, and they gave life expanse that it had never known before. They floated up against the night, and each for a moment hung there clear and visible. Sometimes they mounted poignant and sheer. Sometimes they soared and then, like a bird alighting, fell and brushed earth again.

It was *To the Evening Star*. He finished it and told me. He told me the names of all the other pieces that he played: an *Ave Maria*, *Song of India*, a serenade—all bright through the dark like slow, suspended lightning, chilled sometimes with a glimpse of the unknown. Only for Philip there I could not have endured it. With my senses I clung hard to him—the acrid smell of his cigarettes, the tilted profile daubed with smoky light.

Then abruptly he stood up, as if understanding, and said, "Now we'd better have a march, Tom—to bring us back where we belong. A cornet can be good fun, too, you know. Listen to this one and tell me."

He stood erect, head thrown back exactly like a picture in my reader of a bugler boy, and the notes came flashing gallant through the night until the two of us went swinging along in step with them a hundred thousand strong. For this was another march that did march. It marched us miles. It made the feet eager and the heart brave. It said that life was worth the living and bright as morning shone ahead to show the way.

When he had finished and put the cornet away I said, "There's a field right behind the house that my father started cutting this afternoon. If you like we'll go over now for a few minutes and I'll show you how to stook. . . . You see, if you set your sheaves on top of the stubble they'll be over again in half an hour. That's how everybody does at first but it's wrong. You've got to push the butts down hard, right to the ground—like this, so they bind with the stubble. At a good slant, see, but not too much. So they'll stand the wind and still shed water if it rains."

It was too dark for him to see much, but he listened hard and finally succeeded in putting up a stook or two that to my touch seemed firm enough. Then my mother called, and I had to slip away fast so that she would think I was coming from the bunkhouse. "I hope he stooks as well as he plays," she said when I went in. "Just the same, you should have done as your father told you, and picked a likelier man to see us through the fall."

My father came in from the stable then, and he, too, had been listening. With a wondering, half-incredulous little movement of his head he made acknowledgement.

"Didn't I tell you he could?" I burst out, encouraged to indulge my pride in Philip. "Didn't I tell you he could play?" But with sudden anger in his voice he answered, "And what if he can! It's a man to stook I want. Just look at the hands on him. I don't think he's ever seen a farm before."

It was helplessness, though, not anger. Helplessness to escape his wheat when wheat was not enough, when something more than wheat had just revealed itself. Long after they were both asleep I remembered, and with a sharp foreboding that we might have to find another man, tried desperately to sleep myself. "Because if I'm up in good time," I rallied all my faith in life, "I'll be able to go to the field with him and at least make sure he's started right. And he'll maybe do. I'll ride down after school and help till supper time. My father's reasonable."

Only in such circumstances, of course, and after such a day, I couldn't sleep till nearly morning, with the result that when at last my mother wakened me there was barely time to dress and ride to school. But of the day I spent there I remember nothing. Nothing except the midriff clutch of dread that made it a long day—nothing, till straddling Clipper at four again. I galloped him straight to the far end of the farm where Philip that morning had started to work.

Only Philip, of course, wasn't there. I think I knew—I think it was what all day I had been expecting. I pulled Clipper up short and sat staring at the stooks. Three or four acres of them—crooked and dejected as if he had never heard about pushing the butts down hard into the stubble. I sat and stared till Clipper himself swung round and started for home. He wanted to run, but because there was nothing left now but the half-mile ahead of us, I held him to a walk. Just to prolong a little the possibility that I had misunderstood things. To wonder within the limits of the sane and probable if tonight he would play his cornet again.

When I reached the house my father was already there, eating an early supper. "I'm taking him back to town," he said quietly. "He tried hard enough—he's just not used to it. The sun was hot today; he lasted till about noon. We're starting in a few minutes, so you'd better go out and see him."

He looked older now, stretched out limp on the bed, his face haggard. I tiptoed close to him anxiously, afraid to speak. He pulled his mouth sidewise in a smile at my concern, then motioned me to sit down. "Sorry I didn't do better," he said. "I'll have to come back another year and have another lesson."

I clenched my hands and clung hard to this promise that I knew he couldn't keep. I wanted to rebel against what was happening, against the clumsiness and crudity of life, but instead I stood quiet for a moment, almost passive, then wheeled away and carried out his cornet to the buggy. My mother was already there, with a box of lunch and some ointment for his sunburn. She said she was sorry things had turned out this way, and thanking her politely he said that he was sorry too. My father looked uncomfortable, feeling, no doubt, that we were all unjustly blaming everything on him. It's like that on a farm. You always have to put the harvest first.

And that's all there is to tell. He waved going through the gate; I never saw him again. We watched the buggy down the road to the first turn, then with a quick resentment in her voice my mother said, "Didn't I say that the little he gained would in the long run cost him dear? Next time he'll maybe listen to me—and remember the Sabbath Day."

What exactly she was thinking I never knew. Perhaps of the crop and the whole day's stooking lost. Perhaps of the stranger who had come with his cornet for a day, and then as meaninglessly gone again. For she had been listening, too, and she may have understood. A harvest, however lean, is certain every year; but a cornet at night is golden only once.

Carol Shields, born in 1935 in Oak Park, Illinois, has lived in Canada since 1957. A graduate of Hanover College and the University of Ottawa, where she embarked on a study of the nineteenth-century pioneer memoirist Susanna Moodie, she now lives and writes in Winnipeg, Manitoba. She has published several volumes of fiction, including *Small Ceremonies* (1976), *A Fairly Conventional Woman* (1982), and *Swann: A Mystery*, which was a finalist for the 1987 Governor-General's Award.

"Mrs. Turner Cutting the Grass" was published first in the journal *Arts Manitoba* and then collected in Shields' 1985 volume, *Various Miracles*. The story admirably displays Shields' satiric gifts by showing how inadequate are the assumptions that people make about their neighbours' lives. What the Saschers see they judge to be unfashionable, common, shallow, or peculiar; and perhaps Mrs. Turner is as grotesque a figure as they think, one who lives life erratically. But what Mrs. Turner sees, in her mind's eye, is the reality of a life lived according to a different set of conventions. She is aware that society and its institutions make ethical and esthetic judgments, though she does not always recognize how radically these judgments differ from her own. But is Shields satirizing suburban superficiality here—or the obtuse self-satisfaction of an old woman?

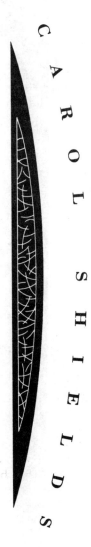

C
A
R
O
L

S
H
I
E
L
D
S

FOR FURTHER READING

Room of One's Own 13, no. 1-2 (July 1989), special Shields issue, including Eleanor Wachtel, "Interview with Carol Shields," pp. 5-45.

Mrs. Turner Cutting the Grass

OH, MRS. TURNER is a sight cutting the grass on a hot afternoon in June! She climbs into an ancient pair of shorts and ties on her halter top and wedges her feet into crepe-soled sandals and covers her red-gray frizz with Gord's old golf cap—Gord is dead now, ten years ago, a seizure on a Saturday night while winding the mantel clock.

The grass flies up around Mrs. Turner's knees. Why doesn't she use a catcher, the Saschers next door wonder. Everyone knows that leaving the clippings like that is bad for the lawn. Each fallen blade of grass throws a minute shadow which impedes growth and repair. The Saschers themselves use their clippings to make compost which they hope one day will be ripe as the good manure that Sally Sascher's father used to spread on his fields down near Emerson Township.

Mrs. Turner's carelessness over the clippings plucks away at Sally, but her husband Roy is far more concerned about the Killex that Mrs. Turner dumps on her dandelions. It's true that in Winnipeg the dandelion roots go right to the middle of the earth, but Roy is patient and persistent in pulling them out, knowing exactly how to grasp the coarse leaves in his hand and how much pressure to apply. Mostly they come up like corks with their roots intact. And he and Sally are experimenting with new ways to cook dandelion greens, believing as they do that the components of nature are arranged for a specific purpose—if only that purpose can be divined.

In the early summer Mrs. Turner is out every morning by ten with her sprinkling can of chemical killer, and Roy, watching from his front porch, imagines how this poison will enter the ecosystem and move by quick capillary surges into his fenced vegetable plot, newly seeded now with green beans and lettuce. His children, his two little girls aged two and four—that they should be touched by such poison makes him morose and angry. But he and Sally so far have said nothing to Mrs. Turner about her abuse of the planet because they're hoping she'll go into an old-folks home soon or maybe die, and then all will proceed as it should.

High-school girls on their way home in the afternoon see Mrs. Turner cutting her grass and are mildly, momentarily repelled by the lapped, striated flesh on her upper thighs. At her age. Doesn't she realize? Every last one of them is intimate with the vocabulary of skin care and knows that what has claimed Mrs. Turner's thighs is the enemy called cellulite, but they can't understand why she doesn't take the trouble to hide it. It makes them queasy; it makes them fear for the future.

The things Mrs. Turner doesn't know would fill the Saschers' new compost pit, would sink a ship, would set off a tidal wave, would make her want to kill herself. Back and forth, back and forth she goes with the electric lawn mower, the grass flying out sideways like whiskers. Oh, the things she doesn't know! She has never heard, for example, of the folk-rock recording star Neil Young, though the high school just around the corner from her house happens to be the very school Neil Young attended as a lad. His initials can actually be seen carved on one of the desks, and a few of the teachers say they remember him, a quiet fellow of neat appearance and always very polite in class. The desk with the initials N.Y. is kept in a corner of Mr. Pring's homeroom, and it's considered lucky—despite the fact that the renowned singer wasn't a great scholar—to touch the incised letters just before an exam. Since it's exam time now, the second week of June, the girls walking past Mrs. Turner's front yard (and shuddering over her display of cellulite) are carrying on their fingertips the spiritual scent, the essence, the fragrance, the aura of Neil Young, but Mrs. Turner is as ignorant of that fact as the girls are that she, Mrs. Turner, possesses a first name—which is Geraldine.

Not that she's ever been called Geraldine. Where she grew up in Boissevain, Manitoba, she was known always—the Lord knows why—as Girlie Fergus, the youngest of the three Fergus girls and the one who got herself in hot water. Her sister Em went to normal school and her sister Muriel went to Brandon to work at Eatons, but Girlie got caught one night—she was nineteen—in a Boissevain hotel room with a local farmer, married, named Gus MacGregor. It was her father who got wind of where she might be and came banging on the door, shouting and weeping, "Girlie, Girlie, what have you done to me?"

Girlie had been working in the Boissevain Dairy since she'd left school at sixteen and had a bit of money saved up, and so, a week after the humiliation in the local hotel, she wrote a farewell note to the family, crept out of the house at midnight and caught the bus to

Winnipeg. From there she got another bus down to Minneapolis, then to Chicago and finally New York City. The journey was endless and wretched, and on the way across Indiana and Ohio and Pennsylvania she saw hundreds and hundreds of towns whose unpaved streets and narrow blinded houses made her fear some conspiratorial, punishing power had carried her back to Boissevain. Her father's soppy-stern voice sang and sang in her ears as the wooden bus rattled its way eastward. It was summer, 1930.

New York was immense and wonderful, dirty, perilous and puzzling. She found herself longing for a sight of real earth which she assumed must lie somewhere beneath the tough pavement. On the other hand, the brown flat-roofed factories with their little windows tilted skyward pumped her full of happiness, as did the dusty trees, when she finally discovered them, lining the long avenues. Every last person in the world seemed to be outside, walking around, filling the streets, and every corner breezed with noise and sunlight. She had to pinch herself to believe this was the same sunlight that filtered its way into the rooms of the house back in Boissevain, fading the curtains but nourishing her mother's ferns. She sent postcards to Em and Muriel that said, "Don't worry about me. I've got a job in the theater business."

It was true. For eight and a half months she was an usherette in the Lamar Movie Palace in Brooklyn. She loved her perky maroon uniform, the way it fit on her shoulders, the way the strips of crinkly gold braid outlined her figure. With a little flashlight in hand she was able to send streams of light across the furry darkness of the theater and onto the plum-colored aisle carpet. The voices from the screen talked on and on. She felt after a time that their resonant declarations and tender replies belonged to her.

She met a man named Kiki her first month in New York and moved in with him. His skin was as black as ebony. *As black as ebony*—that was the phrase that hung like a ribbon on the end of his name, and it's also the phrase she uses, infrequently, when she wants to call up his memory, though she's more than a little doubtful about what *ebony* is. It may be a kind of stone, she thinks, something round and polished that comes out of a deep mine.

Kiki was a good-hearted man, though she didn't like the beer he drank, and he stayed with her, willingly, for several months after she had to stop working because of the baby. It was the baby itself that frightened him off, the way it cried probably. Leaving fifty dollars on the table, he slipped out one July afternoon when Girlie was shopping, and went back to Troy, New York, where he'd been raised.

Her first thought was to take the baby and get on a bus and go find him, but there wasn't enough money, and the thought of the baby crying all the way on the hot bus made her feel tired. She was worried about the rent and about the little red sores in the baby's ears—it was a boy, rather sweetly formed, with wonderful smooth feet and hands. On a murderously hot night, a night when the humidity was especially bad, she wrapped him in a clean piece of sheeting and carried him all the way to Brooklyn Heights where the houses were large and solid and surrounded by grass. There was a house on a corner she particularly liked because it had a wide front porch (like those in Boissevain) with a curved railing—and parked on the porch, its brake on, was a beautiful wicker baby carriage. It was here she placed her baby, giving one last look to his sleeping face, as round and calm as the moon. She walked home, taking her time, swinging her legs. If she had known the word *foundling*—which she didn't—she would have bounded along on its rhythmic back, so airy and wide did the world seem that night.

Most of these secrets she keeps locked away inside her mottled thighs or in the curled pinkness of her genital flesh. She has no idea what happened to Kiki, whether he ever went off to Alaska as he wanted to or whether he fell down a flight of stone steps in the silver-ware factory in Troy, New York, and died of head injuries before his 30th birthday. Or what happened to her son—whether he was bitten that night in the baby carriage by a rabid neighborhood cat or whether he was discovered the next morning and adopted by the large, loving family who lived in the house. As a rule, Girlie tries not to think about the things she can't even guess at. All she thinks is that she did the best she could under the circumstances.

In a year she saved enough money to take the train home to Boissevain. She took with her all her belongings, and also gifts for Em and Muriel, boxes of hose, bottles of apple-blossom cologne, phonograph records. For her mother she took an embroidered apron and for her father a pipe made of curious gnarled wood. "Girlie, my Girlie," her father said, embracing her at the Boissevain station. Then he said, "Don't ever leave us again," in a way that frightened her and made her resolve to leave as quickly as possible.

But she didn't go so far the second time around. She and Gordon Turner—he was, for all his life, a tongue-tied man, though he did manage a proper proposal—settled down in Winnipeg, first in St. Boniface where the rents were cheap and then Fort Rouge and finally the little house in River Heights just around the corner from the high school. It was her husband, Gord, who planted the grass that Mrs. Turner now shaves in the summertime. It was Gord who trimmed and shaped the caragana hedge and Gord who painted the little shutters with the cut-out hearts. He was a man who loved every inch of his house, the wide wooden steps, the oak door with its glass inset, the radiators and the baseboards and the snug sash windows. And he loved every inch of his wife, Girlie, too, saying to her once and only once that he knew about her past (meaning Gus MacGregor and the incident in the Boissevain Hotel), and that as far as he was concerned the slate had been wiped clean. Once he came home with a little package in his pocket; inside was a diamond ring, delicate and glittering. Once he took Girlie on a picnic all the way up to Steep Rock, and in the woods he took off her dress and underthings and kissed every part of her body.

After he died, Girlie began to travel. She was far from rich, as she liked to say, but with care she could manage one trip every spring.

She has never known such ease. She and Em and Muriel have been to Disneyland as well as Disneyworld. They've been to Europe, taking a sixteen-day trip through seven countries. The three of them have visited the south and seen the famous antebellum houses of Georgia, Alabama and Mississippi, after which they spent a week in the city of New Orleans. They went to Mexico one year and took pictures of Mayan ruins and queer shadowy gods cut squarely from stone. And three years ago they did what they swore they'd never have the nerve to do: they got on an airplane and went to Japan.

The package tour started in Tokyo where Mrs. Turner ate, on her first night there, a chrysanthemum fried in hot oil. She saw a village where everyone earned a living by making dolls and another village where everyone made pottery. Members of the tour group, each holding up a green flag so their tour leader could keep track of them, climbed on a little train, zoomed off to Osaka where they visited an electronics factory, and then went to a restaurant to east uncooked fish. They visited more temples and shrines than Mrs. Turner could keep track of. Once they stayed the night in a Japanese hotel where she and Em and Muriel bedded down on floor mats and little pillows stuffed with cracked wheat, and woke up, laughing, with backaches and shooting pains in their legs.

That was the same day they visited the Golden Pavilion in Kyoto. The three-storied temple was made of wood and had a roof like a set of wings and was painted a soft old flaky gold. Everybody in the group took pictures—Em took a whole roll—and bought postcards; everybody, that is, except a single tour member, the one they all referred to as the Professor.

The Professor traveled without a camera, but jotted notes almost continuously into a little pocket scribbler. He was bald, had a trim body and wore Bermuda shorts, sandals and black nylon socks. Those who asked him learned that he really was a professor, a teacher of English poetry in a small college in Massachusetts. He was also a poet who, at the time of the Japanese trip, had published two small chapbooks based mainly on the breakdown of his marriage. The poems, sadly, had not caused much stir.

It grieved him to think of that paltry, guarded nut-like thing that was his artistic reputation. His domestic life had been too cluttered; there had been too many professional demands; the political situation in America had drained him of energy—these were the thoughts that buzzed in his skull as he scribbled and scribbled, like a man with a fever, in the back seat of a tour bus traveling through Japan.

Here in this crowded, confused country he discovered simplicity and order and something spiritual, too, which he recognized as being authentic. He felt as though a flower, something like a lily, only smaller and tougher, had unfurled in his hand and was nudging along his fountain pen. He wrote and wrote, shaken by catharsis, but lulled into a new sense of his powers.

Not surprisingly, a solid little book of poems came out of his experience. It was published soon afterwards by a well-thought-of Boston publisher who, as soon as possible, sent him around the United States to give poetry readings.

Mostly the Professor read his poems in universities and colleges where his book was already listed on the Contemporary Poetry course. He read in faculty clubs, student centers, classrooms, gymnasiums and auditoriums, and usually, part way through a reading, someone or other would call from the back of the room, "Give us your Golden Pavilion poem."

He would have preferred to read his Fuji meditation or the tone poem on the Inner Sea, but he was happy to oblige his audiences, though he felt "A Day At The Golden Pavilion" was a somewhat light piece, even what is sometimes known on the circuit as a 'crowd pleaser.' People (admittedly they were mostly undergraduates) laughed out loud when they heard it; he read it well, too, in a moist, avuncular, amateur actor's voice, reminding himself to pause frequently, to look upward and raise an ironic eyebrow.

The poem was not really about the Golden Pavilion at all, but about three midwestern lady tourists who, while viewing the temple and madly snapping photos, had talked incessantly and in loud, flat-bottomed voices about knitting patterns, indigestion, sore feet, breast lumps, the cost of plastic raincoats and a previous trip they'd made together to Mexico. They had wondered, these three—noisily, repeatedly—who back home in Manitoba should receive a postcard, what they'd give for an honest cup of tea, if there was an easy way to remove stains from an electric coffee maker, and where they would go the following year—Hawaii? They were the three furies, the three witches, who for vulgarity and tastelessness formed a shattering counterpoint to the Professor's own state of transcendence. He had been affronted, angered, half-crazed.

One of the sisters, a little pug of a woman, particularly stirred his contempt, she of the pink pantsuit, the red toenails, the grapefruity buttocks, the overly bright souvenirs, the garish Mexican straw bag containing Dentyne chewing gum, aspirin, breath mints, sun goggles, envelopes of saccharine, and photos of her dead husband standing in front of a squat, ugly house in Winnipeg. This defilement she had spread before the ancient and exquisitely proportioned Golden Pavilion of Kyoto, proving—and here the Professor's tone became grave—proving that sublime beauty can be brought to the very doorway of human eyes, ears and lips and remain unperceived.

When he comes to the end of "A Day At The Golden Pavilion" there is generally a thoughtful half second of silence, then laughter and applause. Students turn in their seats and exchange looks with their fellows. They have seen such unspeakable tourists themselves. There was Old Auntie Marigold or Auntie Flossie. There was that tacky Mrs. Shannon with her rouge and her jewelry. They know—despite their youth they know—the irreconcilable distance between taste and banality. Or perhaps that's too harsh; perhaps it's only the difference between those who know about the world and those who don't.

It's true Mrs. Turner remembers little about her travels. She's never had much of a head for history or dates; she never did learn, for instance, the difference between a Buddhist temple and a Shinto shrine. She gets on a tour bus and goes and goes, and that's all there is to it. She doesn't know if she's going north or south or east or west. What does it matter? She's having a grand time. And she's reassured, always, by the sameness of the world. She's never heard the word *commonality*, but is nevertheless fused with its sense. In Japan she was made as happy to see carrots and lettuce growing in the fields as she was to see sunlight, years earlier, pouring into the streets of New York City. Everywhere she's been she's seen people eating and sleeping and working and making things with their hands and urging things to grow. There have been cats and dogs, fences and bicycles and telephone poles, and objects to buy and take care of; it is amazing, she thinks, that she can understand so much of the world and that it comes to her as easily as bars of music floating out of a radio.

Her sisters have long forgotten about her wild days. Now the three of them love to sit on tour buses and chatter away about old friends and family members, their stern father and their mother who never once took their part against him. Muriel carries on about her children (a son in California and a daughter in Toronto) and she brings along snaps of her grandchildren to pass round. Em has retired from school teaching and is a volunteer in the Boissevain Local History Museum, to which she has donated several family mementos: her father's old carved pipe and her mother's wedding veil and, in a separate case, for all the world to see, a white cotton garment labeled "Girlie Fergus' Underdrawers, handmade, trimmed with lace, circa 1918." If Mrs. Turner knew the word *irony* she would relish this. Even without knowing the word irony, she relishes it.

The professor from Massachusetts has won an important international award for his book of poems; translation rights have been sold to a number of foreign publishers; and recently his picture appeared in the *New York Times*, along with a lengthy quotation from "A Day At The Golden Pavilion." How providential, some will think, that Mrs. Turner doesn't read the *New York Times* or attend poetry readings, for it might injure her deeply to know how she appears in certain people's eyes, but then there are so many things she doesn't know.

In the summer as she cuts the grass, to and fro, to and fro, she waves to everyone she sees. She waves to the high-school girls who timidly wave back. She hollers hello to Sally and Roy Sascher and asks them how their garden is coming on. She cannot imagine that anyone would wish her harm. All she's done is live her life. The green grass flies up in the air, a buoyant cloud swirling about her head. Oh, what a sight is Mrs. Turner cutting her grass and how, like an ornament, she shines.

Born Audrey Callahan in Binghamton, New York, in 1935, Audrey Thomas was educated in the United States, Scotland, and Canada. Interrupting her formal education to spend two years in Ghana, she returned in 1966 to British Columbia, where she now lives. Her first collection of stories, *Ten Green Bottles*, appeared in 1967, and was rapidly followed by several novels, novellas, radio plays, and other story collections. Among her recent books are *Real Mothers* (1981), *Intertidal Life* (1984), and *The Wild Blue Yonder* (1990). Recurrently her writing deals with the difficult relations between men and women, relations that often distinguish men's ostensible objectivity from women's intense, visceral response to sex, children, and death.

"The More Little Mummy in the World" (from *Ladies & Escorts*, 1977) not only documents the break-up of a relationship but also reconstructs in the text the psychological fragmentation that follows. The Mexican setting and the fragments of haltingly translated (or sometimes untranslated) Spanish speech intensify the female narrator's sense of alienation. The external world reads like a projection of her own turmoil. But out of this contact with uncertainty there emerges a sharp sense of the independence she has so painfully won. Preoccupied with death, the woman slowly converts her feelings of personal inadequacy and dependence into an outwardly directed, liberating anger.

FOR FURTHER READING

Anne Archer, "Real Mummies," *Studies in Canadian Literature* 9 (1984): 214-223.

George Bowering, "Snow Red: The Short Stories of Audrey Thomas," *Open Letter*, 3rd series, 5 (1976): 28-39.

Pierre Coupey et al., Interview with Audrey Thomas, *Capilano Review* 7 (Spring 1975): 87-10.

Room of One's Own, special Thomas issue, 10, no. 3-4 (1986).

Audrey Thomas, "Basmati Rice: An Essay About Words," *Canadian Literature* 100 (Spring 1984): 312-17.

The More Little
Mummy in the World

Oscar A. Lempe
  Denver, Color   *U.S. 14-V-1876*
            23-XI-1958

Guanauato, Gto.
  Recuerdo de Su Esposa
  Chijas
  Perpetuidad

Louis Montgomery Allen Sr.
New York City   *Dec. 6-1887*
            Feb. 12-1957

Guanauato, Gto.
  Perpetuidad

Handprints on this one—of whom? *Su esposa? Su hermosa?*
A passing, naughty, unrelated child?

Elisabeth Carnes Allen, D.A.R.

She wandered through the cemetery looking at every stone,
imagining the people, what had brought them there, what
the town had been like nearly a hundred years before. The
lure of what riches? The silver mines perhaps.

Everywhere there were flowers stuck in tins—Mobil Oil
tins, paint tins, tomatoes, green chillies:

Chiles Jalapenos, En Escapbeche

Recuerdo . . . : in memory of his wife/daughters (hijas = daughters)
Su hermosa: his mistress (ie. his 'beautiful')
en escapbeche: in vinegar and oil

She took out her pocket dictionary.

The wind blowing through the cypress trees rattled the tins like bones.

To My Beloved Wife
Maria Concepcion Buchnan

Although there had been a long line-up to see the mummies there were very few people in the Pantheon itself. A young couple with their arms around one another, laughing, exchanging kisses, some old women in black, a gardener. And the dead of course, the multitude of dead stacked six or seven high. The soft brown hills beyond and El Pipla, the boy hero, alone on a hill above the Jardin de la Union, his arm upraised.

Ayer (yesterday). *Hoy* (today).
Mañana

Mother
Lily Mast McBride
Born Sept. 19-1882
Died July 22-1926

A pretty blue-grey stone, this one, beautifully incised.

It was very peaceful here with the wreaths, the plastic flowers and the real—gladioli, lilies—the white ones she saw everywhere here, Easter lilies back home—geraniums, carnations. The flowers dead too of course, or dying, sucking up the last dregs of rusty water from the tins. Still, she liked this place better than the churches with their bleeding Christs, their oppressive smell of hot wax, their plaster damned pleading to her for one last chance at salvation.

Some stones were casually propped against still-occupied cabinets. (They couldn't be called tombs and she couldn't think of a better word than "cabinet"—cabin, verb, to confine in a small space, cramp). She turned one over.

Naci Inocente! . . .
*Muero Ignorante**
Freyre Jose E.
V-7-1925
Perpetuidad

*Naci . . . : born innocent/died ignorant

So much for *perpetuidad*!

She had been thinking of failures and of suicides and had gone to mass on Palm Sunday in the hopes of finding something positive—if only for a second, if only for an instant, if only, even, an aura or a whiff of hope for her salvation.

Buenos dias. Adios.

She straightened a tin of gladioli which had fallen over in the wind.

Outside the Parroquia women and men were braiding palms into elaborate patterns. She bought a small crucifix and went in, covering her head, but the Mass was a disappointment. She stood up. She sat down. She prayed. The priest was way way way up in the chancel. Little bells rang. There was no pageantry, no music, nothing to draw her spirit up and away from the deep well of despair into which it seemed to have fallen. Over the words of the priest a poem of Yeats' kept running through her mind:

> That is no country for old men
> The young in one another's arms
> Fish/flesh/and fowl commend
> all summer long
> Whatever is begotten, born or dies

They had been going to come down here together. Had maps, dreams, destinations. Even a tape:

> *Siento molestarle!*
> *No es ninguna molestia!*
> *Salud!**

How much too much please thank you don't mention it.

Instead he took her out (at her request) the night before she left. To a Greek restaurant (again at her request). She drank a lot of wine, and crumbling a bit of bread between her fingers, told him it was she all along whom he really loved.

"Do you think so?" he said and smiled at her over his wine glass. Then in an offhand manner he asked her if she'd ever been in any of the other Greek restaurants along the street, places where you just walked in and took whatever was going, places where the Greeks themselves went, cheaper places than this. (And he, who never went into a restaurant alone, whom had he lingered with in a small café full of the smell

*Siento . . . . : I'm sorry to bother you/You're not bothering me/hello.

of lamb and garlic and the whine of recorded music. Who? Don't ask, or, as he would have put it, "why humiliate yourself?") He had always been Machiavellian; had always known how to put her in her place.

Once they had been at the house of his best friend and contemporary, Peter:

"I was coming in on the bus from the island," her lover said, "toward sunset—a beautiful evening. Suddenly I looked up and there was this incredible cloud formation—incredible! I said to the fellow next to me, without really thinking about it, you know, 'My God, that looks just like the Mushroom Cloud!' I saw the guy look at me and give a little frown and then I realized with a start that he was younger, younger than the Bomb—that he didn't even know what I was talking about. The only mushroom cloud he knew was psilocybin!"

Peter had laughed appreciatively. He was 35.

"It's true. People talk about the generation gap—as a metaphor I mean—but it seems to me there's a real gap—I almost see it as a physical space—between those born before or during the War and those born after it."

"Yes. There's a point at which Rachel and I just can't communicate; we were born into two different worlds." He had turned to her. "When I talk about Marlene Dietrich I don't know if you even know who I mean."

She was immediately defensive. He had wanted her to be, had set her up.

"Of course I know who Marlene Dietrich is."

"Ah yes—you know her name. But is your Marlene Dietrich the same as mine—I doubt it." Peter nodded and began singing "Lili Marlene." Her lover sat back and lit his pipe.

That night at the Greek restaurant he had given her a handsome present—a shoulderbag with three sections, or pouches, like a saddlebag.

"Now you will have three places to put all your clutter," he said, "instead of just one." ("It's not that she doesn't have a place for everything," he said once, at a party, "it's that she has several places." He was very tidy and they fought about the missing cap to the toothpaste.)

Buenos dias. Adios. No comprendo.

In one place there were freshly-dug graves, four in a row, an accident perhaps. This in a courtyard which led to a view of the city. Bougainvillaea had been splashed against the walls, the original purple and the scarlet, blood-coloured. In the distance she could hear the sound of children's voices.

Estoy esperando un paquete.
Lo tiene usted aqui? *

When he came to get her at the hospital he was very brusque and efficient, annoyed that she was still in bed and crying. His sons were in the car—they were going camping. Yet still she wanted to buy him gifts—an onyx chess set, a heavy silver ring, a blanket for his bed. Things of beauty and whimsy, things that would make him think of her, remember her and want her.

Donde este? Where is?

He had told her there was nothing wrong, that maybe she should see a shrink. The gifts would only embarrass him. When she began to cry at the bus station, he kissed her quickly on the forehead and then walked away. She hated him; no, she loved him.

She had read in the guidebook that if the rent was not kept up on the crypts (yes, that was the word she had been searching for), the bodies were removed after five years and the bones thrown into a common bone-house to make room for new arrivals. But the region was very dry and some of the bodies would be mummified. When they were, they were put into the museum. Directly outside the cemetery were souvenir stands—skeletons, on horseback or playing fiddles or dancing, with springy arms and legs. Postcards of the mummies, earthenware, bone letter-openers and crochet hooks (human bone?). There were mummies of pale beige toffee with raisin eyes. These were wrapped in red or yellow cellophane. As she approached a man had offered her two large ones in one packet, "*Momias Matrimonias*,"** and laughed at her discomfort. Now she was trying to get up enough courage to go into the mummy museum itself.

Death and disease were accepted here. Death was even made fun of, made into toffee to chew or chocolate to lick or tiny plaster figures to decorate, along with gilded pictures of miraculous virgins, the windows and mirrors of buses and cars. She knew now that almost certainly, whenever she saw a street musician, either he was blind or lame or leprous or there was a terribly deformed creature, just out of sight, on behalf of whom he was playing his music.

Her operation had been therapeutic and therefore covered by her insurance. No back streets or borrowed money—things were easier now.

Estoy . . . : I'm waiting for a parcel/Have you got it here?
**Momias . . . :* "married" mummies

Ayer (yesterday). *Hoy* (today).
Mañana

This was a very strange town to walk around in and easy to get lost.
The main road ran underneath the town in places, reappearing above
ground several hundred yards beyond. It was really a stone-arched
tunnel and rather frightening. And there were six or seven main
squares, not just one. She had already, in spite of her map, been lost
several times. The night before, wandering steep alleys full of
wrought-iron balconies, she had stumbled upon a strange religious ceremony in one of the smaller lamplit squares. There were bleachers set
out and many of the people were already seated, men, women and children, facing an old church. The church bell began to ring and then a
priest appeared high up on the church steps, intoning Hail Marys and
Our Fathers. And she understood a bit of it, the history of the week
leading up to the arrest of Jesus. Below the steps stood men in purple
sackcloth and black hoods, very mediaeval and frightening. A lifesized
statue of Christ (looking not unlike the "Jesu Christo Superstare" she
had seen in Mexico City) was brought out of the church by more
hooded men, carried down the steep steps and put on a flower-decked
platform. There was a rope around his neck and it hung down his back,
binding his hands behind him. A child-angel and one of the masked
men climbed up and sat on either side of him. Torches were lit and as
the rest of the masked men shouldered their burden the crowd gave a
deep moan of pity and anticipation. The statue had real hair and
jointed, movable arms. He terrified her, for he hovered somewhere in a
strange space between icon and the living god. The wind blew his hair
across his gentle, accepting face. His gown was purple like the garments of the men but his was of velvet, not hemp. A workman beat a
drum and the entire affair—Christ, angel, masked men, flowers, scaf-
folding, torches, priest—began to move. A young boy followed
behind, playing a simple pipe and the procession slowly moved out
from the small square into the larger one beyond. Behind came small
children, some on tricycles, the women in black, the men, balloon sell-
ers, a thin brown pariah dog. The bowed, bound figure of Christ rode
above them all. It was amateurish in a way but very powerful; she hid
herself in the crowd.

Por que? Why? *No se.* I don't know.
*Perdone.**

It was as though once she had decided she didn't want it he had
washed his hands of the whole affair.

*Perdone: sorry

"Ruth Barnes"

Just a small stone marker with a dried-up geranium obscuring the date. Presumably to be buried in this small courtyard was more expensive than to be deposited on the shelves. The wind blowing rattled the tins like bones.

If he were here he would have struck up a friendship with the gardener, would try out the little Spanish he knew and supplement it with laughter and broad gestures. His energy was one of the first things that had excited her. And his keen intelligence, his learning, the whole sum of his life experience. He had been married (twice), had children (one as old as her youngest sister), had suffered and taken chances.

"I find it impossible to live alone," he had said to her the first night, "and yet somehow I always seem to fuck it up—my relationships with women." He showed her pictures of his sons and took her home to bed.

Dispenseme. Excuse me.
Muchas gracias.

Everywhere down here men followed her and tried to feel her up—a woman alone deserved to be treated that way. Then they gave their paycheques to their mothers and went to mass on Sundays.

Hail Mary Full of Grace Blessed is
The Fruit of Thy Womb Jesus

On the train from Nuevo Laredo she had met a middle-aged man who lived in San Miguel. He said the happiest day of his life was the day when they nailed his wife's coffin shut. Federales came on the train looking for contraband. They wore their revolvers tucked in the back of their pants, Pancho Villa style.

"Watch for the Mordida," the American said.

She shook her head.

"'The Bite.' To force someone to give you a bribe. It's a game between the Federales and the people coming back."

Was that what she had done by getting pregnant? Put the bite on him?

The boy-hero stood unconcerned on the distant hill, his arm upraised forever. Her first day in the town she had followed the crude signs and climbed steep stairs and back alleys until she reached the top of that hill. She had taken some bread and fruit with her and sat in a little summer house just below the enormous figure, eating slices of pineapple and writing in her journal. The boy had set fire to the granary in which the Royalists had barricaded themselves. At his feet it said, in Spanish,

"There are still other castles to burn."

She felt quite happy there, after her climb, the whole town at her feet. But in the evening, at a band concert in the Jardin de la Union, she sat on a wrought-iron bench and longed to have him with her, next to her, observing, commenting, loving. Canaries mocked her from the laurel trees around the square.

Where is? *No comprendo.*

She retraced her steps, back through the main courtyard with all its stacked and silent dead, back through the black iron gate with its simple cross on top. There were very few people in line now so there was no reason not to wait.

He had been quite calm when she told him. Just said, "Well, what do you want to do about it?" He left it entirely up to her. Had she wanted him to be otherwise? Had she wanted to bear his child? She wanted to be a writer, a poet—had he not encouraged her, sung her praises? In Chapultapec Park in Mexico City she sat on the grass one Sunday and watched the fathers spoil their children. They were immaculate—it was the mothers, of course, who saw to that. There were funny animal heads on the trash cans in the children's playground. The children laughed and squealed when they stuck their little heads in.

She paid her five pesos and went into the mummy museum.

In Chapultapec Park she had sat on the grass and wept. She wanted to be six years old in a white dress and riding on her father's shoulders, her small hands tugging at his curly hair. She wanted to be held and to be forgiven. She wanted a red balloon.

Her mother was at home making a delicious Sunday dinner.

Ayer (yesterday). *Hoy* (today).
Mañana.

The mummy museum was really a long artificially-lit corridor with the mummies displayed in glass cases along one side. The corridor was hot and very crowded, so that for a moment she experienced a wave of claustrophobia and almost turned around and ran.

Some of the names and dates on the stones had simply been scrawled in the wet plaster.

Aristo Perez
Manuel Torres M.
Maria de los Angeles Rodriguez

So there were the mummies, in glass cases like curios—which of course they were. Most were without clothes, jaundice-coloured and hideously wrinkled. A few had on mouldy shoes and there was one man who had on a complete suit of tattered black clothes. Very few had hair and this surprised her. Was it just an old wives' tale that the hair would keep on growing?

He read her, one night, from John Donne's "Funerale"

> Whoever comes to shroud me,
>   do not harme
> Nor question much
> That subtile wreathe of hair,
>   which crowns my arme:

and from "A Feaver"

> Oh doe not die, for I shall hate
>   All women so, when thou art gone,
> That thee I shall not celeb.......rate,
>   When I remember, thou wast one.

She got up and cut off a lock of her hair and gave it to him; he kissed her neck and put the lock in the back of his grandfather's gold watch.

Donde este? Where is?

The mummies' faces were full of anger and terror. Shrinkage had pulled their mouths open and their hands were clutched across their empty bellies. Her Spanish was not quick enough to understand everything the guides were saying, but there were abnormalities and tumours and other curious things being pointed out as they moved along. The mummies were tall or short, male and female, the men's papery genitals still visible, the women's wrinkled breasts.

She wrote him letter after letter and tore them all up.

Quiero comprar una postal. I wish to buy a postcard.

As she crossed the street to his car and his waiting sons, she stumbled, still drugged and swollen-eyed, against the curb, and turned her ankle. Suddenly she had to sit down on the grass and put her head between her knees. She knew the boys, his sons, were watching her. What had he said to them? Why had he brought them to the hospital? What was he trying to say?

People with limps, people with no legs, blind people, lepers, pariah dogs. The country swarmed with outcasts and with cripples. The tourists bought silver rings and onyx chess sets and turned their heads away. After all, it was not their problem. Charity begins. . . .

"They hate us," the American man had said. "They want our money but they hate us. They would prefer if we just mailed it down."

Almost at the end of the corridor was a display case full of child mummies—some in christening gowns and bonnets, some naked or wrapped in tiny shrouds. In front of the smallest of these a cardboard sign was propped. She pushed closer, in order to read it, then tugged at the guide's elbow.

"Please. *Por favor.* What does the sign say? *Que quiere decir?*"

"*La Momia Mas Pequena del mundo.*" He smiled at her, showing perfect teeth.

"*Si. Si.* In English. *Habla Usted Inglis?*"

"*Ah. Inglis.*"

He smiled again.

"The more little mummy in the world."

It sat there, no bigger than the rubber babies she had played with as a child.

Where were the parents? Why had these children been removed to this terrible glass limbo? She looked at la momia mas Pequena but it refused to answer.

The American had asked her to come and spend a few days with him in San Miguel.

She pushed her way through the tourists and out the exit door. The sun struck her like a slap. She half-ran, half-walked toward the souvenir stands, rummaged quickly through the cards until she found the one she was looking for, the one she knew was certain to be there.

Back at the apartment he had said, "D'you think you could rustle us up some dinner—we'd like to get away before dark." The boys were looking at her curiously. She went into the bedroom and began to pack, tears running down her face, the little plastic hospital bracelet still locked around her wrist.

Go. Come. Are you ready?
Don't forget.

She fumbled in her bag for the change purse, then headed back down the hill. Tonight, drinking her cho-ko-la-tay in that little restaurant near the Plazuela where she had seen the Christ, she would get out the card and address it.

"Having a wonderful time," she would write.

"Wish you were here."

In a relatively short time John Updike has become one of the most celebrated writers in the United States. A product of the middle America which gives him much of his material, he was born in Shillington, Pennsylvania in 1932, and educated at Harvard and the Ruskin School of Drawing and Fine Art in Oxford, England. After a spell on the staff of the *New Yorker* from 1955 to 1957, Updike became a free-lance writer and journalist, developing a professionalism in his craft ("I would write ads for deodorant or labels for catsup bottles if I had to") which has led at times to a greater concern for surface than for substance, and earned him the charge of superficiality from some critics. Author of numerous novels, short stories, and essays, he writes best (and most frequently) about domestic life, drawing the relationship between husbands and wives, parents and children, with a detailed vividness born of close observation; indeed, many of his stories have an autobiographical basis, and his novel *The Centaur* (1963) is centred on a character modelled after his father. His later work deals increasingly with the domestic crises and emotional traumas accompanying middle age, without any loss of the wit and eloquence characteristic of all his writing. In 1981 his achievement was rewarded with a Pulitzer Prize for his novel *Rabbit is Rich*.

Updike has summarized his major preoccupations as follows: "Domestic fierceness within the middle class, sex and death as riddles for the thinking animal, social existence as sacrifice, unexpected pleasures and rewards, corruption as a kind of evolution. . . . " Sex and death undoubtedly occupy the centre of his imagination, sometimes to morbid excess; *Couples* (1968) at times runs perilously close to refined pornography in its portrait of boredom and sexual decadence in suburban Massachusetts. But Updike is no pornographer; in his fiction he repeatedly shows the deadness of sex without love, and the frailty of domestic love in a society devoid of faith or purpose. In "Giving Blood" (*The Music School*, 1966) he depicts the strains of marriage with compassionate irony, and indicates how the selfish sensuality of contemporary human beings has blinded them to the ancient mystery of love, a mystery we can now apprehend only fleetingly.

FOR FURTHER READING

Robert Detweiler, *John Updike*, rev. ed. (Boston: Twayne, 1984).

Donald J. Greiner, *The Other John Updike: Poems/Short Stories/Prose/Play* (Athens, Ohio: Ohio UP, 1981).

Charles T. Samuels, "The Art of Fiction XLIII: John Updike," *Paris Review* 45 (1968): 84-117.

Giving Blood

The Maples had been married now nine years, which is almost too long.

"Goddammit, goddammit," Richard said to Joan, as they drove into Boston to give blood, "I drive this road five days a week and now I'm driving it again. It's like a nightmare. I'm exhausted. I'm emotionally, mentally, physically exhausted, and she isn't even an aunt of mine. She isn't even an aunt of *yours*."

"She's a sort of cousin," Joan said.

"Well hell, every goddam body in New England is some sort of cousin of yours; must I spent the rest of my life trying to save them *all*?"

"Hush," Joan said. "She might die. I'm ashamed of you. Really ashamed."

It cut. His voice for the moment took on an apologetic pallor. "Well I'd be my usual goddam saintly self if I'd had any sort of sleep last night. Five days a week I bump out of bed and stagger out the door past the milkman and on the one day of the week when I don't even have to truck the blasphemous little brats to Sunday school you make an appointment to have me drained dry thirty miles away."

"Well it wasn't *me*," Joan said, "who had to stay till two o'clock doing the Twist with Marlene Brossman."

"We weren't doing the Twist. We were gliding around very chastely to 'Hits of the Forties.' And don't think I was so oblivious I didn't see you snoogling behind the piano with Harry Saxon."

"We weren't behind the piano, we were on the bench. And he was just talking to me because he felt sorry for me. Everybody there felt sorry for me; you could have at *least* let somebody else dance *once* with Marlene, if only for show."

"Show, show," Richard said. "That's your mentality exactly."

"Why, the poor Matthews or whatever they are looked absolutely horrified."

"Matthiessons," he said. "And that's another thing. Why are idiots like that being invited these days? If there's anything I hate, it's women who keep putting one hand on their pearls and taking a deep breath. I thought she had something stuck in her throat."

"They're a perfectly pleasant, decent young couple. The thing you resent about their coming is that their being there shows us what we've become."

"If you're so attracted," he said, "to little fat men like Harry Saxon, why didn't you marry one?"

"My," Joan said calmly, and gazed out the window away from him, at the scudding gasoline stations. "You honestly *are* hateful. It's not just a pose."

"Pose, show, my Lord, who are you performing for? If it isn't Harry Saxon, it's Freddie Vetter—all these dwarves. Every time I looked over at you last night it was like some pale Queen of the Dew surrounded by a ring of mushrooms."

"You're too absurd," she said. Her hand, distinctly thirtyish, dry and green-veined and rasped by detergents, stubbed out her cigarette in the dashboard ashtray. "You're not subtle. You think you can match me up with another man so you can swirl off with Marlene with a free conscience."

Her reading his strategy so correctly made his face burn; he felt again the tingle of Mrs. Brossman's hair as he pressed his cheek against hers and in this damp privacy inhaled the perfume behind her ear. "You're right," he said. "But I want to get you a man your own size; I'm very loyal that way."

"Let's not talk," she said.

His hope, of turning the truth into a joke, was rebuked. Any implication of permission was blocked. "It's that *smug*ness," he explained, speaking levelly, as if about a phenomenon of which they were both disinterested students. "It's your smugness that is really intolerable. Your stupidity I don't mind. Your sexlessness I've learned to live with. But that wonderfully smug, New England—I suppose we needed it to get the country founded, but in the Age of Anxiety it really does gall."

He had been looking over at her, and unexpectedly she turned and looked at him, with a startled but uncannily crystalline expression, as if her face had been in an instant rendered in tinted porcelain, even to the eyelashes.

"I asked you not to talk," she said. "Now you've said things that I'll always remember."

Plunged fathoms deep into the wrong, his face suffocated with warmth, he concentrated on the highway and sullenly steered. Though they were moving at sixty in the sparse Saturday traffic, he had travelled this road so often its distances were all translated into time, so that they seemed to him to be moving as slowly as a minute hand from one digit to the next. It would have been strategic and dignified of him to keep the silence; but he could not resist believing that just one more pinch of syllables would restore the fine balance which with each wordless mile slipped increasingly awry. He asked, "How did Bean seem to you?" Bean was their baby. They had left her last night, to go to the party, with a fever of 102.

Joan wrestled with her vow to say nothing, but guilt proved stronger than spite. She said, "Cooler. Her nose is a river."

"Sweetie," Richard blurted, "will they hurt me?" The curious fact was that he had never given blood before. Asthmatic and underweight, he had been 4-F, and at college and now at the office he had, less through his own determination than through the diffidence of the solicitors, evaded pledging blood. It was one of those tests of courage so trivial that no one had ever thought to make him face up to it.

Spring comes carefully to Boston. Speckled crusts of ice lingered around the parking meters, and the air, grayly stalemated between seasons, tinted the buildings along Longwood Avenue with a drab and homogeneous majesty. As they walked up the drive to the hospital entrance, Richard nervously wondered aloud if they would see the King of Arabia.

"He's in a separate wing," Joan said. "With four wives."

"Only four? What an ascetic." And he made bold to tap his wife's shoulder. It was not clear if, under the thickness of her winter coat, she felt it.

At the desk, they were directed down a long corridor floored with cigar-coloured linoleum. Up and down, right and left it went, in the secretive, disjointed way peculiar to hospitals that have been built annex by annex. Richard seemed to himself Hansel orphaned with Gretel; birds ate the bread crumbs behind them, and at last they timidly knocked on the witch's door, which said BLOOD DONATION CENTER. A young man in white opened the door a crack. Over his shoulder Richard glimpsed—horrors!—a pair of dismembered female legs stripped of their shoes and laid parallel on a bed. Glints of needles and bottles pricked his eyes. Without widening the crack, the young man passed out to them two long forms. In sitting side by side on the waiting bench, remembering their middle initials and childhood diseases, Mr. and Mrs. Maple were newly defined to themselves. He fought down that urge to giggle and clown and lie that threatened him whenever he was asked—like a lawyer appointed by the court to plead a hopeless case—to present, as it were, his statistics to eternity. It seemed to mitigate his case slightly that a few of these statistics (present address, date of marriage) were shared by the hurt soul scratching beside him, with his own pen. He looked over her shoulder. "I never knew you had whooping cough."

"My mother says. I don't remember it."

A pan crashed to a distant floor. An elevator chuckled remotely. A woman, a middle-aged woman top-heavy with rouge and fur, stepped out of the blood door and wobbled a moment on legs that looked familiar. They had been restored to their shoes. The heels of these shoes clicked firmly as, having raked the Maples with a defiant blue glance, she turned, and disappeared around a bend in the corridor. The young man appeared in the doorway holding a pair of surgical tongs. His noticeably recent haircut made him seem an apprentice barber. He clicked his tongs and smiled. "Shall I do you together?"

"Sure." It put Richard on his mettle that this callow fellow, to whom apparently they were to entrust their liquid essence, was so clearly younger than they. But when Richard stood, his indignation melted and his legs felt diluted under him. And the extraction of the blood sample from his middle finger seemed the nastiest and most needlessly prolonged physical involvement with another human being he had ever experienced. There is a touch that good dentists, mechanics, and barbers have, and this intern did not have it; he fumbled and in compensation was too rough. Again and again, an atrociously clumsy vampire, he tugged and twisted the purpling finger in vain. The tiny glass capillary tube remained transparent.

"He doesn't like to bleed, does he?" the intern asked Joan. As relaxed as a nurse, she sat in a chair next to a table of scintillating equipment.

"I don't think his blood moves much," she said, "until after midnight."

This stab at a joke made Richard in his extremity of fright laugh loudly, and the laugh at last seemed to jar the panicked coagulant. Red seeped upward in the thirsty little tube, as in a sudden thermometer.

The intern grunted in relief. As he smeared the samples on the analysis box, he explained idly, "What we ought to have down here is a pan of warm water. You just came in out of the cold. If you put your hand in hot water for a minute, the blood just pops out."

"A pretty thought," Richard said.

But the intern had already written him off as a clowner and continued calmly to Joan, "All we'd need would be a baby hot plate for about six dollars, then we could make our own coffee too. This way, when we get a donor who needs the coffee afterwards, we have to send up for it while we keep his head between his knees. Do you think you'll be needing coffee?"

"*No*," Richard interrupted, jealous of their rapport.

The intern told Joan, "You're O."

"I know," she said.

"And he's A positive."

"Why that's very good, Dick!" she called to him.

"Am I rare?" he asked.

The boy turned and explained. "O positive and A positive are the most common types." Something in the patient tilt of his closecropped head as its lateral sheen mixed with the lazily bright midmorning air of the room sharply reminded Richard of the days years ago when he had tended a battery of teletype machines in a room much this size. By now, ten o'clock, the yards of copy that began pouring through the machines at five and that lay in great crimped heaps on the floor when he arrived at seven would have been harvested and sorted and pasted together and turned in, and there was nothing to do but keep up with the staccato appearance of the later news and to think about simple things like coffee. It came back to him, how pleasant and secure those hours had been when, king of his own corner, he was young and newly responsible.

The intern asked, "Who wants to be first?"

"Let me," Joan said. "He's never done it before."

"Her full name is Joan of Arc," Richard explained, angered at this betrayal, so unimpeachably selfless and smug.

The intern, threatened in his element, fixed his puzzled eyes on the floor between them and said, "Take off your shoes and each get on a bed." He added, "Please," and all three laughed, one after the other, the intern last.

The beds were at right angles to one another along two walls. Joan lay down and from her husband's angle of vision was novelly foreshortened. He had never before seen her quite this way, the combed crown of her hair so poignant, her bared arm so silver and long, her stocking feet toed in so childishly and docilely. There were no pillows on the beds, and lying flat made him feel tipped head down; the illusion of floating encouraged his hope that this unreal adventure would soon dissolve in the manner of a dream. "You OK?"

"Are you?" Her voice came softly from the tucked-under wealth of her hair. From the straightness of the parting it seemed her mother had brushed it. He watched a long needle sink into the flat of her arm and a piece of moist cotton clumsily swab the spot. He had imagined their blood would be drained into cans or bottles, but the intern, whose breathing was now the only sound within the room, brought to Joan's side what looked like a miniature plastic knapsack, all coiled and tied. His body cloaked his actions. When he stepped away, a plastic cord had been grafted, a transparent vine, to the flattened crook of Joan's extended arm, where the skin was translucent and the veins were faint blue tributaries shallowly buried. It was a tender, vulnerable place where in courting days she had liked being stroked. Now, without visible transition, the pale tendril planted there went dark red. Richard wanted to cry out.

The instant readiness of her blood to leave her body pierced him like a physical pang. Though he had not so much as blinked, its initial leap had been too quick for his eye. He had expected some visible sign of flow, but from the mere appearance of it the tiny looped hose might be pouring blood *into* her body or might be a curved line added, irrelevant as a mustache, to a finished canvas. The fixed position of his head gave what he saw a certain flatness.

And now the intern turned to him, and there was the tiny felt prick of the novocain needle, and then the coarse, half-felt intrusion of something resembling a medium-weight nail. Twice the boy mistakenly probed for the vein and the third time taped the successful graft fast with adhesive tape. All the while, Richard's mind moved aloofly among the constellations of the stained cracked ceiling. What was being done to him did not bear contemplating. When the intern moved away to hum and tinkle among his instruments, Joan craned her neck to show her husband her face and, upside down in his vision, grotesquely smiled.

It was not many minutes that they lay there at right angles together, but the time passed as something beyond the walls, as something mixed with the faraway clatter of pans and the approach and retreat of footsteps and the opening and closing of unseen doors. Here, conscious of a pointed painless pulse in the inner hinge of his arm but incurious as to what it looked like, he floated and imagined how his soul would float free when all his blood was underneath the bed. His blood and Joan's merged on the floor, and together their spirits glided from crack to crack, from star to star on the ceiling. Once she cleared her throat, and the sound make an abrasion like the rasp of a pebble loosened by a cliff-climber's boot.

The door opened. Richard turned his head and saw an old man, bald and sallow, enter and settle in a chair. He was one of those old men who hold within an institution an ill-defined but consecrated place. The young doctor seemed to know him, and the two talked, softly, as if not to disturb the mystical union of the couple sacrificially bedded together. They talked of persons and events that meant nothing—of Iris, of Dr. Greenstein, of Ward D, again of Iris, who had given the old man an undeserved scolding, of the shameful lack of a hot plate to make coffee on, of the rumored black bodyguards who kept watch with scimitars by the bed of the glaucomatous king. Through Richard's tranced ignorance these topics passed as clouds of impression, iridescent, massy—Dr. Greenstein with a pointed nose and almond eyes the color of ivy, Iris eighty feet tall and hurling sterilized thunderbolts of wrath. As in some theologies the proliferant deities are said to exist as ripples upon the featureless ground of Godhead, so these inconstant images lightly overlay his continuous awareness of Joan's blood, like his own, ebbing. Linked to a common loss, they were chastely conjoined; the thesis developed upon him that the hoses attached to them somewhere out of sight met. Testing this belief, he glanced down and saw that indeed the plastic vine taped to the flattened crook of his arm was the same dark red as hers. He stared at the ceiling to disperse a sensation of faintness.

Abruptly the young intern left off his desultory conversation and moved to Joan's side. There was a chirp of clips. When he moved away, she was revealed holding her naked arm upright, pressing a piece of cotton against it with the other hand. Without pausing, the intern came to Richard's side, and the birdsong of the clips repeated, nearer. "Look at that," he said to his elderly friend. "I started him two minutes later than her and he's finished at the same time."

"Was it a race?" Richard asked.

Clumsily firm, the boy fitted Richard's fingers to a pad and lifted his arm for him. "Hold it there for five minutes," he said.

"What'll happen if I don't?"

"You'll mess up your shirt." To the old man he said, "I had a woman in here the other day, she was all set to leave when all of a sudden, pow!—all over the front of this beautiful linen dress. She was going to Symphony."

"Then they try to sue the hospital for the cleaning bill," the old man muttered.

"Why was I slower than him?" Joan asked. Her upright arm wavered, as if vexed or weakened.

"The woman generally is," the boy told her. "Nine times out of ten, the man is faster. Their hearts are so much stronger."

"Is that really so?"

"Sure it's so," Richard told her. "Don't argue with medical science."

"Woman up in Ward C," the old man said, "they saved her life for her out of an auto accident and now I hear she's suing because they didn't find her dental plate."

Under such patter, the five minutes eroded. Richard's upheld arm began to ache. It seemed that he and Joan were caught together in a classroom where they would never be recognized, or in a charade that would never be guessed, the correct answer being Two Silver Birches in a Meadow.

"You can sit up now if you want," the intern told them. "But don't let go of the venipuncture."

They sat up on their beds, legs dangling heavily. Joan asked him, "Do you feel dizzy?"

"With my powerful heart? Don't be presumptuous."

"Do you think he'll need coffee?" the intern asked her. "I'll have to send up for it now."

The old man shifted forward in his chair, preparing to heave to his feet.

"I do *not* want any *coffee*"—Richard said it so loud he saw himself transposed, another Iris, into the firmament of the old man's aggrieved gossip. *Some dizzy bastard down in the blood room, I get up to get him some coffee and he damn near bit my head off.* To demonstrate simultaneously his essential good humor and his total presence of mind, Richard gestured toward the blood they had given—two square plastic sacks filled solidly fat—and declared, "Back where I come from in West Virginia sometimes you pick a tick off a dog that looks like that."

The men looked at him amazed. Had he not quite said what he meant to say? Or had they never seen anybody from West Virginia before?

Joan pointed at the blood, too. "Is that us? Those little doll pillows?"

"Maybe we should take one home to Bean," Richard suggested.

The intern did not seem convinced that this was a joke. "Your blood will be credited to Mrs. Henryson's account," he stated stiffly.

Joan asked him, "Do you know anything about her? When is she—when is her operation scheduled?"

"I think for tomorrow. The only thing on the tab this after is an open heart at two; that'll take about sixteen pints."

"Oh . . . " Joan was shaken. "Sixteen . . . that's a full person, isn't it?

"More," the intern answered, with the regal handwave that bestows largess and dismisses compliments.

"Could we visit her?" Richard asked, for Joan's benefit. ("Really ashamed," she had said; it had cut.) He was confident of the refusal.

"Well, you can ask at the desk, but usually before a major one like this it's just the nearest of kin. I guess you're safe now." He meant their punctures. Richard's arm bore a small raised bruise; the intern covered it with one of those ample, salmon, unhesitatingly adhesive bandages that only hospitals have. That was their specialty, Richard thought—packaging. They wrap the human mess for final delivery. Sixteen doll's pillows, uniformly dark and snug, marching into an open heart: the vision momentarily satisfied his hunger for cosmic order.

He rolled down his sleeve and slid off the bed. It startled him to realize, in the instant before his feet touched the floor, that three pairs of eyes were fixed upon him, fascinated and apprehensive and eager for scandal. He stood and towered above them. He hopped on one foot to slip into one loafer, and then on this foot to slip into the other loafer. Then he did the little shuffle-tap, shuffle-tap step that was all that remained to him of dancing lessons he had taken at the age of seven, driving twelve miles each Saturday into Morgantown. He made a small bow toward his wife, smiled at the old man, and said to the intern, "All my life people have been expecting me to faint. I have no idea why. I never faint."

His coat and overcoat felt a shade queer, a bit slithery and light, but as he walked down the length of the corridor, space seemed to adjust snugly around him. At his side, Joan kept an inquisitive and chastened silence. They pushed through the great glass doors. A famished sun was nibbling through the overcast. Above and behind them, the King of Arabia lay in a drugged dream of dunes and Mrs. Henryson upon her sickbed received like the comatose mother of twins their identical gifts of blood. Richard hugged his wife's padded shoulders and as they walked along leaning on each other whispered, "Hey, I love you. Love love *love* you."

Romance is, simply, the strange, the untried. It was unusual for the Maples to be driving together at eleven in the morning. Almost always it was dark when they shared a car. The oval of her face was bright in the corner of his eye. She was watching him, alert to take the wheel if he suddenly lost consciousness. He felt tender toward her in the eggshell light, and curious toward himself, wondering how far beneath his brain the black pit did lie. He felt no different; but then the quality of consciousness perhaps did not bear introspection. Something certainly had been taken from him; he was less himself by a pint and it was not impossible that like a trapeze artist saved by a net he was sustained in the world of light and reflection by a single layer of interwoven cells. Yet the earth, with its signals and buildings and cars and bricks, continued like a pedal note.

Boston behind them, he asked, "Where should we eat?"

"Should we eat?"

"Please, yes. Let me take you to lunch. Just like a secretary."

"I do feel sort of illicit. As if I've stolen something."

"You too? But what did we steal?"

"I don't know. The morning? Do you think Eve knows enough to feed them?" Eve was their sitter, a little sandy girl from down the street who would, in exactly a year, Richard calculated, be painfully lovely. They lasted three years on the average, sitters; you got them in the tenth grade and escorted them into their bloom and then, with graduation, like commuters who had reached their stop, they dropped out of sight, into nursing school or marriage. And the train went on, and took on other passengers, and itself became older and longer. The Maples had four children: Judith, Richard Jr., poor oversized, angel-faced John, and Bean.

"She'll manage. What would you like? All that talk about coffee has made me frantic for some."

"At the Pancake House beyond 128 they give you coffee before you even ask."

"Pancakes? Now? Aren't you gay? Do you think we'll throw up?"

"Do you feel like throwing up?"

"No, not really. I feel sort of insubstantial and gentle, but it's probably psychosomatic. I don't really understand this business of giving something away and still somehow having it. What is it—the spleen?"

"I don't know. Are the splenetic man and the sanguine man the same?"

"God. I've totally forgotten the humors. What are the others—phlegm and choler?"

"Bile and black bile are in there somewhere."

"One thing about you, Joan. You're educated. New England women are educated."

"Sexless as we are."

"That's right; drain me dry and then put me on the rack." But there was no wrath in his words; indeed, he had reminded her of their earlier conversation so that, in much this way, his words might be revived, diluted, and erased. It seemed to work. The restaurant where they served only pancakes was empty and quiet this early. A bashfulness possessed them both; it had become a date between two people who have little as yet in common but who are nevertheless sufficiently intimate to accept the fact without chatter. Touched by the stain her blueberry pancakes left on her teeth, he held a match to her cigarette and said, "Gee, I loved you back in the blood room."

"I wonder why."

"You were so brave."

"So were you."

"But I'm supposed to be. I'm paid to be. It's the price of having a penis."

"Shh."

"Hey. I didn't mean that about your being sexless."

The waitress refilled their coffee cups and gave them the check.

"And I promise never never to do the Twist, the cha-cha, or the schottische with Marlene Brossman."

"Don't be silly. I don't care."

This amounted to permission, but perversely irritated him. That smugness; why didn't she *fight*? Trying to regain their peace, scrambling uphill, he picked up their check and with an effort of acting, the pretense being that they were out on a date and he was a raw dumb suitor, said handsomely, "I'll pay."

But on looking into his wallet he saw only a single worn dollar there. He didn't know why this should make him so angry, except the fact somehow that it was only *one*. "Goddammit," he said. "Look at that." He waved it in her face. "I work like a bastard all week for you and those insatiable brats and at the end of it what do I have? One goddam crummy wrinkled dollar."

Her hands dropped to the pocketbook beside her on the seat, but her gaze stayed with him, her face having retreated, or advanced, into that porcelain shell of uncanny composure. "We'll both pay," Joan said.

Born in Esterhazy, Saskatchewan, in 1951, Guy Vanderhaeghe now lives in Saskatoon. A contributor to numerous journals, he won the Governor-General's Award for fiction for his first book, the short story collection *Man Descending* (1982). Two novels—*My Present Age* (1984) and *Homesick* (1989)—continue his fictional commentary on living the moral life in the face of private and public pressure to yield or compromise.

Violent in subject and raw in language, "Cages" (from *Man Descending*) depicts how economics, class, intelligence, age, rivalry, desire (for power, for freedom, for love), and responsibility all enclose human beings. The central character, an adolescent on the verge (he thinks) of breaking away, finds himself ultimately as constrained as any other ordinary person. The story stops short of judging or interpreting the protagonist's circumstances; they invite neither pity nor despair—they just are. The condition of being alive, it seems, imposes both connection and conflict; it allows people to aspire and dream, but it also requires them to learn to endure.

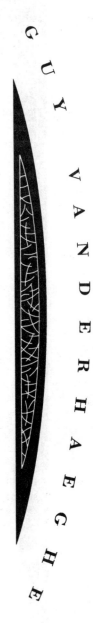

GUY VANDERHAEGHE

FOR FURTHER READING

Guy Vanderhaeghe, "Influences," *Canadian Literature* 100 (Spring 1984): 323-28.

Cages

HERE IT IS, 1967, the Big Birthday. Centennial Year they call it. The whole country is giving itself a pat on the back. Holy shit, boys, we made it.

I made it too for seventeen years, a spotless life, as they say, and for presents I get, in my senior year of high school, my graduating year for chrissakes, a six-month suspended sentence for obstructing a police officer, and my very own personal social worker.

The thing is I don't *need* this social worker woman. She can't tell me anything I haven't already figured out for myself. Take last Wednesday, Miss Krawchuk, who looks like the old widow chicken on the Bugs Bunny Show, the one who's hot to trot for Foghorn Leghorn, says to me: "You know, Billy, your father loves you just as much as he does Gene. He doesn't have a favourite."

Now I can get bullshit at the poolroom any time I want it—and without having to keep an appointment. Maybe Pop *loves* me as much as he does Gene, but Gene is still his favourite kid. Everybody has a favourite kid. I knew that much already when I was only eight and Gene was nine. I figured it out right after Gene almost blinded me.

Picture this. There the two of us were in the basement. It was Christmas holidays and the old man had kicked us downstairs to huck darts at this board he'd give us for a present. Somehow, I must've had horseshoes up my ass, I'd beat Gene six games straight. And was he pissed off! He never loses to me at nothing ever. And me being in such a real unique situation, I was giving him the needle-rooney.

"What's that now?" I said. "Is that six or seven what I won?"

"Luck," Gene said, and he sounded like somebody was slowly strangling him. "Luck. Luck. Luck." He could hardly get it out.

And that's when I put the capper on it. I tossed a bull's-eye. "Read 'er and weep," I told him. That's what the old man says whenever he goes out at rummy. It's his needle-rooney. "Read 'er and weep."

That did it. The straw what broke the frigging camel's back. All I saw was his arm blur when he let fly at me. I didn't even have time to *think* about ducking. Bingo. Dead centre in the forehead, right in the middle of the old noggin he drills me with a dart. And there it stuck. Until it loosened a bit. Then it sagged down real slow between my eyes, hung for a second, slid off of my nose, and dropped at my feet. I hollered bloody blue murder, you better believe it.

For once, Pop didn't show that little bastard any mercy. He took after him from room to room whaling him with this extension cord across the ass, the back of the legs, the shoulders. Really hard. Gene, naturally, was screaming and blubbering and carrying on like it was a goddamn axe murder or something. He'd try to get under a bed, or behind a dresser or something, and get stuck halfway. Then old Gene would really catch it. He didn't know whether to plough forward, back up, shit, or go blind. And all the time the old man was lacing him left and right and saying in this sad, tired voice: "You're the oldest. Don't you know no better? You could of took his eye out, you crazy little bugger."

But that was only justice. He wasn't all that mad at Gene. Me he was mad at. If that makes any sense. Although I have to admit he didn't lay a hand on me. But yell? Christ, can that man yell. Especially at me. Somehow I'm the one that drives him squirrelly.

"Don't you *never*, *never* tease him again!" he bellowed and his neck started to swell. When the old man gets mad you can see it swell, honest. "You know he can't keep a hold of himself. One day you'll drive him so goddamn goofy with that yap of yours he'll do something terrible! Something he'll regret for the rest of his life. And it'll all be your fault!" The old man had to stop there and slow down or a vein would've exploded in his brain, or his arsehole popped inside out, or something. "So smarten, up," he said, a little quieter, finally, "or you'll be the death of me and all my loved ones."

So there you are. I never pretended the world was fair, and I never bitched because it wasn't. But I do resent the hell out of being forced to listen to some dried-up old broad who gets paid by the government to tell me it is. Fuck her. She never lived in the Simpson household with my old man waiting around for Gene to do that *terrible* thing. It spoils the atmosphere. Makes a person edgy, you know?

Of course, Gene has done a fair number of *bad things* while everybody was waiting around for him to do the one great big *terrible thing*; and he's done them in a fair number of places. That's because the old man is a miner, and for a while there he was always telling some foreman to go piss up a rope. So we moved around a lot. That's why the Simpson household has a real history. But Gene's is the best of all. In Elliot Lake he failed grade three; in Bombertown he got picked up for shoplifting; in Flin Flon he broke some snotty kid's nose and got sent home from school. And every grade he goes higher, it gets a little worse. Last year, when we were both in grade eleven, I'm sure the old man was positive Gene was finally going to pull off the *terrible thing* he's been worrying about as long as I can remember.

It's crazy. Lots of times when I think about it, I figure I don't get on with the old man because I treat him nice. That I try too hard to make him like me. I'm not the way Gene is, I respect Pop. He slogs it out, shift after shift, on a shitty job he hates. Really hates. In fact, he told me once he would have liked to been a farmer. Which only goes to show you how crazy going down that hole day after day makes you. Since we moved to Saskatchewan I've seen lots of farmers, and if you ask me, being one doesn't have much to recommend it.

But getting back to that business of being nice to Dad. Last year I started waiting up for him to come home from the afternoon shift. The one that runs from four p.m. in the afternoon until midnight. It wasn't half bad. Most nights I'd fall asleep on the chesterfield with the TV playing after Mom went to bed. Though lots of times I'd do my best to make it past the national news to wait for Earl Cameron and his collection of screwballs. Those guys kill me. They're always yapping off because somebody or something rattled their chain. Most of those characters with all the answers couldn't pour piss out of a rubber boot if they read the instructions printed on the sole. They remind me of Gene; he's got all the answers too. But still, quite a few of them are what you'd call witty. Which Gene is in his own way too.

But most times, as I say, I'd doze off. Let me give you a sample evening. About twelve-thirty the lights of his half-ton would come shooting into the living-room, bouncing off the walls, scooting along the ceiling when he wheeled into the driveway like a madman. It was the lights flashing in my eyes that woke me up most nights, and if that didn't do it there was always his grand entrance. When the old man comes into the house, from the sound of it you'd think he never heard of door knobs. I swear sometimes I'm sure he's taking a battering-ram to the back door. Then he thunks his lunch bucket on the kitchen counter and bowls his hard hat into the landing. This is because he always comes home from work mad. Never once in his life has a shift ever gone right for that man. Never. They could pack his pockets with diamonds and send him home two hours early and he'd still bitch. So every night was pretty much the same. He had a mad on. Like in my sample night.

He flicked on the living-room light and tramped over to his orange recliner with the bottle of Boh. "If you want to ruin your eyes, do it on school-books, not on watching TV in the goddamn dark. It's up to somebody in this outfit to make something of themselves."

"I was sleeping."

"You ought to sleep in bed." *Keerash!* He weighs two hundred and forty-four pounds and he never sits down in a chair. He falls into it. "Who's that? Gary Cooper?" he asked. He figures any movie star on the late show taller than Mickey Rooney is Cooper. He doesn't half believe you when you tell him they aren't.

"Cary Grant."

"What?"

"Cary Grant. Not Gary Cooper. Cary Grant."

"Oh." There he sat in his recliner, big meaty shoulders sagging, belly propped up on his belt buckle like a pregnant pup's. Eyes red and sore, hair all mussed up, the top of his beer bottle peeking out of his fist like a little brown nipple. He has cuts all over those hands of his, barked knuckles and raspberries that never heal because the salt in the potash ore keeps them open, eats right down to the bone sometimes.

"How'd it go tonight?"

"Usual shit. We had a breakdown." He paused. "Where's your brother? In bed?"

"Out."

"Out? Out? *Out?* What kind of goddamn answer is that? Out where?"

I shrugged.

"Has he got his homework done?" That's the kind of question I get asked. *Has your brother got his homework done?*

"How the hell would I know?"

"I don't know why you don't help him with his school-work," the old man said, peeved as usual.

"You mean do it for him."

"Did I say that? Huh? I said help him. Didn't I say that?" he griped, getting his shit in a knot.

He thinks it's that easy. Just screw the top of old Gene and pour it in. No problem. Like an oil change.

"He's got to be around to help," I said.

That reminded him. He jumped out of the chair and gawked up and down the deserted street. "It's almost one o'clock. On a school night. I'll kick his ass." He sat down and watched the screen for a while and sucked on his barley sandwich.

Finally, he made a stab at acting civilized. "So how's baseball going?"

"What?"

"Baseball. For chrissakes clean out your ears. How's it going?"

"I quit last year. Remember?"

"Oh yeah." He didn't say nothing at first. Then he said: "You shouldn't have. You wasn't a bad catcher."

"The worst. No bat and no arm—just a flipper. They stole me blind."

"But you had the head," said the old man. And the way he said it made him sound like he was pissed at me for mean-mouthing myself. That surprised me. I felt kind of good about that. "You had the head," he repeated, shaking his own. "I never told you but Al came up to me at work and said you were smart back there behind the plate. He said he wished Gene had your head."

I can't say that surprised me. Gene is one of those cases of a million-dollar body carrying around a ten-cent head. He's a natural. Flop out his glove and, smack, the ball sticks. He's like Mickey Mantle. You know those stop-action photos where they caught Mickey with his eyes glommed onto the bat, watching the ball jump off the lumber? That's Gene. And he runs like a Negro, steals bases like Maury Wills for chrissake.

But stupid and conceited? You wouldn't believe the half of it. Give him the sign to bunt to move a runner and he acts as if you're asking him to bare his ass in public. Not him. He's a big shot. He swings for the fence. Nothing less. And old Gene is always in the game, if you know what I mean? I don't know what happens when he gets on base, maybe he starts thinking of the hair pie in the stands admiring him or something, but he always dozes off at the wheel. Once he even started to comb his hair at first base. Here it is, a 3 and 2 count with two men out, and my brother forgets to run on the pitch because he's combing his hair. I could have died. Really I could have. The guy is such an embarrassment sometimes.

"He can have my head," I said to Pop. "If I get his girls."

That made the old man wince. He's sure that Gene is going to knock up one of those seat-covers he takes out and make him a premature grandpa.

"You pay attention to school. There's plenty of time later for girls." And up he jumped again and stuck his nose against the window looking for Gene again. Mom has to wash the picture window once a week; he spots it all up with nose grease looking for Gene.

"I don't know why your mother lets him out of the house," he said. "Doesn't she have any control over that boy?"

That's what he does, blames everybody but himself. Oh hell, maybe nobody's to blame. Maybe Gene is just Gene, and there's nothing to be done about it.

"I don't know what she's supposed to do. You couldn't keep him in if you parked a tank in the driveway and strung barbed wire around the lot."

Of course that was the wrong thing to say. I usually say it.

"Go to bed!" he yelled at me. "You're no better than your brother. I don't see you in bed neither. What'd I do, raise alley cats or kids? Why can't you two keep hours like human beings!"

And then the door banged and we knew the happy wanderer was home. Gene makes almost as much noise as the old man does when he comes in. It's beneath his dignity to sneak in like me.

Dad hoisted himself out of the chair and steamed off for the kitchen. He can move pretty quick for a big guy when he wants to. Me, I was in hot pursuit. I don't like to miss much.

Old Gene was hammered, and grinning from ass-hole to ear-lobes. The boy's got a great smile. Even when he grins at old ladies my mother's age you can tell they like it.

"Come here and blow in my face," said my father.

"Go on with you," said Gene. All of a sudden the smile was gone and he was irritated. He pushed past Pop, took the milk out of the fridge and started to drink out of the container.

"Use a glass."

Gene burped. He's a slob.

"You stink of beer," said the old man. "Who buys beer for a kid your age?"

"I ain't drunk," said Gene.

"Not much. Your eyes look like two piss-holes in the snow."

"Sure, sure," said Gene. He lounged, he swivelled over to me and lifted my Players out of my shirt pocket. "I'll pay you back tomorrow," he said, taking out a smoke. I heard that one before.

"I don't want to lose my temper," said Dad, being patient with him as usual, "so don't push your luck, sunshine." The two of them eyeballed it, hard. Finally Gene backed down, looked away and fiddled with his matches. "I don't ride that son of a bitch of a cage up and down for my health. I do it for you two," Dad said. "But I swear to God, Gene, if you blow this year of school there'll be a pair of new work boots for you on the back step, come July 1. Both of you know my rules. Go to school, work, or pack up. I'm not having bums put their feet under my table."

"I ain't scared of work," said Gene. "Anyways, school's a pain in the ass."

"Well, you climb in the cage at midnight with three hours of sleep and see if *that* ain't a pain in the ass. Out there nobody says, please do this, please do that. It ain't school out there, it's life."

"Ah, I wouldn't go to the mine. The mine sucks."

"Just what the hell do you think you'd do?"

"He'd open up shop as a brain surgeon," I said. Of course, Gene took a slap at me and grabbed at my shirt. He's a tough guy. He wasn't really mad, but he likes to prevent uppityness.

"You go to bed!" the old man hollered. "You ain't helping matters!"

So off I went. I could hear them wrangling away even after I closed my door. You'd wonder how my mother does it, but she sleeps through it all. I think she's just so goddamn tired of the three of us she's gone permanently deaf to the sound of our voices. She just don't hear us any more.

The last thing I heard before I dropped off was Pop saying: "I've rode that cage all my life, and take it from me, there wasn't a day I didn't wish I'd gone to school and could sit in an office in a clean white shirt." Sometimes he can't remember what he wants to be, a farmer or a pencil-pusher.

The cage. He's always going on about the cage. It's what the men at the mine call the elevator car they ride down the shaft. They call it that because it's all heavy reinforced-steel mesh. The old man has this cage on the brain. Ever since we were little kids he's been threatening us with it. *Make something of yourself*, he'd warn us, *or you'll end up like your old man, a monkey in the cage!* Or: *What's this, Gene? Failed arithmetic? Just remember, dunces don't end up in the corner. Hell no, they end up in the cage! Look at me!* My old man really hates that cage and the mine. He figures it's the worst thing you can threaten anybody with.

I was in the cage, once. A few years ago, when I was fourteen, the company decided they'd open the mine up for tours. It was likely the brainstorm of some public relations tit sitting in head office in Chicago. In my book it was kind of like taking people into the slaughterhouse to prove you're kind to the cows. Anyway, Pop offered to take us on one of his days off. As usual, he was about four years behind schedule. When we were maybe eleven we might have been nuts about the idea, but just then it didn't thrill us too badly. Gene, who is about as subtle as a bag of hammers, said flat out he wasn't interested. I could see right away the old man was hurt by that. It isn't often he plays the buddy to his boys, and he probably had the idea he could whiz us about the machines and stuff. Impress the hell out of us. So it was up to me to slobber and grin like some kind of half-wit over the idea, to perk him up, see? Everybody suffers when the old man gets into one of his moods.

Of course, like always when I get sucked into this good-turn business, I shaft myself. I'd sort of forgotten how much I don't like tight places and being closed in. When we were younger, Gene used to make me go berserk by holding me under the covers, or stuffing a pillow in my face, or locking me in the garage whenever he got the chance. The jerk.

To start with, they packed us in the cage with twelve other people, which didn't help matters any. Right away my chest got tight and I felt like I couldn't breathe. Then the old cables started groaning and grinding and this fine red dust like chili powder sprinkled down through the mesh and dusted our hard hats with the word GUEST stencilled on them. It was rust. Kind of makes you think.

"Here we go," said Pop.

We went. It was like all of a sudden the floor fell away from under my boots. That cage just dropped in the shaft like a stone down a well. It rattled and creaked and banged. The bare light bulb in the roof started to flicker, and all the faces around me started to dance and shake up and down in the dark. A wind twisted up my pant-legs and I could hear the cables squeak and squeal. It made me think of big fat fucking rats.

"She needs new brake shoes," said this guy beside me and he laughed. He couldn't fool me. He was scared shitless too, in his own way.

"It's not the fall that kills you," his neighbour replied. "It's the sudden stop." There's a couple of horses' patoots in every crowd.

We seemed to drop forever. Everybody got quieter and quieter. They even stopped shuffling and coughing. Down. Down. Down. Then the cage started to slow, I felt a pressure build in my knees and my crotch and my ears. The wire box started to shiver and clatter and shake. *Bang!* We stopped. The cage bobbed a little up and down like a yo-yo on the end of a string. Not much though, just enough to make you queasy.

"Last stop, Hooterville!" said the guide, who thought he was funny, and threw back the door. Straight ahead I could see a low-roofed big open space with tunnels running from it into the ore. Every once in a while I could see the light from a miner's helmet jump around in the blackness of one of those tunnels like a firefly flitting in the night.

First thing I thought was: *What if I get lost? What if I lose the group? There's miles and miles and miles of tunnel under here.* I caught a whiff of the air. It didn't smell like air up top. It smelled used. You could taste the salt. *I'm suffocating,* I thought. *I can't breathe this shit.*

I hadn't much liked the cage but this was worse. When I was in the shaft I knew there was a patch of sky over my head with a few stars in it and clouds and stuff. But all of a sudden I realized how deep we were. How we were sort of like worms crawling in the guts of some dead animal. Over us were billions, no, trillions, of tons of rock and dirt and mud pressing down. I could imagine it caving in and falling on me, crushing my chest, squeezing the air out slowly, dust fine as flour trickling into my eyes and nostrils, or mud plugging my mouth so I couldn't even scream. And then just lying there in the dark, my legs and arms pinned so I couldn't even twitch them. For a long time maybe. Crazy, lunatic stuff was what I started to think right on the spot.

My old man gave me a nudge to get out. We were the last.

"No," I said quickly and hooked my fingers in the mesh.

"We get out here," said the old man. He hadn't caught on yet.

"No, I can't," I whispered. He must have read the look on my face then. I think he knew he couldn't have pried me off that mesh with a gooseneck and winch.

Fred, the cage operator, lifted his eyebrows at Pop. "What's up, Jack?"

"The kid's sick," said Pop. "We'll take her up. He don't feel right." My old man was awful embarrassed.

Fred said, "I wondered when it'd happen. Taking kids and women down the hole."

"Shut your own goddamn hole," said the old man. "He's got the flu. He was up all last night."

Fred looked what you'd call sceptical.

"Last time I take you any place nice," the old man said under his breath.

The last day of school has always got to be some big deal. By nine o'clock all the dipsticks are roaring their cars up and down main street with their goofy broads hanging out their windows yelling, and trying to impress on one another how drunk they are.

Dad sent me to look for Gene because he didn't come home for supper at six. I found him in the poolroom playing dollar-a-hand poker pool.

"Hey, little brother," he waved to me from across the smoky poolroom, "come on here and I'll let you hold my cards!" I went over. He grinned to the goofs he was playing with. "You watch out now, boys," he said, "my little brother always brings me luck. Not that I need it," he explained to me, winking.

Yeah, I always brought him luck. *I* kept track of the game. *I* figured out what order to take the balls down. *I* reminded him not to put somebody else out and to play the next guy safe instead of slamming off some cornball shot. When *I* did all that Gene won—because I brought him luck. Yeah.

Gene handed me his cards. "You wouldn't believe these two," he said to me out of the corner of his mouth, "genuine plough jockeys. These boys couldn't find their ass in the dark with both hands. I'm fifteen dollars to the good."

I admit they didn't look too swift. The biggest one, who was *big*, was wearing an out-of-town team jacket, a Massey-Ferguson cap, and shit-kicker wellingtons. He was maybe twenty-one, but his skin hadn't cleared up yet by no means. His pan looked like all-dressed pizza, heavy on the cheese. His friend was a dinky little guy with his hair designed into a duck's ass. The kind of guy who hates the Beatles. About two feet of a dirty comb was sticking out of his ass pocket.

Gene broke the rack and the nine went down. His shot.

"Dad's looking for you. He wants to know if you passed," I said.

"You could've told him."

"Well, I didn't."

"Lemme see the cards." I showed him. He had a pair of treys, a six, a seven, and a lady. Right away he stopped to pocket the three. I got a teacher who always talks about thought processes. Gene doesn't have them.

"Look at the table," I said. "Six first and you can come around up her." I pointed.

"No coaching," said Pizza Face. I could see this one was a poor loser.

Gene shifted his stance and potted the six.

"What now?" he asked.

"The queen, and don't forget to put pants on her." I paused. "Pop figured you were going to make it. He really did, Gene."

"So tough titty. I didn't. Who the hell cares? He had your suck card to slobber over, didn't he?" He drilled the lady in the side pocket. No backspin. He'd hooked himself on the three. "Fuck."

"The old man is on graveyard shift. You better go home and face the music before he goes to work. It'll be worse in the morning when he needs sleep," I warned him.

"Screw him."

I could see Gene eyeballing the four. He didn't have any four in his hand, so I called him over and showed him his cards. "You can't shoot the four. It's not in your hand."

"Just watch me." He winked. "I've been doing it all night. It's all pitch and no catch with these prizes." Gene strolled back to the table and coolly stroked down the four. He had shape for the three which slid in the top pocket like shit through a goose. He cashed in on the seven. "That's it, boys," he said. "That's all she wrote."

I was real nervous. I tried to bury the hand in the deck but the guy with the runny face stopped me. He was getting tired of losing, I guess. Gene doesn't even cheat smart. You got to let them win once in a while.

"Gimme them cards," he said. He started counting the cards off against the balls, flipping down the boards on the felt. "Three." He nodded. "Six, seven, queen. I guess you got them all," he said slowly, with a look on his face like he was pissing ground glass.

That's when Duck Ass chirped up. "Hey, Marvin," he said, "that guy shot the four. He shot the four."

"Nah," said Gene.

Marvin studied on this for a second, walked over to the table and pulled the four ball out of the pocket. Just like little Jack Horner lifting the plum out of the pie. "Yeah," he said. "You shot the four."

"Jeez," said Gene, "I guess I did. Honest mistake. Look, here's a dollar for each of you." He took two bills out of his shirt pocket. "You got to pay for your mistakes is what I was always taught."

"I bet you he's been cheating all along," said Duck Ass.

"My brother don't cheat," I said.

"I want all my money back," said Marvin. Quite loud. Loud enough that some heads turned and a couple of tables stopped playing. There was what you would call a big peanut gallery, it being the beginning of vacation and the place full of junior high kids and stags.

"You can kiss my ass, bozo," said Gene. "Like my brother here said, I never cheated nobody in my life."

"You give us our money back," threatened Marvin, "or I'll pull your head off, you skinny little prick."

Guys were starting to drift towards us, curious. The manager, Fat Bert, was easing his guts out from behind the cash register.

"Give them their money, Gene," I said, "and let's get out of here."

"No."

Well, that was that. You can't change his mind. I took a look at old Marvin. As I said before, Marvin was *big*. But what was worse was that he had this real determined look people who aren't too bright get when they finally dib on to the fact they've been hosed and somebody has been laughing up his sleeve at them. They don't like it too hot, believe me.

"Step outside, shit-head," said Marvin.

"Fight," somebody said encouragingly. A real clump of ringsiders was starting to gather. "Fight." Bert came hustling up, bumping his way through the kids with his bay window. "Outside, you guys. I don't want nothing broke in here. Get out or I'll call the cops."

Believe me, was I tense. Real tense. I know Gene pretty well and I was sure that he had looked at old Marvin's muscles trying to bust out everywhere. Any second I figured he was going to even the odds by pasting old Marv in the puss with his pool cue, or at least sucker-punching him.

But Gene is full of surprises. All of a sudden he turned peacemaker. He laid down his pool cue (which I didn't figure was too wise) and said: "You want to fight over this?" He held up the four ball. "Over this? An honest mistake?"

"Sure I do," said Marvin. "You're fucking right I do, cheater."

"Cheater, cheater," said Duck Ass. I was looking him over real good because I figured if something started in there I'd get him to tangle with.

Gene shrugged and even kind of sighed, like the hero does in the movies when he has been forced into a corner and has to do something that is against his better nature. He tossed up the four ball once, looked at it, and then reached behind him and shoved it back into the pocket. "All right," he said, slouching a little and jamming his hands into his jacket pockets. "Let's go, sport."

That started the stampede. "Fight! Fight!" The younger kids, the ones thirteen and fourteen, were really excited; the mob kind of swept

Marvin and Gene out the door, across the street and into the OK Economy parking lot where most beefs get settled. There's lots of dancing-room there. A nice big ring.

Marvin settled in real quick. He tugged the brim of his Massey-Ferguson special a couple of times, got his dukes up and started to hop around like he'd stepped right out of the pages of *Ring* magazine. He looked pretty stupid, especially when Gene just looked at him, and kept his hands rammed in his jacket pockets. Marvin kind of clomped from foot to foot for a bit and he said: "Get 'em up."

"You get first punch," said Gene.

"What?" said Marv. He was so surprised his yap fell open.

"If I hit you first," said Gene, "you'll charge me with assault. I know your kind."

Marvin stopped clomping. I suspect it took too much co-ordination for him to clomp and think at the same time. "Oh no," he said, "I ain't falling for that. If I hit *you* first, you'll charge *me* with assault." No flies on Marvin. "*You* get the first punch."

"Fight. Come on, fight," said some ass-hole, real disgusted with all the talk and no action.

"Oh no," said Gene. "I ain't hitting *you* first."

Marvin brought his hands down. "Come on, come on, let fly."

"You're sure?" asked Gene.

"Give her your best shot," said Marvin. "You couldn't hurt a fly, you scrawny shit. Quit stalling. Get this show on the road."

Gene uncorked on him. It looked like a real pansy punch. His right arm whipped out of his jacket pocket, stiff at the elbow like a girl's when she slaps. It didn't look like it had nothing behind it, sort of like Gene had smacked him kind of contemptuous in the mouth with the flat of his hand. That's how it looked. It *sounded* like he'd hit him in the mouth with a ball-peen hammer. Honest to God, you could hear the teeth crunch when they broke.

Big Marvin dropped on his knees like he'd been shot in the back of the neck. His hands flew up to his face and the blood just ran through his fingers and into his cuffs. It looked blue under the parking-lot lights. There was an awful lot of it.

"Get up, you dick licker," said Gene.

Marvin pushed off his knees with a crazy kind of grunt that might have been a sob. I couldn't tell. He came up under Gene's arms, swept him off his feet and dangled him in the air, crushing his ribs in a bear hug.

"*Waauugh!*" said Gene. I started looking around right smartly for something to hit the galoot with before he popped my brother like a pimple.

But then Gene lifted his fist high above Marvin's head and brought it down on his skull, hard as he could. It made a sound like he was banging coconuts together. Marvin sagged a little at the knees and staggered. *Chunk! Chunk!* Gene hit him two more times and Marvin toppled over backwards. My brother landed on top of him and right away started pasting him left and right. Everybody was screaming encouragement. There was no invitation to the dick licker to get up this time. Gene was still clobbering him when I saw the cherry popping on the cop car two blocks away. I dragged him off Marvin.

"Cops," I said, yanking at his sleeve. Gene was trying to get one last kick at Marvin. "Come on, fucker," he was yelling. "Fight now!"

"Jesus," I said, looking at Gene's jacket and shirt, "you stupid bugger, you're all over blood." It was smeared all over him. Marvin tried to get up. He only made it to his hands and knees. There he stayed, drooling blood and saliva on the asphalt. The crowd started to edge away as the cop car bounced up over the curb and gave a long, low whine out of its siren.

I took off my windbreaker and gave it to Gene. He pulled off his jacket and threw it down. "Get the fuck out of here," I said. "Beat it."

"I took the wheels off his little red wagon," said Gene. "It don't pull so good now." His hands were shaking and so was his voice. He hadn't had half enough yet. "I remember that other guy," he said. "Where's his friend?"

I gave him a shove. "Get going." Gene slid into the crowd that was slipping quickly away. Then I remembered his hockey jacket. It was wet with blood. It also had flashes with his name and number on it. It wouldn't take no Sherlock Holmes cop to figure out who'd beat on Marvin. I picked it up and hugged it to my belly. Right away I felt something hard in the pocket. Hard and round. I started to walk away. I heard a car door slam. I knew what was in that pocket. The controversial four ball old Gene had palmed when he pretended to put it back. He likes to win.

I must have been walking too fast or with a guilty hunch to my shoulders, because I heard the cop call, "Hey you, the kid with the hair." Me, I'm kind of a hippy for this place, I guess. Lots of people mention my hair.

I ran. I scooted round the corner of the supermarket and let that pool ball fly as hard as I could, way down the alley. I never rifled a shot like that in my life. If coach Al had seen me trigger that baby he'd have strapped me into a belly pad himself. Of course, a jacket don't fly for shit. The bull came storming around the corner just as I give it the heave-ho. I was kind of caught with shit on my face, if you know what I mean?

Now a guy with half a brain could have talked his way out of that without too much trouble. Even a cop understands how somebody would try to help his brother. They don't hold it too much against you.

And I couldn't really protect Gene. That geek Marvin would have flapped his trap if I hadn't. And it wasn't as if I hadn't done old Gene *some* good. After all, they never found out about that pool ball. The judge would have pinned Gene's ears back for him if he'd known he was going around thwacking people with a hunk of shatter-proof plastic. So Gene came out smelling like a rose, same suspended sentence as me, and a reputation for having hands of stone.

But at a time like that you get the nuttiest ideas ever. I watched them load Marvin in a squad car to drive him to the hospital while I sat in the back seat of another. And I thought to myself: *I'll play along with this. Let the old man come down to the cop shop over me for once. Me he takes for granted. Let him worry about Billy for a change. It wouldn't hurt him.*

So I never said one word about not being the guy who bopped Marvin. It was kind of fun in a crazy way, making like a hard case. At the station I was real rude and lippy. Particularly to a sergeant who was a grade A dink if I ever saw one. It was only when they took my shoelaces and belt that I started to get nervous.

"Ain't you going to call my old man?" I asked.

The ass-hole sergeant gave me a real smile. "In the morning," he said. "All in good time."

"In the morning?" And then I said like a dope: "Where am I going to sleep?"

"Show young Mr. Simpson where he's going to sleep," said the sergeant. He smiled again. It looked like a ripple on a slop pail. The constable who he was ordering around like he was his own personal slave took me down into the basement of the station. Down there it smelled of stale piss and old puke. I kind of gagged. I got a weak stomach.

Boy, was I nervous. I saw where he was taking me. There were four cells. They weren't even made out of bars, just metal strips riveted into a cross hatch you couldn't stick your hand through. They were all empty.

"Your choice," said the corporal. He was real humorous too, like his boss.

"You don't have to put me in one of them, sir," I said. "I won't run away."

"That's what all the criminals say." He opened the door. "Entrez-vous."

I was getting my old crazy feeling really bad. Really bad. I felt kind of dizzy. "I got this thing," I said, "about being locked up. It's torture."

"Get in."

"No—please," I said. "I'll sit upstairs. I won't bother anybody."

"You think you've got a choice? You don't have a choice. Move your ass."

I was getting ready to cry. I could feel it. I was going to bawl in front of a copy. "I didn't do it," I said. "I never beat him up. Swear to Jesus I didn't."

"I'm counting three," he said, " and then I'm applying the boots to your backside."

It all came out. Just like that. *"It was my fucking ass-hole brother, Gene!"* I screamed. The only thing I could think of was, if they put me in there I'll be off my head by morning. I really will. *"I didn't do nothing! I never do nothing! You can't put me in there for him!"*

They called my old man. I guess I gave a real convincing performance. No that I'm proud of it. I actually got sick on the spot from nerves. I just couldn't hold it down.

Pop had to sign for me and promise to bring Gene down in the morning. It was about twelve-thirty when everything got cleared up. He'd missed his shift and his ride in the cage.

When we got in the car he didn't start it. We just sat there with the windows rolled down. It was a beautiful night and there were lots of stars swimming in the sky. This town is small enough that street-lights and neon don't interfere with the stars. It's the only thing I like about this place. There's plenty of sky and lots of air to breathe.

"Your brother wasn't enough," he said. "You I trusted."

"I only tried to help him."

"You goddamn snitch." He needed somebody to take it out on, so he belted me. Right on the snout with the back of his hand. It started to bleed. I didn't try to stop it. I just let it drip on those goddamn furry seat-covers that he thinks are the cat's ass. "They were going to put me in this place, this cage, for him, for that useless shit!" I yelled. I'd started to cry. "No more, Pop. He failed! He failed on top of it all! So is he going to work? You got the boots ready on the back step? Huh? Is he going down in the fucking cage?"

"Neither one of you is going down in the cage. Not him, not you," he said.

"Nah, I didn't think so," I said, finally wiping at my face with the back of my hand. "I didn't think so."

"I don't have to answer to you," he said. "You just can't get inside his head. You were always the smart one. I didn't have to worry about you. You always knew what to do. But Gene . . . " He pressed his forehead against the steering-wheel, hard. "Billy, I see him doing all sorts of stuff. Stuff you can't imagine. I see it until it makes me sick." He looked at me. His face was yellow under the street-light, yellow like a lemon. "I try so hard with him. But he's got no sense. He just does things. He could have killed that other boy. He wouldn't even think of that, you know." All of a sudden the old man's face got all crumpled and creased like paper when you ball it up. "What's going to happen to him?" he said, louder than he had to. "What's going to happen to Eugene?" It was sad. It really was.

I can never stay mad at my old man. Maybe because we're so much alike, even though he can't see it for looking the other way. Our minds work alike. I'm a chip off the old block. Don't ever doubt it.

"Nothing."

"Billy," he said, "you mean it?"

I knew what he was thinking. "Yes," I said. "I'll do my best."

The writings of Kurt Vonnegut (b. 1922) are characterized by a Swiftian sense of despair at the extremes of human folly. His books are about the horrors of war, the dehumanization of modern men and women, the loss of humane values in a society dedicated to technological progress. Though these are now fashionable subjects, Vonnegut's insights derive from personal experience. After serving in the U.S. Infantry during World War II, and witnessing the fire-bombing of Dresden as a prisoner of war, he became a police reporter in Chicago; then he entered the field of public relations, working for the General Electric Company until 1950, when he devoted himself full time to writing. Such a background provided him with ample material for his satire.

Gifted with a Kafka-esque sense of the absurd, Vonnegut works through a mixture of fantasy and realism to depict the deep springs of irrationality which govern human conduct; and he shows how the intellectual genius of modern science has been perverted to base and violent ends by the moral stupidity of the masses and their leaders. A prominent feature of his work is his interest in science fiction, which provides him with images of an automated and impersonal universe, where the individual is of less and less significance. Vonnegut's first novel, *Player Piano* (1952), depicts an America in which government is conducted by computer, and people are of value only as consumers; the futility of human endeavour is set in an even bleaker perspective in *The Sirens of Titan* (1959), which presents human history as subject to control by the inhabitants of a distant planet. Vonnegut's vision is not totally pessimistic; his stories often include at least one character who, aware of the surrounding madness, seeks to restore a measure of sanity; thus the brilliant professor in "Report on the Barnhouse Effect" (1950; *Welcome to the Monkey House*, 1968) and his protegé, the narrator, are determined to turn their amazing discovery to good uses, much to the chagrin of their fellow citizens. But in the novel *Slaughterhouse Five* (1969) Vonnegut is less hopeful, for in his treatment of the Dresden bombing, he suggests that individual effort is powerless to alleviate the misery and suffering of the human condition. The elements of fantasy and science fiction are less evident in his subsequent works, like *Jailbird* (1979), but he has continued his mordant satire of Western materialism and political corruption.

FOR FURTHER READING

D.H. Goldsmith, *Kurt Vonnegut, Fantasist of Fire and Ice* (Bowling Green, Ohio: Bowling Green Popular Press, 1972).

J. Klinkowitz and J. Somer, eds., *The Vonnegut Statement* (New York: Delacorte Press, 1973).

Robert Merrill, ed., *Critical Essays on Kurt Vonnegut* (Boston: G. K. Hall, 1990).

Stanley Schatt, *Kurt Vonnegut, Jr.* (Boston: Twayne, 1976).

Report on the
Barnhouse Effect

Let me begin by saying that I don't know any more about where Professor Arthur Barnhouse is hiding than anyone else does. Save for one short, enigmatic message left in my mail box on Christmas Eve, I have not heard from him since his disappearance a year and a half ago.

What's more, readers of this article will be disappointed if they expect to learn how *they* can bring about the so-called "Barnhouse Effect." If I were able and willing to give away that secret, I would certainly be something more important than a psychology instructor.

I have been urged to write this report because I did research under the professor's direction and because I was the first to learn of his astonishing discovery. But while I was his student I was never entrusted with knowledge of how the mental forces could be released and directed. He was unwilling to trust anyone with that information.

I would like to point out that the term "Barnhouse Effect" is a creation of the popular press, and was never used by Professor Barnhouse. The name he chose for the phenomenon was "*dynamopsychism*," or *force of the mind*.

I cannot believe that there is a civilized person yet to be convinced that such a force exists, what with its destructive effects on display in every national capital. I think humanity has always had an inkling that this sort of force does exist. It has been common knowledge that some people are luckier than others with inanimate objects like dice. What Professor Barnhouse did was to show that such "luck" was a measurable force, which in his case could be enormous.

By my calculations, the professor was about fifty-five times more powerful than a Nagasaki-type atomic bomb at the time he went into hiding. He was not bluffing when, on the eve of "Operation Brainstorm," he told General Honus Barker: "Sitting here at the dinner table, I'm pretty sure I can flatten anything on earth—from Joe Louis to the Great Wall of China."

There is an understandable tendency to look upon Professor Barnhouse as a supernatural visitation. The First Church of Barnhouse in Los Angeles has a congregation numbering in the thousands. He is godlike in neither appearance nor intellect. The man who disarms the world is single, shorter than the average American male, stout, and averse to exercise. His IQ is 143, which is good but certainly not sensational. He is quite mortal, about to celebrate his fortieth birthday, and in good health. If he is alone now, the isolation won't bother him too much. He was quiet and shy when I knew him, and seemed to find more companionship in books and music than in his associations at the college.

Neither he nor his powers fall outside the sphere of Nature. His dynamopsychic radiations are subject to many known physical laws that apply in the field of radio. Hardly a person has not now heard the snarl of "Barnhouse static" on his home receiver. Contrary to what one might expect, the radiations are affected by sunspots and variations in the ionosphere.

However, his radiations differ from ordinary broadcast waves in several important ways. Their total energy can be brought to bear on any single point the professor chooses, and that energy is undiminished by distance. As a weapon, then, dynamopsychism has an impressive advantage over bacteria and atomic bombs, beyond the fact that it costs nothing to use: it enables the professor to single out critical individuals and objects instead of slaughtering whole populations in the process of maintaining international equilibrium.

As General Honus Barker told the House Military Affairs Committee: "Until someone finds Barnhouse, there is no defense against the Barnhouse Effect." Efforts to "jam" or block the radiations have failed. Premier Slezak could have saved himself the fantastic expense of his "Barnhouseproof" shelter. Despite the shelter's twelve-foot-thick lead armor, the premier has been floored twice while in it.

There is talk of screening the population for men potentially as powerful dynamopsychically as the professor. Senator Warren Foust demanded funds for this purpose last month, with the passionate declaration: "He who rules the Barnhouse Effect rules the world!" Commissar Kropotnik said much the same thing, so another costly armaments race, with a new twist, has begun.

This race at least has its comical aspects. The world's best gamblers are being coddled by governments like so many nuclear physicists. There may be several hundred persons with dynamopsychic talent on earth, myself included, but, without knowledge of the professor's technique, they can never be anything but dice-table despots. With the secret, it would probably take them ten years to become dangerous weapons. It took the professor that long. He who rules the Barnhouse Effect is Barnhouse and will be for some time.

Popularly, the "Age of Barnhouse" is said to have begun a year and a half ago, on the day of Operation Brainstorm. That was when dynamopsychism became significantly politically. Actually, the phenomenon was discovered in May, 1942, shortly after the professor turned down a direct commission in the Army and enlisted as an artillery private. Like X-rays and vulcanized rubber, dynamopsychism was discovered by accident.

From time to time Private Barnhouse was invited to take part in games of chance by his barrack mates. He knew nothing about the games, and usually begged off. But one evening, out of social grace, he agreed to shoot craps. It was a terrible or wonderful thing that he played, depending upon whether or not you like the world as it now is.

"Shoot sevens, Pop," someone said.

So "Pop" shot sevens—ten in a row to bankrupt the barracks. He retired to his bunk and, as a mathematical exercise, calculated the odds against his feat on the back of a laundry slip. His chances of doing it, he found, were one in almost ten million! Bewildered, he borrowed a pair of dice from the man in the bunk next to his. He tried to roll sevens again, but got only the usual assortment of numbers. He lay back for a moment, then resumed his toying with the dice. He rolled ten more sevens in a row.

He might have dismissed the phenomenon with a low whistle. But the professor instead mulled over the circumstances surrounding his two lucky streaks. There was one single factor in common: on both occasions, *the same thought train had flashed through his mind just before he threw the dice.* It was that thought train which aligned the professor's brain cells into what has since become the most powerful weapon on earth.

The soldier in the next bunk gave dynamopsychism its first token of respect. In an understatement certain to bring wry smiles to the faces of the world's dejected demagogues, the soldier said, "You're hotter'n a two-dollar pistol, Pop." Professor Barnhouse was all of that. The dice that did his bidding weighed but a few grams, so the forces involved were minute; but the unmistakable fact that there were such forces was earth-shaking.

Professional caution kept him from revealing his discovery immediately. He wanted more facts and a body of theory to go with them. Later, when the atomic bomb was dropped on Hiroshima, it was fear that made him hold his peace. At no time were his experiments, as Premier Slezak called them, "a bourgeois plot to shackle the true democracies of the world." The professor didn't know where they were leading.

In time, he came to recognize another startling feature of dynamopsychism: *its strength increased with use.* Within six months, he was able to govern dice thrown by men the length of a barracks distant. By the time of his discharge in 1945, he could knock bricks loose from chimneys three miles away.

Charges that Professor Barnhouse could have won the last war in a minute, but did not care to do so, are perfectly senseless. When the war ended, he had the range and power of a 37-millimeter cannon, perhaps—certainly no more. His dynamopsychic powers graduated from the small arms class only after his discharge and return to Wyandotte College.

I enrolled in the Wyandotte Graduate School two years after the professor had rejoined the faculty. By chance, he was assigned as my thesis adviser. I was unhappy about the assignment, for the professor was, in the eyes of both colleagues and students, a somewhat ridiculous figure. He missed classes or had lapses of memory during lectures. When I arrived, in fact, his shortcomings had passed from the ridiculous to the intolerable.

"We're assigning you to Barnhouse as a sort of temporary thing," the dean of social studies told me. He looked apologetic and perplexed. "Brilliant man, Barnhouse, I guess. Difficult to know since his return, perhaps, but his work before the war brought a great deal of credit to our little school."

When I reported to the professor's laboratory for the first time, what I saw was more distressing than the gossip. Every surface in the room was covered with dust; books and apparatus had not been disturbed for months. The professor sat napping at his desk when I entered. The only signs of recent activity were three overflowing ash trays, a pair of scissors, and a morning paper with several items clipped from its front page.

As he raised his head to look at me, I saw that his eyes were clouded with fatigue. "Hi," he said, "just can't seem to get my sleeping done at night." He lighted a cigarette, his hands trembling slightly. "You the young man I'm supposed to help with a thesis?"

"Yes, sir," I said. In minutes he converted my misgivings to alarm.

"You an overseas veteran?" he asked.

"Yes, sir."

"Not much left over there, is there?" He frowned. "Enjoy the last war?"

"No, sir."

"Look like another war to you?"

"Kind of, sir."

"What can be done about it?"

I shrugged. "Looks pretty hopeless."

He peered at me intently. "Know anything about international law, the UN and all that?"

"Only what I pick up from the papers."

"Same here," he sighed. He showed me a fat scrapbook packed with newspaper clippings. "Never used to pay any attention to international politics. Now I study them the way I used to study rats in mazes. Everybody tells me the same thing—'Looks hopeless.'"

"Nothing short of a miracle—" I began.

"Believe in magic?" he asked sharply. The professor fished two dice from his vest pocket. "I will try to roll twos," he said. He rolled twos three times in a row. "One chance in about 47,000 of that happening. There's a miracle for you." He beamed for an instant, then brought the interview to an end, remarking that he had a class which had begun ten minutes ago.

He was not quick to take me into his confidence, and he said no more about his trick with the dice. I assumed they were loaded, and forgot about them. He set me the task of watching male rats cross electrified metal strips to get to food for female rats—an experiment that had been done to everyone's satisfaction in the 1930s. As though the pointlessness of my work were not bad enough, the professor annoyed me further with irrelevant questions. His favorites were: "Think we should have dropped the atomic bomb on Hiroshima?" and "Think every new piece of scientific information is a good thing for humanity?"

However, I did not feel put upon for long. "Give those poor animals a holiday," he said one morning, after I had been with him only a month. "I wish you'd help me look into a more interesting problem—namely, my sanity."

I returned the rats to their cages.

"What you must do is simple," he said, speaking softly. "Watch the inkwell on my desk. If you see nothing happen to it, say so, and I'll go quietly—relieved, I might add—to the nearest sanitarium."

I nodded uncertainly.

He locked the laboratory door and drew the blinds, so that we were in twilight for a moment. "I'm odd, I know," he said. "It's fear of myself that's made me odd."

"I've found you somewhat eccentric, perhaps, but certainly not—"

"If nothing happens to that inkwell, 'crazy as a bedbug' is the only description of me that will do," he interrupted, turning on the overhead lights. His eyes narrowed. "To give you an idea of how crazy, I'll tell you what's been running through my mind when I should have been sleeping. I think maybe I can save the world. I think maybe I can make every nation a *have* nation, and do away with war for good. I think maybe I can clear roads through jungles, irrigate deserts, build dams overnight."

"Yes, sir."

"Watch the inkwell!"

Dutifully and fearfully I watched. A high-pitched humming seemed to come from the inkwell; then it began to vibrate alarmingly, and finally to bound about the top of the desk, making two noisy circuits. It stopped, hummed again, glowed red, then popped in splinters with a blue-green flash.

Perhaps my hair stood on end. The professor laughed gently. "Magnets?" I managed to say at last.

"Wish to Heaven it were magnets," he murmured. It was then that he told me of dynamopsychism. He knew only that there was such a force; he could not explain it. "It's me and me alone—and it's awful."

"I'd say it was amazing and wonderful!" I cried.

"If all I could do was make inkwells dance, I'd be tickled silly with the whole business." He shrugged disconsolately. "But I'm no toy, my boy. If you like, we can drive around the neighborhood, and I'll show you what I mean." He told me about pulverized boulders, shattered oaks and abandoned farm buildings demolished within a fifty-mile radius of the campus. "Did every bit of it sitting right here, just thinking—not even thinking hard."

He scratched his head nervously. "I have never dared to concentrate as hard as I can for fear of the damage I might do. I'm to the point where a mere whim is a blockbuster." There was a depressing pause. "Up until a few days ago, I've thought it best to keep my secret for fear of what use it might be put to," he continued. "Now I realize that I haven't any more right to it than a man has a right to own an atomic bomb."

He fumbled through a heap of papers. "This says about all that needs to be said, I think." He handed me a draft of a letter to the Secretary of State.

Dear Sir:

I have discovered a new force which costs nothing to use, and which is probably more important than atomic energy. I should like to see it used most effectively in the cause of peace, and am, therefore, requesting your advice as to how this might best be done.

Yours truly,
A. Barnhouse.

"I have no idea what will happen next," said the professor.

There followed three months of perpetual nightmare, wherein the nation's political and military great came at all hours to watch the professor's trick with fascination.

We were quartered in an old mansion near Charlottesville, Virginia, to which we had been whisked five days after the letter was mailed. Surrounded by barbed wire and twenty guards, we were labeled "Project Wishing Well," and were classified as Top Secret.

For companionship we had General Honus Barker and the State Department's William K. Cuthrell. For the professor's talk of peace-through-plenty they had indulgent smiles and much discourse on practical measures and realistic thinking. So treated, the professor, who had at first been almost meek, progressed in a matter of weeks towards stubbornness.

He had agreed to reveal the thought train by means of which he aligned his mind into a dynamopsychic transmitter. But, under Cuthrell's and Barker's nagging to do so, he began to hedge. At first he declared that the information could be passed on simply by word of mouth. Later he said that it would have to be written up in a long report. Finally, at dinner one night, just after General Barker had read the secret orders for Operation Brainstorm, the professor announced, "The report may take as long as five years to write." He looked fiercely at the general. "Maybe twenty."

The dismay occasioned by this flat announcement was offset somewhat by the exciting anticipation of Operation Brainstorm. The general was in a holiday mood. "The target ships are on their way to the Caroline Islands at this very moment," he declared ecstatically. "One hundred and twenty of them! At the same time, ten V-2s are being readied for firing in New Mexico, and fifty radio-controlled jet bombers are being equipped for a mock attack on the Aleutians. Just think of it!" Happily he reviewed his orders. "At exactly 1100 hours next Wednesday, I will give you the order to *concentrate*; and you, professor, will think as hard as you can about sinking the target ships, destroying the V-2s before they hit the ground, and knocking down the bombers before they reach the Aleutians! Think you can handle it?"

The professor turned gray and closed his eyes. "As I told you before, my friend, I don't know what I can do." He added bitterly, "As for this Operation Brainstorm, I was never consulted about it, and it strikes me as childish and insanely expensive."

General Barker bridled. "Sir," he said, "your field is psychology, and I wouldn't presume to give you advice in that field. Mine is national defense. I have had thirty years of experience and success, Professor, and I'll ask you not to criticize my judgment."

The professor appealed to Mr. Cuthrell. "Look," he pleaded, "isn't it war and military matters we're all trying to get rid of? Wouldn't it be a whole lot more significant and lots cheaper for me to try moving cloud masses into drought areas, and things like that? I admit I know next to nothing about international politics, but it seems reasonable to suppose that nobody would want to fight wars if there were enough of everything to go around. Mr. Cuthrell, I'd like to try running generators where there isn't any coal or water power, irrigating deserts, and so on. Why, you could figure out what each country needs to make the most of its resources, and I could give it to them without costing American taxpayers a penny."

"Eternal vigilance is the price of freedom," said the general heavily.

Mr. Cuthrell threw the general a look of mild distaste. "Unfortunately, the general is right in his own way," he said. "I wish to Heaven the world were ready for ideals like yours, but it simply isn't. We aren't surrounded by brothers, but by enemies. It isn't a lack of food or resources that has us on the brink of war—it's a struggle for power. Who's going to be in charge of the world, our kind of people or theirs?"

The professor nodded in reluctant agreement and arose from the table. "I beg your pardon, gentlemen. You are, after all, better qualified to judge what is best for the country. I'll do whatever you say." He turned to me. "Don't forget to wind the restricted clock and put the confidential cat out," he said gloomily, and ascended the stairs to his bedroom.

For reasons of national security, Operation Brainstorm was carried on without the knowledge of the American citizenry which was footing the bill. The observers, technicians and military men involved in the activity knew that a test was under way—a test of what, they had no idea. Only thirty-seven key men, myself included, knew what was afoot.

In Virginia, the day for Operation Brainstorm was unseasonably cool. Inside, a log fire crackled in the fireplace, and the flames were reflected in the polished metal cabinets that lined the living room. All that remained of the room's lovely old furniture was a Victorian love seat, set squarely in the center of the floor, facing three television receivers. One long bench had been brought in for the ten of us privileged to watch. The television screens showed, from left to right, the stretch of desert which was the rocket target, the guinea-pig fleet, and a section of the Aleutian sky through which the radio-controlled bomber formation would roar.

Ninety minutes before H hour the radios announced that the rockets were ready, that the observation ships had backed away to what was thought to be a safe distance, and that the bombers were on their way. The small Virginia audience lined up on the bench in order of rank, smoked a great deal, and said little. Professor Barnhouse was in his bedroom. General Barker bustled about the house like a woman preparing Thanksgiving dinner for twenty.

At ten minutes before H hour the general came in, shepherding the professor before him. The professor was comfortably attired in sneakers, gray flannels, a blue sweater and a white shirt open at the neck. The two of them sat side by side on the love seat. The general was rigid and perspiring; the professor was cheerful. He looked at each of the screens, lighted a cigarette and settled back, comfortable and cool.

"Bombers sighted!" cried the Aleutian observers.

"Rockets away!" barked the New Mexico radio operator.

All of us looked quickly at the big electric clock over the mantel, while the professor, a half-smile on his face, continued to watch the television sets. In hollow tones, the general counted away the seconds remaining. "Five . . . four . . . three . . . two . . . one . . . *Concentrate!*"

Professor Barnhouse closed his eyes, pursed his lips, and stroked his temples. He held the position for a minute. The television images were scrambled, and the radio signals were drowned in the din of Barnhouse static. The professor sighed, opened his eyes and smiled confidently.

"Did you give it everything you had?" asked the general dubiously.

"I was wide open," the professor replied.

The television images pulled themselves together, and mingled cries of amazement came over the radios tuned to the observers. The Aleutian sky was streaked with the smoke trails of bombers screaming down in flames. Simultaneously, there appeared high over the rocket target a cluster of white puffs, followed by faint thunder.

General Barker shook his head happily. "By George!" he crowed. "Well, sir, by George, by George, by George!"

"Look!" shouted the admiral seated next to me. "The fleet—it wasn't touched!"

"The guns seem to be drooping," said Mr. Cuthrell.

We left the bench and clustered about the television sets to examine the damage more closely. What Mr. Cuthrell had said was true. The ships' guns curved downward, their muzzles resting on the steel decks. We in Virginia were making such a hullabaloo that it was impossible to hear the radio reports. We were so engrossed, in fact, that we didn't miss the professor until two short snarls of Barnhouse static shocked us into sudden silence. The radios went dead.

We looked around apprehensively. The professor was gone. A harassed guard threw open the front door from the outside to yell that the professor had escaped. He brandished his pistol in the direction of the gates, which hung open, limp and twisted. In the distance, a speeding government station wagon topped a ridge and dropped from sight into the valley beyond. The air was filled with choking smoke, for every vehicle on the grounds was ablaze. Pursuit was impossible.

"What in God's name got into him?" bellowed the general.

Mr. Cuthrell, who had rushed out onto the front porch, now slouched back into the room, reading a penciled note as he came. He thrust the note into my hands. "The good man left this billet-doux under the door knocker. Perhaps our young friend here will be kind enough to read it to you gentlemen, while I take a restful walk through the woods."

"Gentlemen," I read aloud, *"As the first superweapon with a conscience, I am removing from your national defence stockpile. Setting a new precedent in*

the behavior of ordnance, I have humane reasons for going off. A. Barnhouse."

Since that day, of course, the professor has been systematically destroying the world's armaments, until there is now little with which to equip an army other than rocks and sharp sticks. His activities haven't exactly resulted in peace, but have, rather, precipitated a bloodless and entertaining sort of war that might be called the "War of the Tattletales." Every nation is flooded with enemy agents whose sole mission is to locate military equipment, which is promptly wrecked when it is brought to the professor's attention in the press.

Just as every day brings news of more armaments pulverized by dynamopsychism, so has it brought rumors of the professor's whereabouts. During the last week alone, three publications carried articles proving variously that he was hiding in an Inca ruin in the Andes, in the sewers of Paris, and in the unexplored lower chambers of Carlsbad Caverns. Knowing the man, I am inclined to regard such hiding places as unnecessarily romantic and uncomfortable. While there are numerous persons eager to kill him, there must be millions who would care for him and hide him. I like to think that he is in the home of such a person.

One thing is certain: at this writing, Professor Barnhouse is not dead. Barnhouse static jammed broadcasts not ten minutes ago. In the eighteen months since his disappearance, he has been reported dead some half-dozen times. Each report has stemmed from the death of an unidentified man resembling the professor, during a period free of the static. The first three reports were followed at once by renewed talk of rearmament and recourse to war. The saber rattlers have learned how imprudent premature celebrations of the professor's demise can be.

Many a stouthearted patriot has found himself prone in the tangled bunting and timbers of a smashed reviewing stand, seconds after having announced that the archtyranny of Barnhouse was at an end. But those who would make war if they could, in every country in the world, wait in sullen silence for what must come—the passing of Professor Barnhouse.

To ask how much longer the professor will live is to ask how much longer we must wait for the blessings of another war. He is of short-lived stock: his mother lived to be fifty-three, his father to be forty-nine; and the life-spans of his grandparents on both sides were of the same order. He might be expected to live, then, for perhaps fifteen years more, if he can remain hidden from his enemies. When one considers the number and vigor of these enemies, however, fifteen years seems an extraordinary length of time, which might better be revised to fifteen days, hours or minutes.

The professor knows that he cannot live much longer. I say this because of the message left in my mailbox on Christmas Eve. Unsigned, typewritten on a soiled scrap of paper, the note consisted of ten sentences. The first nine of these, each a bewildering tangle of psychological jargon and references to obscure texts, made no sense to me at first reading. The tenth, unlike the rest, was simply constructed and contained no large words—but its irrational content made it the most puzzling and bizarre sentence of all. I nearly threw the note away, thinking it a colleague's warped notion of a practical joke. For some reason, though, I added it to the clutter on top of my desk, which included, among other mementos, the professor's dice.

It took me several weeks to realize that the message really meant something, that the first nine sentences, when unsnarled, could be taken as instructions. The tenth still told me nothing. It was only last night that I discovered how it fitted in with the rest. The sentence appeared in my thoughts last night, while I was toying absently with the professor's dice.

I promised to have this report on its way to the publishers today. In view of what has happened, I am obliged to break that promise, or release the report incomplete. The delay will not be a long one, for one of the few blessings accorded a bachelor like myself is the ability to move quickly from one abode to another, or from one way of life to another. What property I want to take with me can be packed in a few hours. Fortunately, I am not without substantial private means, which may take as long as a week to realize in liquid and anonymous form. When this is done, I shall mail the report.

I have just returned from a visit to my doctor, who tells me my health is excellent. I am young, and, with any luck at all, I shall live to a ripe old age indeed, for my family on both sides is noted for longevity.

Briefly, I propose to vanish.

Sooner or later, Professor Barnhouse must die. But long before then I shall be ready. So, to the saber rattlers of today—and even, I hope, of tomorrow—I say: Be advised. Barnhouse will die. But not the Barnhouse Effect.

Last night, I tried once more to follow the oblique instructions on the scrap of paper. I took the professor's dice, and then, with the last, nightmarish sentence flitting though my mind, I rolled fifty consecutive sevens.

Good-by.

Alice Walker's parents were black sharecroppers in Georgia, a fact that has deeply influenced her life and her writing. Born in 1944, she attended Spelman College, Atlanta, and Sarah Lawrence College. She worked for the civil rights movement in Georgia and Mississippi, and in 1967 married a white civil rights lawyer (the marriage was dissolved in 1976). For a time she was employed by the New York City Welfare Department. In 1968 she became a writer-in-residence and a teacher of Black Studies at Jackson State College, and has subsequently taught at a number of universities across the United States. Her publications include several books of poetry and essays, and four novels: *The Third Life of Grange Copeland* (1970), *Meridian* (1976), *The Color Purple* (1982), winner of a Pulitzer Prize and an American Book Award, and *The Temple of My Familiar* (1989). Walker's short stories have been gathered in *In Love and Trouble: Stories of Black Women* (1973) and *You Can't Keep a Good Woman Down* (1981).

Walker writes from a background of racial, social, and sexual discrimination that has significantly shaped her career as an author. She is particularly concerned with the plight of the black woman in America, doubly oppressed by the sexism of her own race and the bigotry of white society. Walker's preoccupation with sexual politics has led some critics to accuse her of stereotyping male characters, but her work rises above simplistic denunciations of male chauvinism to plead for a fulfillment of human potential through a love and an understanding that cross sexual and racial boundaries. As a Southern writer, she has been compared to Faulkner in the evocative richness of her prose, and in her ability to dramatize the sensibility of a naive or uneducated protagonist. In Walker's hands, the ungrammatical syntax of black Americans becomes a powerful, sometimes poetic expression of strong feeling, evoking a history and tradition that are deeply embedded in American consciousness, though often ignored or misrepresented. The uneasy relationship between blacks and whites is subtly explored in "Nineteen Fifty-five" *(You Can't Keep a Good Woman Down)*, in which a white rock-and-roll singer (clearly modelled on Elvis Presley) achieves fame through a song written by a black woman, but searches in vain for the joy in life that the woman has expressed through the song. It may be noted here that Presley's 1956 hit record "Hound Dog" was first recorded in 1953 by Willie Mae ("Big Mama") Thornton.

FOR FURTHER READING

Barbara T. Christian, "Alice Walker," *Dictionary of Literary Biography 33: Afro-American Fiction Writers After 1955* (Detroit: Gale Research, 1984): 258-71.

Mari Evans, ed., *Black Women Writers, 1950-1980* (Garden City: Doubleday, 1984).

Gloria Steinem, "Do You Know This Woman? She Knows You—A Profile of Alice Walker," *Ms* 10 (June 1982): 35-7, 89-94.

Alice Walker, *Living By the Word: Selected Writings 1973-1987* (San Diego: Harcourt Brace Jovanovich, 1988).

Nineteen Fifty-five

1955

The car is a brandnew red Thunderbird convertible, and it's passed the house more than once. It slows down real slow now, and stops at the curb. An older gentleman dressed like a Baptist deacon gets out on the side near the house, and a young fellow who looks about sixteen gets out on the driver's side. They are white, and I wonder what in the world they doing in this neighborhood.

Well, I say to J.T., put your shirt on, anyway, and let me clean these glasses offa the table.

We had been watching the ballgame on TV. I wasn't actually watching, I was sort of daydreaming, with my foots up in J.T.'s lap.

I seen 'em coming on up the walk, brisk, like they coming to sell something, and then they rung the bell, and J.T. declined to put on a shirt but instead disappeared into the bedroom where the other television is. I turned down the one in the living room; I figured I'd be rid of these two double quick and J.T. could come back out again.

Are you Gracie Mae Still? asked the old guy, when I opened the door and put my hand on the lock inside the screen.

And I don't need to buy a thing, said I.

What makes you think we're sellin'? he asks, in that hearty Southern way that makes my eyeballs ache.

Well, one way or another and they're inside the house and the first thing the young fellow does is raise the TV a couple of decibels. He's about five feet nine, sort of womanish looking, with real dark white skin and a red pouting mouth. His hair is black and curly and he looks like a Loosianna creole.

About one of your songs, says the deacon. He is maybe sixty, with white hair and beard, white silk shirt, black linen suit, black tie and black shoes. His cold grey eyes look like they're sweating.

One of my songs?

Traynor here just *loves* your songs. Don't you Traynor? He nudges Traynor with his elbow. Traynor blinks, says something I can't catch in a pitch I don't register.

The boy learned to sing and dance livin' round you people out in the country. Practically cut his teeth on you.

Traynor looks up at me and bites his thumbnail.

I laugh.

Well, one way or another they leave with my agreement that they can record one of my songs. The deacon writes me a check for five hundred dollars, the boy grunts his awareness of the transaction, and I am laughing all over myself by the time I rejoin J.T.

Just as I am snuggling down beside him though I hear the front door bell going off again.

Forgit his hat? asked J.T.

I hope not, I say.

The deacon stands there leaning on the door frame and once again I'm thinking of those sweaty-looking eyeballs of his. I wonder if sweat makes your eyeballs pink because his are sure pink. Pink and gray and it strikes me that nobody I'd care to know is behind them.

I forgot one little thing, he says pleasantly. I forgot to tell you Traynor and I would like to buy up all of those records you made of the song. I tell you we sure do love it.

Well, love it or not, I'm not so stupid as to let them do that without making 'em pay. So I says, Well, that's gonna cost you. Because, really, that song never did sell all that good, so I was glad they was going to buy it up. But on the other hand, them two listening to my song by themselves, and nobody else getting to hear me sing it, give me a pause.

Well, one way or another the deacon showed me where I would come out ahead on any deal he had proposed so far. Didn't I give you five hundred dollars? he asked. What white man—and don't even need to mentioned colored—would give you more? We buy up all your records of that particular song: first, you git royalties. Let me ask you, how much you sell that song for in the first place? Fifty dollars? A hundred, I say. And no royalties from it yet, right? Right. Well, when we buy up all of them records you gonna git royalties. And that's gonna make all them race record shops sit up and take notice of Gracie Mae Still. And they gonna push all them other records of yourn they got. And you no doubt will become one of the big name colored recording artists. And then we can offer you another five hundred dollars for letting us do all this for you. And by God you'll be sittin' pretty! You can go out and buy you the kind of outfit a star should have. Plenty sequins and yards of red satin.

I had done unlocked the screen when I saw I could get some more money out of him. Now I held it wide open while he squeezed through the opening between me and the door. He whipped out another piece of paper and I signed it.

He sort of trotted out to the car and slid in beside Traynor, whose head was back against the seat. They swung around in a u-turn in front of the house and then they were gone.

J.T. was putting his shirt on when I got back to the bedroom. Yankees beat the Orioles 10-6, he said. I believe I'll drive out to Paschal's pond and go fishing. Wanta go?

While I was putting on my pants J.T. was holding the two checks.

I'm real proud of a woman that can make cash money without leavin' home, he said. And I said *Umph*. Because we met on the road with me singing in first one little low-life jook after another, making ten dollars a night for myself if I was lucky, and sometimes bringin' home nothing but my life. And J.T. just loved them times. The way I was fast and flashy and always on the go from one town to another. He loved the way my singin' made the dirt farmers cry like babies and the womens shout Honey, hush! But that's mens. They loves any style to which you can get 'em accustomed.

1956

My little grandbaby called me one night on the phone: Little Mama, Little Mama, there's a white man on the television singing one of your songs! Turn on channel 5.

Lord, if it wasn't Traynor. Still looking half asleep from the neck up, but kind of awake in a nasty way from the waist down. He wasn't doing too bad with my song either, but it wasn't just the song the people in the audience was screeching and screaming over, it was that nasty little jerk he was doing from the waist down.

Well, Lord have mercy, I said, listening to him. If I'da closed my eyes, it could have been me. He had followed every turning of my voice, side streets, avenues, red lights, train crossings and all. It give me a chill.

Everywhere I went I heard Traynor singing my song, and all the little white girls just eating it up. I never had so many ponytails switched across my line of vision in my life. They was so *proud*. He was a *genius*.

Well, all that year I was trying to lose weight anyway and that and high blood pressure and sugar kept me pretty well occupied. Traynor had made a smash from a song of mine, I still had seven hundred dollars of the original one thousand dollars in the bank, and I felt if I could just bring my weight down, life would be sweet.

1957

I lost ten pounds in 1956. That's what I give myself for Christmas. And J.T. and me and the children and their friends and grandkids of all description and just finished dinner—over which I had put on nine and a half of my lost ten—when who should appear at the front door but Traynor. Little Mama, Little Mama! It's that white man who sings—— —— ——. The children didn't call it my song anymore. Nobody did. It was funny how that happened. Traynor and the deacon had bought up all my records, true, but on his record he had put "written by Gracie Mae Still." But that was just another name on the label, like "produced by Apex Records."

On the TV he was inclined to dress like the deacon told him. But now he looked presentable.

Merry Christmas, said he.

And same to you, Son.

I don't know why I called him Son. Well, one way or another they're all our sons. The only requirement is that they be younger than us. But then again Traynor seemed to be aging by the minute.

You looks tired, I said. Come on in and have a glass of Christmas cheer.

J.T. ain't never in his life been able to act decent to a white man he wasn't working for, but he poured Traynor a glass of bourbon and water, then he took all the children and grandkids and friends and whatnot out to the den. After while I heard Traynor's voice singing the song, coming from the stereo console. It was just the kind of Christmas present my kids would consider cute.

I looked at Traynor, complicit. But he looked like it was the last thing in the world he wanted to hear. His head was pitched forward over his lap, his hands holding his glass and his elbows on his knees.

I done sung that song seem like a million times this year, he said. I sung it on the Grand Ole Opry, I sung it on the Ed Sullivan show. I sung it on Mike Douglas, I sung it at the Cotton Bowl, the Orange Bowl. I sung it at Festivals. I sung it at Fairs. I sung it overseas in Rome, Italy, and once in a submarine *underseas.* I've sung it and sung it, and I'm making forty thousand dollars a day offa it, and you know what, I don't have the faintest notion what that song means.

Whatchumean, what do it mean? It mean what it says. All I could think was: these suckers is making forty thousand a *day* offa my song and now they gonna come back and try to swindle me out of the original thousand.

It's just a song, I said. Cagey. When you fool around with a lot of no count mens you sing a bunch of 'em. I shrugged.

Oh, he said. Well. He started brightening up. I just come by to tell you I think you are a great singer.

He didn't blush, saying that. Just said it straight out.

And I brought you a little Christmas present too. Now you take this little box and you hold it until I drive off. Then you take it outside under that first streetlight back up the street aways in front of that green house. Then you open the box and see . . . Well, just *see*.

What had come over this boy, I wondered, holding the box. I looked out the window in time to see another white man come up and get in the car with him and then two more cars full of white mens start out behind him. They was all in long black cars that looked like a funeral procession.

Little Mama, Little Mama, what is it? One of my grandkids come running up and started pulling at the box. It was wrapped in gay Christmas paper—the thick, rich kind that it's hard to picture folks making just to throw away.

J.T. and the rest of the crowd followed me out the house, up the street to the streetlight and in front of the green house. Nothing was there but somebody's gold-grille white Cadillac. Brandnew and most distracting. We got to looking at it so till I almost forgot the little box in my hand. While the others were busy making 'miration I carefully took off the paper and ribbon and folded them up and put them in my pants pocket. What should I see but a pair of genuine solid gold caddy keys.

Dangling the keys in front of everybody's nose, I unlocked the caddy, motioned for J.T. to git in on the other side, and us didn't come back home for two days.

1960

Well, the boy was sure nuff famous by now. He was still a mite shy of twenty but already they was calling him the Emperor of Rock and Roll.

Then what should happen but the draft.

Well, says J.T. There goes all this Emperor of Rock and Roll business.

But even in the army the womens was on him like white on rice. We watched in on the News.

Dear Gracie Mae [he wrote from Germany],

How you? Fine I hope as this leaves me doing real well. Before I came in the army I was gaining a lot of weight and gitting jittery from making all them dumb movies. But now I exercise and eat right and get plenty of rest. I'm more awake than I been in ten years.

I wonder if you are writing any more songs?

Sincerely,
Traynor

I wrote him back:

Dear Son,

We is all fine in the Lord's good grace and hope this finds you the same. J.T. and me be out all times of the day and night in that car you give me—which you know you didn't have to do. Oh, and I do appreciate the mink and the new self-cleaning oven. But if you send anymore stuff to eat from Germany I'm going to have to open up a store in the neighborhood just to get rid of it. Really, we have more than enough of everything. The Lord is good to us and we don't know Want.

Glad to here you is well and gitting your right rest. There ain't nothing like exercising to help that along. J.T. and me work some part of every day that we don't go fishing in the garden.

Well, so long Soldier.

Sincerely,
Gracie Mae

He wrote:

Dear Gracie Mae,

I hope you and J.T. like that automatic power tiller I had one of the stores back home send you. I went through a mountain of catalogs looking for it—I wanted something that even a woman could use.

I've been thinking about writing some songs of my own but every time I finish one it don't seem to be about nothing I've actually lived myself. My agent keeps sending me other people's songs but they just sound mooney. I can hardly git through 'em without gagging.

Everybody still loves that song of yours. They ask me all the time what do I think it means, really. I mean, they want to know just what I want to know. Where out of your life did it come from?

Sincerely,
Traynor

1968

I didn't see the boy for seven years. No. Eight. Because just about everybody was dead when I saw him again. Malcolm X, King, the president and his brother, and even J.T. J.T. died of a head cold. It just settled in his head like a block of ice, he said, and nothing we did moved it until one day he just leaned out the bed and died.

His good friend Horace helped me put him away, and then about a year later Horace and me started going together. We was sitting out on the front porch swing one summer night, dusk-dark, and I saw this great procession of lights winding to a stop.

Holy Toledo! said Horace. (He's got a real sexy voice like Ray Charles.) Look *at* it. He meant the long line of flashy cars and the white men in white summer suits jumping out on the drivers' sides and standing at attention. With wings they could pass for angels, with hoods they could be the Klan.

Traynor comes waddling up the walk.

And suddenly I know what it is he could pass for. An Arab like the ones you see in storybooks. Plump and soft and with never a care about weight. Because with so much money, who cares? Traynor is almost dressed like someone from a storybook too. He has on, I swear, about ten necklaces. Two sets of bracelets on his arms, at least one ring on every finger, and some kind of shining buckles on his shoes, so that when he walks you get quite a few twinkling lights.

Gracie Mae, he says, coming up to give me a hug. J.T.

I explain that J.T. passed. That this is Horace.

Horace, he says, puzzled but polite, sort of rocking back on his heels, Horace.

That's it for Horace. He goes in the house and don't come back.

Looks like you and me is gained a few, I say.

He laughs. The first time I ever heard him laugh. It don't sound much like a laugh and I can't swear that it's better than no laugh a'tall.

He's gitting fat for sure, but he's still slim compared to me. I'll never see three hundreds pounds again and I've just about said (excuse me) fuck it. I got to thinking about it one day an' I thought: aside from the fact that they say it's unhealthy, my fat ain't never been no trouble. Mens always have loved me. My kids ain't never complained. Plus they's fat. And fat like I is I looks distinguished. You see me coming and know somebody's *there*.

Gracie Mae, he says. I've come with a personal invitation to you to my house tomorrow for dinner. He laughed. What did it sound like? I couldn't place it. See them men out there? he asked me. I'm sick and tired of eating with them. They don't never have nothing to talk about. That's why I eat so much. But if you come to dinner tomorrow we can talk about the old days. You can tell me about that farm I bought you.

I sold it, I said.

You did?

Yeah, I said, I did. Just cause I said I liked to exercise by working in a garden didn't mean I wanted five hundred acres! Anyhow, I'm a city girl now. Raised in the country it's true. Dirt poor—the whole bit—but that's all behind me now.

Oh well, he said, I didn't mean to offend you.

We sat for a few minutes listening to the crickets.

Then he said: You wrote that song while you was still on the farm, didn't you, or was it right after you left?

You had somebody spying on me? I asked.

You and Bessie Smith got into a fight over it once, he said.

You *is* been spying on me!

But I don't know what the fight was about, he said. Just like I don't know what happened to your second husband. Your first one died in the Texas electric chair. Did you know that? Your third one beat you up, stole your touring costumes and your car and retired with a chorine to Tuskegee. He laughed. He's still there.

I had been mad, but suddenly I calmed down. Traynor was talking very dreamily. It was dark but seems like I could tell his eyes weren't right. It was like some*thing* was sitting there talking to me but not necessarily with a person behind it.

You gave up on marrying and seem happier for it. He laughed again. I married but it never went like it was supposed to. I never could squeeze any of my own life either into it or out of it. It was like singing somebody else's record. I copied the way it was sposed to be *exactly* but I never had a clue what marriage meant.

I bought her a diamond ring big as your fist. I bought her clothes. I build her a mansion. But right away she didn't want the boys to stay there. Said they smoked up the bottom floor. Hell, there were *five* floors.

No need to grieve, I said. No need to. Plenty more where she come from.

He perked up. That's part of what that song means, ain't it? No need to grieve. Whatever it is, there's plenty more down the line.

I never really believed that way back when I wrote the song, I said. It was all bluffing then. The trick is to live long enough to put your young bluffs to use. Now if I was to sing that song today I'd tear it up. 'Cause I done lived long enough to know it's *true*. Them words could hold me up.

I ain't lived that long, he said.

Look like you on your way, I said. I didn't know why, but the boy seemed to need some encouraging. And I don't know, seem like one way or another you talk to rich white folks and you end up reassuring *them*. But what the hell, by now I feel something for the boy. I wouldn't be in his bed all alone in the middle of the night for nothing. Couldn't be nothing worse than being famous the world over for something you don't even understand. That's what I tried to tell Bessie. She wanted that same song. Overheard me practicing it one day, said, with her hands on her hips: Gracie Mae, I'ma sing your song tonight. I *likes* it.

Your lips be too swole to sing, I said. She was mean and she was strong, but I trounced her.

Ain't you famous enough with your own stuff? I said. Leave mine alone. Later on, she thanked me. By then she was Miss Bessie Smith to the World, and I was still Miss Gracie Mae Nobody form Notasulga.

The next day all these limousines arrived to pick me up. Five cars and twelve bodyguards. Horace picked that morning to start painting the kitchen.

Don't paint the kitchen, fool, I said. The only reason that dumb boy of ours is going to show me his mansion is because he intends to present us with a new house.

What you gonna do with it? he asked me, standing there in his shirt sleeves stirring the paint.

Sell it. Give it to the children. Live in it on weekends. It don't matter what I do. He sure don't care.

Horace just stood there shaking his head. Mama you sure looks *good*, he says. Wake me up when you git back.

Fool, I say, and pat my wig in front of the mirror.

The boy's house is something else. First you come to this mountain, and then you commence to drive and drive up this road that's lined with magnolias. Do magnolias grow on mountains? I was wondering. And you come to lakes and you come to ponds and you come to deer and you come up on some sheep. And I figure these two is sposed to represent England and Wales. Or something out of Europe. And you just keep on coming to stuff. And it's all pretty. Only the man driving my car don't look at nothing but the road. Fool. And then *finally*, after all this time, you begin to go up the driveway. And there's more magnolias—only they're not in such good shape. It's sort of cool up this high and I don't think they're gonna make it. And then I see this building that looks like if it had a name it would be The Tara Hotel. Columns and steps and outdoor chandeliers and rocking chairs. Rocking chairs? Well, and there's the boy on the steps dressed in a dark green satin jacket like you see folks wearing on TV late at night, and he looks sort of like a fat dracula with all that house rising behind him, and standing beside him there's this little white vision of loveliness that he introduces as his wife.

He's nervous when he introduces us and he says to her: This is Gracie Mae Still, I want you to know me. I mean . . . and she gives him a look that would fry meat.

Won't you come in Grace Mae, she says, and that's the last I see of her.

He fishes around for something to say or do and decides to escort me to the kitchen. We go through the entry and the parlor and the breakfast room and the dining room and the servants' passage and finally get there. The first thing I notice is that, altogether, there are five stoves. He looks about to introduce me to one.

Wait a minute, I say. Kitchens don't do nothing for me. Let's go sit on the front porch.

Well, we hike back and we sit in the rocking chairs rocking until dinner.

Gracie Mae, he says down the table, taking a piece of fried chicken from the woman standing over him, I got a little surprise for you.

It's a house, ain't it? I ask, spearing a chitlin.

You're getting *spoiled*, he says. And the way he says *spoiled* sounds funny. He slurs it. It sounds like his tongue is too thick for his mouth. Just that quick he's finished the chicken and is now eating chitlins *and* a pork chop. *Me* spoiled, I'm thinking.

I already got a house. Horace is right this minute painting the kitchen. I bought that house. My kids feel comfortable in that house.

But this one I bought you is just like mine. Only a little smaller.

I still don't need no house. And anyway who would clean it?

He looks surprised.

Really, I think some peoples advance *so* slowly.

I hadn't thought of that. But what the hell, I'll get you somebody to live in.

I don't want other folks living 'round me. Makes me nervous.

You *don't*? It *do*?

What I want to wake up and see folks I don't even know for?

He just sits there downtable staring at me. Some of that feeling is in the song, ain't it? Not the words, the *feeling*. What I want to wake up and see folks I don't even know for? But I see twenty folks a day I don't even know, including my wife.

This food wouldn't be bad to wake up to though, I said. The boy had found the genius of corn bread.

He looked at me real hard. He laughed. Short. They want what you got but they don't want you. They want what I got only it ain't mine. That's what makes 'em so hungry for me when I sing. They getting the flavor of something but they ain't getting the thing itself. They like a pack of hound dogs trying to gobble up a scent.

You talking 'bout your fans?

Right. Right. He says.

Don't worry 'bout your fans, I say. They don't know their asses from a hole in the ground. I doubt there's a honest one in the bunch.

That's the point. Dammit, that's the point! He hits the table with his fist. It's so solid it don't even quiver. You need a honest audience! You can't have folks that's just gonna lie right back to you.

Yeah, I say, it was small compared to yours, but I had one. It would have been worth my life to try to sing 'em somebody else's stuff that I didn't know nothing about.

He must have pressed a buzzer under the table. One of his flunkies zombies up.

Git Johnny Carson, he says.

On the phone? asks the zombie.

On the phone, says Traynor, what you think I mean, git him offa the front porch? Move your ass.

So two weeks later we's on the Johnny Carson show.

Traynor is all corseted down nice and looks a little bit fat but mostly good. And all the women that grew up on him and my song squeal and squeal. Traynor says: The lady who wrote my first hit record is here with us tonight, and she's agreed to sing it for all of us, just like she sung it forty-five years ago. Ladies and Gentlemen, the great Gracie Mae Still!

Well, I had tried to lose a couple of pounds my own self, but failing that I had me a very big dress made. So I sort of rolls over next to Traynor, who is dwarfted by me, so that when he puts his arm around back of me to try to hug me it looks funny to the audience and they laugh.

I can see this pisses him off. But I smile out there at 'em. Imagine squealing for twenty years and not knowing why you're squealing? No more sense of endings and beginnings than hogs.

It don't matter, Son, I say. Don't fret none over me.

I commence to sing. And I sound——wonderful. Being able to sing good ain't all about having a good singing voice a'tall. A good singing voice helps. But when you come up in the Hard Shell Baptist church like I did you understand early that the fellow that sings is the singer. Them that waits for programs and arrangements and letters from home is just good voices occupying body space.

So there I am singing my own song, my own way. And I give it all I got and enjoy every minute of it. When I finish Traynor is standing up clapping and clapping and beaming at first me and then the audience like I'm his mama for true. The audience claps politely for about two seconds.

Traynor looks disgusted.

He comes over and tries to hug me again. The audience laughs.

Johnny Carson looks at us like we both weird.

Traynor is mad as hell. He's supposed to sing something called a love ballad. But instead he takes the mike, turns to me and says: Now see if my imitation still holds up. He goes into the same song, *our* song, I think, looking at his flaky audience. And he sings it just the way he always did. My voice, my tone, my inflection, everything. But he forgets a couple of lines. Even before he's finished the matronly squeals begin.

He sits down next to me looking whipped.

It don't matter, Son, I say, patting his hand. You don't even know those people. Try to make the people you know happy.

Is that in the song? he asks.

Maybe. I say.

1977

For a few years I hear from him, then nothing. But trying to lose weight takes all the attention I got to spare. I finally faced up to the fact that my fat is the hurt I don't admit, not even to myself, and that I been trying to bury it from the day I was born. But also when you git real old, to tell the truth, it ain't as pleasant. It gits lumpy and slack. So one day I said to Horace, I'ma git this shit offa me.

And he fell in with the program like he always try to do and Lord such a procession of salads and cottage cheese and fruit juice!

One night I dreamed Traynor had split up with his fifteenth wife. He said: *You meet 'em for no reason. You date 'em for no reason. You marry 'em for no reason. I do it all but I swear it's just like somebody else doing it. I feel like I can't remember Life.*

The boy's in trouble, I said to Horace.

You've always said that, he said.

I have?

Yeah. You always said he looked asleep. You can't sleep through life if you wants to live it.

You not such a fool after all, I said, pushing myself up with my cane and hobbling over to where he was. Let me sit down on your lap, I said, while this salad I ate takes effect.

In the morning we heard Traynor was dead. Some said fat, some said heart, some said alcohol, some said drugs. One of the children called from Detroit. Them dumb fans of his on a crying rampage, she said. You just ought to turn on the TV.

But I didn't want to see 'em. They was crying and crying and didn't even know what they was crying for. One day this is going to be a pitiful country, I thought.

Winner of several literary awards including the 1973 Nobel Prize, Patrick White (1912-1990) was born in London, brought up in Sydney, Australia, and educated at a British public school and Cambridge University. He served in World War Two; then, after travelling through Western Europe and the United States, and living for a year in Greece, he returned to Australia to write. Dramatist, novelist, and short story writer, he published numerous books, including *The Tree of Man* (1955), *Voss* (1957), *Riders in the Chariot* (1961), and *A Fringe of Leaves* (1976). An observer of tragic depths and spiritual heights in a community that discouraged the display of excessive emotion, he rejected what he considered mediocre in much of Australian society. Out of this rejection grew several hard-edged satires of bourgeois life, including the stories in *The Burnt Ones* (1964).

"Down at the Dump" contrasts the hostilities, envies, and resentments of the conventional adult world with the direct and compelling discovery of adolescent desire. With compassion and humour, White sets the town dump next to the cemetery. He neatly juxtaposes youth and age, rich and poor, life and death, to show the triumph of love even in the most unprepossessing circumstances.

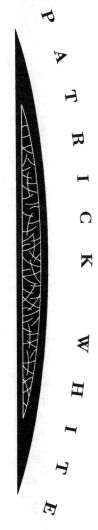

PATRICK WHITE

FOR FURTHER READING

J.F. Burrows, "The Short Stories of Patrick White," *Southerly* 24 (1964): 116-25.

Brian Kiernan, *Patrick White* (London: Macmillan, 1980).

Patrick White, *Flaws in the Glass: a self-portrait* (New York: Viking, 1982).

Down at the Dump

'HI!'

He called from out of the house, and she went on chopping in the yard. Her right arm swung, firm still, muscular, though parts of her were beginning to sag. She swung with her right, and her left arm hung free. She chipped at the log, left right. She was expert with the axe.

Because you had to be. You couldn't expect all that much from a man.

'Hi!' It was Wal Whalley calling again from out of the home.

He came to the door then, in that dirty old baseball cap he had shook off the Yankee disposals. Still a fairly appetizing male, though his belly had begun to push against the belt.

'Puttin' on yer act?' he asked, easing the singlet under his armpits; easy was policy at Whalleys' place.

''Ere!' she protested. 'Waddaya make me out ter be? A lump of wood?'

Her eyes were of that blazing blue, her skin that of a brown peach. But whenever she smiled, something would happen, her mouth opening on watery sockets and the jags of brown, rotting stumps.

'A woman likes to be addressed,' she said.

No one had ever heard Wal address his wife by her first name. Nobody had ever heard her name, though it was printed in the electoral roll. It was, in fact, Isba.

'Don't know about a dress,' said Wal. 'I got a idea, though.'

His wife stood tossing her hair. It was natural at least; the sun had done it. All the kids had inherited their mother's colour, and when they stood together, golden-skinned, tossing back their unmanageable hair, you would have said a mob of taffy brumbies.

'What is the bloody idea?' she asked, because she couldn't go on standing there.

'Pick up a coupla cold bottles, and spend the mornun at the dump.'

'But that's the same old idea,' she grumbled.

'No, it ain't. Not our own dump. We ain't done Sarsaparilla since Christmas.'

She began to grumble her way across the yard and into the house. A smell of sink strayed out of grey, unpainted weather-board, to oppose the stench of crushed boggabri and cotton pear. Perhaps because Whalleys were in the bits-and-pieces trade their home was threatening to give in to them.

Wal Whalley did the dumps. Of course there were the other lurks besides. But no one had an eye like Wal for the things a person needs: dead batteries and musical bedsteads, a carpet you wouldn't notice was stained, wire, and again wire, clocks only waiting to jump back into the race of time. Objects of commerce and mystery littered Whalleys' back yard. Best of all, a rusty boiler into which the twins would climb to play at cubby.

'Eh? Waddaboutut?' Wal shouted, and pushed against his wife with his side.

She almost put her foot through the hole that had come in the kitchen boards.

'Waddabout what?'

Half-suspecting, she half-sniggered. Because Wal knew how to play on her weakness.

'The fuckun *idea*!'

So that she began again to grumble. As she slopped through the house her clothes irritated her skin. The sunlight fell yellow on the grey masses of the unmade beds, turned the fluff in the corners of the rooms to gold. Something was nagging at her, something heavy continued to weigh her down.

Of course. It was the funeral.

'Why, Wal,' she said, the way she would suddenly come round, 'you could certainly of thought of a worse idea. It'll keep the kids out of mischief. Wonder if that bloody Lummy's gunna decide to honour us?'

'One day I'll knock 'is block off,' said Wal.

'He's only at the awkward age.'

She stood at the window, looking as though she might know the hell of a lot. It was the funeral made her feel solemn. Brought the goose-flesh out on her.

'Good job you thought about the dump,' she said, outstaring a red-brick propriety the other side of the road. 'If there's anythun gets me down, it's havin' ter watch a funeral pass.'

'Won't be from 'ere,' he consoled. 'They took 'er away same evenun. It's gunna start from Jackson's Personal Service.'

'Good job she popped off at the beginnun of the week. They're not so personal at the week-end.'

She began to prepare for the journey to the dump. Pulled her frock down a bit. Slipped on a pair of shoes.

'Bet *She*'ll be relieved. Wouldn't show it, though. Not about 'er sister. I bet Daise stuck in 'er fuckun guts.'

Then Mrs Whalley was compelled to return to the window. As if her instinct. And sure enough there She was. Looking inside the letter-box, as if she hadn't collected already. Bent above the brick pillar in which the letter-box had been cemented, Mrs Hogben's face wore all that people expect of the bereaved.

'Daise was all right,' said Wal.

'Daise was all right,' agreed his wife.

Suddenly she wondered: What, if Wal, if Wal had ever . . . ?

Mrs Whalley settled her hair. If she hadn't been all that satisfied at home—and she *was* satisfied, her recollective eyes would admit—she too might have done a line like Daise Morrow.

Over the road Mrs Hogben was calling.

'Meg?' she called. 'Mar*gret*?'

Though from pure habit, without direction. Her voice sounded thinner today.

Then Mrs Hogben went away.

'Once I got took to a funeral,' Mrs Whalley said. 'They made me look in the coffun. It was the bloke's wife. He was that cut up.'

'Did yer have a squint?'

'Pretended to.'

Wal Whalley was breathing hard in the airless room.

'How soon do yer reckon they begin ter smell?'

'Smell? They wouldn't let 'em!' his wife said very definite. 'You're the one that smells, Wal. I wonder you don't think of takin' a bath.'

But she liked his smell, for all that. It followed her out of the shadow into the strong shaft of light. Looking at each other their two bodies asserted themselves. Their faces were lit by the certainty of life.

Wal tweaked her left nipple.

'We'll slip inter the Bull on the way, and pick up those cold bottles.'

He spoke soft for him.

Mrs Hogben called another once or twice. Inside the brick entrance the cool of the house struck at her. She liked it cool, but not cold, and this was if not exactly cold, anyway, too sudden. So now she whimpered, very faintly, for everything you have to suffer, and death on top of all. Although it was her sister Daise who had died, Mrs Hogben was crying for the death which was waiting to carry her off in turn. She called: 'Me-ehg?' But no one ever came to your rescue. She stopped to loosen the soil round the roots of the aluminium plant. She always had to be doing something. It made her feel better.

Meg did not hear, of course. She was standing amongst the fuchsia bushes, looking out from their greenish shade. She was thin and freckly. She looked awful, because Mum had made her wear her uniform, because it was sort of a formal occasion, to Auntie Daise's funeral. In the circumstances she not only looked, but was thin. That Mrs Ireland who was all for sport had told her she must turn her toes out, and watch out—she might grow up knock-kneed besides.

So Meg Hogben was, and felt, altogether awful. Her skin was green, except when the war between light and shade worried her face into scraps, and the fuchsia tassels, trembling against her unknowing cheek, infused something of their own blood, brindled her with shifting crimson. Only her eyes resisted. They were not exactly an ordinary grey. Lorrae Jensen, who was blue, said they were the eyes of a mopey cat.

A bunch of six or seven kids from Second-Grade, Lorrae, Edna, Val, Sherry, Sue Smith and Sue Goldstein, stuck together in the holidays, though Meg sometimes wondered why. The others had come around to Hogbens' Tuesday evening.

Lorrae said: 'We're going down to Barranugli pool Thursday. There's some boys Sherry knows with a couple of Gs. They've promised to take us for a run after we come out.'

Meg did not know whether she was glad or ashamed.

'I can't,' she said. 'My auntie's died.'

'Arrr!' their voices trailed.

They couldn't get away too quick, as if it had been something contagious.

But murmuring.

Meg sensed she had become temporarily important.

So now she was alone with her dead importance, in the fuchsia bushes, on the day of Auntie Daise's funeral. She had turned fourteen. She remembered the ring in plaited gold Auntie Daise had promised her. When I am gone, her aunt had said. And now it had really happened. Without rancour Meg suspected there hadn't been time to think about the ring, and Mum would grab it, to add to all the other things she had.

Then that Lummy Whalley showed up, amongst the camphor laurels opposite, tossing his head of bleached hair. She hated boys with white hair. For that matter she hated boys, or any intrusion on her privacy. She hated Lum most of all. The day he threw the dog poo at her. It made the gristle come in her neck. Ugh! Although the old poo had only skittered over her skin, too dry to really matter, she had gone in and cried because, well, there were times when she cultivated dignity.

Now Meg Hogben and Lummy Whalley did not notice each other even when they looked.

'Who wants Meg Skinny-leg?
I'd rather take the clothes-peg . . . '

Lum Whalley vibrated like a comb-and-paper over amongst the
camphor laurels they lopped back every so many years for firewood. He
slashed with his knife into bark. Once in a hot dusk he had carved I
LOVE MEG, because that was something you did, like on lavatory walls,
and in the trains, but it didn't mean anything of course. Afterwards he
slashed the darkness as if it had been a train seat.

Lum Whalley pretended not to watch Meg Hogben skulking in the
fuchsia bushes. Wearing her brown uniform. Stiffer, browner than for
school, because it was her auntie's funeral.

'Me-ehg?' called Mrs Hogben. 'Meg!'

'Lummy! Where the devil are yer?' called his mum.

She was calling all around, in the woodshed, behind the dunny. Let
her!

'Lum? Lummy, for Chris*sake*!' she called.

He hated that. Like some bloody kid. At school he had got them to
call him Bill, halfway between, not so shameful as Lum, nor yet as
awful as William.

Mrs Whalley came round the corner.

'Shoutin' me bloody lungs up!' she said. 'When your dad's got a nice
idea. We're goin' down to Sarsaparilla dump.'

'Arr!' he said.

But didn't spit.

'What gets inter you?' she asked.

Even at their most inaccessible Mrs Whalley liked to finger her children. Touch often assisted thought. But she liked the feel of them as
well. She was glad she hadn't had girls. Boys turned into men, and you
couldn't do without men, even when they took you for a mug, or got
shickered, or bashed you up.

So she put her hand on Lummy, tried to get through to him. He was
dressed, but might not have been. Lummy's kind was never ever born
for clothes. At fourteen he looked more.

'Well,' she said, sourer than she felt, 'I'm not gunna cry over any
sulky boy. Suit yourself.'

She moved off.

As Dad had got out the old rattle-bones by now, Lum began to clam-
ber up. The back of the ute was at least private, though it wasn't no
Customline.

The fact that Whalleys ran a Customline as well puzzled more unreasonable minds. Drawn up amongst the paspalum in front of Whalleys'
shack, it looked stolen, and almost was—the third payment overdue.
But would slither with ease a little longer to Barranugli, and snooze
outside the Northern Hotel. Lum could have stood all day to admire

their own two-tone car. Or would stretch out inside, his fingers at work on plastic flesh.

Now it was the ute for business. The bones of his buttocks bit into the boards. His father's meaty arm stuck out at the window, disgusting him. And soon the twins were squeezing from the rusty boiler. The taffy Gary—or was it Barry? had fallen down and barked his knee.

'For Chrissake!' Mrs Whalley shrieked, and tossed her identical taffy hair.

Mrs Hogben watched those Whalleys leave.

'In a brick area, I wouldn't of thought,' she remarked to her husband once again.

'All in good time, Myrtle,' Councillor Hogben replied as before.

'Of course,' she said, 'if there are reasons.'

Because councillors, she knew, did have *reasons*.

'But that home! And a Customline!'

The saliva of bitterness came in her mouth.

It was Daise who had said: I'm going to enjoy the good things of life—and died in that pokey little hutch, with only a cotton frock to her back. While Myrtle had the liver-coloured brick home—not a single dampmark on the ceilings—she had the washing machine, the septic, the TV, and the cream Holden Special, not to forget her husband, Les Hogben, the councillor. A builder into the bargain.

Now Myrtle stood amongst her things, and would have continued to regret the Ford the Whalleys hadn't paid for, if she hadn't been regretting Daise. It was not so much her sister's death as her life Mrs Hogben deplored. Still, everybody knew, and there was nothing you could do about it.

'Do you think anybody will come?' Mrs Hogben asked.

'What do you take me for?' her husband replied. 'One of these cleervoyants?'

Mrs Hogben did not hear.

After giving the matter consideration she had advertised the death in the *Herald*:

> MORROW, *Daisy (Mrs), suddenly, at her residence, Showground Road, Sarsaparilla.*

There was nothing more you could put. It wasn't fair on Les, a public servant, to rake up relationships. And the *Mrs*—well, everyone had got into the habit when Daise started going with Cunningham. It seemed sort of natural as things dragged on and on. Don't work yourself up, Myrt, Daise used to say; Jack will when his wife dies. But it was Jack Cunningham who died first. Daise said: It's the way it happened, that's all.

'Do you think Ossie will come?' Councillor Hogben asked his wife slower than she liked.

'I hadn't thought about it,' she said.

Which meant she had. She had, in fact, woken in the night, and lain there cold and stiff, as her mind's eye focused on Ossie's runny nose.

Mrs Hogben rushed at a drawer which somebody—never herself—had left hanging out. She was a thin woman, but wiry.

'Meg?' she called. 'Did you polish your shoes?'

Les Hogben laughed behind his closed mouth. He always did when he thought of Daise's parting folly: to take up with that old scabby deadbeat Ossie from down at the showground. But who cared?

No one, unless her family.

Mrs Hogben dreaded the possibility of Ossie, a Roman Catholic for extra value, standing beside Daise's grave, even if nobody, even if only Mr Brickle saw.

Whenever the thought of Ossie Coogan crossed Councillor Hogben's mind he would twist the knife in his sister-in-law. Perhaps, now, he was glad she had died. A small woman, smaller than his wife, Daise Morrow was large by nature. Whenever she dropped in she was all around the place. Yarn her head off if she got the chance. It go so as Les Hogben could not stand hearing her laugh. Pressed against her in the hall once. He had forgotten that, or almost. How Daise laughed then. I'm not so short of men I'd pick me own brother-in-law. Had he pressed? Not all that much, not intentional anyway. So the incident had been allowed to fade, dim as the brown-linoleum hall, in Councillor Hogben's mind.

'There's the phone, Leslie.'

It was his wife.

'I'm too upset,' she said, 'to answer.'

And began to cry.

Easing his crutch Councillor Hogben went into the hall.

It was good old Horrie Last.

'Yairs . . . yairs . . . ' said Mr Hogben, speaking into the telephone which his wife kept swabbed with Breath-o'-Pine. 'Yairs . . . Eleven, Horrie . . . from Barranugli . . . from Jackson's Personal . . . Yairs, that's decent of you, Horrie.'

'Horrie Last,' Councillor Hogben reported to his wife, 'is gunna put in an appearance.'

If no one else, a second councillor for Daise. Myrtle Hogben was consoled.

What could you do? Horrie Last put down the phone. He and Les had stuck together. Teamed up to catch the more progressive vote. Hogben and Last had developed the shire. Les had built Horrie's home, Lasts had sold Hogbens theirs. If certain people were spreading the rumour that Last and Hogben had caused a contraction of the Green Belt, then certain people failed to realize the term itself implied flexibility.

'What did you tell them?' asked Mrs Last.

'Said I'd go,' her husband said, doing things to the change in his pocket.

He was a short man, given to standing with his legs apart.

Georgina Last withheld her reply. Formally of interest, her shape suggested she had been made out of several scones joined together in the baking.

'Daise Morrow,' said Horrie Last, 'wasn't such a bad sort.'

Mrs Last did not answer.

So he stirred the money in his pocket harder, hoping perhaps it would emulsify. He wasn't irritated, mind you, by his wife—who had brought him a parcel of property, as well as a flair for real estate—but had often felt he might have done a dash with Daise Morrow on the side. Wouldn't have minded betting old Les Hogben had tinkered a bit with his wife's sister. Helped her buy her home, they said. Always lights on at Daise's place after dark. Postman left her mail on the veranda instead of in the box. In summer, when the men went round to read the meters, she'd ask them in for a glass of beer. Daise knew how to get service.

Georgina Last cleared her throat.

'Funerals are not for women,' she declared, and took up a cardigan she was knitting for a cousin.

'You didn't do your shoes!' Mrs Hogben protested.

'I did,' said Meg. 'It's the dust. Don't know why we bother to clean shoes at all. They always get dirty again.'

She stood there looking awful in the school uniform. Her cheeks were hollow from what she read could only be despair.

'A person must keep to her principles,' Mrs Hogben said, and added: 'Dadda is bringing round the car. Where's your hat, dear? We'll be ready to leave in two minutes.'

'Arr, Mum! The hat?'

That old school hat. It had shrunk already a year ago, but had to see her through.

'You wear it to church, don't you?'

'But this isn't church!'

'It's as good as. Besides, you owe it to your aunt,' Mrs Hogben said, to win.

Meg went and got her hat. They were going out through the fuchsia bushes, past the plaster pixies, which Mrs Hogben had trained her child to cover with plastic at the first drops of rain. Meg Hogben hated the sight of those corny old pixies, even after the plastic cones had snuffed them out.

It was sad in the car, dreamier. As she sat looking out through the window, the tight panama perched on her head lost its power to humiliate. Her always persistent, grey eyes, under the line of dark fringe, had taken up the search again: she had never yet looked enough. Along the road they passed the house in which her aunt, they told her, had died. The small, pink, tilted house, standing amongst the carnation plants, had certainly lost some of its life. Or the glare had drained the colour from it. How the mornings used to sparkle in which Aunt Daise went up and down between the rows, her gown dragging heavy with dew, binding with bast the fuzzy flowers by handfuls and handfuls. Auntie's voice clear as morning. No one, she called, could argue they look stiff when they're bunched tight eh Meg what would you say they remind you of? But you never knew the answers to the sort of things people asked. Frozen fireworks, Daise suggested. Meg loved the idea of it, she loved Daise. Not so frozen either, she dared. The sun getting at the wet flowers broke them up and made them spin.

And the clovey scent rose up in the stale-smelling car, and smote Meg Hogben, out of the reeling heads of flowers, their cold stalks dusted with blue. Then she knew she would write a poem about Aunt Daise and the carnations. She wondered she hadn't thought of it before.

At that point the passengers were used most brutally as the car entered on a chain of potholes. For once Mrs Hogben failed to invoke the Main Roads Board. She was asking herself whether Ossie could be hiding in there behind the blinds. Or whether, whether. She fished for her second handkerchief. Prudence had induced her to bring two—the good one with the lace insertion for use beside the grave.

'The weeds will grow like one thing,' her voice blared, 'now that they'll have their way.'

Then she began to unfold the less important of her handkerchiefs.

Myrtle Morrow had always been the sensitive one. Myrtle had understood the Bible. Her needlework, her crochet doilys had taken prizes at country shows. No one had fiddled such pathos out of the pianola. It was Daise who loved flowers, though. It's a moss-rose, Daise had said, sort of rolling it round on her tongue, while she was still a little thing.

When she had had her cry, Mrs Hogben remarked: 'Girls don't know they're happy until it's too late.'

Thus addressed, the other occupants of the car did not answer. They knew they were not expected to.

Councillor Hogben drove in the direction of Barranugli. He had arranged his hat before leaving. He removed a smile the mirror reminded him was there. Although he no longer took any risks in a re-election photograph by venturing out of the past, he often succeeded in the fleshy present. But now, in difficult circumstances, he was exercising his sense of duty. He drove, he drove, past the retinosperas, heavy with their own gold, past the lagerstroemias, their pink sugar running into mildew.

Down at the dump Whalleys were having an argument about whether the beer was to be drunk on arrival or after they had developed a thirst.

'Keep it, then!' Mum Whalley turned her back. 'What was the point of buyin' it cold if you gotta wait till it hots up? Anyways,' she said, 'I thought the beer was an excuse for comin'.'

'Arr, stuff it!' says Wal. 'A dump's business, ain't it? With or without beer. Ain't it? Any day of the week.'

He saw she had begun to sulk. He saw her rather long breasts floating around inside her dress. Silly cow! He laughed. But cracked a bottle.

Barry said he wanted a drink.

You could hear the sound of angry suction as his mum's lips called off a swig.

'I'm not gunna stand by and watch any kid of mine,' said the wet lips, 'turn 'isself into a bloody dipso!'

Her eyes were at their blazing bluest. Perhaps it was because Wal Whalley admired his wife that he continued to desire her.

But Lummy pushed off on his own. When his mum went crook, and swore, he was too aware of the stumps of teeth, the rotting brown of nastiness. It was different, of course, if you swore yourself. Sometimes it was unavoidable.

Now he avoided by slipping away, between the old mattresses, and boots the sun had buckled up. Pitfalls abounded: the rusty traps of open tins lay in wait for guiltless ankles, the necks of broken bottles might have been prepared to gash a face. So he went thoughtfully, his feet scuffing the leaves of stained asbestos, crunching the torso of a celluloid doll. Here and there it appeared as though trash might win. The onslaught of metal was pushing the scrub into the gully. But in many secret, steamy pockets, a rout was in progress: seeds had been sown in the lumps of grey, disintegrating kapok and the laps of burst chairs, the coils of springs, locked in the spirals of wirier vines, had surrendered to superior resilience. Somewhere on the edge of the whole shambles a human ally, before retiring, had lit a fire, which by now the green had almost choked, leaving a stench of smoke to compete with the sicklier one of slow corruption.

Lum Whalley walked with a grace of which he himself had never been aware. He had had about enough of this rubbish jazz. He would have liked to know how to live neat. Like Darkie Black. Everything in its place in the cabin of Darkie's trailer. Suddenly his throat yearned for Darkie's company. Darkie's hands, twisting the wheel, appeared to control the whole world.

A couple of strands of barbed wire separated Sarsaparilla dump from Sarsaparilla cemetery. The denominations were separated too, but there you had to tell by the names, or by the angels and things the RIPs went in for. Over in what must have been the Church of England Alf Herbert was finishing Mrs Morrow's grave. He had reached the clay, and the going was heavy. The clods fell resentfully.

If what they said about Mrs Morrow was true, then she had lived it up all right. Lum Whalley wondered what, supposing he had met her walking towards him down a bush track, smiling. His skin tingled. Lummy had never done a girl, although he pretended he had, so as to hold his own with the kids. He wondered if a girl, if that sourpuss Meg Hogben. Would of bitten as likely as not. Lummy felt a bit afraid, and returned to thinking of Darkie Black, who never talked about things like that.

Presently he moved away. Alf Herbert, leaning on his shovel, could have been in need of a yarn. Lummy was not prepared to yarn. He turned back into the speckled bush, into the pretences of a shade. He lay down under a banksia, and opened his fly to look at himself. But pretty soon got sick of it.

The procession from Barranugli back to Sarsaparilla was hardly what you would have called a procession: the Reverend Brickle, the Hogben's Holden, Horrie's Holden, following the smaller of Jackson's hearses. In the circumstances they were doing things cheap—there was no reason for splashing it around. At Sarsaparilla Mr Gill joined in, sitting high in that old Chev. It would have been practical, Councillor Hogben sighed, to join the hearse at Sarsaparilla. Old Gill was only there on account of Daise being his customer for years. A grocer lacking in enterprise, Daise had stuck to him, she said, because she liked him. Well, if that was what you put first, but where did it get you?

At the last dip before the cemetery a disembowelled mattress from the dump had begun to writhe across the road. It looked like a kind of monster from out of the depths of somebody's mind, the part a decent person ignored.

'Ah, dear! At the cemetery too!' Mrs Hogben protested. 'I wonder the Council,' she added, in spite of her husband.

'All right, Myrtle,' he said between his teeth. 'I made a mental note.' Councillor Hogben was good at that.

'And the Whalleys on your own doorstep,' Mrs Hogben moaned.

The things she had seen on hot days, in front of their kiddies too.

The hearse had entered the cemetery gate. They had reached the bumpy stage toppling over the paspalum clumps, before the thinner, bush grass. All around, the leaves of the trees presented so many grey blades. Not even a magpie to put heart into a Christian. But Alf Herbert came forward, his hands dusted with yellow clay, to guide the hearse between the Methoes and the Presbyterians, onto Church of England ground.

Jolting had shaken Mrs Hogben's grief up to the surface again. Mr Brickle was impressed. He spoke for a moment of the near and dear. His hands were kind and professional in helping her out.

But Meg jumped. And landed. It was a shock to hear a stick crack so loud. Perhaps it was what Mum would have called irreverent. At the same time her banana-coloured panama fell off her head into the tussocks.

It was really a bit confusing at the grave. Some of the men helped with the coffin, and Councillor Last was far too short.

Then Mrs Hogben saw, she saw, from out of the lace handkerchief, it was that Ossie Coogan she saw, standing the other side of the grave. Had old Gill given him a lift? Ossie, only indifferently buttoned, stood snivelling behind the mound of yellow clay.

Nothing would have stopped his nose. Daise used to say: You don't want to be frightened, Ossie, not when I'm here, see? But she wasn't any longer. So now he was afraid. Excepting Daise, Protestants had always frightened him. Well, I'm nothing, she used to say, nothing that you could pigeonhole, but love what we are given to love.

Myrtle Hogben was ropeable, if only because of what Councillor Last must think. She would have like to express her feelings in words, if she could have done so without giving offence to God. Then the ants ran up her legs, for she was standing on a nest, and her body cringed before the teeming injustices.

Daise, she had protested the day it all began, whatever has come over you? The sight of her sister had made her run out leaving the white sauce to burn. Wherever will you take him? He's sick, said Daise. *But you can't*, Myrtle Hogben cried. For there was her sister Daise pushing some old deadbeat in a barrow. All along Showground Road people had come out of homes to look. Daise appeared smaller pushing the wheelbarrow down the hollow and up the hill. Her hair was half uncoiled. *You can't! You can't!* Myrtle called. But Daise could, and did.

When all the few people were assembled at the graveside in their good clothes, Mr Brickle opened the book, though his voice soon suggested he needn't have.

'*I am the resurrection and the life,*' he said.

And Ossie cried. Because he didn't believe it, not when it came to the real thing.

He looked down at the coffin, which was what remained of what he knew. He remembered eating a baked apple, very slowly, the toffee on it. And again the dark of the horse-stall swallowed him up, where he lay hopeless amongst the shit, and her coming at him with the barrow. What do you want? he asked straight out. I came down to the showground, she said, for a bit of honest-to-God manure, I've had those fertilizers, she said, and what are you, are you sick? I live 'ere, he said. And began to cry, and rub the snot from his snivelly nose. After a bit

Daise said: We're going back to my place, What's-yer-Name—Ossie. The way she spoke he knew it was true. All the way up the hill in the barrow the wind was giving his eyes gyp, and blowing his thin hair apart. Over the years he had come across one or two lice in his hair, but thought, or hoped he had got rid of them by the time Daise took him up. As she pushed and struggled with the barrow, sometimes she would lean forward, and he felt her warmth, her firm diddies pressed against his back.

'*Lord, let me know mine end, and the number of my days: that I may be certified how long I have to live,*' Mr Brickle read.

Certified was the word, decided Councillor Hogben looking at that old Ossie.

Who stood there mumbling a few Aspirations, very quiet, on the strength of what they had taught him as a boy.

When all this was under way, all these words of which, she knew, her Auntie Daise would not have approved, Meg Hogben went and got beneath the strands of wire separating the cemetery from the dump. She had never been to the dump before, and her heart was lively in her side. She walked shyly through the bush. She came across an old suspender-belt. She stumbled over a blackened primus.

She saw Lummy Whalley then. He was standing under a banksia, twisting at one of its dead heads.

Suddenly they knew there was something neither of them could continue to avoid.

'I came here to the funeral,' she said.

She sounded, well, almost relieved.

'Do you come here often?' she asked.

'Nah,' he answered, hoarse. 'Not here. To dumps, yes.'

But her intrusion had destroyed the predetermined ceremony of his life, and caused a trembling in his hand.

'Is there anything to see?' she asked.

'Junk,' he said. 'Same old junk.'

'Have you ever looked at a dead person?'

Because she noticed the trembling of his hand.

'No,' he said. 'Have you?'

She hadn't. Nor did it seem probable that she would have to now. Not as they began breathing evenly again.

'What do you do with yourself?' he asked.

Then, even though she would have like to stop herself, she could not. She said: 'I write poems. I'm going to write one about my Aunt Daise, like she was, gathering carnations early in the dew.'

'What'll you get out of that?'

'Nothing,' she said, 'I suppose.'

But it did not matter.

'What other sorts of pomes do you write?' he asked, twisting at last the dead head of the banksia off.

'I wrote one,' she said, 'about the things in a cupboard. I wrote about a dream I had. And the smell of rain. That was a bit too short.'

He began to look at her then. He had never looked into the eyes of a girl. They were grey and cool, unlike the hot, or burnt-out eyes of a woman.

'What are you going to be?' she asked.

'I dunno.'

'You're not a white-collar type.'

'Eh?'

'I mean you're not for figures, and books, and banks and offices,' she said.

He was too disgusted to agree.

'I'm gunna have me own truck. Like Mr Black. Darkie's got a trailer.'

'What?'

'Well,' he said, 'a semi-trailer.'

'Oh,' she said, more diffident.

'Darkie took me on a trip to Maryborough. It was pretty tough goin'. Sometimes we drove right through the night. Sometimes we slept on the road. Or in places where you get rooms. Gee, it was good though, shootin' through the country towns at night.'

She saw it. She saw the people standing at their doors, frozen in the blocks of yellow light. The rushing of the night made the figures for ever still. All around she could feel the furry darkness, as the semi-trailer roared and bucked, its skeleton of coloured lights. While in the cabin, in which they sat, all was stability and order. If she glanced sideways she could see how his taffy hair shone when raked by the burst of electric light. They had brought cases with tooth-brushes, combs, one or two things—the pad on which she would write the poem somewhere when they stopped in the smell of sunlight dust ants. But his hands had acquired such mastery over the wheel, it appeared this might never happen. Nor did she care.

'This Mr Black,' she said, her mouth getting thinner, 'does he take you with him often?'

'Only once interstate,' said Lummy, pitching the banksia head away. 'Once in a while short trips.'

As they drove they rocked together. He had never been closer to anyone than when bumping against Darkie's ribs. He waited to experience again the little spasm of gratitude and pleasure. He would have liked to wear, and would in time, a striped sweatshirt like Darkie wore.

'I'd like to go in with Darkie,' he said, 'when I get a trailer of me own. Darkie's the best friend I got.'

With a drawnout shiver of distrust she saw the darker hands, the little black hairs on the backs of the fingers.

'Oh, well,' she said, withdrawn, 'praps you will in the end,' she said.

On the surrounding graves the brown flowers stood in their jars of browner water. The more top-heavy, plastic bunches had been slapped down by a westerly, but had not come to worse grief than to lie strewn in pale disorder on the uncharitable granite chips.

The heat made Councillor Last yawn. He began to read the carved names, those within sight at least, some of which he had just about forgot. He almost laughed once. If the dead could have sat up in their graves there would have been an argument or two.

'In the midst of life we are in death,' said the parson bloke.

JACK CUNNINGHAM
BELOVED HUSBAND OF FLORENCE MARY,

read Horrie Last.

Who would have thought Cunningham, straight as a silky-oak, would fall going up the path to Daise Morrow's place. Horrie used to watch them together, sitting a while on the veranda before going in to their tea. They made no bones about it, because everybody knew. Good teeth Cunningham had. Always a white, well-ironed shirt. Wonder which of the ladies did the laundry. Florence Mary was an invalid, they said. Daise Morrow liked to laugh with men, but for Jack Cunningham she had a silence, promising intimacies at which Horrie Last could only guess, whose own private life had been lived in almost total darkness.

Good Christ, and then there was Ossie. The woman could only have been at heart a perv of a kind you hadn't heard about.

'Forasmuch as it hath pleased Almighty God of his great mercy to take unto himself the soul . . . ' read Mr Brickle.

As it was doubtful who should cast the earth, Mr Gill the grocer did. They heard the handful rattle on the coffin.

Then the tears truly ran out of Ossie's scaly eyes. Out of darkness. Out of darkness Daise had called: What's up, Ossie, you don't wanta cry. I got the cramps, he answered. They were twisting him. The cramps? she said drowsily. Or do you imagine? If it isn't the cramps it's something else. Could have been. He'd take Daise's word for it. He was never all that bright since he had the meningitis. Tell you what, Daise said, you come in here, into my bed, I'll warm you, Os, in a jiffy. He listened in the dark to his own snivelling. Arr, Daise, I couldn't, he said, I couldn't get a stand, not if you was to give me the jackpot, he said. She sounded very still then. He lay and counted the throbbing of the darkness. Not like that, she said—she didn't laugh at him as he had half expected—besides, she said, it only ever really comes to you once. That way. And at once he was parting the darkness, bumping and shambling, to get to her. He had never known it so gentle. Because Daise wasn't afraid. She ran her hands through his hair, on and on like water flowing. She soothed the cramps out of his legs. Until in the end they were breathing in time. Dozing. Then the lad Ossie Coogan rode again down from the mountain, the sound of the snaffle in the blue air, the smell of sweat from under the saddle-cloth, towards the great, flowing river. He rocked and flowed with the motion of the strong, never-ending river, burying his mouth in brown cool water, to drown would have been worth it.

Once during the night Ossie had woken, afraid the distance might have come between them. But Daise was still holding him against her breast. If he had been different, say. Ossie's throat had begun to wobble. Only then, Daise, Daise might have turned different. So he nuzzled against the warm darkness, and was again received.

'If you want to enough, you can do what you want,' Meg Hogben insisted.

She had read it in a book, and wasn't altogether convinced, but theories sometimes come to the rescue.

'If you want,' she said, kicking a hole in the stony ground.

'Not everything you can't.'

'You can!' she said. 'But you can!'

She who had never looked at a boy, not right into one, was looking at him as never before.

'That's a lot of crap,' he said.

'Well,' she admitted, 'there are limits.'

It made him frown. He was again suspicious. She was acting clever. All those pomes.

But to reach understanding she would have surrendered her cleverness. She was no longer proud of it.

'And what'll happen if you get married? Riding around the country in a truck. How'll your wife like it? Stuck at home with a lot of kids.'

'Some of 'em take the wife along. Darkie takes his missus and kids. Not always, like. But now and again. On short runs.'

'You didn't tell me Mr Black was married.'

'Can't tell you everything, can I? Not at once.'

The women who sat in the drivers' cabins of the semi-trailers he saw as predominantly think and dark. They seldom returned glances, but wiped their hands on Kleenex, and peered into little mirrors, waiting for their men to show up again. Which in time they had to. So he walked across from the service station, to take possession of his property. Sauntering, frowning slightly, touching the yellow stubble on his chin, he did not bother to look. Glanced sideways perhaps. She was the thinnest, the darkest he knew, the coolest of all the women who sat looking out from the cabin windows of the semi-trailers.

In the meantime they strolled a bit, amongst the rusty tins at Sarsaparilla dump. He broke a few sticks and threw away the pieces. She tore off a narrow leaf and smelled it. She would have liked to smell Lummy's hair.

'Gee, you're fair,' she had to say.

'Some are born fair,' he admitted.

He began pelting a rock with stones. He was strong, she saw.

So many discoveries in a short while were making her tremble at the knees.

And as they rushed through the brilliant light, roaring and lurching, the cabin filled with fair-skinned, taffy children, the youngest of whom she was protecting by holding the palm of her hand behind his neck, as she had noticed women do. Occupied in this way, she almost forgot Lum at times, who would pull up, and she would climb down, to rinse the nappies in tepid water, and hang them on a bush to dry.

'All these pomes and things,' he said, 'I never knew a clever person before.'

'But clever isn't any different,' she begged, afraid he might not accept her peculiarity and power.

She would go with a desperate wariness from now. She sensed that, if not in years, she was older than Lum, but this was the secret he must never guess: that for all his strength, all his beauty, she was, and must remain the stronger.

'What's that?' he asked, and touched.

But drew back his hand in self-protection.

'A scar,' she said. 'I cut my wrist opening a tin of condensed milk.'

For once she was glad of the paler seam in her freckled skin, hoping that it might heal a breach.

And he looked at her out of his hard blue Whalley eyes. He liked her. Although she was ugly, and clever, and a girl.

'Condensed milk on bread,' he said, 'that's something I could eat till I bust.'

'Oh, yes!' she agreed.

She did honestly believe, although she had never thought of it before.

Flies clustered in irregular jet embroideries on the backs of best suits. Nobody bothered any longer to shrug them off. As Alf Herbert grunted against the shovelfuls, dust clogged increasingly, promises settled thicker. Although they had been told they might expect Christ to redeem, it would have been no less incongruous if He had appeared out of the scrub to perform on altars of burning sandstone a sacrifice for which nobody had prepared them. In any case, the mourners waited—they had been taught to accept whatever might be imposed—while the heat stupefied the remnants of their minds, and inflated their Australian fingers into foreign-looking sausages.

Myrtle Hogben was the first to protest. She broke down—into the wrong handkerchief. *Who shall change our vile body?* The words were more than her decency could bear.

'Easy on it,' her husband whispered, putting a finger under her elbow.

She submitted to his sympathy, just as in their life together she had submitted to his darker wishes. Never wanting more than peace, and one or two perquisites.

A thin woman, Mrs Hogben continued to cry for all the wrongs that had been done her. For Daise had only made things viler. While understanding, yes, at moments. It was girls who really understood, not even women—sisters, sisters. Before events whirled them apart. So Myrtle Morrow was again walking through the orchard, and Daise Morrow twined her arm around her sister; confession filled the air, together with a scent of crushed, fermenting apples. Myrtle said: Daise, there's something I'd like to do, I'd like to chuck a lemon into a Salvation Army tuba. Daise giggled. You're a nut, Myrt, she said. But never *vile*. So Myrtle Hogben cried. Once, only once she had thought how she'd like to push someone off a cliff, and watch their expression as it happened. But Myrtle had not confessed that.

So Mrs Hogben cried, for those things she was unable to confess, for anything she might not be able to control.

As the blander words had begun falling, *Our Father*, that she knew by heart, *our daily bread*, she should have felt comforted. She should of. Should of.

Where was Meg, though?

Mrs Hogben separated herself from the others. Walking stiffly. If any of the men noticed, they took it for granted she had been overcome, or wanted to relieve herself.

She would have like to relieve herself by calling: 'Margaret Meg wherever don't you hear me Me-ehg?' drawing it out thin in anger. But could not cut across a clergyman's words. So she stalked. She was not unlike a guinea-hen, its spotted silk catching on a strand of barbed-wire.

When they had walked a little farther, round and about, anywhere, they overheard voices.

'What's that?' asked Meg.

'Me mum and dad,' Lummy said. 'Rousin' about somethun or other.'

Mum Whalley had just found two bottles of unopened beer. Down at the dump. Waddayaknow. Must be something screwy somewhere.

'Could of put poison in it,' her husband warned.

'Poison? My arse!' she shouted. 'That's because *I* found it!'

'Whoever found it,' he said, 'who's gunna drink a coupla bottlesa hot beer?'

'I am!' she said.

'When what we brought was good an' cold?'

He too was shouting a bit. She behaved unreasonable at times.

'Who wanted ter keep what we brought? till it got good an' hot!' she shrieked.

Sweat was running down both the Whalleys.

Suddenly Lum felt he wanted to lead this girl out of earshot. He had just about had the drunken sods. He would have liked to find himself walking with his girl over mown lawn, like at the Botanical Gardens, a green turf giving beneath their leisured feet. Statues pointed a way through the glare, to where they finally sat, under enormous shiny leaves, looking out at boats on water. They unpacked their cut lunch from its layers of fresh tissue-paper.

'They're rough as bags,' Lummy explained.

'I don't care,' Meg Hogben assured.

Nothing on earth could make her care—was it more, or was it less?

She walked giddily behind him, past a rusted fuel-stove, over a field of deathly feltex. Or ran, or slid, to keep up. Flowers would have wilted in her hands, if she hadn't crushed them brutally, to keep her balance. Somewhere in their private labyrinth Meg Hogben had lost her hat.

When they were farther from the scene of anger, and a silence of heat had descended again, he took her little finger, because it seemed natural to do so, after all they had experienced. They swung hands for a while, according to some special law of motion.

Till Lum Whalley frowned, and threw the girl's hand away.

If she accepted his behaviour it was because she no longer believed in what he did, only in what she knew he felt. That might have been the trouble. She was so horribly sure, he would have to resist to the last moment of all. As a bird, singing in the prickly tree under which they found themselves standing, seemed to cling to the air. Then his fingers took control. She was amazed at the hardness of his boy's body. The tremors of her flinty skin, the membrane of the white sky appalled him. Before fright and expectation melted their mouths. And they took little grateful sips of each other. Holding up their throats in between. Like birds drinking.

Ossie could no longer see Alf Herbert's shovel working at the earth.

'Never knew a man cry at a funeral,' Councillor Hogben complained, very low, although he was ripe enough to burst.

If you could count Ossie as a man, Councillor Last suggested in a couple of noises.

But Ossie could not see or hear, only Daise, still lying on that upheaval of a bed. Seemed she must have burst a button, for her breasts stood out from her. He would never forget how they laboured against the heavy yellow morning light. In the early light, the flesh turned yellow, sluggish. What's gunna happen to me, Daisy? It'll be decided, Os, she said, like it is for any of us. I ought to know, she said, to tell you, but give me time to rest a bit, to get me breath. Then he got down on his painful knees. He put his mouth to Daise's neck. Her skin tasted terrible bitter. The great glistening river, to which the lad Ossie Coogan had ridden jingling down from the mountain, was slowing into thick, yellow mud. Himself an old, scabby man attempting to refresh his forehead in the last pothole.

Mr Brickle said: '*We give thee hearty thanks for that it hath pleased thee to deliver this our sister out of the miseries of this sinful world.*'

'No! No!' Ossie protested, so choked nobody heard, though it was vehement enough in its intention.

As far as he could understand, nobody wanted to be delivered. Not him, not Daise, anyways. When you could sit together by the fire on winter nights baking potatoes under the ashes.

It took Mrs Hogben some little while to free her *crêpe de Chine* from the wire. It was her nerves, not to mention Meg on her mind. In the circumstances she tore herself worse, and looked up to see her child, just over there, without shame, in a rubbish tip, kissing with the Whalley boy. What if Meg was another of Daise? It was in the blood, you couldn't deny.

Mrs Hogben did not exactly call, but released some kind of noise from her extended throat. Her mouth was too full of tongue to find room for words as well.

Then Meg looked. She was smiling.

She said: 'Yes, Mother.'

She came and got through the wire, tearing herself also a little.

Mrs. Hogben said, and her teeth clicked: 'You chose the likeliest time. Your aunt hardly in her grave. Though, of course, it is only your aunt, if anyone, to blame.'

The accusations were falling fast. Meg could not answer. Since joy had laid her open, she had forgotten how to defend herself.

'If you were a little bit younger'—Mrs Hogben lowered her voice because they had begun to approach the parson—'I'd break a stick on you, my girl.'

Meg tried to close her face, so that nobody would see inside.

'What will they say?' Mrs Hogben moaned. 'What ever will happen to us?'

'What, Mother?' Meg asked.

'You're the only one can answer that. And someone else.'

Then Meg looked over her shoulder and recognized the hate which, for a while, she had forgotten existed. And at once her face closed up tight, like a fist. She was ready to protect whatever justly needed her protection.

Even if their rage, grief, contempt, boredom, apathy, and sense of injustice had not occupied the mourners, it is doubtful whether they would have realized the dead woman was standing amongst them. The risen dead—that was something which happened, or didn't happen, in the Bible. Fanfares of light did not blare for a loose woman in floral cotton. Those who had known her remembered her by now only fitfully in some of the wooden attitudes of life. How could they have heard, let alone believed in, her affirmation? Yet Daise Morrow continued to proclaim.

Listen, all of you, I'm not leaving, except those who want to be left, and even those aren't so sure—they might be parting with a bit of themselves. Listen to me, all you successful no-hopers, all you who wake in the night, jittery because something may be escaping you, or terrified to think there may never have been anything to find. Come to me, you sour women, public servants, anxious children, and old scabby, desperate men. . . .

Physically small, words had seemed too big for her. She would push back her hair in exasperation. And take refuge in acts. Because her feet had been planted in the earth, she would have been the last to resent its pressure now, while her always rather hoarse voice continued to exhort in borrowed syllables of dust.

Truly, we needn't experience tortures, unless we build chambers in our minds to house instruments of hatred in. Don't you know, my darling creatures, that death isn't death, unless it's the death of love? Love should be the greatest explosion it is reasonable to expect. Which sends us whirling, spinning, creating millions of other worlds. Never destroying.

From the fresh mound which they had formed unimaginatively in the shape of her earthly body, she persisted in appealing to them.

I will comfort you. If you will let me. Do you understand?

But nobody did, as they were only human.

For ever and ever. And ever.

Leaves quivered lifted in the first suggestion of a breeze.

So the aspirations of Daise Morrow were laid alongside her small-boned wrists, smooth thighs and pretty ankles. She surrendered at last to the formal crumbling which, it was hoped, would make an honest woman of her.

But had not altogether died.

Meg Hogben had never exactly succeeded in interpreting her aunt's messages, nor could she have witnessed the last moments of the burial, because the sun was dazzling her. She did experience, however, along with a shiver of recollected joy, the down laid against her cheek, a little breeze trickling through the moist roots of her hair, as she got inside the car, and waited for whatever next.

Well, they had dumped Daise.

Somewhere the other side of the wire there was the sound of smashed glass and discussion.

Councillor Hogben went across to the parson and said the right kind of things. Half-turning his back he took a note or two from his wallet, and immediately felt disengaged. If Horrie Last had been there Les Hogben would have gone back at this point and put an arm around his mate's shoulder, to feel whether he was forgiven for unorthodox behaviour in a certain individual—no relation, mind you, but. In any case Horrie had driven away.

Horrie drove, or flew, across the dip in which the dump joined the cemetery. For a second Ossie Coogan's back flickered inside a spiral of dust.

Ought to give the coot a lift, Councillor Last suspected, and wondered, as he drove on, whether a man's better intentions were worth, say, half a mark in the event of their remaining unfulfilled. For by now it was far too late to stop, and there was that Ossie, in the mirror, turning off the road towards the dump, where, after all, the bugger belonged.

All along the road, stones, dust, and leaves, were settling back into normally unemotional focus. Seated in his high Chev, Gill the grocer, a slow man, who carried his change in a little, soiled canvas bag, looked ahead through thick lenses. He was relieved to realize he would reach home almost on the dot of three-thirty, and his wife pour him his cup of tea. Whatever he understood was punctual, decent, docketed.

As he drove, prudently, he avoided the mattress the dump had spewed, from under the wire, half across the road. Strange things had happened at the dump on and off, the grocer recollected. Screaming girls, their long tight pants ripped to tatters. An arm in a sugar-bag, and not a sign of the body that went with it. Yet some found peace amongst the refuse: elderly derelict men, whose pale, dead, fish eyes never divulged anything of what they had lived, and women with blue, metho skins, hanging around the doors of shacks put together from sheets of bark and rusty iron. Once an old downandout had crawled amongst the rubbish apparently to rot, and did, before they sent for the constable, to examine what seemed at first a bundle of stinking rags.

Mr Gill accelerated judiciously.

They were driving. They were driving.

Alone in the back of the ute, Lum Whalley sat forward on the empty crate, locking his hands between his knees, as he forgot having seen Darkie do. He was completely independent now. His face had been reshaped by the wind. He liked that. It felt good. He no longer resented the junk they were dragging home, the rust flaking off at his feet, the roll of mouldy feltex trying to fur his nostrils up. Nor his family—discussing, or quarrelling, you could never tell—behind him in the cabin.

The Whalleys were in fact singing. One of their own versions. They always sang their own versions, the two little boys joining in.

> 'Show me the way to go home,
> I'm not too tired for bed.
> I had a little drink about an hour ago,
> And it put ideas in me head . . . '

Suddenly Mum Whalley began belting into young Gary—or was it Barry?

'Wadda *you* know, eh? Wadda *you?*'

'What's bitten yer?' her husband shouted. 'Can't touch a drop with yer turn nasty!'

She didn't answer. He could tell a grouse was coming, though. The little boy had started to cry, but only as a formality.

'It's that bloody Lummy,' Mrs Whalley complained.

'Why pick on Lum?'

'Give a kid all the love and affection, and waddayaget?'

Wal grunted. Abstractions always embarrassed him.

Mum Whalley spat out of the window, and the spit came back at her.

'Arrrr!' she protested.

And fell silenter. It was not strictly Lum, not if you was honest. It was nothing. Or everything. The grog. You was never ever gunna touch it no more. Until you did. And that bloody Lummy, what with the caesar and all, you was never ever going again with a man.

'That's somethink a man don't understand.'

'What?' asked Wal.

'A caesar.'

'Eh?'

You just couldn't discuss with a man. So you had to get into bed with him. Grogged up half the time. That was how she copped the twins, after she had said never ever.

'Stop cryun, for Chrissake!' Mum Whalley coaxed, touching the little boy's blowing hair.

Everything was sad.

'Wonder how often they bury someone alive,' she said.

Taking a corner in his cream Holden Councillor Hogben felt quite rakish, but would restrain himself at the critical moment from skidding the wrong side of the law.

They were driving and driving, in long, lovely bursts, and at the corners, in semi-circular swirls.

On those occasions in her life when she tried to pray, begging for an experience, Meg Hogben would fail, but return to the attempt with clenched teeth. Now she did so want to think of her dead aunt with love, and the image blurred repeatedly. She was superficial, that was it. Yet, each time she failed, the landscape leaped lovingly. They were driving under the telephone wires. She could have translated any message into the language of peace. The wind burning, whenever it did not cut cold, left the stable things alone: the wooden houses stuck beside the road, the trunks of willows standing round the brown saucer of a dam. Her too candid, grey eyes seemed to have deepened, as though to accommodate all she still had to see, feel.

It was lovely curled on the back seat, even with Mum and Dad in front.

'I haven't forgotten, Margret,' Mum called over her shoulder.

Fortunately Dadda wasn't interested enough to inquire.

'Did Daise owe anything on the home?' Mrs Hogben asked. 'She was never at all practical.'

Councillor Hogben cleared his throat.

'Give us time to find out,' he said.

Mrs Hogben respected her husband for the things which she, secretly, did not understand: Time the mysterious, for instance, Business, and worst of all, the Valuer General.

'I wonder Jack Cunningham,' she said, 'took up with Daise. He was a fine man. Though Daise had a way with her.'

They were driving. They were driving.

When Mrs Hogden remembered the little ring in plaited gold.

'Do you think those undertakers are honest?'

'Honest?' her husband repeated.

A dubious word.

'Yes,' she said. 'That ring that Daise.'

You couldn't very well accuse. When she had plucked up the courage she would go down to the closed house. The thought of it made her chest tighten. She would go inside, and feel her way into the back corners of drawers, where perhaps a twist of tissue-paper. But the closed houses of the dead frightened Mrs Hogben, she had to admit. The stuffiness, the light strained through brown holland. It was as if you were stealing, though you weren't.

And then those Whalleys creeping up.

They were driving and driving, the ute and the sedan almost rubbing on each other.

'No one who hasn't had a migraine,' cried Mrs Hogben, averting her face, 'can guess what it feels like.'

Her husband had heard that before.

'It's a wonder it don't leave you,' he said. 'They say it does when you've passed a certain age.'

Though they weren't passing the Whalleys he would make every effort to throw the situation off. Wal Whalley leaning forward, though not so far you couldn't see the hair bursting out of the front of his shirt. His wife thumping his shoulder. They were singing one of their own versions. Her gums all watery.

So they drove and drove.

'I could sick up, Leslie,' Mrs Hogben gulped, and fished for her lesser handkerchief.

The Whalley twins were laughing through their taffy forelocks.

At the back of the ute that sulky Lum turned towards the opposite direction. Meg Hogben was looking her farthest off. Any sign of acknowledgment had been so faint the wind had immediately blown it off their faces. As Meg and Lummy sat, they held their sharp, but comforting knees. They sank their chins as low as they would go. They lowered their eyes, as if they had seen enough for the present, and wished to cherish what they knew.

The warm core of certainty settled stiller as driving faster the wind payed out the telephone wires the fences the flattened heads of grey grass always raising themselves again again again

Born in 1934 to a Mennonite family in Fairholme, in the hilly wood-lands of northern Saskatchewan, Rudy Wiebe notes in "Passage by Land" that landscape and cultural heritage have always been important to him. Though he did not learn English until he went to school, and did not see a mountain or a plain until he was almost thirteen, he later found language and landscape indissolubly wedded to each other. Encountering the world was a "wandering to find"; and paramount in his work is the sense of wandering that derives from his early experience, expressing itself as a quest for knowledge itself, about ways of knowing. In this story, for example, he does not portray a contrast so much as he enacts one, between the passivity of information and the activity of art.

His Mennonite background features significantly in two of his novels, *Peace Shall Destroy Many* (1964) and *The Blue Mountains of China* (1970); the latter, a modern epic, probes the idealistic impulses behind the sect, traces its spiritual and geographic journeys, and tries to come to terms with the power of the commitment that has impelled so many people to accept its invitation to individual action. His sympathy for human beings takes a different form in *First and Vital Candle* (1966), *The Temptations of Big Bear* (1973), about the Riel Rebellion, and "Where Is the Voice Coming From?" which became the title story of a collection which appeared in 1974. The Indians, Inuit, and Métis who appear in these works are admirably realized characters, and Wiebe has endeavored with great sensitivity to cross the cultural barriers that lie between him and his subject. But he is acutely conscious of the difficulty of being anyone but oneself, of the limitations that one's perspective erects against complete understanding, and of the problems that face the artist and the historian when they try to convey their perceptions of truth or reality. "Where Is the Voice Coming From?" resulted, Wiebe writes, from personal encounters with museum displays and historical accounts of Indian and Royal Canadian Mounted Police history, and from reading in nineteenth-century newspapers and in volume 12 *(Reconsiderations)* of Arnold Toynbee's *A Study of History*. On top of all that is his overpower-ing urge to "make story," for, as he writes in his introduction to an anthology, *The Story-Makers* (1970), a good story seduces "both teller and listener out of their world into its own," illuminating "the world in which teller and listener actually are" and often proving "the more plea-surable as the seduction becomes less immediate: story worth pondering is story doubly enjoyed."

RUDY WIEBE

FOR FURTHER READING

W.J. Keith, *Epic Fiction: The Art of Rudy Wiebe* (Edmonton: University of Alberta Press, 1981).

W.J. Keith, ed., *A Voice in the Land* (Edmonton: NeWest, 1981).

Rudy Wiebe, "Passage by Land," *Canadian Literature* 48 (Spring 1971): 25-47; reprinted in *Writers of the Prairies*, ed. Donald Stephens (Vancouver: U of British Columbia P, 1973): 29-31.

Where Is the Voice Coming From?

The problem is to make the story.

A difficulty of this making may have been excellently stated by Teilhard de Chardin: "We are continually inclined to isolate ourselves from the things and events which surround us ... as though we were spectators, not elements, in what goes on." Arnold Toynbee does venture, "For all that we know, Reality is the undifferentiated unity of the mystical experience," but that need not here be considered. This story ended long ago; it is one of finite acts, of orders, of elemental feelings and reactions, of obvious legal restrictions and requirements.

Presumably all the parts of the story are themselves available. A difficulty is that they are, as always, available only in bits and pieces. Though the acts themselves seem quite clear, some written reports of the acts contradict each other. As if these acts were, at one time, too well known; as if the original nodule of each particular fact had from somewhere received non-factual accretions; or even more, as if, since the basic facts were so clear perhaps there were a larger number of facts than any one reporter, or several, or even any reporter had ever attempted to record. About facts that are still simply told by this mouth to that ear, of course, even less can be expected.

An affair seventy-five years old should acquire some of the shiny transparency of an old man's skin. It should.

Sometimes it would seem that it would be enough—perhaps more than enough—to hear the names only. The grandfather One Arrow; the mother Spotted Calf; the father Sounding Sky; the wife (wives rather, but only one of them seems to have a name, though their fathers are Napaise, Kapahoo, Old Dust, The Rump)—the one wife named, of all things, Pale Face; the cousin Going-Up-To-Sky; the brother-in-law (again, of all things) Dublin. The names of the police sound very much alike; they all begin with Constable or Corporal or Sergeant, but here and there an Inspector, then a Superintendent and eventually all the resonance of an Assistant Commissioner echoes down. More. Herself: Victoria, by the Grace of God etc. etc. QUEEN, Defender of the Faith, etc. etc. and witness "Our Right Trusty and Right Well-beloved Cousin and Councillor the Right Honorable Sir John Campbell Hamilton-Gordon, Earl of Aberdeen; Viscount Formartine, Baron Haddo, Methlic, Tarves and Kellie, in the Peerage of Scotland; Viscount Gordon of Aberdeen, County of Aberdeen, in the Peerage of the United Kingdom; Baronet of Nova Scotia, Knight Grand Cross of Our Most Distinguished Order of Saint Michael and Saint George etc. Governor General of Canada." And of course himself: in the award proclamation named "Jean-Baptiste" but otherwise known only as Almighty Voice.

But hearing cannot be enough: not even hearing all the thunder of A Proclamation: "Now Hear Ye that a reward of FIVE HUNDRED DOLLARS will be paid to any person or persons who will give such information as will lead . . . (etc. etc.) this Twentieth day of April, in the year of Our Lord one thousand eight hundred and ninety-six, and the Fifty-ninth year of our Reign . . . " etc. and etc.

Such hearing cannot be enough. The first item to be seen is the piece of white bone. It is almost triangular, slightly convex—concave actually as it is positioned at this moment with its corners slightly raised—graduating from perhaps a strong eighth to a weak quarter of an inch in thickness, its scattered pore structure varying between larger and smaller on its perhaps polished, certainly shiny surface. Precision is difficult since the glass showcase is at least thirteen inches deep and therefore an eye cannot be brought as close as the minute inspection of such a small, though certainly quite adequate, sample of skull would normally require. Also, because of the position it cannot be determined whether the several hairs, well over a foot long, are still in some manner attached or not.

The seven-pounder cannon can be seen standing almost shyly between the showcase and the interior wall. Officially it is known as a gun, not a cannon, and clearly its bore is not large enough to admit a large man's fist. Even if it can be believed that this gun was used in the 1885 Rebellion and that on the evening of Saturday May 29, 1897 (while the nine-pounder, now unidentified, was in the process of arriving with the police on the special train from Regina), seven shells (all that were available in Prince Albert at that time) from it were sent shrieking into the poplar bluff as night fell, clearly such shelling could not and would not disembowel the whole earth. Its carriage is now nicely lacquered, the perhaps oak spokes of its petite wheels (little higher than a knee) have been recently scraped, puttied and varnished; the brilliant burnish of its brass breeching testifies with what meticulous care charmen and women have used nationally advertised cleaners and restorers.

Though it can also be seen, even a careless glance reveals that the same concern has not been expended on the one (of two) 44 calibre 1866 model Winchesters apparently found at the last in the pit with Almighty Voice. It also is preserved in a glass case; the number 1536735 is still, though barely, distinguishable on the brass cartridge section just below the brass saddle ring. However, perhaps because the case was imperfectly sealed at one time (though sealed enough not to warrant disturbance now), or because of simple neglect, the rifle is obviously spotted here and there with blotches of rust and the brass itself reveals discolorations almost like mildew. The rifle bore, the three long strands of hair themselves, actually bristle with clots of dust. It may be that this museum cannot afford to be as concerned as the other; conversely, the disfiguration may be something inherent in the items themselves.

The small building which was the police guardroom at Duck Lake, Saskatchewan Territory, in 1895 may also be seen. It had subsequently been moved from its original place and used to house small animals, chicken perhaps, or pigs—such as a woman might be expected to have under her responsibility. It is, of course, now perfectly empty, and clean so that the public may enter with no more discomfort than a bend under the doorway and a heavy encounter with disinfectant. The doorjamb has obviously been replaced; the bar network at one window is, however, said to be original; smooth still, very smooth. The logs inside have been smeared again and again with whitewash, perhaps paint, to an insistent point of identity-defying characterlessness. Within the small rectangular box of these logs not a sound can be heard from the streets of the probably dead town.

Hey Injun you'll get hung for stealing that steer
Hey Injun for killing that government cow you'll get
three weeks on the woodpile Hey Injun

The place named Kinistino has disappeared from the map but the Minnechinass Hills have not. Whether they have ever been on a map is doubtful but they will, of course, not disappear from the landscape as long as the grass grows and the rivers run. Contrary to general report and belief, the Canadian prairies are rarely, if ever, flat and the Minnechinass (spelled five different ways and translated sometimes as "The Outside Hill," sometimes as "Beautiful Bare Hills") are dissimilar from any other of the numberless hills that everywhere block out the prairie horizon. They are not bare; poplars lie tattered along their tops, almost black against the straw-pale grass and sharp green against the grey soil of the plowing laid in half-mile rectangular blocks upon their western slopes. Poles holding various wires stick out of the fields, back down the bend of the valley; what was once a farmhouse is weathering into the cultivated earth. The poplar bluff where Almighty Voice made his stand has, of course, disappeared.

The policeman he shot and killed (not the ones he wounded, of course) are easily located. Six miles east, thirty-nine miles north in Prince Albert, the English Cemetery. Sergeant Colin Campbell Colebrook, North West Mounted Police Registration Number 605, lies presumably under a gravestone there. His name is seventeenth in a very long "list of non-commissioned officers and men who have died in the service since the inception of the force." The date is October 29, 1895, and the cause of death is anonymous: "Shot by escaping Indian prisoner near Prince Albert." At the foot of this grave are two others: Constable John R. Kerr, No. 3040, and Corporal C.H.S. Hockin, No. 3106. Their cause of death on May 28, 1897 is even more anonymous, but the place is relatively precise: "Shot by Indians at Min-etch-inass Hills, Prince Albert District."

The gravestone, if he has one, of the fourth man Almighty Voice killed is more difficult to locate. Mr. Ernest Grundy, postmaster at Duck Lake in 1897, apparently shut his window the afternoon of Friday, May 25, armed himself, rode east twenty miles, participated in the second charge into the bluff at about 6:30 P.M., and on the third sweep of that charge was shot dead at the edge of the pit. It would seem that he thereby contributed substantially not only to the Indians' bullet supply, but his clothing warmed them as well.

The burial place of Dublin and Going-Up-To-Sky is unknown, as is the grave of Almighty Voice. It is said that a Métis named Henry Smith lifted the latter's body from the pit in the bluff and gave it to Spotted Calf. The place of burial is not, of course, of ultimate significance. A gravestone is always less evidence than a triangular piece of skull, provided it is large enough.

Whatever further evidence there is to be gathered may rest on pictures. There are, presumably, almost numberless pictures of the policemen in the case, but the only one with direct bearing is one of Sergeant Colebrook who apparently insisted on advancing to complete an arrest after being warned three times that if he took another step he would be shot. The picture must have been taken before he joined the force; it reveals him a large-eared young man, hair brushcut and ascot tie, his eyelids slightly drooping, almost hooded under thick brows. Unfortunately a picture of Constable R.C. Dickson, into whose charge Almighty Voice was apparently placed in that guardroom and who after Colebrook's death was convicted of negligence, sentenced to two months hard labor and discharged, does not seem to be available.

There are no pictures to be found of either Dublin (killed early by rifle fire) or Going-Up-To-Sky (killed in the pit), the two teenage boys who gave their ultimate fealty to Almighty Voice. There is, however, one said to be of Almighty Voice, Junior. He may have been born to Pale Face during the year, two hundred and twenty-one days that his father was a fugitive. In the picture he is kneeling before what could be a tent, he wears striped denim overalls and displays twin babies whose sex cannot be determined from the double-laced dark bonnets they wear. In the supposed picture of Spotted Calf and Sounding Sky, Sounding Sky stands slightly before his wife; he wears a white shirt and a striped blanket folded over his left shoulder in such a manner that the arm in which he cradles a long rifle cannot be seen. His head is thrown back; the rim of his hat appears as a black half-moon above eyes that are pressed shut in, as it were, profound concentration above a mouth clenched thin in a downward curve. Spotted Calf wears a long dress, a sweater which could also be a man's dress coat, and a large fringed and embroidered shawl which would appear distinctly Doukhobor in origin if the scroll patterns on it were more irregular. Her head is small and turned slightly towards her husband so as to reveal her right ear. There is what can only be called a quizzical expression on her crumpled face; it may be she does not understand what is happening and that she would have asked a question, perhaps of her husband, perhaps of the photographer, perhaps even of anyone, anywhere in the world if such questioning were possible for an Indian lady.

There is one final picture. That is one of Almighty Voice himself. At least it is purported to be of Almighty Voice himself. In the Royal Canadian Mounted Police Museum the Barracks Grounds just off Dewdney Avenue in Regina, Saskatchewan it lies in the same showcase, as a matter of fact immediately beside, that triangular piece of skull. Both are unequivocally labeled, and it must be assumed that a police force with a world-wide reputation would not label *such* evidence incorrectly. But here emerges an ultimate problem in making the story.

There are two official descriptions of Almighty Voice. The first reads: "Height about five feet, ten inches, slight build, rather good looking, a sharp hooked nose with a remarkably flat point. Has a bullet scar on the left side of his face about $1\frac{1}{2}$ inches long running from near corner of mouth towards ear. The scar cannot be noticed when his face is painted but otherwise is plain. Skin fair for an Indian." The second description is on the Award Proclamation: "About twenty-two years old, five feet ten inches in height, weight about eleven stone, slightly erect, neat small feet and hands; complexion inclined to be fair, wavy dark hair to shoulders, large dark eyes, broad forehead, sharp features and parrot nose with flat tip, scar on left cheek running from mouth towards ear, feminine appearance."

So run the descriptions that were, presumably, to identify a well-known fugitive in so precise a manner that an informant could collect five hundred dollars—a considerable sum when a police constable earned between one and two dollars a day. The nexus of the problems appears when these supposed official descriptions are compared to the supposed official picture. The man in the picture is standing on a small rug. The fingers of his left hand touch a curved Victorian settee, behind him a photographer's backdrop of scrolled patterns merges to vaguely paradisaic trees and perhaps a sky. The moccasins he wears make it impossible to deduce whether his feet are "neat small." He may be five feet, ten inches tall, may weigh eleven stone, he certainly is "rather good looking" and, though it is a frontal view, it may be that the point of his long and flaring nose could be "remarkably flat." The photograph is slightly over-illuminated and so the unpainted complexion could be "inclined to be fair"; however, nothing can be seen of a scar, the hair is not wavy and shoulder-length but hangs almost to the waist in two thick straight braids worked through with beads, fur, ribbons and cords. The right hand that holds the corner of the blanket-like coat in position is large and, even in the high illumination, heavily veined. The neck is concealed under coiled beads and the forehead seems more low than "broad."

Perhaps, somehow, these picture details could be reconciled with the official description if the face as a whole were not so devastating.

On a cloth-backed sheet two feet by two and one-half feet in size, under the Great Seal of the Lion and the Unicorn, dignified by the names of the Deputy of the Minister of Justice, the Secretary of State, the Queen herself and all the heaped detail of her "Right Trusty and Right Well Beloved Cousin," this description concludes: "feminine appearance." But the picture: any face of history, any believed face that the world acknowledges as *man*—Socrates, Jesus, Attila, Genghis Khan, Mahatma Gandhi, Joseph Stalin—no believed face is more *man* than this face. The mouth, the nose, the clenched brows, the eyes—the eyes are large, yes, and dark, but even in this watered-down reproduction of unending reproductions of original, a steady look into those eyes cannot be endured. It is a face like an axe.

It is now evident that the de Chardin statement quoted at the beginning has relevance only as it proves itself inadequate to explain what has happened. At the same time, the inadequacy of Aristotle's much more famous statement becomes evident: "The true difference [between the historian and the poet] is that one relates what *has* happened, the other what *may* happen." These statements cannot explain the storyteller's activity since, despite the most rigid application of impersonal investigation, the elements of the story have now run me aground. If ever I could, I can no longer pretend to objective, omnipotent disinterestedness. I am no longer *spectator* of what *has* happened or what *may* happen: I am become *element* in what is happening at this very moment.

For it is, of course, I myself who cannot endure the shadows on that paper which are those eyes. It is I who stand beside this broken veranda post where two corner shingles have been torn away, where barbed wire tangles the dead weeds on the edge of this field. The bluff that sheltered Almighty Voice and his two friends has not disappeared from the slope of the Minnechinass, no more than the sound of Constable Dickson's voice in that guardhouse is silent. The sound of his speaking is there even if it has never been recorded in an official report:

hey injun you'll get
hung
for stealing that steer
hey injun for killing that government
cow you'll get three
weeks on the woodpile hey injun

The unknown contradictory words about an unprovable act that move a boy to defiance, an implacable Cree warrior long after the three-hundred-and-fifty-year war is ended, a war already lost the day the Cree watch Cartier hoist his gun ashore at Hochelaga and they begin the retreat west; these words of incomprehension, of threatened incomprehensible law are there to be heard, like the unmoving tableau of the three-day siege is there to be seen on the slopes of the Minnechinass. Sounding Sky is somewhere not there, under arrest, but Spotted Calf stands on a shoulder of the Hills a little to the left, her arms upraised to the setting sun. Her mouth is open. A horse rears, riderless, above the scrub willow at the edge of the bluff, smoke puffs, screams tangle in rifle barrage, there are wounds, somewhere. The bluff is green this spring, it will not burn and the ragged line of seven police and two civilians is staggering through, faces twisted in rage, terror, and rifles sputter. Nothing moves. There is no sound of frogs in the night; twenty-seven policemen and five civilians stand in cordon at thirty-yard intervals and a body also lies in the shelter of a gully. Only a voice rises from the bluff:

We have fought well
You have died like braves
I have worked hard and am hungry
Give me food

but nothing moves. The bluff lies, a bright green island on the grassy slope surrounded by men hunched forward rigid over their long rifles, men clumped out of rifle-range, thirty-five men dressed as for fall hunting on a sharp spring day, a small gun positioned on a ridge above. A crow is falling out of the sky into the bluff, its feathers sprayed as by an explosion. The first gun and the second gun are in position, the beginning and end of the bristling surround of thirty-five Prince Albert Volunteers, thirteen civilians and fifty-six policemen in position relative to the bluff and relative to the unnumbered whites astride their horses, standing up in their carts, staring and pointing across the valley, in position relative to the bluff and the unnumbered Indians squatting silent along the higher ridges of the Hills, motionless mounds, faceless against the Sunday morning sunlight edging between and over them down along the tree tips, down into the shadows of the bluff. Nothing moves. Beside the second gun the red-coated officer has flung a handful of grass into the motionless air, almost to the rim of the red sun.

And there is a voice. It is an incredible voice that rises from among the young poplars ripped of their spring bark, from among the dead somewhere lying there, out of the arm-deep pit shorter than a man; a voice rises over the exploding smoke and thunder of guns that reel back in their positions, worked over, serviced by the grimed motionless men in bright coats and glinting buttons, a voice so high and clear, so unbelievably high and strong in its unending wordless cry.

The voice of "Gitchie-Manitou Wayo"—interpreted as "voice of the Great Spirit"—that is, Almighty Voice. His death chant no less incredible in its beauty than in its incomprehensible happiness.

I say "wordless cry" because that is the way it sounds to me. I could be more accurate if I had a reliable interpreter who would make a reliable interpretation. For I do not, of course, understand the Cree myself.

J. Michael Yates was born in Fulton, Missouri in 1938 and grew up in the United States, emigrating to Canada as an adult. There, he worked in a variety of jobs—writing, editing, and teaching creative writing (he was the founding editor of Sono Nis Press)—and he lived in a variety of places, from West Vancouver to the Queen Charlotte Islands. The range of backgrounds has had its impact on his writing, which transcends borders both political and generic. He writes poetry, drama, fiction, and meditations on existence which embrace features of several different genres. He does not write sociological documentary. Repeatedly, however, he uses the actual forms of literature to require his reader to see the world—and their roles in it—with abrupt clarity. He manages to do so, Andreas Schroeder writes, in his Introduction to *Stories from Pacific & Arctic Canada* (1974), while avoiding the "haven of straight metaphor or fable." Readers may have to suspend the laws of ordinary logic in order to follow Yates's stories, but in doing so they have the opportunity to discover—and surrender to—the inventive logic of the stories themselves.

Among Yates's books are two collections of fiction, *The Abstract Beast* (1971) and *Fazes in Elsewhen* (1977). "The Sinking of the Northwest Passage" comes from the first of these. It coolly portrays a universe of domestic ritual and suburban monomania, whose bizarreness is the more acute for its familiarity.

FOR FURTHER READING

George Bowering, "Introductory Notes" to his ed., *Fiction of Contemporary Canada* (Toronto: Coach House, 1980), pp. 7-9.

Geoff Hancock, "Magic Realism" in his ed., *Magic Realism* (Toronto: Aya, 1980), pp. 7-15.

The Sinking of the
Northwest Passage

*So many of us, alas, were born with
no Northwest Passage to discover.
We spend our lives carrying that
poignant absence inside us wherever
we go, around and around the earth.*

Commodore Eric F.F. Forrer stood in the box of his sail-boat, *The Northwest Passage*, near the base of the bowsprit (whose configuration was most personal, most abstract), arms folded over his still large-calibre chest and shouted: "Eric F.F. Forrer, Commodore!" And then he listened to his echo skittering away among the branches and boles of the scrub-pine.

There was no retort. But as if there had been one, as if there had been a challenge, he continued at the top of his basso: "I am Commodore because I say so. Let any man who doubts come forward and say."

The as-if: "In what navy do you serve, sir?"

The Commodore: "None. Such institutions are for ordinary men."

The as-if: "Such titles as 'Commodore' are earned with valor and conferred in formal and elaborate ceremony."

The Commodore: "Ordinary! Ordinary!"

The as-if: "Nevertheless."

The Commodore: "'Nevertheless' hell! And nuts! Didn't great Caesar place the laurel on his own brow? And what of Tamburlaine? These were great men in history. I am greater than all history!"

The as-if: "Who says so?"

The Commodore: "I say so, you imbecile. Do you doubt it?"

The as-if: "Frankly, yes."

The Commodore: "Frankly, you are a quadrilateral incandescent ordinary gregarious afterbirth of a self-conscious bitch monkey. Why do I waste time talking to you? Name me one, among all past and present commodores, name me one who ever built his own ship with his own hands as I have."

The as-if: "I cannot."

The Commodore: "Of course you can't. I am my own navy, and as head of it, it is fitting and proper that I function as its commodore."

The as-if: "Hmmmmm."

The Commodore: "Further, mister, this may appear an innocuous sailing vessel, but, in fact, it is a cleverly-camouflaged submarine, and if you don't vanish, this instant, I shall cause it to dive, rig for silent running, and sink you with cleverly-concealed torpedos. Do we understand one another?"

The as-if: "Of course, sir. Right away, sir."

The Commodore: "Excellent. Once, while rafting on a lake near Terrace in the wilds of British Columbia, I sank an entire fleet of pleasure craft which annoyed me while I was sun bathing."

Out of the door of the house shuffled a woman hugging herself across her copious bosom against the chill of the northern morning; she yawned, then stood squinting at the tableau of Commodore Eric F.F. Forrer standing in the bow of his sailing ship which stood solid as a monument on its supports in the middle of the smooth asphalt driveway.

"Excellent sailing this morning (pointing to the asphalt of the driveway and the long winding asphalt road which led down the dome toward the town). Not a ripple. But I could wish for more wind, you know?"

"Why all the shouting? There's no one around."

"You'd be surprised, my dear, how many there are around us."

With that he stepped to the port railing and urinated noisily upon the pavement below.

"Oh, don't do that. Someone might see."

"But you just assured me there's no one about."

"Never mind."

He zipped up the fly of his "northern tuxedo" (overalls) with ceremony.

"Come aboard, come aboard, don't just stand there on the surface, can't you see I'm under way?"

She climbed up the ladder still shivering from the chill of the dew-soaked dome.

"Look at that view of Mount Forrer. You can see four hundred miles."

"Yes, it's beautiful. Every day it's the same but not the same."

"Light. Things never look the same on successive days. It's all in how you look at a thing. And every day the light is changing. Wait till you see it up close. We're going to sail right to it, then right up to its summit before we turn again into the Northwest Passage."

"There's no water straight to the mountain."

"Never mind that."

"And you know there's no longer a Northwest Passage to be found."

"Ordinary poppycock. You can come with me, or I'll set you ashore on an island and proceed alone, or leave you here. Whatever you prefer."

"Thank you. We'll think about it again after breakfast. Come on in now."

"Alright. I'll just anchor up now. I won't be a minute."

Over her shoulder she heard the clank of anchor and chain striking the dark asphalt. The boat secured, he followed her into the house.

After his third mug of sourdough wet breakfast (four fingers of overproof rum, honey, cinnamon, lemon juice, and strong black tea—never mixed in that order) he commented: "This is one of the best houses I ever built. It voyages well. Hardly keels at all in the wind."

"Yes."

"But it won't get through the passage. The passage is quite narrow, you know."

"No, I didn't know. How do you know, if it's never yet been discovered?"

"I know these things. It is my affair to know them."

"Yes, of course."

"We'll have to have just the right tide, woman, just the right tide. It may be necessary to wait days, days, or even months for just the right tide . . . and even then it'll be handy to have pikepoles starboard and port to push us off if she goes too close to the sides. But at the right tide, at just the right tide, with the big rollers behind us, we should surf right on through."

"I hope so."

"Probably we won't even need any canvas, much less the engine. No engine is really dependable anyway. Trust the natural stuff—wind and water."

"If you say so."

"I do. Truly."

It was a bright summer morning, light tentacles reaching in through the windows and curling about the legs of the furniture—brilliant as only mornings in the long-lit northern summers can be—when the first foreign, altogether indescribable, sound from the driveway filled their ears.

The Commodore leapt to the screen door and scowled out into the dazzling sunlight.

"What is it?"

"Nothing I can see. Ship's riding easily at anchor."

"What a strange noise."

" . . . Yes . . . "

The sound again.

"It's coming from the boat."

"Is she breaking up?"

"I built it."

"Silly of me."

"Extremely."

"Why don't you go out and look around?"

"I guess I'd better."

He turned from the door and began placing dishes in a cupboard.

"Then go."

He first withdrew his pocket-watch from the upper left-hand pocket of his overalls and glanced at the time, then replaced it, then gazed slowly around the kitchen and through the doorway to the living room which framed a magnificent view of Mount Forrer, then pushed out the door and strode slowly down the asphalt driveway. She watched from the door and the house slowly filled with her ineffable dread. She could see nothing unusual—only the driveway with the boat on its supports filling it, and Commodore Eric F.F. Forrer nearing the source of the noise which was growing louder and continuous now.

"What do you see? Can you see anything?"

"The ship looks fine."

Then he was bending over examining the supports.

"Is it too heavy for them? Are they breaking?"

"No."

"Then what is it?"

"Eh . . . here!"

He was looking at the cross-members on the pavement.

"What?"

"The supports seem to be sinking through the pavement. Funny they've been here in this same position for such a long time . . . all these years . . . same weight, same conditions . . . why would they wait until this moment to begin sinking?"

She came up beside him and bent over too, examining. "I don't know. Maybe it's the heat."

"Can't be. It's not hot out."

"It's been much hotter than this on other days and it had no effect. Don't you remember the hot scorcher of a summer we had about nine years ago? If the supports were ever going to sink through the asphalt, they would have done so then."

"Well, it's right in front of your eyes, woman . . . sinking . . . there, look!"

As if on cue, the back cross-member vanished and the stern of the vessel settled to the ground. It gave the whole vehicle a strange lurching look—as if climbing a great swell on the high seas. The lines of the craft had become so familiar to them, and now the deck was almost at a thirty degree angle with the horizon.

"And look under here, the keel's more than halfway submerged."

"Yes."

"Blast it, blast the blasted luck!"

"What now?"

"Quick, help me put those planks over there under the hull."

Soon an assortment of weather-silvered two by sixes and two by eights were neatly formed into a protective bed beneath the middle and forward hull.

"We've got to keep her from keeling over; it'll smash the ribbing and ruin everything. I'll never find yellow cedar of that quality again. They don't even replant that stuff after they cut it."

They braced the boat from pavement to gunwales with four by fours.

"Where are you going?"

"To get jacks, jack her up, and build another platform under the stern."

"How did this happen? Do such things happen?"

"No."

The Commodore was fretfully pulling out hairs of his blonde moustache, a growth that couldn't be seen at a distance greater than a few feet. One could always tell when he enjoyed a book: its pages were full of hairs from his moustache.

"On the other hand, seamanship is a tricky science and a difficult art. There are strange currents, woman, strange currents which sink great ships even in the fairest of surface conditions. Tides change. Sea-floors rearrange themselves. A man can never know too much about navigation—although there are things a man can know far too much about. I'll get the jacks."

Behind him he heard the sound begin again, and even before he turned he knew the bow support and remaining keel had disappeared under the surface of the asphalt.

"Oh dear, now the bow is down."

"I have eyes. I . . . have . . . eyes."

"Will the planks keep it afloat?"

"Who can be certain of such things? No sense trying the jacks now. There's nothing forward or astern skookum enough to take leverage against that weight. I have no intention of cracking ribs and breaking off her railings to get purchase. Better *The Northwest Passage* go down just as I made her, than go down broken and maimed."

"But wouldn't it be better to save even . . . "

"No."

"Can't you do something?"

"Possibly I could tunnel in two places beneath the ship, run belts under, then hire a crane to yard her up while I build new supports under her."

"Yes, do that. But you would have to ruin the driveway, wouldn't you?"

"Yes."

He went in through the screen door then emerged a few minutes later carrying two kitchen chairs.

"What are those for?"

"We'll sit and keep a close watch. She's sailing high and easy now on the planks. Maybe something will occur to us."

"Did you call about the crane?"

"Yes."

"What did they say?"

"Either there is no elevation company listed in the yellow pages, or there is no crane this far north large enough for the job, or it would require two smaller cranes (and likely the two operators couldn't coordinate their lifting: suppose a bee flew into the cab of one of them at a crucial moment. And everyone knows that two machines cannot be perfectly harmonized . . . even by a third machine; there are two many variables). If one failed, not only would all that effort be in vain, but much money would go for nothing; all our money is riding on the planks before us there. If one broke down in mid-lift (even without damage to the vessel, let us hopefully suppose), then where would we be? We would pay for men and machines alike by the hour nevertheless, if we could pay. They would have to send for a mechanic and then for parts which must be flown in from the outside. Or, since all of them are on tracks, it would take a long time to get up here from their present job-sites, if, indeed, they could be spared at all. This is the building season, and all things and all men are under contract. In fact, they wouldn't be allowed to come up here on tracks, they would scar the pavement, and there are ordinances. They would have to bring them on low-beds and it would be necessary to add the cost of the trucks and their drivers. If they came on trucks, there would be far too much weight per axle for the myriad small bridges between the city and this driveway. There are ordinances, always ordinances to protect the forms of civilisation. They aren't fond, you know, of small and extraordinary jobs like this one and avoid them at all costs. Or the line was busy. Or out of order. Or they wouldn't believe me."

"I'd forgotten."

"Why do women forget such things?"

"I'm not women; I'm singular; and I don't know why I forget such things."

"Sit down. I'm sorry."

"Thank you. I'm sorry too. Can you use the ship's radio to call for help?"

"No, there are too many domes and ridges for sending signals from here. And there are no charts for this extremity of north; no one sails here."

"How about sending up a flare?"

"Too dry. The forest fire hazard is too high. I won't risk burning the ship; too much of my life is in her seams."

"I suppose so."

"Believe it."

They sat, she still hugging herself, he with his left arm across the back of her chair, and both gazing at the soft line where the keel touched the pavement.

"Possibly it was only the night air. It might have somehow weakened the supports."

"There was nothing wrong with the supports. They sank without giving way."

"Ah, that's right. But it's not sinking now."

"I'm afraid you're wrong. Since the forward support disappeared, it's been sinking steadily."

"I can't hear it. And it doesn't look like it to me."

"Look closely. Don't you see how the planks we set underneath are gradually floating out beyond the sides?"

"Yes . . . I see it now. But why do we hear nothing?"

"Not all sinking is sensory. It sometimes goes on through the nights and days without our noticing at all. By the time we've grown cognizant of it, there is no bilge-pump strong enough to save us. Probably *The Northwest Passage* began to sink the moment I touched pencil to paper to design her."

"Do you think so?"

"Yes."

"And, knowing this, it made no difference?"

"No."

"I think I wouldn't have gone through with it, if such a suspicion occurred to me."

"I could have preferred things otherwise . . . but without boats to build . . . there wouldn't be anything."

The ship was settling evenly, gracefully, now, toward the waterline. Without sound. Not far away a grouse drummed. A ptarmigan strode across the asphalt road. And a black bear was nosing a blueberry bush absent of berries. High sun strummed through the well-strung rigging of the mast and cross-spars, then darted here and there among the polished brass fittings.

"Soon she'll hit the water-line."

"Yes."

"Then, who knows?"

"Say, I just thought of something. Maybe *The Northwest Passage* simply has a mind of her own and is trying to tell us something by launching herself. She'll stop at the water-line. I think I'll go inside for a bottle of champagne to christen her, just in case."

"That sparkling muscatel?"

"Don't be coarse. It's twenty a magnum."

"Ships should be christened with rum. Bring the rum."

"Where's your sense of ceremony?"

"In my insides—where that rum is going."

She brought the rum.

"There's the water-line!"

"Good. Now we'll see."

"I have the champagne near the door."

"Very well, if she stops at the water-line, you have my leave to ruin my stern varnish with that belly-rot."

"Later you'll be glad I christened her properly."

The mast stood like a sundial, wavering only slightly in the breeze and the almost imperceptible silent settlings below. It marked the passing of high noon and cast its crossed shadows in the direction of evening and the dark which never seems to arrive in the summer north, but suddenly is upon you.

"So much for my water-line." He tossed the empty rum bottle into the bushes which lined the driveway.

"Yes, nothing showing of it at all. I'll only have to pick up that bottle and discard it later."

"So you will. So you will."

Before she could protest, he leapt from his chair, raced to the ladder at the side of the vessel, climbed it, and drew the ladder up on the deck.

"What do you think you can accomplish from up there?"

No answer. He was drawing up the anchor. The anchor secured, he began pacing around the decks, the bill of his sailing cap pulled low against the vanishing rays of the strange northern sun. He paused to check this fitting, then that, gave a turn-buckle a couple of turns, then went inside to his compass, charts, and wheel.

"Don't you think you ought to come down?"

His head appeared around the frame of the cabin door. He glared at her with fraudulent anger.

"I mean, you never know what might happen."

"You never know."

He unlashed the mainsail and pulled it determinedly up the mast, secured the boom, then returned to the wheelhouse. A weak breeze over the dome-top began to luff the canvas erratically. He emerged again quickly, leapt to the bow, cupped his hands, and: "In the name of Boreas and all inspiration . . . MORE GODDAM WIND!!"

And you could hear it in the distant trees like a locomotive nearing.

"There's always breeze in the late afternoon and evening. You know it as well as I do."

"Never mind. Where's my line now?"

"About midway between water-line and gunwale, I guess."

The mainsail was full now. The Commodore went forward and ran up the jib which stiffened until it looked like the blade of a knife held aloft.

"Alright now, alright, we'll see what we'll see." And into the cabin we went again. Below on the driveway she paced round and round the craft, hugging herself against the chill and wind rising. The vessel heaved back and forth in the pavement and the noise had returned—grating and grating of the cedar ribs against the stone layers and permafrost into which it was sinking.

The Commodore again came out of the cabin, and, struggling against the winds mounting to gale force, managed to get the deep green spinnaker up. It required almost super-human effort. The canvas ballooned and burgeoned like the throat-sac of a monster frog.

The noise now was truly stupendous. It overwhelmed even the sound of the careering wind. She stood in the draft of the vessel, but not too close: it pitched now side to side and forward and aft, as if in the highest of seas. Anything might have happened—sails might have split, the boat might have broken up, or might even have rolled free. But these things did not occur; simply the violent motion accelerated the sinking.

Commodore Eric F.F. Forrer stood, legs rooted substantially far apart, knees bending rhythmically to absorb the shocks of the listing and pitching, there in the wheelhouse at the wheel until, at a dramatic moment toward late evening, the bowsprit nosed under and the wind expired as if there had never been wind, and the forward decks were awash with asphalt.

"You see? It didn't work."

The Commodore standing on the slant amidships, cap in his left hand, mopping his brow with his right sleeve: "On the contrary, woman, on the contrary."

Another lurch. The stern and aft decking sank from sight. He sprang to the roof of the cabin. The sails hung limp from their rigging.

"This is the best ship I ever made. See how she sinks evenly instead of going stern or bow first. You can tell the character of a boat by the way she dies."

"I see."

"Plenty of time for all hands to abandon."

"Plenty."

"Better stand back and clear. Sometimes the last suction can be fierce."

"Very well. Have all abandoned?"

"Yes, I gave the order some time ago."

"I didn't hear it."

"Doubtless it was the big wind and the sound of the sinking."

"Yes, I suppose."

The surface of the driveway was now level with the flat roof of the wheelhouse. No wind, and darkness closing like the shutter of a camera.

"I'll get a light."

She returned with a glass lantern, brilliant and hissing.

"Is there any more rum?" he asked as he began climbing the rigging toward the cross-spar.

"No. I'm sorry."

He sat, legs dangling on either side of the mast, and holding the tip of the mast near the flag with one hand.

The light of the lantern lit one side of his profile so brightly that his features seemed almost washed out. The other side of his face, like the moon which had now risen over the scrub-timber at the crest of the dome, erased itself in darkness. Up the mast crept the asphalt like mercury in a barometer. There was little sound now, so smooth was the surface of the mast, save the occasional crinkle of new canvas going under.

When the surface met the corrugated soles of his deck shoes, he stood upon the cross-spar, drew himself to his full height, inhaled the darkness deeply, and shouted:

"Eric F.F. Forrer, Commodore!"

There was no retort. Nor did he begin to polemicize as if there had been one.

She held the light closer as the asphalt gathered in his broad shoulders.

His last words were: "Blow that damned thing out."

She did.

And there was not a trace, not a ripple, not even a small indentation in the dark surface of the driveway. She spent some minutes looking after she re-lit the lamp (not difficult in the windless darkness; there was still plenty of pressure in it).

And then she went inside where the bottle of champagne still stood waiting; she replaced it in the liquor cupboard. She would fetch the empty rum bottle in the morning and throw it in the trash.

As she switched out the lights from room to room and began to prepare for bed, the house rolled a little ... like a large boat at a calm mooring. But she hardly noticed the motion; miniature earth tremors are so very usual in that precinct of the world.

Appendix

HOW TO READ A SHORT STORY

There is no single form of short fiction; and there is no single acceptable way of responding to the art of this genre. Reading is a creative, not a mechanical act; it requires imaginative participation, not passive receptivity. But involvement of this kind does not permit readers to decide that a story may mean whatever they want it to mean. Writers arrange their words to engage their readers in quite particular ways, and use a variety of techniques—some familiar, some unusual or obscure—to shape and guide our responses. One of the challenges facing a reader is to sort out the how and why of a story's structure: how is it put together in order to create the effects it achieves? why did the writer choose that way, rather than another? why did the writer select these particular words, and arrange them in this particular order? Ideally, finding answers to such questions adds to the pleasure of reading; the reader ends up, not merely with a grasp of the story's content, but with a greater appreciation of the writer's verbal and organizational skills, and of the sophisticated art by means of which the writer has cast a fresh light on human behaviour.

You can identify many of the techniques of short fiction by asking particular questions about any story that you read, and the paragraphs that follow attempt to suggest the kinds of questions that may be appropriate. However, two points should be borne in mind here: first, the use of any given technique is no indication of a story's quality; a writer may use a web of complex symbols, or an intricate plot pattern, without producing a good story; and conversely, the absence of these or other techniques does not necessarily make a story weak. Secondly, not all the questions or points listed below will be applicable to every story; the artists have each made a choice and selected only those elements of the story-teller's art that will most effectively render character, scene, or action, and thus fulfil their purpose.

1. What happens?

Answers to this question involve an understanding of the plot, the sequence of events in the narrative. Who does what to whom? How do the events that take place, and the order in which they occur, affect the outcome of the story? (For example, in melodramatic stories dire events often occur because something goes missing—a letter, a mortgage deed—at an inopportune time.)

How does the story *begin*: at the beginning of the action or part-way through? How does it *develop*: in chronological order or in flashback; at one moment in time, or over an extended period? Is there a *climax*, a high point of the action when all the threads of the story come together? If the story has no discernible climax, why not? Is there any *suspense*, and how is it created? Is the outcome of the action a surprise? How does the story come to an end—does it close off the action with some kind of resolution, or leave it open and indeterminate? Does the ending offer a general comment about the world at large, or does it focus on the feelings of an individual character?

2. Where does the story happen, and when?

These questions ask about the *setting*, which involves both *place* and *time*. A story may make extensive use of scenic description; remember, however, that in well-written stories such descriptions are never ornamental: they are a means of telling the reader something about the characters or the action. Some stories rely on your making either general or specific associations with details of setting: what comes to mind when you think of an Arctic winter, a day in May, the year 1867, the date 11 November 1918, a railway station, the American South, Middle Earth, a small-town diner, the star-ship "Enterprise"? Each of these is a "setting"; some are specific in their historical or geographical reference, others fantastic or imaginary; still others call on traditional associations common to human experience.

Why does the author set the action in a given place or at a given time? Are there political or cultural or social ramifications to the setting? What details of setting throw light on the actions or feelings of the characters? How are the characters formed or influenced by their physical environment? Does the writer want readers to make conventional associations with a particular setting (a spring day suggesting possibility and hope, a crossroads pointing to a moment of decision)? Or does the story somehow subvert such conventional associations (the spring day leading to disaster, the crossroads offering merely an illusion of choice)?

Note that in some stories there may not be a conventional setting at all; the action may take place in a character's mind or imagination. Or the setting may be the printed page, itself a "field" on which words assemble, in patterns suggestive of action or meaning.

3. Who is the story about?

This question concerns both *character* and the techniques of *characterization* by which an author creates character. Who is the main character (the protagonist) in the story, and what does the reader learn about that character's identity, appearance, and background? How are the principal characters revealed: through what they say and do? through their thoughts? by the way that others react to them, or by what the author says about them? Do the characters undergo any kind of change in the course of the story? Do they come to some illumination or new understanding of the world (James Joyce called such a moment an "epiphany"), or are they unaffected by their experience?

Does the story include a "foil" for the main character—an enemy or "antagonist" who opposes the main character's progress or thwarts success? Such a foil does not always have to be human: it can be an aspect of nature (like a beast or a rugged landscape), imaginary (like a creature of nightmare), mythic (supernatural figures or deities), or even abstract and intangible (like the forces of time).

Does the story contain a "double" of the main character—that is, a character who in some way embodies or reflects an aspect of the main character's personality, possibly something that has lain hidden or suppressed? How do the experiences and problems of the minor characters reflect on those of the protagonist? Do they suggest alternative courses of action, or reveal options or solutions that the main character should, or should not, choose?

Some stories have first-person narrators. The "I" who tells a story may be the protagonist, or a minor character acting as an observer, or a *persona* (Latin, "mask") of the author; whatever the case, the "I" is as much a character in the narrative as any of the other characters, and you should ask the same kinds of questions about this "I" as you would apply to the other actors in the story. (See the next section, on "Who tells the story?")

Remember that characters are not "people"—that is, a story is not "real life," no matter how much it may create that illusion, and no matter how it may resemble the situations that we know happen in real life. Therefore we can know only as much about a character as the story reveals, and must form our judgments accordingly.

4. Who tells the story?

This question asks you not simply to give a name to the narrator, but to figure out the strategy of narration.

Is the story told in the *first person* by a participant in the action, or by an invisible narrator who records everything in the *third person*? Is the first-person narrator wholly reliable, or does that narrator betray some bias or prejudice that might slant his or her interpretation of events? If the story is in third-person, does the narrator intrude with comments or explanations, or does the story appear to unfold by itself, without any interpretive comment?

By the choice of narrative angle, the author can significantly influence our understanding of the story. For example, a story in which the narrator is *omniscient*—that is, knows all and tells all—will likely cast the reader in the role of observer of the action; readers may be sympathetic to the characters, but remain essentially uninvolved, sharing a viewpoint that distances them from the action. In a first-person narration, on the other hand, the speaker is likely to be limited in knowledge, and this very limitation may create a stronger bond with the reader: because we are forced to see things from one character's point of view, we are more likely to identify with that character's feelings and responses. In such cases, we should ask ourselves whether the narrator is telling us all he or she knows, or concealing something to mislead us. Sometimes narrators are unconsciously revealing something about themselves that they might not wish others to know, or showing a side of themselves that they are unaware of.

In some stories the author may use the third person, but filter the events through the consciousness of the main character. What is the effect of such a strategy?

5. What is your reaction to the story?

The issue addressed by this question is that of *tone*. Tone is related to point-of-view, because it is a way of characterizing the attitude of mind conveyed by the style of narration. In conversation, a speaker's tone of voice helps the listener to interpret his or her meaning and feelings; similarly in fiction, the tone of the narration guides the reader's response and understanding. You will react differently to a story that you know is told in jest from one that is told angrily or sadly. How does a writer establish (and control) the tone of a story? Is the tone dependent just on the overt subject, or is it somehow linked with language (could you write a sad story about a comic event)? Is the story sad, funny, sarcastic, ironic, tragic, satiric, witty, playful, bitter, passionate, cool, or something else—and how do you know? What effect does the tone have on the way you respond emotionally or intellectually to the events of the story?

6. What form does the story take?

This is a question about the kinds and effects of various verbal patterns, and should really be thought of as three more specific questions, concerning (a) the *style*, or the shape, pattern, and rhythm of words, phrases, and sentences; (b) the design and function of separate *scenes*; and (c) the organization and shape of the story as a whole, its *narrative pattern*.

(a) *style*: The questions to be asked about style in fiction are the same as those we use in the analysis of any kind of prose. Is the language *formal* or *informal*, or some combination of these? Is the vocabulary simple and direct, or complex and ornate? Why did the author choose these particular words, and arrange them in this particular order? (It can be instructive to substitute synonyms in a passage, to see the difference in effect that *word choice* can make.) The study of *syntax* (the way in which words are put together to form phrases and sentences) is equally important. Are the sentences short or long; *simple, compound*, or *complex*; cast in the *active* or the *passive*, the *affirmative* or the *negative*? Do they follow a standard order (subject-verb-object), or is this order altered in key places?

What contributions do word choice and syntax make to the story? The way that characters speak is an important clue to their social background, their attitudes, and their feelings. *Repetitions* of phrase or form can emphasize a particular attitude or reflect a speaker's obsessions; *fragmented* or *incomplete* sentences or *exclamations* may convey incoherent thoughts, sudden impulses, or strong emotions. In passages of narration or description, repetition may be used to suggest the cyclic nature of an event, or to draw attention to similarities between different parts of the story. Even *silence* can communicate an attitude or express an idea. Writers sometimes use a character's silences or incomplete utterances to suggest inarticulacy or powerlessness, or conversely to indicate a character's refusal to yield to the power of others.

A writer may use *figurative language* to add layers of meaning to the narrative. *Metaphor, symbol*, and *metonymy* extend the literal meaning of an object or event by introducing another level or range of associations and enlarging the story's frame of reference. The use of *simile* is a means of stressing the likenesses between things. Another method of making comparisons is *allusion*; the story that makes repeated allusions to figures in history or myth, or to other works of literature, may be asking you to recognize the way it parallels, or echoes, or modifies some other work.

All writers use *images*, words or phrases that recreate the physical world by appealing to the senses (words, for example, like rose, flag, thunder, heave, gritty). Such images can take on figurative meaning, depending on their function and their context. An image that is used repeatedly in a story may acquire symbolic force, or become a kind of *motif* associated with a particular mood or setting or character.

(b) *Scenes*: Just as the structure of individual sentences can reflect aspects of character or elements of meaning, so the structure of individual scenes in a story can sometimes contain in small the issues and the tensions that the story as a whole explores on a larger scale. A scene which dramatizes an individual moment of temptation, for example, might constitute an intrinsic part of a story that concerns itself with the problem of moral choice in a fallen world. Or a scene in which is shown an act of petty cruelty might reflect the story's broader treatment of the injustices characterizing a hierarchical society.

Individual scenes play an important role in the development of plot and character. Some of the following questions may be relevant in considering the relation of scenes to overall plot structure: how does the scene contribute to the main action? Is it part of the story's exposition, laying the groundwork for what follows? Does it introduce a complication (the arrival of a new character, the announcement of some unexpected news, for instance)? Does it form the climax of the story, bring a conflict to a head, show the protagonist making a crucial decision? Does it form a conclusion to the narrative, embody a resolution of the central conflict, untangle any narrative knots *(dénouement)*? What aspect of the main character is revealed in the scene? If the scene occurs early in the story, does it offer clues about the main character's motives or future conduct?

(c) *Narrative pattern*: A writer may draw on any one of a variety of traditional patterns, or forms, to structure (i.e., organize) the narrative as a whole. The story can be constructed to read as a *memoir*, an *allegory*, a *documentary*, a *history*, a *fairy-tale*, an *adventure*, a *romance*, a *character sketch*, a *journal*, a *myth*, a *fable*, a *parable*; each of these forms has its own set of conventions and associations. The critical reader must ask: what is the form that the author has chosen for the story, and what is the effect on the story of that choice? Clearly, the writer who casts a work of fiction as a documentary journal wants the fiction to give the illusion of being a faithful record of experience; the writer who presents a fable set in modern life may well be making an ironic comment on contemporary morality, drawing effects from an implicit comparison with traditional fables and their appeal to conventional virtues. Ask yourself whether the story you are reading follows a pattern of this kind. Is it presented as a tall tale? an heroic quest? a rite of initiation? a myth of death and resurrection, or of seasonal and cyclical return?

Some stories fall into the category of *metafiction*, fiction about the workings of fiction; such stories may include any of the forms noted above, or variants of these forms, in order to explore the character of verbal artifice itself.

7. Does the story have a central subject?

This is a difficult question, not least because it is often misleading. It sometimes takes other forms—"What is the story *about?*" "What does the story *say?*" "What is the *meaning* of the story?" Such questions suggest that hidden at the heart of a story, waiting to be sprung loose like a jack-in-the-box, is a secret "message." But good stories don't work that way; instead, they use narrative as a process to draw the reader into an appreciation of the complexities (and sometimes the simplicities) of human behaviour, motivation, and value. Sometimes they deliberately defer meaning, resisting the idea of completion, of conclusion or "closure." The reader must then participate with the text to explore a variety of possibilities.

However, because they do select from and focus upon particular aspects of human experience, stories inevitably have *subjects* or *themes*; they concern themselves with politics and ethics, with life and death, youth and age, continuity and change, with war and peace, hate and love, science and nature, words and feelings—with everything that embodies or expresses our humanity. But simply to say that a story is "about war" or "about nature" is not enough. The effective reader seeks to discover how all the elements in a given story—character, plot, setting, language, tone—work together, whether to create a sense of a "whole," or to emphasize the fragmentary nature of experience and understanding. Though there may be times when you want to express a story's main concerns or themes in a sentence or two, remember that by doing so you run the risk of oversimplifying the author's complex creation. You should also look for those occasions when a story isn't concerned so much with conventional "themes" as with the nature of language, the very process of storytelling itself; such stories are a reminder that fiction is artifice, and that however "real" a story may seem, it can only take shape and meaning when writer and reader actively collaborate on the plane of the imagination.

FOR FURTHER READING

John Bayly, *The Short Story* (Brighton: Harvester, 1988).

Helmut Bonheim, *The Narrative Modes* (Cambridge: D.S. Brewer, 1982).

Suzanne Ferguson, "Defining the Short Story: Impressionism and Form," *Modern Fiction Studies* 28, no. 1 (Spring 1982): 13-24.

Gerald Gillespie, "Novella, Novelle, Novella, Short Novel? A Review of Terms," *Neophilologus* 55 (1967): 117-27, 225-30.

Graham Good, "Notes on the Novella," *Novel* 10, no. 3 (Spring 1977): 197-211.

Clare Hanson, *Short Stories & Short Fictions 1880-1990* (London: Macmillan, 1985).

———, ed., *Re-reading the Short Story* (London: Macmillan, 1989).

Susan Lohafer, *Coming to Terms with the Short Story* (Baton Rouge: Louisiana State UP, 1983).

—— and Jo Ellyn Clarey, eds., *Short Story Theory at a Crossroads* (Baton Rouge: Louisiana State UP, 1990).

Charles E. May, ed., *Short Story Theories* (Athens, Ohio: Ohio UP, 1978).

W.H. New, *Dreams of Speech and Violence: The Art of The Short Story in Canada and New Zealand* (Toronto: U of Toronto P, 1987).

Mary Louise Pratt, "The Short Story: The Long and the Short of It," *Poetics* 10, nos. 2/3 (June 1981): 175-94.

Ian Reid, *The Short Story* (London: Methuen, 1977).

Hollis Summers, ed., *Discussions of the Short Story* (Boston: D.C. Heath, 1963).

An honest attempt has been made to secure permission for all material used, and if there are errors or omissions, these are wholly unintentional and the Publisher will be grateful to learn of them.

Civil Peace from *Girls at War and other stories* by Chinua Achebe. Copyright © 1972, 1973 by Chinua Achebe. Used by permission of Doubleday, A Division of Bantam Doubleday Dell Publishing Group, Inc., and by permission of Harold Ober Associates Incorporated.

Scarlet Ibis from *Bluebeard's Egg* by Margaret Atwood: Copyright © 1983, 1986 by O. W. Toad, Ltd. Reprinted by permission of Houghton Mifflin Company, and by permission of the Canadian Publishers, McClelland & Stewart, Toronto.

The Persimmon Tree from *The Persimmon Tree and other stories* by Marjorie Barnard. Copyright © by Curtis Brown (Pty) Ltd. of Australia. Used by permission.

Report from *Unspeakable Practices, Unnatural Acts* by Donald Barthelme. Copyright © 1968 by Donald Barthelme. Used by permission of Wylie, Aitken & Stone.

Eyes from *A North American Education* by Clark Blaise. Copyright © 1973 by Clark Blaise. Reprinted by permission.

Allal copyright © 1979 by Paul Bowles. Reprinted from *Collected Stories* with the permission of Black Sparrow Press.

Two Fishermen from *Morley Callaghan's Stories* by Morley Callaghan. Reprinted by permission of Macmillan of Canada, A Division of Canada Publishing Corporation.

"Do You Love Me?" from *War Crimes* by Peter Carey. Copyright © 1979 by Peter Carey. Reprinted by permission of University of Queensland Press.

The Country Husband from *The Stories of John Cheever* by John Cheever. Copyright © 1954 by John Cheever. Reprinted by permission of Alfred A. Knopf, Inc.

Ko-ishin-mit and the Shadow People from *Son of a Raven, Son of a Deer* by George Clutesi. Used by permission of the author's estate.

Dry September from *Collected Stories of William Faulkner* by William Faulkner. Copyright © 1930 and renewed 1958 by William Faulkner. Reprinted by permission of Random House Inc.

The Road from Colonus from *The Collected Tales of E. M. Forster* by E. M. Forster. Published 1947 by Alfred A. Knopf, Inc. Reprinted by permission of the publisher and of Sidgwich and Jackson as the literary representatives of the Estate of E. M. Forster.

No Place Like from *Selected Stories* by Nadine Gordimer. Copyright © 1971 by Nadine Gordimer. Reprinted by permission of Viking Penguin, A Division of Penguin Books USA Inc.

ACKNOWLEDGEMENTS

Brother Copyright © 1949 by Graham Greene, renewed 1977 from *Collected Stories* by Graham Greene. Used by permission of Viking Penguin, A Division of Penguin Books USA Inc., and by permission of Laurence Pollinger Limited.

Slow Dissolve from *The Bearded Lady* by Kate Grenville. Published by University of Queensland Press. Used by permission of the publisher.

Letters from the Samantha from *Ellis Island & other stories* by Mark Helprin. Reprinted by permission of Dell Publishing Co., Division of Bantam Doubleday Dell Publishing Group Inc.

Hills Like White Elephants reprinted with permission of Charles Scribner's Sons, an imprint of Macmillan Publishing Company, from *Men Without Women* by Ernest Hemingway. Copyright © 1927 by Charles Scribner's Sons; copyright renewed 1955 by Ernest Hemingway.

The Lepers' Squint from *The Barclay Family Theatre* by Jack Hodgins. Copyright © 1981. Reprinted by permission of Macmillan of Canada, A Division of Canada Publishing Corporation.

The Monkey's Paw from *The Lady of the Barge* was originally published by Harper and Brothers, Publishers, in 1902.

The Boarding House from *Dubliners* by James Joyce. Originally published by B. W. Huebsch in 1916. Definitive text copyright © 1967 by The Estate of James Joyce. Reprinted by permission of Viking Penguin, A Division of Penguin Books USA Inc.

Mrs. Putnam at the Planetarium by Janice Kulyk Keefer is reprinted from *The Paris Napoli Express* by permission of Oberon Press.

Joe the Painter and the Deer Island Massacre by Thomas King originally published in *Whetstone*, 1985. This version used by permission of the author.

The Merchant of Heaven from *The Tomorrow Tamer* by Margaret Laurence. Copyright © by The Estate of Margaret Laurence. Reprinted by permission.

The Horse Dealer's Daughter from *The Complete Short Stories of D. H. Lawrence*. Copyright 1922 by Thomas B. Seltzer, Inc., renewed 1950 by Frieda Lawrence. Reprinted by permission of Viking Penguin, A Division of Penguin Books USA Inc., and by Laurence Pollinger Limited.

The Doll's House from *The Short Stories of Katherine Mansfield* by K. Mansfield. Copyright © 1923 by Alfred A. Knopf, Inc. and renewed 1951 by John Middleton Murry. Reprinted by permission of Alfred A. Knopf, Inc.

Swimming Lessons from *Tales from Firozsha Baag*. Copyright © Rohinton Mistry, 1987. Reprinted by permission of Penguin Books Canada Limited.

Thanks for the Ride from *Dance of the Happy Shades* by Alice Munro. Copyright © 1968 by Alice Munro. Originally published by McGraw-Hill Ryerson Limited. Reprinted by arrangement with Virginia Barber Literary Agency. All rights reserved.

My Aunt Gold Teeth from *A Flag on the Island* by V.S. Naipaul. Published by André Deutsch. Reprinted by permission.

Miracle at Indian River from *Miracle at Indian River* by Alden Nowlan. Copyright © by Irwin Publishing. Reprinted by permission Stoddart Publishing Co. Limited.

In the Region of Ice from *The Wheel of Love* by Joyce Carol Oates. Reprinted by permission.

A Good Man Is Hard to Find from *A Good Man is Hard to Find* by Flannery O'Connor. Copyright © 1953 by Flannery O'Connor and renewed 1981 by Regina O'Connor. Reprinted by permission of Harcourt Brace Jovanovich, Inc.

He from *Flowering Judas and other stories* by Katherine Anne Porter. Copyright © 1930, renewed 1958 by Katherine Anne Porter. Reprinted by permission of Harcourt Brace Jovanovich, Inc.

Cornet at Night from *The Lamp at Noon and other stories* by Sinclair Ross. Used by permission of the Canadian Publishers, McClelland & Stewart, Toronto.

Mrs. Turner Cutting the Grass from *Various Miracles* by Carol Shields. Reprinted by permission of Stoddart Publishing Co. Limited.

The More Little Mummy in the World from *Ladies and Escorts* by Audrey Thomas. Used by permission of the author.

Giving Blood from *The Music School* by John Updike. Copyright © 1963 by John Updike. Reprinted by permission of Alfred A. Knopf, Inc. Originally appeared in the *New Yorker*.

Cages from *Man Descending* by Guy Vanderhaeghe. Copyright © 1982. Reprinted by permission of Macmillan of Canada, A Division of Canada Publishing Corporation.

Report on the Barnhouse Effect from *Welcome to the Monkey House* by Kurt Vonnegut. Reprinted by permission of Dell Publishing Co., Division of Bantam Doubleday Dell Publishing Group Inc.

Nineteen Fifty-five from *You Can't Keep a Good Woman Down* by Alice Walker. Copyright © 1981 by Alice Walker. Reprinted by permission of Harcourt Brace Jovanovich, Inc.

Down at the Dump from *The Burnt Ones* by Patrick White. Copyright © 1964 by Patrick White. Reprinted by permission of Viking Penguin, A Division of Penguin Books USA Inc.

Where is the Voice Coming From? by Rudy Wiebe is printed in *The Angel of the Tar Sands and other stories* published by McClelland & Stewart, 1982. Reprinted by permission of the author.

The Sinking of the Northwest Passage from *The Abstract Beast* by J. Michael Yates. Reprinted by permission of Sono Nis Press, A Division of Morriss Publishing Ltd.